What Works in Offender Rehabilitation

What Works in Offender Rehabilitation

An Evidence-Based Approach to Assessment and Treatment

Edited by

Leam A. Craig

Forensic Psychology Practice Ltd, The Willows Clinic, UK
University of Birmingham, UK

Louise Dixon

University of Birmingham, UK

Theresa A. Gannon

University of Kent, UK

A John Wiley & Sons, Ltd., Publication

Library of Congress Cataloging-in-Publication Data

What works in offender rehabilitation : an evidence-based approach to assessment and treatment / edited by Leam A. Craig, Louise Dixon, Theresa A. Gannon.
     pages   cm
  Includes bibliographical references and index.
  ISBN 978-1-119-97457-4 (cloth) – ISBN 978-1-119-97456-7 (pbk.)   1. Criminals–Rehabilitation.
I. Craig, Leam, editor   II. Dixon, Louise, editor   III. Gannon, Theresa A. editor
  HV9275.W427 2013
  365'.661–dc23

                                                    2012050028

A catalogue record for this book is available from the British Library.

Contents

About the Editors

Leam A. Craig, BA (Hons), MSc, PhD, MAE, CSci, CPsychol, AFBPsS, EuroPsy, is a Consultant Forensic and Clinical Psychologist and Partner at Forensic Psychology Practice Ltd. He is Professor of Forensic Psychology at the Centre for Forensic and Criminological Psychology, University of Birmingham, UK. He is a Chartered and Registered (Forensic and Clinical) Psychologist, a Chartered Scientist and holder of the European Certificate in Psychology, permitting practice throughout the European Union. His current practice includes direct services to forensic adult mental health and learning disability hospitals and consultancy to prison and probation services throughout England and Wales and Northern Ireland. He acts as an expert witness to civil and criminal courts in the assessment of sexual and violent offenders and in matters of child protection. He has published over 70 research articles and chapters in a range of research and professional journals. He has also published five books: an authored book entitled *Assessing Risk in Sex Offenders: A Practitioners Guide* (2008), and four edited books, *Assessment and Treatment of Sex Offenders: A Handbook* (2009), *Assessment and Treatment of Sexual Offenders with Intellectual Disabilities: A Handbook* (2010), *International Perspectives on the Assessment and Treatment of Sexual Offenders* (2011) and *Assessments in Forensic Practice: A Handbook* (2013), all published with Wiley-Blackwell. He is currently working on a *Major Reference Work on Assessing and Treating Sexual Offenders* with Drs Douglas Boer and Martin Rettenberger. He sits on the editorial boards of several journals, including *International Journal of Offender Therapy and Comparative Criminology, Journal of Sexual Aggression, Journal of Aggression, Conflict and Peace Research* and *The Open Criminology Journal*.

Louise Dixon, BSc (Hons), MSc, PhD, CPsychol, is a Forensic Psychologist and Senior Lecturer in Forensic Psychology at the Centre for Forensic and Criminological Psychology, University of Birmingham, UK. She is the Course Director of the Continued Professional Development route to the Doctorate in Forensic Psychology Practice. Louise enjoys an active research and publication profile and is involved in the wider international research scene. She is on the editorial board of internationally peer-reviewed journals *Child Maltreatment, Journal of Aggression Conflict and Peace Research* and *British Journal of Forensic Practice*. She is the E-bulletin Editor for the International Family Aggression Society (IFAS) and is Vice Chair of the West Midlands branch of the British Association for the Study and Prevention of Child Abuse and Neglect (BASPCAN). Her research interests centre on family and intimate partner violence and the role of group aggression in understanding and preventing street gang affiliation and offending. She has published numerous articles and book chapters in these domains. Louise also practises as a Forensic Psychologist, specializing in the assessment and intervention of violent adult offenders.

Theresa A. Gannon, DPhil, CPsychol (Forensic), is Director of the Centre for Research and Education in Forensic Psychology (CORE-FP) and Professor of Forensic Psychology at the University of Kent, UK. Theresa also works as a Chartered Consultant Forensic Psychologist specializing in sexual offenders and firesetters for Kent Forensic Psychiatry Services, UK. Theresa has published numerous chapters, articles, books and other scholarly works in the areas of male- and female-perpetrated sexual offending and firesetting. She is particularly interested in research relating to both the treatment needs and overall rehabilitation of sexual offenders. Theresa is Lead Editor of several books, including *Aggressive Offenders' Cognition: Theory, Research, and Treatment* (John Wiley & Sons) along with Professor Tony Ward, Professor Anthony Beech and Dr Dawn Fisher, and *Female Sexual Offenders: Theory, Assessment and Treatment* (Wiley-Blackwell) along with Franca Cortoni. Theresa serves on the editorial boards of *Aggression and Violent Behavior, British Journal of Forensic Practice, International Journal of Offender Therapy and Comparative Criminology, Sexual Abuse: A Journal of Research and Treatment* and is Associate Editor of *Journal of Sexual Aggression*.

About the Contributors

Julia Babcock, PhD, is an Associate Professor and Co-director of the Center for Couples Therapy at the University of Houston. She conducts observational and psychophysiological research on intimate partner violent couples. She has published over 30 articles on the topic of intimate partner violence and batterers' interventions. She has received federal funding for her projects and is the recipient of Texas Psychological Association 2011 Outstanding Contribution to Science Award. She also maintains a private practice specializing in couples therapy and domestic abuse.

Josilyn Banks is a Clinical Psychology PhD candidate specializing in the study of intimate relationships at the University of Houston. Her current research interests include intimate partner violence, minority relationships and the effects of intimate partner violence on children. Currently she is investigating possible ethnic biases in observational coding systems. Josilyn received a Bachelor of Arts degree in Psychology from Northwestern University where her research included intimate relationships and the aetiology and treatment of anxiety disorders in children and families.

Anthony R. Beech, DPhil, CSci, FBPsS, CPsychol, is a Professor and the Head of the Centre for Forensic and Criminological Psychology at the University of Birmingham, UK. He has authored over 140 peer-reviewed articles, 40 book chapters and 6 books in the area of forensic science/criminal justice. His particular research interests are centred on the assessment, theoretical understanding and treatment of sex offenders. In 2009, he received the Significant Achievement Award from the Association for the Treatment of Sexual Abusers in Dallas, Texas, and the Senior Award from the Division of Forensic Psychology, British Psychological Society, for recognition of his work in this area.

James Bonta, PhD, received his PhD in Clinical Psychology in 1979 and began his career as a Psychologist at a maximum security remand centre, and later as Chief Psychologist. In 1990, he joined Public Safety Canada, and he is presently Director of Corrections Research. Dr Bonta is a Fellow of the Canadian Psychological Association and recipient of the Criminal Justice Section's Career Contribution Award for 2009. His interests are in the areas of risk assessment and offender rehabilitation. He has co-authored, with the late D. A. Andrews, *The Psychology* *of Criminal Conduct* (now in its fifth edition). He is also a co-author of the various Level of Service risk/need instruments that have been translated into five languages and used by correctional systems throughout the world.

Charles M. Borduin, PhD, is a Professor of Psychology at the University of Missouri and Director of the Missouri Delinquency Project. He is the Co-developer of multisystemic therapy, which has extensive empirical support in the treatment of violence and other serious antisocial behaviours in adolescents. His research has been funded by the National Institute of Mental Health and the National Institute on Alcohol Abuse and Alcoholism. Dr Borduin has published more than 100 journal articles, chapters and books on the development and validation of effective mental health services for youth, and he has served as a National and International Consultant to government and private agencies on the reform of children's mental health services.

Fiona Clark is a Consultant Clinical Psychologist and Lead Psychologist working within the Mental Illness Directorate, Broadmoor Hospital, West London Mental Health Trust, UK. Fiona has worked as a Clinical Psychologist in high-secure forensic services for 24 years providing a range of clinical interventions to mentally disordered offenders. As part of that role, she has also run an assessment and group treatment service for firesetters with complex mental health problems.

Rachael M. Collie, MA, PGDipClinPsyc, is a Member of the Center for Learning Innovation Teaching Faculty at the University of Minnesota, Rochester, USA. She has a background in clinical psychology in New Zealand, previously working for Victoria University of Wellington, Department of Corrections, and in private practice. Areas of clinical and research interest include narcissistic personality disorder, violent offender rehabilitation and the Good Lives Model. Teaching interests include development of active-based and integrated learning curricula.

Franca Cortoni, PhD, received her PhD in clinical and forensic psychology from Queen's University at Kingston, Ontario. Since 1989, she has worked with and conducted research on male and female sexual offenders in a variety of Canadian and Australian penitentiaries and community settings. In addition, she has provided consultancy and training services in the assessment, treatment and management of sexual offenders in Canada, Australia, the United States and the United Kingdom. After many years with the Correctional Service of Canada, Dr Cortoni joined the School of Criminology at the Université de Montréal in 2007 where she is Associate Professor of Clinical Criminology. She has published and made numerous presentations at national and international conferences on issues related to the development of sexual offending behaviour, risk assessment and treatment of both male and female sexual offenders.

Leam A. Craig, BA (Hons), MSc, PhD, MAE, CSci, CPsychol, AFBPsS, EuroPsy, is a Consultant Forensic Clinical Psychologist and Partner at Forensic Psychology Practice Ltd. He is Professor (Hon) of Forensic Psychology at the Centre for Forensic and Criminological Psychology, University of Birmingham, UK. His practice includes services to forensic adult mental health units and consultancy to courts, prisons and probation services. He has extensive academic publications including five books: an authored book entitled *Assessing Risk in Sex Offenders: A Practitioners Guide* (2008), and four edited books, *Assessment and Treatment of Sex Offenders: A Handbook* (2009), *Assessment and Treatment of Sexual Offenders with*

Intellectual Disabilities: A Handbook (2010), *International Perspectives on the Assessment and Treatment of Sexual Offenders* (2011) and *Assessments in Forensic Practice: A Handbook* (2013), all published with Wiley-Blackwell. (See About the Editors section for more detail.)

Francis T. Cullen is a Distinguished Research Professor of Criminal Justice and Sociology at the University of Cincinnati, USA. His recent works include *Unsafe in the Ivory Tower: The Sexual Victimization of Women*, the *Encyclopedia of Criminological Theory*, *The Origins of American Criminology* and *Correctional Theory: Context and Consequences*. His current research focuses on the organization of criminological knowledge and on rehabilitation as a correctional policy. He is a Past President of both the American Society of Criminology and the Academy of Criminal Justice Sciences.

Andrew Day is Professor in Forensic Psychology and Director of the Forensic Psychology Centre at Deakin University, Australia. He has a clinical background, previously working as a Clinical and Forensic Psychologist in both the United Kingdom and Australia and is particularly interested in the application of psychological thought and practice to the correctional setting. Andrew is a Fellow of the Australian Psychological Society and a Member of the Colleges of Clinical and Forensic Psychology. His current research interests centre around the development of therapeutic regimes within prison settings, effective practice in Australia with offenders from Aboriginal and Torres Strait Islander cultural backgrounds and the role that anger plays in aggressive and violent behaviour.

Louise Dixon, BSc (Hons), MSc, PhD, CPsychol (Forensic), is a Senior Lecturer in Forensic Psychology at the Centre for Forensic and Criminological Psychology, University of Birmingham, UK. She is the Course Director of the Continued Professional Development route to the Doctorate in Forensic Psychology Practice. Louise enjoys an active research and publication profile and is involved in the wider international research scene. She is on the editorial board of internationally peer-reviewed journals *Child Maltreatment*, *Journal of Aggression Conflict and Peace Research* and *British Journal of Forensic Practice*. She is the E-bulletin Editor for the International Family Aggression Society (IFAS) and is Vice Chair of the West Midlands branch of the British Association for the Study and Prevention of Child Abuse and Neglect (BASPCAN). Her research interests centre on family and intimate partner violence and the role of group aggression in understanding and preventing street gang affiliation and offending. She has published numerous articles and book chapters in these domains. Louise also practises as a Forensic Psychologist, specializing in the assessment and intervention of violent adult offenders.

Rebekah Doley, BA (Hons), Grad Dip Psych Prac MSc (Inv Psy), MPsych (Clin), PhD, MAPS, MCC, AMFC, is a Clinical and Forensic Psychologist specializing in the psychology of serial firesetting. In addition to lecturing domestically and internationally on this issue, Rebekah has developed a screening instrument for firefighters which has been introduced nationally in New Zealand. Rebekah is an Assistant Professor in Psychology at Bond University, Gold Coast, Queensland, where she is the Director of the Clinical and Forensic Psychology Programs. She teaches postgraduate courses in forensic and clinical psychology, undertakes research and supervises probationary psychologists. In addition, Rebekah is Co-director of the Australian Centre for Arson Research and Treatment and also runs a successful private community-based psychology practice.

Alex R. Dopp, BA, is a doctoral student in the clinical child psychology programme at the University of Missouri. He received his Bachelor's degree in Psychology from the University of Michigan. His interests include the implementation, dissemination and economic analysis of evidence-based interventions, particularly services for the treatment and prevention of juvenile delinquency.

Deirdre D'Orazio is a Clinical Psychologist in private practice as the CEO of Central Coast Clinical and Forensic Psychology Services located in California. She has extensive experience in the Sexually Violent Predator (SVP) arena, providing treatment, assessment, training and programme consultation and development. She formerly held the position of the Director of Evaluation and Development Services, overseeing the treatment programme and forensic services for the California SVP program at Coalinga State Hospital. She is a Member of the California state SVP forensic evaluator panel. She is a Member of the Board of Directors for the California Coalition on Sexual Offending (CCOSO) as the Chairperson of the Civil Commitment Committee and the Lead Author of the CCOSO paper on the California SVP system. Dr D'Orazio's SVP-related research presently includes studies within the areas of diagnosis, risk assessment, criminogenic need and physiological indicators of psychopathy.

Vincent Egan obtained a Bachelor's degree (Hons) in Psychology from the University of London in 1984, a PhD in Psychology from the University of Edinburgh in 1991 and a Doctorate in Clinical Psychology from the University of Leicester in 1996. He is a Clinical and Forensic Psychologist. He has over 80 academic publications, is a Fellow of the British Psychological Society and a Director of the International Society for the Study of Individual Differences. The Central Nottinghamshire Health Service NHS Trust at the East Midlands Centre for Forensic Mental Health previously employed him as a Clinical Psychologist, where he worked for three years as Lead Psychologist on a personality disorder unit. He has written over 340 court reports. Previously a Director of the MSc in Forensic Psychology at Glasgow Caledonian University, he is now Course Director of the MSc in Forensic Psychology at the University of Leicester.

Katarina Fritzon, MA (Hons), MSc (Inv Psy), PhD, MAPS, AMCC, MFC, is an Associate Professor at Bond University on the Gold Coast, Australia. Katarina's research interests include the psychology of firesetting, the links between personality characteristics and offending behaviour, and female offenders. Katarina is a Co-director of the Australian Centre for Arson Research and Treatment, which has recently received funding from the Commonwealth Attorney-General's Department to develop a pilot treatment programme for firesetters, which will be the first such programme in Australia. Katarina teaches postgraduate and undergraduate programmes and supervises probationary psychologists.

Theresa A. Gannon, DPhil, CPsychol (Forensic), is Director of the Centre for Research and Education in Forensic Psychology (CORE-FP) and Professor in Forensic Psychology at the University of Kent, UK. Theresa also works as a Chartered Consultant Forensic Psychologist specializing in sexual offenders and firesetters for Kent Forensic Psychiatry Services, UK. She has published numerous chapters, articles, books and other scholarly works in the areas of male- and female-perpetrated sexual offending and firesetting. She is particularly interested in research relating to both the treatment needs and overall rehabilitation of sexual offenders. Theresa is Lead Editor of several books, including *Aggressive Offenders' Cognition: Theory, Research, and Treatment* (John Wiley & Sons) along with Professor Tony Ward, Professor Anthony Beech and Dr Dawn Fisher, and *Female Sexual Offenders: Theory, Assessment and Treatment* (Wiley-Blackwell) along with Franca Cortoni. She serves on the editorial boards of *Aggression and Violent Behavior*, *British Journal of Forensic Practice*, *International Journal of Offender Therapy and Comparative Criminology*, *Sexual Abuse: A Journal of Research and Treatment*, is Associate Editor of *Journal of Sexual Aggression* and Editor of *Psychology, Crime & Law*.

R. Karl Hanson, **PhD**, **CPsych**, is a Senior Research Scientist, Public Safety Canada and Adjunct Professor, Psychology Department, Carleton University. Dr Hanson is one of the leading researchers in the field of sexual offender risk assessment and treatment. He has published more than 130 articles, including several highly influential reviews, and is the lead author of the Static-99 and STABLE-2007 sexual offender risk assessment tools. He is a Fellow of the Canadian Psychological Association and the 2002 recipient of Significant Achievement Award from the Association for the Treatment of Sexual Offenders.

Leigh Harkins, **PhD**, is a Registered Psychologist with the UK's Health Professions Council and a Forensic Psychologist with the British Psychological Society. Dr Harkins is a Lecturer at the Centre for Forensic and Family Psychology at the University of Birmingham. She has published a number of reports, papers and book chapters, primarily in the area of sexual offender treatment effectiveness. Leigh also has experience working in forensic practice settings in the United Kingdom and Canada. Her research interests include sexual offending and group aggression.

Andrew J.R. Harris, **PhD**, **CPsych**, is Director of the Forensic Assessment Group, Ottawa, Ontario, Canada. Dr Harris did his doctoral research on the intersection of Hare's conception of criminal psychopathy and high levels of sexual deviance as assessed in a probation and parole sample. Previously employed in both research and clinical capacities at the Oak Ridge (Maximum Security) Penetanguishene Mental Health Centre, and by the Correctional Service of Canada as a Clinician at Workworth penitentiary, Dr Harris speaks and teaches extensively on the history of prison architecture, static and dynamic risk assessment, psychopathy and risk to re-offend among developmentally delayed and high-risk violent offenders.

Ruth M. Hatcher, **PhD**, is a Lecturer of Forensic Psychology in the School of Psychology at the University of Leicester, UK. Her main research interest concerns interventions for offenders delivered to offenders within community and custodial settings and their impact. In particular, she is interested in attrition from offending behaviour programmes, the reasons for it and how it impacts on offender outcomes, for example, reconviction. She is an author of the textbook *Criminal Psychology: A Beginner's Guide* (2009, 2nd edition, Oneworld) and has also written numerous book chapters and other academic publications in this and related fields.

Sarah Hilder is a Senior Lecturer at De Montfort University, extensively involved in the trainee Probation Officer programmes and Criminological Teaching at undergraduate and postgraduate levels. A former Senior Probation Officer, her practice specialism is centred on the management of high-risk offenders, court work and race equality issues. Moving across to academia in 2004, her research interests and publications have included an examination of multi-agency work with black and minority ethnic offenders, sex offender registration and public disclosure and best practice in working with victims of domestic abuse.

Sheilagh Hodgins, BA, MA, MSc, PhD (CLPsych), FRSC, has been studying antisocial and violent behaviour among people with schizophrenia for many years. Initially, she conducted investigations of large birth cohorts, showing that persons with schizophrenia were at increased risk, as compared to the general population, to engage in both non-violent and violent crimes. Subsequently, she undertook studies to identify both proximal and distal factors associated with criminality among people with schizophrenia and evaluations of treatment programmes that aimed to reduce and prevent crime. She has published numerous articles in scientific journals, books and book chapters. She currently holds faculty positions at the Institute of Psychiatry, King's College London, the Département de Psychiatrie at the Université de Montréal, and directs a research centre in Stockholm, Sweden.

Clive R. Hollin is a Professor of Criminological Psychology in the School of Psychology at The University of Leicester, UK. He wrote the best-selling textbook *Psychology and Crime: An Introduction to Criminological Psychology* (1989, Routledge), the 2nd edition of which is due to appear in 2012. In all, he has published 21 books alongside over 300 other academic publications, and he is a former editor of the journal *Psychology, Crime & Law*. Alongside his various university appointments, he has worked as a Psychologist in prisons, the Youth Treatment Service, special hospitals and regional secure units. In 1998, he received The Senior Award for Distinguished Contribution to the Field of Legal, Criminological and Forensic Psychology from The British Psychological Society.

Cheryl Lero Jonson is an Assistant Professor of Criminal Justice at Xavier University. She recently received her PhD from the University of Cincinnati, USA. She has co-authored *Correctional Theory: Context and Consequences* and co-edited *The Origins of American Criminology*. Her recent work has appeared in *Crime and Justice: A Review of Research*, *Criminology and Public Policy* and *Victims and Offenders*. Her research interests include public opinion, the criminogenic effects of incarceration, early intervention and correctional rehabilitation.

Hazel Kemshall is a Professor of Community and Criminal Justice at De Montfort University. She has research interests in risk assessment and management of offenders, effective work in multi-agency public protection and implementing effective practice with high-risk offenders. Hazel teaches and consults extensively on public protection and high-risk offenders. She has also completed research for the Economic and Social Research Council, the Home Office, Ministry of Justice, the Scottish Government and the Risk Management Authority. She has numerous publications on risk, including *Understanding Risk in Criminal Justice* (2003, Open University Press). She is the lead author of the CD *Risk of Harm Guidance and Training Resource* for the English and Welsh National Offender Management Service, and for the *Assessment and Management of Risk* CD in Scotland for the Risk Management Authority. She was recently appointed to the Parole Board Review Committee. Her most recent book, *Understanding the Community Management of High Risk Offenders*, was published by the Open University in 2008.

Sheetal Kini is a Clinical Psychology PhD candidate specializing in the study of emotions in marriage and intimate relationships at the University of Houston. Her current research interests include intimate partner violence and the impact of domestic violence on children. Empirical projects include typologies of the functions of men's violence. Sheetal received a Bachelor of Science degree in Psychology from College of William and Mary where her research included aggression in intimate relationships and marriage and family therapy.

Nathan Kolla, BA, BSc (Med), MA, MSc, MD, FRCP(C), is a Staff Forensic Psychiatrist at the Centre for Addiction and Mental Health in Toronto and a Lecturer in Psychiatry at the University of Toronto. He recently completed subspecialty training in forensic psychiatry at New York University following general psychiatry residency training at the University of Toronto. Dr Kolla received his undergraduate and medical degrees both with great distinction from the University of Saskatchewan. When he received his Bachelor's degree, he was awarded the President's Medal as the University's most distinguished graduate. Dr Kolla has a Master's degree in Sociology from the University of Toronto and a Master's degree in Forensic Mental Health Science from the Institute of Psychiatry, King's College London. He holds a Canadian Institute of Health Research Phase I Clinician Scientist Award and a research fellowship from the American Psychiatric Association.

William R. Lindsay, PhD, CPsychol, FBPsS, is a Consultant Forensic Clinical Psychologist and Lead Clinician in Scotland for Castlebeck Care. He was previously Head of Psychology (LD) in NHS Tayside and a Consultant with the State Hospital, Carstairs. He is Professor of Learning Disabilities and Forensic Psychology at the University of Abertay, Dundee, and Visiting Professor at the University of Northumbria, Newcastle. He has published over 200 research articles and book chapters and given many presentations and workshops on cognitive therapy and the assessment and treatment of offenders with intellectual disabilities. His recent publications include *Assessment and Treatment of Sexual Offenders with Intellectual Disabilities: A Handbook* (Craig, Lindsay and Browne, 2011), *The Treatment of Sex Offenders with Developmental Disabilities: A Practice Workbook* (2009) and *Offenders with Developmental Disabilities* (Lindsay, Taylor and Sturmey, 2004), all by Wiley-Blackwell.

Jennifer L. Lux is a PhD candidate in Criminal Justice at the University of Cincinnati, where she also holds the position of Research Associate in the Corrections Institute. She has recently published on the empirical status of multisystemic therapy and on public support for rehabilitation. Her research interests include evidence-based corrections and effective offender intervention in community settings.

Liam E. Marshall, PhD, has been treating and conducting research on offenders for more than 15 years. He has been a therapist for and helped design a variety of programmes for adult and juvenile sexual offenders, as well as anger management, domestic violence, gambling, pro-social attitudes and lifestyle programmes. Liam is an award-winning author and has many publications including three books. He has made numerous international conference presentations on sexual offending, violence, aging and pathological gambling issues. Liam is an Associate Editor for the *Journal of Sexual Offender Treatment*, is on the editorial boards of the *Journal of Sexual Aggression* and *Sexual Addiction and Compulsivity* and is an Invited

Reviewer for the journals *Sexual Abuse: A Journal of Research and Treatment*, the *Journal of Sexual Medicine* and *Journal of Gambling Studies*. He is currently a Therapist and Training and Research Director for Rockwood Psychological Services, a Consultant to the Royal Ottawa Health Care Group and Evaluation and Intervention Consultant for the St. Lawrence Youth Association, Canada. Liam has delivered more than 70 trainings for therapists who work with sexual and violent offenders in 15 countries worldwide.

William L. Marshall, **OC**, **FRSC**, **PhD**, has been involved in research and treatment of sexual offenders for 42 years. He is on, or has been on, the editorial boards of 19 international scientific journals and has over 370 publications including 18 books. Bill has been Consultant to and/or provided training for prison services and sexual offender programmes in over 20 countries, and to seven Sexual Violent Predator or Civil Commitment Programmes in the United States. Bill was President of the Association for the Treatment of Sexual Abusers (ATSA) from 1999 to 2001 and is currently President of the International Association for the Treatment of Sexual Offenders. In 1993, Bill was given a Significant Achievement Award of ATSA; in 1999, he was recipient of the Santiago Grisolia Prize awarded by the Queen Sophia Centre in Spain for his significant worldwide contributions to the reduction of violence; in 2000, Bill was appointed a Fellow of the Royal Society of Canada for his contributions to science; in 2003, he was given the Pope John Paul medal for his assistance to the Vatican's Academia Pro Vita's design of a protocol for dealing with sexual abuse committed by clergy and religious members of the Catholic Church; and in 2006, Bill was appointed an Officer of the Order of Canada for his national and international contributions to making society safer.

Flora I. Matheson, **PhD**, is a Research Sociologist with a Doctorate from the University of Toronto. Dr Matheson specializes in crime, deviance and socio-legal studies. She has extensive experience in research focusing on marginalized populations, specifically offenders and illicit drug users. Dr Matheson uses a gender lens when examining social determinants of health and problem behaviours. She is a Research Scientist at the Centre for Research on Inner City Health at The Keenan Research Centre in the Li Ka Shing Knowledge Institute of St. Michael's Hospital. She is also an Adjunct Scientist in the Primary Care and Population Health and the Mental Health and Addictions Programs at the Institute for Clinical and Evaluative Sciences. Dr Matheson is also an Assistant Professor with the Dalla Lana School of Public Health, University of Toronto.

James McGuire, **PhD**, **CPsychol**, **AFBPsS**, is a Professor of Forensic Clinical Psychology and Director of the Doctorate in Clinical Psychology at the University of Liverpool. He also holds an Honorary Consultant post with Mersey Care NHS Trust. He previously worked in a high-security hospital and has carried out psycho-legal work involving assessment of individuals for criminal courts, for the Mental Health Review Tribunal, Parole Board and Criminal Cases Review Commission. He has conducted research in probation services, prisons and other settings on aspects of psychosocial rehabilitation with offenders, has published widely on this and related issues and has acted as a Consultant to criminal justice agencies in a number of countries.

Amanda M. Michie, **PhD**, is Head of Clinical Psychology Services in Lothian NHS Learning Disability Service. She has completed research in the assessment and treatment of social and community living skills and in the last 10 years has worked with offenders with learning disabilities. Her clinical and research interests include sex offenders, anger management and cognitive-behavioural therapy.

Andrea E. Moser, PhD, is qualified in Clinical/Counselling Psychology from York University and is currently the Director of the Addictions Research Centre, Correctional Service of Canada (CSC). Dr Moser started her career with CSC in 1993 as a Psychologist working with offenders with mental disorders at the Regional Treatment Centre in Ontario. She has been at CSC National Headquarters since 1997 and has held a variety of positions, including National Manager of Substance Abuse Programs, National Drug Strategy Coordinator, National Manager of Violence Prevention Programs and National Coordinator of Institutional and Community Mental Health Initiatives. Dr Moser has published several articles and presented in the areas of mental health, substance abuse treatment and effective correctional programming.

Raymond W. Novaco, PhD, is Professor of Psychology and Social Behavior at the University of California, Irvine, USA. He pioneered the cognitive-behavioral treatment of anger, for which he received the Best Contribution Award from the International Society for Research on Aggression in 1978. Funded by the MacArthur Foundation Research Network on Mental Health and the Law in 1991–1993, he developed anger assessment procedures for use with mentally disordered persons, which have been extended to those with intellectual disabilities. He received the Distinguished Contributions to Psychology Award from the California Psychological Association in 2000 and the Distinguished Academic Contributions Award from the Division of Forensic Psychology of the British Psychological Society in 2009. His ongoing research includes assessment and treatment studies in England and Scotland forensic hospitals, with US military combat veterans, and with women and children in domestic violence facilities.

Matt D. O'Brien, MSc, CPsychAssoc, has worked with sexual offenders for the past 17 years. He is currently a Therapist for Rockwood Psychological Services' Preparatory, Regular, Deniers and Maintenance programmes for sexual offenders in two Canadian Federal prisons. He also provides clinical supervision for community mental health staff working with juvenile offenders at St. Lawrence Youth Association, Canada. Matt previously worked in the delivery and design of offending behaviour programmes, primarily with sexual offenders, in Her Majesty's Prison Service (of England and Wales) for 10 years. Matt has many publications including being Co-author of a recent book on sexual offender treatment. He has presented at numerous international conferences and trained and consulted with staff in a number of different jurisdictions. Matt's specific topics of interest include healthy sexuality and Internet offending.

Emma J. Palmer, PhD, is a Reader in Forensic Psychology in the School of Psychology at the University of Leicester, UK. Her research interests include the design and effectiveness of interventions with offenders, offender risk and needs assessments and the development of offending. She has published extensively in these areas in academic journals and book chapters. She is the author of the text *Offending Behaviour: Moral Reasoning, Criminal Conduct and the Rehabilitation of Offenders* (2003; Willan Publishing) and Co-editor (with

Clive Hollin) of the book *Offending Behaviour Programmes: Development, Application and Controversies* (2006; John Wiley & Sons).

Geris A. Serran, PhD, has worked in treatment and research with sexual offenders for 12 years and is currently employed at Rockwood Psychological Services as the Clinical Director of the sexual offender treatment programmes at Bath Institution (a medium-security federal penitentiary), Canada. She has 43 publications, has co-edited and co-authored two books, has presented at numerous international conferences and has consulted internationally. She is on the editorial board for the *Journal of Sexual Aggression*. Geris' research interests include therapeutic processes, coping strategies, maladaptive schemas and treatment of sexual offenders. Geris is also a part-time Faculty Member at St. Lawrence College, Canada, where she provides supervision for student projects and teaches behavioural counselling.

Richard Shuker is a Forensic Psychologist and Head of Psychology and Research at HMP Grendon, a therapeutic community prison for personality-disordered offenders. He has managed cognitive-behavioural treatment programmes within adult and young offender prisons and is Lead Clinician on the assessment unit at Grendon. His research interests needs assessment and treatment of high-risk offenders. He is Series Editor for the book series *Issues in Forensic Psychology* and has publications in the areas of risk assessment, treatment outcome and therapeutic communities. He has recently co-edited a book on Grendon's work, research and outcomes.

Erin K. Taylor, MA, is a doctoral student in the clinical child psychology programme at the University of Missouri. She received her Master's degree in Clinical Psychology from the University of Missouri and her Bachelor's degree with a Research Concentration in Psychology from Vanderbilt University. Her research interests include gender differences in psycho-pathology and juvenile offending as well as family therapy process and outcome.

Jenny Tew is a Registered Psychologist with the UK's Health Professions Council and a Chartered Forensic Psychologist with the British Psychological Society. Jenny works for the National Offender Management Service in the United Kingdom and is the Lead for psycho-pathy and the PCL-R. She has worked in both custody and community forensic settings in the United Kingdom, including HMP Grendon therapeutic community prison. Jenny is currently undertaking a PhD in the assessment and treatment of psychopathy with the Centre for Forensic and Criminological Psychology at the University of Birmingham.

Jo Thakker, PhD, is a Senior Lecturer in psychology at the University of Waikato in Hamilton, New Zealand. She received her PhD in psychology from Canterbury University in New Zealand in 1997 and has since worked in both clinical and university settings. Most of her clinical work has been with offenders in prisons in Australia and New Zealand. Her key research areas include cultural psychology, substance use and abuse and sexual offenders. She also has a background in theoretical research.

David Thornton, PhD, is currently Treatment Director for the Wisconsin SVP programme, a position he has held for about a decade. Prior to that, he worked in the United Kingdom facilitating the development of assessment and treatment programmes for offenders. As part of this, he was involved in the creation of evidence-based accreditation standards for correctional programmes. He carries out research into sexual and violent offenders. He is also an Advisor to the DSM-5 workgroup developing the next generation of diagnostic criteria for paraphilias.

Tony Ward, PhD, DipClinPsyc, is a Professor of Clinical Psychology at Victoria University of Wellington, New Zealand. He has authored over 310 academic publications. Professor Ward is the developer of the Good Lives Model (GLM) and has published numerous books, book chapters and academic articles on this model since 2002. He is currently working on a research project with Dr Gwenda Willis and Dr Jill Levenson investigating the degree to which North American treatment programmes for sex offenders adhere to the basic conceptual underpinnings of the GLM. His most recent book, *Desistance from Sex Offending: Alternatives to Throwing Away the Keys* (2011, Guilford Press: co-authored with Richard Laws), presents an integration of the GLM with desistance theory and research.

John R. Weekes, PhD, has worked in corrections, criminal justice and forensic psychology for over 25 years. Dr Weekes is trained as both a Clinical and Research Psychologist and holds a Doctorate in Quantitative Experimental Psychology from Ohio University. Since 1994, he has been Adjunct Professor of Forensic Psychology and Addictions at Carleton University in Ottawa, Ontario. He teaches courses in forensic psychology and addictions and supervises students. Dr Weekes has consulted widely in Canada and elsewhere, including England, Ireland, the United States and Scandinavia. Between 2003 and 2006, he was Senior Researcher for the Canadian Centre on Substance Abuse. Dr Weekes has published and presented extensively on a range of issues, including substance abuse, forensic psychology, psychopathology, motivation, evidence-informed treatment and treatment-outcome research.

Michael Wheatley is a registered, qualified Social Worker and experienced Commissioner employed by the National Offender Management Service (NOMS) to lead NOMS Offender Services Co-Commissioning Group on prison substance misuse commissioning. In this role, he works with government ministers, other government departments, other NOMS directorates, prison governors, local health commissioners and service providers to support the design, development and implementation of bespoke substance misuse services. Previously, Michael was a Senior Manager responsible for delivering, co-ordinating and supporting the commissioning of interventions designed to reduce reoffending in high-security prisons. He has also worked as a Community Probation Officer. Michael has a BA in Applied Social Studies, a Certificate in Qualified Social Work (Sheffield Hallam University) and an MSt in Applied Criminology, Penology and Prison Management from Cambridge University.

Gwenda M. Willis is a Research Fellow at Deakin University, Australia, and a registered Clinical Psychologist. Her research focuses on the tertiary prevention of sexual offending and canvasses sex offender treatment, community re-entry and community/policy responses to sex offenders. Gwenda has received numerous awards and accolades for her research, including the Association for the Treatment of Sexual Abusers (ATSA) Graduate Research Award (2007), a MacDiarmid Young Scientists of the Year Award (2008) and a Fulbright Senior Scholar Award (2010).

J. Stephen Wormith is a Professor in the Psychology Department at the University of Saskatchewan (United States) and Director of the Centre of Forensic Behavioural Science and

moral community are entitled to adequate ...
offenders' decisions that arguably affect them how ...
assist offenders to desist and live socially acceptable ...
value laden enterprise ... ...
resources and an obligation only for recovering ...
involve legal, social and moral norms and institutions ...
from incarceration to community reintegration.

What follows from these observations ... Well, for one ...
what types of programmes work best to reduce offending ...
Alongside these questions it is also important to consider whether ...
or not the entitlements and interests of key stakeholders ...
and members of the community alike ... ... a role ... Clinicians are experts in which specific technology best reduce ...
in ethical, social and legal terms. We need to cast aside the ...
that draws from cultural, social, legal ... moral understanding ...

*... ... ... within their own expertise and expertise
Assessment and Treatment ... ... this unique demand their ... ...
exactly that. It is a comprehensive and ...*

... Blackwell for their patience and encouraging ...
... thank you to those ... ... support ...
treatment, and others that touch upon ... the attitudes ... ...
tion. Many of the chapters emphasis integrative, eclectic ...
of assessment and treatment approaches to individuals ...
book is the sheer diversity of theoretical perspectives ...
of the necessity to evaluate treatment programmes and ...
also a recognition that empirical adequacy matters, ...
programme's value. Finally, the editors should be ...
established and young researchers and clinicians an ...
ness and intellectual experience. What this book offers ...
while pointing the way to future developments. I believe ...
likely to be adopted by numerous trainee clinicians ...
as a resource for practitioners already working in the ...

References

Andrews, D. and Bonta, J. (2010) *The Psychology of Criminal* ...
  Newark ...
Laws, D.R. and Ward, T. (2011) *Desistance from Sexual Offending* ...
  Key, The Guilford Press, New York.
McNeill, F. (2012) Four forms of offender rehabilitation ...
  Legal and Criminological Psychology, 17, 18 ...
Polaschek, D.L.L. (2012) An appraisal of the risk-need-responsivity ...
  itation and its application to treatment ... *Legal* ...
Ward, T. and Maruna, S. (2007) *Rehabilitation*, Routledge, ...

Part I
Introduction

1

Overview and Structure of the Book

Leam A. Craig[1,2], Louise Dixon[2] and Theresa A. Gannon[3]

[1]Forensic Psychology Practice Ltd, UK
[2]University of Birmingham, UK
[3]University of Kent, UK

Introduction

The concept and public perception of offender rehabilitation has had a chequered history, influenced by the social and political climate of the day. From the early introduction of penitentiary, public and government opinion has had to strike a balance between punishment and rehabilitation (see Reynolds, Craig and Boer, 2009). Early research suggests there is a 'duality' to the public's sanctioning ideology – 'although citizens clearly want offenders punished, they continue to believe that offenders should be rehabilitated' (Cullen, Cullen and Wozniak, 1988, p. 305). The public juxtaposition is one of getting tough on crime and that punishment should be accompanied by rehabilitation, that treatment can work and that prison inmates should be given the opportunity to reform themselves. This two-pronged finding, support for the 'just deserts' theory of punishment along with the 'need for rehabilitation', suggests that public attitudes towards crime are not one-dimensional. Instead, underlying the need for retribution is an element of optimism for offenders to reform and become participating members of society.

However, the concept of change and rehabilitation took a blow during the 1970s following the publication of Martinson's (1974) much-cited review in which he believed education or therapeutic intervention programmes cannot overcome the tendency for offenders to continue to engage in criminal behaviour. This was followed by the work of Lipton, Martinson and Wilks (1975) and Brody (1976) who suggested, due to poor methodologies and research designs, that the evidence for offender rehabilitation cannot be relied upon.

In response to the assumption that 'nothing works' in rehabilitation and reducing tendencies in offenders to continue criminal behaviour, the 1980s and 1990s witnessed a resurgence of research activity into offender assessment and treatment, and a number of theoretical advances have been made progressing our understanding of offender rehabilitation. New techniques such as meta-analyses marked a turning point in the understanding of reducing reoffending

What Works in Offender Rehabilitation: An Evidence-Based Approach to Assessment and Treatment,
First Edition. Edited by Leam A. Craig, Louise Dixon and Theresa A. Gannon.
© 2013 John Wiley & Sons, Ltd. Published 2013 by John Wiley & Sons, Ltd.

(Andrews *et al.*, 1990). This methodology allowed for the analysis of data from multiple studies identifying significant factors associated with offending from which treatment targets could be identified.

Addressing the methodological concerns raised by Lipton, Martinson and Wilks (1975) and Brody (1976), research into offender rehabilitation has culminated in a 'what works' research literature – *The Psychology of Criminal Conduct* (Andrews and Bonta, 1994, 1998, 2003, 2006, 2010), *What Works: Reducing Reoffending* (McGuire, 1995), *Offender Rehabilitation and Treatment: Effective Programmes and Policies to Reduce Reoffending* (McGuire, 2002), *Offender Rehabilitation in Practice: Implementing and Evaluating Effective Programmes* (Bernfield, Farrington and Leschied, 2001) and *Offending Behaviour Programmes: Development, Application and Controversies* (Hollin and Palmer, 2006) – the emphasis of which was evidence-based practice and empirical rigour.

Evaluating Offender Rehabilitation

'Rehabilitation' means literally 're-enabling' or 'making fit again' (from the Latin *rehabilitare*). Some argue that it is, in part, the definitional ambiguities of the concept of 'rehabilitation' which have contributed to the difficulties faced in criminal justice settings. As McNeill (2012) highlights, rehabilitation in the work of eighteenth-century Classicists (e.g., Beccaria, 1764[1963]) who argued for the use of punishment as a way of 'requalifying individuals' (p. 22) suggests a *utilitarian* concept of rehabilitation.

The term 'rehabilitation', we suggest, in the prison context means readying prisoners to rejoin society, as useful and law-abiding members of the wider community. With an ever-expanding prison population, the successful rehabilitation of offenders is often considered the 'holy grail' of criminal justice systems around the world. The number of offenders in prison in England and Wales reached a record high of 88 179 prisoners on 2 December 2011, approximately 1100 places below the useable operational capacity of the prison estate (Berman, 2012). The number of people in Scottish prisons passed 8000 for the first time in August 2008 and reached its record level of 8301 on 7 November 2011 (Berman, 2012).

As part of the push towards reducing reoffending and offender rehabilitation, a number of countries have begun to introduce structured intervention programmes in prison and probation services. The introduction of programmes has been accompanied by an 'accreditation' process to select the programmes thought most likely to achieve good results, and an elaborate system of monitoring standards of delivery and evaluating outcomes has been developed.

With the American Psychological Association (APA), Chambless and colleagues (Chambless and Hollon, 1998; Chambless and Ollendick, 2001; Chambless *et al.*, 1998) developed a methodology of examining the quality of evidence from outcome studies on the effectiveness of psychological therapy. One outcome of the APA criteria was that treatment should be supported by a manual to ensure consistency and standardization across sites.

In a report to the US Congress, Sharman *et al.* (1997) developed a 'levels' system for reviewing the quality of evidence supporting any given intervention in the field of criminal behaviour. They developed and employed the Maryland Scale of Scientific Methods ranking each study from Level I (weakest) to Level V (strongest) on overall internal validity. Level I represents correlation between a crime prevention programme and a measure of crime, or crime risk factors, at a single point in time. Level II represents a temporal sequence between the programme and the crime or risk outcome clearly observed, or the presence of a comparison group without demonstrated comparability to the treatment group. Level III represents a comparison between two or more comparable units of analysis, one with and one without the programme. Level IV represents comparison between multiple units with and without the programme, controlling for other factors, or using comparison units that evidence only minor differences. Level V represents random assignment and analysis of comparable units to programme and comparison groups. As part of the evaluation, they categorized programmes into 'what works', 'what does not work', 'what is promising' and 'what is unknown'. They identified 15 programmes (including vocational training, rehabilitation programmes with risk-focused treatments and therapeutic community treatment programmes) on the list of 'what works' and 23 on the list of 'what does not'. The longest list, however, is the 30 'promising programmes'. They argued that if even half of these programmes were found effective with one additional Level III impact evaluation, the number of programmes known to prevent crime through the scientific standards included in their review would double.

The Cochrane Collaboration created in 1993 has been influential in the United Kingdom in categorizing evidence on the effectiveness of psychological and pharmaceutical interventions from different studies. The Cochrane Database of Systematic Reviews has led to the Cochrane Library (www.thecochranelibrary.com) which lists relevant research studies and treatment evaluations.

In England and Wales, the *Crime Reduction Programme* (2000) was introduced as part of an initiative into large-scale offender rehabilitation. As part of a review of correctional services in England and Wales, Carter (2003) concluded that rehabilitation has an important role to play in the prison regime:

> well-designed, well-run and well-targeted rehabilitation programmes can reduce reconviction rates by 5–10 per cent… The maximum effect is achieved when programmes target a spectrum of risk factors – employment and education, along with behavioural or cognitive programmes. Although drug treatment is difficult, evidence suggests that it can be cost-effective in reducing crime and social harms. (p. 16)

However, Carter's optimism of the success of offender change programmes was measured against the concerns of the scalability of some rehabilitative programmes and the extent to which pilot programmes can be maintained on a large scale. Indeed, the Carter report also highlighted systematic failures in the implementation of the programmes, and in response to the review in 2004, the UK government announced the development of the National Offender Management Service (NOMS) which would have the twin aims of reducing reoffending and providing end-to-end management of offenders. As part of a gradual introduction of structured programmes in prison and probation services, a set of criteria was drawn up to assess the structure and delivery of intervention programmes. These criteria were based on what the research has identified to be those most reliably associated with better results in terms of reducing reoffending. A Correctional Services Accreditation Panel (CSAP), made up of independent group of experts, was appointed to examine and 'accredit' prospective programmes. The CSAP is a non-statutory body that helps the Ministry of Justice develop and implement high-quality 'accredited' offender change programmes. The measure that enabled the accreditation process to be brought in-house was included in the Offender Management Act which received Royal Assent in July 2007. This initiative led to the development of 'accredited offender change programmes'. As part of the accreditation process, emphasis was placed on treatment efficacy and revaluation, often recorded as a reduction in reconviction. Programmes such as Think First, Reasoning and Rehabilitation (R&R) and Enhanced Thinking Skills (ETS) have been empirically reviewed and evaluated (McDougall, 2009; Palmer *et al.*, 2007), demonstrating a reduction in reoffending behaviour. Positive results have also been reported for other structured interventions such as the Cognitive Self Change Programme (CSCP) (Baro, 1999; Dowden and Andrews, 2000) and the Sex Offender Treatment Programme (SOTP) (Beech, Mandeville-Norden and Goodwill, 2012; Harkins and Beech, 2007). In a review of intervention programmes, 11 different interventions for violent offenders showed that they led to reductions in both general and violent reconviction (Jolliffe and Farrington, 2007). Comparing those offenders who participated in interventions to those who did not, there was an 8–11% reduction in general reconviction and 7–8% in violent reconviction. The review showed that interventions using cognitive-behavioural approaches were more effective than those which did not. Well-designed, high-intensity cognitive-behavioural programmes have been shown to reduce recidivism by at least 20% (Dowden and Andrews, 2000).

Theoretical Underpinnings of Offender Rehabilitation

The development of accredited programmes was based on the theoretical underpinning that offending behaviour could be predicted based on known associated risk factors, the treatment of which would reduce the likelihood of reoffending. One of the more influential models is that of the Risk–Need–Responsivity model (RNR; Andrews and Bonta, 2003; Andrews, Bonta and Wormith, 2006; Andrews and Dowden, 2006; Andrews *et al.*, 1990; Gendreau and Andrews, 2001) of offender rehabilitation. Operationalized throughout the world, including Canada, the United States, the United Kingdom, Europe, Australia and New Zealand, the RNR model represents an evolution in offender assessment and treatment. As an empirically driven approach, the model represents a methodology of risk and classification of offenders for treatment, based on the concept that early criminal behaviour can be predicted, that risk interacts with level of treatment intensity and targets in influencing treatment outcome (i.e., recidivism) and that these factors interact with offender-based factors in influencing outcome (Andrews and Bonta, 2003).

The model considers three core principles, risk, need and responsivity, designed to guide offender rehabilitation. The risk principle suggests that offenders at higher risk for reoffending will benefit most from higher levels of intervention, including high-intensity treatment, and that lower-risk offenders should receive minimal, routine or no intervention. The need principle refers to targets for change and proposes that only those factors associated with reductions in recidivism (i.e., criminogenic needs) should be targeted in intervention. Such factors include: antisocial attitudes, antisocial associates, antisocial temperament/personality, history of diverse antisocial behaviour, family/marital circumstances, social/work, leisure/recreation and substance use, identified from meta-analytical results (Andrews and Bonta, 1994, 1998). Finally, the responsivity principle states that intervention programmes should be matched to offender characteristics such as learning style, level of motivation and the individual's personal and interpersonal circumstances. The model suggests that the first two principles (risk and need) are used to select treatment intensity and targets, and the whole set is used to guide the way practice is actually implemented. A fourth principle, that of professional discretion, allows for clinical judgement to override the three principles if circumstances warrant. There is a well-established literature on the effectiveness of the RNR model in targeting offenders based on levels of risk and matching them with treatment intensity (Beech, Mandeville-Norden and Goodwill, 2012).

However, the assumption that the RNR model is the most effective way to successfully tackle offending behaviour is starting to be questioned (Polaschek, 2012). Recently, Ward, Mann and Gannon (2007) note that current approaches regarding the identification of risk factors in treatment reduce the level of these risk factors akin to a pincushion approach, where 'each risk factor constitutes a pin and treatment focuses on the removal of each risk factor' (p. 88). Therefore, what has been rarely considered in this work are the relative strengths that individuals have to prevent themselves reoffending. New methods for treatment targeting specific offence pathways are also starting to be described (Ward, Yates and Long, 2006). Ward and colleagues (i.e., Ward and Gannon, 2006) have suggested an alternative to the more traditional approaches to treatment, that is termed the 'Good Lives Model' (GLM) approach, which is concerned with taking a positivistic approach to treatment. Ward and Gannon (2006) note that in the GLM, an individual is hypothesized to commit criminal offences because he lacks the opportunities and/or the capabilities to realize valued outcomes in personally fulfilling and socially acceptable ways. The GLM suggests that human beings are naturally inclined to seek certain types of experiences or 'human goods' and experience high levels of well-being if these goods are obtained. Ward and Maruna (2007) note that primary goods are defined as states of affairs, states of mind, personal characteristics, activities or experiences that are sought for their own sake and are likely to achieve psychological well-being if achieved.

There are three levels or components to the GLM: (i) a set of general principles and assumptions that specify the values underlying rehabilitation practice and the kind of overall aims for which clinicians should be striving; (ii) the implications of these general assumptions for explaining and understanding (sexual) offending and its functions and (iii) the treatment implications of a focus on goals (goods), self-regulation strategies and ecological variables.

Therefore, the positive psychology approach attempts to promote human welfare by concentrating on strengths in an individual rather than focusing on deficits (Ward, Polaschek and Beech, 2006). Or to put it more succinctly, the application of positive psychology is the optimization of human functioning (Linley and Joseph, 2004). Ward, Polaschek and Beech also note that those taking a positive psychology approach (see Snyder and Lopez, 2005) contend that human beings are naturally predisposed to seek out things that make them feel good, and that it is the expression of essential human qualities such as love, work, interpersonal skills, aesthetic sensibilities, perseverance, courage, forgiveness, originality, spirituality, talents and wisdom that yields happiness, psychological well-being and fulfilment. Thus, the attainment of these goals is important to concentrate on in work with individuals. Here, a number of authors have focused on different aspects of positive psychology, such as: strengths-based approaches (e.g., human and environmental), emotion-focused work (e.g., resilience, happiness, self-esteem within individuals), cognition-focused work (e.g., creativity, well-being, self-efficacy), self-based (e.g., the pursuit of authenticity, uniqueness seeking and humility), interpersonal (e.g., compassion, empathy and altruism), biological (e.g., toughness) and specific adaptive coping approaches (e.g., the search for meaning, humour and spirituality in life). Therefore, even though positive psychology is a relatively new discipline, a number of books have already been written on the subject (see Aspinall and Stadinger, 2003; Joseph and Linley, 2006; Linley and Joseph, 2004; Snyder and Lopez, 2005).

This approach resonates with the developing movement of 'desistance' from offending, which is defined as an event, or a process emerging from maturational development, or shifts in personal narratives and cognitive transformation (Laws and Ward, 2011). Desistance is centred around an individual carrying out a fundamental, and intentional, shift in their sense of self (e.g., cognitive transformation) and their place in society (Maruna, 2001). This process of 'making good' involves: (i) establishing the 'real me', (ii) having an optimistic perception of self-control over one's destiny and (iii) the desire to be productive and give something back to society. Therefore, important determinants of desisting are an overall increase in acceptance of responsibility for one's actions, an increased optimism and an ability to find positives in negative situations. This emphasizes the importance of an individual's strengths in terms of positive psychological characteristics, such as self-efficacy and an internal locus of control (Craig, Browne and Beech, 2008).

From a desistance perspective, effective interventions involve the reintegration of offenders into the community, and the various skills they acquire while in therapy help in this process. Laws and Ward (2011) have integrated the research on desistance with the GLM of offender rehabilitation in the sex offender literature. Farmer, Beech and Ward (2012) recently considered the process of desistance in two groups of child molesters: one group was deemed to be *desisting* and the other group was deemed as being still potentially *active* offenders. Desisters appeared to be moderately more confident in their own self-efficacy. Pre-existing themes of *Redemption, Communion* and *Agency* clearly identified the desisting group compared to the (potentially) active offender group. The desisting group also demonstrated a greater sense of Agency (i.e., higher internal locus of control), which may also be important in explaining their apparent refusal to further offend. The desisting group also showed more belief in their own personal efficacy and their ability to control events in their lives. They were vocal about how things had changed for the better, and were able to talk about the way their views of themselves and their lives had changed in clinically significant ways.

Arguably most of the decisive rehabilitation work is done outside therapy, with the assistance of friends, community agencies and educational personnel. Essentially, this rehabilitation work involves the utilization of social and cultural resources and societal reactions to the stigmatization of convictions (Maruna, 2011), known as social capital. This resonates with McNeill (2012) and McNeill and Weaver (2010) who suggest that rehabilitation is a social project as well as a personal one, insufficiently explained, but nevertheless supported, by models such as RNR. Desistance research that focuses on social bonds has consistently shown that important life events such as obtaining a job, marriage, having supportive peers, receiving training or an education are decisive factors in individuals desisting from crime. As McNeill (2012) argues, rehabilitative interventions are important but *supporting* roles in the wider enterprise of desistance. That is to say, rehabilitative interventions do not cause change but they may support it.

In light of the theoretical and empirical advancements being made, the field of offender rehabilitation is a rapidly expanding area of interest. There is growing evidence that correctional programmes are effective, and there is an increasing literature on the effectiveness of rehabilitative programmes for juvenile offenders (e.g., Borduin *et al.*, 2011; Dowden and Andrews, 1999), violent offenders (e.g., Polaschek and Dixon, 2001) and sexual offenders (e.g., Beech, Mandeville-Norden and Goodwill, 2012; Hall, 1995; Hanson *et al.*, 2002). A growing sense of optimism may be warranted, given the 'nothing works' sentiments of the 1970s, from the preponderance of effectiveness data in the late 1990s and early 2000s.

Structure of the Book

The book is divided into a number of parts as follows.

Part One: Introduction

Chapter 2 of the introductory part of the book is by James McGuire who provides a historical overview of the 'what works' movement. He begins by surveying what has become a sizeable corpus of research findings that has amassed, the largest proportion of which concentrates on intervention programmes and whether or not they have 'worked', that is, reduced subsequent recidivism. He describes the review of 91 meta-analyses or systematic reviews of individually focused treatment-outcome studies on reducing criminal recidivism or antisocial behaviour, the majority of the results of which demonstrate positive effect sizes in reducing reoffending. He goes on to examine the fate of some of the policy impacts of the earlierphase of 'what works' findings before considering the research on extra-programmatic factors, related to risk assessment and allocation, attrition, programme integrity, quality of delivery and other organizational dimensions that were neglected during the initial phase of applying the findings of research reviews. He highlights the importance of four inter-related levels, respectively pertaining to the *client, programme, organization* and *society* as part of a systemic change. McGuire concludes by considering the treatment of psychopaths and the field of cognitive and social neuroscience as a method to further advance our understanding of cognitive processes and behavioural change.

This is followed by Chapter 3 by Cheryl Jonson, Francis Cullen and Jennifer Lux who examine the importance of public support regarding offender rehabilitation. Jonson and colleagues begin by reviewing the results of opinion polls suggesting that the public are punitive in their response to offenders (e.g., by showing support for capital punishment). They then examine research suggesting that, although the public will endorse punitive sanctions when questioned in a particular manner, they also appear to hold more progressive attitudes towards rehabilitation. It seems that when questioning is purposefully broad, the public's attitudes are revealed as being somewhat more complex, and somewhat more pro-rehabilitation across a diverse range of offenders (i.e., juveniles, non-violent offenders, sexual offenders). Jonson and colleagues argue that policy makers generally overestimate the public's punitive attitudes regarding offender rehabilitation and that researchers should continue to design rigorous research and disseminate this research to show policy makers the true extent of the public's attitudes. In Jonson and colleagues' own words, doing so 'creates the ideological space needed to propose and implement policies'.

Part Two: What Works in Offender Assessment

This part begins with Chapter 4 where James Bonta and Stephen Wormith explore the RNR principles in aiding offender assessment. Here they describe the history of offender risk assessment and provide an overview of the role of theory and the RNR model. They go onto describe the Level of Service instruments as a practical application of RNR before discussing future challenges and potential solutions in this area. The authors conclude that although major advances in the accuracy and usefulness of risk assessment technology have been made, further improvement is possible. They suggest that a General Personality and Cognitive Social Learning theory, and the theory-driven RNR model, can pioneer these improvements.

This is followed by Chapter 5 in which Leam Craig, Anthony Beech and Franca Cortoni review best practices and 'what works' in assessing risk in sexual and violent offenders. The authors consider the development of risk assessment technologies such as structured guided assessments and actuarial measures used in the assessment of sexual and violent offenders.

They provide a detailed summary of the relative strengths, weakness and predictive accuracy of the various methods before considering a convergent approach to risk assessment – the methodology of combining estimations of actuarial static risk with assessments of stable dynamic psychological factors to assess the level of risk and treatment need of offenders. This is demonstrated by mapping static risk factors onto the four risk domains associated with reoffending. They conclude that with an emphasis on discovering 'what works' in offender risk assessment, a number of promising actuarial and structured approaches to sexual and violent risk assessment have been developed and evaluated.

Part Three: What Works in Offender Rehabilitation

Clive Hollin, Emma Palmer and Ruth Hatcher begin this part with Chapter 6 with a review of some of the cognitive skills programmes which have been developed within the criminal justice system in England and Wales such as Straight Thinking on Probation (STOP), ETS and R&R. They describe the introduction of the accreditation process used to examine the integrity of programmes and the programme audit. They address some of the methodological criticisms which dogged early programme evaluations (Lipton, Martinson and Wilks, 1975) and provide a detailed description of the programme evaluation process, research designs and measures of change. They conclude that the evidence from the outcome research shows that completion of cognitive-behavioural programmes has a positive effect on reoffending, with a concurrent negative effect of non-completion as compared to no-treatment comparison groups.

In Chapter 7, Jenny Tew, Leigh Harkins and Louise Dixon address the question of 'what works' in reducing violence in psychopathic offenders. After considering the concept of psychopathy, they move on to review the empirical literature considering the efficacy of treatment with offenders with high levels of psychopathic traits. They challenge the apparent belief that people with psychopathic personality disorder are 'untreatable' or possibly even made worse by treatment (D'Silva, Duggan and McCarthy, 2004), something which is often traced back to early evaluations in high-security institutions (Rice, Harris and Cormier, 1992). They discuss the specific assessment and treatment needs of this group within the RNR framework. They suggest that targeting traits within Factor 1 or Factor 2 for treatment (e.g., responsivity) may help reduce problematic behaviours. For example, they suggest individuals scoring highly on the Factor 2 item 'poor behavioural controls' may benefit from some sort of anger management training to reduce their risk of violence. They argue that the focus of research into the treatment of those scoring high in psychopathy has shifted from considering whether they are able to benefit from treatment on the whole, to trying to identify principles for treatment that would maximize engagement and successful outcomes. They conclude that the next stage is to evaluate recently accredited programmes in order to better understand the treatment needs of individuals with high psychopathy.

Continuing the theme of 'what works' with people with personality disorders, Vincent Egan, in Chapter 8, considers current best practice to treat personality-disordered offenders. First, the parameters and complexities of personality disorder are addressed, as these issues inform an exploration of the theory and practice of interventions with personality-disordered offenders. The therapeutic approaches considered are those which combine clinical practice and experience with academic content. This chapter highlights the clinical nature of much therapeutic work with this offender population, and the specific approaches aimed at managing interpersonal and impulsive aspects of personality disorder.

Josilyn Banks, Sheetal Kini and Julia Babcock review the evidence on 'what works' in reducing male intimate partner violence recidivism in Chapter 9. The authors state that they 'aim to educate the reader about the current "go to" interventions used in the rehabilitation of batterers, and the theoretical frameworks that shape these interventions'. They begin with a discussion of their research that has demonstrated the small effect of batterer interventions on partner violence recidivism. As such, they argue there is great room for improvement in developing such interventions. They go onto provide a review of commonly administered battering intervention programmes, exploring the efficacy of therapeutic strategies such as motivational interviewing and RNR. Finally, they consider typologies of batterers and their role in the future of rehabilitation with this offender population. They conclude, based on the underwhelming results of current batterer interventions, there is a need to generate and test the efficacy of new and novel programmes.

In Chapter 10, William L. Marshall, Liam E. Marshall, Geris A. Serran and Matt D. O'Brien examine 'what works' in reducing sexual reoffending. Marshall and colleagues begin the chapter with an examination of punitive treatment approaches and conclude that treatment for any offender, in the context of punitive measures, is unlikely to be successful. Marshall and colleagues suggest that due to the inherent variability across sexual offender treatment programmes, it makes sense to ask the question '*Can* treatment of sexual offenders be effective?' since this can lead professionals to carefully investigate the underlying principles guiding successful programmes. Marshall and colleagues review contemporary meta-analyses and conclude that sexual offender treatment *can* be effective in some cases. They move on to discuss principles that they believe bring about positive effects in reducing sexual reoffending and describe – in detail – their own sexual offender treatment programme along with associated outcome data relating to its effectiveness. Marshall and colleagues conclude that strengths-based sexual offender treatment targeting criminogenic needs can often be effective, although they recognize that the knowledge base in this area is constantly expanding.

Turning to the treatment needs of violent juvenile offenders, Charles Borduin, Alex Dopp and Erin Taylor discuss in Chapter 11 the juvenile justice intervention programmes that have proven most effective. They note that although large-scale progress has been slow, several interventions have proven effective over the past 20 years in reducing the criminal activity of serious juvenile offenders, and recent efforts to disseminate these evidence-based interventions have been very promising. They begin by outlining the criteria for selection before detailing Multisystemic Therapy (MST), Multidimensional Treatment Foster Care (MTFC) and Functional Family Therapy (FFT). They explain the theoretical and clinical foundations of each intervention before reporting research outcomes. Each of the three interventions produced positive results in decreases in adolescent antisocial behaviour, association with deviant peers and significantly lower recidivism rates for status offences. Borduin, Dopp and Taylor argue that when taken together, these studies suggest that changes in caregiver discipline practices and youth association with deviant peers are critical factors in the attenuation of antisocial behaviour in youths. They highlight the most important goal of future research in this area should be to determine the specific components of treatment (e.g., in-session behaviours, protocols) that lead to improved caregiver discipline and disengagement of youths from deviant peers.

In Chapter 12, Raymond W. Novaco provides a comprehensive review of focused anger treatment studies with offender populations. He begins by setting the origins of understanding of anger citing Roman and Greek philosophers who make reference to rage, wrath and madness as indicators of anger. Novaco highlights anger is neither necessary nor sufficient for violence, but it is part of the confluence of multi-level risk factors affecting violent behaviour. Having discussed the mechanism of anger and emotional dysregulation, he provides a chronological narrative of illustrative studies with control groups giving attention to important issues, topical content, types of intervention, populations (adult and juvenile, male and female) and settings (prison, psychiatric). The review of studies reveals that cognitive-behavioural treatment of anger has been shown to have applicability to a wide range of client populations and many clinical disorders. Prisoners and hospitalized patients with long-standing aggression histories, mental disorder and even intellectual disabilities (ID) can be engaged in cognitive behavioural therapy (CBT) anger treatment and have been shown to benefit. Novaco points out that although some studies with prisoners have not found anger reductions to follow anger control interventions, the illustrative studies reviewed have demonstrated that self-reported anger does decline following intervention programmes. He suggests that one can say with reasonable confidence that anger management or anger treatment interventions are successful in reducing anger levels in offender populations, provided that the treatment recipients have certified anger regulatory problems. When anger treatment is applied to persons for whom the treatment target is absent, the outcome evaluation enterprise is dubious. He cautions, regarding whether therapeutic interventions for anger have been successful in reducing aggressive behaviour, the evidence is less clear. One first must be mindful that a *behavioural* criterion is something independent of the subject's self-report; for example, 'physical aggression' scales on self-report instruments are not *behaviour*. He argues many studies exclusively assess anger by self-report instruments, and, of those, few studies have a measurement set that provides a look at whether there is convergence in multiple validated self-report instruments. Anger is a construct having cognitive, somatic and behavioural referents. He concludes, beyond anger control, if the aim is to reduce violent offending, an elaborated account of the complexities and the prospects of anger should be considered.

In Chapter 13, John Weekes, Flora Matheson, Andrea Moser and Michael Wheatley address 'what works' in reducing substance-related offending. The authors note the importance of this topic considering the well-established link between the use and abuse of substances and offending behaviour and provide the reader with a theory- and research-driven integrated model for the assessment and treatment of offenders' substance abuse problems. They begin the discussion of 'what works' with a brief review of the prevalence and dynamics of substance abuse problems in incarcerated populations, and the relationship between substance abuse and criminal offending. A focus on substance abusing female offenders and the role of trauma in the genesis of substance abuse problems is provided. They go on to consider the important role of assessment and highlight the need to consider specific client characteristics in the development of an individualized treatment plan. Finally, the authors describe theoretically based, evidence-informed, intervention models before presenting evidence showing the efficacy of some treatment models and approaches in reducing the likelihood of future problematic use of alcohol and other drugs.

Turning to 'what works' in reducing arson-related offending, in Chapter 14 Kate Fritzon, Rebekah Doley and Fiona Clark synthesize the key theory and treatment approaches that have been used by professionals to treat individuals who have set fires. Fritzon and colleagues note that a lack of knowledge about this group and a lack of rigourous treatment evaluations have greatly restricted professionals' knowledge about 'what works' with individuals who set fires. However, Fritzon and colleagues are able to cite some ongoing UK work aimed at rectifying this issue (Gannon, Lockerbie and Tyler, 2012) and – through piecing together current theory and research findings – make some valuable proposals regarding the potential dynamic risk factors associated with firesetting. However, Fritzon and colleagues note that this particular area is relatively under-researched and 'sparse', making it difficult for professionals to move forward in an empirically informed manner. However, they conclude positively by noting that professionals in the United Kingdom and Australia are moving forward in their efforts to further understand this phenomenon fully.

Similarly to Chapter 14, there has long been a distinct lack of knowledge concerning 'what works' with female sexual offenders. However, Franca Cortoni and Theresa A. Gannon begin Chapter 15 by noting that they feel there is now enough information in this field to make some recommendations on what is *likely* to work with female sexual offenders. Using the RNR principles (Andrews and Bonta, 2010), Cortoni and Gannon examine what is known, and what can reasonably be concluded, about risk and treatment need for female sexual offenders regarding each principle. In particular, Cortoni and Gannon highlight important gender differences that should be taken into account by any consulting professional (e.g., differences in baseline recidivism rates, women's greater need for emotional connections with others, women's severe victimization at the hands of males). Cortoni and Gannon conclude by urging professionals to stay abreast of the constantly updating research literature and not to be tempted to fall back on the more established male sexual offender literature during professional practice with female sexual offenders.

In Chapter 16, William Lindsay and Amanda Michie consider 'what works' for offenders with ID, specifically relating to anger control, sexually inappropriate behaviour and social problem solving and offence-related thinking. They begin by providing a detailed description of an Anger Management Treatment (AMT) which includes behavioural relaxation, understanding of the person's own and others' emotion, understanding the construction of anger and stress inoculation. They present a number of case studies on group and individual AMT on people with ID as well as the results from recent random control trials demonstrating positive outcomes from treatments using AMT principles. They move on to consider 'what works' in the treatment of sexually inappropriate behaviour in people with ID. They argue that CBT techniques have become the predominant approach for the treatment of sex offenders in the last 20 years, including the treatment of those with ID. Using specialist psychometric measures designed for people with ID, they provide evidence for significant improvements on a range of cognitive assessments relating to attitudes to offending, sexual knowledge, victim empathy and measures of locus of control. However, they note due to pressures from courts or criminal justice services not to delay treatment, there have been no evaluations of sex offender treatment in this client group using a randomized control trial or waiting list controlled trial. They note other interventions such as the Social Problem Solving and Offence Related Thinking (SPORT) programme have also had success in sexual and violent offender groups. In conclusion, they note although treatments for AMT, inappropriate sexual behaviour, firesetting and criminal thinking have all been conducted with some success, there is clearly a need for better controlled research in this field.

In Chapter 17, Gwenda M. Willis and Tony Ward examine whether adhering to the GLM actually 'works' and review preliminary evidence regarding this most recent rehabilitation model. They begin by outlining the main tenets of the model as well as the clinical implications of the GLM. They move on to assess existing empirical research examining rehabilitation programmes that use the GLM's overarching framework or incorporate at least some Good Lives principles. The majority of research, as Willis and Ward point out, has focused largely on sexual offender populations since the GLM was first developed and applied to this forensic group. Although only a small amount of studies to date have examined rehabilitation programmes using the GLM as an overall framework, Willis and Ward conclude that evidence supporting the GLM is accumulating. In particular, Willis and Ward note that the striking difference between classical RNR and Good Lives rehabilitation is the engagement of the client in the change or desistance process, and the ability of the GLM to promote positive pro-social ways of living a crime-free life.

Part Four: What Works in Secure Settings

In exploring the role of secure settings on offender behaviour, Nathan Kolla and Sheilagh Hodgins, in Chapter 18, consider what the empirical literature tells us about the efficacy of services and treatment that aims to prevent antisocial and aggressive behaviour among persons with schizophrenia living in the community. The authors present a brief review of the pathways through which individuals with schizophrenia and a history of offending come to receive psychiatric care. Differences between general and forensic psychiatric services are highlighted. They go onto discuss different subtypes of offenders with schizophrenia before finally considering specific interventions for reducing aggressive behaviour in this population. It is concluded that the evidence base on effective treatments for offenders with schizophrenia is small, yet greatly needed. Therefore, current policy and practice regarding the treatment of this population is not based on empirical evidence.

Next, in Chapter 19, Richard Shuker considers the role and efficacy of therapeutic communities (TCs) in treating UK offenders, which, as Shuker asserts, have provided intervention for this population of offenders for over half a century. The chapter first outlines the origins, recent developments and contribution of TCs to forensic practice. It outlines their treatment approach and methods and addresses the issue of TCs as a model of risk reduction, before addressing the opportunities that they provide for risk assessment and engagement in a safe and collaborative treatment process. Finally, it explores an analysis of the evidence base for TCs. It is concluded that TCs provide a key position in addressing risk and treatment of offenders.

In Chapter 20, David Thornton and Deirdre D'Orazio discuss best practice in sexually violent predator (SVP) treatment programmes, from initial assessment and detention criteria to treatment programme targets and strategies for managing risk on release. They begin by offering a historical overview of the development of SVP laws before providing a detailed analysis of the important treatment philosophy and the challenges faced by professionals and detainees within civil commitment legislation. They emphasize the importance of individualized treatment targets and highlight the difficulties that treatment participants face as part of the change process. In contrast to less-developed SVP treatment programmes, from which there have been few or no releases, Thortnon and D'Orazio recognize the important progress that has been made with more recent SVP treatment programmes which have improved assessment and treatment methodologies and theoretical underpinnings leading to a significant number of persons committed under SVP laws having been returned to the community.

Part Five: Cultural Factors and Individualized
Approaches to Offender Rehabilitation

Jo Thakker begins this part of the book with Chapter 21 by examining the complex role of culture within offender rehabilitation. Thakker begins the chapter by defining culture as a concept and discusses how contemporary rehabilitation/treatment models (i.e., the RNR and GLM) conceptualize and integrate the concept of culture. Following this, Thakker outlines what is known about the effectiveness of 'culture-inclusive' treatment programmes for offenders. In particular, she focuses on programmes in Canada (e.g., The Tupiq Program for Inuit Sexual Offenders), Australia (e.g., The Indigenous Family Violence Offender Program) and New Zealand (e.g., The Te Piriti Special Treatment Unit). Thakker notes throughout this chapter that very few research evaluations of culturally inclusive programmes result in peer-reviewed publication, and many are instead published 'in-house' as governmental reports (often with ill-matched comparison groups). Consequently, although the preliminary evidence looks promising, there are many questions that remain unanswered in this field. In particular, Thakker suggests that future research needs to provide more convincing information about the additional benefit of incorporating a strong cultural component to treatment since it is often unclear whether treatment – in the absence of a cultural component – would have been equally effective. Furthermore, if the cultural aspect of treatment *is* highly important for treatment effectiveness, researchers need to establish exactly why this is the case.

In Chapter 22, Andrew Day and Rachael M. Collie examine the Australasian approach to offender rehabilitation. They begin the chapter by providing an overview of the distinguishing features of Australia and New Zealand in terms of demographic and jurisdictional features. Following this, they examine, in detail, the rehabilitation programmes provided in each country and discuss the dearth of research examining the effectiveness of these programmes. Similarly to Chapter 21, Day and Collie note that many of the treatment evaluations currently available in each country are based on in-house government reports and do not appear to meet the study design standards required for international peer review. Day and Collie conclude that although Australasian offender rehabilitation programme development has paralleled developments observed in other countries, Australasia holds some unique challenges as a context for the development of successful rehabilitation. In particular, challenges are faced particularly in Australia where treatment providers are required to provide services to very large rural areas. Furthermore, Day and Collie note that the development of methodologically sound, peer-reviewed research examining treatment effectiveness must represent a crucial aim for both New Zealand and Australian researchers if the field is to progress.

In Chapter 23, R. Karl Hanson and Andrew Harris consider the criminogenic needs of sexual offenders on community supervision. They begin by considering psychologically meaningful risk factors for sexual recidivism and the results of a programme of research known as the Dynamic Supervision Project (DSP) from 2000 to 2007. They describe how, following the results of the DSP, two new measures were revised and created – STABLE-2007 and ACUTE-2007. These were developed to address the dynamic (changeable) risk factors of sexual offenders on community supervision. STABLE-2007 is a structured rating scheme containing 13 risk items and is completed by the evaluator based on file review and an interview with the offender. In contrast to stable factors, the seven items in ACUTE-2007 include factors based on current behaviour, which, in practice, means behaviour during the past month, or less (if the offender was seen more recently). T items were developed from previous studies of high-risk behaviours and the immediate precursors of sexual reoffending. Hanson and Harris provide encouraging support for the psychometric properties of the STABLE-2007 and ACUTE-2007 and the scales ability to discriminate between recidivists and non-recidivists. However, they note such research is in the early stages, and further research is required to determine the conditions under which meaningful changes in STABLE-2007 can be observed. In conclusion, they note that although initial results with these measures are encouraging, further research is needed to: (i) clarify the constructs assessed by these measures and (ii) determine the extent to which these constructs function as genuinely *dynamic* risk factors.

In Chapter 24, Hazel Kemshall and Sarah Hilder consider multi-agency approaches to effective risk management of high-risk offenders in the community in England and Wales. The chapter aims to summarize current issues associated with these approaches, post a 2007 evaluation. It begins by explaining the history of Multi-Agency Public Protection Arrangements (MAPPA) and goes on to discuss improvements in standards of risk management, engaging high-risk offenders in risk management plans and responding to issues of diversity. Important issues for the future development of MAPPA are also discussed. It is concluded that it is a challenging time for MAPPA, and although the system has expanded since its inception, it must now explicitly prove its worth. This can be achieved through increased attention to quality, effective risk management and positively evaluated outcomes.

In Chapter 25, Geris A. Serran, William L. Marshall, Liam E. Marshall and Matt D. O'Brien discuss whether individual or group therapy is the most effective mode for the treatment of sexual offenders. Serran and colleagues begin by examining what is known about the relative effectiveness of individual versus group treatment in the general clinical literature. They note that the general clinical research literature suggests that either treatment approach is more effective than no treatment provision at all. Moving on to discuss the sexual offending literature, Serran and colleagues note that group treatment appears, by far, to be the preferred treatment modality for sexual offender professionals (see the 2003 Survey of North American Programmes; McGrath, Cumming and Burchard, 2003). Consequently, there appears to be very little research literature examining the effectiveness of individual versus group treatment. However, of the scant research available, Serran and colleagues draw similar conclusions to those drawn in the general clinical literature. In short, both types of treatment are likely to be more effective than no treatment at all. Serran and colleagues argue that the most important consideration is *how* individual or group-based work is implemented (i.e., therapeutic process). They then outline what makes group or individual therapy effective drawing upon both the general and sexual offender therapeutic process literature. On the basis of their review, Serran and colleagues conclude that professionals should not feel limited to group therapy and should consider engaging a client in individual therapy when this seems most appropriate.

References

Andrews, D.A. and Bonta, J. (1994) *The Psychology of Criminal Conduct*, Anderson Publishing Co., Cincinnati.

Andrews, D.A. and Bonta, J. (1998) *The Psychology of Criminal Conduct*, 2nd edn, Anderson Publishing Co., Cincinnati.

Andrews, D.A. and Bonta, J. (2003) *The Psychology of Criminal Conduct*, 3rd edn, Anderson Publishing Co., Cincinnati.

Andrews, D.A. and Bonta, J. (2006) *The Psychology of Criminal Conduct*, 4th edn, Anderson Publishing Co., Cincinnati.

Andrews, D.A. and Bonta, J. (2010) *The Psychology of Criminal Conduct*, 5th edn, Anderson Publishing Co., Cincinnati.

Andrews, D.A. and Dowden, C. (2006) Risk principle of case classification in correctional treatment: a meta-analytic investigation. *International Journal of Offender Therapy and Comparative Criminology*, 50, 88–100.

Andrews, D.A., Zinger, I., Hoge, R.D. *et al.* (1990) Does correctional treatment work? A clinically relevant and psychologically informed meta-analysis. *Criminology*, 28, 369–404.

Andrews, D.A., Bonta, J. and Wormith, J.S. (2004) *The Level of Service/Case Management Inventory (LS/CMI)*, Multi-Health Systems, Toronto.

Andrews, D.A., Bonta, J. and Wormith, J.S. (2006) The recent past and near future of risk and/or need assessment. *Crime & Delinquency*, 52, 7–27.

Aspinall, L.G. and Staudinger, U.M. (2003) *A Psychology of Human Strengths: Fundamental Questions and Future Directions for Positive Psychology*, American Psychological Association, Washington, DC.

Baro, A.L. (1999) Effects of a cognitive restructuring programme on inmate institutional behaviour. *Criminal Justice and Behaviour*, 26, 466–484.

Beccaria, C. (1764[1963]) *On Crimes and Punishment* (trans. H. Pallouci), Bobbs-Merrill, Indianapolis.

Beech, A.R., Mandeville-Norden, R. and Goodwill, A. (2012) Comparing recidivism rates of treatment responders/nonresponders in a sample of 413 child molesters who had completed community-based sex offender treatment in the United Kingdom. *International Journal of Offender Therapy and Comparative Criminology*, 56 (1), 29–49.

Berman, G. (2012) Prison Population Statistics. House of Commons. Section, Social and General Statistics. *Standard Note: SN/SG/4334.* http://www.parliament.uk/briefing-papers/SN04334.pdf (accessed 26 December 2012).

Bernfeld, G.A., Farrington, D.P. and Leschied, A.W. (eds) (2001) *Offender Rehabilitation in Practice: Implementing and Evaluating Effective Programmes*, John Wiley & Sons, Ltd, Chichester.

Borduin, C.M., Munschy, R.J., Wagner, D.V. and Taylor, E.K. (2011) Multisystemic therapy with juvenile sexual offenders: development, validation and dissemination, in *International Perspectives on the Assessment and Treatment of Sexual Offenders: Theory, Practice and Research* (eds D.P. Boer, R. Eher, L.A. Craig *et al.*), Wiley-Blackwell, Oxford, pp. 263–286.

Brody, S. (1976) The Effectiveness of Sentencing. *Home Office Research Study No. 35*, Her Majesty's Stationery Office, London.

Carter, P. (2003) *Managing Offenders, Reducing Crime.* Home Office, London, http://www.thelearningjourney.co.uk/Patrick_Carter_Review.pdf/file_view (accessed 26 December 2012).

Chambless, D.L. and Hollon, S.D. (1998) Defining empirically supported therapies. *Journal of Consulting and Clinical Psychology*, 66, 7–18.

Chambless D. and Ollendick, T. (2001) Empirically supported psychological interventions: controversies and evidence. *Annual Review of Psychology*, 52, 685–716.

Chambless, D.L., Baker, M., Baucom, D.H. *et al.* (1998) Update on empirically validated therapies, II. *The Clinical Psychologist*, 51 (1), 3–16.

Craig, L.A., Browne, K.D. and Beech, A.R. (2008) *Assessing Risk in Sex Offenders: A Practitioner's Guide*, John Wiley & Sons, Ltd, Chichester.

Cullen, F.T., Cullen, J.B. and Wozniak, J.F. (1988) Is rehabilitation dead? The myth of the punitive public. *Journal of Criminal Justice*, 16: 303–317.

Dowden, C. and Andrews, D.A. (1999) What works in young offender treatment: a meta-analysis. *Forum on Corrections Research*, 11, 21–24.

Dowden, C. and Andrews, D.A. (2000) Effective correctional treatment and violent re-offending: a meta analysis. *Canadian Journal of Criminology*, 42, 449–467.

D'Silva, K., Duggan, C. and McCarthy, L. (2004) Does treatment really make psychopaths worse? A review of the evidence. *Journal of Personality Disorders*, 18, 163–177.

Farmer, M., Beech, A.R. and Ward, T. (2012) Assessing desistance in child molesters: a qualitative analysis. *Journal of Interpersonal Violence*, 27 (5), 930–950.

Gannon, T.A., Lockerbie, L. and Tyler, N. (2012) A long time coming? The Firesetting Intervention Programme for Mentally Disordered Offenders (FIP-MO). *Forensic Update*, 106, 1–16.

Gendreau, P. and Andrews, D.A. (2001) *Correctional Program Assessment Inventory – 2000 (CPAI-2000)*, University of New Brunswick, Saint John.

Hall, G.C.N. (1995) Sexual offender recidivism revisited: a meta-analysis of recent treatment studies. *Journal of Consulting and Clinical Psychology*, 63, 802–809.

Hanson, R.K., Gordon, A., Harris, A.J.R. *et al.* (2002) First report of the collaborative outcome data project on the effectiveness of psychological treatment for sex offenders. *Sexual Abuse: A Journal of Research and Treatment*, 14 (2), 169–194.

Harkins, L. and Beech, A.R. (2007) Measurement of the effectiveness of sex offender treatment. *Aggression and Violent Behaviour*, 12 (1), 36–44.

Hollin, C.R. and Palmer, E.J. (2006) *Offending Behaviour Programmes: Development, Application, and Controversies*, John Wiley & Sons, Ltd, Chichester.

Jolliffe, D. and Farrington, D.P. (2007) A Systematic Review of the National and Interventional Evidence on the Effectiveness of Interventions with Violent Offenders. *Research Series 16/07*. Ministry of Justice, London.

Joseph, S. and Linley, P.A. (2006) *Positive Therapy: A Meta-theory for Positive Psychological Practice*, Routledge, London.

Laws, D.R. and Ward, T. (2011) *Desistance from Sex Offending: Alternatives to Throwing Away the Keys*, Guilford Press, New York.

Linley, P.A. and Joseph, S. (2004) *Positive Psychology in Practice*, John Wiley and Sons, Inc., Hoboken.

Lipton, D.S., Martinson, R. and Wilks, J. (1975) *The Effectiveness of Correctional Treatment: A Survey of Treatment Evaluation Studies*, Praeger, New York.

Martinson, R. (1974) What works? – questions and answers about prison reform. *Public Interest*, 10, 22–54.

Maruna, S. (2001) *Making Good: How Ex-Convicts Reform and Rebuild Their Lives*, American Psychological Association, Washington, DC.

Maruna, S. (2011) Judicial rehabilitation and the 'Clean Bill of Health' in criminal justice, *European Journal of Probation*, 3, 97–117.

McDougall, C., Perry, A.E., Clarbour, J. *et al.* (2009) *Evaluation of HM Prison Service Enhanced Thinking Skills Programme: Report on the Outcomes from a Randomised Controlled Trial*, Ministry of Justice, London. http://www.reclassering.nl/documents/Rapport%20ETS.pdf (accessed 24 December 2012).

McGrath, R.J., Cumming, G.F. and Burchard, B.L. (2003) *Current Practices and Trends in Sexual Abuser Management: Safer Society 2002 Nationwide Survey*, Safer Society Press, Brandon.

McGuire, J. (1995) *What Works: Reducing Reoffending: Guidelines from Research and Practice*, John Wiley & Sons, Ltd, Chichester.

McGuire, J. (2002) *Offender Rehabilitation and Treatment: Effective Programmes and Policies to Reduce Reoffending*, John Wiley & Sons, Ltd, Chichester.

McNeill, F. (2012) Four forms of 'offender' rehabilitation: towards an interdisciplinary perspective. *Legal and Criminological Psychology*, 17, 18–36.

McNeill, F. and Weaver, B. (2010) Changing Lives? Desistance Research and Offender Management. *Report no. 03/2010*, Scottish Centre for Crime and Justice Research, Glasgow. http://www.krus.no/upload/PDF-dokumenter/England%20artikkel%20ved%20Fergus%20McNeill.pdf (accessed 26 December 2012).

Palmer, E.J., McGuire, J., Hounsome, J.C. *et al.* (2007) Offending behaviour programmes in the community: the effects on reconviction of three programmes with adult male offenders. *Legal and Criminological Psychology*, 12, 251–264.

Polaschek, D.L.L. (2012) An appraisal of the risk-need-responsivity (RNR) model of offender rehabilitation and its application in correctional treatment. *Legal and Criminological Psychology*, 17, 1–17.

Polaschek, D.L.L. and Dixon, B.G. (2001) The violence prevention project: the development and evaluation of a treatment programme for violent offenders. *Psychology, Crime & Law*, 7, 1–23.

Reynolds, N., Craig, L.A. and Boer, D.P. (2009) Public attitudes towards offending, offenders, and reintegration, in *Public Opinion and Criminal Justice* (eds J.L. Wood and T.A. Gannon), Wilan Publishing, Cullompton, pp. 166–186.

Rice, M.E., Harris, G.T. and Cormier, C.A. (1992) An evaluation of a maximum security therapeutic community for psychopaths and other mentally disordered offenders. *Law and Human Behaviour*, 16, 399–412.

Sharman, L.W., Gottfredson, D., MacKenzie, D.L. *et al.* (1997) Preventing Crime: What Works, What Doesn't, What's Promising, U.S. Department of Justice, National Institute of Justice, Washington, DC. https://www.ncjrs.gov/pdffiles/171676.PDF (accessed 26 December 2012).

Snyder, C.R. and Lopez, J.S. (2005) *The Handbook of Positive Psychology*, Oxford University Press, Oxford.

Ward, T. and Gannon, T.A. (2006) Rehabilitation, etiology, and self-regulation: the comprehensive good lives model of treatment for sexual offenders. *Aggression and Violent Behaviour*, 11, 77–94.

Ward, T. and Maruna, S. (2007) *Rehabilitation*, Routledge, London.

Ward, T., Polaschek, D.L.L. and Beech, A.R. (2006) *Theories of Sexual Offending*, John Wiley & Sons, Ltd, Chichester.

Ward, T., Yates, P. and Long, C. (2006) *The Self-Regulation Model of the Offence and Relapse Process*. vol. 2. Treatment. Pacific Psychological Assessment Corporation, Victoria.

Ward, T., Mann, R. and Gannon, T.A. (2007) The good lives model of rehabilitation: clinical implications. *Aggression and Violent Behaviour*, 12, 87–107.

2

'What Works' to Reduce Re-offending
18 Years On

James McGuire
University of Liverpool, UK

Introduction

In a sweeping overview of the history of criminal justice endeavours published towards the end of the last century, Gaes (1998, p. 713) characterized 'a 150-year-old era of optimism about the possibilities of reforming the offender'. That period can be dated approximately from the advent of the penitentiary circa 1820 until the emphasis and tone of policy and practice changed, at least in Anglophone countries, from approximately 1975 onwards. In other words, for a century and a half, people in the business of criminal justice intervention or 'corrections' had a generally positive expectation that persons who had repeatedly broken the law also had the capacity to change that behaviour, and to adjust to living their lives in a more socially acceptable ('good and useful') way. Of course the processes believed to engender such changes altered markedly over that timescale. But the period since then has been one of more rapid swings in what we might call the criminal justice temperament. At a time when the predominant ethos appears once again to emphasize punitive sanctions over all else, when a justice minister who proposes to halt or very marginally reverse the relentless rise in prison numbers is disparaged by the media (and some of his colleagues) for doing so, it is useful to recapitulate what we have learnt about how best to address the problem of recurrent offending behaviour.

Remembrance of things (not long) past

The change of direction that occurred in the mid-1970s is often ascribed to the publication of research reports and literature reviews by Martinson (1974), Brody (1976), and von Hirsch (1976) who, erroneously as it transpired, cast doubt on the possibility of doing anything constructive in this sphere. The temper of the age may of course have been mutating in any case for entirely different reasons, and some authors have identified an assortment of other factors that may have been at work in the move towards 'get tough' policies (Smith, Gendreau and Swartz, 2009). But the rapidity and pervasiveness with which those pessimistic messages took hold and were diffused stands in stark contrast to the considerable effort that was later needed, and continues to be

What Works in Offender Rehabilitation: An Evidence-Based Approach to Assessment and Treatment,
First Edition. Edited by Leam A. Craig, Louise Dixon and Theresa A. Gannon.
© 2013 John Wiley & Sons, Ltd. Published 2013 by John Wiley & Sons, Ltd.

needed, to disconfirm them and set the record straight. We should not of course lose sight of the point that the aforementioned reviewers cast as much doubt on the value of imprisonment as they did on the likelihood of treatment success, and they urged restrictions on its use – a part of their message to which far less attention was paid. Nor should it be forgotten that there were dissenting voices during that period which called into question the unwarranted dismissal of evidence that had taken place (Cullen and Gilbert, 1982; Gendreau and Ross, 1980; Palmer, 1975).

The allegorical law-and-order pendulum then swung slowly back and a phase ensued in which confidence in the possibility of 'offender rehabilitation' was at least partially restored. The extent to which this was facilitated by the increasing difficulty of ignoring a mounting body of evidence on positive effects of programmatic interventions, which eventually achieved a kind of critical mass, is difficult to gauge. Several more sanguine reviews published in the United Kingdom in the second half of the 1990s (Goldblatt and Lewis, 1998; McGuire, 1995; Vennard, Sugg and Hedderman, 1997) reinforced by similar messages emanating from Canada, and doubts about the 'death of rehabilitation' in the United States, collectively appeared to induce policy changes. Psychologically based work with offenders lifted off on a scale never previously witnessed.

Within the latter phase, however, there have also been some seemingly paradoxical trends. Whilst there has been a growing engagement with more constructive approaches to intervention in many jurisdictions, there has also been – in parallel and in some of the same places – a dramatic rise in the use of imprisonment. The question was posed, whether 'what works' leads to a more oppressive approach in criminal justice (Boone, 2004). In England and Wales, for example, the prison population rose more steeply after 1990 than at any other time in the twentieth century (Berman, 2010). Criminal justice is swayed by many influences, and it would be best not to delude ourselves into believing that outcome data generated by social scientists plays a particularly large part in it. But that need not be a permanent state of affairs, and as the ethos of 'evidence-based practice' slowly strengthens and it becomes incrementally harder for decision-makers to ignore massive datasets, perhaps research will become steadily more influential. Meanwhile, it seems more likely that the adoption of 'what works' research evidence and the contemporaneous growth in prison numbers were both functions of a rising 'managerialism' within criminal justice, rather than having a cause–effect relationship.

The double paradox here is the now more solid than ever evidence on the futility of punitive sanctions as a solution to the problem of criminal recidivism. Despite the failures of earlier 'short sharp shock' experiments, there was further experimentation with boot camps before they were again found to have failed. In dismal sequence, other initiatives such as 'smart sentencing', 'scared straight', wilderness/challenge programmes, exercise and physically demanding regimes and the inception of 'three strikes' laws, one after another in tedious succession, were deployed in fearful response to baying newspaper headlines. If it is true that history repeats itself, this may be nowhere more vividly illustrated than in the dreary perseveration of the scientifically discredited idea that the problem of crime can be solved if we simply increase the severity of penalties. One wonders how many more times maxims such as 'back-to-basics', 'bang-them-up', 'hit-them-hard', 'show-less-understanding', 'turn-up-the-heat' and 'they showed-no-mercy-why-should-we' have to be tested and their pointlessness demonstrated before their adherents accept the futility and vacuity of their approach.

Chapter objectives

In this chapter, an attempt will be made to cover three broad issues with respect to the present-day position regarding what is colloquially known as 'what works' in the field of criminal justice or 'correctional treatment'. First, we will survey what has been consolidated from the now very sizeable corpus of research findings that has amassed, the largest proportion of which concentrates on intervention programmes and whether or not they have 'worked', that is, reduced subsequent recidivism. Second, we will examine the fate of some of the policy impacts of the earlier phase of 'what works' findings. Third, we will summarize some of the research on extra-programmatic factors, related to risk assessment and allocation, attrition, programme integrity, quality of delivery and other organizational dimensions, that were neglected during the initial phase of applying the findings of research reviews.

Reviews Update

A proportion of research reviews continue to use the traditional narrative method, and for some purposes (e.g., where the number of studies located is small, or the study designs, participant populations or intervention methods are very heterogeneous) that is still the most appropriate course of action. However, meta-analysis has come to be recognized and extensively used in both psychology and criminology (Lipsey and Cullen, 2007; Smith, Gendreau and Swartz, 2009; Wilson, 2001). As more research has accumulated, the number of research reviews has gone on increasing (Lipsey, 2009; MacKenzie, 2006; McGuire, 2002, 2008, 2009). Some have followed the model of systematic review which differs from meta-analysis and may or may not incorporate integrative statistical methods (McGuire, 2011). So first let us consider a brief update on the 'state of the art' (or the science), a kind of review of reviews.

It is not easy to define and demarcate a firm line for deciding what to include or exclude for this purpose, as there are numerous overlaps between the objectives of different reviews and across adjacent fields of interest. But the count of relevant meta-analyses and systematic reviews of 'tertiary prevention' measures, that is, ones carried out with adjudicated offenders in criminal justice or closely allied settings, has now reached 100. These studies focus on an evaluated intervention where the basic, initial 'unit of analysis' is the behaviour of the individual who has broken the law. Such individuals have been included in a study cohort (sometimes involving group-based work) with evaluative results being reported in primary studies, and where some time later those results have been incorporated in a meta-analysis or systematic review.

Conversely, for present purposes, interventions of some other types are excluded, such as those that entailed changes in legal procedures (e.g., curfews, drug courts, problem-solving courts), in sentencing practices (e.g., court-mandated methods entailing no direct psychological intervention, such as electronic monitoring) and in situational crime-preventive measures (improved street lighting, installation of CCTV, Neighbourhood Watch). Reviews that focus purely on medical interventions are excluded, but some of the included reviews address both pharmacological and psychologically based methods (e.g., Hockenhull *et al.*, 2010; Lösel and Schmucker, 2005). The majority of reviews of treatment of substance abuse, which are generally conducted in healthcare rather than justice settings, are also excluded. However, reviews that approached this from a criminal justice perspective (e.g., Holloway, Bennett and Farrington, 2005; Pearson and Lipton, 1999) are included, and we should keep in mind some large clinical trials, such as the United Kingdom's National Treatment Outcome Research Study, which have shown the possibility of reducing criminal recidivism through health-service-based substance abuse treatment (Gossop *et al.*, 2005). Also excluded are studies of interventions focused solely or primarily on children below the age of criminal responsibility, whose antisocial behaviour is of concern and is thought to be a likely precursor of later delinquency, but who have not yet made contact with the criminal justice system.

Again note, however, that there are some encouraging reviews of that area (Dretzke *et al.*, 2009; Kaminski *et al.*, 2008; Serketich and Dumas, 1996). Grietens and Hellinckx (2004) have collated findings of several meta-analyses, and Knorth *et al.* (2008) have reported a further meta-analysis concerning the impact of residential childcare treatment on children's and adolescents' externalizing behaviour.

Table 2.1 lists the 100 source publications that remain after these exclusions, organized chronologically from the first pioneering review by Garrett (1985). Those reported in each subsequent year are arranged alphabetically by first author. The second column gives a very brief outline of the designated subject area, and the third gives basic information on the number of effect-size tests that were reported. This sometimes differs from the number of studies found, as some projects measure more than one effect. Clearly, set beside the gargantuan efforts involved in carrying out these reviews, attempting to summarize them in this highly condensed way is fairly primitive by comparison. It is strongly recommended therefore to go to the original sources. The final column shows key effect-size results. The majority of effect sizes reported are correlation coefficients (Pearson r or Φ), with a smaller proportion using standardized mean difference statistics (Cohen's d or Hedges' g). Where these effect sizes are quoted, a+sign indicates that the outcome favoured the experimental sample (i.e., its level of recidivism was lower than that of controls). However, some effect sizes are reported as odds ratios (OR), and here the direction varies according to how the analysis was done in the denoted review. Where column four reads *na* (not available/not applicable), this is where, for varying reasons, no average effect size was computed, or alternatively the overall result is not a comparison between treated and untreated groups, but a set of correlations between either an independent or moderator variable and recidivism outcomes.

We should bear in mind that there is sometimes quite extensive duplication amongst the studies reviewed, with some appearing under more than one heading or incorporated in more than one review. But even taking that into account, this is a very substantial body of literature. The volume of work here is commensurate with or in many cases exceeds that available on many other public policy questions. In providing an overview of outcome research, the basic studies and the reviews cited here can be classified in a number of ways. At risk of some over-simplification, we can divide the reviews listed in Table 2.1 into five main categories according to the principal aims of the researchers when they embarked on their work:

- In an initial phase, many focused on the general question: Does intervention ('offender treatment') work? Virtually every review pays some (however brief) attention to that issue.
- As differential outcomes were noted from the outset, other reviews explicitly focused on comparing methods of intervention (or 'treatment modalities') to test not just whether some worked better than others but whether they did so reliably.
- Reviews progressively emerged focusing on selected target groups, usually defined by type of principal or most frequent category of offence (e.g., general, acquisitive, sexual, violent, substance abuse).
- Some reviews were conducted to test for the effects of moderator variables (e.g., gender, age, ethnicity), often entailing what might be called secondary meta-analysis, that is, reiteration of the work done in a review but testing for variations in effect sizes by subgroup or as a function of other factors (e.g., rigour of research design, date of publication, role of principal investigator). In a small number of reviews, qualitative, process-oriented studies were also included.
- As evidence regarding structured programmes became more firmly established, but researchers noted variations in effects according to context, other reviews investigated non-programmatic variables, such as participant risk levels, background and skills of front-line staff, quality or integrity of delivery of interventions and the impact of attrition.

Table 2.1 Summary information from 100 meta-analyses or systematic reviews of individually focused treatment outcome studies on reducing criminal recidivism or antisocial behaviour published in the period 1985–2013

Source	Focus of review	Number of effect-size tests (k)	Mean effect size(s) reported
Garrett (1985)	Young offenders in residential placements	121	+0.18
Gensheimer *et al.* (1986)	Diversion schemes for young offenders	31	+0.26
Mayer *et al.* (1986)	Social-learning-based interventions with youth	17	+0.33
Gottschalk *et al.* (1987a)	Community-based interventions with youth	61	+0.22
Gottschalk *et al.* (1987b)	Behavioural interventions with youth	14	+0.25
Lösel and Koferl (1989)	Socio-therapeutic prison regimes in Germany	16	+0.12
Whitehead and Lab (1989)	Young offenders: general	50	+0.13
Andrews *et al.* (1990)	Testing a model of 'human service principles'	Types of service: 'Appropriate' 54 'Unspecified' 32 'Inappropriate' 38 'Deterrence' 30	+0.30 +0.13 −0.06 −0.07
Izzo and Ross (1990)	Cognitive versus non-cognitive interventions	46	Ratio of mean ESs (cog: non-cog)=2.5:1
Roberts and Camasso (1991)	Young offenders: general	46	na
Lipsey (1992, 1995)	Offenders aged 12–21	397	+0.10
Hall (1995)	Sexual offending	12	+0.12
Wells-Parker *et al.* (1995)	Drunk-driving offences	215	8–9% reduction
Gendreau and Goggin (1996)	Deterrence and intermediate punishment	138	0.00
Cleland *et al.* (1997)	Impact of age as moderator variable	659	na
Pearson, Lipton and Cleland (1997)	CDATE Project: comprehensive review	846	na
Redondo, Garrido and Sánchez-Meca (1997)	European structured programmes	57	+0.12
Lipsey and Wilson (1998)	Serious violent and sexual offending by youth	Institutional 83 Community 117	+0.10 +0.14
Marsch (1998)	Methadone maintenance for opiate dependence	24	r=+0.23, d=+0.54
Alexander (1999)	Sexual offending	79	+0.10
Dowden and Andrews (1999a)	Programmes for women offenders	24	na
Dowden and Andrews (1999b)	Young offenders: general	229	+0.09
Gallagher *et al.* (1999)	Sexual offending	25	d=+0.43

Table 2.1 (*cont'd*)

Source	Focus of review	Number of effect-size tests (k)	Mean effect size(s) reported
Pearson and Lipton (1999)	Substance abuse treatment and offending	30	na
Polizzi, MacKenzie and Hickman (1999)	Sexual offending	13	na
Redondo, Sánchez-Meca and Garrido (1999)	European structured programmes	32	+0.12
Dowden and Andrews (2000)	Interventions for violent offenders	52	+0.07
Egg *et al.* (2000)	Treatment programmes in Germany	25	r=+0.12, OR=1.9
Petrosino, Turpin-Petrosino and Finckenauer (2000)	'Scared straight' programmes	9	−0.01
Prendergast, Podus and Chang (2000)	Treatment of drug dependence (treatment-comparison studies only)	28 17	Drug use +0.29 Crime +0.17
Wilson, Gallagher and MacKenzie (2000)	Educational and vocational programmes, adults	53	OR=1.52
Wilson and Lipsey (2000)	'Wilderness challenge' programmes	22	+0.18
Gendreau *et al.* (2001)	Intermediate punishment	140	0.00
Latimer (2001)	Family treatment	50	+0.15
Lipsey, Chapman and Landenberger (2001)	Cognitive-behavioural interventions	14	OR=0.66
MacKenzie, Wilson and Kider (2001)	Correctional boot camps	44	OR=1.02
Wilson, Gottfredson and Najaka (2001)	School-based interventions	40	d=+0.04
Hanson *et al.* (2002)	Sexual offending	43	OR=0.81
Lipton *et al.* (2002a)	Therapeutic communities	35	+0.14
Lipton *et al.* (2002b)	Behavioural and cognitive-behavioural interventions	68	+0.12
Prendergast *et al.* (2002)	Programme factors in treating drug dependence	78 25	Drug use g+0.33 Crime g+0.13
Redondo, Sánchez-Meca and Garrido (2002)	European structured programmes	23	+0.21
Salekin (2002)	Treatment of personality disorders	42	na
Woolfenden, Williams and Peat (2002)	Family-based interventions	5	OR=0.66
Dowden and Andrews (2003)	Family-based interventions	53	+0.21
Dowden, Antonowicz and Andrews (2003)	Effectiveness of relapse prevention	40	+0.15
Farrington and Welsh (2003)	Family-based interventions	40	+0.32
Lösel and Beelman (2003)	Child skills training	135	Post-test d+0.38 Follow-up d+0.28

(*continued*)

Table 2.1　(*cont'd*)

Source	Focus of review	Number of effect-size tests (k)	Mean effect size(s) reported
Wilson, Lipsey and Derzon (2003)	School-based intervention programmes	522	+0.25
Wilson, Lipsey and Soydan (2003)	Impact of ethnicity as moderator variable	305	na
Babcock, Green and Robie (2004)	Domestic violence/ programmes for abusers	36	na
Dowden and Andrews (2004)	Influence of staff practice and related variables	273	na
Nugent, Williams and Umbreit (2004)	Victim–offender mediation (young offenders)	15	OR=0.70
Walker *et al.* (2004)	Adolescent sex offenders	10	+0.26
Andrews and Dowden (2005)	Programme and treatment integrity as moderator	273	na
Feder and Wilson (2005)	Domestic violence, court-ordered treatment programmes	RCTs 7 QEs 4	RCTs: for official reports d=+0.26 QEs: for official reports d = −0.14 Combined: for victim reports d=+0.01
Holloway, Bennett and Farrington, (2005)	Impact of drug treatment on criminal recidivism	28	OR=1.41–1.56
Latimer, Dowden and Muise (2005)	Restorative justice	32	+0.07
Lösel and Schmucker (2005) and Schmucker and Lösel (2008)	Sexual offending	80	+0.29
Visher, Winterfield and Coggeshall (2005)	Employment programmes (community-based)	10	+0.03
Wilson, Bouffard and MacKenzie (2005)	Cognitive-behavioural group programmes	74	Range: +0.16 to +0.49
Wilson, MacKenzie and Mitchell (2005)	Correctional boot camps	43	OR=1.02
Andrews and Dowden (2006)	Test of 'risk-needs' principles of case classification	374	Significant support found
Aos, Miller and Drake (2006)	A wide range of programmes in adult corrections: boot camps, intensive supervision, TCs, CBT, drug treatment programmes	291	ES (d) adjusted for design quality ranged from 0.00 to –0.23. Equivalent to reductions in re-offending from 0% to 31.2%

Table 2.1 (*cont'd*)

Source	Focus of review	Number of effect-size tests (k)	Mean effect size(s) reported
Bilby, Brooks-Gordon and Wells (2006)	Treatment of sexual offending (systematic review, QEs only)	17	Significant reductions in offending: $k=7$ No significant findings: $k=10$
Bradshaw, Roseborough and Umbreit (2006)	Victim offender mediation (juveniles)	15	+0.34
Brooks-Gordon, Bilby and Wells (2006)	Treatment of sexual offending (systematic review, RCTs only)	9	Outcome data mainly psychometric; + effects for CBT at 1 year; – effect in one 10-year FU
French and Gendreau (2006)	Reducing prison misconducts	104	+0.14
Lowenkamp, Latessa and Holsinger (2006)	Risk level as basis of allocation to correctional programmes in Ohio	Residential: 53 Non-residential: 44	Regression model incorporating elements of allocation by risk level: adjusted $R^2=0.27$
Lowenkamp, Latessa and Smith (2006)	Programme integrity and quality of delivery evaluated using the CPAI	38	CPAI total× re-offence: +0.35 CPAI total× return to prison: +0.42
McCart *et al.* (2006)	Relative effects of behavioural parent training (BPT) and cognitive-behavioural therapy (CBT)	BPT 32 CBT 45	+0.47 +0.35
Reitzel and Carbonell (2006)	Juvenile sex offenders	9	OR=0.43
Tong and Farrington (2006)	Reasoning and rehabilitation programme	25	OR=1.16
Garrido and Morales (2007)	Institutionally based interventions, violent youth	Recidivism 30 Serious offence 15	OR=1.13 OR=1.35
Jolliffe and Farrington (2007)	Programmes for adults convicted of violence	11	FE d=+0.16, RE d=+0.21
Limbos *et al.* (2007)	Effectiveness of interventions to reduce youth violence	41 of which RCTs=15	No mean ES reported; 49% of interventions effective
Lipsey, Landenberger and Wilson (2007)	Treatment factors, cognitive-behavioural programmes	58	OR=1.53 'best practices' OR=2.86

(continued)

Table 2.1   (*cont'd*)

Source	Focus of review	Number of effect-size tests (k)	Mean effect size(s) reported
Tanasichuk and Wormith (2007)	Comparison between treated and untreated psychopaths	3	Criminality −0.10 Violence +0.03
Bonta *et al.* (2008)	Effectiveness of probation supervision	26	General +0.022 Violence +0.004
Cheliotis (2008)	Prison temporary release (home leave or work-release schemes, some TC-linked)	Home leave 5 Work release 12 Project CREST 6	na but 4/5 effects + mixed effects but mainly + effects mainly −
Doren and Yates (2008)	Treatment of psychopathic sexual offenders	10 evaluations from 4 sites	Only one study with comparison group; results inconclusive
Parhar *et al.* (2008)	Impact of coercion in offender treatment, i.e., comparing mandated with voluntary participation	Mandated 46 Non-mandated 83	Larger effect sizes for voluntary than mandated treatment, moderated by setting: main effect for level of coercion $p=0.006$
Hanson *et al.* (2009)	Sex offender treatment	22 (sexual offence) 13 (any re-offence)	OR (sexual): 0.66; (general) 0.61; RNR-adherent programmes: 0.21
Lipsey (2009)	Wide range of intervention types with young offenders	548	+0.062
McMurran (2009)	Motivational interviewing with offenders	9 (for offence behaviour)	No overall ES Results varied by offence
Perry *et al.* (2009a)	Substance-abusing offenders; systematic review	24 RCTs, of which 13 meta-analysed	+ effects for TCs (OR=0.37) For intensive supervision, surveillance, ORs=0.88–2.09
Perry *et al.* (2009b)	Interventions with 'persistent and prolific' offenders: rapid evidence assessment	20 meta-analysed	ORs: Prison-based TCs: 0.66 Community drug treatment: 0.62 Cognitive skills programmes: 0.74

Table 2.1 (*cont'd*)

Source	Focus of review	Number of effect-size tests (k)	Mean effect size(s) reported
Stover, Meadows and Kaufman (2009)	Interventions to reduce partner abuse, RCTs only	7	na; large variations in outcomes
Tolan *et al.* (2008)	Mentoring of young offenders	RCTs 22 QEs 17	For *k*=21 outcomes on delinquency: mean weighted ES (*d*)=+0.25
Andrews and Bonta (2010a)	Restorative justice	67	+0.07
Andrews and Bonta (2010b)	Analysis of relationship between needs targeted and outcome effect sizes	374	Significant correlations found: Antisocial cognition/skill deficits 0.39; interpersonal/ family/peer 0.37; matching of needs 0.30 (all *p*<0.001)
Lowenkamp *et al.* (2010)	Comparison of intervention philosophy (treatment versus deterrence)	58 programmes	Mean ES ranged from: −0.16 for deterrence-based to +0.17 for RNR-based programmes
DuBois *et al.* (2011)	Mentoring programmes for young offenders	82 study samples; 7 with follow-up	For conduct problems (*k*=39) at post-test: ES=+0.23 For follow-up studies ES=+0.17 (across various outcomes)
Olver, Stockdale and Wormith (2011)	Attrition from structured programmes	96	Significant predictors of attrition: Criminal history, antisocial personality (+) Age, intelligence, motivation (−)
Hockenhull *et al.* (2012)	Reduction of violence in mental health settings (RCTs only, dependent variable psychometrics or ward behaviour)	Total *k*=51 (includes some inter-drug comparisons)	Pharmacological (*k*=16) OR=0.17 Psychological (*k*=9) OR=0.53

(*continued*)

Table 2.1 (*cont'd*)

Source	Focus of review	Number of effect-size tests (k)	Mean effect size(s) reported
Schwalbe *et al.* (2012)	Diversion for young offenders, various components	45 (RCTs=27)	OR=0.83 Family treatment OR=0.57
Martin *et al.* (2012)	Interventions for offenders with major mental disorders	37	d=0.19
Mitchell, Wilson and MacKenzie (2012)	Incarceration-based drug treatment	74	OR=1.34
Morgan *et al.* (2012)	Treatment of offenders with mental illness	26 Re-offending 4	No overall ES computed Criminal recidivism d=0.11
James *et al.* (2013)	Aftercare programmes for juvenile and young adult offenders	22	d=0.12

CBT = cognitive behavioural therapy or training; CDATE = Correctional Drug Abuse Treatment Effectiveness; CPAI = *Correctional Program Assessment Inventory*; ES = effect size; FE = fixed effects model; FU = follow-up; na = not available/no mean effect size reported; QE = quasi-experimental design; OR = odds ratio; RCT = randomized controlled trial; RE = random effects model; RNR = risk-need-responsivity model; TC = therapeutic community.

On the basis of the findings from this accumulated body of research, several conclusions are warranted. First, as can be seen from Table 2.1, almost all effect sizes are positive, and whilst some are close to 0 the majority are in the small or moderate range, following the conventional descriptors proposed by Cohen (1992). Thus, there are firm grounds for arguing that we can be more confident than ever that there is a range of methods which 'work' to bring about reductions in rates of criminal recidivism. Second, there are systematic and replicable variations in effect sizes. These emerge with sufficient consistency to allow identification of features of more effective interventions, to the extent that they can be used to derive a model of 'best practice' for maximizing the impact of criminal justice intervention. Third, to recap what was anticipated earlier, the only recurrently negative mean effect sizes reported to date are those obtained from criminal sanctions or deterrence-based methods. Punitive sanctions repeatedly emerge as a failed strategy in altering offenders' behaviour. Fourth, not evident from Table 2.1 but briefly discussed later, there is also mounting evidence that such approaches can be cost-effective and in addition to their impact on recidivism can result in lower criminal justice costs.

At an earlier stage of research in this field, on the basis of a then relatively small number of meta-analytic reviews, Lösel (1995) estimated the 'grand mean' effect size across all studies, expressed as a correlation coefficient, to be in the region of 0.10. Such a figure may not be intuitively easy to interpret as it stands, and it may be useful to translate it into different terms. Imagine that on average, across all the data sets available on punishment or treatment of offenders, the mean recidivism rate at follow-up was 50%. Using this as a benchmark, the average finding obtained from the meta-analyses corresponds to recidivism rates of 45% for experimental groups and 55% for control groups, respectively.

Does this finding tell us anything meaningful in practical or policy terms? One way of acquiring a perspective on this is to consider the distinction between what Rosenthal (1994) called *statistical* and *practical* significance. The mean effect just described, although fairly modest, is statistically significant, and it compares reasonably well with those found in other applied fields. Some healthcare interventions that are generally regarded as producing worthwhile benefits have similar, but sometimes lower, mean treatment effects. McGuire (2002), drawing partly on Rosenthal (1994), composed a list of relevant comparisons with findings obtained from research on healthcare interventions. For example, the mean effect size for aspirin in reducing myocardial infarctions (heart attack) is 0.04; of chemotherapy for breast cancer it is 0.8–0.11; and of heart bypass surgery in reducing coronary thrombosis it is 0.15. Set against that background, an average effect size of 0.10 cannot be dismissed as merely trivial. A 10% reduction in crime rates would represent an enormous benefit to any community.

Trends and Variations in Effects

What counts for far more, however, are the variations in observed effect sizes. It is consistently found that there is considerable heterogeneity amongst individual study effect sizes: there is '… an enormous amount of between-study variability' (Lipsey, 2009, p. 130). That would be impossible to decode, and probably meaningless if the results were random or entropic, but there are regular and consistent patterns within the variation. This observation is considerably more important than the average effect for the purpose of selecting and planning interventions that have the best chance of achieving good effects. There is now a widespread consensus that it is possible to maximize effect sizes, that is, produce larger reductions in recidivism, by combining a number of elements in treatment and intervention services (Andrews, 2001). Expert reviewers agree that there are certain features of criminal justice interventions that maximize the likelihood of securing a practical, meaningful impact in terms of reduced re-offending. The major findings that arise from this, and which have emerged repeatedly over time, include the following:

Risk level

It is generally regarded as good practice to assess risk of future offending and allocate individuals to different levels of service accordingly. Risk assessment is usually based on information about an individual's criminal history, such as the age at which he or she was first convicted and the total number of convictions to date, though it can be supplemented with other information about an individual's personal attributes and functioning. The most intensive types of intervention should be reserved for those individuals assessed as posing the highest risk of re-offending. This pattern was originally labelled the 'risk principle', and the volume of evidence concerning its importance is now fairly substantial (Andrews, Bonta and Wormith, 2006; Lowenkamp, Latessa and Holsinger, 2006).

Risk factors as targets of change ('criminogenic needs')

Research on the emergence of delinquency suggests that certain patterns of social interaction, egocentric attitudes, poor social or cognitive skills and other factors are associated with its onset and maintenance. If work with offenders is to make a difference to their prospects of re-offending, those same factors should be its outcome targets. They are therefore called *dynamic risk factors*, and there are clear reasons for prioritizing them in rehabilitation services, with strong evidence of an association between the extent to which they are addressed and the size of outcome effects (Andrews and Bonta, 2010a). These factors have often been referred to as 'criminogenic needs', which has given rise to debate concerning the relationship between them and broader frameworks of human motivation and needs analysis (Ward and Stewart, 2003).

Responsivity

There are certain methods or approaches that have a superior record in engaging, motivating and helping participants in criminal justice interventions to change (Andrews, 2001; Andrews, Bonta and Wormith, 2006). There are two aspects of this. First, the concept of *general responsivity* suggests that rehabilitative efforts will work better if they have clear, concrete objectives, their contents are structured and there is a focus on activity and the acquisition of skills. Personnel involved in providing this should possess high-quality interpersonal skills and foster supportive, collaborative relationships within clearly explained boundaries. They will also possess skills for developing effective working alliances with service users and for stimulating and enhancing their treatment motivation (McMurran, 2002). Second, the concept of *specific responsivity* suggests that it is vital to adapt intervention strategies to accommodate diversity amongst participants with respect to age, gender, ethnicity, sexuality, language, culture and learning styles. This is not a matter of changing the methods that have been found to work, rather one of modifying their delivery or presentation to maximize engagement and participation.

The preceding three features (*risk, need* and *responsivity*) were initially identified in what remains one of the most influential and seminal meta-analyses, reported by Andrews *et al.* (1990). In that review, Andrews and his associates first pinpointed those features that contributed separately to enhancing effect size, but then found that the combination of them produced an additive effect. Dividing a set of 154 outcome studies into four categories, the category ('appropriate service') possessing most of the features yielded an average reduction in recidivism rates of 53%. So, although the mean effect size across all studies as denoted earlier is not particularly remarkable in itself, when interventions are suitably designed and delivered, it is possible to secure far larger gains. What were originally known as 'human service principles' (Andrews, 2001) developed from these results have continued to be tested, and the initial findings are now supported by a steadily expanding body of evidence. It has repeatedly been found that the same features are associated with the most beneficial outcomes. For example, in a meta-analysis of cognitive-behavioural programmes by Lipsey, Landenberger and Wilson (2007), whereas the mean OR for all 58 studies they reviewed was 1.53 (corresponding to a reduction in recidivism of 25%), amongst those that most closely adhered to applying these principles, the mean OR was 2.86. This is equivalent to a reduction in recidivism amongst experimental as compared to control groups of 52%. The basic precepts of this model, which might be regarded as a template for 'best practice', have progressively evolved into what has since been re-formulated as the *risk–need–responsivity* (RNR) model (Andrews and Bonta, 2010a, b; Andrews, Bonta and Wormith, 2006).

Multiple targets

Given the multiplicity of factors known to contribute to criminal activity, there is virtual unanimity amongst researchers that more effective interventions will contain a number of elements, addressing a mixture of the criminogenic risks and needs. Interventions that successfully do this are termed *multimodal*. When individuals with extensive criminal histories re-offend, it is often because of a build-up of difficulties in their lives, and a resort to ill-considered attempts at problem solving that instead result in a further offence (Zamble and Quinsey, 1997). Thus, working with a group of persistent offenders might involve training them in cognitive and social skills, helping them to acquire self-control of impulses and providing support for these changes through supervision or mentoring. Equally it might be accompanied by giving assistance with accommodation, employment and other basic practical problems, although remedying such everyday problems alone has not been reliably found to have a significant impact on rates of re-conviction.

Theory and evidence base

In a famous maxim, Kurt Lewin noted that 'there is nothing more practical than a good theory'. Intervention efforts are more likely to succeed if they are based on a conceptual model of criminal behaviour that is both conceptually sound and has firm empirical support. This provides a rationale for the methods that are used and the method of change believed to be at work when an individual participates. For example, if he or she is expected to desist from offending, will this be accomplished by learning new skills, changing attitudes, improving ability to communicate, increasing self-knowledge, solving problems, overcoming bad feelings, or some permutation from within these ingredients? Most of the structured programmes currently employed in criminal justice services use methods derived from cognitive social learning theory (*cognitive-behavioural* interventions). Whilst this is by no means the only theoretical option available, to date it has the most consistent record in yielding positive outcomes. It is erroneous and misleading to suggest that this field is atheoretical, an ideational vacuum, or that offender treatment is a 'black box' with only inputs and outputs and an absence of proposals concerning what goes on inside (McGuire, 2000).

Treatment integrity

Lipsey (1995) and other meta-analysts noted some time ago that intervention services appeared to work better when they were being actively monitored and evaluated by a researcher. Regular collection of data on how an intervention is delivered sustains its clarity of purpose, and its adherence to the theory and methods it was intended to apply and to evaluate. This feature is called the *integrity* or *fidelity* of an intervention (Hollin, 1995), and in the best intervention services it is routinely measured and checked.

To provide the most favourable conditions for the delivery of the kinds of services described earlier, many other ingredients also need to be in place. All of the assessments carried out, and procedures for integrating their results, should be founded on the best-validated methods currently available. This applies equally to processes for recording integrity and evaluating outcomes. It applies also at a strategic level, in the management and co-ordination of the portfolio of programmes and allied services within a criminal justice agency or ministry (Andrews, 2001).

One of the most widely propagated initiatives to have emerged from the 'what works' findings has been the assembly of methods and materials into a number of pre-arranged formats known as *programmes*. Strictly defined, a programme consists simply of a planned sequence of learning opportunities that can be reproduced on successive occasions (McGuire, 2001). Used in criminal justice settings, its general objective is to reduce participants' subsequent criminal recidivism. Within that context, the typical programme is a pre-arranged set of activities, has clearly stated objectives and comprises a number of elements interconnected according to a planned design. Usually, its overall shape and the contents of separate sessions will be recorded in a specially designed manual specifying in detail how the programme should be delivered. Manuals may vary with respect to how prescriptive they are, with some allowing considerably more scope than others for practitioners to adapt aspects of the materials for different groups with whom they are working (McMurran and Duggan, 2005).

A Step Towards Evidence-Based Practice?

Most of the primary studies analysed in the reviews itemized in Table 2.1 were conducted on a comparatively modest scale, and often, though by no means always, under reasonably well-controlled conditions. The question therefore arises as to whether similar findings will be obtained when interventions of this type are disseminated on a larger scale and become assimilated into routine practice, assuming that can be achieved. Impressed by the sorts of findings just surveyed, criminal justice departments of several countries embarked on policy experiments in which specially designed programmes or other services were introduced into prison, probation or youth justice agencies.

In England and Wales, this took the form of a large-scale policy initiative, the *Crime Reduction Programme*, which was put into practice from 2000 onwards. It involved the gradual introduction of structured programmes at many prison and probation sites. It was accompanied by an 'accreditation' process to select the programmes thought most likely to achieve good results and an elaborate system of monitoring standards of delivery and evaluating outcomes (National Probation Service, 2004). A dedicated set of criteria was drawn up for assessing the appropriateness and monitoring the delivery of programmes to be provided. These *Accreditation Criteria* were based closely on the list of features, reproduced earlier, that research has shown to be those most reliably associated with better results in terms of reductions in recidivism. The process was overseen by a specially appointed, independent group of experts, known then as the Correctional Services Accreditation Panel (CSAP; the name has since then been altered to Correctional Services Advisory and Accreditation Panel (CSAAP)). For programmes to be approved by the Panel, they need to be accompanied by a considerable quantity of supporting documentation. Each submission requires five manuals: (i) a Theory Manual, which describes the intervention model and evidence supporting it; (ii) the Programme Manual itself, describing the content, exercises and materials used; (iii) an Assessment and Evaluation Manual; (iv) a Management and Operational Manual; and (v) a Staff Training Manual. Programmes are then carefully scrutinized to judge whether they should be awarded accredited status. An 'inside story' of the Panel's activity has been given by some of its key members (Maguire *et al.*, 2010).

The number of programmes available has gone on expanding steadily (for more details on some of them, see McGuire, 2005, 2006, 2007). In its most recent annual report, the CSAP, which evaluates proposals for the introduction of programmes in both prison and probation services, listed a total of 42 programmes then approved for implementation. Amongst them, 18 we for use in prisons, 14 for probation and 10 for use in both settings (Correctional Services Accreditation Panel, 2009).

To date, the results of these initiatives have however been rather mixed and not entirely conclusive. Evaluation studies reported some significant reductions in recidivism following participation in prison programmes, notably *Reasoning and Rehabilitation* (R&R) and its briefer equivalent *Enhanced Thinking Skills* (ETS), the two most widely used in that setting (Friendship *et al.*, 2002). However, other evaluations conducted along similar lines have shown only marginal evidence of positive outcomes (Cann *et al.*, 2003).

Results in community settings were on the whole more positive, but a major obstacle to evaluation in that setting was the very high attrition rate amongst those allocated to attend programmes, at least during the initial years after their inception (Hatcher *et al.*, 2011). Fortunately there was evidence of steady and significant improvements in attendance thereafter, with completion rates doubling over a five-year period (National Probation Service, 2007). Evaluations of the probation *Pathfinder* programmes showed that those who completed programmes were significantly less likely to re-offend than the comparison sample not allocated to attend (Hollin *et al.*, 2008; Palmer *et al.*, 2007). Whilst the evaluations could not be based on randomized experimental trials, the studies were designed in accordance with the principles of the Transparent Reporting of Evaluations with Non-randomized Designs (TREND) statement for high-quality quasi-experimental studies (Des Jarlais *et al.*, 2004). Further analysis showed that the observed effects could not be explained solely in terms of prior features of the participants (McGuire *et al.*, 2008), discerning a difference that was most likely an effect of treatment.

Official statistics too are suggestive of positive effects resulting from participation in many probation programmes. This is not however based on either experimental or quasi-experimental evaluation designs, but on comparisons between predicted and actual re-offending rates over a two-year follow-up period (Hollis, 2007). The risk assessment instrument employed for this purpose, the *Offender Group Reconviction Scale* (OGRS) was developed and tested by Copas and Marshall (1998) and has one of the highest levels of predictive validity amongst methods of this type (Farrington, Jolliffe and Johnstone, 2008). Analysis of data on over 25 000 offenders by Hollis (2007) showed that there were statistically significant, and sometimes quite large, reductions in re-offending amongst those who had completed probation programmes.

The British government's Crime Reduction Programme remains one of the largest-scale initiatives ever undertaken in applying evidence-based practice to an area of public policy. Whilst many practitioners and researchers welcomed its arrival, it is also true that others had considerable reservations concerning it. Some were ideologically opposed from the outset, seeing it as a species of the soulless, target-driven managerialism mentioned earlier, an approach propelled primarily by targets and paying little if any regard to the social circumstances that form the background to much crime. Other commentators were sceptical from the outset and highlighted the gradually widening gap between the levels of recidivism reduction that were anticipated and what actually occurred (Stanley, 2009). Even amongst those who supported the departure in principle, the scale and pace of its dissemination took many by surprise. Possibly the biggest challenge, however, arose from the fact that the entire process was instituted in parallel alongside a number of other major organizational changes, which may have been a factor in weakening the results (Hollin, 2006; Raynor, 2004). Thus, the waters into which the CRP was launched were metaphorically speaking fairly rough, and perhaps not the most favourable for conducting a scientifically sound test of the potential effectiveness of offending behaviour programmes.

Economic evaluations

Apart from their demonstrable impact on recidivism and related indicators, there is another reason why intervention programmes of the kind just described should be attractive to criminal justice departments, to government finance departments and to the public at large. This centres on economic considerations, and the relationship between the expenses incurred in running such programmes relative to the sums that can be saved by preventing further crimes.

The outcome variable used to evaluate this aspect of effectiveness is called the *benefit–cost ratio*. There are several ways of computing this, all of which require some fairly complex accounting, but they all revolve around the comparison between two sets of figures. The first is the sum of all the costs involved in delivering an intervention programme. That entails adding together the amounts for staff salaries, premises, utilities, equipment, manuals, transport and indirect costs such as insurance. On the other side of the equation are the costs that arise when an individual commits an offence; they include police work, court hearings, legal personnel, property repairs, victim support, potentially hospital treatment of victims, and costs of imprisonment or supervision. The effect size of the intervention (its impact on re-offending) is then factored in. The result can be expressed as a ratio *per capita* of the amount of money saved to the amount of money spent.

An early example of this is the work of Prentky and Burgess (1990) who carried out an exercise of this kind in relation to a high-security institution, the Massachusetts Treatment Center (MTC), which specializes in working with men who have committed sexual offences. Follow-up studies showed that the group discharged from the MTC had a re-offence rate 15% lower than that of a comparable group released from prison. Prentky and Burgess showed that for each man sent to the MTC as compared to prison, the State of Massachusetts saved $68 000.

Other reviews of economic outcomes have since concluded that there are sizeable financial savings to be made from investment in direct interventions across both youth and adult correctional services. Aos *et al.* (2001) undertook a series of comparisons between different interventions in their benefit–cost ratios. They identified several that both lowered crime *and* reduced costs. Whilst the savings from some programmes were modest, several others such as *Aggression Replacement Training* (Goldstein *et al.*, 2004) emerged with very high benefit–cost ratios. Other evaluators (McDougall *et al.*, 2003; Welsh and Farrington, 2000) have reported a range of benefit–cost ratios for criminal justice interventions.

Monetary savings can be made even when reductions in crime are quite small. As a kind of corollary to this, Weisburd, Lum and Yang (2003) have noted that even if a programme evaluation does not produce statistically significant findings in the orthodox sense, this does not necessarily mean it has not 'worked'. Even a small change might be enough for the intervention to have paid for itself. That could be taken as an indicator of a minimal requirement or 'bottom line' in judging the net worth of a programme.

Change Methods and Contextual Factors

In the earlier phase of assembling and interrogating the evidence from meta-analytic reviews, when extracting messages from it that might be used to inform practice, there was an emphasis on methods of change and their compilation into the structured formats that came to be known as programmes. The focus therefore tended to be on the design and contents of such activities. Certainly, programmes are extremely valuable, and have arguably transformed the capacity of criminal justice services to discharge their appointed duties. Evidence such as that summarized earlier was sometimes taken to imply that all that had to be done to make the criminal justice system more effective was to install or develop a portfolio of well-chosen programmes and disseminate them throughout the system. Regrettably, that has been shown to be a rather naïve underestimation of the complexity of the task.

It is widely acknowledged today that when programmes were being widely adopted and applied, some other core aspects of high-quality intervention remained only poorly understood. This was despite the distinction forwarded by Palmer (1995) between *programmatic* and *non-programmatic* aspects of intervention, and his insistence that attention needed to be given to both. In the immediately ensuing years, the latter issues were almost certainly neglected (Gendreau, Goggin and Smith, 1999), and it was only following this that researchers turned more attention to the question of implementation of interventions. The weaker than expected effects of the methods disseminated through the Crime Reduction Programme may, at least in part, have been a consequence of insufficient understanding of, or attention paid to, these issues. It is now well established that many other elements need to be in place in order to ensure that programme activities are adequately supported, and that they are delivered in an appropriate way.

A helpful formulation first proposed by Bernfeld, Blase and Fixsen (1990) was revisited and offered as a framework for placing programmes in a wider context and directing attention to the other processes that needed to be occurring to embark on and sustain effective, evidence-based service improvements. This suggested that systemic change was only likely to be successful when adequate attention was paid to each of four interrelated levels, respectively, pertaining to the *client, programme, organization* and *society*. Often, well-intended and well-designed innovations have failed to flourish because their instigators or managers devoted efforts to one or two of these levels whilst ignoring the remainder. This set of concepts was given practical illustration in an influential book (Bernfeld, Farrington and Leschied, 2001) containing numerous real-world examples of how success or failure had been differentially influenced by contextual influences and organizational forces.

These areas have now been better researched, though given the intricacy and sometimes sensitivity of the issues to be explored, many questions remain unanswered. But there is a steadily evolving grasp of the connections between a programme's theory and design, on the one hand, and the factors that can optimize its chances of success (or alternatively militate against them), on the other (Bourgon *et al.*, 2010). There is firm evidence that contextual and other aspects of service delivery have a close association with outcomes. Dowden and Andrews (2004) reviewed the relationship between a variety of staff skills and practices, the nature of agency policies in delivering programmes and the resultant impact on recidivism. In declining order of the correlations obtained, they found that: (i) the use of structured learning procedures, (ii) levels of staff interpersonal skill, (iii) effective use of modelling, (iv) application of problem-solving approaches, (v) establishment of positive relationships, (iv) use of effective reinforcement and (vi) of disapproval where needed and (vii) effective use of authority were all significantly associated with the effect sizes of interventions. These findings have been expanded and substantiated in a more recent review of the area by Andrews and Bonta (2010a). With reference to the relational aspects, some primary studies in this area have suggested that a balanced combination of usage of authority with openness and what might be called 'Rogerian' qualities produces better effects than either an autocratic, rule-oriented style or a highly sensitive, but unboundaried approach, in working with criminal justice service users (Paparozzi and Gendreau, 2005; Skeem *et al.*, 2007).

Lowenkamp, Latessa and Holsinger (2006) reviewed evidence on the *risk principle*, the predicted relationship between assessed likelihood of future offending and actual outcomes. They surveyed evaluations of a series of 53 residential and 44 non-residential programmes in the state of Ohio, with a cumulative sample of 13 676 participants. They found that the extent to which services incorporated elements of allocation by risk level had a substantial impact on the extent to which recidivism was reduced. Andrews and Dowden (2005) and Lowenkamp, Latessa and Smith (2006) surveyed research on the importance of treatment integrity, and on quality of delivery, as factors influencing the relative success (or failure) of criminal justice programmes. The latter authors used the *Correctional Program Assessment Inventory* (CPAI-2000), a specially designed tool for appraising the extent to which a programme or agency fulfils evidence-based criteria of 'good correctional practice' (Gendreau and Andrews, 2001). The CPAI yields a series of component scores, and both these and its overall total were significantly correlated with rates of new offences, with numbers of technical violations and with proportions of samples returned to prison (an indirect measure of offence seriousness). Many programmes did not meet basic standards of effective intervention specified in the CPAI, and many of the programmes that were audited were simply not effective. However, as additional CPAI criteria were met, correlations with a reducing-recidivism effect increased from −0.05 to +0.18 (for residential programmes) and from −0.14 to +0.09 (for non-residential programmes).

Other recent meta-analytic reviews have studied and thrown light on a range of equally searching questions regarding contextual or extra-programmatic factors. Parhar *et al.* (2008) examined the possible impact of coercion in offender treatment, that is, comparing court-mandated with voluntary participation in programmes. They found larger outcome effect sizes for voluntary than mandated treatment: the main effect for level of coercion in both community and institutional settings was highly significant, but overall effects were moderated by setting, with larger effect sizes in the community. Whilst some might comment that this should be obvious (people are more likely to do well in something they have chosen to do), it had not been empirically tested in this way, and other evidence from research on substance abuse programmes has found equivocal results on the role of coercion in treatment effects (McSweeney *et al.*, 2007). Olver, Stockdale and Wormith (2011) investigated factors associated with attrition (dropout) from criminal justice programmes. Significant predictors of attrition were criminal history, antisocial personality (positively correlated), age, intelligence and motivation (negatively correlated). Given the frequently challenging nature of this problem in criminal justice service delivery (and its sometimes pivotal position in public relations), this review generates some potential guidance for improving programme take-up and completion rates.

Andrews (2011) has summarized progress on these questions and described a framework for synthesizing what is known about programmes themselves with what is known about organizational environments and other non-programmatic factors. This affords a clearer understanding of why, despite the availability of what appear (on the basis of other research) to be sound methods of intervention, under some circumstances programmes nevertheless perform less well than expected, and results fall below levels that were obtained elsewhere.

Conclusions

To conclude this chapter, it is worthwhile turning attention, even if only briefly, to three aspects of this field, superficially disparate, but more closely connected than they might first seem. Collectively (at least in this writer's opinion), they may have potentially far-reaching implications.

The first is concerned with the treatment of 'psychopaths' in the sense defined by Hare (1996). There is an apparently prevalent belief that some or all of those categorized in this way are 'untreatable' or possibly even made worse by treatment (D'Silva, Duggan and McCarthy, 2004). The latter suggestion is often traced to an evaluation of the regime at Penetanguishene, a high-security institution in Ontario (Rice, Harris and Cormier, 1992), following release from which 'treated psychopaths' committed more violent offences than untreated controls. But the treatment was of a highly dubious nature: groups of men were coerced into spending up to 11 days in each other's company, in a state of nakedness, in an experience known as the 'total encounter capsule'. It is hardly a surprise that these already high-risk men were made riskier as a result. In recent years, several findings have emerged that call into question the conclusions drawn from this. It must be acknowledged that this remains a highly controversial issue (Harris and Rice, 2006); there is as yet no definitive trial showing a clear treatment effect, and some reviews have remained inconclusive (Doren and Yates, 2008). However, there is also tentative evidence from several sources of responsiveness to treatment (see Chapter 7). Some of it comes from the review by Salekin (2002), whilst there are also more recent reports showing indicators of positive short-term effects (Skeem, Monahan and Mulvey, 2002; Wong *et al.*, 2006). Possibly the strongest findings to date come from the Mendota Youth Treatment Center, Wisconsin, addressing the needs of young offenders with 'psychopathic traits', with a four-year follow-up showing a very large treatment effect (Caldwell *et al.*, 2007). This regime, incidentally, was also economically effective, yielding a benefit–cost ratio of 7:1 (Caldwell, Vitacco and Van Rybroek, 2006).

Second, within many of the reviews listed in Table 2.1, covering interventions such as boot camps, scared straight interventions, demanding regimes, intensive surveillance and other explicitly punitive interventions – all grounded in deterrence theory – there is voluminous evidence that the standard approach to 'disposal' of offenders in the criminal justice system is either wholly ineffective or actually counterproductive. To this could be added many other types of information, from official statistics on reconviction rates to reviews of the outcomes of curfews (Adams, 2003) or the evaluation of 'three strikes' legislation in California, which produced effects directly opposite to those intended (Center on Juvenile and Criminal Justice, 2008). To endorse the conclusions of Andrews and Bonta (2010a, p. 369): '...specific deterrence may be declared to be empirically indefensible as a rationale for increasing the severity of the penalty'. Thus, the changes that are so frequently called for in 'law and order' debates are precisely the ones that are least likely to make any constructive difference (von Hirsch *et al.*, 1999). Psychological theory can offer a perfectly plausible explanation why punishment, applied in the manner it has to be in the criminal justice system, is virtually bound to fail (McGuire, 2004). Despite this clear evidence, and advice to act creatively to 're-invest' in a new approach to criminal justice (House of Commons Justice Committee, 2010), there remains an implacable intransigence and inertia on the part of governments to apply the knowledge so gained. Meaningful change to the status quo seems to remain persistently elusive. Psychologists have been urged to be more outspoken concerning issues such as the currently gross overuse of imprisonment (Haney, 1999, 2005), and whilst the prospects may remain forlorn, it is to be hoped that this set of findings could also become influential in a future direction of justice policy.

Third, and not as far removed from the previous points as it might sound, there are gradually developing links between the theories that underpin the most effective types of intervention programmes and the field of cognitive and social neuroscience. As brain imaging becomes progressively more refined, the cognitive-emotional systems that underpin action are being gradually, even if slowly and haltingly, elucidated. Already, some criminologists, a group of professionals not generally renowned for their enthusiasm for purportedly biological models, have noted the connections between research on the outcomes of cognitive-behavioural programmes and evidence concerning brain plasticity and the neural correlates of skill acquisition (Vaske, Galyean and Cullen, 2011). This converges with the models of cognitive social learning theory and person–situation interactionism that have underpinned and informed the development of many offending behaviour programmes. Other researchers have built conceptual bridges between those models and the advancing knowledge from neuroscience (Barrett, Mesquita and Smith, 2010). Some psycho-legal experts have been resistant to the suggestion that this carries significant implications for the law, and, in particular, for concepts of criminal responsibility and how offenders should be dealt with. However, as amply illustrated by Greene and Cohen (2011), there are more convincing arguments to the effect that the emerging research has potentially profound repercussions for the use of rehabilitative as opposed to punitive strategies in attempting to secure behavioural change.

References

Adams, K. (2003) The effectiveness of juvenile curfews at crime prevention. *Annals of the American Academy of Political and Social Science*, 587, 136–159.

Alexander, M.A. (1999) Sexual offender treatment efficacy revisited. *Sexual Abuse: Journal of Research and Treatment*, 11, 101–116.

Andrews, D.A. (2001) Principles of effective correctional programs, in *Compendium 2000 on Effective Correctional Programming* (eds L.L. Motiuk and R.C. Serin), Correctional Service Canada, Ottawa, pp. 9–17.

Andrews, D.A. (2011) The impact of nonprogrammatic factors on criminal-justice interventions. *Legal and Criminological Psychology*, 16, 1–23.

Andrews, D.A. and Bonta, J. (2010a) *The Psychology of Criminal Conduct*, 5th edn, Anderson Publishing Co., Cincinnati.

Andrews, D.A. and Bonta, J. (2010b) Rehabilitating criminal justice policy and practice. *Psychology, Public Policy, and Law*, 16, 39–55.

Andrews, D.A. and Dowden, C. (2005) Managing correctional treatment for reduced recidivism: a meta-analytic review of programme integrity. *Legal and Criminological Psychology*, 10, 173–187.

Andrews, D.A. and Dowden, C. (2006) Risk principle of case classification in correctional treatment: a meta-analytic investigation. *International Journal of Offender Therapy and Comparative Criminology*, 50, 88–100.

Andrews, D.A., Zinger, I., Hoge, R.D. *et al.* (1990) Does correctional treatment work? A clinically relevant and psychologically informed meta-analysis. *Criminology*, 28, 369–404.

Andrews, D.A., Bonta, J. and Wormith, J.S. (2006) The recent past and near future of risk and/or need assessment. *Crime & Delinquency*, 52, 7–27.

Aos, S., Miller, M. and Drake, E. (2006) *Evidence-Based Adult Corrections Programs: What Works and What Does Not*, Washington State Institute for Public Policy, Olympia.

Aos, S., Phipps, P., Barnoski, R. and Lieb, R. (2001) The comparative costs and benefits, in *Sentencing and Criminal Justice*, 4th edn (ed. A. Ashworth), Cambridge University Press, Cambridge.

Babcock, J.C., Green, C.E. and Robie, C. (2004) Does batterers' treatment work? A meta-analytic review of domestic violence treatment. *Clinical Psychology Review*, 23, 1023–1053.

Barrett, L.F., Mesquita, B. and Smith, E.R. (2010) The context principle, in *The Mind in Context* (eds B. Mesquita, L.F. Barrett and E.R. Smith), Guilford Press, New York, pp. 1–22.

Berman, G. (2010) *Prison Population Statistics*, House of Commons Library, London.

Bernfeld, G.A., Blase, K.A. and Fixsen, D.L. (1990) Towards a unified perspective on human service delivery systems: application of the teaching-family model, in *Behavioral Disorders of Adolescence* (eds R.J. McMahon and R. DeV. Peters), Plenum Press, New York, pp. 191–205.

Bernfeld, G.A., Farrington, D.P. and Leschied, A.W. (eds) (2001) *Offender Rehabilitation in Practice: Implementing and Evaluating Effective Programmes*, John Wiley & Sons, Ltd, Chichester.

Bilby, C., Brooks-Gordon, B. and Wells, H. (2006) A systematic review of psychological interventions for sexual offenders II: quasi-experimental and qualitative data. *Journal of Forensic Psychiatry & Psychology*, 17, 467–484.

Bonta, J., Rugge, T., Scott, T. *et al.* (2008) Exploring the black box of community supervision. *Journal of Offender Rehabilitation*, 47, 248–270.

Boone, M. (2004) Does what works lead to less repression? The justification of punishment according to what works. Paper presented at the Societies of Criminology 1st Key Issues Conference, Paris, May.

Bourgon, G., Bonta, J., Rugge, T. *et al.* (2010). The role of program design, implementation, and evaluation in evidence-based "real world" community supervision. *Federal Probation*, 77, 2–15.

Bradshaw, W., Roseborough, D. and Umbreit, M. (2006) The effect of victim offender mediation on juvenile offender recidivism: a meta-analysis. *Conflict Resolution Quarterly*, 24, 87–98.

Brody, S. (1976) The Effectiveness of Sentencing. *Home Office Research Study no. 35*, Her Majesty's Stationery Office, London.

Brooks-Gordon, B., Bilby, C. and Wells, H. (2006) A systematic review of psychological interventions for sexual offenders I: randomised control trials. *Journal of Forensic Psychiatry & Psychology*, 17, 442–466.

Caldwell, M.F., Vitacco, M. and Van Rybroek, G.J. (2006) Are violent delinquents worth treating? A cost–benefit analysis. *Journal of Research in Crime and Delinquency*, 43, 148–168.

Caldwell, M.F., McCormick, D.J., Umstead, D. and Van Rybroek, G.J. (2007) Evidence of treatment progress and therapeutic outcomes among adolescents with psychopathic features. *Criminal Justice and Behavior*, 34, 573–587.

Cann, J., Falshaw, L., Nugent, F. and Friendship, C. (2003) Understanding What Works: Accredited Cognitive Skills Programmes for Adult Men and Young Offenders. *Findings 226*, Home Office Research, Development and Statistics Directorate, London.

Center on Juvenile and Criminal Justice (2008) Research Update: Does More Imprisonment Lead to Less Crime? www.cjcj.org (accessed 12 December 2012).

Cheliotis, L. K. (2008) Reconsidering the effectiveness of temporary release: a systematic review. *Aggression and Violent Behavior*, 13, 153–168.

Cleland, C.M., Pearson, F.S., Lipton, D.S. and Yee, D. (1997) Does age make a difference? A meta-analytic approach to reductions in criminal offending for juveniles and adults. Paper presented at the Annual Meeting of the American Society of Criminology, San Diego, November.

Cohen, J. (1992) A power primer. *Psychological Bulletin*, 112, 155–159.

Copas, J. and Marshall, P. (1998) The offender group reconviction scale: a statistical reconviction score for use by probation officers. *Applied Statistics*, 47, 159–171.

Correctional Services Accreditation Panel (2009) *Report 2008–2009*, Ministry of Justice, Correctional Services Accreditation Panel Secretariat, London.

Cullen, F.T. and Gilbert, K.E. (1982) *Reaffirming Rehabilitation*, Anderson Publishing Co., Cincinnati.

Des Jarlais, D.C., Lyles, C., Crepaz, N. and the TREND Group (2004) Improving the reporting quality of nonrandomized evaluations of behavioral and public health interventions: the TREND statement. *American Journal of Public Health*, 94, 361–366.

Doren, D.M. and Yates, P.M. (2008) Effectiveness of sex offender treatment for psychopathic sexual offenders. *International Journal of Offender Therapy and Comparative Criminology*, 52, 234–245.

Dowden, C. and Andrews, D.A. (1999a) What works for female offenders: a meta-analytic review. *Crime & Delinquency*, 45, 438–452.

Dowden, C. and Andrews, D.A. (1999b) What works in young offender treatment: a meta-analysis. *Forum on Corrections Research*, 11, 21–24.

Dowden, C. and Andrews, D.A. (2000) Effective correctional treatment and violent reoffending: a meta-analysis. *Canadian Journal of Criminology and Criminal Justice*, 42, 449–467.

Dowden, C. and Andrews, D.A. (2003) Does family intervention work for delinquents? Results of a meta-analysis. *Canadian Journal of Criminology and Criminal Justice*, 45, 327–342.

Dowden, C. and Andrews, D.A. (2004) The importance of staff practice in delivering effective correctional treatment: a meta-analytic review of core correctional practice. *International Journal of Offender Therapy and Comparative Criminology*, 48, 203–214.

Dowden, C., Antonowicz, D. and Andrews, D.A. (2003) The effectiveness of relapse prevention with offenders: a meta-analysis. *International Journal of Offender Therapy and Comparative Criminology*, 47, 516–528.

Dretzke, J., Davenport, C., Frew, E. *et al.* (2009) The clinical effectiveness of different parenting programmes for children with conduct problems: a systematic review of randomised controlled trials. *Child and Adolescent Psychiatry and Mental Health*, 3, 7. http://www.capmh.com/content/3/1/7 (accessed 12 December 2012).

D'Silva, K., Duggan, C. and McCarthy, L. (2004) Does treatment really make psychopaths worse? A review of the evidence. *Journal of Personality Disorders*, 18, 163–177.

DuBois, D.L., Portillo, N., Rhodes, J.E. *et al.* (2011). How effective are mentoring programs for youth? A systematic review of the evidence. *Psychological Science in the Public Interest*, 12, 57–91.

Egg, R., Pearson, F.S., Cleland, C.M. and Lipton, D.S. (2000) Evaluations of correctional treatment programs in Germany: a review and meta-analysis. *Substance Use and Misuse*, 35, 1967–2009.

Farrington, D.P. and Welsh, B.C. (2003) Family-based prevention of offending: a meta-analysis. *Australian and New Zealand Journal of Criminology*, 36, 127–151.

Farrington, D.P., Jolliffe, D. and Johnstone, L. (2008) *Assessing Violence Risk: A Framework for Practice*, Risk Management Authority, Paisley.

Feder, L. and Wilson, D.B. (2005) A meta-analytic review of court-mandated batterer intervention programs: can courts affect abusers' behaviour? *Journal of Experimental Criminology*, 1, 239–262.

French, S.A. and Gendreau, P. (2006) Reducing prison misconducts: What works! *Criminal Justice and Behavior*, 33, 185–218.

Friendship, C., Blud, L., Erikson, M. and Travers, R. (2002) An Evaluation of Cognitive-Behavioural Treatment for Prisoners. *Findings 161*, Home Office Research, Development and Statistics Directorate, London.

Gaes, G.G. (1998) Correctional treatment, in *The Handbook of Crime and Punishment* (ed. M. Tonry), Oxford University Press, Oxford, pp. 712–738.

Gallagher, C.A., Wilson, D.B., Hirschfield, P. *et al.* (1999) A quantitative review of the effects of sexual offender treatment on sexual reoffending. *Corrections Management Quarterly*, 3, 19–29.

Garrett, C.G. (1985) Effects of residential treatment on adjudicated delinquents: a meta-analysis. *Journal of Research in Crime and Delinquency*, 22, 287–308.

Garrido, V. and Morales, L.A. (2007) *Serious (Violent and Chronic) Juvenile Offenders: A Systematic Review of Treatment Effectiveness in Secure Corrections*, Campbell Collaboration Reviews of Intervention and Policy Evaluations (C2-RIPE), Philadelphia. DOI: 10.4073/csr.2007.7 accessed on 19/02/2013

Gendreau, P. and Andrews, D.A. (2001) *Correctional Program Assessment Inventory (CPAI-2000)*, 7th edn, University of New Brunswick, New Brunswick.

Gendreau, P. and Goggin, C. (1996) Principles of effective correctional programming. *Forum on Corrections Research*, 8, 38–41.

Gendreau, P. and Ross, R.R. (1980) Effective correctional treatment: bibliotherapy for cynics, in *Effective Correctional Treatment* (eds R.R. Ross and P. Gendreau), Butterworths, Toronto, pp. 3–36.

Gendreau, P., Goggin, C. and Smith, P. (1999) The forgotten issue in effective correctional treatment: program implementation. *International Journal of Offender Therapy and Comparative Criminology*, 43, 180–187.

Gendreau, P., Goggin, C., Cullen, F.T. and Andrews, D.A. (2001) The effects of community sanctions and incarceration on recidivism, in *Compendium 2000 on Effective Correctional Programming* (eds L.L. Motiuk and R.C. Serin), Correctional Services Canada, Ottawa, pp. 18–26.

Gensheimer, L.K., Mayer, J.P., Gottschalk, R. and Davidson, W.S. (1986) Diverting youth from the juvenile justice system: a meta-analysis of intervention efficacy, in *Youth Violence: Program and Prospects* (eds S.A. Apter and A.P. Goldstein), Pergamon Press, Elmsford, pp. 39–57.

Goldblatt, P. and Lewis, C. (1998) Reducing Offending: An Assessment of Research Evidence on Ways of Dealing with Offending Behaviour. *Home Office Research Study no. 187*, Home Office, London.

Goldstein, A.P., Nensén, R., Daleflod, B. and Kalt, M. (eds) (2004) *New Perspectives on Aggression Replacement Training*, John Wiley & Sons, Ltd, Chichester.

Gossop, M., Trakada, K., Stewart, D. and Witton, J. (2005) Reduction in criminal convictions after addiction treatment: 5-year follow-up. *Drug and Alcohol Dependence*, 79, 295–302.

Gottschalk, R., Davidson, W.S., Gensheimer, L.K. and Mayer, J.P. (1987a) Community-based interventions, in *Handbook of Juvenile Delinquency* (ed. H.C. Quay), John Wiley & Sons, Inc., New York, pp. 266–289.

Gottschalk, R., Davidson, W.S., Mayer, J. and Gensheimer, L.K. (1987b) Behavioral approaches with juvenile offenders: a meta-analysis of long-term treatment efficacy, in *Behavioral Approaches to Crime and Delinquency* (eds E.K. Morris and C.J. Braukmann), Plenum Press, New York, pp. 399–422.

Greene, J. and Cohen, J. (2011) For the law, neuroscience changes nothing and everything, in *Why Punish? How Much? A Reader on Punishment* (ed. M. Tonry), Oxford University Press, Oxford, pp. 293–314.

Grietens, H. and Hellinckx, W. (2004) Evaluating effects of residential treatment for juvenile offenders by statistical metaanalysis: a review. *Aggression and Violent Behavior*, 9, 401–415.

Hall, G.C.N. (1995) Sexual offender recidivism revisited: a meta-analysis of recent treatment studies. *Journal of Consulting and Clinical Psychology*, 63, 802–809.

Haney, C. (1999) Ideology and crime control. *American Psychologist*, 54, 786–788.

Haney, C. (2005) *Reforming Punishment: Psychological Limits to the Pains of Imprisonment*, American Psychological Association, Washington, DC.

Hanson, R.K., Gordon, A., Harris, A.J.R. *et al.* (2002) First report of the Collaborative Outcome Data Project on the effectiveness of psychological treatment for sex offenders. *Sexual Abuse: A Journal of Research and Treatment*, 14, 169–194.

Hanson, R.K., Bourgon, G., Helmus, L. and Hodgson, S. (2009). The principles of effective correctional treatment also apply to sexual offenders: a meta-analysis. *Criminal Justice and Behavior*, 36, 865–891.

Hare, R.D. (1996) Psychopathy: a clinical construct whose time has come. *Criminal Justice and Behavior*, 23, 25–54.

Harris, G.T. and Rice, M.E. (2006) Treatment of psychopathy: a review of empirical findings, in *Handbook of Psychopathy* (ed. C. Patrick), Guilford Press, New York, pp. 555–572.

Hatcher, R.M., Palmer, E.J., McGuire, J. and Hollin, C.R. (2011) An investigation of the relationships between dosage, appropriateness of selection, and reconviction amongst completers and non-completers of community-based offender interventions in England and Wales. Paper presented at the 2nd North American Correctional and Criminal Justice Psychology Conference, Sheraton Centre Hotel, Toronto.

Hockenhull, J.C., Whittington, R., Leitner, M., Barr, W., McGuire, J., Cherry, M.G., et al. (2012) A systematic review of prevention and intervention strategies for populations at high risk of engaging in violent behaviour: update 2002–8. *Health Technology Assessment*, 16(3).

Hollin, C.R. (1995) The meaning and implications of program integrity, in *What Works: Reducing Reoffending: Guidelines from Research and Practice* (ed. J. McGuire), John Wiley & Sons, Ltd, Chichester, pp. 195–208.

Hollin, C.R. (2006) Offending behaviour programmes and contention: evidence-based practice, manuals, and programme evaluation, in *Offending Behaviour Programmes: Development, Application, and Controversies* (eds C.R. Hollin and E.J. Palmer), John Wiley & Sons, Ltd, Chichester, pp. 33–67.

Hollin, C.R., McGuire, J., Hatcher, R.M. *et al.* (2008) Cognitive skills offending behavior programs in the community: a reconviction analysis. *Criminal Justice and Behavior*, 34, 269–283.

Hollis, V. (2007) *Reconviction Analysis of Interim Accredited Programmes Software (IAPS) Data*, Research Development Statistics, National Offender Management Service, London.

Holloway, K., Bennett, T. and Farrington, D. (2005) The Effectiveness of Criminal Justice and Treatment Programmes in Reducing Drug Related Crime: A Systematic Review. *Home Office Online Rep. no. 26/05*, Home Office, London.

House of Commons Justice Committee (2010) Cutting Crime: The Case for Justice Reinvestment. *First Report for Session 2009–2010*. The Stationery Office Limited, London.

Izzo, R.L. and Ross, R.R. (1990) Meta-analysis of rehabilitation programmes for juvenile delinquents. *Criminal Justice and Behavior*, 17, 134–142.

James, C., Stams, G.J.J.M., Asscher, J.J. *et al.* (2013). Aftercare programs for reducing recidivism among juvenile and young adult offenders: a meta-analytic review. *Clinical Psychology Review*, 33, 263–274.

Jolliffe, D. and Farrington, D.P. (2007) A Systematic Review of the National and International Evidence on the Effectiveness of Interventions with Violent Offenders. *Ministry of Justice Research Ser. 16/07*, Ministry of Justice, Research Development Statistics, London.

Kaminski, J.W., Valle, L.A., Filene, J.H. and Boyle, C.L. (2008) A meta-analytic review of components associated with parent training program effectiveness. *Journal of Abnormal Child Psychology*, 36, 567–589.

Knorth, E.J., Harder, A.T., Zandberg, T. and Kendrick, A.J. (2008) Under one roof: a review and selective meta-analysis on the outcomes of residential child and youth care. *Children and Youth Services Review*, 30, 123–140.

Latimer, J. (2001) A meta-analytic examination of youth delinquency, family treatment, and recidivism. *Canadian Journal of Criminology*, 43, 237–253.

Latimer, J., Dowden, C. and Muise, D. (2005) The effectiveness of restorative justice practices: a meta-analysis. *Prison Journal*, 85, 127–144.

Limbos, M.A., Chan, L.S., Warf, C. *et al.* (2007). Effectiveness of interventions to prevent youth violence: a systematic review. *American Journal of Preventive Medicine*, 33, 65–74.

Lipsey, M.W. (1992) Juvenile delinquency treatment: a meta-analytic inquiry into the variability of effects *Meta-Analysis for Explanation: A Casebook* (eds T. Cook, D. Cooper, H. Corday *et al.*), Russell Sage Foundation, New York, pp. 83–127.

Lipsey, M.W. (1995) What do we learn from 400 studies on the effectiveness of treatment with juvenile delinquents? in *What Works: Reducing Re-Offending: Guidelines from Research and Practice* (ed. J. McGuire), John Wiley & Sons, Ltd, Chichester, pp. 63–78.

Lipsey, M.W. (2009) The primary factors that characterize effective interventions with juvenile offenders: a meta-analytic overview. *Victims and Offenders*, 4, 124–147.

Lipsey, M.W. and Cullen, F.T. (2007) The effectiveness of correctional rehabilitation: a review of systematic reviews. *Annual Review of Law and Social Science*, 3, 297–320.

Lipsey, M.W. and Wilson, D.B. (1998) Effective intervention for serious juvenile offenders: a synthesis of research, in *Serious and Violent Juvenile Offenders: Risk Factors and Successful Interventions* (eds R. Loeber and D.P. Farrington), Sage Publications, Thousand Oaks, pp. 313–345.

Lipsey, M.W., Chapman, G.L. and Landenberger, N.A. (2001) Cognitive-behavioral programs for offenders. *Annals of the American Academy of Political and Social Science*, 578, 144–157.

Lipsey, M.W., Landenberger N.A. and Wilson, S.J. (2007) Effects of cognitive-behavioral programs for criminal offenders. *Campbell Systematic Reviews*, 2007, 6.

Lipton, D.S., Pearson, F.S., Cleland, C.M. and Yee, D. (2002a) The effects of therapeutic communities and milieu therapy on recidivism, in *Offender Rehabilitation and Treatment: Effective Programmes and Policies to Reduce Re-Offending* (ed. J. McGuire), John Wiley & Sons, Ltd, Chichester, pp. 39–77.

Lipton, D.S., Pearson, F.S., Cleland, C.M. and Yee, D. (2002b) The effectiveness of cognitive-behavioural treatment methods on recidivism, in *Offender Rehabilitation and Treatment: Effective Programmes and Policies to Reduce Re-Offending* (ed. J. McGuire), John Wiley & Sons, Ltd, Chichester, pp. 79–112.

Lösel, F. (1995) The efficacy of correctional treatment: a review and synthesis of meta-evaluations, in *What Works: Reducing Re-Offending: Guidelines from Research and Practice* (ed. J. McGuire), John Wiley & Sons, Ltd, Chichester, pp. 79–111.

Lösel, F. and Beelman, A. (2003) Effects of child skills training in preventing antisocial behaviour: a systematic review of randomized evaluations. *Annals of the American Academy of Political and Social Science*, 587, 84–109.

Lösel, F. and Koferl, P. (1989) Evaluation research on correctional treatment in West Germany: a meta-analysis, in *Criminal Behavior and the Justice System: Psychological Perspectives* (eds H. Wegener, F. Lösel and J. Haisch), Springer-Verlag, New York, pp. 334–355.

Lösel, F. and Schmucker, M. (2005) The effectiveness of treatment for sexual offenders: a comprehensive meta-analysis. *Journal of Experimental Criminology*, 1, 117–146.

Lowenkamp, C.T., Latessa, E.J. and Holsinger, A.M. (2006) The risk principle in action: what have we learned from 13,676 offenders and 97 correctional programs? *Crime & Delinquency*, 52, 77–93.

Lowenkamp, C.T., Latessa, E.J. and Smith, P. (2006) Does correctional program quality really matter: the impact of adhering to the principles of effective intervention. *Criminology and Public Policy*, 5, 201–220.

Lowenkamp, C.T., Flores, A.W., Holsinger, A.M., Makarios, M.D. and Latessa, E.J. (2010). Intensive supervision programs: does program philosophy and the principles of effective intervention matter? *Journal of Criminal Justice*, 38, 368–375.

MacKenzie, D.L. (2006) *What Works in Corrections: Reducing the Criminal Activities of Offenders and Delinquents*, Cambridge University Press, Cambridge.

MacKenzie, D.L., Wilson, D.B. and Kider, S.B. (2001) Effects of correctional boot camps on offending. *Annals of the American Academy of Political and Social Science*, 578, 126–143.

Maguire, M., Grubin, D., Lösel, F. and Raynor, P. (2010) 'What Works' and the Correctional Services Accreditation Panel: taking stock from an insider perspective. *Criminology and Criminal Justice*, 10, 37–58.

Marsch, L.A. (1998) The efficacy of methadone maintenance interventions in reducing illicit opiate use, HIV risk behaviour and criminality: a meta-analysis. *Addiction*, 93, 515–532.

Martin, M.S., Dorken, S.K., Wamboldt, A.D. and Wootten, S.E. (2012). Stopping the revolving door: a meta-analysis on the effectiveness of interventions for criminally involved individuals with major mental disorders. *Law and Human Behavior*, 36, 1–12.

Martinson, R. (1974) What works? – questions and answers about prison reform. *Public Interest*, 10, 22–54.

Mayer, J.P., Gensheimer, L.K., Davidson, W.S. and Gottschalk, R. (1986) Social learning treatment within juvenile justice: a meta-analysis of impact in the natural environment, in *Youth Violence: Programs and Prospects* (eds S.A. Apter and A.P. Goldstein), Pergamon Press, Elmsford, pp. 24–38.

McCart, M.R., Priester, P.E., Davies, W.H. and Azen, R. (2006) Differential effectiveness of behavioural parent-training and cognitive-behavioral therapy for antisocial youth: a meta-analysis. *Journal of Abnormal Child Psychology*, 34, 527–543.

McDougall, C., Cohen, M.A., Swaray, R. and Perry, A. (2003) The costs and benefits of sentencing: a systematic review. *Annals of the American Academy of Political and Social Science*, 587, 160–177.

McGuire, J. (ed.) (1995) *What Works: Reducing Reoffending: Guidelines from Research and Practice*, John Wiley & Sons, Ltd, Chichester.

McGuire, J. (2000) *Cognitive-Behavioural Approaches: An Introduction to Theory and Research*, Home Office, London.

McGuire, J. (2001) Defining correctional programs, in *Compendium 2000 on Effective Correctional Programming* (eds L.L. Motiuk and R.C. Serin), Correctional Service Canada, Ottawa, pp. 1–8.

McGuire, J. (2002) Criminal sanctions versus psychologically-based interventions with offenders: a comparative empirical analysis. *Psychology, Crime & Law*, 8, 183–208.

McGuire, J. (2004) *Understanding Psychology and Crime: Perspectives on Theory and Action*, Open University Press/McGraw-Hill Education, Buckingham.

McGuire, J. (2005) The Think First Programme, in *Social Problem Solving and Offending: Evidence, Evaluation and Evolution* (eds M. McMurran and J. McGuire), John Wiley & Sons, Ltd, Chichester, pp. 183–206.

McGuire, J. (2006) General offending behaviour programmes, in *Offending Behaviour Programmes: Development, Application, and Controversies* (eds C.R. Hollin and E.J. Palmer), John Wiley & Sons, Ltd, Chichester, pp. 69–111.

McGuire, J. (2007) Programmes for probationers, in *Developments in Social Work with Offenders*. Research Highlights in Social Work Series (eds G. McIvor and P. Raynor), Jessica Kinglsey, London, pp. 153–183.

McGuire, J. (2008) A review of effective interventions for reducing aggression and violence. *Philosophical Transactions of the Royal Society B*, 363, 2577–2597.

McGuire, J. (2009) Reducing personal violence: risk factors and effective interventions, in *The Neurobiological Basis of Violence: Science and Rehabilitation* (eds S. Hodgins, E. Viding and A. Plodowski), Oxford University Press, Oxford, pp. 287–327.

McGuire, J. (2011) Treatment and rehabilitation evaluation and large-scale outcomes, in *Research in Practice for Forensic Professionals* (eds K. Sheldon, J. Davies and K. Howells), Routledge, London/New York, pp. 283–300.

McGuire, J., Bilby, C.A.L., Hatcher, R.M. *et al.* (2008) Evaluation of structured cognitive-behavioural programs in reducing criminal recidivism. *Journal of Experimental Criminology*, 4, 21–40.

McMurran, M. (ed.) (2002) *Motivating Offenders to Change: A Guide to Enhancing Engagement in Therapy*, John Wiley & Sons, Ltd, Chichester.

McMurran, M. (2009) Motivational interviewing with offenders: a systematic review. *Legal and Criminological Psychology*, 14, 83–100.

McMurran, M. and Duggan, C. (2005) The manualisation of a treatment programme for personality disorder. *Criminal Behaviour and Mental Health*, 15, 17–27.

McSweeney, T., Stevens, A., Hunt, N. and Turnbull, P.J. (2007) Twisting arms or a helping hand? Assessing the impact of 'coerced' and comparable 'voluntary' drug treatment options. *British Journal of Criminology*, 47, 470–490.

Mitchell, O., Wilson, D.B. and MacKenzie, D.L. (2012) The effectiveness of incarceration-based drug treatment on criminal behaviour: a systematic review. *Campbell Systematic Reviews*, 2012, 18. DOI: 10.4073/csr.2012.18 accessed on 19/02/2013

Morgan, R.D., Flora, D.B., Kroner, D.G. *et al.* (2012). Treating offenders with mental illness: a research synthesis. *Law and Human Behavior*, 36, 37–50.

National Probation Service (2004) *General Offending Behaviour/Cognitive Skills Programmes: Evaluation Manual and Scoring Supplement*, Home Office, National Probation Directorate, London.

National Probation Service (2007) *Annual Report for Accredited Programmes 2006–2007*, National Offender Management Service Interventions and Substance Abuse Unit, London.

Nugent, W.R., Williams, M. and Umbreit, M.S. (2004) Participation in victim-offender mediation and the prevalence of subsequent delinquent behaviour: a meta-analysis. *Research on Social Work Practice*, 14, 408–416.

Olver, M.E., Stockdale, K.C. and Wormith, J.S. (2011) A meta-analysis of predictors of offender treatment attrition and its relationship to recidivism. *Journal of Consulting and Clinical Psychology*, 79, 6–21.

Palmer, T. (1975) Martinson re-visited. *Journal of Research in Crime and Delinquency*, 12, 133–152.

Palmer, T. (1995) Programmatic and nonprogrammatic aspects of successful intervention: new directions for research. *Crime & Delinquency*, 41, 100–131.

Palmer, E.J., McGuire, J., Hounsome, J.C. *et al.* (2007) Offending behaviour programmes in the community: the effects on reconviction of three programmes with adult male offenders. *Legal and Criminological Psychology*, 12, 251–264.

Paparozzi, M.A. and Gendreau, P. (2005) An intensive supervision program that worked: service delivery, professional orientation, and organizational supportiveness. *Prison Journal*, 85, 445–466.

Parhar, K.K., Wormith, S.J., Derkzen, D.M. and Beauregard, A.M. (2008) Offender coercion in treatment: a meta-analysis of effectiveness. *Criminal Justice and Behavior*, 35, 1109–1135.

Pearson, F.S. and Lipton, D.S. (1999) A meta-analytic review of the effectiveness of corrections-based treatments for drug abuse. *Prison Journal*, 79, 384–410.

Pearson, F.S., Lipton, D.S. and Cleland, C.M. (1997) Rehabilitative programs in adult corrections: CDATE meta-analyses. Paper presented at the Annual Meeting of the American Society of Criminology, San Diego, November.

Perry, A.E., Darwin, C., Godfrey, C. *et al.* (2009a) The effectiveness of interventions for drug-using offenders in the courts, secure establishments and the community: a systematic review. *Substance Use and Misuse*, 44, 374–400.

Perry, A.E., Newman, M., Hallam, G. *et al.* (2009b) A Rapid Evidence Assessment of the Effectiveness of Interventions with Persistent/Prolific Offenders in Reducing Re-Offending. *Ministry of Justice Research Ser. no.12/09*. Ministry of Justice, Research Development Statistics, London.

Petrosino, A., Turpin-Petrosino, C. and Finckenauer, J.O. (2000) Well-meaning programs can have harmful effects! Lessons from experiments of programs such as Scared Straight. *Crime & Delinquency*, 46, 354–379.

Polizzi, D.M., MacKenzie, D.L. and Hickman, L.J. (1999) What works in adult sex offender treatment? A review of prison- and non-prison-based treatment programs. *International Journal of Offender Therapy and Comparative Criminology*, 43, 357–374.

Prendergast, M.L., Podus, D. and Chang, E. (2000) Program factors and treatment outcomes in drug dependence treatment: an examination using meta-analysis. *Substance Use and Misuse*, 35, 1931–1965.

Prendergast, M.L., Podus, D., Chang, E. and Urada, D. (2002) The effectiveness of drug abuse treatment: a meta-analysis of comparison group studies. *Drug and Alcohol Dependence*, 67, 53–72.

Prentky, R.A. and Burgess, A.W. (1990) Rehabilitation of child molesters: a cost-benefit analysis. *American Journal of Orthopsychiatry*, 60, 108–117.

Raynor, P. (2004) The probation service 'pathfinders': finding the path and losing the way? *Criminal Justice*, 4, 309–325.

Redondo, S., Garrido, V. and Sánchez-Meca, J. (1997) What works in correctional rehabilitation in Europe: a meta-analytical review, in *Advances in Psychology and Law: International Contributions* (eds S. Redondo, V. Garrido, J. Pérez and R. Barberet), Walter de Gruyter, Berlin, pp. 499–523.

Redondo, S., Sánchez-Meca, J. and Garrido, V. (1999) The influence of treatment programmes on the recidivism of juvenile and adult offenders: an European meta-analytic review. *Psychology, Crime & Law*, 5, 251–278.

Redondo, S., Sánchez-Meca, J. and Garrido, V. (2002) Crime treatment in Europe: a review of outcome studies, in *Offender Rehabilitation and Treatment: Effective Programmes and Policies to Reduce Re-Offending* (ed. J. McGuire), John Wiley & Sons, Ltd, Chichester, pp. 113–141.

Reitzel, L.R. and Carbonell, J.L. (2006) The effectiveness of sexual offender treatment for juveniles as measured by recidivism: a meta-analysis. *Sexual Abuse: A Journal of Research and Treatment*, 18, 401–421.

Rice, M.E., Harris, G.T. and Cormier, C.A. (1992) An evaluation of a maximum security therapeutic community for psychopaths and other mentally disordered offenders. *Law and Human Behaviour*, 16, 399–412.

Roberts, A.R. and Camasso, M.J. (1991) The effect of juvenile offender treatment programs on recidivism: a meta-analysis of 46 studies. *Notre Dame Journal of Law, Ethics and Public Policy*, 5, 421–441.

Rosenthal, R. (1994) Parametric measures of effect size, in *Handbook of Research Synthesis* (eds H. Cooper and L.V. Hedges), Russell Sage Foundation, New York, pp. 231–244.

Salekin, R.T. (2002) Psychopathy and therapeutic pessimism: clinical lore or clinical reality? *Clinical Psychology Review*, 22, 79–112.

Schmucker, M. and Lösel, F. (2008) Does sexual offender treatment work? A systematic review of outcome evaluations. *Psicothema*, 20, 10–19.

Schwalbe, C.S., Gearing, R.E., MacKenzie, M.J. et al. (2012). A meta-analysis of experimental studies of diversion programs for juvenile offenders. *Clinical Psychology Review*, 32, 26–33.

Serketich, W.J. and Dumas, J.E. (1996) The effectiveness of behavioural parent training to modify antisocial behaviour in children: a meta-analysis. *Behavior Therapy*, 27, 171–186.

Skeem, J.L., Monahan, J. and Mulvey E.P. (2002) Psychopathy, treatment involvement, and subsequent violence among civil psychiatric patients. *Law and Human Behavior*, 26, 577–603.

Skeem, J.L., Louden, J.E., Polaschek, D. and Camp, J. (2007) Assessing relationship quality in mandated community treatment: blending care with control. *Psychological Assessment*, 19, 397–410.

Smith, P., Gendreau, P. and Swatrz, K. (2009) Validating the principles of effective intervention: a systematic review of the contributions of meta-analysis in the field of corrections. *Victims and Offenders*, 4, 148–169.

Stanley, S. (2009) What works in 2009: progress or stagnation? *Probation Journal*, 56, 153–174.

Stover, C.S., Meadows, A.L. and Kaufman, J. (2009) Interventions for intimate partner violence: review and implications for evidence-based practice. *Professional Psychology: Research and Practice*, 40, 223–233.

Tanasichuk, C.L. and Wormith, S.J. (2007) Does treatment make psychopaths worse? A meta-analytic review. Paper presented at the North American Criminal Justice and Correctional Psychology Conference, The Westin Ottawa, Ottawa, June.

Tolan, P., Henry, D., Schoeny, M. and Bass, A. (2008) Mentoring interventions to affect juvenile delinquency and associated problems. *Campbell Systematic Reviews*, 2008, 16 DOI: 10.4073/csr.2008.16.

Tong, L.S.J. and Farrington, D.P. (2006) How effective is the "Reasoning and Rehabilitation" programme in reducing re-offending? A meta-analysis of evaluations in three countries. *Psychology, Crime & Law*, 12, 3–24.

Vaske, J., Galyean, K. and Cullen, F.T. (2011) Toward a biosocial theory of offender rehabilitation: why does cognitive-behavioral therapy work? *Journal of Criminal Justice*, 39, 90–102.

Vennard, J., Sugg, D. and Hedderman, C. (1997) Changing Offenders' Attitudes and Behaviour: What Works? *Home Office Research Study no. 171*. Her Majesty's Stationery Office, London.

Visher, C.A., Winterfield, L. and Coggeshall, M.B. (2005) Ex-offender employment programs and recidivism: a meta-analysis. *Journal of Experimental Criminology*, 1, 295–315.

von Hirsch, A. (1976) *Doing Justice: The Choice of Punishments. Report of the Committee for the Study of Incarceration*, Hill & Wang, New York.

von Hirsch, A., Bottoms, A.E., Burney, E. and Wikström, P.O. (1999) *Criminal Deterrence and Sentencing Severity: An Analysis of Recent Research*, Hart Publishing, Oxford.

Walker, D.F., McGovern, S.K., Poey, E.L. and Otis, K.E. (2004) Treatment effectiveness for male adolescent sexual offenders: a meta-analysis and review. *Journal of Child Sexual Abuse*, 13, 281–293.

Ward, T. and Stewart, C. (2003) Criminogenic needs and human needs: a theoretical model. *Psychology, Crime & Law*, 9, 125–143.

Weisburd, D., Lum, C.M. and Yang, S.-M. (2003) When can we conclude that treatments or programs "don't work"? *Annals of the American Academy of Political and Social Science*, 587, 31–48.

Wells-Parker, E., Bangert-Drowns, R., McMillen, R. and Williams, M. (1995) Final results from a meta-analysis of remedial interventions with drink/drive offenders. *Addiction*, 9, 907–926.

Welsh, B.C. and Farrington, D.P. (2000) Correctional intervention programs and cost benefit analysis. *Criminal Justice and Behavior*, 27, 115–133.

Whitehead, J.T. and Lab, S.P. (1989) A meta-analysis of juvenile correctional treatment. *Journal of Research in Crime and Delinquency*, 26, 276–295.

Wilson, D.B. (2001) Meta-analytic methods for criminology. *Annals of the American Academy of Political and Social Science*, 578, 71–89.

Wilson, D.B., Gallagher, C.A. and MacKenzie, D.L. (2000) A meta-analysis of corrections-based education, vocation and work programs for adult offenders. *Journal of Research in Crime and Delinquency*, 37, 568–581.

Wilson, D.B., Gottfredson, D.C. and Najaka, S.S. (2001) School-based prevention of problem behaviors: a meta-analysis. *Journal of Quantitative Criminology*, 17, 247–272.

Wilson, D.B., Bouffard, L.A. and Mackenzie, D.L. (2005) A quantitative review of structured, group-oriented, cognitive-behavioral programs for offenders. *Criminal Justice and Behavior*, 32, 172–204.

Wilson, D.B., MacKenzie, D.L. and Mitchell, F.N. (2005) *Effects of Correctional Boot Camps on Offending*, Campbell Collaboration Systematic Review, Philadelphia. DOI: 10.4073/csr.2003.1 accessed on 19/02/2013

Wilson, S.J. and Lipsey, M.W. (2000) Wilderness challenge programs for delinquent youth: a meta-analysis of outcome evaluations. *Evaluation and Program Planning*, 23, 1–12.

Wilson, S.J., Lipsey, M.W. and Derzon, J.H. (2003) The effects of school-based intervention programs on aggressive behaviour: a meta-analysis. *Journal of Consulting and Clinical Psychology*, 71, 136–149.

Wilson, S.J., Lipsey, M.W. and Soydan, H. (2003) Are mainstream programs for juvenile delinquency less effective with minority youth than majority youth? A meta-analysis of outcomes research. *Research on Social Work Practice*, 13, 3–26.

Wong, S.C.P., Witte, T.D., Gordon, A. *et al.* (2006) Can a treatment program designed primarily for violent risk reduction reduce recidivism in psychopaths? Poster presentation at the Annual Convention of the Canadian Psychological Association, Calgary.

Woolfenden, S.R., Williams, K. and Peat, J.K. (2002) Family and parenting interventions for conduct disorder and delinquency: a meta-analysis of randomised controlled trials. *Archives of Disease in Childhood*, 86, 251–256.

Zamble, E. and Quinsey, V. (1997) *The Criminal Recidivism Process*, Cambridge University Press, Cambridge.

3

Creating Ideological Space
Why Public Support for Rehabilitation Matters

Cheryl Lero Jonson[1], Francis T. Cullen[2]
and Jennifer L. Lux[2]

[1]Xavier University, USA
[2]University of Cincinnati, USA

For four decades, the core reality of crime policy in the United States has been what Clear (1994) calls the 'penal harm movement' (see also Currie, 1998; Gottschalk, 2006; Pratt, 2009). This movement has been characterized by elected officials voicing harsh rhetoric and promising to 'get tough' on crime and, most significantly, by the enthusiastic embrace of mass imprisonment. On any given day, over 2.2 million Americans sit behind bars – an astounding 1 in 100 of the country's adults (Cullen and Jonson, 2012; Pew Center on the States, 2008). Furthermore, unlike the nations in the European Union, more than two-thirds of the states in America still claim the legal right to use the death penalty (Garland, 2010).

In this context, it seems reasonable to conclude that a punitive culture exists in the United States and has an iron grip on crime policy – a linkage sometimes called 'penal populism' (Pratt, 2007). In this view, whether due to beliefs arising from the threat of crime or to manipulation by elected officials, the American citizenry wants its criminals 'locked up and the keys thrown away'. Politicians who dare to ignore the 'will of the people' will rightly be punished by the 'punitive public' at the polls by being denied re-election.

Notably, this belief in the hegemony of punitiveness is part of the professional ideology of criminologists (Matthews, 2005; see also Listwan *et al.*, 2008). Their embrace of the 'myth of punitiveness', as Matthews (2005) has provocatively called it, is understandable. They rarely see citizens marching in the streets in a campaign to reduce sentence lengths. By contrast, when heinous crimes occur, public calls for harsh justice can flare. For example, in December 2010, a parolee in Massachusetts shot and killed a police officer during a department store hold-up. In response to 'public outrage' and in an effort 'to restore public confidence', the state's governor terminated the parole officials from their positions (Finucane, 2011). Legislation was also filed to toughen parole-release standards for career offenders.

What Works in Offender Rehabilitation: An Evidence-Based Approach to Assessment and Treatment,
First Edition. Edited by Leam A. Craig, Louise Dixon and Theresa A. Gannon.
© 2013 John Wiley & Sons, Ltd. Published 2013 by John Wiley & Sons, Ltd.

Thus, an important kernel of truth is captured by the view that the public harbours punitive sentiments about crime control. But criminologists play an integral role in socially constructing the 'myth of punitiveness' when they portray citizen attitudes as being *exclusively* harsh on crime-related issues. This depiction rests, we suspect, on an implicit tautology: The very existence of punitive policies means that the public is punitive, which in turn helps to explain why punitive policies exist. In fact, a close inspection of public opinion polls and academic studies of citizen attitudes reveals a far more complex picture.

In short, the 'punitive public' is rivalled by the 'rehabilitative public'. To be sure, at the far tails of the ideological Bell Curve, it is possible to find Americans who only want to punish or who only want to save the criminally wayward. But in the giant centre, research shows that individuals hold a duality of beliefs, wanting offenders to be appropriately punished *and* to be appropriately corrected (Unnever *et al.*, 2010). The punch line here is that the 'myth of punitiveness' risks creating a context that is inhospitable to progressive, effective approaches to crime control. It thus is essential to engage in honest scholarship that illuminates the complexity of public attitudes towards crime. Good scholarship has the potential to be a wedge that splits apart the punitive myth and, in turn, that creates much-needed ideological space in which progressive policies might be seen as realistic and favoured by the public.

With this goal in mind, we begin by documenting the reality of the extent to which the public is punitive. We then proceed to deconstruct this myth of public punitiveness. In particular, we present evidence showing that the public has a complex understanding of the causes of crime and, consistent with these beliefs, supports a complex solution to the crime problem. Thus, although a 'punitive public' exists, so too does a 'progressive public'. We then focus specifically on public opinion polls and academic studies that demonstrate the persistence of the 'rehabilitative public' – that is, of the enduring belief among citizens that offenders should be the objects of correction. Our cautiously optimistic discussion adds a caveat, however, when we identify a potentially growing danger in the United States and in Europe – the 'prejudiced public' – that involves the use of racial and ethnic animus to excite punitive sentiments and policies. We conclude by emphasizing the importance of using public opinion research to create the ideological space for the development of effective correctional policies.

Before proceeding, we must add two points – a policy insight and a qualification, respectively. First, for four decades, the idea that nothing works to reform offenders has been a widely held and influential belief in corrections (Cullen and Smith, 2013). Due to the efforts of a small number of scholars at first but an increasing number now (Cullen, 2005), a wealth of evidence exists showing the effectiveness of treatment interventions (Andrews and Bonta, 2010; Smith, Gendreau and Swartz, 2009). Still, programme effectiveness is only one of the ingredients needed to achieve a policy transformation. Such a recipe for change also must include a clear demonstration to elected officials that the rehabilitation of offenders is an expression of the public will. Public opinion data thus play a potentially crucial role in facilitating a more therapeutic correctional enterprise. They provide an assurance to policymakers that advocating the rehabilitative enterprise will not evoke untoward repercussions and may well expand their political capital.

Second, except for the latter part of this essay, our analysis is confined to assessing public opinion in the United States. We must confess that this focus is due largely to the myopia of our expertise; we are US criminologists who have conducted and/or read surveys on crime-related attitudes in America. Even so, we suspect that much of what we have to say about the United States differs from other advanced Western nations more by degree than by kind.

The Punitive Public

The belief that offenders, especially those who break the law seriously and repeatedly, should be punished harshly for their wrongdoings is prevalent in today's society (Cullen, Fisher and Applegate, 2000; McCorkle, 1993; Reynolds, Craig and Boer, 2009; Roberts and Stalans, 2000). As discussed in the following section, opinion polls demonstrate that the public supports a harsh criminal justice system. Nevertheless, although a healthy reservoir of public punitiveness exists, these sentiments are often overestimated by traditional public opinion research.

Perceptions of the courts and criminal justice system

One common way to assess punitiveness is to ask survey respondents if they believe that the criminal justice system, particularly the courts, are 'tough enough' on criminals (Roberts *et al.*, 2003). Numerous surveys have reached similar results: The public does not believe that the criminal justice system is sufficiently stringent with lawbreakers.

A prominent poll that has tapped this issue for over three decades is the General Social Survey (GSS). Since 1972, the GSS has asked the following question: 'In general, do you think the courts in this area deal too harshly or not harshly enough with criminals'? As Cullen, Fisher and Applegate (2000) clearly demonstrated, from 1972 to 1998, the GSS found that the feeling that lawbreakers were getting off too easily was expressed by anywhere from 65 to 87% of the respondents. Eight years later, similar sentiments were found in the 2006 GSS. More than 82% of individuals indicated that they believed that the courts did not deal harshly enough with offenders. Only 5.2% stated that the courts were too harsh, and 12.2% stated that the courts dealt with offenders about right. The results of the GSS were echoed in a recent Gallup poll. Americans were asked if the criminal justice system was tough enough on criminals. Almost two-thirds (65%) answered that the criminal justice system was not tough enough, with only 6% claiming the system was too tough on offenders (Gallup Poll, 2004). These results confirmed Applegate, Cullen and Fisher's (2002) finding from a study of Ohio residents that the majority of those surveyed believed that the courts were not harsh enough with offenders, with 70.2% of women and 68.6% of men in their sample expressing this sentiment.

When dealing with the actual sentencing of offenders, the public also appears to express dissatisfaction in the harshness of sanctions given to offenders. The GSS (2006) asked respondents to state their level of agreement with the following item: 'People who break the law should be given stiffer sentences'. More than 8 in 10 of the respondents (85.8%) agreed with that statement, with more than 4 in 10 strongly agreeing. Thus, when general or 'global' questions about the punishment of offenders are used, the public often conveys that offenders are treated too leniently and that more punitive measures should be implemented.

Support for three-strikes   Three-strikes laws quickly spread across the United States in the early 1990s in response to the tragic murders of Polly Klaas and Kimber Reynolds (Schiraldi, Colburn and Lotke, 2004). Although there are variations in these laws across states, the basic premise is that once a person who has two prior violent felony convictions is convicted of a third felony, the offender is given a life sentence (or, in some cases, a minimum of 25 years in prison). Proposed as a foolproof way to remove the most dangerous offenders from society, a high proportion of the public supported the passage of these laws. In 1994, for example, California passed their three-strikes law with 72% of the votes (Wood, 2006).

Support for the life imprisonment of habitual offenders was also found in the Midwest (Applegate *et al.*, 1996). In a survey of 237 Ohioans, Applegate and his colleagues found that 88.4% approved three-strikes laws, with 52.1% strongly supporting such legislation. Such support did not vary by respondent characteristics. Furthermore, even though the willingness of politicians to implement three-strikes laws has declined in recent years, a large majority of the public continues to endorse mandatory lifetime imprisonment for habitual offenders (see Johnson, 2009).

Prisons as the preferred sanction Punitiveness can also be assessed by examining the public's support for the use of imprisonment as a means to punish offenders. For example, Jacoby and Cullen (1998) asked respondents in a national survey to assign sanctions in crime vignettes that included 24 offence types ranging from drunk driving to homicide. Across all vignettes, the sentence of jail or prison was assigned, on average, by 71% of the respondents. Even more telling, for 23 of the 24 offence types, jail or prison was chosen as the preferred sanction. Only for larceny under $10 was jail or prison not the most preferred sanction, falling only second to restitution.

Additionally, Jacoby and Cullen reported that those surveyed favoured relatively long prison sentences, with the mean prison sentences chosen by the respondents ranging from a little more than two years (27 months) for a $10 burglary from a building to more than 34 years (416 months) for a fatal rape offence. Thus, even for minor crimes (e.g., low-level burglaries and larcenies under $100), those surveyed wanted multiple-year sentences in prison for these lawbreakers.

Similarly, Turner *et al.* (1997) demonstrated the public's preference for offenders to be incarcerated for their wayward behaviour. For two types of robbery (no injury and with an injury) and two types of burglary (of $250 and $1000), the percent of respondents favouring a sanction with an imprisonment component (e.g., shock incarceration or straight imprisonment) ranged from 51.7 to 57.9. By contrast, few respondents favoured lenient sentences, with only 6.2–12.5% supporting regular probation across the four offence types.

Further, in a national sample of 804 adults, Hart Research Associates (2002) found that 71% strongly agreed that prisons should be the sanction used to punish violent offenders. An additional 20% somewhat agreed with this sentiment. However, among these same respondents, three-quarters favoured giving non-violent offenders community sanctions instead of imprisonment. This finding mirrors the results found in Hartney and Marchionna's (2009) survey of 1049 likely voters. Thus, the surveys show a strong commitment to imprisonment for violent offenders, but with the qualification that imprisonment is not necessary for non-violent offenders.

Support for capital punishment Unlike other Western nations – capital punishment is banned in the European Union, for example – the United States continues to put offenders to death. At present, 33 states have the death penalty, with 1321 executions having occurred since 1976 and another 3146 inmates sitting on death row (Death Penalty Information Center, 2013). The case for such 'American exceptionalism' is often justified as an expression of the public will – as democracy in action (Roberts and Stalans, 2000).

Public attitudes towards capital punishment have been researched more than any other criminal justice policy (Cullen *et al.*, 2009; Roberts and Stalans, 2000; Unnever and Cullen, 2010). Since 1953, Gallup has examined whether or not the public was supportive of capital punishment, asking the broad question: 'Are you in favour of the death penalty for a person convicted of murder?' (Cullen *et al.*, 2002, p. 32). For the past 57 years, Gallup has found that a large percentage of the US population is in favour of capital punishment. Support dipped below 50% to a low of 42% in 1966, but this proved to be an anomaly – an expression of a unique period in US history. Indeed, those endorsing the death penalty rose to a high of 80% in 1994, with support not falling below 60% since 1976. In the last decade, support has ranged from 64% to 70% (Gallup Poll, 2010b). This level of support is found across numerous studies examining multiple populations (Cullen *et al.*, 2009; Sandys and McGarrell, 1995; Unnever, Cullen and Jonson, 2008; Unnever, Cullen and Roberts, 2005). Consequently, when assessed with broad, global measures, it is apparent that a majority of the American public has endorsed the use of capital punishment.

Even more telling, over the past 10 years, Gallup polls have also found that the public expresses that they want the death penalty imposed in more cases. Responding to the question, 'In your opinion, is the death penalty imposed…', 49% responded 'not enough' (Gallup Poll, 2010b). Only 18% expressed that the sanction was being used 'too often'. Thus, not only do the majority of Americans hold favourable opinions concerning the death penalty, but roughly half of those polled also want the sanction to be used more frequently.

Punitive attitudes are not only seen in the general favourability to the death penalty, but are also seen in the reasons people state for justifying their support of capital punishment. In a 2003 Gallup poll, 40% of respondents stated retribution as their reason for supporting capital punishment. This justification was more popular than deterrence, cost concerns and incapacitation and has been replicated in numerous studies (Roberts and Stalans, 2000). Consequently, it appears that among a strong minority of the public, support for capital punishment is based more on a desire for justice or revenge.

The tempering of punitive attitudes   Although the public clearly harbours punitive tendencies, research has found that the strength of these sentiments is tempered by three major factors (Gromet, 2009; Hough and Roberts, 1999; Hutton, 2005; Stalans, 2009). This means that conclusions about the level of the public's punitiveness will be misleading if these contingencies are not fully understood. The research seems to show that while the public often initially reacts in a punitive fashion, the allegiance to these views wanes when they are given the opportunity to render a judgement based on more specifics.

First, the magnitude of the punitiveness varies by the type of question asked in the survey. For example, many public opinion polls tap global attitudes or sentiments by asking over-arching questions that tap impulsive, superficial views on a subject (Cullen *et al.*, 2009; Gromet 2009). These questions are very general and broad (e.g., 'Do you favour or oppose the death penalty?'), as was seen in the Gallup poll question presented earlier. When global questions are presented, the public tends to express punitive tendencies. However, when more specific questions are asked of the respondents that provide detailed information about the crime and/or offender, less punitive responses are often elicited.

This phenomenon is clearly revealed in the support for three-strikes laws. As shown earlier, when asking the global question about whether an individual approved of the laws, 88% supported the legislation (Applegate *et al.*, 1996). However, Applegate and colleagues also included on the survey instrument vignettes in which offenders were described as committing a third offence that, under an existing state law, would make them eligible for a three-strikes sanction. When such vignettes (giving specifics of the crime and offender) were presented to the respondents, support for three-strikes laws diminished substantially. In fact, only 16.9% selected a life imprisonment sentence for the offenders described in the vignettes, while the majority of individuals preferred the offender be sentenced from 5 to 15 years. Consequently, it is apparent that the degree of punitiveness substantially decreases when moving from global questions to specific questions that provide more details about the offence and/or offender.

Second, the strength of punitive ideals often diminishes when the respondents are given response sets with multiple sentencing options rather than a dichotomous (e.g., favour or oppose/yes or no) choice (Cullen *et al.*, 2009; Gromet, 2009; Roberts and Stalans, 2000; Unnever and Cullen, 2009). When individuals are forced to support or not support a particular criminal sanction, they often favour such measures because they are, in effect, comparing that option to doing nothing with the offender or letting them go free. Thus, citizens appear to be more punitive than if they were given alternative sanctions from which to choose.

This methodological artefact is clearly demonstrated in the research concerning capital punishment. For example, in the National Crime Policy Survey, Cullen *et al.* (2009) found that 74% of the respondents favoured the death penalty when asked the global question, 'Do you favour or oppose capital punishment – that is, the death penalty – in cases where people are convicted of murder'? Taken alone, this measure appears to show that Americans overwhelmingly approve the use of the death penalty. However, when the respondents were asked whether they prefer the death penalty or the life imprisonment of the offender without the possibility of parole, support for the death penalty waned substantially, with 53.5% choosing capital punishment and 46.5% selecting life imprisonment. Even more telling, when given the option of life imprisonment without parole and restitution to the family, only 39% chose the death penalty, with 61% preferring the alternative sanction for convicted murders. This tempering of punitive attitudes when presented with alternatives suggests that the American public's support of capital punishment is not static, but rather will vary depending on the alternatives presented (see Cullen *et al.*, 2009).

A third factor is that many Americans express a willingness to impose community sanctions, especially for non-violent offenders as studies cited earlier revealed. Even when expressing that imprisonment would be an appropriate sanction for many lawbreakers, members of the public are simultaneously willing to approve of a non-incarcerative sanction for these same offenders. Thus, the public is not so wed to incarceration that its members will not tolerate less harsh punishments for some types of offenders.

This tolerance for non-incarcerative sanctions was revealed in Turner *et al.*'s (1997) survey assessing the public's preferred sanctions for burglary and robbery offenders. As was stated earlier, over half of the respondents preferred a custodial sanction for these offenders. However, Turner and colleagues took this analysis further and asked the respondents to indicate whether or not they would find a variety of community alternatives to imprisonment (e.g., probation, strict probation, house arrest and halfway houses) as acceptable sanctions, even if imprisonment was their initial preference. They discovered that 64.8% and 73.3%, respectively, were willing to tolerate community sanctions for burglary and robbery. Consequently, this suggests that citizens are not so rigidly punitive as to completely resist community sanctions. Rather, these findings demonstrate that Americans are open to the idea of using less restrictive sentences when punishing lawbreakers.

The Progressive Public

As was shown earlier, clear evidence exists that the American public is punitive. However, substantial evidence exists to suggest that a vast number of Americans support the prevention of crime through social welfare policies and the early intervention of at-risk youth

(Unnever *et al.*, 2010). Consequently, favourable attitudes for two seemingly opposing ideals – a punitive and a progressive approach to crime control – are simultaneously held among Americans (Cullen, Fisher and Applegate, 2000; Cullen *et al.*, 2007; Unnever *et al.*, 2010). This coexisting support arises from the fact that Americans have a multifaceted understanding of crime causation. The public believes crime's sources lie in a variety of factors, both dispositional and situational, and thus that a single solution will not solve the problem. In this section, we discuss the public's complex view of the causes of crime and support for related policy proposals.

Complex causes of crime

Even if not always clearly understood and articulated, how individuals explain crime influences what they think should be done to reduce such conduct. This is a core thesis of what has become known as attributional theory (Miller, Smith and Uleman, 1981). In general, this social psychological approach distinguishes two attributional styles – one that justifies punitive policies and one that justifies progressive social welfare policies.

A *dispositional view* sees crime as caused by factors that lie *within the individual*. In such instances, people choose to go into crime because they think it pays or because they lack morals. Logically, the solution is to punish such waywardness so that these deviant souls will learn that crime does not pay. A bit of fuzziness arises if the dispositional trait is biological. But even here, a harsh policy is suggested: If offenders are marked by some immutable trait, then all one can do is to selectively incapacitate them. By contrast, a *situational view* sees crime as caused by factors that lie *outside the individual*. The fault thus rests not with the individual but with the fact that the person has lost life's birth lottery and been consigned to grow up in areas marked by disorganized families, ineffective schools, physical deterioration, economic deprivation and a criminal culture. Stopping crime thus requires social welfare programmes that mitigate these social disadvantages and interventions that insulate youngsters from these conditions (Unnever *et al.*, 2010).

Numerous studies have shown empirically this hypothesized relationship between the public's attribution of crime causation and its approval of various crime control strategies (Cochran, Boots and Heide, 2003; Cullen *et al.*, 1985; Grasmick and McGill, 1994; Johnson, 2009; Mascini and Houtman, 2006). For example, Cochran, Boots and Heide (2003) discovered that respondents who believed that crime was caused by dispositional factors were more likely to support capital punishment for adult, juvenile, mentally retarded and mentally incompetent offenders, while those who attributed crime to situational factors were less likely to support the death penalty for juveniles and adults. This finding was echoed by Mascini and Houtman (2006) who showed that people who endorse internal attributes were more likely to support repressive sanctions and less likely to support rehabilitative measures, while those attributing crime to external factors were more likely to support rehabilitative initiatives to control crime. Even more recently, Johnson (2009) similarly found support for a positive relationship between those who attribute crime to dispositional factors and punitiveness. Thus, it appears that Americans' perceptions of the causes of crime often dictate the level of support they have for punitive or progressive crime policies.

Research has recently discovered, however, that there may not be an absolute inverse relationship between dispositional and situational attribution styles (Unnever *et al.*, 2010). In other words, just because an individual may attribute crime to dispositional factors does not necessarily mean that same individual cannot still believe that situational factors also play a role in the causation of crime. Rather, people can hold both views (Unnever *et al.*, 2010).

Thus, even if they believe dispositional factors play a strong role in crime causation, they can still support progressive crime control policies. Unnever *et al.* (2010) empirically tested this proposition and found that situational and dispositional attributions were actually positively correlated, meaning those who endorsed the idea that crime was caused by factors internal to the individual also believed that crime had causes that were external to the individual. This suggests that Americans see crime as a complex phenomenon that can be explained by a variety of both internal and external factors. Consequently, it should not be surprising to learn that while the public does hold punitive attitudes towards criminals, they are also in favour of more progressive crime control policies.

Attacking the social causes of crime

Despite their support for punitive crime control strategies, recent surveys have found that the public is very supportive of policies that seek to attack the social causes of crime. For example, since 1989, Gallup polls have asked the following question: 'Do you think more money and effort should go to attacking the social and economic problems that lead to crime through better education and job training or more money and effort should go to deterring crime by improving law enforcement with more prisons, police, and judges'? Regardless of the year, respondents' support for attacking social problems has never fallen under 51%. In fact, support for attacking social problems has hovered around 65% for the last decade (Gallup Poll, 2010a). Interestingly, support for spending money on law enforcement has not exceeded 33% in the last 10 years. Thus, an overwhelming majority favour the more progressive approach to solving the crime problem.

These findings coincided with those found in a comprehensive survey of the public's attitudes towards a variety of criminal justice policies conducted by Hart Associates (2002). In this survey, conducted from May to December 2001, Hart Associates found that a variety of progressive policies were supported by the public. When asked what should be done to alleviate the crime problem, 63% agreed with a strategy that included providing job and vocational skills, providing counselling and increasing neighbourhood activities. Only 35% agreed with a strategy that included stricter sentencing, capital punishment and fewer parolees. Even more telling is that the respondents expressed concern that harsh punishments might increase the criminal behaviour of offenders. When asked about the current state of prisons, over 50% of the respondents agreed that prisons are more likely to train criminals to become better criminals rather than they are to reform them.

Furthermore, Hart Associates (2002) found that the public viewed progressive policies as being cost-effective. For example, 77% of the respondents agreed that 'expanding after-school programmes and other crime prevention programmes would save money in the long run by reducing the need for prison'. These same respondents also stated that they would be most willing to cut funding to prisons to save the state money rather than cut spending for education, job training, health care or terrorism prevention. Thus, despite its so-called punitiveness, the American public is willing to spend less on harsh crime control policies and instead invest in more progressive policies aimed at the prevention rather than the punishment of crime.

Support for early intervention

Over the past 20 years, life-course criminology has shown that important risk factors for later criminal behaviour often are manifested in early childhood (Loeber and Farrington, 2011; Wright, Tibbetts and Daigle, 2008). Thus, if interventions are undertaken early in a child's life – even at the prenatal stage – it is possible to have a substantial impact on the future criminal behaviour of that individual (Farrington, 1994). Numerous studies have found that early intervention is effective in reducing later criminal behaviour (Farrington and Coid, 2003; Farrington and Welsh, 2007; Greenwood, 2006). And, fortunately, not only is early intervention effective, but the public is also very supportive of and willing to spend money on early intervention initiatives (Cullen *et al.*, 2007).

One way to assess the public's attitudes towards early intervention programmes is to ask survey respondents whether they would spend their money on incarcerating offenders or on programmes that try to prevent crime by intervening with high-risk youths (Cullen *et al.*, 1998, 2002). The results from these studies have been quite consistent, with approximately 80% choosing the early intervention option (Cullen *et al.*, 1998, 2002). Furthermore, in three studies, it was discovered that the public overwhelmingly supported various early intervention strategies, ranging from expanding preschool programmes, to providing parental training, to school programmes, to rehabilitation programmes, even if it meant that their taxes would increase (Cullen *et al.*, 1998, 2002; Moon, Cullen and Wright, 2003). For all seven strategies presented to the respondents, no programme had less than 77% of the public supporting it.

In a unique study, Nagin *et al.* (2006) assessed how much members of the public were willing to pay for a rehabilitation programme, an extra year of incarceration for offenders, and for the nurse home visitation early intervention programme (an initiative where experienced nurses help young, single, at-risk mothers to avoid unhealthy conduct, such as smoking or taking drugs during pregnancy, and to use nurturing child-rearing techniques after giving birth; see Olds, 2007). A full two-thirds of the Pennsylvania adults surveyed (65.4%) were willing to pay at least $100 for rehabilitation, while only about half (51.8%) were willing to pay that same amount for an extra year of incarceration. Garnering even more support was the early intervention programme. More than 56% of the respondents were willing to pay $150 for the nurse home visitation programme, with 65.1% willing to pay at least $75 for the programme. When examining the average amount that the respondents were willing to spend on each of these three programmes, the results were as follows: the Pennsylvania adults were willing to spend the most on the nurse home visitation programme ($125.71), the second most on rehabilitation programmes ($98.10), and the least on an extra year of incarceration ($80.97). Thus, Americans not only seem to support early intervention programmes, but they are also willing to spend money on these initiatives in order keep these at-risk youth from engaging in a lifetime of criminal behaviour.

The Rehabilitative Public

Rehabilitation has had a long history in the United States. Beginning with the 1870 National Congress on Penitentiary and Reformative Discipline, the idea of individualized treatment and rehabilitation came into dominance in the United States (Rothman, 1980; Wines, 1910). This notion that the criminal justice system had the ability to reform lawbreakers into law-abiders was the guiding philosophy of the correctional system for nearly 100 years. However, in the 1970s, during a time of much social turmoil, rehabilitation came under attack from both liberals, who viewed rehabilitation as victimizing offenders through unequal punishments, and conservatives, who argued the discretion that accompanied rehabilitation victimized society by imposing lenient sentences and allowing the early release of dangerous offenders (Cullen, 2006; Cullen and Gilbert, 1982). This abandonment of rehabilitation as a guiding philosophy contributed to the rise of the 'get tough' movement in the United States that promoted the harsh punishment of offenders. However, in the past decade, 'cracks' have developed in this penal harm movement, with more progressive and rehabilitative solutions to the crime problem being endorsed (Listwan *et al.*, 2008).

Since the attack on rehabilitation occurred, it has often been assumed that the public not only harboured punitive sentiments but also had come to reject correctional rehabilitation. It is a 'remarkable criminological fact', however, that despite the punitive rhetoric, the rise of mass incarceration and critiques of offender treatment, citizens' support for rehabilitation – for the idea of 'corrections' – has persisted over the past several decades (Cullen, 2006). In this section, we document the extent of the public's desire for rehabilitation to be a defining feature of the correctional system.

Rehabilitation as the main goal of the criminal justice system

Since 1968, Americans have been surveyed about their views on the goals of imprisonment, or what they believe should be the main purpose of prisons (Harris, 1968). These early polls found that almost three-quarters of respondents selected rehabilitation over punishment and protecting society (Cullen, Fisher and Applegate, 2000). Although support for rehabilitation declined from particularly high levels following the late 1960s – a period of progressive reform – subsequent surveys have demonstrated that a large proportion of Americans continue to endorse rehabilitation as a major goal for prisons. For example, in a forced choice question, Cullen *et al.* (1990) asked residents of Cincinnati and Columbus to select what 'should be the main emphasis of prison'. For the two cities, respectively, 54.7% and 58.7% chose 'rehabilitating the individual so that he or she could return to society as a productive citizen'. Support for the punitive options were 5.7% and 6.7% for 'punishing the convicted of a crime' and 35.3% and 29.7% for 'protecting society from future crimes he or she might commit' (4.3% and 5.0% were 'not sure'). Further, over 80% of those surveyed in each city stated that they would favour expanding the rehabilitation programmes currently utilized in the prison. These results are notable because they occurred at the height of America's 'get tough' era and prior to major declines in the United States' crime rate (Blumstein and Wallman, 2000). Further, similar results were found in a 1996 survey of Ohio residents where, once again, rehabilitation was chosen as the preferred goal of imprisonment (Applegate, Cullen and Fisher, 1997).

The same forced-choice question was used in a 2001 national survey, which reported that 55% believed that the treatment of offenders should be the main purpose of prisons (Cullen *et al.*, 2002). Those endorsing rehabilitation were far more numerous than those who chose either punishment (14%) or protect society (25%). Additionally, the respondents were asked to rate the importance of each goal separately (i.e., one at a time rather than in a forced-choice format where only the goal most favoured is selected). Notably, 87% rated rehabilitation as being either important or very important. The respondents also were asked to judge whether 'it is a good idea to provide treatment for offenders who are in prison'. In this case, 92% expressed agreement with this statement.

In both 2002 and 2003, the Pew Research Center (2004) found that roughly 72% of those participating in a national poll agreed with the statement, 'The criminal justice system should try to rehabilitate criminals, not just punish them'. Similarly, Krisberg and Marchionna (2006) conducted a national public opinion poll examining attitudes towards rehabilitation. Only 11% approved of a prison system that should be strictly based on punishment where no rehabilitation is offered to inmates during their time behind bars or after their release. On the other hand, 81% endorsed the provision of state-funded treatment services while inmates are incarcerated. Thus, it has been clearly shown that since the late 1960s, Americans have expressed a desire to include rehabilitation as an integral component of the correctional enterprise.

Support for rehabilitation across gender, offender types and modalities   It is well established that Americans express a strong desire for rehabilitation to be the predominate goal of corrections when assessed with broad, global questions. Notably, similar support is still found when respondents are polled about more specific attitudes towards the treatment of offenders. For example, studies have shown that the public supports the provision of treatment for both male and female offenders as well as for various types of offenders (particularly those who are non-violent) and endorses a wide range of treatment programmes. Support of rehabilitation is more than a superficial reaction to a general question, but remains firm even when respondents are probed more specifically about their opinions about treatment.

Gender   The public appears to endorse rehabilitation as an appropriate correctional response for men and women alike. When presented with the statements – one for men and one for women – that 'We should try to rehabilitate men/women who have broken the law', almost an equal percentage of respondents expressed agreement. In this nationwide survey of 1000 respondents, Cullen *et al.* (2002) found that 92% supported rehabilitation for men and 93% for women. These findings confirm those of Applegate, Cullen and Fisher (1997). In their survey of 1000 Ohio residents, 87.4% advocated the use of treatment with men, while 90% of those surveyed expressed approval of treatment with women. Consequently, regardless of gender, it appears that Americans are steadfast proponents of correctional intervention with offenders.

Offender types   The public appears to support rehabilitation for a variety of offenders, particularly non-violent offenders. For example, in a survey of Ohio residents, Cullen *et al.* (1990) found that 84.4% of the public believed that rehabilitation would be helpful or very helpful with non-violent offenders. More telling, however, is the public's perception of the ability of rehabilitation to be effective with violent offenders. A majority (54.7%) stated that rehabilitation would be at least 'slightly helpful' with violent offenders. These findings were largely replicated by Sundt *et al.* (1998) around 10 years later. In this later survey, 89.5% perceived rehabilitation to be at least 'slightly helpful' for non-violent offenders and 41.4% believed treatment to be 'slightly helpful' for violent offenders. Although a modest decline occurred in the percentage indicating treatment is helpful for violent offenders, a significant minority of people nonetheless believed that rehabilitation can be effective with dangerous offenders. Furthermore, Sundt *et al.* discovered that rehabilitation was perceived as being helpful by over two-thirds of respondents for drug offenders and by 47.7% of those surveyed for sexual offenders. Notably, this result for sexual offenders suggests that about half the public rejects the often-repeated notion that all sexual offenders are beyond redemption. Research shows positive findings for treatment programmes for sexual offenders (see Hanson and Morton-Bourgon, 2005, or Chapter 10, this volume). Evidence exists that interventions that adhere to the principles of effective intervention achieve the higher reductions in sexual offenders' general and sexual recidivism rates (Andrews and Bonta, 2010, p. 484).

Also relevant is the research of Applegate, Cullen and Fisher (1997) who found that 54.2% of Ohio respondents agreed with the following statement: 'Rehabilitation programs should be available even for offenders who have been involved in a lot of crime in their lives'. This same question was asked in a national survey, with even more respondents (69%) indicating support for treating chronic offenders (Cullen *et al.*, 2002). Taken together, these findings suggest that even for career criminals who have been caught up in the revolving door of justice, rehabilitation is still seen as a worthwhile endeavour by the American public.

Treatment modalities   Americans appear willing to treat offenders using a variety of modalities. For example, the American public supports educational and vocational programs for offenders as a way to reform them into prosocial individuals (Applegate, Cullen and Fisher, 1997; Cullen, Cullen and Wozniak, 1988; Cullen, Fisher and Applegate, 2000; Cullen *et al.*, 1998; Hart Associates, 2002; Krisberg and Marchionna, 2006; Sundt *et al.*, 1998). In the numerous studies examining the public's support for job and educational programmes for offenders, support has ranged from 37% to 89%. Additionally, Americans have shown support for helping offenders with their emotional, attitudinal and/or mental health issues that may be contributing to their criminal behaviour. For example, in a national survey, Cullen *et al.* (2002) discovered that 88% of the respondents agreed with the following statement: 'The best way to rehabilitate offenders is to try to help them change their values and to help them with the emotional problems that caused them to break the law'. Note that studies do not analyse the data to show how many different treatment modalities each respondent advocates. But given the high level of support manifested across types of programmes, it is safe to conclude that most Americans embrace the use of multiple interventions with a variety of offenders. As such, ideological space would appear to exist for the multimodal treatment of offenders with diverse problems and for individualizing treatments for offenders beset with specific risk factors.

Support for juvenile rehabilitation   The public's support for the rehabilitation of juveniles not only has remained steadfast but also exceeds their support for the treatment of adult offenders. In fact, the support for juvenile rehabilitation is so strong that Cullen *et al.* (2007) have termed it a 'habit of the heart' for Americans – an enduring cultural belief. In various opinion polls, it has been shown that the public strongly believes that the main emphasis of juvenile sentencing and prisons should be rehabilitation, that the public considers treatment to be more effective with younger rather than adult offenders, and that Americans endorse various educational, vocational and counselling programmes for juveniles and are willing to do so even if it means increasing their taxes. No matter what method is used to ask or answer the question, the extant research confirms that Americans are firmly supportive of reforming wayward youth.

Public opinion polls have shown that Americans unequivocally support rehabilitation as the main purpose of juvenile corrections (Applegate, Cullen and Fisher, 1997; Applegate, Davis and Cullen, 2009; Cullen *et al.*, 2002). For example, in a forced choice question that included punitive options, Moon *et al.* (2000) reported that 63.3% of Tennessee respondents indicated that rehabilitation should be the main emphasis of juvenile prisons. Even more impressive, Cullen *et al.*'s (2002) nationwide survey found that 80% of the public stated that rehabilitation should be the overarching goal of juvenile corrections. Applegate, Davis and Cullen (2009) also demonstrated that 94.7% of those surveyed stated that rehabilitation is an important goal of juvenile sentencing. Consequently, the desire for the juvenile justice system to rehabilitate and treat wayward youth is a strongly held sentiment among the American public.

When examining the importance that the American public places on the rehabilitation of juvenile offenders, very strong support is found. Both Applegate, Cullen and Fisher (1997) and Cullen *et al.* (2002) asked respondents to indicate whether they agreed or disagreed with the following statement: 'It is important to try to rehabilitate juveniles who have committed crimes and are now in the correctional system'. In each survey, over 96% of those surveyed agreed. Similarly, Moon *et al.* (2000) found that 94.5% of respondents stated that having rehabilitation as the main goal was important or extremely important.

Furthermore, the American public is more likely to believe that rehabilitation is effective or 'helpful' with juvenile offenders than with adult offenders. When asking Ohioans in 1986 how helpful rehabilitation is with juvenile offenders, Cullen *et al.* (1990) found that 94% believed that rehabilitation would be useful for juvenile offenders as opposed to 85.6% stating treatment would be helpful for adults. In their replication nine years later, Sundt *et al.* (1998) found similar results. This sentiment was also confirmed in Piquero *et al.*'s (2010) survey of Pennsylvania residents, where 77.2% of respondents stated that juveniles will benefit more from rehabilitation than adult offenders. Thus, the public has much faith in the ability of rehabilitation to exact change in young criminals and turn them into law-abiding and productive young adults.

Moreover, just as the public supports various treatment programmes for adult offenders, Americans are open to a variety of interventions for juvenile delinquents. For example, strong support (96%) has been found for the placement of both the youth and their parents in rehabilitation programmes in order to address and correct the root of the child's problems (Cullen, Fisher and Applegate, 2000). The public also supports helping young offenders deal with their emotional problems that are contributing to their criminal behaviour (92.9%), providing vocational skills (89.3%) and offering educational programmes (76.5%) (Moon *et al.*, 2000). Finally, Moon *et al.* (2000) also found that Americans are still incredibly supportive of these treatment programmes even if their taxes increased. Specifically, 94.5% approved of rehabilitation programmes for both the youth and their parents regardless of the increase in taxes that the intervention may cause. These findings lend credence to the conclusion that the public not only endorses juvenile rehabilitation but is also willing to pay for it.

The Prejudiced Public

Thus far, our analysis has struck a cautiously optimistic chord, suggesting that the manifest pool of punitive sentiments is balanced by a less celebrated sea of progressive and rehabilitative beliefs. Still, one factor, unmentioned thus far, can play a dynamic role in fuelling support for punitiveness: racial prejudice, including the dislike of minorities and negative stereotypes (Unnever and Cullen, 2012). In the United States, minorities are less punitive, with a substantial gap in support for the death penalty (over 25 percentage points) existing between Whites and African Americans (Unnever and Cullen, 2007b). Further, racism among Whites – harbouring animus towards minority groups – is a strong predictor of punitiveness, accounting for a meaningful amount of this gap (Unnever and Cullen, 2007a). These sentiments are important because evidence exists that they have been exploited by politicians when they engage in 'wars on crime' in hopes of courting support among White racist voters. By intermingling race and crime – with minorities depicted as the 'criminal other' – elected officials are able to justify harsh policies, such as mass imprisonment, that disproportionately impact African Americans and similarly disadvantaged groups (see Tonry, 2011; Wacquant, 2009).

Importantly, these trends also can be seen in Europe where animus towards immigrants and migrant workers has been rising (Pettigrew, 1998). To be sure, the United States remains exceptional in the four-decade penal harm movement that has been marked by harsh rhetoric voiced by political elites and by increasing mass incarceration (Cullen and Jonson, 2012; Pratt, 2009). Even so, research reveals that in European nations, racial and ethnic animus is, as was found in the United States, a robust predictor of punitive sentiments (Unnever and Cullen, 2010; Unnever, Cullen and Jonson, 2008). This reservoir of resentment can be exploited by politicians – especially those on the right wing – that seek to identify minorities with crime, thus legitimating the crackdown on immigrant groups under the veil of 'public safety'. In these circumstances, a 'prejudiced public' can result in 'penal populism' – that is, in the growth of punitiveness and the call to 'get tough' with immigrant-criminals that are seen to threaten dominant group hegemony (see Pratt, 2007).

Again, discussions of the prejudiced public should not be pushed too far – it should be only identified as one source of public punitiveness that can intensify under certain conditions (e.g., economic downturns, terrorist attacks). These views must be seen as part of a broader, complex set of attitudes that are rooted in long-standing ideas about the government's social welfare obligations. Rather, the point to be made is that the prejudice public is a dynamic risk factor for punitiveness – a latent source of hostility that can be tapped to justify harsh crime control policies. Accordingly, awareness of its existence should be a sobering reminder that even in the twenty-first century, the effects of racial and ethnic prejudice can be a barrier to progressive approaches to reducing criminal conduct (see also Unnever and Cullen, 2010).

Conclusion: Creating Ideological Space

Similar to any stereotypes, myths about crime can capture an element of reality. The difficulty is that they convey beliefs that are exclusive and exaggerated – that treat a kernel of truth as the whole truth and that deny the truth of the other side of the coin. In this context, correctional rehabilitation has faced two difficult myths that eroded its legitimacy and placed its advocates on the defensive for more than three decades.

The first myth is that 'nothing works' to rehabilitate offenders (Cullen and Smith, 2013; Raynor and Robinson, 2009). Robert Martinson's (1974) classic review of evaluation studies popularized the conclusion that no treatment modality could reliably change lawbreakers into law-abiders. This so-called nothing works doctrine damaged the credibility of correctional rehabilitation and contributed to the movement to make punishment the sole, or main, goal of sentencing in the United States. This pessimism lingers, but it has been substantially rebutted by a wealth of empirical studies identifying promising strategies to achieve offender change (Andrews and Bonta, 2010; Brayford, Cowe and Deering, 2010; Cullen, 2005; MacKenzie, 2006; McGuire, 1995). Research also has demonstrated that punitive correctional interventions (e.g., boot camps, control-oriented intensive probation supervision) are ineffective. As a result, advocates of progressive, evidence-based corrections are able to 'cite the data' in their efforts to elevate rehabilitation's claim to be a central goal of offender intervention.

But showing that something 'works' is not all that is involved in policy formation. What the public thinks – or what policymakers think the public thinks – also matters. As Woods (2009, p. 34) notes, such opinion 'sets the limits or borders within which the public will support or tolerate a policy'. Garland (2010, p. 67) puts it this way: 'In the United States there are few claims more powerful than that of the democratic will'. In this context, it becomes apparent why it is so essential to combat the myth of the punitive public – the idea that all that citizens desire is to inflict pain on and 'warehouse' offenders (Cullen, Cullen and Wozniak, 1988; Cullen *et al.*, 2009). To the extent that elected officials are convinced that the public demands punitive solutions to crime – that is, that the will of the citizens is to 'get tough' – a strong disincentive exists to consider crime-control strategies that are more oriented towards social welfare.

These can be foreclosed with the simple retort that 'the public will not support them'. Although not plentiful, existing research indicates that policymakers generally overestimate the public's punitiveness (see Gottfredson and Taylor, 1984; Riley and Rose, 1980; Roberts and Stalans, 2000; Roberts *et al.*, 2003; Stalans, 2009).

Importantly, the need exists not simply to argue the negative – that the public is not exclusively punitive – but to put the matter in *positive terms* – that the public strongly supports a diverse response to crime control that includes correctional rehabilitation. As Garland (2010, p. 67) states, 'a social practice that can claim the support of a popular majority avails itself of an authority that is hard to challenge, whatever criticisms can be made of the way the practice is carried out'. Being able to argue that the public supports a given policy thus is consequential. In our terms, it *creates the ideological space* needed to propose and implement policies.

Showing that the public supports rehabilitation matters. Thus, it is critical for scholars using different methods and from different disciplines to continue to produce rigorous studies illuminating the nature and extent of public support for offender treatment. High-quality national studies are perhaps most compelling, but local studies are also salient because policymakers are often most concerned with what their particular constituencies favour. Furthermore, once studies exist – and are compiled in essays of this sort (see also Cullen, Fisher and Applegate, 2000) – efforts also must be made at knowledge dissemination. Deconstructing the punitive myth and actively creating ideological space for rehabilitation will not progress too far if scholars simply write for one another and publish results in journals read only by a narrow academic audience.

We close with one more cautionary remark: Hubris must be avoided. Again, to claim that the public is open to rehabilitation is not to say that a large reservoir of punitive sentiments does not exist. In the end, the public favours a *responsible* approach to crime control. Offenders must suffer a just measure of pain and must be controlled in a way commensurate with their risk of dangerousness. A mature approach to offender corrections should not ignore these aspects of the public will and, in so doing, hope to construct a myth of the rehabilitative public. Rather, honesty is the best policy. We must recognize the public's legitimate concern over just deserts and safety, while also educating policymakers of people's desire to see offenders return to society less criminogenic and more capable of being contributing citizens.

References

Andrews, D.A. and Bonta, J. (2010) *The Psychology of Criminal Conduct*, 5th edn, Anderson/LexisNexis, New Providence.

Applegate, B.K., Cullen, F.T., Turner, M.G. and Sundt, J.L. (1996) Assessing public support for three-strikes-and-you're out laws: global versus specific attitudes. *Crime & Delinquency*, 42, 517–534.

Applegate, B.K., Cullen, F.T. and Fisher, B.S. (1997) Public support for correctional treatment: the continuing appeal of the rehabilitative ideal. *Prison Journal*, 77, 237–258.

Applegate, B.K., Cullen, F.T. and Fisher, B.S. (2002) Public views toward crime and correctional policies: is there a gender gap? *Journal of Criminal Justice*, 30, 89–100.

Applegate, B.K., Davis, R.K. and Cullen, F.T. (2009) Reconsidering child saving: the extent and correlates of public support for excluding youths from the juvenile court. *Crime & Delinquency*, 55, 51–77.

Blumstein, A. and Wallman, J. (eds) (2000) *The Crime Drop in America*, Cambridge University Press, New York.

Brayford, J., Cowe, F. and Deering, J. (eds) (2010) *What Else Works? Creative Work with Offenders*, Willan, Cullompton.

Clear, T.R. (1994) *Harm in American Penology: Offenders, Victims, and Their Communities*, State University of New York Press, Albany.

Cochran, J.K., Boots, D.P. and Heide, K.M. (2003) Attribution styles and attitudes toward capital punishment for juveniles, the mentally incompetent, and the mentally retarded. *Justice Quarterly*, 20, 65–93.

Cullen, F.T. (2005) The twelve people who saved rehabilitation: how the science of criminology made a difference—the American Society of Criminology 2004 presidential address. *Criminology*, 43, 1–42.

Cullen, F.T. (2006) It's time to reaffirm rehabilitation: reaction essay. *Criminology and Public Policy*, 5, 665–672.

Cullen, F.T. and Gilbert, K.E. (1982) *Reaffirming Rehabilitation*, Anderson, Cincinnati.

Cullen, F.T. and Jonson, C.L. (2012) *Correctional Theory: Context and Consequences*, Sage, Thousand Oaks.

Cullen, F.T. and Smith, P. (2013) The myth that correctional rehabilitation does not work, in *Demystifying Crime and Criminal Justice*, 2nd edn (eds R.M. Bohm and J.T. Walker), Oxford University Press, New York, pp. 296–310.

Cullen, F.T., Clark, G.A., Cullen, J.B. and Mathers, R.A. (1985) Attribution, salience, and attitudes toward criminal sanctioning. *Criminal Justice and Behavior*, 12, 305–331.

Cullen, F.T., Cullen, J.B. and Wozniak, J.F. (1988) Is rehabilitation dead? The myth of the punitive public. *Journal of Criminal Justice*, 16, 303–317.

Cullen, F.T., Skovron, S.E., Scott, J.E. and Burton, V.S. (1990) Public support for correctional treatment: the tenacity of rehabilitative ideology. *Criminal Justice and Behavior*, 17, 6–18.

Cullen, F.T., Wright, J.P., Brown, S. et al. (1998) Public support for early intervention programs: implications for a progressive policy agenda. *Crime & Delinquency*, 44, 187–204.

Cullen, F.T., Fisher, B.S. and Applegate, B.K. (2000) Public opinion about punishment and corrections, in *Crime and Justice: A Review of Research*, vol. 14 (ed. M. Tonry), University of Chicago Press, Chicago, pp. 1–79.

Cullen, F.T., Pealer, J.A., Fisher, B.S. et al. (2002) Public support for correctional rehabilitation in America: change or consistency, in *Public Support for Correctional Rehabilitation in America* (eds J. Roberts and M. Hough), Willan, Cullompton, pp. 128–147.

Cullen, F.T., Vose, B.A., Jonson, C.N.L. and Unnever, J.D. (2007) Public support for early intervention: is child saving a "habit of the heart"? *Victims and Offenders*, 2, 109–124.

Cullen, F.T., Unnever, J.D., Blevins, K.R. *et al.* (2009) The myth of public support for capital punishment, in *Public Opinion and Criminal Justice* (eds J. Wood and T.A. Gannon), Willan, Cullompton, pp. 73–95.

Currie, E. (1998) *Crime and Punishment in America*, Metropolitan Books, New York.

Death Penalty Information Center. (2013) *Facts About the Death Penalty*, Death Penalty Information Center, Washington, DC.

Farrington, D.P. (1994) Early developmental prevention of juvenile delinquency. *Criminal Behavior and Mental Health*, 4, 209–227.

Farrington, D.P. and Coid, J.W. (eds) (2003) *Early Prevention of Adult Antisocial Behavior*, Cambridge University Press, Cambridge.

Farrington, D.P. and Welsh, B.C. (2007) *Saving Children from a Life of Crime: Early Risk Factors and Effective Interventions*, Oxford University Press, New York.

Finucane, M. (2011) In Wake of Officer's Slaying, Mass. gov. Shakes Up Parole Board. http://www.boston.com/news/local/breaking_news/2011/01/governor_announ_2.html (accessed 24 December 2012).

Gallup Poll. (2004) Public on Justice System: Fair, But Still Too Soft. http://www.gallup.com/poll/10474/public-justice-system-fair-still-too-soft.aspx (accessed 24 December 2012).

Gallup Poll. (2010a) Crime. http://www.gallup.com/poll/1603/Crime.aspx (accessed 24 December 2012).

Gallup Poll. (2010b) Death Penalty. http://www.gallup.com/poll/1606/death-penalty.aspx (accessed 24 December 2012).

Garland, D. (2010) *Peculiar Institution: America's Death Penalty in an Age of Abolition*, Belknap/ Harvard University Press, Cambridge, MA.

General Social Survey. (2006) *National Opinion Research Center*, Chicago.

Gottfredson, S.D. and Taylor, R.B. (1984) Public policy and prison populations: measuring opinions about reform. *Judicature*, 68 (4–5), 190–201.

Gottschalk, M. (2006) *The Prison and the Gallows: The Politics of Mass Incarceration in America*, Cambridge University Press, New York.

Grasmick, H.G. and McGill, A.L. (1994) Religion, attribution style, and punitiveness toward juvenile offenders. *Criminology*, 30, 21–45.

Greenwood, P.W. (2006) *Changing Lives: Delinquency Prevention as Crime-Control Policy*, University of Chicago Press, Chicago.

Gromet, D.M. (2009) Psychological perspectives on the place of restorative justice in criminal justice systems, in *Social Psychology of Punishment of Crime* (eds M.E. Oswald, S. Bieneck and J. Hupfeld-Heinemann), John Wiley & Sons, Ltd, Chichester, pp.39–54.

Hanson, R.K. and Morton-Bourgon, K.E. (2005) The characteristics of persistent sexual offenders: a meta-analysis of recidivism studies. *Journal of Consulting and Clinical Psychology*, 73, 1154–1163.

Harris, L. (1968) Changing public attitudes toward crime and corrections. *Federal Probation*, 32 (4), 9–16.

Hart Associates. (2002) *The New Politics of Criminal Justice*, Hart Associates, Washington, DC.

Hartney, C. and Marchionna, S. (2009) *Attitudes of US Voters Toward Nonserious Offenders and Alternatives to Incarceration*, National Council on Crime and Delinquency, Oakland.

Hough, M. and Roberts, J.V. (1999) Sentencing trends in Britain: public knowledge and public opinion. *Punishment and Society*, 1, 7–22.

Hutton, N. (2005) Beyong populist punitiveness? *Punishment and Society*, 7, 243–258.

Jacoby, J.E. and Cullen, F.T. (1998) The structure of punishment norms: applying the Rossi-Berk model. *Journal of Criminal Law and Criminology*, 89, 245–312.

Johnson, D. (2009) Anger about crime and support for punitive criminal justice practices. *Punishment and Society*, 11, 51–66.

Krisberg, B. and Marchionna, S. (2006) *Attitudes of US Voters Toward Prisoner Rehabilitation and Reentry Policies*, National Council on Crime and Delinquency, Oakland.

Listwan, S.J., Jonson, C.L., Cullen, F.T. and Latessa, E.J. (2008) Cracks in the penal harm movement: evidence from the field. *Criminology and Public Policy*, 7, 423–465.

Loeber, R. and Farrington, D.P. (2011) *Young Homicide Offenders and Victims: Risk Factors, Prediction, and Prevention from Childhood*, Springer, New York.

MacKenzie, D.L. (2006) *What Works in Corrections: Reducing the Criminal Activities of Offenders and Delinquents*, Cambridge University Press, New York.

Martinson, R. (1974) What works? Questions and answers about prison reform. *Public Interest*, 35, 22–54.

Mascini, P. and Houtman, D. (2006) Rehabilitation and repression: reassessing their ideological emeddedness. *British Journal of Criminology*, 46, 822–836.

Matthews, R. (2005) The myth of punitiveness. *Theoretical Criminology*, 9, 175–201.

McCorkle, R.C. (1993) Research note: punish and rehabilitate? Public attitudes toward six common crimes. *Crime & Delinquency*, 39, 500–513.

McGuire, J. (ed.) (1995) *What Works: Reducing Offending*, John Wiley & Sons, Ltd, Chichester.

Miller, F.D., Smith, E.R. and Uleman, J. (1981) Measurement and interpretation of situational and dispositional attributions. *Journal of Experimental Social Psychology*, 17, 80–95.

Moon, M.M., Sundt, J.L., Cullen, F.T. and Wright, J.P. (2000) Is child saving dead? Public support for juvenile rehabilitation. *Crime & Delinquency*, 46, 38–60.

Moon, M.M., Cullen, F.T. and Wright, J.P. (2003) It takes a village: public willingness to help wayward youths. *Youth Violence and Juvenile Justice*, 1, 32–45.

Nagin, D.S., Piquero, A.R., Scott, E.S. and Steinberg, L. (2006) Public preferences for rehabilitation versus incarceration of juvenile offenders: evidence from a contingent valuation survey. *Criminology and Public Policy*, 5, 627–672.

Olds, D.L. (2007) Preventing crime with prenatal and infancy support of parents: the nurse-family partnership. *Victims and Offenders*, 2, 205–225.

Pettigrew, T.F. (1998) Reactions toward the new minorities of Western Europe. *Annual Review of Sociology*, 24, 77–103.

Pew Center on the States. (2008) *One in 100: Behind Bars in America 2008*, Pew Charitable Trusts, Washington, DC.

Pew Research Center for the People and the Press. (2004) *The 2004 Political Landscape: Evenly Divided and Increasingly Polarized*, Pew Charitable Trusts, Washington, DC.

Piquero, A.R., Cullen, F.T., Unnever, J.D. *et al.* (2010) Never too late: public optimism about juvenile rehabilitation. *Punishment and Society*, 12, 187–207.

Pratt, J. (2007) *Penal Populism*, Routledge, London.

Pratt, T.C. (2009) *Addicted to Incarceration: Corrections Policy and the Politics of Misinformation in the United States*, Sage, Thousand Oaks.

Raynor, P. and Robinson, G. (2009) *Rehabilitation, Crime and Justice*, Rev. and updated edn, Palgrave Macmillan, Hampshire.

Reynolds, N., Craig, L.A. and Boer, D.P. (2009) Public attitudes towards offending, offenders, and reintegration, in *Public Attitudes Towards Crime, Victims and Offenders: Myths and Realities*, Willan, Cullompton, pp. 166–186.

Riley, P.J. and Rose, V.M. (1980) Public vs. elite opinion in correctional reform: implications for social policy. *Journal of Criminal Justice*, 8, 345–356.

Roberts, J.V. and Stalans, L.J. (2000) *Public Opinion, Crime, and Criminal Justice*, Westview, Boulder.

Roberts, J.V., Stalans, L.J., Indermaur, D. and Hough, M. (2003) *Penal Populism and Public Opinion*, Oxford University Press, New York.

Rothman, D.J. (1980) *Conscience and Convenience: The Asylum and Alternatives in Progressive America*, Little, Brown, Boston.

Sandys, M. and McGarrell, E.F. (1995) Attitudes toward capital punishment: preference for the penalty or mere acceptance? *Journal of Research in Crime and Delinquency*, 32, 191–213.

Schiraldi, V., Colburn, J. and Lotke, E. (2004) Three Strikes and You're Out: An Examination of the Impact of Strikes Laws 10 Years After Their Enactment, Justice Policy Institute, Washington, DC. soros.org/initiatives/justice/articles_publications/publications/threestrikes_20040923/three_strikes.pdf (accessed on 24 December 2012).

Smith, P., Gendreau, P. and Swartz, K. (2009) Validating the principles of effective intervention: a systematic review of the contributions of meta-analysis in the field of corrections. *Victims and Offenders*, 4, 148–169.

Stalans, L.J. (2009) Measuring attitudes to sentencing and sentencing goals, in *Social Psychology of Punishment of Crime* (eds M.E. Oswald, S. Bieneck and J. Hupfeld-Heinemann), John Wiley & Sons, Ltd, Chichester, pp. 231–254.

Sundt, J.L., Cullen, F.T., Applegate, B.K. and Turner, M.G. (1998) The tenacity of the rehabilitative ideal revisited: have offender attitudes toward offender treatment changed? *Criminal Justice and Behavior*, 25, 426–442.

Tonry, M. (2011) *Punishing Race: A Continuing American Dilemma*, Oxford University Press, New York.

Turner, M.G., Cullen, F.T., Sundt, J.L. and Applegate, B.K. (1997) Public tolerance for community sanctions. *Prison Journal*, 77, 6–26.

Unnever, J.D. and Cullen, F.T. (2007a). The racial divide in support for the death penalty: does white racism matter? *Social Forces*, 85, 1281–1301.

Unnever, J.D. and Cullen, F.T. (2007b). Reassessing the racial divide in support for capital punishment: the continuing significance of race. *Journal of Research in Crime and Delinquency*, 44, 124–158.

Unnever, J.D. and Cullen, F.T. (2009) Public opinion and the death penalty, in *Social Psychology of Punishment of Crime* (eds M.E. Oswald, S. Bieneck and J. Hupfeld-Heinemann), John Wiley & Sons, Ltd, Chichester, pp. 113–133.

Unnever, J.D. and Cullen, F.T. (2010) The social sources of Americans' punitiveness: a test of three competing models. *Criminology*, 48, 99–129.

Unnever, J.D. and Cullen, F.T. (2012). White perceptions of whether African Americans and Hispan-
ics are prone to violence and support for the death penalty. *Journal of Research in Crime and
Delinquency*, 49, 519–544.

Unnever, J.D., Cullen, F.T. and Roberts, J.V. (2005) Not everyone strongly supports the death penalty:
assessing weakly-held attitudes about capital punishment. *American Journal of Criminal Justice*,
29, 187–216.

Unnever, J.D., Cullen, F.T. and Jonson, C.L. (2008) Race, racism, and support for capital punishment,
in *Crime and Justice: A Review of Research*, vol. 37 (ed. M. Tonry), University of Chicago Press,
Chicago, pp. 45–96.

Unnever, J.D., Cochran, J.K., Cullen, F.T. and Applegate, B.K. (2010) The pragmatic American:
attributions of crime and the hydraulic relation hypothesis. *Justice Quarterly*, 27, 431–457.

Wacquant, L. (2009) *Punishing the Poor: The Neoliberal Government of Social Insecurity*, Duke University
Press, Durham.

Wines, E.C. (1910) Declaration of principles promulgated at Cincinnati, Ohio, 1870, in *Prison Reform:
Correction and Prevention* (ed. C.R. Henderson), Russell Sage, New York, pp. 39–63.

Wood, D.B. (2006). State Rethinks the Three-Strikes Law: Proposed Initiatives in California Would
Give Judges more Leeway in Sentencing. *Christian Science Monitor*, February 28.csmonitor.
com/2006/0228/p01s03-usju.html (accessed on 24 December 2007).

Wood, J. (2009) Why public opinion of the criminal justice system is important, in *Public Attitudes
Towards Crime, Victims and Offenders: Myths and Realities* (eds J. Wood and T. Gannon), Willan,
Cullompton, pp. 33–48.

Wright, J.P., Tibbetts, S.G. and Daigle, L.E. (2008) *Criminals in the Making: Criminality Across the
Life-Course*, Sage, Thousand Oaks.

Part II
What Works in Offender Assessment

4

Applying the Risk–Need–Responsivity Principles to Offender Assessment

James Bonta[1] and J. Stephen Wormith[2]

[1]Public Safety, Canada
[2]University of Saskatchewan, Canada

Offender assessment is a fundamental activity in the criminal justice system that impacts the offender, staff within the system and the general public. Courts, parole boards and probation and parole officers make decisions affecting the personal liberties of offenders and community safety. Prison staff assign inmates to differing levels of security to ensure the safety of staff and other inmates, and offenders are placed into different treatment programmes as a result of offender evaluations. These activities also impact financial and human resources. The consequences of offender assessments can truly be enormous.

This chapter describes how we have conducted the assessment of offenders over the past decades, how we continue to do so today and the challenges facing us. We have taken significant strides in the accuracy and usefulness of our risk assessment technology but there remains substantial room for improvement. It is our view that a General Personality and Cognitive Social Learning theory, and in particular the Risk–Need–Responsivity (RNR) model derived from the theory, can lead the way to significant improvements. We begin this chapter with a brief history of offender risk assessment followed by an overview of the role of theory and the RNR model. The chapter then continues with a description of the Level of Service (LS) instruments as a practical application of RNR. Finally, we end the chapter with the challenges before us and offer suggestions to address these challenges.

The Evolution of Offender Risk Assessment

When asked the question, 'How does one know that offender risk assessment works?' the answer is almost always related to the issue of predictive accuracy. Although predictive accuracy is important, it should not be the sole criterion for judging whether or not an assessment 'works'. The answer must also include the criterion of risk reduction. An assessment with high predictive accuracy may assist decisions on incarceration, custodial placement and community supervision, thereby balancing the freedoms of individual offenders with public

What Works in Offender Rehabilitation: An Evidence-Based Approach to Assessment and Treatment,
First Edition. Edited by Leam A. Craig, Louise Dixon and Theresa A. Gannon.
© Public Safety Canada 2013. Published 2013 by John Wiley & Sons, Ltd.

safety. However, this balance also requires the reduction of offender risk and the most effective way to reduce this risk is through treatment. Thus, offender assessment should also inform rehabilitative efforts in the reduction of offender risk.

Actuarial risk assessment

Most readers would be familiar with the clinical judgement versus actuarial debate around offender assessment. Clinical judgement is the unstructured gathering of information about the offender by a professional trained in understanding human behaviour. Clinical judgement is a highly individualized approach to assessment that may vary from client to client and is open to considerable personal bias. On the other hand, an actuarial-based assessment is highly structured. All clients are asked the same empirically based questions. The test administrator gathers the equivalent file information, organizes it into a quantitative mode and interprets it in a uniform manner.

Research comparing the two approaches has been conducted for decades and the findings are unequivocal. When it comes to predictive accuracy, actuarial assessment outperforms clinical judgement whether it pertains to offender risk assessment (Andrews, Bonta and Wormith, 2006; Hilton, Harris and Rice, 2006) or to assessments in general psychology (Ægisdóttir *et al.*, 2006; Grove *et al.*, 2000). So, what is it about actuarial assessment that makes it work better and are some actuarial assessments better than others?

The simple answer to the first part of our question is that actuarial assessment is evidence-based. The individual items or total scores based on the items are empirically related to future criminal behaviour. Clinical judgement is more dependent upon personal experience and perhaps because it is so individualized, unstructured and non-quantitative, rarely performs much better than chance. Clinical judgement is also subject to personal biases that are often unintended and usually go undetected without detailed research (Garb, 1997). However, not all actuarial assessments are equivalent. Offender assessments have been categorized by Bonta and his colleagues (Andrews, Bonta and Wormith, 2006; Bonta, 1996) into four 'generations'. First-generation assessment refers to clinical judgement. The remaining three are all actuarial assessments. Briefly, second-generation instruments consist mostly of static items, third-generation assessments include mostly dynamic risk factors, and fourth-generation instruments add theoretically important risk factors along with a case management strategy. We will now examine these generations of assessment tools in more detail.

Second-generation assessment: static risk

Second-generation offender assessment began with Burgess' (1928) pioneering research on the prediction of failure while on parole. He followed over 3000 offenders released on parole from three Illinois prisons for a minimum of two and one-half years. Each offender was scored as falling above (one point) or below (zero point) the base rate on 21 items (e.g., type of offence, marital status, psychiatric prognosis). The outcome criterion was parole success (i.e., no parole violation or a new arrest). Burgess then created an expectancy table of parole success. Those with the highest scores (16–21) had an expected success rate of 98.5% and offenders in the lowest category had an expected success rate of only 24%.

Surprisingly, second-generation risk scales did not enjoy widespread use until 1973 when the US Parole Commission adopted the Salient Factor Score (SFS) to assist in parole release decisions (Hoffman and Beck, 1974). Originally, the SFS consisted of nine items and it was subsequently reduced to six (Hoffman and Beck, 1985). The six items were entirely static (e.g., history of heroin/opiate dependence) unless the item 'recent commitment free period (three years)' is considered to be dynamic. The SFS demonstrated good predictive validity with point–biserial correlations in the range of 0.28–0.32 (e.g., Hoffman, 1994; Hoffman, Stone-Meierhoefer and Beck, 1978).

At approximately the same time, Canada developed the Statistical Information on Recidivism (SIR; Nuffield, 1982). The SIR consists of 15 items, most of which are static with a few potentially dynamic items (e.g., marital status). Fifteen years later, the United Kingdom developed the six-item Offender Group Reconviction Scale (OGRS; Copas and Marshall, 1998). These three instruments predicted recidivism in the range of $r = 0.24$–0.45 (Bonta *et al.*, 1996; Hoffman, 1994; Hoffman and Beck, 1985). Although the SFS has fallen by the wayside with the advent of third-generation risk assessments, the SIR is still in use by the Correctional Service of Canada. In the United Kingdom, the OGRS still appears sporadically in some research studies (Gray *et al.*, 2004), although it too has been largely replaced by third-generation risk assessment, the Offender Assessment System (OASys; Debidin, 2009).

Probably the most widely used second-generation risk instrument today is the 12-item Violence Risk Appraisal Guide (VRAG; Harris, Rice and Quinsey, 1993). We have three observations to make on the VRAG. First, as with all second-generation risk instruments, the items are static but produce satisfactory predictive validity. In fact, the developers of the VRAG have argued that static risk assessment is sufficient for the prediction of long-term risk (Rice, Harris and Hilton, 2010). We are not sure if this reflects a view that treatment is largely ineffective, thereby discounting a need for including dynamic risk factors typical of third-generation assessments. Our position is that limiting ourselves to prediction places constraints on the usefulness of an assessment instrument (i.e., risk reduction). Second, despite the term 'Violence' in the title of the instrument, the VRAG predicts violence no better than other instruments, even those that were developed to predict general recidivism (Campbell, French and Gendreau, 2009). Finally, unlike the other second-generation assessments that are strictly atheoretical, the VRAG incorporates a theoretically based item – the Psychopathy Checklist. We will say more about theory shortly.

Third-generation assessment: risk and needs

Third-generation assessments go beyond the measurement of static factors to include the assessment of offender needs. One of the earliest examples is the Wisconsin risk and needs assessment instruments (Baird, Heinz and Bemus, 1979). The 11-item risk assessment form consisted of mostly static items whereas the 12-item needs form tapped into the problems presented by the offender. There was no theory to suggest which needs were important. The need items were derived from suggestions by probation officers involved in the development of the form. The highest score from either instrument was used to make decisions on the supervision of offenders in the community.

One of the anomalies of the early research on the Wisconsin classification instruments is that only the risk form was subjected to any empirical validation (Baird, 1981, 1991). In 1994, Bonta, Parkinson, Pang, Barkwell, and Wallace-Capretta undertook a validation study of both of the Wisconsin instruments. The results were disappointing. Six of the items on the need form showed either no relationship with recidivism or exceedingly low base rates (less than 10%). As a consequence of their analysis, many of the need items were dropped and the need items that did predict outcomes were merged into the risk scale to produce one instrument.

This combination of static risk factors and dynamic risk factors into one instrument was not new. In the province of Ontario, the Level of Supervision Inventory (Andrews, 1982), a precursor to the Level of Service Inventory-Revised (LSI-R: Andrews and Bonta, 1995), did exactly this and it was introduced into probation in 1981. This merging of risk factors was not only efficient from an administration perspective but also made a great deal of sense from a theoretical perspective as we describe in 'Theory and Risk Assessment'.

Fourth-generation assessment: enhancing usefulness

Most correctional jurisdictions use some type of evidence-based classification system. Correctional staff is trained in the administration of various instruments; they dutifully record the results and make some basic decisions based on the results (e.g., frequency of contact, institutional security placement). With the assessment of criminogenic needs afforded by third-generation assessment instruments, staff is also expected to develop and implement a case management plan. Whether or not staff produce a workable case management plan was a question unanswered until 2008.

In a study by Bonta and his colleagues (Bonta *et al.*, 2008), the case management practices of 62 probation officers were examined. Three important findings emerged from this study. First, there was a weak relationship between the risk level of the probationers as measured by the agency's classification instrument and frequency of contact. Second, the formulation of a specific case plan for an identified need varied. For example, 79.5% of adult probationers with a substance abuse problem had a written case plan that addressed substance abuse, but only 10% of those with employment difficulties had a case plan that addressed employment. Third, within the audiotaped sessions, addressing criminogenic needs of the offenders also varied ranging from 3% for attitudes to 90% for family/marital issues. To sum, it appeared that the assessments conducted were used unevenly in formulating and implementing case management practices.

Fourth-generation assessments integrate aspects of case management into the assessment process. For example, in the Level of Service/Case Management Inventory (LS/CMI; Andrews, Bonta and Wormith, 2004), the case management goals and monitoring of activities to achieve these goals are part and parcel of the assessment document. By embedding case management information into the same document as the risk/need assessment, the chance that correctional staff will lose sight of the relationship between the offender's risk and needs and the case plan is diminished.

Theory and Risk Assessment

Many assessment instruments are borne out of 'dustbowl empiricism' and are atheoretical. Easily available, existing information about the offender (e.g., type of offence, number of prior convictions) is recorded at time A and examined as to whether the information predicts criminal behaviour at time B. There is no reason as to why particular information is selected at time A, other than it is available, or as to why the information predicts behaviour – it simply does. Examples from our previous discussion are the SFS and the SIR. Other assessment instruments are theory driven.

Two different theoretical perspectives have influenced the development of offender assessment instruments – forensic mental health and social learning theory. Forensic mental health perspectives view criminal behaviour as a product of psychological dysfunction and/or personality disorder. Therefore, assessment should focus on indicators of pathology (anxiety, thought disturbance, mood swings, etc.) and personality traits conducive to criminal behaviour. Offender assessment in the forensic mental health tradition has a long and varied history. Certainly, for psychologists and psychiatrists the Minnesota Multiphasic Personality Inventory (MMPI; Hathaway and McKinley, 1951) has been a staple in their assessment battery for years. Originally designed to assist the clinician in making a diagnosis (e.g., Schizophrenia, Psychopathic), the MMPI has changed over the years and was widely used in corrections up to the turn of this century (Boothby and Clements, 2000). Despite efforts to make the MMPI more relevant to criminal offenders (e.g., the Megargee-MMPI classification system; Megargee and Bohn, 1979), many have come to recognize that, except for Scale 4 of the MMPI (the old Psychopathic Deviate scale), the MMPI is a poor predictor of criminal behaviour (Motiuk, Bonta and Andrews, 1986).

Other assessment systems based on forensic mental health theories include Quay's (1965) Four-Factor Personality Typology, Grant and Grant's (1959) Interpersonal Maturity (I-Level) system, and Hunt and Hardt's (1965) Conceptual Level system. All three assessment systems stress the importance of inappropriate psychological functioning in criminal behaviour. What is noteworthy about the forensic mental health-based assessments, including the Megargee-MMPI, is that each has attached to it a framework for delivering rehabilitation programmes. This is something that assessments developed from dustbowl empiricism do not provide. Although these assessment systems were extremely popular in the 1970s and 1980s, the lack of predictive validity with respect to recidivism and the development of new assessments with better evidence have resulted in their almost total disappearance from the correctional landscape.

Before moving on, no overview of forensic mental health perspectives would be complete without a discussion of the Psychopathy Checklist-Revised (PCL-R; Hare, 2003). If it was not for Hare's development of the PCL-R, traditional forensic mental health assessment would have become a quaint, historical footnote. The PCL-R is comprised of 20 items and although some of the items are dynamic, the PCL-R is viewed as a static risk instrument consistent with the theory that psychopaths are largely unchangeable. However, Hare has recently moderated his position on the treatability of psychopaths. While acknowledging that no treatment programme has yet demonstrated a reduction in recidivism among psychopaths, it is possible that a programme designed upon what we know about effective programmes among general offenders could work with psychopaths (Wong and Hare, 2005).

Social learning theory and particularly the General Personality and Cognitive-Social Learning (GPCSL) described by Andrews and his colleagues (Andrews and Bonta, 2010a, b; Andrews, Bonta and Wormith, 2011) have been influential in developing offender assessment instruments. GPCSL posits multiple risk factors of varying degrees of importance associated with criminal behaviour. Table 4.1 summarizes what is referred to as the Central Eight risk/ need factors and at the top are the Big Four (the best predictors of criminal behaviour). Of special note is that mental health indicators, central in forensic mental health theories, do not appear on the list. An important hypothesis from GPCSL is that it is a *general* theory of criminal conduct. That is, the Central Eight are viewed as applicable to a wide variety of offenders. If the evidence supports the generality of the theory, then the need for specialized offender instruments for specific groups may be lessened.

Observe from Table 4.1 that seven of the eight risk/need factors are dynamic factors that can change bi-directionally (e.g., one can start taking drugs and one can also stop). Criminal

Table 4.1 The Central Eight risk/need factors in a general personality and cognitive social learning theory

Risk/need factor	Description
Criminal history	Early onset of antisocial behaviour, high frequency, variety of antisocial acts
Procriminal attitudes	Thoughts, values and sentiments supportive of criminal conduct
Antisocial personality pattern	Low self-control, hostile, pleasure/thrill seeking, disregard for others, callous
Procriminal associates	Friends and acquaintances who model, encourage and support criminal behaviour and thoughts
Education/employment	Difficulties in school and work settings with peers and authority, poor performance, lack of interest and ambition
Family/marital	Marital instability, poor parenting skills, criminality within the family and marital relationship
Substance abuse	Alcohol and/or drug abuse, substance abuse interfering with positive behaviours and relationships within the context of school, work and family
Leisure/recreation	Lack of prosocial pursuits

History is the exception – one can only increase criminal history. GPCSL theory outlines what should be assessed but it is important to note that these dynamic risk factors play another important function in the assessment of offenders. They direct service delivery. Reductions in risk can be achieved by addressing the dynamic risk factors or the criminogenic needs of offenders. In our case, GPCSL theory informs not only the content of assessments but also the practicalities of effective interventions (referring back to the risk reduction criterion).

The RNR model flows from GPCSL theory (see Andrews and Bonta, 2010a for a fuller explanation). Although the RNR principles are now numbering between 17 and 19, depending on whether one includes sub-principles (Andrews and Bonta, 2010a; Andrews, Bonta and Wormith, 2011; Bonta and Andrews, 2007), the following three original principles (Andrews, Bonta and Hoge, 1990) remain at the core:

Risk principle Match the LS to the offender's risk level. Provide more treatment to the higher risk offender and less to the lower risk offender.
Need principle Treatment should have as its major targets the dynamic risk factors or criminogenic needs of the offender.
Responsivity principle Match the style and mode of treatment to the offender's learning style and abilities. In general, cognitive-behavioural interventions work best but treatment should also pay attention to the biopsychosocial and cultural characteristics of the offender.

From a practice perspective, the Risk and Need principles imply that assessments should be repeated since there is an expectation that an offender's dynamic risk could change with the right intervention. Even without systematic intervention, an offender's life circumstances can change affecting their risk to re-offend. In addition, the Responsivity principle calls for the assessment of specific biosocial, cultural factors that can moderate the effects of treatment. There are relatively few offender assessment instruments developed from any theoretical perspective and even fewer based on GPCSL and informed by the RNR model. One of the few assessment tools that does exist is the LS family of instruments.

The Level of Service instruments: theoretically informed and evidence-based

GPCSL and RNR would be of little value if they did not offer something concrete to the criminal justice system and this is precisely where these two theoretical concepts really shine. As Kurt Lewin, the father of modern social psychology, mused, 'There is nothing so practical as a good theory' (Lewin, 1951, p. 169). The LS instruments allow clinicians, practitioners and researchers to bring these principles to reality.

Third-generation LS　In the early 1980s, Andrews (1982) began to draw from social learning theory, personality theory and the empirical research describing common attributes of offenders to create a checklist of risk/need factors. After trying various combinations of items with adult probationers in Ontario, the checklist was originally introduced as the LSI-VI (Andrews, 1982). The 54-item instrument covered a range of historical items such as criminal, educational, employment and substance abuse history, the so-called static items. Yet, true to its roots, LSI-VI also tapped into an array of items that are subject to change over time, some slowly, but others much more quickly. These 'dynamic' items included current educational, employment and recreational activities; family and companion relationships; financial; accommodation; emotional status; and substance use. A theme that ran through the items was the concept of behaving in an antisocial manner contrary to the laws and morals of traditional society. Because of their capacity to change, often with intervention or treatment, these dynamic items are also known as criminogenic needs. It is this latter feature that qualified LSI-VI as a third-generation instrument and gave it added utility to correctional agencies and their practitioners.

LSI-VI was quickly validated by showing strong correlations with recidivism (Andrews and Robinson, 1984; Andrews *et al.*, 1986). This in turn led to an explosion of LSI research, in Canada, the United States and beyond and the demand for a more accessible, formally published version, the LSI-R (Andrews and Bonta, 1995). Today, the LSI-R is one of the most researched and widely used offender assessment instruments in the world (Andrews, Bonta and Wormith, 2010; Interstate Commission for Adult Offender Supervision, 2007).

A downward extension of LS led to the development of a youth version based on the same set of theories and principles. The Youth Level of Service Inventory (YLSI; Andrews, Robinson and Hoge, 1984) was designed for adolescent offenders and includes the same kind of static and dynamic items, but also takes the psychosocial developmental stage through which adolescents must navigate into consideration. First developed with and then applied to young offenders on probation in Ontario, it has since been researched and applied to many correctional agencies internationally (see Olver, Stockdale and Wormith, 2009).

If one reflects on the origins and aetiology of the LS scales, their capacity to travel should come as no surprise. LS is based on the fundamental principle that criminal behaviour is primarily a function of individual characteristics of the offender and less so the social location in which one resides. These characteristics and their relationship with crime are extremely robust, if not universal, across communities, cultures and social classes. Similarly, the process of social learning, which is in part responsible for acquiring many of these attributes, is an aspect of the human condition to be found across all reaches of humanity. So it is only logical to find a tool like the LS, which is based on an empirically defensible theory, to be effective across legal jurisdictions and national boundaries (Andrews *et al.*, 2011; Yang, Wong and Coid, 2010). Yet in an effort to realize its full potential in the field, LS went through yet again another revision.

Fourth-generation LS   One application of risk assessment is to aid decision-making: Who should be released from prison? Who requires greater supervision in the community? A second application in keeping with RNR is to determine what kind of intervention should be provided and who should it take. One might reasonably think that a theoretically sound and empirically validated third-generation risk assessment instrument would be sufficient to ensure appropriate services to the offender. This indeed was the expectation with implementation of the LSI-R. Presumably, a clinician or case worker, such as a probation officer, parole officer or youth worker, would, first, assess the offender on the instrument, second, derive a score and a corresponding risk level, third, review the instrument to determine what criminogenic needs were revealed and, if the degree of risk warranted intervention (i.e., at least moderate), develop and implement an appropriate case plan that would target the identified criminogenic needs.

Sadly, the Nike approach, 'just do it', is woefully inadequate. Even with training on the importance of addressing criminogenic needs in one's correctional plan, correctional workers easily drift away from the rigour that is required to apply RNR in their routine work with offenders. This drift has been found not only with LS (Luong and Wormith, 2011; Simon, 2008), but other third-generation risk assessment tools such as the Client Management Classification (CMC), which is based on the Wisconsin Scales (e.g., Harris, Gingerich and Whittaker, 2004).

It also became apparent that in their zeal to focus on criminogenic needs as presented in LSI-R and YLSI, which we applauded, correctional workers were ignoring other important attributes of their clientele. This included individually specific factors that might put their clients at added risk, other kinds of (noncriminogenic) needs that merit attention such as social, medical and humanitarian services to the offender, offender strengths and specific responsivity considerations. Moreover, experienced practitioners and correctional administrators pleaded for a more comprehensive assessment protocol that would fully meet their agency needs, while at the same time would strategically place their organization in a position to implement RNR-based practices more effectively on an agency-wide basis. In response to these needs, the fourth generation of risk/need was born with the release of the LS/CMI (Andrews, Bonta and Wormith, 2004) and the Youth Level of Service/Case Management Inventory (YLS/CMI; Hoge and Andrews, 2002). Once again, their publications followed an extensive validational phase with the instruments administered to thousands of offenders in Ontario and researched in terms of their predictive validity prior to being made publically available (Girard and Wormith, 2004; Jung and Rowana, 1999).

Three key features characterize the latest generation of LS tools. First, the instrument was theoretically and psychometrically re-organized. Items from LSI-R and YLSI that were redundant to other items or had no direct correlation with recidivism were eliminated and the remaining items were re-organized into eight domains in the general risk/need section of the LS/CMI and YLS/CMI. These eight domains coincide with the Central Eight.

Second, a format and protocol for the case management of the offender was directly linked to the assessment document. Although the risk/need assessment–case management document is not foolproof, it does provide a direct linkage between assessment and case management and therefore between identified criminogenic needs and intervention and supervision practices. Simply put, case notes pertaining to the offender's status, intervention activities and progress are written with routine reference to the previously conducted risk/need assessment of the offender.

Third, the assessment itself was extended beyond the stripped down risk/need assessment to take on a more holistic clinical perspective of the offender. For example, sections were added on responsivity issues and noncriminogenic needs that although unrelated to criminal behaviour per se, may require attention prior to addressing the assessed criminogenic need through a traditional intervention. Similarly, the assessment of strengths or protective factors was made explicit and intended for use to build case plans.

By capitalizing on the three key features of the fourth-generation LS instruments, practitioners and the agencies they represent are much better positioned to offer a more comprehensive kind of service, one that many critics believe is missing in RNR and by extension in LS (e.g., Ward and Maruna, 2007). In our view, these features were never missing. They simply had not been articulated or formalized to the extent that they should have been to ensure their use by practitioners (Andrews, Bonta and Wormith, 2011).

Efforts to Reconcile First- and Third-Generation Instruments

Structured professional judgement – a step backward

Although there is ample evidence that statistically based approaches to offender risk assessment are superior to subjective, clinical approaches in the prediction of recidivism, there is continued interest in the clinical tradition. One means of accommodating clinical judgement is the structured professional (or clinical) judgement (SPJ) approach popularized in the 1990s. SPJ structures the process of clinical judgement by ensuring that the assessor systematically considers an array of risk factors, ensuring that each of them is reviewed in a thorough clinical fashion. Ultimately, however, the final assessment of offender risk is left to the discretion of the assessor. There is no quantitative summation of risk factors, or if there is, there is no direct or required correspondence to the degree of risk that is declared by the assessor. Consequently, SPJ differs from unstructured clinical judgement in that it requires the assessor to consider a preset list of risk factors, most or all of which have been derived from the same empirical literature as statistically based measures of offender risk. However, SPJ differs from statistically based approaches in that it does not include a numerical scoring of items or predetermined rules to convert the number and degree of risk present to a descriptive risk score or level.

The classification of SPJ in terms of generations of risk assessment presents an interesting challenge. Proponents of SPJ describe three types of risk assessment: clinical, actuarial and SPJ, which is described as a melding of the two (Douglas and Reeves, 2010; Douglas, Cox and Webster, 1999). We would describe SPJ as a variant of third-generation instruments because it certainly includes both static and dynamic risk factors. Secondly, its timing in the sequence of emerging instruments is in keeping with the wave of third-generation tools, although it is a more recent example. However, its failure to employ any quantitative scoring scheme or pre-defined criteria for levels of declared risk is most reminiscent of first-generation, clinically based prediction. SPJ's content and systematic organization is very third generation, while its process is very first generation. In our view, SPJ is a regressive step. It is particularly problematic in many correctional settings where risk assessments are not conducted by trained professional clinicians but by paraprofessionals who are considerably less trained in clinical assessment procedures.

In its effort to accommodate both approaches to offender risk assessment, SPJ has become particularly popular in forensic mental health settings. A number of instruments are now available and perhaps the best known and well-established instrument is the Historical-Clinical-Risk Management-20 (HCR-20; Webster *et al.*, 1997), which was designed for the purpose of violence risk assessment. As is implicit in its name, this instrument combines items derived from three different sources. Historical items address issues of the offender's past including previous offences and diagnoses. Clinical items focus on current attitudes and symptoms. Risk management items pertain to the offender's future plans, support and compliance.

A number of specialized SPJ assessment protocols have also been developed. For domestic abusers there is the Spousal Abuse Risk Assessment (SARA; Kropp *et al.*, 1995) that samples general criminal history, psychosocial adjustment, spousal assault history and the current offence. For sexual offenders, there are the Sexual Violent Risk 20 (SVR-20; Boer *et al.*, 1997) and its successor the Risk for Sexual Violence Protocol (RSVP; Hart *et al.*, 2003). These scales measure a range of factors from psychosocial adjustment to sexual deviation. Finally, two examples of SPJ for youth are the Structured Assessment of Violence in Youth (SAVRY; Borum, Bartel and Forth, 2002) and the Estimate of Risk of Adolescent Sexual Offender Recidivism (ERASOR; Worling and Curwen, 2001).

To our knowledge, there have been three reviews of the predictive validity of the SPJ approach with offender risk prediction. One review was a narrative summary of 13 studies finding 11 studies predicting violent recidivism (Heilbrun, Yasuhara and Shah, 2010). The remaining two reviews were meta-analyses. Hanson and Morton-Bourgon's (2009) review of 118 prediction studies on sexual offenders found SPJ (average $r = 0.13$) to outperform unstructured clinical judgement ($r = 0.05$) but not purely actuarial instruments ($r = 0.25$; all conversions to r based on Cohen's d reported in the article). In a review of 108 examinations of SPJ conducted with a mix of offenders, Guy (2008) found a modest effect size ($r = 0.32$) for any antisocial behaviour. Moderator analyses revealed that some SPJ schemes fared better than others. For example, summary SPJ ratings demonstrated better validity when predicting violent, including sexually violent, behaviour than they did for general antisocial behaviour ($r = 0.47$ and 0.44, respectively), which may not be surprising since SPJ instruments are typically designed to address general, sexual or domestic violence.

One advantage of SPJ is that it lends itself nicely to subsequent clinical work and case management with the offender. Having identified the high risk characteristics or circumstances of the offender, one can devise a plan for intervention. Thus, it has a distinct advantage over the second-generation instruments that are based solely on static risk factors. In spite of this presumed advantage, there is very little research that has shown dynamic predictive validity (i.e., changes in assessment results correspond to changes in recidivism) and provide directions for subsequent intervention which are related to actual reductions in offender risk.

Professional discretion or override

Another means of accommodating the wisdom of clinical professionals is to include an 'override' mechanism whereby the correctional worker may adjust the assessment of risk derived directly from the score of any quantitative risk assessment tool. This is similar to the SPJ approach, but is a step closer to strictly actuarially based schemes in that a score and corresponding degree of risk are actually determined and then adjusted in either direction depending on additional information that is not captured in the original risk assessment scheme. The information justifying an override could be of a personal, historical, clinical or even environmental/situational nature. We have acknowledged the importance of specific, possibly idiosyncratic, features of the offender that truly merit overriding the score-derived risk level. In addition to the original RNR principles, Andrews and colleagues also emphasized a role for professional discretion (Andrews, 1989; Andrews, Bonta and Hoge, 1990) and still do acknowledge that one may deviate from RNR and LS-based recommendations with sufficient reason (Andrews *et al.*, 2011).

This provision was available in the LSI-R, but achieves a more prominent position in LS/ CMI as we have come to accept the possibility of different kinds of overrides. First, as described earlier, we included professional overrides whereby the risk level is adjusted for some clinical or client-specific reason. Second, overrides may be initiated as a matter of correctional policy by a criminal justice agency. A common example is that some jurisdictions must declare all sex offenders, at least initially, as high risk. Similarly, the type of sentence, such as a life sentence, may be used to override offender risk in the security placement of a prisoner. Overrides may even be dictated by the judiciary if, for example, a court-ordered condition requires that the offender be treated in a specific manner that is not derived from, or consistent with, the risk/ need assessment. Although these decisions may not be supported empirically, we acknowledge that there are other considerations that a correctional agency may require in the management of its offender population.

These provisions should add incremental validity to the assessment process of offenders, particularly if one has gone to great length and expense to acquire specialized clinical or forensic training. However, there is very little, if any, systematic evidence that this is an effective practice, at least in terms of predictive validity (Heilbrun, Yasuhara and Shah, 2010). Again, we acknowledge that there may be other socially, clinically or legally 'valid' reasons for exercising the override function. In fact, studies that systematically monitor the use of the professional override show a slight decrement in predictive validity after the override option is made available to assessors (Hanson and Morton-Bourgon, 2007; Quinsey *et al.*, 2006; Rice, Harris and Hilton, 2010).

The detrimental impact of the professional override on predictive accuracy is evidenced in our work with Ontario's provincial correctional agency. The automated version of the LS instrument captures both the 'initial' risk level based strictly on predetermined cut-off scores and the 'final' risk level after the override option is allowed. An initial study where 3% of cases were overridden found a slight increment in predictive validity for general ($r = 0.37$–0.38) and violent recidivism (0.25–0.26), as well as re-offence severity (0.39–0.40; Girard and Wormith, 2004).

With time, however, the override function increased to 15% usage. Not surprisingly, due to the inherently cautious nature of correctional organizations, assessors were much more likely to override cases to a higher risk level than to a lower risk level (13% versus 3%; Wormith and Sheppard, 2003). Moreover, the override had a slight, but consistent, negative effect on the predictive validity of the instrument. Brews (2009) found that the predictive validity fell from 0.44 to 0.41 on a large sample of female offenders after the override provision was applied. The difference is particularly apparent in the assessment of sexual offenders where the predictive validity correlation decreased from 0.45 to 0.26 for general recidivism (Wormith, Hogg and Guzzo, 2012). This finding is not surprising, given the heightened concern about sexual offenders in the community and pressure on case managers to respond accordingly. However, in our opinion, the override function should only be exercised sparingly and with documented justification.

Persistent and Emerging Challenges to Offender Assessment

There are numerous complex issues that are inherent in the process of offender assessment. Some are related to the demands that the criminal justice system has placed, either explicitly or implicitly, on the process. Others are related to the changing profile of crime and the offenders who perpetrate it. Consequently, the business of offender assessment is constantly evolving and the instruments on which it is based are in a seemingly never-ending struggle to meet the needs of demanding professionals and criminal justice agencies. The following is a brief synopsis of seven persistent or emerging issues that are faced by correctional practitioners and administrators and some of the answers that researchers have offered.

Working with limited resources

Although it may sound trite to suggest that correctional jurisdictions are under continued, if not increasing, pressure to apply human and financial resources in a most judicious fashion, we are constantly faced with this reality when communicating with our colleagues in the field. Variations on this theme include 'doing more with less' and 'maximizing benefit while minimizing costs'. This is particularly true in the United States where, in spite of falling crime rates, correctional populations continue to grow in many jurisdictions, while pressure to reduce spending intensifies because of shrinking financial resources. It is a truism that larger caseloads translate to less time and attention that can be devoted to any one offender. It is not surprising that a reduction in the quality of risk assessment, or even its elimination, can become a victim of increasingly scarce human resources.

It is quite likely, however, that fiscal decisions designed solely to achieve year-end financial objectives in an office or local agency are likely to be short-sighted in the long run and in the bigger criminal justice picture. The kinds of saving that may be generated by sound offender assessment, coupled with specifically targeted interventions that in turn reduce recidivism, lower costs and improve human productivity, are not only better for the individual offender, but for the community in which he or she lives. Cost-benefit and cost-effective studies (e.g., Aos *et al.*, 2011) are required to clearly demonstrate the fiscal soundness of offender assessments that have the potential for what is described as 'tertiary' crime prevention in the future.

A compromise strategy that may yet prove to be quite efficient is the concept of screening offenders for a more detailed assessment investigation. A number of instruments including the LS and the PCL-R (Hart, Cox and Hare, 1995) have developed brief screening versions of their instruments, which allow an assessor to obtain a reasonably accurate representation of an offender's degree of risk. For example, the LS screener (LSI-R; SV; Andrews and Bonta, 1998) and the full version of the LS are highly correlated for probationers ($r = 0.84$) and prisoners ($r = 0.85$). Consequently, it is no surprise to find this eight-item screening version correlating very respectably with general recidivism for probationers ($r = 0.33$) and prisoners ($r = 0.30$) (Andrews and Bonta, 1998). Using a screening instrument, the assessor may then determine which offenders merit a more detailed investigation. For example, offenders who score low risk on the screening tool may be passed over for the full assessment and triaged to low security, low supervision, and no treatment, all of which makes good clinical and financial sense. Since treatment is not recommended, in accordance with the risk principle, one need not engage in a detailed examination to determine what criminogenic needs might otherwise merit intervention. At the other extreme, offenders who score high risk on a screening tool may then be administered the full instrument in order to determine which criminogenic needs are most deserving of attention and in what order they might be addressed.

Single versus multiple assessments

Ironically, the opposite kind of dilemma is faced by other clinicians who have a plethora of instruments from which to choose and an appreciable amount of time to complete them. This leads to the question, 'Is more better?' Opinion is divided. On the one hand, the use of multiple instruments for the same purpose may confuse the issue because it is unlikely that the results of multiple instruments will be identical. This then allows the assessor to 'cherry pick' the assessment that corresponds to his or her personal impression of the client and to emphasize certain results, either knowingly or not, in the formation of the overall assessment. Using the LSI-R, along with the PCL-R, VRAG and the SIR, Mills and Kroner (2006) demonstrated that predictive accuracy can decrease when the projections of multiple instruments are discordant with each other. They also refer to the clinical judgement involved in rating certain items (e.g., marital relationships, lack of empathy) from the LSI-R, PCL-R and the VRAG as a source of the discordance in predictive accuracy among the instruments. That is, because each scale may evaluate a particularly shared construct slightly differently (e.g., marital relationship), the chances of discrepancies in the assessment are more likely. Thus, it may be better to stay with one instrument and not become confused when multiple instruments are used.

Alternatively, the use of multiple instruments for the same or similar purposes may strengthen one's ultimate impression of the case (e.g., Banks *et al.*, 2004). Related to the geometric concept of triangulation, the use of multiple assessments has an intuitive appeal as it conjures images of forest rangers honing in on the precise location of a forest fire based on multiple sightings from different vantage points. Unlike mapping, however, risk assessment is not a two-dimensional task. Moreover, no two risk assessment tools are exactly alike. Although popular tools such as the LS and the PCL-R are highly correlated ($r = 0.79$; Wormith *et al.*, 2007), each has its own theoretical basis and methodological aetiology. This leaves the assessor with the challenge of reconciling any differences in prognostication that may come from multiple instruments. Although the use of multiple assessment tools for the same purpose sounds like a reasonable prospect, we know of no research that has demonstrated its incremental validity, with the possible exception of combining the static risk of one tool (Static-99) with the dynamic risk of another tool (Stable-2007) to produce a sex offender risk/need assessment battery that mimics the risk/need structure of LS for general offenders (Eher *et al.*, 2012; Hanson *et al.*, 2007).

The preceding scenario should not be confused with the strategy of using multiple assessment tools for different reasons. An example would be the case whereby an offender might be in need of an assessment for criminal risk as well as suicidal risk. Where the predicted outcomes are distinct, multiple assessment tools are required as the validating research behind individual tools is unlikely to provide any instruction for such diverse outcome measures. Similarly, one might consider multiple assessment tools for related outcome behaviour, for example, general, violent and sexual recidivism. Although it seems uncanny how well the LS predicts general recidivism for sexual offenders, with correlations as high as 0.44 (Girard and Wormith, 2004), comparative studies would suggest that one would want to supplement a general risk assessment tool, such as LS, with a specialized instrument such as the STATIC-99 (Hanson and Thornton, 2000) when predicting sexual recidivism.

This is because predictive validities for specialized outcomes are stronger for specialized assessment protocols (Hanson and Morton-Bourgon, 2009).

The application of a common instrument to other offence-based subgroups of offenders is yet again another variation of this important and widely debated topic. Opinion on this matter is also divided. Some practitioners express concern about applying a generic risk/need assessment tool, such as LS, to other special offender groups prematurely without the necessary empirical validation. One the one hand, there is the universality of the Central Eight in the production of antisocial behaviour, regardless of its manifestation. Some have assumed the position that the aetiology of some criminal behaviour is unique to that specific type of crime and, therefore, specialized instruments are required. The prediction of domestic violence with instruments such as the SARA (Kropp *et al.*, 1995) and the Ontario Domestic Assault Risk Assessment (ODARA; Hilton, Harris and Rice, 2010) is a particular example. Yet, LS research has demonstrated a reasonable predictive validity coefficient with a sample of domestic violence offenders ($r = 0.31$; Girard and Wormith, 2004). Thus far, the research on the generality of the Central Eight risk/need factors derived from GPCSL has been positive and this is most clearly demonstrated in the next section.

Gender-specific or generic instruments

Risk assessment tools that were constructed for and validated on cohorts of general offender populations were done so largely on male offenders. This is a reasonable result given that men constitute approximately 75% of most offender populations (Kong and AuCoin, 2008). This history, however, has led to a debate about the applicability of generic instruments to women offenders. There is the contention that these tools are gender neutral, in part because they were developed with and for the *total* offender population and in part because some correctional theories (e.g., GPCSL; Andrews and Bonta, 2010a) and the related empirical literature, have repeatedly found that the Central Eight risk/need factors are equally relevant to both males and females. It follows that a risk tool built around these factors will be equally applicable to both male and female offenders (Andrews *et al.*, 2011).

A second position is that some, perhaps many, female offenders come by their criminality via a series of pathways, some of which are different from those typically followed by male offenders (e.g., Hannah-Moffatt, 2009). Examples of these pathways include histories of abuse, partner-initiated crime and economically driven crime, although some of these factors are also present, but allegedly to a weaker degree, among male offenders. Consequently, it is maintained that the traditional risk assessment tools cannot be generalized to women offenders. Moreover, given the lower rates of recidivism among women offenders, traditional instruments may over-classify them to a higher degree of risk than they deserve.

Considerable effort has been devoted to the gender issue in offender risk assessment over the last decade, with only some resolution between competing positions. One conceptually reasonable approach is to build upon a generic risk assessment tool with a women-specific supplement to capture the gendered pathways related to female crime (Van Voorhis *et al.*, 2010). However, the incremental validity of this approach has yet to be demonstrated in a replicable and convincing manner. In reviews of the LS research, the findings have stood up very well in simple tests of predictive validity with correlations comparable, and in some cases superior, to what are found for males in the same cohort, assessed in the same manner and measured against a common database for recidivism outcome (Andrews *et al.*, 2012; Smith, Cullen and Latessa, 2009).

Yet at the same time, a couple of patterns have emerged in the LS studies. It has been repeatedly demonstrated that the substance abuse domain is a particularly powerful predictor of female offender recidivism, even more so than it is for males. The implication of this finding is that the instrument might be modified to give more attention to the substance abuse domain, either by adding items or weighting this domain by some mathematical factor, in the calculation of the total risk score. Secondly, there is some suggestion that women who score in the low-risk range on the LS scales actually recidivate at a lower rate than their male counterparts, suggesting that for at least these women the instrument may be over-predicting their degree of risk (Andrews *et al.*, 2011).

There are two easily achieved solutions to this latter concern. First, the different recidivism rates for men and women may be declared so that users of the instrument appreciate there is a small but possibly significant difference in the likelihood of recidivism for a female offender who is classified to a low or very low risk group. Second, the so-called cut-off scores for women could be increased such that more of them are classified as being low risk. Consequently, by adding slightly higher-risk women to these categories, the percentage of women who recidivate would increase to a rate that coincides with the recidivism rate for males classified to the same risk level, but on the basis of lower cut-off scores.

Ethnic and cultural variation in offender population

The same issues that pertain to women offenders are equally relevant to ethnic or racial minorities. It is standard procedure in the application of any psychometric instrument to a group on which the instrument has not been validated to air a voice of caution. With more ethnic and cultural variation in North American and European states, and the over-representation of many of these cultures under correctional supervision, concerns are mounting about the use of instruments on these groups. With greater reliance on risk assessment measures for correctional decisions and case planning, these concerns will only increase. Consequently, there is pressure to validate these instruments on the many cultural groups that are now found under correctional care. This no longer includes only African-American, Latino and Aboriginal or Native-American offenders who so disproportionately populate correction agencies, but also the numerous immigrant groups from Asia, Africa, Eastern Europe and the Caribbean.

Research has begun to examine the predictive validity of the LS with some of these racial and cultural groups. Most notably, a number of studies have been conducted with Aboriginal offenders in Canada, who in some jurisdictions make up more than half of the offender population. In the province of Ontario, the LS has consistently demonstrated comparable predictive validity coefficients among Aboriginal ($r = 0.38$) and African-American offenders ($r = 0.42$) in comparison to non-Aboriginal offenders ($r = 0.42$), and across gender within these racial groups except for Aboriginal offenders (Hogg, 2011). In a meta-analysis of risk/need factors, Gutierrez, Wilson, Rugge *et al.* (2013) found the Central Eight to predict similarly for both Aboriginal and non-Aboriginal offenders. Furthermore, the mean correlation coefficient for the LS total score was 0.28 among Aboriginal offenders ($k = 10$, $N = 18\ 619$). Once again, this was to be expected given the generality of the GPCSL perspective of criminal behaviour.

In the United States, the results of studies with African-American, Latino, and Native-American offenders have been less impressive and mixed (Schlager and Simourd, 2007), including a non-significant relationship with recidivism for Native-American women (Holsinger, Lowenkamp and Latessa, 2003, 2006). The lower correlations between the

LS and recidivism outside of Canada appear to be consistent with meta-analytic comparisons (Andrews *et al.*, 2011; Yang, Wong and Coid, 2010). This has led to speculations about the accuracy of both the predictor variable, by means of high-quality training and quality assurance in the field, and the recidivism outcome variable, by means of a national offender database.

Changing face of crime and criminals

Another nagging question concerns the changing nature of crime in the twenty-first century. Understandably, correctional administrators and practitioners have begun to ask whether instruments developed and validated in the 1980s and 1990s are still relevant in the 2010s. In many ways, this question is similar to queries about gender and ethnicity in that it is a principle of psychometric theory that any instrument should be validated on the desired outcome with a sample of the target population before it is put to practice.

There are also two competing views about this question. One is the contention that an underlying theme of antisocial people cuts across a wide swath of criminal behaviours and those who perpetrate it. Consequently, generic tools for antisocial behaviour, such as LS, are capable of identifying these people and providing a metric as to the extent to which they are at risk of perpetrating criminal behaviour, regardless of the specific type. Studies demonstrating the predictive validity of LS with sexual offenders perpetrating both sexual and non-sexual offences illustrate this point (Hanson and Morton-Bourgon, 2009).

The other view is that the dramatic technological and cultural developments which have emerged over the last decade are of such substance and magnitude that one wonders about the capacity of assessment tools based on GPCSL and RNR to maintain their utility and predictive value. Would these theoretical models remain relevant when faced with emerging trends such as Internet crime, extremism and terrorism? Our view is that modern electronic crime is simply an extension to the kind of white collar crime that has been in evidence for more than a century. With computers and smart phones in every home, it is simply more accessible to those who would be predisposed to such offending. As such, one would expect that assessments of those at risk would show a history of committing electronic crime, attitudes supportive of electronic crime, association with others who engage in electronic crime and a personality and lifestyle that is consistent with committing electronic crime.

The same might be said about extremist and terrorist crime being based, at least in part, on the Central Eight risk/need factors (e.g., associations with other terrorists, history of anti-government attacks), and other elements of social learning theory (Bandura, 1998). Notably, terrorism and extremism invoke the concept of ideology, which is not captured in traditional measures such as LS (Krueger, 2007), but is closely related to the risk/need factor of attitudes. Although, some extremists appear to be otherwise law-abiding and conventional in their attitudes and lifestyle, many of the Central Eight constructs may be quite applicable if they are made more specific to extremist activities. For example, instead of assessing attitudes supportive of criminal behaviour as generally viewed ('It is alright to steal; they are insured'), one may look for attitudes supportive of terrorist behaviour ('It is O.K. to bomb the American embassy because we are being oppressed by foreigners'). To this end, researchers are working on specialized assessment protocols that are designed to capture the unique features that may be related to terrorism but missing in traditional risk/need instruments (Loza, 2007; Pressman, 2009). True to our respect for data, the test will come from the difficult but important research that has yet to be conducted.

The mentally disordered offender

In recent years, there has been an explosive growth in the number of mentally ill offenders in Canada, the United States and the United Kingdom. For example, one recent report estimates that 24% of inmates in American state prisons have a diagnosable mental disorder (James and Glaze, 2006). These offenders pose significant challenges for correctional systems that have limited experience in managing individuals with serious psychological problems. The assessment of the mentally disordered offender (MDO) is an area where traditional forensic mental health assessment instruments play a role. Instruments that facilitate making a diagnosis of a major mental disorder are important for symptom management and other treatment decisions, but is there a role for third- and fourth-generation instruments? We certainly think so. The MDO may have significant psychological difficulties that need to be addressed but there is also an element of antisociality, and this is where assessments of the Central Eight risk/need factors come into the picture.

In an early meta-analysis, Bonta, Law and Hanson (1998) found that having a major mental disorder or evidencing clinical symptoms was unrelated to recidivism ($r = -0.02$, $k = 44$, $N = 11$ 156). They also found that some of the Central Eight risk/need factors predicted recidivism in approximately the same manner as for non-mentally disordered offenders (e.g., criminal history, employment and family problems). Unfortunately, at the time Bonta and his colleagues could not conduct a test of most of the Central Eight risk/need factors because of a lack of studies.

In an update to the 1998 meta-analysis, Blais, Wilson and Bonta (2011) recoded the studies reviewed in the 1998 report to align them with the Central Eight and added 20 new longitudinal studies published to the end of 2010. Antisocial personality pattern was the best predictor of recidivism ($r = 0.22$), followed by criminal history ($r = 0.19$). Three Central Eight risk/need factors could not be coded because of their infrequency (a minimum of three studies was required to be included in the meta-analysis). The three unreported factors were procriminal attitudes, criminal companions and leisure/recreation. However, the remaining five factors were all predictive of recidivism. While not a meta-analysis, a single study found that the LS/CMI general risk/need score correlated with general recidivism among MDOs (0.39) at a rate that approximated the rate for general offenders (0.41), but fared less well for violent recidivism (0.18 versus 0.32 for general offenders; Girard and Wormith, 2004).

Facilitating prisoner re-entry and reintegration into the community

The last decade has witnessed the emergence of prisoner re-entry into the community as a crucial event in the rehabilitation of the offender. This is certainly not a new concept. The very act of parole is largely based on the understanding that the transition from prison to community is dramatic and for some offenders, particularly long-term offenders, a scary proposition. Known as 'after care' in the traditional lexicon of correctional practice, re-entry (or some use 'reintegration') is really a new emphasis to an old, but important practice (Petersilia, 2002). The challenge faced by a correctional agency and case managers is how to attend to a prisoner's re-entry into the community (Seiter and Kadela, 2003).

In our view, knowledge of the offender's RNR characteristics is vital to assisting with the re-entry process. Specifically, which offenders are high risk and therefore likely to need more re-entry services? What kind of criminogenic needs should be targeted to best facilitate re-entry? And how should both the prison and community caseworker offer services? LS/CMI and YLS/CMI are nicely positioned to facilitate re-entry for three reasons. First, they are designed to answer the RNR questions that should guide planning for re-entry. Secondly, they were designed, and are now being used, both in custodial and community settings. Thus, when the offender moves from a prison to community setting, the use of a single instrument facilitates communication between the institution and community worker and allows for the measurement of progress along a common metric. Finally, as fourth-generation tools, LS/CMI and YLS/CMI specifically direct the case management team to plan and implement re-entry in keeping with the theoretically sound and empirically demonstrated principles of RNR.

Conclusions

It is somewhat unfortunate that we have for many years used the term 'risk assessment' to describe a process that so fundamentally impacts the offender. The term immediately communicates a picture of the offender as unmalleable and who poses a threat to the community. Undoubtedly, this is a reflection of the history of offender assessment that began with a need to differentiate those offenders who pose a risk to society from those who are less threatening. The proliferation of static second-generation risk instruments in the 1970s and 1980s and the 'nothing works' ideology certainly reinforced the view that the assessment of offenders can be frozen in time and efforts to provide human services were unnecessary.

Today, the picture of offender assessment is dramatically different. Although many challenges lie ahead, we now have convincing evidence that treatment can work if the RNR principles are followed. However, to deliver effective services first requires an assessment that follows the RNR model. Yes, we need to know the offender's probability of re-offending, but it is not because we want to simply decide upon whether the offender should be paroled, housed in maximum security or supervised more closely. We need this information to guide the intensity of treatment services. We also need an assessment of criminogenic needs for this serves as the basis for targeting treatment services. At least third-generation risk/*need* instruments are required to do this. In the twenty-first century, there is no excuse for any modern correctional agency to use second-generation risk instruments. To continue to do so does a disservice to the offender (i.e., ignores treatment needs) and the community (i.e., fails to provide services that diminishes the offender's risk).

We now have fourth-generation instruments that assess responsivity factors, specific risk/need factors and personal strengths and organize this information in a way that facilitates case management. Over the past 50 years, we have moved considerably away from the notion that offender assessment is simply a matter of risk to the community. The third- and fourth-generation instruments integrate assessment with treatment. In the fourth-generation LS instruments, these two functions are almost inseparable. This integration has led to 'risk/need' assessment as the new lexicon and we eagerly await what new terminology for offender assessment will emerge in the future.

References

Ægisdóttir, S., White, M.J., Spengler, P.M. *et al.* (2006) The meta-analysis of clinical judgment project: fifty-six years of accumulated research on clinical versus statistical prediction. *Counseling Psychologist*, 34, 341–382.

Andrews, D.A. (1982) The Level of Supervision Inventory (LSI): The First Follow-Up, Ontario Ministry of Correctional Services, Toronto.

Andrews, D.A. (1989) Recidivism is predictable and can be influenced: using risk assessments to reduce recidivism. *Forum of Correction Research*, 1, 11–18.

Andrews, D.A. and Bonta, J. (1995) The Level of Service Inventory-Revised: User's Manual, Multi-Health Systems Inc., Toronto.

Andrews, D.A. and Bonta, J. (1998) The Level of Service Inventory-Revised: Screening Version. User's Manual, Multi-Health Systems Inc., Toronto.

Andrews, D.A. and Bonta, J. (2010a) The Psychology of Criminal Conduct, 5th edn, LexisNexis Matthew Bender, New Providence.

Andrews, D.A. and Bonta, J. (2010b) Rehabilitating criminal justice policy and practice. *Psychology, Public Policy, and Law*, 16, 39–55.

Andrews, D.A. and Robinson, D. (1984) The Level of Supervision Inventory: Second Report, Ontario Ministry of Correctional Services, Toronto.

Andrews, D.A., Robinson, D. and Hoge, R.D. (1984) Manual for the Youth Level of Service Inventory, Department of Psychology, Carleton University, Ottawa.

Andrews, D.A., Kiessling, J.J., Mickus, S. and Robinson, D. (1986) Some convergent and divergent validities of the LSI. Paper presented to the annual meeting of the Canadian Psychological Association, Winnipeg, June.

Andrews, D.A., Bonta, J. and Hoge, R.D. (1990) Classification for effective rehabilitation: rediscovering psychology. *Criminal Justice and Behavior*, 17, 19–52.

Andrews, D.A., Bonta, J. and Wormith, J.S. (2004) The Level of Service/Case Management Inventory (LS/CMI), Multi-Health Systems Inc., Toronto.

Andrews, D.A., Bonta, J. and Wormith, J.S. (2006) The recent past and near future of risk/need assessment. *Crime & Delinquency*, 52, 7–27.

Andrews, D.A., Bonta, J. and Wormith, J.S. (2010) The Level of Service (LS) assessment of adults and older adolescents, in Handbook of Violence Risk Assessment (eds R.K. Otto and K. Douglas), Routledge, New York, pp. 199–225.

Andrews, D.A., Bonta, J. and Wormith, J.S. (2011) The risk-need-responsivity model: does adding the good lives model contribute to effective crime prevention? *Criminal Justice and Behavior*, 38, 735–755.

Andrews, D.A., Bonta, J., Wormith, J.S. *et al.* (2011) Sources of variability in estimates of predictive validity: a specification with level of service general risk/need. *Criminal Justice and Behavior*, 38, 413–432.

Andrews, D.A., Guzzo, L., Raynor, P. *et al.* (2012) Are the major risk/need factors predictive of both female and male reoffending? A test with the eight domains of the level of service/case management inventory. *International Journal of Offender Therapy and Comparative Criminology*, 56, 113–133.

Aos, S., Lee, S., Drake, E. *et al.* (2011) Return on Investment: Evidence-Based Options to Improve Statewide Outcomes (Document no. 11-07-1201), Washington State Institute for Public Policy, Olympia.

Baird, C. (1981) Probation and parole classification: the Wisconsin model. *Corrections Today*, 43, 36–41.

Baird, C. (1991) Validating Risk Assessment Instruments Used in Community Corrections, National Council on Crime and Delinquency, Madison.

Baird, S.C., Heinz, R.C. and Bemus, B.J. (1979) A Two Year Follow-Up. *Project Rep. no.* 14, Department of Health and Social Services, Case Classification/Staff Deployment Project, Bureau of Community Corrections, Madison.

Bandura, A. (1998). Mechanism of moral disengagement, in Origins of Terrorism (ed. W. Reich), Woodrow Wilson Center Press, Washington, DC, pp. 161–191.

Banks S., Robbins, P.C., Silver, E. *et al.* (2004) A multiple-models approach to violence risk assessment among people with mental disorder. *Criminal Justice and Behavior*, 31, 324–340.

Blais, J., Wilson, H. and Bonta, J. (2011) The prediction of criminal and violent recidivism among mentally disordered offenders: an updated meta-analysis. Presentation at the Annual Conference of the Canadian Psychological Association, Toronto, June 4.

Boer, D.P., Hart, S.D., Kropp, P.R. and Webster, C.D. (1997) Manual for the Sexual Violence Risk-20: Professional Guidelines for Assessing Risk of Sexual Violence, Mental Health, Law, and Policy Institute, Vancouver.

Bonta, J. (1996) Risk-needs assessment and treatment, in Choosing Correctional Options that Work: Defining the Demand and Evaluating the Supply (ed. A.T. Harland), Sage, Thousand Oaks, pp. 18–32.

Bonta, J. and Andrews, D.A. (2007) Risk-Need-Responsivity Model for Offender Assessment and Rehabilitation. User Rep. no. 2007-06, Public Safety Canada, Ottawa.

Bonta, J., Parkinson, R., Pang, B. *et al.* (1994) The Revised Manitoba Classification System, Solicitor General Canada, Ottawa.

Bonta, J., Harman, W.G., Hann, R.G. and Cormier, R.B. (1996) The prediction of recidivism among federally sentenced offenders: a re-validation of the SIR scale. *Canadian Journal of Criminology*, 38, 61–79.

Bonta, J., Law, M. and Hanson, K. (1998) The prediction of criminal and violent recidivism among mentally disordered offenders: a meta-analysis. *Psychological Bulletin*, 123, 123–142.

Bonta, J., Rugge, T., Scott, T. *et al.* (2008) Exploring the black box of community supervision. *Journal of Offender Rehabilitation*, 47, 248–270.

Boothby, J.L. and Clements, C.B. (2000) A national survey of correctional psychologists. *Criminal Justice and Behavior*, 27, 716–732.

Borum, R., Bartel, P. and Forth, A. (2002) Manual for the Structured Assessment for Violence Risk in Youth (SAVRY): Consultation Version, Florida Mental Health Institute, University of South Florida, Tampa.

Brews, A.L. (2009) The level of supervision inventory and female offenders: addressing issues of reliability and predictive ability. Unpublished Master thesis. University of Saskatchewan, Saskatoon.

Burgess, E.W. (1928) Factors determining success or failure on parole, in The Workings of the Indeterminate-Sentence Law and the Parole System in Illinois (eds A.A. Bruce, A.J. Harno, E.W. Burgess and J. Landesco), State Board of Parole, Springfield.

Campbell, M.A., French, S. and Gendreau, P. (2009) The prediction of violence in adult offenders: a meta-analytic comparison of instruments and methods of assessment. *Criminal Justice and Behavior*, 36, 567–590.

Copas, J. and Marshall, P. (1998) The offender group reconviction scale: a statistical reconviction score for use by probation officers. *Journal of the Royal Statistical Society*, 47, 159–171.

Debidin, M. (ed.) (2009) A Compendium of Research and Analysis on the Offender Assessment System (OASys) 2006–2009, Ministry of Justice, London.

Douglas, K.S. and Reeves, K. (2010) Historical-Clinical-Risk Management-20 (HCR-20) violence risk assessment scheme: rationale, application, and empirical overview, in Handbook of Violence Risk Assessment (eds R. Otto and K.S. Douglas), Routledge/Taylor & Francis, Oxford, pp. 147–185.

Douglas, K.S., Cox, D.N. and Webster, C. (1999) Violence risk assessment: science and practice. *Legal and Criminological Psychology*, 4, 149–184.

Eher, R., Matthes, A., Schilling, F. *et al.* (2012) Dynamic risk assessment in sexual offenders using STABLE-2000 and the STABLE-2007: an investigation of predictive incremental validity. *Sexual Abuse: A Journal of Research and Treatment*, 24 (1), 5–28.

Garb, H.N. (1997) Race bias, social class bias, and gender bias in clinical judgement. *Clinical Psychology: Science and Practice*, 4, 99–120.

Girard, L. and Wormith, J.S. (2004) The predictive validity of the level of service inventory-Ontario revision on general and violent recidivism among various offender groups. *Criminal Justice and Behaviour*, 31, 150–181.

Grant, J.D. and Grant, M.Q. (1959) A group dynamics approach to the treatment of nonconformists in the navy. *Annals of the American Academy of Political and Social Science*, 322, 126–135.

Gray, N.S., Snowden, R.J., MacCulloch, S. *et al.* (2004) Relative efficacy of criminological, clinical, and personality measures of future risk of offending in mentally disordered offenders: a comparative study of HCR-20, PCL: SV, and OGRS. *Journal of Consulting and Clinical Psychology*, 72, 523–530.

Grove, W.M., Zald, D.H., Lebow, B.S. *et al.* (2000) Clinical vs. mechanical prediction: a meta-analysis. *Psychological Assessment*, 12, 19–30.Gutierrez, L., Wilson, H., Rugge, T., and Bonta, J. (2011) The Prediction of Recidivism with Aboriginal Offenders: A Quantitative and Theoretically Informed Review. Unpublished manuscript, Public Safety Canada, Ottawa.

Gutierrez, L., Wilson, H.A., Rugge, T. and Bonta, J. (2013) The prediction of recidivism with Aboriginal Offenders: A theoretically informed meta-analysis. *Canadian Journal of Criminology and Criminal Justice*, 55, 55–99.

Guy, L.S. (2008) Performance indicators of the structured professional judgment approach for assessing risk for violence to others: a meta-analytic survey. Unpublished doctoral dissertation. Simon Fraser University, Burnaby.

Hannah-Moffat, K. (2009) Gridlock or mutability: reconsidering "gender" and risk assessment. *Criminology and Public Policy*, 8, 209–219.

Hanson, R.K. and Morton-Bourgon, K.E. (2007) The Accuracy of Recidivism Risk Assessments for Sexual Offenders: A Meta-Analysis. Corrections User Rep. no. 2007-05, Public Safety Canada, Ottawa.

Hanson, R.K. and Morton-Bourgon, K.E. (2009) The accuracy of recidivism risk assessments for sexual offenders: a meta-analysis of 118 prediction studies. *Psychological Assessment*, 21, 1–21.

Hanson, R.K. and Thornton, D. (2000) Static-99: improving risk assessments for sex offenders: a comparison of three actuarial scales. *Law and Human Behavior*, 24, 119–136.

Hanson, R.K., Harris, J.R., Scott, T.-L. and Helmus, L. (2007) Assessing the Risk of Sexual Offenders on Community Supervision: The Dynamic Supervision Project, Public Safety Canada, Ottawa.

Hare, R.D. (2003) The Psychopathy Checklist – Revised, 2nd edn, Multi-Health Systems Inc., Toronto.

Harris, G.T., Rice, M.E. and Quinsey, V.L. (1993) Violent recidivism of mentally disordered offenders: the development of a statistical prediction instrument. *Criminal Justice and Behavior*, 20, 315–335.

Harris, P.M., Gingerich, R. and Whittaker, T.A. (2004) The "effectiveness" of differential supervision. *Crime & Delinquency*, 50, 235–271.

Hart, S.D., Cox, D. and Hare, R.D. (1995) Manual for the Psychopathy Checklist: Screening Version (PCL: SV), Multi-Health Systems Inc., Toronto.

Hart, S.D., Kropp, P.R., Laws, D.R. *et al.* (2003) The Risk for Sexual Violence Protocol (RSVP), Mental Health, Law, and Policy Institute of Simon Fraser University, Burnaby.

Hathaway, S. and McKinley, J.C. (1951) The Minnesota Multiphasic Personality Inventory, Psychological Corporation, New York.

Heilbrun, K., Yasuhara, K. and Shah, S. (2010) Violence risk assessment tools: overview and critical analysis, in Handbook of Violence Risk Assessment (eds R.K. Otto and K. Douglas), Routledge, New York, pp. 1–17.

Hilton, Z.N., Harris, G.T. and Rice, M.E. (2006) Sixty-six years of research on the clinical versus actuarial prediction of violence. *Counseling Psychologist*, 34, 400–409.

Hilton, Z.N., Harris, G.T. and Rice, M.E. (2010) Risk Assessment for Domestically Violent Men: Tools for Criminal Justice, Offender Intervention, and Victim Services, American Psychological Association, Washington, DC.

Hoffman, P.B. (1994) Twenty years of operational use of a risk prediction instrument: the United States parole commission's salient factor score. *Journal of Criminal Justice*, 22, 477–494.

Hoffman, P.B. and Beck, J.L. (1974) Parole decision-making: a salient factor score. *Journal of Criminal Justice*, 2, 195–206.

Hoffman, P.B. and Beck, J.L. (1985) Recidivism among released federal prisoners: salient factor score and five-year follow-up. *Criminal Justice and Behavior*, 12, 501–507.

Hoffman, P.B., Stone-Meierhoefer, B. and Beck, J.L. (1978) Salient factor score and release behavior: three validational samples. *Law and Human Behavior*, 2, 47–63.

Hoge, R.D. and Andrews, D.A. (2002) Youth Level of Service/Case Management Inventory: User's Manual, Multi-Health Systems Inc., Toronto.

Hoge, R.D., Andrews, D.A. and Leschied, A.W. (1995) The Risk/Need Inventory, Ministry of Community and Social Services, Toronto.

Hogg, S.M. (2011) The level of service inventory (Ontario Revision) scale validation for gender and ethnicity: addressing issues of reliability and predictive validity. Unpublished Master thesis. Department of Psychology, University of Saskatchewan, Saskatoon.

Holsinger, A.M., Lowenkamp, C.T. and Latessa, E.J. (2003) Ethnicity, gender, and the level of service inventory-revised. *Journal of Criminal Justice*, 31, 309–320.

Holsinger, A.M., Lowenkamp, C.T. and Latessa, E.J. (2006) Exploring the validity of the level of service inventory–revised with Native American offenders. *Journal of Criminal Justice*, 34, 331–337.

Hunt, D.E. and Hardt, R.H. (1965) Development stage, delinquency, and differential treatment. *Journal of Research in Crime and Delinquency*, 2, 20–31.

Interstate Commission for Adult Offender Supervision. (2007) SO Assessment Information Survey 4-2007. http://www.interstatecompact.org/resources/surveys/survey_results/SexOffender_Assessment_042007.pdf (accessed 19 December 2012).

James, D.J. and Glaze, L.E. (2006) Mental Health Problems of Prison and Jail Inmates. Statistics Special Rep. no. NCJ 213600, Department of Justice, Washington, DC.

Jung, S. and Rawana, E.P. (1999) Risk-need assessment of juvenile offenders. *Criminal Justice and Behavior*, 26, 69–89.

Kong, R. and AuCoin, K. (2008) Female offenders in Canada. *Juristat*. Statistics Canada. Catalogue no. 85-002-XIE, vol. 28, no. 1, January.

Kropp, P.R., Hart, S.D., Webster, C.D. and Eaves, D. (1995) Manual for the Spousal Assault Risk Assessment Guide, 2nd edn, British Columbia Institute on Family Violence, Vancouver.

Krueger, A.B. (2007) What Makes a Terrorist? Economics and the Roots of Terrorism, Princeton University Press, Princeton.

Lewin, K. (1951) Field Theory in Social Science; Selected Theoretical Papers, Harper & Row, New York.

Loza, W. (2007) Psychology of extremism and terrorism: a middle-eastern perspective. *Aggression and Violent Behavior*, 12, 141–155.

Luong, D. and Wormith, J.S. (2011) Applying risk/need assessment to probation practice and its impact on the recidivism of young offenders. *Criminal Justice and Behavior*, 38, 1177–1199.

Megargee, E.I. and Bohn, M.J., Jr. (1979) Classifying Criminal Offenders: A New System Based on the MMPI, Sage, Beverly Hills.

Mills, J.F. and Kroner, D.G. (2006) The effect of discordance among violence and general recidivism risk estimates on predictive accuracy. *Criminal Behaviour and Mental Health*, 16, 155–166.

Motiuk, L.L., Bonta, J. and Andrews, D.A. (1986) Classification in correctional halfway houses: the relative and incremental predictive criterion validities of the Megargee-MMPI and LSI Systems. *Criminal Justice and Behavior*, 13, 33–46.

Nuffield, J. (1982) Parole Decision-Making in Canada: Research Towards Decision Guidelines, Solicitor General of Canada, Ottawa.

Olver, M.E., Stockdale, K.C. and Wormith, J.S. (2009) Risk assessment with young offenders: a meta-analysis of three assessment measures. *Criminal Justice and Behavior*, 36, 329–353.

Petersilia, J. (2002) Reforming Probation and Parole in the 21st Century, American Correctional Association, Lanham.

Pressman, E. (2009) Risk Assessment Decisions for Violent Political Extremists. User Rep. no. 2009-01, Public Safety Canada, Ottawa.

Quay, H.C. (1965) Psychopathic personality as pathological stimulus-seeking. *American Journal of Psychiatry*, 122, 180–183.

Quinsey, V.L., Harris, G.T., Rice, M.E. and Cormier, C.A. (2006) Violent Offenders: Appraising and Managing Risk, 2nd edn, American Psychological Association, Washington, DC.

Rice, M.E., Harris, G.T. and Hilton, Z.N. (2010) The violence risk appraisal guide and sex offender risk appraisal guide for violence risk assessment and the Ontario domestic assault risk assessment and domestic violence risk appraisal guide for wife assault risk assessment, in Handbook of Violence Risk Assessment (eds R.K. Otto and K. Douglas), Routledge, New York, pp. 99–119.

Schlager, M.D. and Simourd, D.J. (2007) Validity of the level of service inventory – revised among African American and Hispanic offenders. *Criminal Justice and Behavior*, 34, 545–554.

Seiter, R.P. and Kadela, K.R. (2003) Prisoner reentry: what works, what does not, and what is promising. *Crime & Delinquency*, 49, 360–388.

Simon, T.L. (2008) Effectiveness of the Probation and Parole Service Delivery Model (PPSDM) in reducing recidivism. Unpublished Master thesis, University of Saskatchewan, Saskatoon.

Simourd, L. and Andrews, D.A. (1994) Correlates of delinquency: a look at gender differences. *Forum on Corrections Research*, 6, 26–31.

Smith, P., Cullen, F.T. and Latessa, E.J. (2009) Can 14,373 women be wrong? A meta-analysis of the LSI-R and recidivism for female offenders. *Criminology and Public Policy*, 8, 183–208.

Van Voorhis, P., Wright, E.M., Salisbury, E. and Bauman, A. (2010) Women's risk factors and their contributions to existing risk/needs assessment: the current status of a gender-responsive supplement. *Criminal Justice and Behavior*, 37, 261–288.

Ward, T. and Maruna, S. (2007) Rehabilitation: Beyond the Risk Paradigm, Routledge, New York.

Webster, C.D., Douglas, K.S., Eaves, D. and Hart, S.D. (1997) HCR-20: Assessing the Risk for Violence (Version 2), Simon Fraser University, Mental Health, Law, and Policy Institute, Vancouver.

Wong, S. and Hare, R.D. (2005) Guidelines for a Psychopathy Treatment Program, Multi-Health Systems Inc., Toronto.

Worling, I.R. and Curwen, T. (2001) Estimate of risk of adolescent sexual offense recidivism (ERASOR; Version 2.0), in Juveniles and Children Who Sexually Abuse: Frameworks for Assessment, 2nd edn (ed. M.C. Calder), Russell House Publishing, Dorset, pp. 372–397.

Wormith, J.S., Hogg, S. and Guzzo, L. (2012) The predictive validity of a general risk/needs assessment inventory on sexual offender recidivism and an exploration of the professional override. *Criminal Justice and Behavior*, 39, 1511–1538.

Wormith, J.S. and Sheppard, M. (2003) Standardized risk assessment in corrections from an organizational perspective. *Canadian Psychology*, 44(2a), 21.

Wormith, J.S., Olver, M., Stevenson, H. and Girard, L. (2007) The long term prediction of offender recidivism using diagnostic, personality and risk/need approaches to offender assessment. *Psychological Services*, 4, 287–305.

Yang, M., Wong, S.C.P. and Coid, J. (2010) The efficacy of violence prediction: a meta-analytic comparison of nine risk assessment tools. *Psychological Bulletin*, 136, 740–767.

5

What Works in Assessing Risk in Sexual and Violent Offenders

Leam A. Craig[1,2], Anthony R. Beech[2] and Franca Cortoni[3]

[1]Forensic Psychology Practice Ltd, The Willows Clinic, UK
[2]University of Birmingham, UK
[3]Université de Montréal, Canada

Introduction

In response to the assumption that 'nothing works' in the assessment and rehabilitation designed to reduce tendencies in offenders to engage in criminal behaviour (Lipton, Martinson and Wilks, 1975; Martinson, 1974), the past four decades have seen an explosion of research produced in these areas. In accordance with the work of Andrews and Bonta (2010), who advocate the use of *risk*, *need* and *responsivity* principles in determining the course of treatment for a particular individual, the accurate assessment of risk of reoffending is often the first stage of assessment in determining treatment need as well as informing community management and supervision arrangements (see Chapter 4). The aim of this chapter is to consider the development of risk assessment methodologies such as structured guided assessments and actuarial measures used in the assessment of sexual and violent offenders.

Risk Assessment Methodologies

Identification of the risks posed by sexual or violent offenders and the factors associated with their recidivism are crucial to an understanding of appropriate and effective interventions to prevent future assaultive behaviour. Professionals working with sexual and violent offenders are often asked to assess the risk they present. These assessments are normally concerned with the risk of further sexual offences or with the risk of future violence of any kind. To carry out this task, the professional typically uses a combination of actuarial scales and (structured) clinical judgement (Craig, Browne and Beech, 2008).

What Works in Offender Rehabilitation: An Evidence-Based Approach to Assessment and Treatment,
First Edition. Edited by Leam A. Craig, Louise Dixon and Theresa A. Gannon.
© 2013 John Wiley & Sons, Ltd. Published 2013 by John Wiley & Sons, Ltd.

Actuarial risk assessment instruments (ARAIs) are often made up of static (historical) risk items. A static risk factor is something that is useful for evaluating long-term risk, but because it is historical in nature, it cannot be used to assess changes in levels of risk over time (e.g., Static-99, Hanson and Thornton, 2000). ARAIs share a number of characteristics. Each include 'predictor' items that were selected because they were found to be highly correlated with sexual recidivism. A sum of the risk items produces an overall 'risk score' which translates into a 'risk category' (low, medium, high or very high). Although some items may be weighted more heavily than others (such as age risk item), individuals who score positively on many items typically obtain total scores that place them in a high-risk group, while those who score positively on a few items obtain low-risk scores. In most cases, the scale developers have compiled 'experience tables' (Ohlin, 1951) from retrospective (often meta-analytical) studies of released offenders that show the percentage of offenders in each risk category who have recidivated in a given cohort. Validation studies for these instruments have also consistently demonstrated predictive accuracy on these measures across samples and countries (for review see Craig, Browne and Beech, 2008).

While actuarial assessment of risk can have some benefits in the correct context, it has limitations in regard to the consequent management of the offender, as an understanding of the more changeable elements of risk is not provided. As such, a greater focus on understanding the dynamic assessment of risk has to be of substantial consideration. Structured clinical judgement (SCJ) protocols are not 'scored' actuarially but allow for a measured approach to the identification of relevant risk factors by considering 'static' and 'dynamic' factors. Dynamic factors are enduring features linked to the likelihood of offending that can be changed following intervention. Dynamic factors can be subdivided into *stable* and *acute* factors. Stable dynamic risk factors are those which are relatively persistent characteristics of the offender which are subject to change such as levels of responsibility, cognitive distortions and sexual arousal. Acute dynamic factors are rapidly changing factors such as substance misuse, isolation and negative emotional states, the presence of which increases risk (Hanson and Harris, 1998).

With the advent of actuarial risk scales, criminal justice professionals have increasingly endorsed actuarial measures of risk as the most reliable predictive instruments for decision making (Archer *et al.*, 2006; Ericson and Haggerty 1997; Hannah-Moffat and Shaw, 2001). Within the field, the relative merits of predictive accuracy of actuarial versus clinical judgement have been hotly debated, but it is now widely accepted that the former have shown to be superior in predicting recidivism compared with the latter (Hanson and Morton-Bourgon, 2009; Harris, Rice and Cormier, 2002). It can be argued that actuarial prediction is an objective approach, while SCJ is subjective and can be influenced by the individual's own feelings and prejudices. Over 10 years ago, Doren (1998), for example, noted that clinical judgement of risk typically under-predicts (sexual) violence because the great majority of sexual offenders are classified as non-recidivists. Doren's conclusion was based on an analysis, which assumed that the maximum prediction rate for sexual violence ranged from 0.6% to 12%, while actual long-term recidivism was much higher, from 39% for rapists to 52% for child abusers.

The evidence base for actuarial scales is such that in North America and the UK, ARAIs have permeated the entire criminal justice system. Many states in the US have enacted legislation allowing for the post-prison civil commitment of sex offenders as *sexually violent predators* (SVP; Covington, 1997; Doren, 2002; Miller, Amenta and Conroy, 2005). The sexually violent predator laws establish procedures for the civil commitment of persons who, due to a 'mental abnormality' or 'personality disorder', are likely to engage in 'predatory acts of sexual violence'. The criteria for commitment consider three aspects: that the individual has engaged in harmful sexual conduct in the past, that the individual currently suffers from a mental disorder and that the individual will likely engage in future acts of harmful sexual misconduct (Janus and Meehl, 1997). With regard to assessing the likelihood the individual will engage in future acts of harmful sexual misconduct, the US judicial system relies heavily on the opinions of expert witnesses within the field. These witnesses often base their opinions on actuarial tests for the prediction of sexual recidivism at commitment hearings (Wollert, 2006).

In Canada, the National Parole Board (NPB, 2004) note, '...[that] There are numerous actuarial risk assessment instruments that exist and which the Board must consider in its decision-making process' (p. 20). In England and Wales, in the Secretary of State's directions (issued August 2004) to the Parole Board under Section 32(6) of the Criminal Justice Act 1991, it is noted that regarding the release and recall back to prison of life sentence prisoners, the Parole Board must take into account '...any indication of predicted risk as determined by a validated actuarial risk predictor model or any other structured assessment of risk and treatment needs' (Criminal Justice Act, 1991, Annex B, 6 K, p. 2).

The attraction for clinicians in using actuarial risk scales is, in part, related to their ease of use and simplicity. It is often a simple matter of translating risk scores into risk categories from which it is possible to extract risk tables (usually expressed in percentages) indicating future risk level. Hence, some have argued (e.g., Grove and Meehl, 1996; Quinsey *et al.*, 2006) that failure to conduct actuarial risk assessment, or consider its results, is irrational, unscientific, unethical and unprofessional.

The applicability of ARAIs, based on group data, to produce risk estimates in individual cases has been widely debated, with some arguing that the individual confidence intervals for the Static-99 and the Violence Risk Appraisal Guide (VRAG; Quinsey *et al.*, 2006) are so great as to render the scale virtually useless (Hart, Michie and Cooke, 2007). However, several authors have taken issue with these conclusions (Doren, 2007; Harris, Rice and Quinsey, 2007; Mossman and Sellke, 2007), highlighting methodological limitations in the research (for a review see Craig and Beech, 2010). Harris, Rice and Quinsey (2007) note that the statistical argument by Hart, Michie and Cooke (2007) does not refute the empirical results supporting the accuracy of ARAIs, and that to view 'individual risk' as something different from 'group risk' is a mistake. Harris, Rice and Quinsey (2007) argue by conventional standards, average predictive effects of ARAIs (in terms of the sensitivity-specificity tradeoff) are large and are distributed as expected by psychometric principles. Of course, ARAIs are not without their weaknesses, and practitioners using actuarial scales must do so with a thorough understanding of methodological limitations of the technology and possible errors and inaccuracies of reporting actuarial risk estimates in individual cases (see Craig and Beech, 2010).

However, by the nature of the scales' *apparent* simplicity, the use of actuarial scales can lead to misuse of data and, in turn, the misinterpretation and misrepresentation of the results, particularly when actuarial data is heavily relied upon in decision making. A developing risk assessment methodology, referred to as a 'convergent approach' to risk assessment (Boer, 2006; Craig *et al.*, 2004), utilizes both actuarial and structured clinical judgement. The application of actuarial risk scales follows a *nomothetic* approach to risk assessment (i.e., searching for general traits of personality), as typically used in risk assessment approaches. This is in comparison to SCJ, which follows an i*diographic* approach (i.e., measuring the uniqueness of the individual through clinical assessment) (Windelband, 1904). The convergent approach uses an appropriate ARAI to provide a 'baseline estimate' of risk and adjusts this risk estimate based on clinically relevant factors. Before considering convergent approaches to risk assessment, we will first examine the predictive validity of ARAIs and SCJ.

Risk Assessment in Sexual Offenders

Actuarial risk assessment

In the last 10–15 years, the literature has witnessed a proliferation of actuarial sexual and violent offender risk assessment instruments that typically examine static risk factors, including: Static-99 (Hanson and Thornton, 2000), Static-2002R (Hanson and Thornton, 2003), Risk Matrix 2000 (RM2000/S; Thornton *et al.*, 2003), the Sex Offender Risk Appraisal Guide (SORAG: Quinsey *et al.*, 2006) and the Violence Risk Scale-Sex Offender version (VRS-SO; Wong *et al.*, 2003) used in the UK (see Table 5.1).

The *Static-99* is perhaps one of the most widely used and researched ARAIs with more than 13 000 cases and has been shown to produce large predictive effects (Harris, Rice and Quinsey, 2007). The best reported predictive accuracy for the Static-99, expressed as an Area Under the Curve (AUC) of the Receiver Operating Characteristic, is AUC of 0.91 (Thornton and Beech, 2002). The predecessor to the Static-99 was the Rapid Risk Assessment for Sexual Offence Recidivism (RRASOR; Hanson, 1997) which was developed in Canada using predominantly North American samples but has since been validated in England and Wales using a prison sample. RRASOR contains four items: past sexual offences, age at commencement of risk, extra-familial victims and male victims. Hanson recommends that the use of RRASOR be discontinued.

Accurate multiple-instrument interpretation requires prior knowledge of the degree to which different scales assess each of the multiple aetiological dimensions (Doren, 2002). In examining the dual dimension to sexual offending, Doren (2002) and Roberts, Doren and Thornton (2002) investigated the inter-relationships between several actuarial sex and violent risk measures including the RRASOR, Static-99, the Minnesota Sex Offender Screening Tool-Revised (MnSOST-R; Epperson, Kaul and Hesselton, 1998), VRAG and the Psychopathy Checklist-Revised (PCL-R; Hare, 1991) and revealed two distinct dimensions relating to sexual reconviction: 'deviant sexual interests' and 'antisocial/violent personality characteristics'. On the basis of their findings, the authors argue that there are two underlying drives towards sexual recidivism: (i) *Pedophilic Deviance/Sexual Repetitiveness*, diagnosable and illegal sexual desires, and (ii) *General Criminality/Antisocial-Violence*. They suggest that RRASOR and Static-99 may actually measure different aspects of sexual and violent offending. The RRASOR tended to correlate with sexual deviance dimensions and deviant profiles using penile plethysmography) but not with antisocial behaviour, whereas exclusive (i.e., non RRASOR) Static-99 items correlated with diagnosable antisocial personality disorder and high PCL-R scores but negatively correlated with paedophilia. The RRASOR scale tended to correlate with sexual deviance dimensions, whereas other actuarial instruments tended to correlate with the general violence dimension.

Doren's (2002) and Roberts, Doren and Thornton's (2002) suggestion is that the RRASOR and Static-99 tap into aspects of sexual deviance and antisociality risk. Indeed, this is consistent with RM2000 (Thornton *et al.*, 2003) risk scales. RM2000 system has two scales: one for measuring risk of sexual recidivism – Risk Matrix 2000/Sexual (RM2000/S) – and one for measuring risk of non-sexual violent recidivism – Risk Matrix 2000/Violent (RM2000/V) – in sexual offenders. Both the RM2000/S and RM2000/V have been shown to demonstrate good predictive accuracy (for a review, see Craig, Browne and Beech, 2008).

Further support for the dual dimension of sexual violent offending can be seen in Parent, Guay and Knight's (2011) evaluation of the predictive accuracy of nine ARAIs and SCJ measures which revealed clear distinctions in risk between rapists and child molesters. In the

Table 5.1 ARAIs for sexual offenders

Risk instrument	Scale description
Static-99 (Hanson and Thornton, 2000)	The Static-99 is an actuarial risk tool for evaluating the risk of sexual and violent recidivism among adult male sexual offenders. The Static-99 consists of 10 items (including the 4 items of the RRASOR): prior sex offences, prior sentencing occasions, convictions for non-contact sex offences, index non-sexual violence, prior non-sexual violence, unrelated victims, stranger victims, male victims, lack of a long-term intimate relationship and if the offender is aged under 25 on release (or now, if the offender is in the community). There is also an updated Static-99R that assigns different weights to age categories. Additional information on the Static-99R is available on www.static99.org The revised 2003 coding rules for Static-99 are available at http://www.static99.org/pdfdocs/static-99-coding-rules_e.pdf
Static-2002 (Hanson and Thornton, 2003)	The Static-2002 also evaluates the risk of sexual and violent recidivism among adult male sexual offenders, but it is a separate instrument from the Static-99. Static-2002 predicts sexual, violent and any recidivism as well as other actuarial risk tools commonly used with sexual offenders and has slightly improved predictive accuracy over that of Static-99. Static-2002 is intended to assess some theoretically meaningful characteristics presumed to be the cause of recidivism risk (persistence of sexual offending, deviant sexual interests, general criminality). Static-2002 has 14 items, with some items modified from Static-99. Static-2002 items are grouped into five domains: age, persistence of sex offending, deviant sexual interests, relationship to victims and general criminality. Total scores can range from 0 to 14. There is also an updated Static-2002R that assigns different weights to age categories. Additional information on the Static-2002R is available on www.static99.org The scoring manual for the Static-2002 is available online from http://www.static99.org/pdfdocs/static2002codingrules.pdf
Risk Matrix 2000 (Thornton *et al.*, 2003)	This scale has separate indicators for risk of sexual recidivism (RM2000/S) and overall violence (RM2000/V), and can be combined to give a composite risk of reconviction for sexual or non-sexual assaults – Risk Matrix 2000/ Combined (RM2000/C). This scale is used in prison, probation and other mental health settings in the UK, as it is a widely cross-validated, static risk assessment for sex offenders. An individual's level of sexual violence risk (low, medium, high, very high) is ascertained by a two-stage process. The first stage involves scoring individuals on three items: (i) age at commencement of risk, (ii) sexual appearances, (iii) total criminal appearances. The second stage of RM2000 contains four aggravating factors that contribute to elevated risk: (i) male victim, (ii) stranger victim, (iii) non-contact sexual offences and (iv) lack of a long-term intimate relationship. In a cross validation study, the RM2000/S obtained moderate (AUC = 0.68) accuracy in predicting sexual reconviction whereas the RM2000/V obtained good accuracy in predicting violent and sexual/violent (combined) (AUC = 0.87 and 0.76) reconviction (Craig, Beech and Browne, 2006). The RM2000 scoring guide is available at http://www.cfcp.bham.ac.uk/Extras/SCORING%20GUIDE%20FOR%20RISK%20MATRIX%202000.9-%20SVC%20-%20(ver.%20Feb%202007).pdf

Table 5.1   (*cont'd*)

Risk instrument	Scale description
Sex Offender Risk Appraisal Guide (SORAG) (Quinsey *et al.*, 2006)	SORAG was designed to predict at least one reconviction for a sexual offence and is developed from a version used for violent offenders (Violent Risk Appraisal Guide (VRAG), see Quinsey *et al.*, 2006). SORAG contains 14 static risk factors: lived with biological parents, elementary school maladjustment, alcohol problems, marital status, criminal history for violent offences, criminal history for non-violent offences, history of sexual offences, sexual offences against girls under 14 years, failure of prior conditional release, age at index offence, DSM criteria for any personality disorder, schizophrenia, phallometric test results and psychopathy scores
Violence Risk Scale-Sex Offender version (VRS-SO) (Wong *et al.*, 2003)	The VRS-SO is a dynamic actuarial instrument for assessing pre- and post-treatment risk for sexual offenders. It consists of 7 static items and 17 dynamic items organized into three factors: Sexual Deviance, Criminality and Treatment Responsivity. VRS-SO ratings produce several scale component scores: VRS-SO Static, pre-treatment Dynamic and Total scores (i.e., Static plus pre-treatment Dynamic), post-treatment Dynamic and Total scores and pre- and post-treatment scores on each of the three Dynamic factors. VRS-SO Total scores can be translated into four risk categories: low (score of 0–20), moderate-low (21–30), moderate-high (31–40) and high (41–72)

child molester sample, the RRASOR (AUC = 0.74), Static-99 (AUC = 0.75), Static-2002 (AUC = 0.74), SORAG (AUC = 0.72) and RM2000/S (AUC = 0.72) were better at predicting sexual recidivism compared with the VRAG (AUC = 0.74), SORAG (AUC = 0.71), RM2000/V (AUC = 0.73) and PCL-R (AUC = 0.73) which were better at predicting violent recidivism in the rapists sample.

The SORAG (Quinsey *et al.*, 2006) has also shown promising results in predicting sexual recidivism. The SORAG differs from the VRAG with the addition of two risk items: history of sexual offences (against girls under 14 years) and phallometric test results. Dempster, Hart and Boer (2002) found an AUC of 0.77 for the SORAG for sexual recidivism but 0.88 for violent recidivism (including sexual) for the same group of offenders.

Derived from the Violence Risk Scale (VRS; Wong and Gordon, 2006), the *Violence Risk Scale-Sex Offender* version (VRS-SO; Wong *et al.*, 2003) was designed as a comprehensive actuarial risk instrument for sexual offenders and includes both static and dynamic risk factors that are empirically or theoretically related to sexual recidivism. Apart from predicting recidivism risk, the VRS-SO was also designed to integrate risk assessment with treatment by identifying criminogenic needs as potential treatment targets, to evaluate readiness to change on each identified need according to the Transtheoretical Change Model (Prochaska, DiClemente and Norcross, 1992) and to assess changes in risk following treatment. The developers of the VRS-SO carried out initial analyses of the psychometric properties of the measure on a sample of 321 men who completed a treatment programme for sexual offenders in a maximum-security forensic unit (Olver *et al.*, 2007). The inter-rater reliability, concurrent validity and predictive validity of the measure were evaluated, as well as the relationship between change on the dynamic items and sexual recidivism. Analysis of the dynamic items revealed a three-factor structure: Sexual Deviance, Criminality and Treatment Responsivity.

The VRS-SO Static scale, pre- and post-treatment Dynamic scale and pre- and post-treatment Total scale scores all had significant positive correlations with the Static-99. The Sexual Deviance (AUC = 0.63) factor outperformed the PCL-R (AUC = 0.61) predicting any new sexual conviction (Olver and Wong, 2006). The VRS-SO Static scale, pre- and post-treatment Dynamic scale and pre- and post-treatment Total scale scores were all significantly correlated with sexual recidivism over an average 10-year follow-up (Olver *et al.*, 2007). AUC values from 0.66 to 0.74 are comparable with the predictive validity of the Static-99. The VRS-SO Dynamic scale has demonstrated incremental validity in the prediction of sexual recidivism over the VRS-SO Static scale and over the Static-99. In a cross validation study of 218 sexual offenders who had completed treatment in New Zealand, the predictive accuracy of the VRS-SO Total (pre-treatment AUC = 0.79), Static scale (AUC = 0.70), Dynamic scale (AUC = 0.78) and Sexual Deviance factor (pre-treatment AUC = 0.72) were comparable with that of the Static-99 (AUC = 0.72) (Beggs and Grace, 2010). The VRS-SO, as a measure of treatment change, has demonstrated convergent and predictive validity, which suggests that effective treatment that targets dynamic risk factors leads to a reduction in sexual recidivism (Beggs and Grace, 2011).

Structured clinical judgement

Unlike the actuarial field, the development of structured clinical guidelines for assessment of risk in sexual offenders has been slow, with only a few instruments of note.

The *Sexual Violence Risk-20* (SVR-20; Boer *et al.*, 1997) assesses the risk of sexual violence by selecting 20 factors, from an extensive list, that could be comprehensively divided into three main sections to formulate the SVR-20. Factors include: (i) *Psychological Adjustment* – sexual deviation, victim of child abuse, cognitive impairment, suicidal/homicidal ideation, relationship/employment problems, previous offence history (non-sexual violent, non-violent), psychopathy, substance use problems and past supervision failure; (ii) *Sexual Offending* – such as high-density offences, multiple offences, physical harm to victims, use of weapon, escalation and cognitive distortions; and (iii) *Future Plans* – whether the offender lacks realistic plans and has negative attitudes towards instruction. Boer *et al.* (1997) developed the SVR-20 more as a set of guidelines to improve assessments of risk for sexual violence. The authors note that the SVR-20 risk factors are not intended to be used as an actuarial scale. Instead, they suggest that evaluators should consider the SVR-20 and any other case-specific factors deemed important and should integrate them in an unstructured or clinical manner (p. 336). The AUC indices for the SVR-20 in predicting sexual reconviction range from 0.48 to 0.77, although Craig *et al.* (2006a, b) and Sjöstedt and Långström (2002) both found that the SVR-20 was a better predictor of violent reconviction than of sexual reconviction. Barbaree *et al.* (2008) reported an AUC of 0.63 in a sample of 468 Canadian sexual offenders, while Rettenberger *et al.* (2010) reported an AUC of 0.71 in a sample of 394 Austrian sexual offenders.

Rettenberger, Boer and Eher (2011) examined the predictive accuracy and psychometric properties of the SVR-20 in a sample of 493 male sexual offenders assessed between 2001 and 2007 at the Federal Evaluation Centre for Violent and Sexual Offenders in the Austrian Prison System. Sexual reconviction data was examined over a three- and five-year period. Findings indicate good predictive accuracy for the prediction of sexual recidivism for the total sample (AUC = 0.72) as well as for the rapist subgroup (*n* = 221, AUC = 0.71) and the child molester subsample (*n* = 249, AUC = 0.77). Of the three subscales, the Psychosocial Adjustment scale produced the most promising results significantly predicting general sexual recidivism (AUC

= 0.67) for the entire sample. However, when the sample were grouped by offence category, rapist or child molester, the accuracy of this subscale in predicting sexual recidivism in the rapist only sample (AUC = 0.63) performed less well when compared to the child molester sample (AUC = 0.72). In contrast, the Sexual Offences subscale performed better in the rapists sample (AUC = 0.77) compared to the child molester sample (AUC = 0.65) in predicting general sexual recidivism.

The SVR-20 is currently under revision (Boer, 2011). The revised SVR-20 (second edition) follows a clear multidimensional focus, all items having both dynamic and static features and all items having variable components (i.e., a continuum exists within items and issues within items interact to produce the complexities we see in the individual case – with some examples within and between items) (Boer, 2011). A convergent approach is recommended – using an appropriate actuarial baseline to provide an anchor for structured clinical evaluation. Many of the original 20 items remain, although some items have changed or been replaced, allowing for the inclusion of new items. As Boer (2011) notes, given the existing research base for the original SVR-20, to change the scale beyond recognition would invalidate much of the research base. In the Psychosocial Adjustment section, new items 'sexual health problems' and 'past non-sexual offending' have been included, the latter replacing 'past non-sexual violent' and 'past non-violent offences'. The item 'past supervision failure' has been moved to the Future Plans section and renamed. In describing the changes to the Psychosocial Adjustment section, Boer (2011) argues it is common for 'sexual health problems' to decrease risk, and it is also common that sexual desire and ability decrease with age. Thus, this item measures *normal* decreases in risk with aging for all individuals. There are also some individuals who have sexual health disorders that increase their risk if a sexual assault occurs, for example, HIV. HIV+persons are not at any greater risk to offend than anyone else, but if an HIV+person does sexually offend, the victim may be lethally affected. Boer argues there are some unique cases in which older individuals offend in non-sexual ways due to impotence, and there are some individuals who actually do not start offending until they are much older. Within the Sexual Offences section, a new item 'diversity of sexual offending' replaces 'multiple offence types', 'actual or threatened physical harm to victim' replaces 'physical harm to victim(s)' and 'psychological coercion in sexual offences' replaces 'use of weapons of threats of death'. It is argued that persons who have committed multiple types (as determined by differing victim characteristics and varying in nature) of sexual offences are at increased risk for sexual recidivism. This is a risk factor that likely reflects the presence of sexual deviation and attitudes that support or condone sexual violence. Psychological coercion refers to coercive tactics ranging from grooming of victims through the use of gifts or additional privileges to threats of family separation or abandonment – all of which serve to provide the offender with victim access while protecting the offender's behaviour from discovery. Boer (2011) notes this item is supported more by the clinical treatment literature than from the meta-analyses per se. This is a risk factor that likely reflects the presence of sexual deviation (e.g., sadism) and attitudes that support or condone sexual violence. The Future Plans section includes three items (instead of two in the 1997 version). As well as continuing to have 'realistic future plans' and 'negative attitudes towards intervention', a new item, 'negative attitudes towards supervision', has been added. It is argued that non-compliance with supervision is related to recidivism of a general, violent and sexually violent nature, and persons who reject or do not comply with supervision are at increased risk for criminality and violence. Such attitudes may be related to future sexual violence by resulting in inadequate professional support, leading to increasing sexual deviance, increased distress or increased risk for exposure to destabilizing influences such as drugs, alcohol or potential victims. The scoring system has also altered to reflect changes (reductions, no change or increases) in a risk-relevant item over a specified period of time.

The *Risk for Sexual Violence Protocol* (RSVP, Hart *et al.*, 2003) can be seen as a variation and evolution of earlier SCJ scales. Like the *Historical, Clinical, Risk Management-20* (HCR-20) and SVR-20, the RSVP does not employ actuarial or statistical methods to support decision making about risk. Rather, it offers a set of guidelines for collecting relevant information and making structured risk formulations. The RSVP protocol is an evolved form of the SVR-20 and is based on a rejection of actuarial approaches to the assessment of risk of sexual violence. Similar to the SVR-20, the RSVP identifies the potential risk factors (presence) and makes a determination of their importance to future offending (relevance). However, in addition to the SVR-20, the RSVP provides explicit guidelines for risk formulation, such as risk scenarios and management strategies.

The inclusion of risk formulation adds to the likely completion time for the RSVP and, as such, may take much longer to complete than other guided risk measures. The RSVP assumes that risk must be defined in the context in which it occurs and regards the primary risk decision as preventative, and considers steps which are required to minimize any risks posed by the individual. Laws (2006) emphasizes the RSVP is not a predictor tool but rather a system that permits the management of current risk that includes both static and dynamic risk factors. According to the authors, the target populations for the RSVP are males aged 18 years or more with a known or suspected history of sexual violence, older male adolescents (16–17 years) and women with known or suspected history. It is important to note here that the claim the RSVP is suitable for females is made without any empirical evidence that the risk factors predictive of sexual recidivism in males are applicable to females. In fact, the risk factors for females are as of yet unknown, although one study has shown that a history of child maltreatment appears related to sexual recidivism among females (Sandler and Freeman, 2009). The protocol is not suitable for children or young adolescents. The RSVP is a 22-item protocol divided into five domains including sexual violence history, psychological adjustment, mental disorder, social adjustment and manageability. The RSVP should not be used to determine whether someone committed an act(s) of sexual violence in the past, and it does not provide an estimate of specific likelihood or probability that someone will commit acts of sexual violence in the future. The test authors suggest that the RSVP is designed to highlight information relating to clinical problems rather than producing an overall risk score. Information is structured in a number of steps: case information, presence of risk factors, relevance of risk factors, risk scenarios (possible futures), risk management strategies and summary judgements. The RSVP has good inter-rater agreement and concurrent validity but should only be used as a long-term measure to inform case management as there is little empirical study into the predictive accuracy of this scale (e.g., Kropp, 2000).

ARAIs and SCJ evaluation

A number of studies have evaluated the predictive accuracy and psychometric properties of both ARAIs and SCJ measures. In a meta-analytical comparison between ARAIs (e.g., Static-99) and SCJ (e.g., SVR-20), Hanson and Mortnon-Bourgon (2009) found that actuarial measures designed for sexual recidivism produced the greatest effect size ($d = 0.67$) while SCJ produced an effect size of $d = 0.46$. Although the SVR-20 produced the largest average association with sexual recidivism, the authors note this was only based on three studies ($n = 245$).

More recently, Blacker *et al.* (2011) compared ARAIs (RRASOR and RM2000/V) and SCJ (SVR-20) in a sample of 88 offenders (44 mainstream and 44 sexual offenders with special needs). In predicting sexual reconviction, the SVR-20 (AUC = 0.73) outperformed the RM2000/V (AUC = 0.56) and RRASOR (AUC = 0.60) for the mainstream sample, with the Psychosocial Adjustment section of the SVR-20 producing a large effect (AUC = 0.72).

Parent, Guay and Knight (2011) evaluated the predictive accuracy of nine instruments (VRAG, SORAG, RRASOR, Static-99, Static-2002, RM2000, MnSOST-R, SVR-20, PCL-R) on 590 sexual offenders who had been evaluated at the Massachusetts Treatment Center for Sexually Dangerous Persons in Bridgewater, Massachusetts, across a 15-year follow-up. There was little difference between the ARAIs in predicting sexual recidivism ranging from AUC = 0.71 for the Static-99 to AUC = 0.68 for the RM2000/S and MnSOST-R, with the SVR-20 producing AUC = 0.66. However, in respect of violent recidivism, the RM2000/V and VRAG outperformed all other scales producing AUCs of 0.71 and 0.70, respectively.

Convergence of risk assessment approaches

Where concern relates to tailoring treatment to the needs of the offender, then static actuarial assessments should be combined with a functional analysis assessment (Ireland and Craig, 2011), plus the assessment of stable (psychological) dynamic risk factors: ((deviant) sexual interests, pro-offending attitudes, poor socio-emotional functioning, emotional/behavioural dysregulation problems) (see Craig, Browne and Beech, 2008). These problems can be assessed, to a greater or lesser degree, by the following: Stable 2007 (Hanson *et al.*, 2007, also see Chapter 23, this volume), Beech's Deviancy system (Beech, 1998) or the Structured Assessment of Risk and Need (SARN; Thornton, 2002). As Harkins and Beech (2007) suggest, common among the three frameworks of assessing stable dynamic risk factors are the four overarching domains: sexual interests/sexual self-regulation, distorted attitudes/ attitudes tolerant of sexual offending, socio-affective functioning/intimacy deficits and self-management/self-regulation problems (Craig and Beech, 2010) (Table 5.2).

In an attempt to improve actuarial accuracy, several researchers have considered additional risk factors such as pro-offending attitudes (Hudson *et al.*, 2002) and other dynamic measures (Dempster and Hart, 2002; Thornton, 2002) which have increased predictive accuracy when combined with static risk factors. Thornton and Beech (2002) examined the extent to which psychological *deviance* predicts sexual recidivism as well as compared the predictive accuracy of dynamic and static risk assessments. Here, they compared the accuracy of the deviancy assessment (dynamic risk factors) to the Static-99 (static risk factors – Hanson and Thornton, 2000) on two samples of sex offenders (121 men assessed prior to participating on a brief cognitive-behavioural prison programme in England and Wales and 53 adult male sex offenders assessed prior to participating in brief community treatment programme) (Beech *et al.*, 2002). Thornton and Beech found that as a predictor of sexual recidivism, problems in the number of dysfunctional domains obtained moderate accuracy (AUC ranging from 0.83 to 0.85) compared with Static-99 (AUC ranging from 0.91 to 0.75) over a four-year follow-up period.

More recently, Craig *et al.* (2007) considered the effectiveness of psychometric markers of risk in approximating the *deviancy* domains, and how these measures of dynamic risk could be used to predict sexual reconviction compared with actuarial risk. A Psychological Deviance Index (PDI) was calculated by standardizing each of the scale scores for a domain. A domain was counted as dysfunctional if its average standard score was greater than 0. This means the total number of dysfunctional domains index could be calculated running from 0 (indicating no

Table 5.2 Stable dynamic risk factors for sexual offenders

Stable dynamic risk factors/ deviancy domains	Beech deviancy classification (Beech et al., 1998/2002)	STABLE-2007 (Hanson et al., 2007)	SARN (Thornton, 2002)
Sexual interests	Sexually obsessed Sex deviance patterns (child molestation) marked	Sexual preoccupation/ sex drive Sex as a coping strategy Deviant sexual interests	Sexual preoccupation (obsession) Sexual preference for children Sexualized violence Other offence-related sexual interests (fetish)
Attitudes supportive of sexual assault	Distorted attitudes about children and children's sexuality Distorted attitudes about own victims Justifications for sexual deviance	Sexual entitlement Pro-rape attitudes Child molester attitudes	Adversarial sexual attitudes Sexual entitlement Child abuse supportive beliefs Belief women are deceitful
Intimacy deficits	Emotional identification with children Low self-esteem Emotional loneliness Under-assertiveness Personal distress Locus of control	Lack of lovers/intimate partners Emotional identification with children Hostility towards women General social rejection/loneliness Lack of concern for others	Personal inadequacy (low self-esteem, external locus of control, passive victim stance, suspiciousness) Emotional congruence with children (feeling more comfortable with children than adults) Grievance stance (being suspicious, angry and vengeful with other people) Emotional loneliness (lack of intimate relationships, difficulty or unwillingness to create intimate relationships)
General self-regulation		Impulsive acts Poor cognitive problem-solving skills Negative emotionality/ hostility	Lifestyle impulsiveness – impulsive, unstable lifestyle Poor problem solving (poor problem recognition, poor consequential thinking, rigidity in thinking Poor emotional control (tendency to explosive outbursts or other behavioural expression of emotional impulses)

dysfunctional domains) to 4 (indicating four dysfunctional domains). The examination of the risk assessment properties of the four dynamic risk domains showed that the Sexual Interests domain obtained a large effect in predicting sexual reconviction over two-year (AUC = 0.86) and five-year follow-up periods (AUC = 0.72). The Self Management factor obtained moderate results (AUC = 0.71) in predicting sexual reconviction at two years. However, the Distorted Attitudes (AUC = 0.62) and the Socio-Affective Functioning (AUC = 0.69) domains were less promising at two-year follow-up. In comparison, Static-99 obtained moderate accuracy in predicting sexual reconviction at two-year (AUC = 0.66) and five-year (AUC = 0.60) follow-up periods. When the PDI was grouped into Low (0), Moderate (1–2) and High (3+) categories, it was found the degree of PDI and rates of sexual reconviction were linear at 3%, 18% and 40%, respectively. When the PDI and Static-99 were entered into a logistic regression analysis, it was found that the PDI made a statistically significant contribution to prediction of sexual reconviction independent of the Static-99 scores at five-year follow-up.

To examine the relationship between static and dynamic domains, Craig *et al.* (2007) organized the Static-99 into three sub-scales: *Sexual Deviance* (prior sexual convictions, male victims, non-contact sexual offences, non-relative and stranger victims), *General Criminality* (index non-sexual violence, prior non-sexual violence and four or more sentencing occasions) and *Immaturity* (young age at offending). They found that these actuarial domains correlated with different aspects of the psychological risk factors. Specifically, the *Sexual Interests* domain correlated with the *Sexual Deviance* subscale of Static-99, the *Socio-Affective* domain correlated with the *Immaturity* Static-99 subscale and the *Self Management* domain correlated with both the *General Criminality* and the *Immaturity* subscales of Static-99.

Table 5.3   Actuarial markers and dynamic risk domains for sexual offenders

	Static-99/RM2000 markers	SORAG markers	SVR-20 markers
Domain 1: Sexual interests	Non-contact sexual offences Unrelated victims Stranger victims Male victims Prior sex offences	Previous sexual convictions Male or male + female victims Deviant sexual preferences (phallometric results)	High frequency of sex offences Range of sex offences Escalation in frequency and severity of sex offences
Domain 2: Distorted attitudes			Extreme minimization or denial of offences
Domain 3: Socio-affective functioning	Lack of long-term intimate relationship (<2 years) or single	Never married	Relationship problems
Domain 4: Self-management	Index non-sexual violence Prior non-sexual violence Prior sentencing Occasions/criminal appearances Age at time of risk assessment	Violent criminality Non-violent criminality Failure on conditional release	Violent non-sexual offences General criminality

These studies support the methodology of combining estimations of actuarial static risk with assessments of stable dynamic psychological factors to assess the level of risk and treatment need of sexual offenders. The argument can be most clearly made by the mapping of static risk factors, described in some of the better known risk schedules, onto the four risk domains described in the preceding paragraph (Table 5.3).

Table 5.3 clearly indicates that Static-99, SORAG and the SVR-20 contain items that are historical risk markers of *sexual interests* and *self-management* problems, indicating that they are proxy measures of the level of these problems in the offender's history. However, Table 5.3 also clearly indicates that these schedules contain no historical items measuring distorted attitudes, although the SVR-20 does contain a clinical item that indicates it is important to measure current level of pro-offending attitudes, and a few items tap into levels of socio-affective functioning. This is not surprising, as there would not appear to be many historical items that could actually assess attitudes. We would note that this mapping exercise illustrates how *static* and *dynamic* factors are to some extent two aspects of what we would term psychological vulnerability (Beech and Ward, 2004), with static risk factors identifying strong evidence of (deviant) *sexual interests* and *self-management* problems in an individual's past, and the assessment of the four dynamic risk factors indicating an individual's current levels of problems.

Risk Assessment in Violent Offenders

Actuarial risk assessment

Unlike the field of actuarial risk assessment in sexual offenders, the literature on the actuarial assessment of violent offenders appears dominated by only a couple of scales.

Actuarial scales of note include the *Violence Risk Appraisal Guide* (VRAG; Quinsey *et al.*, 2006) and the *Violence Risk Scale* (Wong and Gordon, 2000). The VRAG is a 12-item actuarial prediction instrument that includes variables related to childhood history, adult adjustment index offence characteristics, PCL-R scores and DSM III criteria for personality disorder and schizophrenia. There is substantial empirical support for the VRAG with AUCs ranging from 0.73 to 0.77 in predicting violent recidivism (Quinsey *et al.*, 2006). The VRAG has also shown to perform well with offenders with intellectual disabilities (Camilleri and Quinsey, 2011; Gray *et al.*, 2007).

The *Violence Risk Scale 2 Edition* (VRS-2; Wong and Gordon, 2000, 2006) is a 26-item measure, which was developed and validated in a regional forensic unit in Canada designed to facilitate violence assessment, prediction and treatment planning. Similar to the HCR-20 (Webster *et al.*, 1997), the VRS-2 reflects a *risk, needs* approach (Bonta and Andrews, 2007); that is, both include items (i.e., the Clinical and Risk Management scales of the HCR-20 and the Dynamic Factors scale on the VRS-2) focused on characteristics and situational changes over time that are hypothesized to correspond to a change in the likelihood of recidivism and that can be targeted in treatment. The most recent version of the VRS-2 consists of 6 static risk factors (e.g., age at first violent conviction, prior release failures/escapes, stability of family upbringing) and 20 dynamic risk factors (e.g., criminal attitudes, insight into cause of violence, substance use, cognitive distortion) which are scored 0–3 producing an overall score. Like the VRS-SO, the dynamic items from the VRS can be coded at pre- and post-treatment stages. Part A of the VRS-2 is the pre-treatment assessment, obtained by summing the value of all ratings on both static and dynamic items, while Part B is the assessment of response to treatment, which is measured by change in ratings on individual dynamic risk factors.

The VRS-2 is reported to have good psychometric properties (Wong and Gordon, 2006). In a UK cross validation sample of 136 male medium secure psychiatric inpatients, Dolan and Fullam (2007) examined the validity of the VRS-2 and the HCR-20. There were highly significant correlations between the scales on the rating of items measuring comparable variables. Both the HCR-20 and the VRS-2 could distinguish between violent and non-violent subgroups with reasonable effect sizes. In a second study, Dolan *et al.* (2008) compared the VRS-2 and the Psychopathy Checklist: Screening Version (PCL:SV; Hart, Cox and Hare, 1995) in a sample of 147 male psychiatric patients on inpatient aggression. The VRS-2 and the PCL:SV were only modest predictors of inpatient aggression. In predicting any aggressive incident, the VRS-2 total score (AUC = 0.68), static subscale score (AUC = 0.60) and dynamic subscale score (AUC = 0.70) were broadly comparable to the PCL:SV total (AUC = 0.67), PCL:SV interpersonal subscale score (AUC = 0.66) and PCL:SV social deviance sub-scale score (AUC = 0.65). However, the VRS-2 putative 'dynamic' items showed the highest predictive accuracy.

Structured clinical assessment

The HCR-20 (Webster *et al.*, 1997) is a 20-item risk assessment checklist developed for the purpose of assisting the SCJ in violence risk assessments. The HCR-20 was developed to structure the clinical assessment of risk for violence and to guide treatment planning among violent offenders and psychiatric patient populations. It consists of 20 items: 10 historical items (previous violence, young at first violent incident, relationship instability, employment problems, substance misuse, major mental illness, psychopathy, early maladjustment, personality disorder and prior supervision failure); 5 clinical (stable dynamic) items (lack of insight, negative attitudes, active symptoms of mental illness, impulsivity and response to treatment) and 5 (acute dynamic) risk management items (feasibility of plans, exposure to destabilizers, lack of personal support, non-compliance and stress). The predictive validity and psychometric qualities of the HCR-20 have been examined extensively (for a review, see Douglas *et al.*, 2010). As part of the revision of the HCR-20 (Version 3), Guy and Wilson (2007) conducted a comprehensive review of the published literature; this revised HCR-20 is currently under testing.

Coid *et al.* (2007) recently reported a community follow-up study of adult male offenders in the UK who were at risk for reoffending over a mean time of 1.97 years post release. These authors evaluated the predictive qualities of the HCR-20, the VRAG, the RM2000/V and the PCL-R (Hare, 2003) in a sample of 1396 adult male offenders serving determinate sentences of a minimum of two years for sexual ($n = 119$ sexual offences against adults and $n = 206$ sexual offences against children) or violent offences (including violence and robbery). The RM2000/V (AUC = 0.68), the VRAG (AUC = 0.70), the HCR-20 (AUC = 0.64) and the PCL-R (AUC = 0.64) all significantly predicted violent recidivism. Of the subscales of the HCR-20, the Historical subscale obtained the most promising results (AUC = 0.67).

However, in a sample of 1353 male prisoners in England and Wales, Coid *et al.* (2011) found most items contained in the VRAG, PCL-R and HCR-20 were not independently predictive of recidivism. They argue that the predictive power of the PCL-R, VRAG and HCR-20 is actually based only on a small number of their items. This may partly explain the 'glass-ceiling' effect beyond which further improvement cannot be achieved.

In a prospective evaluation, Langton *et al.* (2009) compared the predictive accuracy of the HCR-20, VRS, Static-99 and RM2000 in a sample of 44 male offenders admitted to a Dangerous and Severe Personality Disorder (DSPD) unit at a high-security forensic psychiatric hospital. Among the sample, the most common personality disorder diagnoses were for Antisocial PD (73%), Borderline PD (41%) and Narcissistic PD (16%). Using the recommended UK cutoff score of 28 on the PCL-R (Cooke *et al.*, 2005), 49% of the sample met criteria for psychopathy. All patients had been charged with or convicted of a criminal offence, and 89% had committed one or more violent offences. Outcome was measured against incidents of aggression, including damage to property, verbal aggression and interpersonal physical aggression directed to staff or other patients.

Langton *et al.* (2009) found that the HCR-20 total score (AUC = 0.68) and the 'structured final risk judgement' (AUC = 0.80) obtained the most promising results in predicting interpersonal physical aggression compared to the RM2000/V (AUC = 0.38), VRS total (AUC = 0.62) and Static-99 (AUC = 0.33). Interestingly, the acute HCR-20 Risk items also obtained good results in predicting interpersonal physical aggression (AUC = 0.70) and damage to property (AUC = 0.74).

Similarly, Arbach-Lucioni *et al.* (2011) conducted a prospective study examining the predictive validity of the HCR-20 and the PCL:SV in a sample of 78 mentally disordered high-risk population. The HCR-20 (AUC = 0.69–0.77) outperformed the PCL:SV (AUC = 0.61–0.70) in predicting violent incidents. Patients scoring above the HCR-20 mean were 2.1–2.5 times more likely to be violent than those scoring below the mean.

Bonta *et al.* (1996) have demonstrated the use of the *Statistics Information on Recidivism Scale* (SIR) for prevalence decisions by the Correctional Services of Canada. This 15-item scale related to criminality, first conviction, age at conviction, mental status and social functioning was constructed using a sample summation technique, where weighting an item was based on the difference between the recidivism rate for offenders with that particular characteristic and the overall recidivism rate. The scale has proved useful as a measurement of risk for general recidivism among sexual offenders but is less effective at predicting sexual offending. This indicates that different sets of factors are involved in predicting sexual recidivism than those which predict general and non-sexual violent recidivism (Hanson and Bussière, 1998). Moreover, the SIR is composed of static risk factors, so it is limited in its provisions regarding potential for treatment intervention, while risk level changes may go undetected.

Other risk procedures have been recommended to include changeable (dynamic) factors (e.g., *Level of Service Inventory-Revised* (LSI-R); Andrews and Bonta, 1995). The LSI-R is a 54-item assessment divided into 10 domains. Unlike most ARAIs which are usually atheoretical (e.g., Static-99), the LSI-R is supported by general behavioural theories, including social learning theories, and the 'personal, interpersonal and community-reinforcement perspective' (Andrews, 1982; Andrews and Bonta, 1995, 2006). According to Andrews and Bonta (2006), deviant behaviours are not aberrations from normal behaviours but share similar triggers, cognitive logics and repercussions. There is a growing body of research supporting the use of the LSI-R to assess risk of *general* recidivism (but not *sexual* recidivism) for different offender groups, including violent offenders (Hollin, Palmer and Clark, 2003; Lowenkamp, Holsinger and Latessa, 2001; Loza and Simourd, 1994; Mills, Jones and Kroner, 2005; Mills and Kroner, 2006), female offenders (Coulson *et al.*, 1996; Palmer and Hollin, 2007), sex offenders (Gentry, Dulmus and Theriot, 2005; Girard and Wormith, 2004; Simourd and Malcolm, 1998), juvenile offenders (Nee and Ellis, 2005; Shields and Simourd, 1991) and offenders with different racial and cultural backgrounds (Allan and Dawson, 2004; Rugge, 2006; Schlager and Simourd, 2007; Whiteacre, 2006). The literature has thus indicated that the LSI-R is capable of identifying specific general criminogenic need patterns, or profiles, for specific offender groups. The LSI-R has now been revised into the LS-CMI to include case management strategies (Andrews, Bonta and Wormith, 2004).

Conclusions

With an emphasis on discovering 'What Works' in offender assessment and rehabilitation, a number of promising actuarial and structured approaches to sexual and violent risk assessment have been developed and evaluated. In relation to assessing risk in sexual offenders, measures of sexual deviance (pre-occupation/obsessions with sex), intimacy deficits and affect dysregulation have consistently identified sexual recidivists. Sexual (deviant) interest continues to be one of the strongest predictors of sexual recidivism. In contrast, for violent offenders the expression of antisocial attitudes, values and beliefs; rule violation; poor insight into offending; impulsivity; and substance misuse risk factors have repeatedly identified the violent recidivist.

References

Allan, A. and Dawson, D. (2004) Assessment of the risk of reoffending by indigenous male violent and sexual offenders. *Trends and Issues in Crime and Criminal Justice*, 280, 1–6.

Andrews, D.A. (1982) *A Personal, Interpersonal and Community-Reinforcement Perspective on Deviant Behaviour (PIC-R)*, Ontario Ministry of Correctional Services, Toronto.

Andrews, D.A. and Bonta, J. (1995) *LSI-R: The Level of Service Inventory-Revised*, Multi-Health Systems, Toronto.

Andrews, D.A. and Bonta, J. (2006) *The Psychology of Criminal Conduct*, 4th edn, Anderson, Cincinnati.

Andrews, D.A. and Bonta, J. (2010) *The Psychology of Criminal Conduct*, 5th edn, Lexis Nexis, New Providence.

Andrews, D.A., Bonta, J.L. and Wormith, J.S. (2004) *LS/CMI Level of Service/Case Management Inventory: An Offender Assessment System, User's Manual*, Multi-Health Systems, Toronto.

Arbach-Lucioni, K., Andres-Pueyo, A., Pomarol-Clotet, E. and Gomar-Sones, J. (2011) Predicting violence in psychiatric inpatients: a prospective study with the HCR-20 violence risk assessment scheme. *Journal of Forensic Psychiatry & Psychology*, 22, 203–222.

Archer, R.P., Buffington-Vollum, J.K., Stredny, R.V. and Handel, R.W. (2006) A survey of psychological test use patterns among forensic psychologists. *Journal of Personality Assessment*, 87, 84–94.

Barbaree, H.E., Langton, C.M., Blanchard, R. and Boer, D.P. (2008) Predicting recidivism in sex offenders using the SVR-20: the contribution of age-at-release. *International Journal of Forensic Mental Health*, 7, 47–64.

Beech, A.R. (1998) A psychometric typology of child abusers. *International Journal of Offender Therapy and Comparative Criminology*, 42, 319–339.

Beech, A.R. and Ward, T. (2004) The integration of etiology and risk in sexual offenders: a theoretical framework. *Aggression and Violent Behavior*, 10, 31–63.

Beech, A.R., Friendship, C., Erikson, M. and Hanson, R.K. (2002) The relationship between static and dynamic risk factors and reconviction in a sample of U.K. child abusers. *Sexual Abuse: A Journal of Research and Treatment*, 14 (2), 155–167.

Beggs, S.M. and Grace, R.C. (2010) Assessment of dynamic risk factors: an independent validation study of the violence risk scale: sexual offender version. *Sexual Abuse: A Journal of Research and Treatment*, 22, 234–251.

Beggs, S.M. and Grace, R.C. (2011) Treatment gain for sexual offenders against children predicts reduced recidivism: a comparative validity study. *Journal of Consulting and Clinical Psychology*, 79, 182–192.

Blacker, J., Beech, A.R., Wilcox, D.T. and Boer, D.P. (2011) The assessment of dynamic risk and recidivism in a sample of special needs sexual offenders. *Psychology, Crime & Law*, 17, 75–92.

Boer, D.P. (2006) Sexual offender risk assessment strategies: is there a convergence of opinion yet? *Sexual Offender Treatment*, 1, 2. http://www.sexual-offender-treatment.org/43.html (accessed 24 December 2012).

Boer, D.P. (2011) SVR-20 Version 2: Item Descriptions. New Directions in Sex Offender Practice Conference University of Birmingham, UK, October 24.

Boer, D.P., Hart, S.D., Kropp, P.R. and Webster, C.D. (1997) *Manual for the Sexual Violence Risk – 20 Professional Guidelines for Assessing Risk of Sexual Violence*, Mental Health, Law, and Policy Institute, Simon Frazer University, Vancouver.

Bonta, J. and Andrews, D.A. (2007) Risk-Need-Responsivity Model for Offender Assessment and Rehabilitation. *User Rep. no. 2007_06*. Public Safety Canada, Ottawa. http://www.publicsafety.gc.ca/res/cor/rep/_fl/Risk_Need_2007-06_e.pdf (accessed on 17 January 2013).

Camilleri, J.A. and Quinsey, V.L. (2011) Appraising the risk of sexual and violent recidivism among intellectually disabled offenders. *Psychology, Crime & Law*, 17, 59–74.

Coid, J., Yang, M., Ullrich, S. *et al.* (2007) Predicting and Understanding Risk of Re-Offending: The Prisoner Cohort Study. *Research Summary 6*. Ministry of Justice, London. http://pdprogramme.wswtest.com/news/wp-content/uploads/MofJResearchSummary6 (accessed on 17 January 2013).

Coid. J.W., Yang, M., Ullrich, S. *et al.* (2011) Most items in structured risk assessment instruments do not predict violence. *Journal of Forensic Psychiatry & Psychology*, 22, 3–21.

Cooke, D.J., Michie, C., Hart, S.D. and Clark, D. (2005) Assessing psychopathy in the UK: concerns about cross-cultural generalisability. *British Journal of Psychiatry*, 186, 335–341.

Coulson, G., Ilacqua, G., Nutbrown, V. *et al.* (1996) Predictive utility of the LSI for incarcerated female offenders. *Criminal Justice and Behavior*, 23, 427–439.

Covington, J.R. (1997) Preventive detention for sex offenders. *Illinois Bar Journal*, 85, 493–498.

Craig, L.A. and Beech, A.R. (2010) Towards a best practice in conducting actuarial risk assessments with adult sexual offenders. *Aggression and Violet Behavior*, 15, 278–293.

Craig, L.A., Browne, K.D., Hogue, T.E. and Stringer, I. (2004) New directions in assessing risk for sex offenders, in *Risk Assessment and Management: Issues in Forensic Psychology* (eds G. Macpherson and L. Jones), British Psychological Society, Leicester, pp. 81–99.

Craig, L.A., Browne, K.D., Beech, A.R. and Stringer, I. (2006a) Psychosexual characteristics of sexual offenders and the relationship to reconviction. *Psychology, Crime & Law*, 12, 231–244.

Craig, L.A., Browne, K.D., Beech, A.R. and Stringer, I. (2006b) Personality characteristics and recidivism rates in sex, violent and general offenders. *Criminal Behaviour and Mental Health*, 16, 183–194.

Craig, L.A., Thornton, D., Beech, A. and Browne, K.D. (2007) The relationship of statistical and psychological risk markers to sexual reconviction in child molesters. *Criminal Justice and Behavior*, 34, 314–329.

Craig, L.A., Browne, K.D. and Beech, A.R. (2008) *Assessing Risk in Sex Offenders: A Practitioner's Guide*, John Wiley & Sons, Ltd, Chichester.

Criminal Justice Act 1991 (2004) Office of Public Sector Information. Home Office, issued August 2004. http://www.opsi.gov.uk/ACTS/acts1991/ukpga_19910053_en_4 (accessed on 26 December 2012).

Dempster, R.J. and Hart, S.D. (2002) The relative utility of fixed and variables risk factors in discriminating sexual recidivists and non-recidivists. *Sexual Abuse: A Journal of Research and Treatment*, 14, 121–138.

Dempster, R.J., Hart, S.D. and Boer, D.P. (2002) *Prediction of Sexually Violent Recidivism: A Comparison of Risk Assessment Instruments*. Unpublished manuscript.

Dolan, M. and Fullam, R. (2007) The validity of the Violence Risk Scale Second Edition (VRS-2) in a British forensic inpatient sample. *Journal of Forensic Psychiatry & Psychology*, 18, 381–393.

Dolan, M., Fullam, R., Logan, C. and Davies, G. (2008) The Violence Risk Scale Second Edition (VRS-2) as a predictor of institutional violence in a British forensic inpatient sample. *Psychiatry Research*, 158, 55–65.

Doren, D.M. (1998) Recidivism base rates, predictions of sex offender recidivism, and the "sexual predator" commitment laws. *Behavioral Sciences and the Law*, 16, 97–114.

Doren, D.M. (2002) *Evaluating Sex Offenders: A Manual for Civil Commitments and Beyond*, Sage Publications Inc., Thousand Oaks.

Doren, D. (2007) A critique of Hart, Michie, and Cooke. *The Precision of Actuarial Risk Instruments.* Unpublished manuscript.

Douglas, K.S., Blanchard, A.J.E., Guy, L.S. *et al.* (2010) HCR-20 Violence risk assessment scheme: overview and annotated bibliography (current up to September 1, 2010). http://kdouglas. wordpress.com (accessed on 26 December 2012).

Epperson, D.L., Kaul, J.D. and Hesselton, D. (1998) Final report on the development of the Minnesota Sex Offender Screening Tool-Revised (MnSOST-R). Paper presented at the 17th Annual Conference of the Association for the Treatment of Sexual Abusers, Vancouver, October 14–17.

Ericson, R.V. and Haggerty, K.D. (1997) *Policing the Risk Society,* University of Toronto Press, Toronto/ Oxford University Press, Oxford.

Gentry, A.L., Dulmus, C.N. and Theriot, M.T. (2005) Comparing sex offender risk classification using the Static-99 and LSI-R assessment instruments. *Research on Social Work Practice,* 15, 557–563.

Girard, L. and Wormith, J.S. (2004) The predictive validity of the Level of Service Inventory–Ontario Revision on general and violent recidivism among various offender groups. *Criminal Justice and Behavior,* 31, 150–181.

Gray, N.S., Fitzgerald, S., Taylor, J. *et al.* (2007) Predicting future reconviction in offenders with intellectual disabilities. The predictive efficacy of VRAG, PCL-R and the HCR-20. *Psychological Assessment,* 19 (4), 474–479.

Grove, W.M. and Meehl, P.E. (1996) Comparative efficiency of informal (subjective, impressionistic) and formal (mechanical, algorithmic) prediction procedures: the clinical-statistical controversy. *Psychology, Public Policy, and Law,* 2, 293–323.

Guy, L.S. and Wilson, C.M. (2007) *Empirical Support for the HCR-20: A Critical Analysis of the Violence Literature,* Mental Health, Law, and Policy Institute, Simon Fraser University, Burnaby. http:// kdouglas.files.wordpress.com/2006/04/hcr-20-report-2007.pdf (accessed on 26 December 2012).

Hannah-Moffat, K. and Shaw, M. (2001) *Taking Risks: Incorporating Gender and Culture into the Classification and Assessment of Federally Sentenced Women in Canada,* Status of Women Canada, Ottawa.

Hanson, R.K. (1997) The Development of a Brief Actuarial Risk Scale for Sexual Offence Recidivism. *User Rep. no. 1997–04.* Department of the Solicitor General of Canada, Ottawa. http://www. publicsafety.gc.ca/res/cor/rep/_fl/1997-04-dbarssor-eng.pdf (accessed on 17 January 2013).

Hanson, R.K. and Bussière, M.T. (1998) Predicting relapse: a meta-analysis of sexual offender recidivism studies. *Journal of Consulting and Clinical Psychology,* 66 (2), 348–362.

Hanson. R.K. and Harris. A. (1998) Dynamic Predictors of Sexual Recidivism. Corrections Research. Department of the Solicitor General Canada, Ottawa. http://www.publicsafety.gc.ca/res/cor/ rep/1998-01-dpsr-eng.aspx (accessed on 17 January 2013).

Hanson, R.K. and Morton-Bourgon, K. (2009) The accuracy of recidivism risk assessments for sexual offenders: a meta-analysis of 118 prediction studies. *Psychological Assessment,* 21, 1–21.

Hanson, R.K. and Thornton, D. (2000) Improving risk assessment for sex offenders: a comparison of three actuarial scales. *Law and Human Behavior,* 24, 119–136.

Hanson, R.K. and Thornton, D. (2003) Notes on the Development of a Static-2002. *Corrections Research User Rep. no. 2003-01.* Department of the Solicitor General of Canada, Ottawa. http:// www.publicsafety.gc.ca/res/cor/rep/_fl/2003-01-not-sttc-eng.pdf (accessed on 17 January 2013).

Hanson, R.K., Harris, A.J.R., Scott, T.-L. and Helmus, L. (2007) Assessing the Risk of Sexual Offenders on Community Supervision: The Dynamic Supervision Project. *User Rep. no. 2007–05.* Public Safety Canada, Ottawa. http://www.publicsafety.gc.ca/res/cor/rep/_fl/crp2007-05-en.pdf (accessed 24 December 2012).

Hare, R.D. (1991) *The Hare Psychopathy Checklist – Revised,* Multi Health Systems, Toronto.

Harkins, L. and Beech, A. (2007) A review of the factors that can influence the effectiveness of sexual offender treatment: risk, need, responsivity and process issues. *Aggression and Violent Behavior,* 12, 615–627.

Harris, G.T., Rice, M.E. and Cormier, C.A. (2002) Prospective replication of the violent risk appraisal guide in predicting violent recidivism among forensic patients. *Law and Human Behavior*, 26, 377–394.

Harris, G.T., Rice, M.E. and Quinsey, V.L. (2007) Abandoning evidence-based risk appraisal in forensic practice: comments on Hart *et al. British Journal of Psychiatry*, 190, s60–s65.

Hart, S.D., Cox, D.N. and Hare, R.D. (1995) *Manual for the Psychopathy Checklist: Screening Version (PCL:SV)*, Multi-Health Systems, Toronto.

Hart, S.D., Kropp, P.R., Laws, D.R. *et al.* (2003) *The Risk for Sexual Violence Protocol (RSVP): Structured Professional Guidelines for Assessing Risk of Sexual Violence*, Simon Fraser University, Mental Health, Law, and Policy Institute, Burnaby.

Hart, S.D., Michie, C. and Cooke, D.J. (2007) Precision of actuarial risk assessment instruments: evaluating the 'margins of error' of group v. individual predictions of violence. *British Journal of Psychiatry*, 190 (Suppl. 49), 60–65.

Hollin, C.R., Palmer, E.J. and Clark, D.A. (2003) The level of service inventory – revised profile of English prisoners. *Criminal Justice and Behavior*, 30, 422–440.

Hudson, S.M., Wales, D.S., Bakker, L. and Ward, T. (2002) Dynamic risk factors: the Kia Marama evaluation. *Sexual Abuse: A Journal of Research and Treatment*, 14 (2), 103–119.

Ireland, C.A. and Craig, L.A. (2011) Adult sex offender assessment, in *International Perspectives on the Assessment and Treatment of Sexual Offenders: Theory, Practice and Research* (eds D.P. Boer, R. Eher, M.H. Miner and F. Pfafflin), Wiley-Blackwell, Oxford, pp. 13–34.

Janus, E.A. and Meehl, P.E. (1997) Assessing the legal standard for predictions of dangerousness in sex offender commitment proceedings. *Psychology, Public Policy, and Law*, 3, 33–64.

Kropp, P.R. (2000) The Risk for Sexual Violence Protocol (RSVP). Paper presented at the 26th Annual Research and Treatment Conference of the Association for the Treatment of Sexual Abusers, San Diego, November.

Langton, C.M., Hogue, T.E., Daffern, M. *et al.* (2009) Prediction of institutional aggression among personality disordered forensic patients using actuarial and structured clinical risk assessment tools: prospective evaluation of the HCR-20, VRS, Static-99, and Risk Matrix 2000. *Psychology, Crime & Law*, 15, 635–659.

Laws, D.R. (2006) *Risk for Sexual Violence Protocol*. 16th Annual Conference: National Organisation for the Treatment of Sexual Abusers, York University, 20–22 September 2006.

Lipton, D., Martinson, R. and Wilks, J. (1975) *The Effectiveness of Correctional Treatment: A Survey of Treatment Evaluation Studies*, Prager, New York.

Lowenkamp, C., Holsinger, A. and Latessa, E. (2001) Risk/need assessment, offender classification, and the role of childhood abuse. *Criminal Justice and Behavior*, 28, 543–563.

Loza, W. and Simourd, D.J. (1994) Psychometric evaluation of the Level of Supervision Inventory (LSI) among male Canadian federal offenders. *Criminal Justice and Behavior*, 21, 468–480.

Martinson, R. (1974) What works? – questions and answers about prison reform. *Public Interest*, 10, 22–54.

Mills, J.F. and Kroner, D.G. (2006) The effect of base-rate information on the perception of risk for re-offence. *American Journal of Forensic Psychology*, 24, 45–56.

Mills, J.F., Jones, M.N. and Kroner, D.G. (2005) An examination of the generalizability of the LSI-R and VRAG probability bins. *Criminal Justice and Behavior*, 32, 565–585.

Miller, H.A., Amenta, A. and Conroy, M. (2005) Sexually violent predator evaluations: empirical evidence, strategies for professionals, and research directions. *Law and Human Behavior*, 29, 29–54.

Mossman, D. and Sellke, T.M. (2007) Avoiding errors about 'margins of error'. *British Journal of Psychiatry*, July 5. Electronic letters sent to the journal. http://bjp.rcpsych.org/cgi/eletters/190/49/s60#5674 (accessed on 26 December 2012).

National Parole Board (2004) Evaluation Report for the National Parole Board's Effective Corrections and Citizen Engagement Initiatives 2000–2003. http://pbc-clcc.gc.ca/rprts/pdf/ecce_2000_2003/01-eng.shtml (accessed on 18 January 2013).

Nee, C. and Ellis, T. (2005) Treating offending children: what works? *Legal and Criminological Psychology*, 10, 133–148

Ohlin, L.E. (1951) *Selection for Parole: A Manual of Parole Prediction*, Russell Sage Foundation, New York.

Olver, M.E. and Wong, S.C.P. (2006) Psychopathy, sexual deviance, and recidivism among sex offenders. *Sexual Abuse: A Journal of Research and Treatment*, 18, 65–82.

Olver, M.E., Wong, S.C.P., Nicholaichuk, T. and Gordon, A. (2007) The validity and reliability of the Violence Risk Scale-Sexual Offender version: assessing sex offender risk and evaluating therapeutic change. *Psychological Assessment*, 19, 318–329.

Palmer, E.J. and Hollin, C.R. (2007) The Level of Service Inventory – Revised with English women prisoners: a needs and reconviction analysis. *Criminal Justice and Behavior*, 34, 971–984.

Parent, G., Guay, J.-P. and Knight, R.A. (2011) An assessment of long-term risk of recidivism by adult sex offenders: one size doesn't fit all. *Criminal Justice and Behavior*, 38, 188–209.

Prochaska, J.O., DiClemente, C.C. and Norcross, J.C. (1992) In search of how people change: applications to the addictive behaviors. *American Psychologist*, 47, 1102–1114.

Quinsey, V.L., Harris, G.T., Rice, M.E. and Cormier, C.A. (2006) *Violent Offenders: Appraising and Managing Risk*, 2nd edn, American Psychological Association, Washington, DC.

Rettenberger, M., Matthes, A., Boer, D.P. and Eher, R. (2010) Prospective actuarial risk assessment: a comparison of five risk assessment instruments in different sexual offender subtypes. *International Journal of Offender Therapy and Comparative Criminology*, 54, 169–186.

Rettenberger, M., Boer, D.P. and Eher, R. (2011) The predictive accuracy of risk factors in the Sexual Violence Risk-20 (Svr-20). *Criminal Justice and Behavior*, 38, 1009–1027.

Roberts, C.F., Doren, D.M. and Thornton, D. (2002) Dimensions associated with assessments of sex offender recidivism risk. *Criminal Justice and Behavior*, 29, 596–589.

Rugge, T. (2006) Risk Assessment of Male Aboriginal Offenders: A 2006 Perspective. *User Rep. 2006-01*. Public Safety Canada, Ottawa.

Sandler, J.C. and Freeman, N.J. (2009) Female sex offender recidivism: a large-scale empirical analysis. *Sexual Abuse: A Journal of Research and Treatment*, 21, 455–473.

Schlager, M.D. and Simourd, D.J. (2007) Validity of the Level of Service Inventory-Revised (LSI-R) among African American and Hispanic male offenders. *Criminal Justice and Behavior*, 34, 545–554.

Shields, I.W. and Simourd, D.J. (1991) Predicting predatory behavior in a population of incarcerated young offenders. *Criminal Justice and Behavior*, 18, 180–194.

Simourd, D.J. and Malcolm, P.B. (1998) Reliability and validity of the Level of Service Inventory-Revised among federally incarcerated sex offenders. *Journal of Interpersonal Violence*, 3, 261–274.

Sjöstedt, G. and Långström, N. (2002) Assessment of risk for criminal recidivism among rapists: a comparison of four different measures. *Psychology, Crime & Law*, 8, 25–40.

Thornton, D. (2002) Constructing and testing a framework for dynamic risk assessment. *Sexual Abuse: A Journal of Research and Treatment*, 14, 139–153.

Thornton, D. and Beech, A.R. (2002) Integrating statistical and psychological factors through the structured risk assessment model. Paper presented at the 21st Annual Research and Treatment Conference, Association of the Treatment of Sexual Abusers, Montreal, October 2–5.

Thornton, D., Mann, R., Webster, S. *et al.* (2003) Distinguishing and combining risks for sexual and violent recidivism (in *Understanding and Managing Sexually Coercive Behavior* (eds R. Prentky, E. Janus and M. Seto). *Annals of the New York Academy of Sciences*, 989, 225–235.

Webster, C.D., Douglas, K.S., Eaves, D. and Hart, S.D. (1997) *HCR-20: Assessing Risk for Violence, Version 2*, Simon Fraser University, Burnaby.

Whiteacre, K.W. (2006) Testing the Level of Service Inventory-Revised (LSI-R) for racial/ethnic bias. *Criminal Justice Policy Review*, 17, 330–342.

Windelband, W. (1904) *Theories in Logic*, Philosophical Library, New York.

Wong, S. and Gordon, A. (2000) *Violence Risk Scale*, Department of Psychology, University of Saskatchewan, Saskatoon. Available at http://www.psynergy.ca (accessed on 17 January 2013)

Wong, S.C.P. and Gordon, A. (2006) The validity and reliability of the Violence Risk Scale: a treatment friendly violence risk assessment tool. *Psychology, Public Policy, and Law*, 12, 279–309.

Wong, S., Olver, M.E., Nicholaichuk, T.P. and Gordon, A.E. (2003) *The Violence Risk Scale – Sexual Offender Version (VRS-SO)*, Department of Psychology and Research, Regional Psychiatric Centre, Saskatoon.

Wollert, R. (2006) Low base rates limit expert certainty when current actuarial tests are used to identify sexually violent predators: an application of Bayes's theorem. *Psychology, Public Policy, and Law*, 12, 56–85.

Part III

What Works in Offender Rehabilitation

6

Efficacy of Correctional Cognitive Skills Programmes

Clive R. Hollin, Emma J. Palmer and Ruth M. Hatcher

University of Leicester, UK

Introduction

The growth in the use of cognitive skills programmes in correctional services can be directly traced to two areas of research. The first, which can be seen in the general context of the expansion of cognitive psychology in the 1980s, is found in a range of studies concerned with the cognitive functioning of offenders (Ross and Fabiano, 1985). This research highlighted a range of cognitive styles such as poor interpersonal problem solving, impulsivity and a lack of self-control, and limited perspective-taking skills, that are characteristic of some offenders.

Reasoning and Rehabilitation (R&R)

It was a short step from research to practice as seen with the development of programmes that aimed to reduce reoffending by helping the offender to develop their cognitive skills. The first such cognitive skills programme to be used on a large scale was *R&R* developed in Canada by Ross and Fabiano (Ross, Fabiano and Ross, 1989). *R&R* is an evidence-based, structured cognitive-behavioural programme employing techniques such as role-playing, rehearsal, modelling and reinforcement that aims to promote alternative ways of thinking and so assist the offender in the development of ways of thinking which will encourage prosocial behaviour. *R&R* was designed to be delivered by trained correctional staff, not just professional therapists, and has been used in a number of jurisdictions in both institutional and community settings (Tong and Farrington, 2006).

The development of *R&R* coincided with the second line of research which clarified 'What Works' in reducing offending.

'What Works'

The statistical technique of meta-analysis provides a review of a large number of primary research studies and identifies trends in the accumulated data. Meta-analysis can control for variations and potential biases in the primary studies and produce a quantifiable treatment

What Works in Offender Rehabilitation: An Evidence-Based Approach to Assessment and Treatment,
First Edition. Edited by Leam A. Craig, Louise Dixon and Theresa A. Gannon.
© 2013 John Wiley & Sons, Ltd. Published 2013 by John Wiley & Sons, Ltd.

effect. Since the first reported meta-analysis of the offender treatment literature (Garrett, 1985), there have been over 50 meta-analytic studies of offender treatment incorporating hundreds of primary research studies including different types of offenders and offences (McGuire, 2002, 2008). The meta-analyses reported by Andrews *et al.* (1990) and Lipsey (1992) have proved to be of particular influence.

The meta-analyses gave remarkably consistent findings: the interventions which are effective in reducing offending are cognitive-behavioural in nature, are structured with specific aims and objectives, are conducted with offenders who have a high risk of reoffending, are delivered by trained staff and have high treatment integrity. Andrews, Bonta and Hoge (1990) condensed these findings into a model of appropriate correctional service based on three principles: first, the *Risk principle* whereby services are directed towards medium- to high-risk offenders; second, the *Needs principle* by which interventions target needs known to be related to offending (i.e., *criminogenic needs*, sometimes referred to as dynamic risk factors); third, the *Responsivity principle* by which interventions are matched to the offenders' individual characteristics such as age and gender. This tripartite model has become known as the Risk–Needs–Responsivity (RNR) model (see Chapter 4).

Thus, guided by an enhanced understanding of 'What Works' and the associated RNR model, there was an increase in interventions, often in the form of an Offending Behaviour Programme (OBP; Hollin and Palmer, 2006a), aimed at improving offenders' cognitive skills and ultimately reducing offending (McGuire, 2006).

Cognitive Skills Programmes

A number of cognitive skills programmes have been developed within the criminal justice system in England and Wales including: *Straight Thinking on Probation (STOP)*, *Enhanced Thinking Skills (ETS)* and *Think First (TF)*.

STOP. In the UK, Mid-Glamorgan Probation Service in Wales led the way by adapting *R&R* in the form of the *STOP* programme for offenders in the community (Knott, 1995). This innovation was soon followed by two other cognitive skills programmes.

Enhanced Thinking Skills (ETS). ETS was developed by the English and Welsh Prison Service and addresses similar targets to *R&R* (Clark, 2000). *ETS* was first used by the Prison Service then later by the Probation Service in England and Wales.

Think First (TF). TF, also developed for the criminal justice system in England and Wales, is similar in design to both R&R and ETS but with a more explicit focus on criminal behaviour (McGuire, 2006). *TF* was also initially used in the Prison Service and later in the Probation Service.

Maintaining Good Practice

The RNR model and the findings from the meta-analysis were applied to define the principles of effective practice. However, no matter how well a programme is designed, its effectiveness depends on the quality of delivery: effective programme management is therefore critically important (Bernfield, 2001). The issue of how to maintain practitioner adherence to a set of methodological principles, often referred to as 'treatment integrity', is a common one in practice (Hollin, 1995) and is important with respect to both effective practice and reliable evaluation (Andrews and Dowden, 2005). The way to ensure high-quality programme design and content lies in the processes of programme *accreditation* and *programme audit*.

Accreditation and accreditation criteria

In the mid-1990s, the English and Welsh Prison Service developed a set of Accreditation Criteria to facilitate an independent review of the design of OBPs (Lipton *et al.*, 2000). Ten Accreditation Criteria were defined to determine how well a given programme fits the *What Works* template:

1. *Model of change* Programmes should have a clearly articulated model of change based on the theoretical and empirical literature, which explains the principles by which the programme functions.
2. *Selection of offenders* There should be clear criteria for the selection of offenders to participate in the programme (including inclusion and exclusion criteria).
3. *Target a range of dynamic risk factors* Dynamic risk factors are the psychological and social features of an offender's functioning that are related to their offending and are amenable to change. As criminal behaviour is likely to be associated with a number of risk factors, programmes should address a range of dynamic risk factors.
4. *Effective methods* The methods used to change the dynamic risk factors should be supported by empirical evidence.
5. *Skills oriented* Alongside cognitive change, programmes should aim to develop associated life and social skills that will help to avoid criminal behaviour and promote prosocial behaviour.
6. *Sequencing, intensity and duration* In keeping with the risk principle, the level and intensity of the programme should match the offenders' level of risk.
7. *Engagement and motivation* Attention should be paid to offenders' engagement and motivation. Programme attendance and completion rates should be monitored, along with monitoring the reasons for programme non-attendance and non-completion.
8. *Continuity of programmes and services* Programmes should take place in the context of a clear sentence planning process, encompassing procedures both within and across services.
9. *Maintaining integrity* Strategies should be in place to monitor programme integrity. These strategies should include providing staff with constructive feedback on their practice.
10. *Evaluation* There should be continual monitoring and evaluation of programmes, both process and outcome, with regard to their effectiveness.

The force of the Accreditation Criteria is that they set high standards for the development, implementation and maintenance of OBPs. These standards give a clear platform for organizations seeking to develop programmes to meet the needs of their particular client group (Hollin, 2001).

Programme audit

The purpose of programme audit is to ensure the highest possible levels of quality in programme delivery (Goggin and Gendreau, 2006). This process may be facilitated by the use of instruments such as *The Correctional Programme Assessment Inventory* (CPAI; Gendreau, Goggin and Smith, 2002).

The introduction of programme audit to ensure high levels of treatment integrity was made by the Prison Service in England and Wales in the mid-1990s (Blud *et al.*, 2003). The wider therapeutic literature describes three threats to programme integrity (Hollin, 1995): first, *programme drift* which is a gradual shift with time in the aims and practice of a programme, perhaps as practitioners come and go and focus is blurred; second, *programme reversal* is active practitioner resistance as seen in efforts to oppose and undermine the workings of the programme; third, *programme non-compliance* which is where practitioners decide unilaterally to change the programme by, for example, adding new sessions and dropping others, bringing in new treatment techniques and changing the targets for change. In all three instances, the outcome is the same – the programme's integrity is lost and its likely effectiveness diminished.

Regular programme audit can facilitate the early detection of active threats to integrity. Hollin (1995) describes three sources of information that can be used to help monitor integrity: first, independent observation of practice during the programme; second, client reporting of their experience; third, practitioner self-report. These three methods may be used in combination to provide a wealth of information.

The Prison Service audit was carried out through an annual visit to prisons running OBPs and looked at four areas. These four are: (i) *institutional support* with reference to the prison's management of the programme, (ii) *treatment support* including the selection of prisoners for the programme (Palmer *et al.*, 2009) and the staff to deliver it, (iii) continuity of *throughcare* across other services, (iv) *quality of delivery* in terms of dropout and completion rates and as assessed by the use of video-monitoring (Blud *et al.*, 2003).

Responsivity

A programme's effectiveness is dependent upon the degree to which an offender participates and engages in the programme. The responsivity principle holds that programme design and delivery style should be congruent with the offenders' characteristics so as to increase their engagement (Redondo, Sánchez-Meca and Garrido, 2002). Andrews (2001) made the distinction between *internal* and *external* responsivity factors. Internal responsivity refers to the offender's characteristics – such as their age, gender, ethnicity and intellectual functioning – which may affect their ability to participate in a programme. Sensitive programme design can ensure that the content and pace of programmes are appropriate to these offender characteristics. External responsivity refers to organizational factors such as the staff who deliver the programme and the setting in which programme sessions take place.

The majority of apprehended offenders are adult males, and most programmes are intended for this group. It cannot be assumed, however, that young offenders and women offenders will be responsive to programmes designed for men. This same point extends to offenders from different ethnic and cultural groups. As criminogenic needs may vary according to the personal, cultural and social factors, so programme content must ensure that the content is appropriate to the specific offender (Bonta, 1995). The process of establishing the criminogenic needs of different offender groups can be a complex task (Hollin and Palmer, 2006b; Palmer and Hollin, 2007).

Adaptations for different populations

The responsivity principle suggests that the content of interventions should be congruent with the abilities and characteristics of the offenders taking part in the intervention. Different types of offenders may present with different criminogenic needs, so programmes must accommodate these variations. Thus, programmes have been developed for different types of offenders including violent offenders (Polaschek, 2006) and sex offenders (Mann and Fernandez, 2006) as well as for offenders with substance-abuse problems (McMurran, 2006), women offenders; (Andrews and Dowden, 1999; Blanchette and Brown, 2006; Dowden and Andrews, 1999a), young offenders (Dowden and Andrews, 1999b) and mentally disordered offenders (Young and Ross, 2007; Young, Chick and Gudjonsson, 2010). Young and colleagues have adapted *R&R* (*R&R2M*) for mentally disordered offenders incorporating a module on cognitive impairments (attention, memory, planning) and a *manualized coaching paradigm* where individual mentoring sessions, conducted between group sessions, focus on the application of the programme to everyday life.

Manuals

The growth in the use of programmes has seen rise in the use of programme manuals. At its most complete, a programme may have five manuals: a *Theory Manual* that provides the theory and supporting research evidence which informs the programme's model of change; a *Programme Manual* which gives full details of every session; an *Assessment and Evaluation Manual* that provides full details of all the measures used for monitoring and evaluation; a *Management Manual* that gives the procedures for staff selection, training and support, the programme's selection criteria, the minimum operating conditions for the programme, procedures for monitoring and evaluation and staff roles and responsibilities; and, finally, a *Staff Training Manual* that details the training, competency and review procedures for all staff involved in programme delivery. This emphasis on manuals has generated considerable professional debate (Hollin, 2009; Mann, 2009; Marshall, 2009).

Programme Structure

The majority of cognitive skills interventions are intended for delivery to a group of 8–12 offenders under the leadership of 2 or 3 group facilitators. The structure and content of the programme and its sessions, as in the programme manual, are tailored to the risk and needs of the specific offenders for whom the programme is intended. For example, in England and Wales, the more recently developed *Thinking Skills Programme* (*TSP*) is for medium- to high-risk offenders and comprises 19 two-hour sessions. On the other hand, *R&R* is designed for high-risk offenders and, in line with the risk principle, consists of 38 two-hour sessions.

Some programmes, such as *R&R*, have sessions that are completed in sequence from first to last, while others have several modules without a prescribed order. The structure of *TSP* consists of three modules of four sessions, each focusing on a different area of need – self-control, problem solving and positive relationships – with the remaining sessions delivered on a one-to-one basis at the start of the programme and after completion of each module. This variation in the mode of delivery from group to individual permits close monitoring of each offender's learning and engagement.

The development of modular programmes provides the opportunity for delivery on a *rolling* basis. While *closed* programmes maintain the same group of offenders from start to finish – notwithstanding the likelihood, especially when delivered in the community, of offender dropout – *rolling* programmes allow offenders to join and leave the programme at different points. Thus, with the TSP modules, one offender may commence at the start of the self-control module while another starts with the positive relationships module.

The advantage of a modular system is that offenders can start as soon as a place is available without waiting until a programme is scheduled and a full group assembled. However, there are concerns about the impact of rolling programmes on the group dynamic and whether the therapeutic environment is disturbed by the changes. A research project comparing the delivery mode (rolling versus closed) of the TSP is currently under consideration (Travers, 2011, personal communication).

Methods of Bringing About Change

The majority of OBPs are based on cognitive social learning theory (Bandura, 1977, 2001). Cognitive social learning theory proposes that criminal behaviour has its origins in socialization, group interaction and interpersonal influences (McGuire, 2006) and is learnt through both imitation and differential reinforcement (Akers, 1973). There is empirical evidence to support the view that offenders and non-offenders differ with regard to some aspects of cognitive functioning, particularly problem-solving skills (McMurran and McGuire, 2005; Ross and Fabiano, 1985). Offenders are typically more impulsive, more rigid in their thinking patterns, less likely to consider the consequences of their actions and less likely to consider alternative behavioural options (Ross and Fabiano, 1985).

Evaluation

Do cognitive skills programmes work? Does the *process* bring about cognitive change? Is the *outcome* reduced offending? Is the enterprise worth the financial costs?

Process: clinical versus statistical change

Cognitive skills programmes typically aim to change the offender's cognitive and emotional functioning. These changes may be assessed using psychometric tests that are administered pre and post programme. Any pre-post changes on these measures are examined using statistical significance testing usually against a comparison group who did not participate in the programme. As noted by Borenstein (1997), statistically significant change at a group level is not the only criterion of effectiveness. Does the degree of change have any clinical importance or significance? Clinical significance relies on establishing whether any change has moved an individual into a normal level of functioning on a given assessment (Jacobson *et al.*, 1999). Further, the change should be so substantial as not to be attributed to measurement error (Jacobson and Truax, 1991).

Thus, following an intervention, an individual who has shown positive change can be considered as being *recovered* as seen in statistically reliable change from the dysfunctional to functional range, *improved but not yet recovered* with a statistically reliable change in a positive direction but remaining within the dysfunctional range, or *unchanged* in that any change is not statistically reliable. It is also possible that an individual might deteriorate over the course of the intervention; however, clinical significance does not allow for this outcome.

Testing for clinically significant change has been used to evaluate treatment effectiveness with various clinical populations but it has been used less often with offenders. Several studies have examined the clinical effectiveness of interventions with sex offenders (e.g., Beech, Fisher and Beckett, 1999; Beech and Ford, 2006; Mandeville-Norden, Beech and Hayes, 2008). Nunes, Babchishin and Cortoni (2011) reported an evaluation of a Canadian sex offender programme examining change at both group and individual levels on measures of cognitive distortions associated with sexual offending, intimacy, loneliness, and risk of reoffending. Using the clinical significance approach, they reported a moderate level of significant change at a group level and slightly lower levels of change at an individual level. Overall, they found that around one-third of the offenders showed reliable change and moved into the functional range across the five outcome measures.

Outcome: research designs

The critical issue is whether cognitive skills programmes reduce offending. From a research perspective, there are several available research designs, varying in strength as judged by their internal validity (Farrington *et al.*, 2002). It appears that high-quality quasi-experimental designs and experimental designs provide the best options for evaluation of cognitive skills programmes (Hollin, 2008). These two designs produce broadly comparable findings when used to assess the outcome of OBPs, including cognitive skills programmes (Babcock, Green and Robie, 2004; Lipsey, Chapman and Landenberger, 2001; Lösel and Schmucker, 2005; Wilson, Bouffard and MacKenzie, 2005).

Another issue in evaluation lies in the analysis strategy with respect to those offenders who fail to complete programmes. One approach is to compare the outcome of those allocated to a programme group, regardless of whether they complete (or even start) the programme, with a comparison group. This approach is analogous to Intention to Treat (ITT) analysis within a clinical trial. However, given that cognitive skills programmes are designed to be completed, attrition is an important consideration with regard to outcome if a sizeable proportion of offenders fail to complete. The alternative is Treatment Received (TR) analysis, in which outcome is measured by comparing the outcome for offenders who complete the programme with a comparison group.

In fact, ITT and TR analyses point to different outcomes: ITT analysis evaluates the effect of the policy of offering intervention, while TR analysis determines what happens when the offer is taken up and the treatment is delivered in the prescribed manner (Sherman, 2003).

The question of using ITT or TR is important, given the research that shows that programme non-completion is associated with a significantly *greater* rate of reoffending (Olver, Stockdale and Wormith, 2011). A high rate of non-completion can have a disproportionate effect on the results of an ITT analysis (see Hatcher *et al.*, 2012). Thus, some evaluations report both analysis strategies, along with information about the rate of non-completion (cf. Hollin *et al.*, 2008; Palmer *et al.*, 2007; Van Voorhis *et al.*, 2004).

Effects of misallocation   Alongside methodological issues, programme implementation issues may also impact on the findings of outcome studies. In particular, misallocation of offenders to programmes has been shown to be important. Cognitive skills programmes have clear selection criteria to ensure that the targets, methods and dosage correspond with the offenders' needs. The selection of offenders who are not appropriate for a cognitive skills programme may skew the outcome and so give rise to misleading evaluation results.

The effects of misallocation are demonstrated in studies of the effectiveness of cognitive-behavioural programmes in the Probation Service in England and Wales (Palmer *et al.*, 2008, 2009). One of the selection criteria for these programmes was that, in line with the risk principle (Andrews, 2001), offenders had a medium risk of reconviction as assessed by Offender Group Reconviction Scale-2 (OGRS2; Taylor, 1999). However, the data for the offenders allocated to programmes indicated that there were substantial numbers allocated to programmes whose OGRS2 scores were above and below the medium risk range. The programme evaluations showed a significant reduction in reconviction among programme completers (Hollin *et al.*, 2008; Palmer *et al.*, 2007); however, examination of the reconviction outcomes by appropriateness of allocation gave some interesting results (Palmer *et al.*, 2008, 2009). It was found that about one-half of the offenders in the programme group had OGRS2 scores outside the selection criteria (mainly too high risk). There was a differential programme effect on reconviction by allocation group (too low risk, appropriately allocated, too high risk). For appropriate offenders, there was a good size treatment effect, with completers having a significantly lower rate of reconviction than the comparison group and offenders who did not complete the programme. However, for inappropriately allocated low-risk offenders there was no significant treatment effect, while for the inappropriately allocated high-risk offenders there was a very high non-completion rate (cf. Olver, Stockdale and Wormith, 2011), although when these offenders did complete, there was a significant treatment effect.

Reducing reconviction Evidence from meta-analyses suggests that cognitive skills programmes can be effective in reducing reoffending (McGuire, 2002, 2008). While meta-analyses are useful in identifying trends from a large body of evaluation studies, it is still necessary to continue to evaluate individual programmes. A meta-analysis of 16 studies conducted in four countries reported positive effects on reconviction of *R&R* among adult male offenders (Tong and Farrington, 2006). In England and Wales, several large-scale evaluations have been conducted, in prison and community settings, of *R&R*, *ETS* and *TF*. The evaluations of *R&R* and *ETS* in the Prison Service reported significant treatment effects in terms of reducing reconviction among adult male offenders at a two-year follow-up (Friendship *et al.*, 2003), although this finding was not replicated by Falshaw *et al.* (2003). Cann *et al.* (2003) used a cohort of adult and young offender prisoners and found a significant treatment effect on reconviction at a one-year follow-up for both age groups when programme dropouts were excluded from the analysis. This effect was not maintained at a two-year post-release follow-up.

An evaluation of the same three programmes, *ETS*, *R&R* and *TF*, within the English and Welsh Probation Service has been reported (Hollin *et al.*, 2008; McGuire *et al.*, 2008; Palmer *et al.*, 2007). These studies employed a TR approach with a high-level quasi-experimental design to compare the reconviction rates of completers, non-completers and a comparison group. The results showed that the three programmes were broadly comparable in terms of reconviction outcome, with completers having a significantly lower rate of reconviction compared to non-completers and the comparison group.

Following these and similar findings, attention has focused on the group of offenders who start but do not complete a programme. A significant negative effect of non-completion on reconviction, when compared to both programme completers and to no-treatment comparison groups, has been demonstrated in individual studies (Hollin *et al.*, 2008; Palmer *et al.*, 2007; Van Voorhis *et al.*, 2004) and in a meta-analysis of 114 studies (Olver, Stockdale and Wormith, 2011). It remains to be established whether this 'non-completion effect' is best explained by risk of reconviction, given that many of the factors, such as younger age, a greater number of previous convictions, lower levels of education and substance abuse, that predict non-completion are also associated with reoffending.

Financial costs Romani *et al.* (2012) used the articles included in the meta-analysis of correctional services reported by Andrews *et al.* (1990) to look at the costs associated with service provision. The original articles were reconsidered according to the maximum financial cost of the service provision. Romani *et al.* reported that correctional services which adhered to the RNR principles were no more expensive than inappropriate services which did not adhere to RNR, or more expensive than traditional criminal sanctions. There was, however, a cost difference between appropriate and inappropriate correctional services such that inappropriate services attracted an *increased* cost. Thus, the gains in terms of reduced recidivism that come from services based on RNR principles are not at any additional cost.

Conclusion

Overall, the evidence from the outcome research shows that completion of cognitive-behavioural programmes has a positive effect on reoffending, with a concurrent negative effect of non-completion as compared to no-treatment comparison groups. Further, the gains in terms of reduced recidivism that follow appropriate service provision do not come at an exorbitant cost and, indeed, may actually produce savings over the longer term.

References

Akers, R.L. (1973) *Deviant Behavior: A Social Learning Approach*, Wadsworth, Belmont.

Andrews, D.A. (2001) Principles of effective correctional programs, in *Compendium 2000 on Effective Correctional Programming* (eds L.L. Motiuk and R.C. Serin), Correctional Service Canada, Ottawa, pp. 9–17.

Andrews, D.A. and Dowden, C. (1999) A meta-analytic investigation into effective correctional intervention for female offenders. *Forum on Correctional Research*, 11, 18–21.

Andrews, D.A. and Dowden, C. (2005) Managing correctional treatment for reduced recidivism: a meta-analytic review of programme integrity. *Legal and Criminological Psychology*, 10, 173–187.

Andrews, D.A., Bonta, J. and Hoge, R.D. (1990) Classification for effective rehabilitation: rediscovering psychology. *Criminal Justice and Behavior*, 17, 19–52.

Andrews, D.A., Zinger, I., Hoge, R.D. *et al.* (1990) Does correctional treatment work? A clinically relevant and psychologically informed meta-analysis. *Criminology*, 28, 369–404.

Babcock, J.C., Green, C.E. and Robie, C. (2004) Does batterers' treatment work? A meta-analytic review of domestic violence treatment. *Clinical Psychology Review*, 23, 1023–1053.

Bandura, A. (1977) *Social Learning Theory*, Prentice-Hall, New York.

Bandura, A. (2001) Social cognitive theory: an agentic perspective. *Annual Review of Psychology*, 52, 1–26.

Beech, A.R. and Ford, H. (2006) The relationship between risk, deviance, treatment outcome and sexual reconviction in a sample of child sexual abusers completing residential treatment for their offending. *Psychology, Crime & Law*, 12, 685–701.

Beech, A.R., Fisher, D. and Beckett, R.C. (1999) An Evaluation of the Prison Sex Offender Treatment Programme. *Research Findings no. 79*, Home Office, London.

Bernfield, G.A. (2001) The struggle for treatment integrity in a "dis-integrated" service delivery system, in *Offender Rehabilitation in Practice: Effective Programs and Policies to Reduce Re-offending* (eds G.A. Bernfield, D.P. Farrington and A.W. Leschied), John Wiley & Sons, Ltd, Chichester, pp. 168–188.

Blanchette, K. and Brown, S.L. (2006) *The Assessment and Treatment of Women Offenders: An Integrative Process*, John Wiley & Sons, Ltd, Chichester.

Blud, L., Travers, R., Nugent, F. and Thornton, D.M. (2003) Accreditation of offending behaviour programmes in HM Prison Service: 'what works' in practice. *Legal and Criminological Psychology*, 8, 69–81.

Bonta, J. (1995) The responsivity principle and offender rehabilitation. *Forum on Corrections Research*, 7, 34–37.

Borenstein, M. (1997) Hypothesis testing and effect size estimation in clinical trials. *Annals of Allergy, Asthma, and Immunology*, 78, 5–11.

Cann, J., Falshaw, L., Nugent, F. and Friendship, C. (2003) Understanding What Works: Accredited Cognitive Skills Programmes for Adult Men and Young Offenders. *Research Findings no. 226*, Home Office, London.

Clark, D.A. (2000) Theory Manual for Enhanced Thinking Skills. Prepared for the Joint Prison Probation Accreditation Panel, Home Office, London.

Dowden, C. and Andrews, D.A. (1999a). What works for female offenders: a meta-analytic review. *Crime & Delinquency*, 45, 438–452.

Dowden, C. and Andrews, D.A. (1999b). What works in young offender treatment: a meta-analysis. *Forum on Corrections Research*, 11, 21–24.

Falshaw, L., Friendship, C., Travers, L. and Nugent, F. (2003) Searching for What Works: An Evaluation of Cognitive Skills Programmes. *Research Findings no. 206*, Home Office, London.

Farrington, D.P., Gottfredson, D.C., Sherman, L.W. and Welsh, B.C. (2002) The Maryland Scientific Methods Scale, in *Evidence-Based Crime Prevention* (eds L.W. Sherman, D.P. Farrington, B.C. Welsh and D.L. MacKenzie), Routledge, London, pp. 13–21.

Friendship, C., Blud, L., Erikson, M. *et al.* (2003) Cognitive-behavioural treatment for imprisoned offenders: an evaluation of HM Prison Service's cognitive skills programmes. *Legal and Criminological Psychology*, 8, 103–114.

Garrett, C.J. (1985) Effects of residential treatment on adjudicated delinquents: a meta-analysis. *Journal of Research in Crime and Delinquency*, 22, 287–308.

Gendreau, P., Goggin, C. and Smith, P. (2002) Implementation guidelines for correctional programs in the "real world", in *Offender Rehabilitation in Practice: Implementing and Evaluating Effective Programmes* (eds G.A. Bernfeld, D.P. Farrington and A.W. Leschied), John Wiley & Sons, Ltd, Chichester, pp. 228–268.

Goggin, C. and Gendreau, P. (2006) The implementation and maintenance of quality services in offender rehabilitation programmes, in *Offending Behaviour Programmes: Development, Application, and Controversies* (eds C.R. Hollin and E.J. Palmer), John Wiley & Sons, Ltd, Chichester, pp. 209–246.

Hatcher, R.M., McGuire, J., Bilby, C.A.L. *et al.* (2012) Methodological considerations in the evaluation of offender interventions: the problem of attrition. *International Journal of Offender Therapy and Comparative Criminology*, 56, 447–464.

Hollin, C.R. (1995) The meaning and implications of "programme integrity", in *What Works: Reducing Reoffending* (ed. J. McGuire), John Wiley & Sons, Ltd, Chichester, pp. 195–208.

Hollin, C.R. (2001) The role of the consultant in developing effective practice, in *Offender Rehabilitation in Practice: Implementing and Evaluating Effective Programmes* (eds G.A. Bernfeld, D.P. Farrington and A.W. Leschied), John Wiley & Sons, Ltd, Chichester, pp. 269–281.

Hollin, C.R. (2008) Evaluating offending behaviour programmes: does only randomisation glister? *Criminology and Criminal Justice*, 8, 89–106.

Hollin, C.R. (2009) Treatment manuals: the good, the bad, and the useful. *Journal of Sexual Aggression*, 15, 133–137.

Hollin, C.R. and Palmer, E.J. (eds) (2006a) *Offending Behaviour Programmes: Development, Application, and Controversies*, John Wiley & Sons, Ltd, Chichester.

Hollin, C.R. and Palmer E.J. (2006b) Criminogenic need and women offenders: a critique of the literature. *Legal and Criminological Psychology*, 11, 179–195.

Hollin, C.R., McGuire, J., Hounsome, J.C. *et al.* (2008) Cognitive skills offending behavior programs in the community: a reconviction analysis. *Criminal Justice and Behavior*, 35, 269–283.

Jacobson, N.S. and Truax, P. (1991) Clinical significance: a statistical approach to defining meaningful change in psychotherapy research. *Journal of Consulting and Clinical Psychology*, 59, 12–19.

Jacobson, N.S., Roberts, L.J., Berns, S.B. and McGlinchey, J.B. (1999) Methods for defining and determining the clinical significance of treatment effects: description, application, and alternatives. *Journal of Consulting and Clinical Psychology*, 67, 300–307.

Knott, C. (1995) The STOP programme: Reasoning and Rehabilitation in a British setting, in *What Works: Reducing Reoffending* (ed. J. McGuire), John Wiley & Sons, Ltd, Chichester, pp. 115–126.

Lipsey, M.W. (1992) Juvenile delinquency treatment: a meta-analytic inquiry into the variability of effects, in *Meta-analysis for Explanation: A Casebook* (eds T. Cook, D. Cooper, H. Corday *et al.*), Russell Sage Foundation, New York, pp. 83–127.

Lipsey, M.W., Chapman, G.L. and Landenberger, N.A. (2001) Cognitive-behavioral programs for offenders. *Annals of the American Academy of Political and Social Science*, 578, 144–157.

Lipton, D.S., Thornton, D.M., McGuire, J. *et al.* (2000) Program accreditation and correctional treatment. *Substance Use and Misuse*, 35, 1705–1734.

Lösel, F. and Schmucker, M. (2005) The effectiveness of treatment for sexual offenders: a comprehensive meta-analysis. *Journal of Experimental Criminology*, 1, 117–146.

Mandeville-Norden, R., Beech, A.R. and Hayes, E. (2008) Examining the effectiveness of a UK community-based sexual offender treatment programme for child abusers. *Psychology, Crime & Law*, 14, 493–512.

Mann, R.E. (2009) Sex offender treatment: the case for manualization. *Journal of Sexual Aggression*, 15, 121–131.

Mann, R.E. and Fernandez, Y.M. (2006) Sex offender programmes: concept, theory, and practice, in *Offending Behaviour Programmes: Development, Application, and Controversies* (eds C.R. Hollin and E.J. Palmer), John Wiley & Sons, Ltd, Chichester, pp. 155–177.

Marshall, W.L. (2009) Manualization: a blessing or a curse? *Journal of Sexual Aggression*, 15, 109–120.

McGuire, J. (2002) Integrating findings from research reviews, in *Offender Rehabilitation and Treatment: Effective Programmes and Policies to Reduce Re-offending* (ed. J. McGuire), John Wiley & Sons, Ltd, Chichester, pp. 3–38.

McGuire, J. (2006) General offending behaviour programmes: concept, theory, and practice, in *Offending Behaviour Programmes: Development, Application, and Controversies* (eds C.R. Hollin and E.J. Palmer), John Wiley & Sons, Ltd, Chichester, pp. 69–111.

McGuire, J. (2008) A review of effective interventions for reducing aggression and violence. *Philosophical Transactions of the Royal Society B*, 363, 2577–2597.

McGuire, J., Bilby, C.A.L., Hatcher, R.M. *et al.* (2008) Evaluation of structured cognitive-behavioral treatment programs in reducing criminal recidivism. *Journal of Experimental Criminology*, 4, 21–40.

McMurran, M. (2006) Drug and alcohol programmes: concept, theory, and practice, in *Offending Behaviour Programmes: Development, Application, and Controversies* (eds C.R. Hollin and E.J. Palmer), John Wiley & Sons, Ltd, Chichester, pp. 179–207.

McMurran, M. and McGuire, J. (eds) (2005) *Social Problem Solving and Offending: Evidence, Evaluation and Evolution*, John Wiley & Sons, Ltd, Chichester.

Nunes, K.L., Babchishin, K.M. and Cortoni, F. (2011) Measuring treatment change in sex offenders. *Criminal Justice and Behavior*, 38, 157–173.

Olver, M.E., Stockdale, K.C. and Wormith, J.S. (2011) A meta-analysis of predictors of offender treatment attrition and its relationship to recidivism. *Journal of Consulting and Clinical Psychology*, 79, 6–21.

Palmer, E.J. and Hollin, C.R. (2007) The Level of Service Inventory-Revised with English women prisoners: a needs and reconviction analysis. *Criminal Justice and Behavior*, 34, 971–984.

Palmer, E.J., McGuire, J., Hounsome, J.C. *et al.* (2007) Offending behaviour programmes in the community: the effects on reconviction of three programmes with adult male offenders. *Legal and Criminological Psychology*, 12, 251–264.

Palmer, E.J., McGuire, J., Hatcher, R.M. *et al.* (2008) The importance of appropriate allocation to offending behavior programs. *International Journal of Offender Therapy and Comparative Criminology*, 52, 206–221.

Palmer, E.J., McGuire, J., Hatcher, R.M. *et al.* (2009) Allocation to offending behaviour programmes in the English and Welsh probation service. *Criminal Justice and Behavior*, 36, 909–922.

Polaschek, D.L.L. (2006) Violent offender programmes: concept, theory, and practice, in *Offending Behaviour Programmes: Development, Application, and Controversies* (eds C.R. Hollin and E.J. Palmer), John Wiley & Sons, Ltd, Chichester, pp. 113–154.

Redondo, S., Sánchez-Meca, J. and Garrido, V. (2002) Crime treatment in Europe: a review of outcome studies, in *Offender Rehabilitation and Treatment: Effective Programmes and Policies to Reduce Re-offending* (ed. J. McGuire), John Wiley & Sons, Ltd, Chichester, pp. 113–141.

Romani, C.J., Morgan, R.D., Gross, N.R. and McDonald, B.R. (2012) Treating criminal behavior: is the bang worth the buck? *Psychology, Public Policy, and Law*, 18, 144–165.

Ross, R.R. and Fabiano, E.A. (1985) *Time to Think: A Cognitive Model of Delinquency Prevention and Offender Rehabilitation*, Institute of Social Sciences and Arts, Johnson City.

Ross, R.R., Fabiano, E.A. and Ross, B. (1989) *Reasoning and Rehabilitation: A Handbook for Teaching Cognitive Skills*, Cognitive Centre, Ottawa.

Sherman, L.W. (2003) Misleading evidence and evidence-led policy: making social science more experimental. *Annals of the American Academy of Social and Political Science*, 589, 6–19.

Taylor, R. (1999) Predicting Reconvictions for Sexual and Violent Offences Using the Revised Offender Group Reconviction Scale. *Research Findings no. 104*, Home Office, London.

Tong, L.S.J. and Farrington, D.P. (2006) How effective is the "Reasoning and Rehabilitation" programme in reducing re-offending? A meta-analysis of evaluations in four countries. *Psychology, Crime & Law*, 12, 3–24.

Van Voorhis, P., Spruance, L.M.P., Ritchey, N. *et al.* (2004) The Georgia cognitive skills experiment: a replication of reasoning and rehabilitation. *Criminal Justice and Behavior*, 31, 282–305.

Wilson, D.B., Bouffard, L.A. and MacKenzie, D.L. (2005) A quantitative review of structured, group-oriented, cognitive-behavioral programs for offenders. *Criminal Justice and Behavior*, 32, 172–204.

Young, S. and Ross, R. (2007) *R&R2 for Youths and Adults with Mental Health Problems: A Prosocial Competence Training Program*, Cognitive Centre of Canada, Ottawa.

Young, S., Chick, K. and Gudjonsson, G. (2010) A preliminary evaluation of reasoning and rehabilitation 2 in mentally disordered offenders (R&R2M) across two secure forensic settings in the United Kingdom. *Journal of Forensic Psychiatry & Psychology*, 21, 336–349.

7

What Works in Reducing Violent Re-offending in Psychopathic Offenders

Jenny Tew, Leigh Harkins and Louise Dixon

University of Birmingham, UK

Introduction

Psychopathy is recognized as a significant issue for the criminal justice system as it negatively impacts re-offending (Dolan and Doyle, 2000; Salekin, Rogers and Sewell, 1996), compliance with institutional rules and regimes (Dolan and Davies, 2005), inpatient interpersonal aggression in secure settings (Langton *et al.*, 2011) and responses to treatment (Ogloff, Wong and Greenwood, 1990).

As identified by Bonta and Wormith (see Chapter 4), best practice in treatment planning for offenders is guided by the principles of risk, need and responsivity (RNR) (Andrews and Bonta, 2003). These principles have been shown to be greatly impacted by psychopathy (e.g., Abracen, Looman and Langton, 2008; Harkins and Beech, 2007; Langton, 2007; Looman, Dickie and Abracen, 2005), thus affecting the likelihood that treatment will be successful for individuals with high levels of psychopathic traits.

The aim of this chapter is to provide an overview of how the most commonly used measure to assess psychopathy, the Psychopathy Checklist-Revised (PCL-R; Hare, 2003), can be used to inform the assessment and treatment of offenders with high levels of psychopathic traits. We consider the concept and measurement of psychopathy before moving on to review the empirical literature considering the efficacy of treatment with offenders with high levels of psychopathic traits. We will then discuss the specific assessment and treatment needs of this group within the RNR framework. Finally we consider possible directions for future research and practice.

Defining and Assessing Psychopathy

Defining psychopathy has caused much debate across a range of disciplines over many decades. Although there is still some debate about specific details (e.g., the exact factor structure, whether psychopathy is a categorical or continuous construct), it is generally accepted that

What Works in Offender Rehabilitation: An Evidence-Based Approach to Assessment and Treatment,
First Edition. Edited by Leam A. Craig, Louise Dixon and Theresa A. Gannon.
© 2013 John Wiley & Sons, Ltd. Published 2013 by John Wiley & Sons, Ltd.

there are a variety of specific affective, interpersonal and behavioural characteristics of psychopathy which impact on a person's social interactions and general lifestyle, and which define the concept. People labelled as 'psychopaths' are experienced as being superficially charming, lacking in guilt and remorse, emotionally and socially empty in dealing with others, insincere and manipulative and having shallow emotional affect and poor insight. Behaviourally they can be impulsive, demonstrate a failure to learn from experience and are irresponsible and often law breaking (Cleckley, 1976).

The most commonly used tool to assess psychopathy is the PCL-R (Hare, 2003). This is a 20-item scale used to assess psychopathy in a range of settings. It uses interviews, files and information from third parties to assess personality traits and behaviours related to the concept of psychopathy. No single PCL-R item is considered necessary or sufficient for diagnosis, and no item is weighted more heavily than any other. This means that people with high levels of psychopathic traits, as measured by the PCL-R, form a heterogeneous group with different needs and difficulties.

There has been some debate over the years about the factor structure of the PCL-R. Hare (2003) advocates the use of a two-factor, four-facet model. Factor 1 is characterized by selfishness, callousness and remorseless use of others, and Factor 2 is characterized by a chronic unstable and anti-social lifestyle and social deviance. Factor 1 is further divided into two facets: Facet 1 containing the interpersonal items and Facet 2 containing the affective items. Factor 2 also divides into two further facets: Facet 3 containing the lifestyle items and Facet 4 containing the anti-social items. As an alternative to the two-factor model, Cooke and Michie (2001) propose a three-factor model where Factor 1 refers to arrogant and deceitful interpersonal style, Factor 2 deficient affective experience and Factor 3 impulsive and irresponsible behaviour. They have removed items from the model that relate directly to anti-social behaviour, namely, Facet 4 items from the Hare model, as they believe that anti-social behaviour is a symptom of psychopathy rather than a core feature of the disorder. However, in practice, scores on Hare's (2003) two-factor or four-facet model are usually reported.

There has also been debate as to whether the concept of psychopathy defines a distinct category of individuals or if the traits that make up the disorder run on a continuum for all members of society (see Skeem *et al.*, 2003). The PCL-R allows for both theoretical perspectives. Total and factor scores produce a continuum of trait strength with a higher score more closely resembling a prototypical psychopath, whereas cut scores (e.g., 25[1] or 30) are often used to classify people as 'psychopaths' or 'non-psychopaths'. This is particularly useful for research purposes (Cooke and Michie, 1999; Cooke *et al.*, 2005; Hare, 1991), although this cut-off is sometimes used in practice to make decisions (e.g., at sentencing, for treatment planning and release from custody). This highlights the importance of ensuring accurate and responsible use of the PCL-R.

At present, the PCL-R is one of the most widely used and respected measures of psychopathy with considerable supporting research (Hare, 2003). However, it is not the only measure available for assessing psychopathy. Within the PCL family of assessments, there is also a screening version; the PCL:SV (Hart, Cox and Hare, 1995) which is a 12-item scale based on a subset of PCL-R items, the P-SCAN (Hare and Hervé, 2001) which is a non-clinical tool providing a rough screen of the possible presence of psychopathic traits and the PCL:YV

---

[1]   A score of 30 on the PCL-R is used as a cut-off to indicate psychopathy (Hare, 2003). However, there is evidence to support the use of a lower cut-off of 25 in the United Kingdom in that the same level of psychopathy as observed in the United States was found to be associated with lower scores on the PCL-R in the United Kingdom (Cooke & Michie, 1999).

(Forth, Kosson and Hare, 2003) which is a 20-item scale providing an assessment of psychopathic traits in offenders between 12 and 18 years old.

In addition to these tools, while it may seem counterintuitive to use self-report measures to assess a concept characterized in part by conning and manipulative behaviour, several such measures exist. Dedicated self-report measures of psychopathy include the Psychopathic Personality Inventory (PPI; Lilienfield and Andrews, 1996), the Psychopathic Personality Inventory Revised (PPI-R; Lilienfeld and Widows, 2005), the Levenson Primary and Secondary Psychopathy scales (LPSP; Levenson, Kiehl and Fitzpatrick, 1995) and the Self-Report Psychopathy Scales (SRP; Hare, 1985, SRP II; Hare, Hemphill and Paulhus, 2002). These assessments provide insight into an individual's view of themselves and are often used in the community where a lack of collateral information may mean a PCL-R assessment is not possible.

The assessments noted so far are not designed to measure change over time in psychopathic traits. This is a potentially important area when considering issues such as responses to treatment. In response to this gap, Cooke *et al.*, (2004) developed the Comprehensive Assessment of Psychopathic Personality (CAPP). This is a semi-structured clinical interview that evaluates psychopathic traits independent of criminal behaviour. According to this measure, psychopathic personality disorder is split into six domains, the self, attachment, emotional, behavioural, dominance and cognitive domains, each containing several symptoms that are assessed. The CAPP is primarily developed for research and is still undergoing validation. That said, it assesses the symptoms of psychopathic personality disorder over discrete time periods and is capable of measuring change in clinical presentation over time. As research into this tool develops, it is hoped its use as a dynamic assessment of psychopathic traits will increase.

The remainder of this chapter will focus on psychopathy as assessed by the PCL-R as the measure providing the most robust evidence base.

Psychopathy and Treatment Response

Before considering the RNR factors associated with psychopathy in more detail, we first consider the general question of whether individuals with high levels of psychopathic traits are considered capable of benefiting from treatment.

Although quite a bit has been written about psychopathy and treatment, Hemphill and Hart (2002) comment, 'far more has been written about the subject than is actually known about it' (p. 198). It is clear that there has been some debate over the impact of treatment on those with high levels of psychopathic traits through the years, a debate which has significantly impacted on clinical practices (Barbaree, 2005; Langton *et al.*, 2006; Rice, Harris and Cormier, 1992; Seto and Barbaree, 1999). Evidence assessing the efficacy of treatment often comes from meta-analytic studies. These studies combine the results of a number of smaller studies which do not provide conclusive evidence on their own, sometimes due to small effect sizes or non-significant results. Thus, they can provide stronger evidence about treatment efficacy than individual studies (DerSimonian and Laird, 1986). Garrido, Esteban and Molero (1996) and Salekin (2002) both conducted meta-analyses looking at the response of individuals classified as 'psychopaths' to treatment and noted that while 'psychopaths' tended to do worse than 'non psychopaths', they did seem to benefit from treatment. Looking more closely at these meta-analyses though, there were methodological problems with the studies they included such as lack of appropriate control groups, differences in the conceptualization of psychopathy and unclear treatment aims.

Indeed, it has been argued that the quality of the research in this area thus far has been questionable. In fact, D'Silva, Duggan and McCarthy (2004) reported that they were not able to conduct a meta-analysis as they could not find one research paper that met their standards for review (i.e., having an appropriate control group, using the Hare model of psychopathy to focus treatment, appropriate outcome variables and an adequate follow-up period). Both they and Thornton and Blud (2007) critically reviewed the available literature in the area and came to similar conclusions, namely, that higher PCL-R scorers tend not to do as well in treatment as lower PCL-R scorers, and that the response of individuals to treatment is quite diverse, but on the whole, high PCL-R scorers do seem able to benefit from treatment. Hemphill and Hart (2002) concluded as a result of their review of the literature that 'psychopathic' offenders engaged in more disruptive behaviour, were less likely to stay in treatment and were re-convicted faster than 'non psychopaths'. Despite this, they also concluded that there was no good evidence that psychopathy was untreatable.

Consistent amongst these reviews is the opinion that level of psychopathy does impact on response to treatment (Abracen *et al.*, 2008; Hemphill and Hart, 2002; Thornton and Blud, 2007), but, possibly due in part to the heterogeneity of those with high levels of psychopathic traits, this impact differs in both strength and type. As such, it seems possible that some offenders with high levels of psychopathic traits can benefit from some treatment programmes. It is worth considering that even if one is of the belief that treatment makes those with high levels of psychopathy worse, as some studies suggest (e.g., Rice, Harris and Cormier, 1992; Seto and Barbaree, 1999), then it cannot be the case that these individuals cannot change (even if it is for the worse). This too would suggest that the right treatment approach needs to be found in order to work effectively with people with high levels of psychopathic traits. As Wong and Hare (2009) note, it is not that treatment makes psychopaths worse but that the *wrong* treatment makes them worse. It seems crucial that psychopathy is considered when planning treatment, and therefore should be considered within each of the RNR principles so that treatment engagement is maximized and risk of reoffending can be reduced.

Psychopathy Within the RNR Framework (Assessment and Treatment Needs)

As noted earlier, when considering appropriate interventions for offenders, clinicians are advised to consider their level of risk, treatment needs and any pertinent responsivity issues (see Chapter 4 for a detailed description of the RNR framework). Andrews and Bonta (2003) developed these three principles as important elements to a successful treatment pathway for offenders. They found that effective treatment matched the intensity of the intervention to the risk level of the offender, with higher-risk offenders requiring longer, more intense treatment programmes than lower-risk offenders in order to gain the same benefits (i.e., Risk principle). The concept of treatment need is intuitive and states that for a treatment to be effective in reducing risk of re-offending, it needs to target those changeable areas that are relevant to a person's offending. These needs are termed 'criminogenic needs' (hence the term 'Need principle') and form the dynamic part of an offender's level of risk (Hollin, 2002). According to the Responsivity principle, for an individual to be responsive to treatment, it should be delivered in a way that takes account of factors that can influence their engagement. These responsivity factors include issues such as motivation, personality characteristics and treatment modality.

When we consider that psychopathy has been found to be a relevant factor in risk of re-offending (Campbell, French and Gendreau, 2009; Gendreau, Goggin and Smith,

2002) and response to treatment (Garrido, Esteban and Molero, 1996; Salekin, 2002), then it may be even more critical that treatment be carefully planned for offenders with high levels of psychopathic traits. We will now consider psychopathy in terms of each of the RNR principles.

Risk

It follows that for offenders to be matched to treatment of appropriate duration and intensity, accurate assessment of risk is necessary (Hollin, 2002). The PCL-R was not designed as a risk assessment tool; however, numerous researchers have considered its link to recidivism and institutional misconduct and found evidence of a relationship (Hare, 2003; Hare *et al.*, 2000; Hemphill, Hare and Wong, 1998; Sjostedt and Langstrom, 2000; Walsh and Kosson, 2008; Walters *et al.*, 2008).

Meta-analytic studies provide overwhelming evidence for the relationship between psychopathy and risk, with high scorers on the PCL-R consistently representing a high-risk group (Campbell, French and Gendreau, 2009; Gendreau, Goggin and Smith, 2002; Yang, Wong and Coid, 2010). Results across the meta-analyses also suggest that the two factors of the PCL-R (Hare, 2003) correlate differently with measures of recidivism, with Factor 2 being a stronger predictor of violent and general recidivism than Factor 1 (Hemphill, Hare and Wong 1998; Yang, Wong and Coid, 2010). However, many who have reported these relationships also note that the effect size of Factor 1 is not trivial (Leistico *et al.*, 2008; Salekin, Rogers and Sewell, 1996; Walters, 2003), ranging from 0.15 to 0.37, representing a small to medium effect size. Studies have shown that the interaction between the two factors is important, as they form one higher order factor of psychopathy (Hare and Neumann, 2008; Walsh and Kosson, 2008). As such, it is not advised to simply consider each factor in isolation.

Considering the relationship between the PCL-R and tools designed to assess risk, the meta-analytic research shows that the PCL-R performs as well as other tools, such as the Level of Service Inventory-Revised (LSI; Andrews and Bonta, 1995) and Historical Clinical Risk Assessment-20 (HCR-20; Webster *et al.*, 1997), designed to assess risk (Gendreau, Goggin and Smith, 2002; Gray *et al.*, 2004). It should also be remembered that low PCL-R scores do not necessarily mean low risk (Hare, 1998), that psychopathy would need to be seen as dimensional rather than categorical construct and that psychopathy should be considered within the context of other risk assessments and risk-related information.

Based on the literature reviewed previously, it appears that different combinations of traits on the PCL-R do not relate to the same level or type of risk (Salekin, Rogers and Sewell, 1996). Thus, one person who receives a particular score on the PCL-R could present a very different type of risk of re-offending than another individual who has the same overall score, but for whom this score is made up from different levels of Factor 1 and Factor 2 items.

In line with the Risk principle, it follows that those who score more highly on the PCL-R are at a higher risk of recidivism; thus, higher PCL-R scorers are likely to require longer (Lösel, 1998) and more intensive (Salekin, 2002) treatment programmes to reduce their risk of re-offending. Once it has been established that an individual has high levels of psychopathic traits (either in total or on either factor), and therefore a higher associated risk of re-offending, we then need to consider what this intensive treatment programme should address.

Treatment need

In considering the treatment needs of offenders with high levels of psychopathic traits, we need to be clear about what the aims of treatment are. Within the criminal justice system, the focus of rehabilitation is on the prevention of crime, and as such treatment should focus on addressing the areas relevant to a person offending. Treatment targets should not merely be symptoms of psychopathy, although the reduction of symptoms may be important to improving the offender's quality of life (Serin, 1995) and amenability to treatment.

It is clear that those with high levels of psychopathy are not a homogeneous group, and, although they are a high-risk group, not all of them re-offend. Wong and Burt (2007) used the Violence Risk Scale (VRS; Wong, 2004) to show that similar static variables (i.e., age at release, age at first conviction, number of juvenile convictions, violent lifestyle and stability when young) and similar dynamic variables (particularly violence while incarcerated, interpersonal aggression and release to a high-risk situation) distinguish re-offending and non-re-offending individuals with high levels of psychopathy, just as they do recidivists and non-recidivists in the general offender population. This would support the idea that the risk of recidivism for offenders with high levels of psychopathic traits could be reduced in the same way as with offenders with low levels of psychopathic traits, by addressing their individual criminogenic needs. This work is supported by that of Olver and Wong (as cited in Hare, 2003), who also found correlations between the PCL-R and the VRS, and Douglas and Webster (1999) who found correlations between the PCL-R and the HCR-20, both of which contain dynamic risk factors for violence. Research has also shown links between the PCL-R and the Psychological Inventory of Criminal Thinking (PICTS; Walters, 1995), a measure assessing criminal thinking styles. All of this work suggests that there is a link between psychopathy and level of criminogenic needs, with more psychopathic individuals having higher levels of criminogenic need. Given this, an important part of assessing suitability for treatment is developing an understanding of what factors contribute to an individual's offending and how.

Given these differences within and between individuals, there is a need to identify the specific criminogenic factors relevant to an offender. The PCL-R includes both static and dynamic factors and so may offer clinicians useful information regarding treatment needs. However, its use in respect of assessing criminogenic need is much less firmly established than its use as a risk predictor (Hollin, 2002). Focusing on the individual PCL-R items may help clinicians identify needs that are highlighted in the wider literature as being potential criminogenic needs for particular offenders. Research suggests that Factor 2 on the PCL-R is more strongly associated with risk of recidivism than Factor 1 (Hemphill, Hare and Wong 1998; Yang, Wong and Coid, 2010); therefore, it would be logical for treatment to reduce re-offending by focusing on addressing those problems highlighted within Factor 2 of the PCL-R for it to be most effective.

In support of this idea, Brown and Forth (1997) looked at factors linked to offending in 'psychopathic' and 'non psychopathic' rapists. They concluded that 'psychopathic' rapists would get more benefit from treatment strategies aimed at reducing impulsive lifestyle and improving their poor behavioural controls, rather than ones more commonly targeted in sex offender treatment aimed at identifying negative emotions and offence cycles.

Individuals who have a high PCL-R score but low scores on the impulsivity and behavioural control items in Factor 2 could be more likely to commit violent acts that are purposeful rather than uncontrolled and therefore require treatment aimed at finding more pro-social ways of achieving their aims and improving their problem-solving abilities (e.g., generating alternatives). Individuals scoring highly on the Factor 2 item 'poor behavioural controls' may benefit from some sort of anger management training to reduce their risk of violence.

While focusing on needs identified within Factor 2 of the PCL-R might be beneficial, Factor 1 items also offer us some important information. Shine and Hobson (1997) found that the PCL-R Factor 1 scores did not significantly correlate with most sub-scales in a psychometric test battery used to inform suitability for treatment in a democratic therapeutic community. They found that the test battery tapped the anti-social behavioural aspect of psychopathy covered by Factor 2 of the PCL-R, but the interpersonal aspects (Factor 1) were missed. The added value of the PCL-R in the assessment of treatment needs may therefore be gained from Factor 1 items.

Scoring highly specifically on affective items of Factor 1 (i.e., Facet 2) may mean an individual lacks the capacity for empathy, rather than preventing themselves from experiencing this through cognitive distortions. Thornton and Blud (2007) suggest that for these individuals, treatment aimed at challenging their distortions to increase empathy may not be relevant. Interventions that intend to increase offenders' empathy for victims or have them process emotional experiences may be contraindicated for individuals scoring highly in Facet 2 (Lösel, 1998). Such interventions may actually help to improve their skills at 'faking' emotions in interpersonal situations and using this to deceive and manipulate (Hart and Hare, 1997). Conversely, low scores on the empathy and guilt-type items of Facet 2 could be seen as indicators of a potential positive response to treatments based on developing moral reasoning and concern for others.

Following an assessment of risk and of the relevant criminogenic needs that treatment should address, our attention turns to considering factors that might have an impact on an individual's engagement in that treatment.

Responsivity

Given that offenders with high levels of psychopathic traits are more likely to drop out of treatment than those with lower levels of psychopathy (Olver and Wong, 2009; Seto and Barbaree, 1999), and do not seem to gain as much benefit from treatment they do attend compared to offenders with lower levels of psychopathic traits (Garrido, Esteban and Molero, 1996; Salekin, 2002), responsivity is clearly an important factor to consider for this group.

Those with high levels of psychopathic traits have a particular style of interpersonal interaction and manner of processing information that should be considered a responsivity issue for treatment (Looman, Dickie and Abracen, 2005; Olver and Wong, 2009; Serin, 1995). However, this group have different traits and trait combinations, individuals may differ in their problems in treatment. Identifying the high PCL-R scorers and why they are scoring highly may help treatment providers identify individual's responsivity issues.

The literature in this area again suggests that the two factors of the PCL-R have different impacts on the response of individuals to treatment and therefore what type of treatment is likely to be most effective for an individual. Factor 1 has been found to be more associated with treatment behaviours and outcome than Factor 2 (Hare *et al.*, 2000; Hobson, Shine and Roberts, 2000; Looman, 2003). Different traits within Factor 1 may have different impacts on responsivity. For example, individuals may be quite grandiose, focusing on a need for status and responding aggressively to perceived challenges to their status (Hemphill and Hart, 2002; Hobson, Shine and Roberts, 2000). They may be quite egocentric (Serin, 1995), and see little reason to change (Losel, 1998; Ogloff, Wong and Greenwood, 1990; Thornton and Blud, 2007). They may also more likely be skilled at using treatment to con and manipulate others, being unlikely to give accurate accounts of their attitudes and behaviour but being skilled at presenting themselves in a positive light. Those scoring highly on Factor 1 may also have difficulties in forming attachments which would impact on their ability to develop a working alliance, seen as important for treatment success (Martin, Garske and Davis, 2000).

The challenge for treatment providers is to find ways to address these responsivity issues. They may, for example, work with high levels of grandiosity and egocentricity by focusing on satisfying the individuals' own needs (Thornton and Blud, 2007; Wong and Hare, 2009) and encourage them to see 'what's in it for them' by changing their behaviour. Treatment may highlight offending as low status, with the intention of appealing to an individuals desire for status as a potential motivator for change. Also, interventions may work with their desire for control by offering treatment that focuses on giving individuals choices and encouraging them to take responsibility for their behaviour (Harris, Attrill and Bush, 2005).

Wong and Hare (2009) stress the importance of developing motivation and aiming treatment towards the appropriate stage of change for the individual as ways of maximizing treatment engagement and reducing resistance. This may be particularly true for those scoring highly on the PCL-R Factor 1 items, who may well already possess the skills that treatment would typically try to teach offenders but lack the motivation to use them positively. Considering the issue of treatment alliance, Wong and Hare (2009) suggest focusing on developing a professional and respectful working relationship aimed at working together to achieve tasks and not on developing an affective bond, which may be viewed as a sign of weakness by those with high levels of psychopathic traits and used to manipulate individuals or situations.

Traits making up Factor 2 on the PCL-R may also offer us important clues about the difficulties an individual may face in treatment. Hobson, Shine and Roberts (2000) found that Factor 2 scores correlated with early disruptive behaviour on the therapeutic community. Individuals scoring more highly in some of these traits may find it harder to see treatment through until the end, to complete tasks and to achieve goals set in treatment (Thornton and Blud, 2007). They are more likely to get bored easily and be impulsive in their decision making and actions. This may mean they are likely to struggle to comply with the requirements of an intervention, breaking rules and pushing boundaries (Thornton and Blud, 2007). It may also make them more likely to miss sessions and less likely to apply what they are doing in treatment to their everyday life.

In line with the responsivity principle, the characteristics could be addressed by setting clear short-term goals that appeal to the individuals' own self-interests and which are exciting and challenging. This may help individuals remain focused and interested in treatment. Treatment should also have clear boundaries, and where possible behaviours should be made the focus of treatment rather than be an obstacle to it.

It is clear that those with many psychopathic traits experience a range of difficulties engaging in and benefiting from treatment. It is worth considering, however, that they may also have personality traits that may be seen as positives to treatment engagement and success. For example, they may have good self-control, great interpersonal skills or be keen to try out new things. Treatment may be more beneficial for these individuals if it aims to make use of these strengths.

There has been an increasing focus within the general treatment literature on interventions building on individuals' strengths to help reduce re-offending (Linley and Joseph, 2004; Ward and Maruna, 2007; Ward and Stewart, 2003), and developing treatment for those with high levels of psychopathic traits should be no exception to this. This focus also increases the potential for constructive positive reinforcement which may be particularly effective with individuals who are quite grandiose.

Future Directions

The focus of research into the treatment of those with high levels of psychopathy has shifted from considering whether they are able to benefit from treatment on the whole to trying to identify principles for treatment that would maximize engagement and successful outcomes. Our knowledge in this area is still growing through the development of interventions which now require evaluation.

Efforts have been extended to designing interventions specifically for offenders with high levels of psychopathic traits. Wong and Hare (2009) have published 'Guidelines for a psychopathy treatment programme'. In 2004, the Chromis programme became accredited by the Correctional Services Accreditation Panel (CSAP) in the United Kingdom and started to run within one of their prison service Dangerous and Sever Personality Disorder (DSPD) units. The Chromis programme has been specifically designed to address risk of violence in men with high levels of psychopathic traits. This programme is informed by the research on RNR issues relevant for those with high levels of psychopathic traits and is currently under evaluation.

Across the research considered here, there are numerous methodological factors that can influence research findings. These include how psychopathy and psychopathic traits are assessed, how recidivism is defined, how treatment success is defined, what an intervention's aims and methods entail, the research sample, how the data is defined and what statistical analysis is conducted. Considering these factors, the research relating to psychopathy and risk is far more advanced than that of psychopathy and treatment. There is a limited body of quality literature that examines types of treatment programmes with psychopaths and which approaches are most effective (Salekin, 2002; Thornton and Blud, 2007). More work is needed to further developments in this area.

One thing that should be noted is that many of the treatments studied within the psychopathy and treatment literature are very different in form and content to contemporary interventions. For example, within the United Kingdom, interventions are now accredited via the CSAP and meet a range of standards considered good practice in treatment design and delivery. Therefore, interventions such as modern democratic therapeutic communities are very different to those discussed in previous research on the effectiveness of treatment for those with high levels of psychopathic traits (e.g., Rice, Harris and Cormier, 1992). There is a lack of sound research regarding the response of offenders with high levels of psychopathic traits to current treatment practices.

Conclusions

Psychopathy is clearly an important concept in determining risk of violent re-offending and for treatment designed to reduce that risk. Looking across the literature, while some of the finer points are being researched and debated, it seems that those with high levels of psychopathic traits are considered to be a high risk of re-offending and difficult to treat. This is not a positive outlook. It is therefore important that we invest in understanding these individuals with a view to improving treatment engagement and reducing risk of re-offending.

Psychopathy is an important factor in considering someone's risk of recidivism. The PCL-R is correlated with recidivism (Leistico *et al.*, 2008; Walters, 2003) and with other tools specifically designed to assess risk of re-offending (Campbell, French and Gendreau, 2009; Yang, Wong and Coid, 2010). Psychopathy is also relevant to identifying successful interventions to address this risk. As one component of an assessment protocol, the PCL-R can assist with screening, programme implementation and decision making throughout the course of treatment (Loving, 2002). Research is unclear about *how* offenders with high levels of psychopathic traits can benefit from *which* interventions, but it is known that they are a difficult group to engage in treatment and who have complex treatment needs. Factor 2 of the PCL-R seems to be more directly associated with risk of recidivism than Factor 1, but Factor 1 may be at least as relevant as Factor 2 when considering treatment planning to address that risk. Harpur and Hare (1994) found that while Factor 2 scores declined with age, Factor 1 scores remained stable. Walters (2004) states that characteristics assessed by Factor 1 of PCL-R also appear more stable across situations than Factor 2. The impact of psychopathic traits on treatment engagement may therefore continue to remain significant, while its impact on risk may reduce over time or be more situationally dependent. These are all issues that need to be further researched, and so the debates continue.

References

Abracen, J., Looman, J. and Langton, C.M. (2008) Treatment of sexual offenders with psychopathic traits: recent research developments and clinical implications. *Trauma, Violence and Abuse: A Review Journal*, 19, 144–166.

Andrews, D.A. and Bonta, J. (1995) *The Level of Service Inventory – Revised*, Multi-Health Systems Inc., Toronto.

Andrews, D.A. and Bonta, J. (2003) *The Psychology of Criminal Conduct*, 3rd edn, Anderson Publishing, Cincinnati.

Barbaree, H.E. (2005) Psychopathy, treatment behavior, and recidivism: an extended follow-up of Seto and Barbaree. *Journal of Interpersonal Violence*, 20 (9), 1115–1131.

Brown, S.L. and Forth, A.E. (1997) Psychopathy and sexual assault: static risk factors, emotional precursors, and rapist subtypes. *Journal of Consulting and Clinical Psychology*, 65, 848–857.

Campbell, M.A., French, S. and Gendreau, P. (2009) The prediction of violence in adult offenders: a meta-analytic comparison of instruments and methods of assessment. *Criminal Justice and Behavior*, 36 (6), 567–590.

Cleckley, H. (1976) *The Mask of Sanity*, 5th edn, Mosby, St. Louis.

Cooke, D.J. and Michie, C. (1999) Psychopathy across cultures: North America and Scotland compared. *Journal of Abnormal Psychology*, 108 (1), 58–68.

Cooke, D.J. and Michie, C. (2001) Refining the construct of psychopathy: toward a hierarchical model. *Psychological Assessment*, 13, 171–188.

Cooke, D.J., Hart, S.D., Logan, C. and Michie, C. (2004) *Comprehensive Assessment of Psychopathic Personality – Institutional Rating Scale (CAPP IRS)*. Unpublished manuscript.

Cooke, D.J., Michie, C., Hart, S.D. and Clark, D. (2005) Assessing psychopathy in the UK: concerns about cross-cultural generalisability. *British Journal of Psychiatry*, 186, 335–341.

DerSimonian, R. and Laird, N. (1986) Meta-analysis in clinical trials. *Controlled Clinical Trials*, 7, 177–188.

Dolan, M. and Davies, G. (2005) Psychopathy and institutional outcome in patients with schizophrenia in forensic settings in the UK. *Schizophrenia Research*, 81, 277–281.

Dolan, M. and Doyle, M. (2000) Violence risk prediction. *British Journal of Psychiatry*, 177, 303–311.

Douglas, K.S. and Webster, C.D. (1999) The HCR-20 violence risk assessment scheme: concurrent validity in a sample of incarcerated offenders. *Criminal Justice and Behavior*, 26, 3–19.

D'Silva, K., Duggan, C. and McCarthy, L. (2004) Does treatment really make psychopaths worse? A review of the evidence. *Journal of Personality Disorders*, 18, 163–177.

Forth, A., Kosson, D. and Hare, R.D. (2003) *Hare Psychopathy Checklist: Youth Version*. Multi-Health Systems Inc., Toronto.

Garrido, V., Esteban, C. and Molero, C. (1996) The effectiveness in the treatment of psychopathy: a meta-analysis. *Issues in Legal and Criminological Psychology*, 24, 57–59.

Gendreau, P., Goggin, C. and Smith, P. (2002) Is the PCL-R really the "unparalleled" measure of offender risk? A lesson in knowledge cumulation. *Criminal Justice and Behaviour*, 29 (4), 397–426.

Gray, N.S., Snowden, R.J., MacCulloch, S. *et al.* (2004) Relative efficacy of criminological, clinical, and personality measures of future risk of offending in mentally disordered offenders: a comparative study of HCR-20, PCL:SV, and OGRS. *Journal of Consulting and Clinical Psychology*, 72, 523–530.

Hare, R.D. (1985) A comparison of procedures for the assessment of psychopathy. *Journal of Consulting and Clinical Psychology*, 53, 7–16.

Hare, R.D. (1991) *Hare Psychopathy Checklist-Revised (PCL-R)*, Multi-Health Systems Inc., Toronto.

Hare, R.D. (1998) The Hare PCL-R: some issues concerning its use and misuse. *Legal and Criminological Psychology*, 3 (1), 101–119.

Hare, R.D. (2003) *Hare Psychopathy Checklist-Revised (PCL-R)*, 2nd edn, Multi-Health Systems Inc., Toronto.

Hare, R.D. and Hervé, H.F. (2001) *Hare Psychopathy – SCAN Research Version*, Multi-Health Systems Inc., Toronto.

Hare, R.D. and Neumann, C.S. (2008) Psychopathy as a clinical and empirical construct. *Annual Review of Clinical Psychology*, 4, 217–246.

Hare, R.D., Clark, D., Grann, M. and Thornton, D. (2000) Psychopathy and the predictive validity of the PCL-R: an international perspective. *Behavioural Sciences and the Law*, 18, 623–645.

Hare, R.D., Hemphill, J.F. and Paulhus, D. (2002) *The Self-Report Psychopathy Scale-II (SRP II)*, Multi-Health Systems Inc., Toronto.

Harkins, L. and Beech, A.R. (2007) A review of the factors that can influence the effectiveness of sexual offender treatment: risk, need, responsivity, and process issues. *Aggression and Violent Behavior*, 12, 616–627.

Harpur, T.J. and Hare, R.D. (1994) The assessment of psychopathy as a function of age. *Journal of Abnormal Psychology*, 103, 604–609.

Harris, D., Attrill, G. and Bush, J. (2005) Using choice as an aid to engagement and risk management with violent psychopathic offenders. *Issues in Forensic Psychology*, 5, 144–151.

Hart, S.D. and Hare, R.D. (1997) Psychopathy: assessment and association with criminal conduct, in *Handbook of Antisocial Behaviour* (eds D.M. Stoff, J. Breiling and J.D. Master), John Wiley & Sons, Inc., New York, pp. 22–35.

Hart, S.D., Cox, D.N. and Hare, R.D. (1995) *Manual for the Hare Psychopathy Checklist: Screening Version*. Multi-Health Systems Inc., Toronto.

Hemphill, J.F. and Hart, S.D. (2002) Motivating the unmotivated: psychopathy, treatment, and change, in *Motivating Offenders to Change: A Guide to Enhancing Engagement in Therapy* (ed. M. McMurran), John Wiley & Sons, Ltd, Chichester, pp. 193–219.

Hemphill, J.F., Hare, R.D. and Wong, S. (1998) Psychopathy and recidivism: a review. *Legal and Criminological Psychology*, 3, 139–170.

Hobson, J., Shine, J. and Roberts, R. (2000) How do psychopaths behave in a prison therapeutic community? *Psychology, Crime & Law*, 6 (2), 139–154.

Hollin, C.R. (2002) Risk – needs assessments and allocation to offender programmes, in *Offender Rehabilitation and Treatment: Effective Programmes and Policies to Reduce Re-offending* (ed. J.M. McGuire), John Wiley & Sons, Ltd, Chichester, pp 309–332.

Langton, C.M. (2007) Assessment implications of "what works research for dangerous and severe personality disorder (DSPD) service evaluation. *Psychology, Crime & Law*, 13 (1), 97–111.

Langton, C.M., Barbaree, H.E., Harkins, L. and Peacock, E.J. (2006) Sexual offenders' response to treatment and its association with recidivism as a function of psychopathy. *Sexual Abuse: A Journal of Research and Treatment*, 18, 99–120.

Langton, C.M., Hogue, T.E., Daffern, M. *et al.* (2011) Personality traits as predictors of inpatient aggression in a high-security forensic psychiatric setting: prospective evaluation of the PCL-R and

IPDE dimension rating. *International Journal of Offender Therapy and Comparative Criminology*, 55 (3), 392–415.

Leistico, A.R., Salekin, R.T., DeCoster, D. and Rogers, R. (2008) A large-scale meta-analysis relating the hare measures of psychopathy to antisocial conduct. *Law and Human Behaviour*, 32, 28–45.

Levenson, M.R., Kiehl, K.A. and Fitzpatrick, C.M. (1995) Assessing psychopathic attributes in a non-institutionalized population. *Journal of Personality and Social Psychology*, 68, 151–158.

Lilienfield, S.O. and Andrews, B.P. (1996) Development and preliminary validation of a self report measure of psychopathic personality traits in noncriminal populations. *Journal of Personality Assessment*, 66, 488–524.

Lilienfeld, S.O. and Widows, M. (2005) *Psychopathic Personality Inventory – Revised: Professional Manual*. Psychological Assessment Resources Inc., Lutz.

Linley, P.A. and Joseph, S. (eds) (2004) *Positive Psychology in Practice*, John Wiley & Sons, Inc., Hoboken.

Looman, J. (2003) PCL-R factor scores and treatment outcome. Unpublished raw data, in Looman, J., Dickie, I. and Abracen, J. (2005) Responsivity issues in the treatment of sexual offenders. *Trauma Violence Abuse*, 6, 330–353, 339.

Looman, J., Dickie, I. and Abracen, J. (2005) Responsivity issues in the treatment of sexual offenders. *Trauma Violence Abuse*, 6, 330–353.

Lösel, F. (1998) Treatment and management of psychopaths, in, *Psychopathy: Theory, Research, and Implications for Society* (eds D.J. Cooke, A.E. Forth and R.D. Hare), Kluwer Academic, Dordrecht, pp. 303–354.

Loving, J.L. (2002) Treatment Planning with the Psychopathy Checklist–Revised (PCL-R). *International Journal of Offender Therapy and Comparative Criminology*, 46, 281–293.

Martin, D.J., Garske, J.P. and Davis, M.K. (2000) Relation of the therapeutic alliance with outcome and other variables: a meta-analytic review. *Journal of Consulting and Clinical Psychology*, 68, 438–450.

Ogloff, J.R.P., Wong, S. and Greenwood, A. (1990) Treating criminal psychopaths in a therapeutic community program. *Behavioral Sciences and the Law*, 8, 181–190.

Olver, M.E. and Wong, S.C.P. (2009) Therapeutic responses of psychopathic sexual offenders: treatment attrition, therapeutic change, and long-term recidivism. *Journal of Consulting and Clinical Psychology*, 77 (2), 328–336.

Rice, M.E., Harris, G.T. and Cormier, C.A. (1992) An evaluation of a maximum security therapeutic community for psychopaths and other mentally disordered offenders. *Law and Human Behavior*, 16, 399–412.

Salekin, R.T. (2002) Psychopathy and therapeutic pessimism. *Clinical lore or clinical reality? Clinical Psychology Review*, 22 (1), 79–112.

Salekin, R.T., Rogers, R. and Sewell, K.W. (1996) A review and meta-analysis of the psychopathy checklist and psychopathy checklist-revised: predictive validity of dangerousness. *Clinical Psychology Science and Practice*, 3, 203–215.

Serin, R.C. (1995) Treatment responsivity in criminal psychopaths. *Forum on Corrections Research*, 7, 23–26. http://www.csc-scc.gc.ca/text/pblct/forum/e073/e073h-eng.shtml (accessed 18 December 2012).

Seto, M.C. and Barbaree, H.E. (1999) Psychopathy, treatment behavior, and sex offender recidivism. *Journal of Interpersonal Violence*, 14 (12), 1235–1248.

Shine, J. and Hobson, J. (1997) Construct validity of the hare psychopathy checklist, revised, on a UK prison population. *Journal of Forensic Psychiatry*, 8 (3), 546–561.

Sjostedt, G. and Langstrom, N. (2000) Actuarial assessment of sex offender recidivism risk: a cross-validation of the RRASOR and Static-99 in Sweden. *Law and Human Behavior*, 25 (6), 629–645.

Skeem, J.L., Poythress, N.G., Edens, J.F. *et al.* (2003) Psychopathic personality or personalities? Exploring potential variants of psychopathy and their implications for risk assessment. *Aggression and Violent Behavior*, 8, 513–546.

Thornton, D. and Blud, L. (2007) The influence of psychopathic traits on response to treatment, in *The Psychopath: Theory, Research and Practice* (eds H. Hervé and J.C. Yuille) Lawrence Erlbaum Associates Inc., Mahwah, pp. 141–170.

Walsh, Z. and Kosson, D.S. (2008) Psychopathy and violence: the importance of factor level interactions. *Psychological Assessment*, 20, 114–120.

Walters, G.D. (1995) The psychological inventory of criminal thinking styles; Part I Reliability and preliminary validity. *Criminal Justice and Behavior*, 22, 307–325.

Walters, G.D. (2003) Predicting institutional adjustment and recidivism with the psychopathy checklist factor scores: a meta-analysis. *Law and Human Behaviour*, 27 (5), 541–558.

Walters, G.D. (2004) The trouble with psychopathy as a general theory of crime. *International Journal of Offender Therapy and Comparative Criminology*, 48, 133–148.

Walters, G.D., Knight, R.A., Grann, M. and Dahle, K.P. (2008) Incremental validity of the psychopathy checklist facet scores: predicting release outcome in six samples. *Journal of Abnormal Psychology*, 117 (2), 396–405.

Ward, T. and Maruna, S. (2007) *Rehabilitation: Beyond the Risk Paradigm*, Routledge, London.

Ward, T. and Stewart, C.A. (2003) The treatment of sex offenders: risk management and the good lives model. *Professional Psychology: Research and Practice*, 34, 353–360.

Webster, C.D., Douglas, K.S., Eaves, D. and Hart, S.D. (1997) *HCR-20 – Assessing Risk for Violence* (Version 2), Multi-Health Systems Inc., Toronto.

Wong, G.A. (2004) *Violence Risk Scale*, Multi-Health Systems Inc., Toronto.

Wong, S.C.P. and Burt, G. (2007) The heterogeneity of incarcerated psychopaths: differences in risk, need, recidivism and management approaches, in *The Psychopath: Theory, Research and Practice* (eds H. Hervé and J.C. Yuille), Lawrence Erlbaum Associates Inc., Mahwah, pp. 141–170.

Wong, S.C.P. and Hare, R.D. (2009) *Guidelines for a Psychopathy Treatment Programme*. Multi-Health Systems Inc., Toronto.

Yang, M., Wong, S.C.P. and Coid, J. (2010) The efficacy of violence prediction: a meta-analytic comparison of nine risk assessment tools. *Psychological Bulletin*, 136, 740–767.

8

What Works for Personality-Disordered Offenders?

Vincent Egan
University of Leicester, UK

Personality disorders are pervasive, persistent and problematic. Their effects and treatment require substantial resources, and seriously burden society and care systems (McCrone, Dhanasiri and Patel, 2008). This chapter discusses current best-practice methods to treat personality-disordered offenders, combining clinical practice and experience with academic content. In order to explore the theory and practice of interventions with personality-disordered offenders, it is necessary to understand the parameters of the disorder itself, and the complexities involved. The first part of this chapter addresses this issue, before moving on to consider therapeutic approaches to personality disorder. Much therapeutic work with this group is generically clinical, with more specific approaches related to managing interpersonal and impulsive aspects of personality disorder.

The Parameters of Personality Disorder

Personality disorder: diagnostic systems

The main psychiatric diagnostic systems are DSM-IV (American Psychiatric Association, 1994, 2000) and ICD-10 (World Health Organization, 1992). These descriptive, atheoretical and positivist systems are used by appropriately trained professionals, and largely map onto one another (Table 8.1). Up to quite recently, personality-disordered persons were sometimes explicitly and wrongly excluded from services due to their being 'untreatable'. However, personality disorder is more like a systemic illness, in that it is manageable provided the individual and the care team can follow a constructive informed treatment plan. Personality disorders, especially antisocial (ASPD) and borderline personality disorder (BPD), and psychopathy underlie much antisocial behaviour and are strong predictors of violent offending (Egan, 2011; Hemphill, Hare and Wong, 1998).

Personality disorder classification is being substantially revised for the fifth edition of DSM (DSM-V; Skodol et al., 2011). The revised model reduces the personality disorders down from 10 to 6 (see Table 8.1) and increases recognition of their dimensional and general nature.

What Works in Offender Rehabilitation: An Evidence-Based Approach to Assessment and Treatment,
First Edition. Edited by Leam A. Craig, Louise Dixon and Theresa A. Gannon.
© 2013 John Wiley & Sons, Ltd. Published 2013 by John Wiley & Sons, Ltd.

Table 8.1 Classification schemes for personality disorder: DSM-IV, ICD-10 and proposed revisions for DSM-V

Psychiatry DSM-IV	Psychiatry ICD-10	DSM-V
American Psychiatric Association	**World Health Organization**	**(Proposed)**
Axis II		
Cluster A ('odd' or 'bizarre')		
Paranoid	Paranoid	
Schizoid	Schizoid	
Schizotypal spectrum	Schizophrenic	Schizotypal
Cluster B ('dramatic')		
Antisocial	Dissocial	Antisocial
Borderline	Impulsive	Borderline
Histrionic	Histrionic	
Narcissistic		Narcissistic
Cluster C ('neurotic')		
Avoidant	Avoidant	Avoidant
Dependent	Dependent	
Obsessive-compulsive	Anankastic	Obsessive-compulsive

The revisions propose a person must be deemed to have significant impairment in two areas of personality functioning – how they see themselves and live their lives (i.e., the self) and how they relate to and understand others (i.e., interpersonal functioning). Superimposed on these generic continua are six retained (and more tightly diagnosed) disorders: schizotypy, ASPD, BPD, narcissistic, avoidant and obsessive-compulsive. These conditions are less clinically ambiguous, and while some comorbidity of disorders remains, it is reduced relative to the 10-disorder model.

Demographics and epidemiology

All three personality disorder clusters can be seen in nascent forms in adolescents, as childhood personality developmental disorder is a risk factor for later personality disorder, even if some diagnoses are not formally made until a patient is 18; such presentation is not attributable to gender, class, ethnicity or co-morbid mental illness (Johnson *et al.*, 2000; Zoccolillo *et al.*, 1992). Some degree of personality disorder burnout is apparent with ageing; older persons are significantly less likely than younger persons to have any personality disorder (6.6% versus 10.5%); specific disorders that are rather less prevalent in older persons are ASPD and histrionic personality disorders (Cohen *et al.*, 1994). As with the diagnosis and operationalization of any phenomena, incidence varies with how strictly the construct is defined. Epidemiological statistics for the incidence of personality disorder in the community suggest that some 5.9% of the US population meet narrow criteria for the diagnosis (9.3% if the exact diagnosis is loosened by one diagnostic criterion). Men have higher rates of personality disorder than women, and persons with unstable relationships the highest rates. Persons with more personality disorder symptoms and diagnoses are more likely to have sexual dysfunction, alcohol/drug use disorders and suicidal thoughts (Samuels *et al.*, 1994). Narrower criteria suggest incidences of 1.3%, 1.5% and 2.5% for specific Cluster A odd, B dramatic or C neurotic disorders (Mattia and Zimmerman, 2001). If these criteria are relaxed, up to 13% of the population can be so diagnosed, males being more inclined to Cluster A and women Cluster B. The largest epidemiological study from the United Kingdom thus far comprised a study of 626 persons aged 16–74 years , and found a personality disorder prevalence in the UK of 4.4% (95% confidence interval = 2.9–6.7%). Rates of personality disorder were highest among men, and for separated and unemployed participants living in urban locations (Coid *et al.*, 2006).

Personality disorder in offender populations

The high incidence of personality-disordered persons in healthcare and prison systems is confounded by concurrent (co-morbid) mental illness and substance misuse in these groups. Of all personality disorder clusters, it is the dramatic/emotional/erratic Cluster B disorders that are most associated with early institutional care and criminality (Coid *et al.*, 2006). Such disorders are sometimes co-morbid with conditions on DSM Axis 1 (mental illness, learning disability, substance use). Personality disorders are particularly common in prisoners: a large survey of psychiatric morbidity in England and Wales found 78% male remand prisoners had personality disorder, 64% of sentenced males and 50% of sentenced females (Singleton, Meltzer and Gatward, 1998). A more systematic review by Fazel and Danesh (2002) found 65% of males and 42% of female offenders had some type of personality disorder; of this cohort, 47% of the males had ASPD and 15% BPD; for females these proportions were 21% and 25% for ASPD and BPD, respectively. These results show female offending is disproportionately related to problems associated with BPD, relative to males.

Comorbidity of mental illness and personality disorder

Comorbidity of Axis I (mental illness) and Axis II (personality disorder) pathology is common (APA, 1994). These patterns of association mirror what might be anticipated in terms of the neurotic nature of many mental disorders; thus, mood disorders, phobias, anxiety and panic, and eating disorders are all associated with avoidant and borderline personality disorder. Persons with obsessive-compulsive problems are also commonly diagnosed with avoidant and paranoid personality disorder, as well as obsessive-compulsive personality disorder; persons with schizophrenia have an affinity for schizotypal and paranoid personality disorders; and substance misusers commonly have ASPD and BPD. These associations should not dictate a misapprehension that causality runs from mental disorder to offending; a study of 280 Swedish offenders were compared for mental illness, psychopathy, substance use and criminal offending. Psychopathic, but otherwise non-mentally ill, offenders committed more number of offences per year when at liberty to do so than persons with schizophrenia alone. Persons with concurrent psychosis and psychopathy committed more offences than persons with schizophrenia alone, and substance misuse did not increase the number of offences committed by either group (Tengström *et al.*, 2004).

Another way of considering the importance of personality disorder relative to more generic mental illness in dually diagnosed offenders is to follow probands longitudinally. Psychotic patients with comorbid personality disorder were significantly more likely to be violent when followed prospectively over two years (Moran *et al.*, 2003). The salience of personality disorder also follows for persons released from high-security British hospitals (e.g., Broadmoor, Ashworth and Rampton). Of 223 conditionally discharged patients from high-security hospitals followed up after release, 74 (38%) were reconvicted, 26% for serious offences. All 10 multiple re-offenders (persons who committed nine or more offences) were male. Those diagnosed with personality disorder were seven times more likely than a person with mental illness to be convicted of a serious offence on release (Jamieson and Taylor, 2004).

A psychological approach

Symptom behaviours Categorized diagnoses are not necessarily genuine natural classes (Kendell and Jablensky, 2003; Williamson and Allman, 2011). Nevertheless, by examining a disorder's symptoms, it is possible to infer where the typical difficulties with a particular syndrome lie. Black *et al.* (2007) screened newly convicted offenders for BPD, and found the frequencies of some symptoms more salient than others; thus, 87% admitted to having impulsive problems, 63% being excessively angry, 48% having unstable mood, 32% having suicidal thoughts and behaviour, 29% having paranoid thoughts, 25% having interpersonal problems, 23% feeling empty, 20% having frantic efforts to avoid abandonment and 10% having identity disturbance. Common symptoms, for example, impulsivity (Gordon and Egan, 2011), are not specific to particular disorders, whereas less-frequent symptoms may effectively differentiate.

Due to disjunctive diagnostic labels, two people with the same personality disorder diagnosis can have differing apparent symptoms. This is because when diagnosis is based on a person having *x* symptoms out of *y* diagnostic signs (e.g., four of seven symptoms), two persons may have only one symptom in common. This can lead to over-broad classification, and is a consequence of the equal weighting given to particular symptoms (Krueger *et al.*, 2011). The method of Rasch scaling personality disorder symptoms enables certain symptoms to be recognized as more central to a clinical problem, rather than all symptoms being equally weighted. When Rasch analysis is employed in this way, generic aspects of personality disorder (e.g., impulsivity) become less central, and a more rational five-dimensional structure emerges (Parker and Hadzi-Pavlovic, 2001).

Personality disorders as extremes of normal behaviour Classically, it is difficult to discern where general extremes of personality begin and end relative to clinical problems, as self-reported and interview-diagnosed personality disorders both appear dimensional and related to broad personality traits (Parker and Barrett, 2000). The aforementioned co-morbidity of personality disorders is common, and suggests discrete personality disorders reflect a smaller set of underlying constructs (Costa and Widiger, 2002; Widiger and Mullins-Sweatt, 2009). Some have called this model the '4As' (*A*ntisocial (or criminal and hostile), *A*social (odd and withdrawn), *A*esthenic (inclined to personal distress) and *A*nankastic (obsessive-compulsive)). The 4As explain most of the variance shared between the 10 core DSM-IV personality disorders (Livesley, Jackson and Schroeder, 1992). A joint factor analysis of the IPDE-SR and the NEO-FFI (which measures the five-factor model of personality, that is, Neuroticism (N), Extraversion (E), Openness (O), Agreeableness (A) and Conscientiousness (C); Costa and McCrae, 1992) on 162 mentally disordered offenders from the United Kingdom found the 4As model loaded rationally with these personality dimensions. The Antisocial dimension (defined by a loading of 0.83 on ASPD, with lower loadings of 0.49 and 0.47 for paranoid and histrionic personality disorder) had loadings of −0.75 and −0.40 for A and C, respectively; for the Asocial dimension (comprising schizotypal, avoidant and paranoid personality disorders), the correlations were 0.64, −0.85 and −0.55 for N, E and C, respectively; for the Aesthenic dimension (histrionic, BPD and avoidant personality disorders), N loaded at 0.44. Finally, the Anankastic dimension (defined by compulsive, narcissistic and paranoid personality disorders) did not show significant loadings for general personality traits (perhaps because such variance was already taken up for the other disorders) (Egan *et al.*, 2003). While O is not generally associated with personality disorder, it is functionally relevant to practice. Piedmont *et al.* (2009) noted that patients unable to consider ideas and feelings can be as much a problem for therapists as a client over-valuing ideas and feelings to the extent that they dominate life and hinder practical functioning. They described this construct as 'experiential permeability', and developed a scale to measure this comprising four dimensions: odd and eccentric interests (intellectual egotism), unrestricted self (autonomy over social rules), rigidity (rules and unreflective routine) and superficiality (unreflective and closed). The first two were positively related to O, whereas the second pair negatively related to O. Greater intellectual egotism and unrestricted sense of self was related to dramatic/emotional/erratic (Cluster B) disorders.

Outcomes in personality disorder

Evidence for the long-term outcome of personality disorder depends partially upon whether the disorder is treatment-seeking or treatment-rejecting (Tyrer *et al.*, 2003). Stone (1993) observed that the best information derives from long-term institutionalized, 'bothersome' conditions that involve some kind of custodial involvement. Less immediately troublesome (to the community) conditions with externalizing ('other-blaming') personality disorders (e.g.,paranoid personality disorder) are inherently hard to follow up, as unless obliged, paranoid or withdrawn persons generally eschew official monitoring. Broadly speaking, persons with 'odd/eccentric' personality disorders (i.e., Cluster A conditions like schizoid or schizotypal personality disorder) tend to remain isolated, marginal and vulnerable to mental illness, perhaps because of the behavioural and genetic continuity between schizotypy and schizophrenia (Fanous *et al.*, 2001). For Cluster B conditions like BPD or ASPD, a wide range of outcomes is possible. Mehlum *et al.* (1994) followed up such patients over 10–25 years, finding 50–60% of persons with a previous diagnosis of BPD made some kind of 'recovery' (relative to the individual's needs and effectiveness). However, another 3–9% of the persons followed up committed suicide, whether intentional or as a consequence of self-harming. Mehlum *et al.* found IQ and creativity were protective factors, perhaps because the individual had some way of articulating or expressing their feelings, whereas a serious history of past abuse was ominous. If emotional flashbacks associated with abuse become overwhelming, the person may seek to harm themselves. Persons with ASPD often show some remission and 'cooling down' (sometimes called 'antisocial burnout'), but this does not occur for those persons who have ASPD and psychopathy (Huchzermeier *et al.*, 2008). The outcomes for persons with narcissistic personality disorder are somewhat similar to those with BPD, in that they are highly variable, with more intelligent and creative persons being able to learn to live with themselves and others. Narcissists present a risk to themselves should they become suicidal from the narcissistic injuries caused by their identity-maintaining false beliefs being exposed by reality and failure (Kohut, 1972). Persons with narcissistic personality disorder make more effective lethal suicidal gestures than impulsive parasuicides generally (Blasco-Fontecilla *et al.*, 2009).

Treatment or Management?

The current view is that it is possible to treat and manage – or at least manage – persons with personality disorder. This is a considerable improvement from when the phrase 'untreatable personality disorder' could be used to exclude a person from psychiatric services, it being reasoned that such patients were best contained by the criminal justice system, and so effectively neglecting duty of care (Maden, 1999). While many physical and mental illnesses are not 'treatable', they remain manageable; IQ cannot be raised in the learning disabled, and alcoholics can relapse after 25 years of sobriety; but both the learning disabled and the alcoholic can, with care, live meaningful lives despite their respective difficulties. Personality-disordered offenders also present specific challenges, for example, poor treatment compliance, shifting problems and goals, and therapeutic focus being sabotaged by regular crises. In such a climate, demoralization can emerge on both sides of the dialogue, evoking the much misunderstood observation that 'nothing works', rather than the subsequent, more nuanced observation, 'something works' (Martinson, 1974, 1979).

Target identification of problematic behaviours

Many aspects of a personality-disordered person's narrative are historic, static and unchangeable; these over-predict behaviour. The past cannot be undone, so it is clinically prudent to target dynamic (i.e., changeable) factors. Finding treatable central targets that give rise to the client's problems is vital, for example, substance misuse, impulse control (addressed in prison 'Stop & Think!' and 'Reasoning and Rehabilitation' programmes (Friendship *et al.*, 2003)), constructive problem-solving strategies (Huband *et al.*, 2007), recognizing triggers to offending, identifying motivations to change lifestyle and reviewing criminogenic cognitions that implicitly maintain the antisocial schema and expectancies that lead a client to present a risk to others (Egan *et al.*, 2000). Whilst criminal cognitions come in many forms, they are easiest classified into 'thoughtless' versus 'callous' types; a person can be made more thoughtful, whereas callousness is more difficult to treat, as it reflects more cruel and sadistic qualities.

One issue in the assessment and treatment of personality-disordered persons is how pathological behaviour within closed or custodial conditions can be assessed. Behavioural approaches to psychological assessment and treatment in the personality-disordered sometimes speak of 'analogue behaviour' arising from functional analyses of an individual (Haynes, 2001; Nelson-Gray and Farmer, 1999). This is sometimes called offence-paralleling behaviour (Jones, 2004), and could be seen in a schizotypal person's search for esoteric information to confirm their magical-supernatural model of the world, or within-custody criminal activity committed by a person with ASPD. Extrapolation from offence to context reflects dispositional attributional assumptions, but contextual factors are also relevant (Daffern *et al.*, 2008, 2009).

A broad-spectrum approach

No treatment approach has a clear monopoly on effectiveness. Duggan *et al.* (2007) provide a conceptual model that suggests professionals start by considering what therapeutic tasks are core to the treatment process for the individual (although all personality-disordered persons (and maybe all patients) require a therapist who provides 'a secure base' to manage attachment problems (Agrawal *et al.*, 2004; Romano, Fitzpatrick and Janzen, 2008)). Grencavage and Norcross (1990) suggested that whatever the favoured clinical model, the focus has to be on the need for change and how this can occur. Moreover, all require the development of a therapeutic alliance, an opportunity for the client to vent and share their experience, to acquire and rehearse new behaviours and, the inculcation of a belief in the client that some kind of positive change is possible. Much of therapy is generic; all involve an intense, emotionally charged relationship with person/group; a rationale or myth explaining the distress and methods of dealing with this distress; provision of new information about the future, the source of the problem and possible alternatives giving hope of relief; non-specific methods of boosting self-esteem; the provision of success experiences; the facilitation of emotional arousal and control; and all take place in a locale designated as a place of healing (Frank, 1985). Whatever the client or the disorder, a good therapist helps develop and maintain a therapeutic alliance, helps an individual deal with any behavioural disturbance they have (e.g., self-harming behaviour, violence), and helps the individual integrate the different aspects of their self in a more effective way.

The evidence base

One problem with psychological treatments is the nature of the evidence base. Controlled trials lend themselves more effectively to some kinds of intervention than others; they are hard to do in psychotherapy, but there are plenty of studies demonstrating the effectiveness of cognitive-behavioural interventions. Absence of evidence is not evidence of absence, so little evidence for a particular intervention does not mean a particular treatment is ineffective. However, a person proposing that a therapeutic approach works needs to demonstrate proof of this over other approaches. Research into psychotherapy is not easy; persons with personality disorder are inherently hard to study and follow up over time, and interventions may be complex and multifaceted. Patients may engage with a therapist and treatment or not; clinically, priority must be for persons with pressing difficulties, and the unprincipled (or perhaps pragmatic) clinical researcher may recruit amenable and biddable patient participants to minimize cohort attrition. In such circumstances, the basic principle to avoid experimental confounding – random allocation to conditions – may be compromised. Lastly, there is the question of outcome; behavioural outcome provides one criterion endpoint, self-report on a questionnaire another.

One can structure systematic reviews in the area of personality disorder in terms of PICO: *P*opulation, *I*ntervention type, *C*omparator (controls/comparison to data norms) and *O*utcome (self-report, clinical, behavioural). Duggan *et al.*'s (2007) review of PICOed research into the effectiveness of treatment for personality-disordered persons focussed on the *sine qua non* of good methodology, the randomized control trial. They found 27 studies meeting Cochrane criteria for a systematic review (e.g., define the clinical problem, do a proper search of all relevant papers starting from electronic databases, maximally eliminate sources of bias and integrate the results statistically, ideally using meta-analysis). Attachment-based work with partial hospitalization worked best for persons with BPD; psychoeducation was generically helpful; combined therapies (cognitive-behavioural therapies plus appropriate medication) helped persons with multiaxial disorders (i.e., mental illness and personality disorder); dialectical behaviour therapy (DBT), emotion regulation work, schema-focussed work, cognitive-behavioural therapies and manualized therapies were all broadly equivalent in effectiveness for BPD, neurosis and parasuicide; and cognitive-behavioural therapies worked best for ASPD and substance misuse. Roth and Fonagy (2004) similarly show that psychotherapy (in particular, structured interventions based around cognitive-behavioural therapy) is effective for managing and treating aspects of neurotic and behavioural disorders.

Working with persons with personality disorder

Health professionals ideally seek to understand, respect, care for, positively support, accept and maintain an unconditional positive regard for a client. These intentions can be profoundly challenged when working with personality-disordered offenders. It takes a special kind of person and unusual skills to find rapport and an effective working relationship with a child molester, rapist, wife-beater or killer. Not everyone can focus on the problematic behaviour of such clients and remain respectful. However, as personality-disordered offenders are generally very aware of what they have done and how they are perceived, one limits oneself by adopting an overt moral position, as frank communication during a session is hindered. Transparency of intent is crucial for a personality disorder service, as is a good structure, theoretically coherent treatment models, and a clear treatment alliance between therapist and patient. Services should integrate with other necessary services and provide long-term follow up. McMurran and Duggan (2005) systematized the treatment process within one specialist UK unit for the care of personality-disordered offenders into three broad areas: psychoeducation, the control of behaviour and emotions via structured manualized interventions (akin to those used in the UK Prison Service to make people 'Stop & Think!', control angry aggression, address substance use, criminal thinking and beliefs), and generic social skills. This structure optimizes evidence-based practice, ensuring treatment integrity and replicability. Within this setting, interpersonal work and treatment implementation also occurs. For example, clients can put into practice competencies discussed in therapeutic sessions (e.g., learning to tolerate themselves, their triggers, and the demands placed on tolerance by living alongside other personality-disordered offenders). As an individual becomes more stable, they form a more internal locus of control (Newton, 1998). With more time, the offender comes to understand how they create their own environment, and how this transacts with their own identity (Anderson, Buckley and Carnegey, 2008; Dolan, Warren and Norton, 1997). This process of insight necessitates the offender integrating an awareness of their personality disorder into their self-schema so they can be mindful of their own behaviour and their effect on others – and start to behave differently.

Starting work with such patients

The practicalities of a treatment process for a personality-disordered offender depend upon the context in which the professional is based and the resources available. However, all work should commence with the collation of a thorough history based on official records as well as a clinical interview; discrepancies can be approached as areas to discuss. Appropriate formal assessment is helpful so any diagnostic issues can be resolved, along with, if necessary, any specialist medical services or detoxification. Next, one should discuss behaviours that may have caused problems for the client. They may or may not acknowledge their difficulties. This awareness enables you to position them within the 'Stages of Change' model (pre-contemplation, contemplation, planning, action, maintenance; Prochaska and Norcross, 2001) and nudge the person through the stages using motivational interviewing techniques (Miller and Rollnick 2002). Therapies helpful with personality-disordered persons include DBT, which addresses impulse control and risk reduction needs, the ever-popular (and effective) cognitive-behavioural therapy, schema-focussed therapies (mostly for BPD) and mentalization-based treatments (Bateman and Fonagy, 2008). Therapeutic interactions/interventions with personality-disordered offenders are psychosocial. All seek to engender hope, coaching skills and competencies; facilitate motivation to change; increase the ability of the client to speak comfortably about their difficulties; and maybe face some unpleasant memories and responsibilities. All seek a client to become competent at evaluating the positives and negatives of a situation, rather than avoiding any discussion of such behaviour.

Substance misuse: relapses and abstinence violation effects

As persons become more reflective and open, offence- and risk-related interventions become increasingly feasible, for example, alcohol and substance misuse work (or, if this remains somewhat ambitious given where the client is in their process of change, harm reduction strategies). This can be a good time to explore a client's beliefs about their substance use, which is often rather more ambivalent than it would seem; once persons have acquired a chemical tolerance, they no longer enjoy drug use as much, and may spend much time chasing increasingly elusive highs. Diminishing returns from drug use along with the behavioural chaos of the hard-drug-using community often prompt older drug users to tire of the lifestyle. Typically, progress with a client is followed by an episode of backsliding. While this can be perceived as catastrophic by the client or the therapist, lapse is not relapse so much as an opportunity to review skills and motivation: '*What happened?*' '*What went wrong?*' '*What could you do better next time?*', '*Is anything else needed?*' Many lapses start with 'apparently (or seemingly) irrelevant decisions' and overwhelming desires for their problematic pleasure ('the problem of immediate gratification'). The precarious reasoning involved in such decisions is always worthy of exploration, particularly as it can lead to an 'abstinence violation effect', whereby a lapse becomes a genuine relapse. When lapse occurs, it is important that the client understands what happened that led to their slip, and how things could be done differently to better manage comparable future risks (Brandon, Vidrine and Litvin, 2007).

Stages of change and motivational interviewing

The 'Stages of Change' model (Prochaska and Norcross, 2001) is deservedly well-regarded for its ability to encompass the dynamics of change for populations as disparate as dieters and drug misusers. Persons not countenancing change and happy functioning with whatever problem requires change are said to be 'pre-contemplative'. Those who acknowledge their problem and discuss it (even if they do not take any action) are said to be at the 'contemplative' stage. Persons who move from discussing the problem to preparing to act and planning (e.g., a person who, feeling plump after Christmas, buys a gym membership in January) is said to be at the 'preparation' stage. Putting the plan into action is known as the 'action' stage. Many persons who buy a gym membership in January cease going to the gym by March, demonstrating that action can be hard to sustain; thus, the model also has a 'maintenance' stage, which focuses on maintaining any gains made. A once plump person who does not maintain their dietary and exercise regime will regain weight, and a violent person who resumes substance misuse greatly increases their risk of future violent offending. Thus, maintenance is key to consolidating personal advances. The final stage of the Stages of Change model is 'termination' – where the problem is extinguished. This is a somewhat hypothetical position, as without maintenance, relapse to the problem behaviour is always possible; having beaten a four-year heroin addiction in the 1950s, jazz musician Miles Davis succumbed to a further decade of heroin and cocaine addiction that led to him spending most of the 1970s as a recluse. The 'Stages of Change' model has typical 'stage' model problems; for example, there are no real 'stages', so much as overlapping continua; it is not causal so much as descriptive. Nevertheless, if one can work collaboratively with a client and give them ownership of the change sought, and a desire for improvement, there is at least some hope of progress; meta-analysis of the theory of planned behaviour (common in health psychology interventions) suggests that perceived behavioural control and intention significantly improves the change process (Armitage and Conner, 2001).

Movement between stages of change can be difficult. One method is to use motivational interviewing (Miller and Rollnick, 2002). This involves techniques such as expressing empathy with a person without sympathizing (and thus becoming complicit with some of the maladaptive strategies that may have been used in their past). A good therapist not only sees the world as it is but becomes meta-cognitive in their ability to also see the person as they see themselves; in developing discrepancies between how a person is and how they present themselves, cognitive dissonance can be manipulated, such that the person becomes more insightful. Developing discrepancies must be done tactfully, as the professional should avoid argument; reflexive psychological reactance – and particularly a personality-disordered person's reactance – means if told to *not* do something, they will quite possibly do what they were asked to refrain from with maximum prejudice and provocation, irrespective of how unhelpful and self-destructive it is. Rather than arguing, motivational interviewing advises 'roll with the resistance', for example, putting the questions and behaviour they generate back to the client as another way of getting them to discuss their difficulties and generate their own solutions. Persons who generate workable solutions need their self-efficacy supported. Personality-disordered offenders often have considerable interpersonal incompetence; so if a person makes behavioural adjustments that prove effective, such advances must be consolidated (Bandura, 2001). The technique apparently works: meta-analysis of motivational interviewing methods show a moderate effect size in facilitating change within substance misusers (Burke, Arkowitz and Menchola, 2003).

'Going inside'

While change can be facilitated, personality disorders are not treated in a couple of brief sessions of psychotherapy. One task is to enable clients to tolerate difficult emotions (distress tolerance), for example, being able to constructively discuss painful topics and experiences (including how they may have hurt other people). Providing individuals with the verbal tools and knowledge to recognize, differentiate and label different types of emotional states enables the client to better articulate their feelings, improving self-talk and monitoring. Individuals with poor social problem-solving skills need practice to become more competent in their coping abilities, and therapeutic sessions are often helpful for rehearsing and reviewing such processes. Mindfulness techniques (i.e., observing one's thoughts and physical feelings) help create conscious awareness where once was unthinking reaction. When exploring the nature of this reaction, it is crucial to differentiate assertive, aggressive and passive-aggressive, which can reduce the hostility the patient apparently presents, whether intentionally or inadvertently. Thinking through the interpersonal problems they face, the personality-disordered offender may become better able to generate feasible solutions without resorting to aggression.

Maintaining rapport under difficult circumstances

Whatever approach is adopted with a personality-disordered offender, therapeutic rapport is needed. There are a number of ways a therapeutic rapport can complicate the interpersonal process between a personality-disordered client and the therapist. If a therapy is a mandatory part of their treatment, attending sessions may reflect compulsion more than a genuine wish to change; this is incompatible with the ideal of engagement reflecting collaborative work and accepted treatment targets. The patient may have polarized expectations of therapy; many have been seeing professionals of various kinds since they were small children, so remain realistically cynical, whereas others might over-idealize a therapist they find inspiring, expecting greater improvement than is likely. These expectations reflect the denigration–idealization continuum of personality disorder. Clients who have been subject to unfavourable reports may be cautious about disclosing information in an interview, limiting engagement. Others are ambivalent about the need for help, apparently liking their lives and lifestyles. Some realistically worry that becoming less violent or intimidating will lead to retaliatory violence from persons they have previously harmed, or that becoming more emotionally open will make them less able to cope with their memories and conscience. People may create personal myths to help explain their lives, and disabusing patients of their expedient fictions may be traumatic. Over-idealism followed by failure helps maintain a patient's mistrust and nihilism regarding the therapeutic process. Lastly, there is transference and boundaries; both have two sides, and patients and therapists may push them in either direction, sabotaging the interpersonal process personality disorder treatment requires.

Cognitive and dialectical behaviour therapy approaches

Evidence-based therapeutic approaches to personality disorder build on the cognitive-behavioural traditions of clinical psychology. The guidelines produced by the UK's National Institute of Clinical Excellence on ASPD and BPD exemplify this literature (NICE, 2009a, b). Effective care recognizes that thoughts mediate and maintain feelings and behaviours (even if, in many cases, persons may not be aware of or able to articulate their mental lives, e.g., the anankastic). In principle, given time and therapy, patients come to understand how their behaviours maintain attitudes towards themselves and the world outside. However, one difficulty with personality-disordered patients is their disorder; by the time they are being seen by a clinician within a forensic setting, their behaviour has been sufficiently troublesome to draw the attention of criminal justice and mental health systems. This may require different types of intervention. The development and implementation of DBT (Linehan, 1993a, b) has increased a practitioner's ability to facilitate change in disordered behaviour, as the therapy inherently recognizes many of a personality-disordered individual's problems are maladroit attempts to cope with emotional arousal (anger, distress, shame, misplaced affection, etc.). The focus of DBT on teaching and inculcating behavioural skills related to emotion regulation and improved interpersonal competency is thus a critical step in treatment of the personality-disordered offender with BPD.

Linehan's model of personality disorder (Linehan, 1993a) recognizes that individuals have heritable difficulties that give rise to difficulties regulating emotions (interestingly, BPD and ASPD share a common genetic basis; Torgersen *et al.*, 2008). These distressing emotions are real to the client, but sometimes exaggerated such that others may not appreciate the intensity of the feelings of the patient. As such, a personality-disordered person's feelings are often invalidated by their social environment, their feelings being 'dismissed' and 'denied'; at worst, they may be told what they should think and feel about a situation, further distorting their affective experience. In extremely invalidating environments, a patient may experience abusive acts (whether emotional, physical or sexual, or, not infrequently, all three) that are not stopped or adequately penalized. I have seen clients who were variously sexually abused in religious boarding schools as well as children's homes. The victims appealed to official and familial carers, who said priests or registered social workers would not do such things. The abuse continued, and the victims learnt to not trust people who professed to care for them, their only way to manage assaults and abuse being to dissociate. In this way, already disturbed attachments are further sabotaged, and the client becomes an adult who trusts nobody, scorns those who affect to care, the inconsistency of law enforcement, and becomes able to detach from feelings that would provide somatic markers of emotional arousal.

DBT is a highly structured programmatic approach. It encourages the person to better label their experiences, better regulate their emotions, and to accept their experience as one possible (if not ideal or fixed) response to events. The therapy combines generic elements from behavioural therapy, for example, self-monitoring, and focuses on skills and enhancing capabilities to overcome practical difficulties, rather than an infinite regress of explanations and interpretations that still leave the patient unable to respond to day-to-day life. Some cognitive work also occurs; emotional attributions need to be changed, attention needs to be refocussed and constructive emotions must be recognized; anger can be a motivator under the right conditions. DBT also allows some therapeutic irreverence. This is the idea that humour and irony can get to places an earnest and sombre approach cannot, and that judicious use of humour arising from the dark farce of life may lead to a moment of genuine connection between client and therapist.

DBT is an eclectic mix, and, like many psychological therapies using a variety of approaches, it is sometimes unclear what is the active element in the treatment, or whether it is some synergy of elements, some active and some inert. Inhibitions to change are explored, as are the cognitions and reinforcement contingencies behind such inhibition (or engagement). Like all skills-oriented cognitive therapies, DBT seeks the generalization of acquired skills in therapeutic sessions to the patient's natural environment through rehearsed strategies and behavioural experiments, enabling new competencies. The work is also collaborative; patient and therapist have to mutually agree on treatment goals and methods. A therapist using DBT is encouraged to approach the client with 'radical genuineness', whereby they occasionally give their natural response (rather than passively accept or reflect everything they hear). One could argue radical genuineness, whereby one seeks to see a patient as a 'normal' person, is indeed radical. In the rush to 'care', the normality of patients is sometimes missed. Patients often have lives beyond their difficulties, and may relate effectively and functionally in many ways. This partial competency may provide a basis from which to build.

A great psychological truth indicative of theory of mind is that you should see people as they see themselves, even if their self-deceptions are also apparent; human life is difficult without such double-think. Thus, DBT advises that the therapist recognize that a person's (mis)perceptions may be true for them at some level. Obvious efforts to try to change somebody's mind often provoke psychological reactance (a negative emotional reaction to impositions challenging our autonomy; Brehm and Brehm, 1981). Partially accepting how the person sees the world facilitates better communication, as the client is not so heavily censoring from the therapist what they really mean and feel. This approach avoids over-simplifying issues and ignoring the patient's view. The vast majority of mentally disordered offenders come from very poor material, emotional and social conditions, and expecting an over-intellectualized model of any kind to help them shows a massive ignorance and disrespect for the difficult lives our clients have, and which we are largely unable to change. Lastly, the therapist helps patients become better able to anticipate, recognize and tolerate potentially distressing situations and problems. This is the first step in resolving problems more effectively. Ultimately DBT seeks to inculcate 'mindfulness' in patients. This is a concept which derives from Buddhist approaches to psychotherapy in which one seeks to not judge; to observe, describe, participate and focus in the world; and to be practical in one's engagement. The evidence for DBT is promising; meta-analyses show that patients are less likely to drop out of treatment (Barnicot *et al.*, 2011), and that DBT is particularly effective in reducing suicidal and self-injurious behaviour (Kliem, Kröger and Kosfelder, 2011); integrated reviews show that DBT is now the preferred treatment for BPD and impulsivity-related difficulties (Lynch *et al.*, 2007). Though DBT has not proved so effective for other personality disorders, BPD and ASPD are the most common, and present some of the most pressing clinical needs. DBT is thus a good basis from which to build future therapeutic developments.

Problems: the presumptions of psychotherapy

It is nevertheless legitimate to ask whether the assumptions of CBT and DBT are necessarily compatible with persons who have personality disorder. Much CBT research derives from motivated patients who have good premorbid functioning and healthy, stable personalities; some clinical trials actively seek persons who do not have co-morbid conditions, and research from the United States is quite often done by practitioners with private patients. This is incomparable with typically socially excluded, unemployed and uneducated milieu which defines most mentally disordered offenders. CBT builds on practical, positive beliefs that encourage progress like 'I can trust my therapist' and 'I can make changes in my life that can make things better'. With such positives *in situ*, the patient can be taught about distorted thinking, dysfunctional behaviour and problem solving, and examine the schema that lead to negative automatic thoughts, unhelpful expectancies and cognitive biases. This can only be done if a good therapeutic rapport exists.

Whatever theoretical orientation you take with personality-disordered offenders, you need to gear intervention to clear, shared and collaborative target problems, as clients need to have ownership of their own problems and the potential solutions. Personality-disordered clients have problems that typically emerge in social interactions. For this reason, you need to ensure the quality and integrity of the therapist–client relationship. The disturbed attachments fundamental to personality-disordered persons make such clients sensitive to superficial concern, and providing the 'secure base' from which the client may make some recovery necessitates your genuine engagement; services which emphasize fast throughput and short sessions are unlikely to be very helpful for such persons. A corollary of being with a client for a longer run of sessions is that the earlier stages should not involve their extensive self-disclosure, as they need time to learn to trust, and for you to understand them. In discussing plans with the client, try to identify and address the client's fears before implementing changes; a person who has derived his identity and security (and possibly livelihood) from violence may be very ambivalent about becoming more empathic (which will reduce their ability to be violent effectively) or less violent (which may mean they become subject to reprisals).

An inability to recognize the context the person comes from (and will most likely return to) is endemic in blithe therapeutic approaches to offenders, and probably contributes to unsuccessful interventions. The assumption that a person will complete homework tasks may work with some, but for mentally disordered offenders you need to gear homework to what is quick and tractable. Be realistic about what can be achieved, and avoid setting someone up to fail; better a cumulative percentage improvement in the right direction than a yo-yoing of responses. Slow but genuine reliable change aggregates over time, and can be very effective, as problematic behaviour often only occurs once a person's criterion for distress or agitation is met. Reducing the probability of reaching this critical criterion is itself a key clinical target.

Conclusion

This chapter has sought to cover a large literature from a somewhat pragmatic perspective. Healing and helping personality-disordered offenders is not an intellectual game for professionals to have their pet theories confirmed, so much as a way to create a practical change in an individual who becomes better able to live with themselves and others, and to thus have less recourse to hurting others as they live their lives or manage their distress. There is much the therapist cannot do; the economic traps people are in cannot be solved by psychology; though people can be helped to live with their traumatic childhoods, this is rather less satisfactory than having avoided abuse in the first place. The hurt an offender has caused cannot be undone, and victim(s) are generally given less care and support than assailants. Such matters reflect the remit of society; how it decides to allocate resources, and how people choose to live their lives.

Acknowledgement

Many thanks to Elaine Fehrman of Rampton Hospital for her kind comments on an earlier version of this chapter.

References

Agrawal, H.R., Gunderson, J., Holmes, B.M. and Lyons-Ruth, K. (2004) Attachment studies with Borderline patients: a review. *Harvard Review of Psychiatry*, 12, 94–104.

Anderson, C.A., Buckley, K.E. and Carnagey, N.L. (2008) Creating your own hostile environment: a laboratory examination of trait aggressiveness and the violence escalation cycle. *Personality and Social Psychology Bulletin*, 34, 462–473.

American Psychiatric Association (1994) *Diagnostic and Statistical Manual of Mental Disorders*, 4th edn, American Psychiatric Press, Washington, DC.

American Psychiatric Association (2000) *Diagnostic and Statistical Manual of Mental Disorders*, 4th edn, text rev., American Psychiatric Press, Washington, DC.

Armitage, C.J. and Conner, M. (2001) Efficacy of the theory of planned behaviour: a meta-analytic review. *British Journal of Social Psychology*, 40, 471–499.

Bandura, A. (2001) Social cognitive theory: an agentic perspective. *Annual Review of Psychology*, 52, 1–26.

Barnicot, K., Katsakou, C., Marougka, S. and Priebe, S. (2011) Treatment completion in psychotherapy for borderline personality disorder – a systematic review and meta-analysis. *Acta Psychiatrica Scandinavica*, 123, 327–338.

Bateman, A.W. and Fonagy, P. (2008) Comorbid antisocial and borderline personality disorders: mentalization-based treatment. *Journal of Clinical Psychology*, 64, 181–194.

Black, D.W., Guntera, T., Allena, J. *et al.* (2007) Borderline personality disorder in male and female offenders newly committed to prison. *Comprehensive Psychiatry*, 48, 400–405.

Blasco-Fontecilla, H., Baca-Garcia, E., Dervic, K. *et al.* (2009) Specific features of suicidal behavior in patients with narcissistic personality disorder. *Journal of Clinical Psychiatry*, 70, 1583–1587.

Brandon, T.H., Vidrine, J.I. and Litvin, E.B. (2007) Relapse and relapse prevention. *Annual Review of Clinical Psychology*, 3, 257–284.

Brehm, J.W. and Brehm, S.S. (1981) *Psychological Reactance: A Theory of Freedom and Control*, Academic Press, San Diego.

Burke, B.L., Arkowitz, H. and Menchola, M. (2003) The efficacy of motivational interviewing: a meta-analysis of controlled clinical trials. *Journal of Consulting and Clinical Psychology*, 71, 843–861.

Cohen, B.J., Nestadt, G., Samuels, J.F. *et al.* (1994) Personality disorder in later life: a community study. *British Journal of Psychiatry*, 165, 493–499.

Coid, J., Yang, M., Tyrer, P. *et al.* (2006) Prevalence and correlates of personality disorder in Great Britain. *British Journal of Psychiatry*, 188, 423–431.

Costa, P.T. and McCrae, R.R. (1992) *The NEO PI-R Professional Manual*, Psychological Assessment Resources, Odessa.

Costa, P.T. and Widiger, T.A. (2002) *Personality Disorders and the Five Factor Model of Personality*, American Psychological Association, Washington, DC.

Daffern, M., Howells, K., Stacey, J. *et al.* (2008) Is sexually abusive behaviour in personality disordered inpatients analogous to sexual offences committed prior to hospitalization? *Journal of Sexual Aggression*, 14, 123–133.

Daffern, M., Howells, K., Mannion, A. and Tonkin, M. (2009) A test of methodology intended to assist detection of aggressive offence paralleling behaviour within secure settings. *Legal and Criminological Psychology*, 14, 213–226.

Dolan, B., Warren, F. and Norton, K. (1997) Change in borderline symptoms one year after therapeutic community treatment for severe personality disorder. *British Journal of Psychiatry*, 171, 274–279.

Duggan, C., Huband, N., Smailagic, N. *et al.* (2007) The use of psychological treatments for people with personality disorder: a systematic review of randomised control trials. *Personality and Mental Health*, 1, 95–125.

Egan, V. (2011) Individual differences and antisocial behavior, in *Handbook of Individual Differences* (eds A. Furnham, S. von Stumm and K. Petredies), Wiley-Blackwell, Oxford, pp. 512–537.

Egan, V., McMurran, M., Richardson, C. and Blair, M. (2000) Criminal cognitions and personality: what does the PICTS really measure? *Criminal Behaviour and Mental Health*, 10, 170–184.

Egan, V., Austin, E., Elliot, D. *et al.* (2003) Personality traits, personality disorders and sensational interests in mentally disordered offenders. *Legal and Criminological Psychology*, 8, 51–62.

Fanous, A., Gardner, C., Walsh, D. and Kendler, K.S. (2001) Relationship between positive and negative symptoms of schizophrenia and schizotypal symptoms in non-psychotic relatives. *Archives of General Psychiatry*, 58, 669–673.

Fazel, S. and Danesh, J. (2002) Serious mental disorder in 23000 prisoners: a systematic review of 62 surveys. *Lancet*, 359, 545–550.

Frank, J. (1985) Therapeutic components shared by all psychotherapies, in *Cognition and Psychotherapy* (eds M. Mahoney and A. Freeman), Plenum, New York, pp. 49–79.

Friendship, F., Blud, L., Erikson, M. *et al.* (2003) Cognitive behavioural treatment for imprisoned offenders: an evaluation of HM Prison Service's cognitive skills programmes. *Legal and Criminological Psychology*, 8, 103–114.

Gordon, V. and Egan, V. (2011) What self-report impulsivity measure best predicts criminal convictions and prison breaches of discipline? *Psychology, Crime & Law*, 17, 305–318.

Grencavage, L.M. and Norcross, J.C. (1990) Where are the commonalities among the therapeutic common factors? *Professional Psychology: Research and Practice*, 21, 372–378.

Haynes, S.N. (2001) Clinical applications of analogue behavioral observation: dimensions of psychometric evaluation. *Psychological Assessment*, 13, 73–85.

Hemphill, J.F., Hare, R.D. and Wong, S. (1998) Psychopathy and recidivism: a review. *Legal and Criminological Psychology*, 3, 139–170.

Huband, N., McMurran, M., Evans, C. and Duggan, C. (2007) Social problem-solving plus psychoeducation for adults with personality disorder: a pragmatic randomised controlled trial. *British Journal of Psychiatry*, 190, 307–313.

Huchzermeier, C., Geiger, F., Köhler, D. *et al.* (2008) Are there age-related effects in antisocial personality disorders and psychopathy? *Journal of Forensic and Legal Medicine*, 15, 213–218.

Jamieson, L. and Taylor, P.J. (2004) A reconviction study of (high security) hospital patients. *British Journal of Criminology*, 44, 783–802.

Johnson, J.G., Cohen, P., Kasen, S. *et al.* (2000) Age-related change in personality disorder trait levels between early adolescence and adulthood: a community-based longitudinal investigation. *Acta Psychiatrica Scandinavica*, 102, 265–275.

Jones, L.F. (2004) Offence Paralleling Behaviour (OPB) as a framework for assessment and interventions with offenders, in *Applying Psychology to Forensic Practice* (eds A. Needs and G. Towl), Blackwell, Oxford, pp. 34–63.

Kendell, R. and Jablensky, A. (2003) Distinguishing between the validity and utility of psychiatric diagnoses. *American Journal of Psychiatry*, 160, 4–12.

Kliem, S., Kröger, C. and Kosfelder, J. (2011) Dialectical behavior therapy for borderline personality disorder: a meta-analysis using mixed-effects modeling. *Journal of Consulting and Clinical Psychology*, 78, 936–951.

Kohut, H. (1972) Thoughts on narcissism and narcissistic rage, in *The Search for the Self*, vol. 2, International Universities Press, New York, pp. 615–658.

Krueger, R.F., Eaton, N.R., Clark, L.A. *et al.* (2011) Deriving an empirical structure of personality pathology for DSM-5. *Journal of Personality Disorders*, 25, 170–191.

Linehan, M.M. (1993a) *Cognitive-Behavioral Treatment of Borderline Personality Disorder*, Guildford Press, New York.

Linehan, M.M. (1993b) *Skills Training Manual for Treating Borderline Personality Disorder*, Guilford Press, New York.

Livesley, W.J., Jackson, D.N. and Schroeder, M.L. (1992) Factorial structure of traits delineating personality disorders in clinical and general population samples. *Journal of Abnormal Psychology*, 101, 432–440.

Lynch, T.R., Trost, W.T., Salsman, N. and Linehan, M.M. (2007) Dialectical behaviour therapy for borderline personality disorder. *Annual Review of Clinical Psychology*, 3, 181–205.

Maden, T. (1999) Treating offenders with personality disorder. *Psychiatric Bulletin*, 23, 707–710.

Martinson, R. (1974) What works? – questions and answers about prison reform. *Public Interest*, 35, 22–54.

Martinson, R. (1979) New findings, new reviews: a note of caution regarding sentencing reform. *Hofstra Law Review*, 7, 243–258.

Mattia, J.I. and Zimmerman, M. (2001) Epidemiology, in *Handbook of Personality Disorder* (ed. J.W. Livesley), Guilford Press, New York.

McCrone, P., Dhanasiri, S. and Patel, A. (2008) *Paying the Price: The Cost of Mental Health Care in England to 2026*, King's Fund, London.

McMurran, M. and Duggan, C. (2005) The manualization of a treatment programme for personality disorder. *Criminal Behaviour and Mental Health*, 15, 17–27.

Mehlum, L., Friis, S., Vaglum, P. and Karterud, S. (1994) The longitudinal pattern of suicidal behaviour in borderline personality disorder: a prospective follow-up study. *Acta Psychiatrica Scandinavica*, 90, 124–130.

Miller, W.R. and Rollnick, S. (2002) *Motivational Interviewing: Preparing People for Change*, 2nd edn, Guilford Press, New York.

Moran, P., Walsh, E., Tyrer, P. *et al.* (2003) Impact of comorbid personality disorder on violence in psychosis: report from the UK700 trial. *British Journal of Psychiatry*, 182, 129–134.

National Institute of Health and Clinical Excellence (2009a) *Borderline Personality Disorder: Treatment and Management*, National Institute of Health and Clinical Excellence, London.

National Institute of Health and Clinical Excellence (2009b) *Antisocial Personality Disorder: Treatment, Management and Prevention*, National Institute of Health and Clinical Excellence, London.

Nelson-Gray, R.O. and Farmer, R.F. (1999) Behavioral assessment of personality disorders. *Behaviour Research and Therapy*, 37, 347–368.

Newton, M. (1998) Changes in measures of personality, hostility and locus of control during residence in a prison therapeutic community. *Legal and Criminological Psychology*, 3, 209–223.

Parker, G. and Barrett, E. (2000) Personality and personality disorder: current issues and directions. *Psychological Medicine*, 30, 1–9.

Parker, G. and Hadzi-Pavlovic, D. (2001) A question of style: refining the dimensions of personality disorder style. *Journal of Personality Disorders*, 15, 300–318.

Piedmont, R.L., Sherman, M.F., Dy-Liacco, G. *et al.* (2009) Using the five-factor model to identify a new personality disorder domain: the case for experiential permeability. *Journal of Personality and Social Psychology*, 96, 1245–1258.

Prochaska, J.O. and Norcross, J.C. (2001) Stages of change. *Psychotherapy: Theory, Research, Practice, Training*, 38, 443–448.

Romano, V., Fitzpatrick, M. and Janzen, J. (2008) The secure-base hypothesis: global attachment, attachment to counselor, and session exploration in psychotherapy. *Journal of Counseling Psychology*, 55, 495–504.

Roth, A. and Fonagy, P. (2004) *What Works for Whom? A Critical Review of Psychotherapy Research*, 2nd edn, Guilford Press, New York.

Samuels, J.F., Nestadt, G., Romanoski, A.J. *et al.* (1994) DSM-III personality disorders in the community. *American Journal of Psychiatry*, 151, 1055–1062.

Singleton, N., Meltzer, H. and Gatward, R, (1998) *Psychiatric Morbidity among Prisoners in England and Wales*, Stationary Office, London.

Skodol, A., Bender, D.S., Morey, L.C. *et al.* (2011) Personality disorder types proposed for DSM-5. *Journal of Personality Disorders*, 25, 136–169.

Stone, M. (1993) Long-term outcome in personality disorders. *British Journal of Psychiatry*, 162, 299–313.

Tengström, A., Hodgins, S., Grann, M. *et al.* (2004) Schizophrenia and criminal offending: the role of psychopathy and substance use disorders. *Criminal Justice and Behaviour*, 31, 367–391.

Torgersen, S., Czajkowski, N., Jacobson, K.T. *et al.* (2008) Dimensional representations of DSM-IV cluster B personality disorders in a population-based sample of Norwegian twins: a multivariate study. *Psychological Medicine*, 14, 1–9.

Tyrer, P., Mitchard, S., Methuen, C. and Ranger, M. (2003) Treatment-rejecting and treatment-seeking personality disorders: Type R and Type S. *Journal of Personality Disorders*, 17, 265–270.

Widiger, T.A. and Mullins-Sweatt, S.N. (2009) Five-factor model of personality disorder: a proposal for DSM-V. *Annual Review of Clinical Psychology*, 5, 197–220.

Williamson, P. and Allman, J. (2011) *The Human Illnesses*, Oxford University Press, Oxford.

World Health Organization (1992) *International Statistical Classification of Diseases and Related Health Problems, Tenth Revision (ICD-10)*, World Health Organization, Geneva.

Zoccolillo, M., Pickles, A., Quinton, D. and Rutter, M. (1992) The outcome of childhood conduct disorder: implications for defining adult personality disorder and conduct disorder. *Psychological Medicine*, 22, 971–986.

9

Interventions that Work to Stop Intimate Partner Violence

Josilyn Banks, Sheetal Kini and Julia Babcock

University of Houston, USA

In the United States, intimate partner violence (IPV) has become a public health epidemic, affecting about four million women each year (Greenfeld *et al.*, 1998). Battered women experience aggression in varied ways ranging from acts such as pushing, grabbing or slapping to more severe forms such as being hit with a fist or being choked (Straus and Gelles, 1990). The lifetime prevalence rates indicate that approximately 25% of women suffer from physical aggression or sexual assault at the hands of their husbands or intimate partners (Browne, 1993; Tjaden and Thoennes, 2000). While men may be victimized by their partners, about 92% of the crimes are committed by men against women (Tjaden and Thoennes, 2000). However, while these statistics are important to consider, community surveys, such as the National Family Violence Surveys conducted in the United States, suggest that physical IPV perpetration rates are approximately equal for men and women (Straus, 1985, 1990; Straus, Gelles and Steinmetz, 1980). Nevertheless, the majority of research into IPV intervention has focused on male perpetrators. This chapter will review the evidence in this domain, and will therefore provide a focus on male offenders.

The criminal justice system has a history of using social science research to inform their handling of IPV. In the 1970s, lawsuits were brought against police departments for negligence and failure to provide equal protection to female victims from IPV, for example, *Bruno vs. Codd* (1977), *Scott vs. Hart* (1976) and *Thurman vs. City of Torrington* (1984). In each of these cases, the police department discriminated against the assaulted women due to the domestic nature of their complaints. For instance, in the case of *Bruno vs. Codd* (1977), 12 women were denied police assistance despite being assaulted by their partners, with one of the women being assaulted in front of police personnel. Similarly, in *Scott vs. Hart* (1976), four women were denied police protection by receiving close to no response to their attempts of seeking assistance against physical assault. In *Thurman vs. City of Torrington* (1984), estranged wife Tracey Thurman was assaulted by her husband Charles Thurman over a two-year period before the police arrested him and took serious action against him.

Results of the Minneapolis domestic violence experiment (Sherman and Berk, 1984a, b) suggested arrest thwarts IPV recidivism. Replication studies on the effect of arrest on recidivism

What Works in Offender Rehabilitation: An Evidence-Based Approach to Assessment and Treatment, First Edition. Edited by Leam A. Craig, Louise Dixon and Theresa A. Gannon.
© 2013 John Wiley & Sons, Ltd. Published 2013 by John Wiley & Sons, Ltd.

were conducted in six different cities (Berk *et al.*, 1991; Dunford, Huizinga and Elliott, 1990; Hirschel *et al.*, 1990); Pate and Hamilton, 1992; Sherman, Schmidt and Rogan, 1992). While the effects of arrest on IPV recidivism have been re-evaluated and sometimes contradicted, the bottom line appears to be that arrest does indeed lead to fewer police calls and future arrests for IPV (Maxwell, Garner and Fagan, 2002). However, arrest had a deterrent effect only for *employed* men who were batterers (Berk *et al.*, 1992; Sherman, Schmidt and Rogan, 1992). Among unemployed perpetrators, arrest was associated with a significant *increase* in assaults at the six-month follow-up (Pate and Hamilton, 1992). Sherman and colleagues concluded that the data consistently showed that for men with a greater stake in conformity, whom they called the 'socially bonded' men, arrest made them less violent (Sherman *et al.*, 1992). For those with a lesser stake in conformity, or the 'socially marginal' men, arrest made them more violent (Sherman, Schmidt and Rogan, 1992).

Informed by the data, most jurisdictions have implemented a mandatory or 'preferred' arrest policy (Hirschel *et al.*, 2007) and defer adjudication of misdemeanour arrests if the perpetrator attends a comprehensive, state-certified battering intervention programme (Austin and Dankwort, 1999). The goals of this coordinated system are multifaceted: (i) rehabilitation, (ii) punishment and (iii) avoiding overcrowding of jails. Channelling perpetrators into battering intervention programmes also saves taxpayers' money. For example, in one jurisdiction, if the court mandated 30 days in jail plus one year's probation, the cost to taxpayers is approximately $2130. However, by mandating rehabilitation, the cost is $264 to complete a 12-week programme, with 50% of the fee billed to the batterer (Jones, 2000). While the goals and cost savings are laudable, whether this hybrid judicial/therapeutic system is effective in reducing recidivism is a matter of debate.

Some scholars and most practitioners in the field argue that the system is working to reduce IPV and keep women safe (Gondolf, 2007). We argue that there is great room for improvement in developing interventions that function to reduce IPV recurrence. Our meta-analysis of the empirical research on battering intervention programmes, entitled 'Does Batterers' Treatment Work?' (Babcock, Green and Robie, 2004), concluded that, overall, batterer intervention programmes have only a small effect on reducing IPV recidivism. No differences in recidivism were found based on the type of intervention or treatment length. We also surmised that the *better* designed the research study, the *worse* the outcomes were likely to be. Tightly controlled, randomized clinical trials where judges mandate batterers into a battering intervention programme versus no treatment, or an alternative sanction, are rare because they are expensive, difficult to conduct and rife with politics. Across the five controlled, randomized clinical trials conducted before 2004, battering interventions led to 5% more men stopping violence as compared to men who did not attend treatment ($D < 0.13$; $D < 0.50$ = 'small'). Since then, only one more randomized clinical trial of battering interventions has been conducted (Labriola, Rempel and Davis, 2008), with similar disappointing results. Comparing a Duluth model battering intervention programme to judicial monitoring, there was slight decrease in recidivism based on victim report ($D = 0.11$) and a slight increase in recidivism based on police reports ($D = -0.12$). In general, non-controlled programme evaluations found a larger impact on recidivism, although regardless of the type of study, the impact of battering interventions on recidivism remains small ($D < 0.35$). Adding extrajudicial monitoring does not appear to make the intervention more effective (Rempel, Labriola and Davis, 2008).

What to make of the small impact of battering intervention programmes on subsequent violence? Perhaps our outcome measures of cessation of violence, that is, no re-occurrence of IPV as reported by the partner and no arrests for IPV during the follow-up period, were too stringent.

One could argue that a decrease in the frequency of being abused is good enough. Or perhaps battering intervention programmes, as they typically are administered in the United States, are insufficient. Just as arrest works only for some batterers, so too may battering intervention programmes. We will argue that arrest is sufficient for the 'socially bonded' subset of batterers, and battering intervention has no additive effect. Yet, ironically, our existing interventions may be geared towards these men who are unlikely to benefit. For batterers who are unmotivated to change, are hardened criminals and have psychopathic traits, existing interventions may be insufficient or even be counterproductive. We aim to educate the reader about the current 'go to' interventions used in the rehabilitation of batterers, and the theoretical frameworks that shape these interventions. Furthermore, we analyse the efficacy of therapeutic strategies such as motivational interviewing (MI) and Risk–Need–Responsivity (RNR)-based approaches that improve existing batterer interventions. Additionally, we discuss a relatively new classification system of batterers, and how this classification system could shape the future of batterer rehabilitation. We will begin by reviewing the commonly administered battering intervention programmes here.

Current Batterer Interventions

The two dominant interventions sanctioned by most states are the cognitive behavioural therapy (CBT) and feminist psychoeducation approach known as the Duluth model (Pence and Paymar, 1993). These two models have been used separately and in combination generally in group formats. Manuals have been published on both models, but every agency has the freedom to modify and blend modes of intervention, so much so that the distinction between the CBT and Duluth model may be lost at the practical level.

Cognitive behavioural therapy

At the philosophical level, CBT broadly assumes that IPV is caused by (i) cognitive distortions about self and partner and (ii) a lack of skills to appropriately express and process feelings leading to maladaptive expressions of anger. CBT is used for partner-abusive individuals through a combination of methods: most commonly, assertiveness training, relaxation training and some cognitive therapies (Edleson and Tolman, 1992; Ganley, 1981; Saunders, 1984; Sonkin and Durphy, 1989; Stordeur and Stille, 1989). Cognitive approaches are based on the notion that irrational thoughts and cognitive distortions may contribute to anger arousal. This anger then develops into physical or verbal aggression. The cognitive framework assumes that men's need for superiority and sense of privileged status are cognitive distortions that can be rectified. These therapies incorporate tools such as homework, lectures and cognitive rehearsal to help batterers internalize the treatment strategies they learn in therapeutic sessions (Wexler, 2000). While cognitive approaches are based on certain assumptions about distorted cognitions and irrational beliefs, the behavioural approaches are different in the way they perceive the attribution of violent tendencies. Subsequently, the ways in which these approaches are executed are also somewhat different.

Behavioural approaches attribute aggression to deficits in interpersonal skills or to a heightened sensitivity to certain events leading instantaneously to anger arousal (Wexler, 2000). Such an interpersonal skill deficit is targeted through modelling and behavioural rehearsal; the heightened sensitivity to specific cues is dealt with through systematic desensitization (Wexler, 2000). These approaches thus target how and when aggression arises. In situations where individuals do not confront initial anger cues and let them build up, assertiveness training is offered. In situations where there is a low tolerance to anger cues such that they fly off the handle easily, systematic desensitization may be used.

While addressing learning history, anger and interpersonal skills in battering intervention may sound reasonable; many CBT proponents are loudly criticized for addressing emotions and psychopathology. Many battered women's advocates are trained in social work, and have been taught to eschew the 'medical model' approach (Eckhardt and Schram, 2000). Explanations blaming internal deficits may displace responsibility for the violence and reinforce batterers' tendency to project blame and accountability, as a loss of control that led them to 'snap' and accidentally became violent (Gondolf, 2007).

The Duluth model

The Duluth model, so called because it was developed in Duluth, Minnesota, in the 1980s, is a psychoeducational model (re-educating and changing beliefs) as opposed to a psychotherapeutic one (helping and healing). The Duluth model was influenced theoretically and politically by feminist and sociological analyses of IPV (Day *et al.*, 2009). It focuses on re-educating violent men on their beliefs about IPV and women, anger and stress management, relationship skills training and gender role resocialization (Pence and Paymar, 1993). Furthermore, feminist models hold that patriarchy supports male dominance and entitlement, thus using IPV as a method of controlling female partners (Lawson, Brossart and Shefferman, 2010). Growing from a grass roots movement beginning with interviewing and advocating for women in battered women shelters, the Duluth model places a strong emphasis on the needs and safety of victims. This feminist approach views IPV as a result of gender power imbalances; thus, the Duluth model's higher-order goal is societal change more so than offender rehabilitation (Day *et al.*, 2009). It primarily addresses re-education to confront the core belief system of masculinity (Pence and Paymar, 1993). However, it also integrates some features of cognitive-behavioural work such as relapse prevention (Gondolf, 2007).

While some criticize the Duluth model for effectively removing the psychology of violence from intervention and replacing it with gender politics (Dutton and Corvo, 2006), the feminist approach to batterers' intervention may be more theoretically compatible with a criminal justice perspective than the CBT psychotherapeutic approach (Healey, Smith and O'sulivan, 1998). First, it clearly views IPV as criminal behaviour, not as the result of a personality disorder or a deficit in couple communication or other relational skills. Second, the goal is accepting responsibility and becoming accountable for one's own violence as opposed to blaming early childhood experiences or some dysfunctional interaction with the victim. Finally, because the cause of battering stems from a societal problem of misogynist and sexist attitudes, rather than from individual psychopathology, batterer programmes focus on re-educating men rather than providing them with therapy (Austin and Dankwort, 1999).

Both the Duluth model and CBT have made a significant contribution towards batterer interventions. They set philosophical frameworks that guide clinical work with offenders and moti-vate the agency staff. Unfortunately, the empirical research finds that both models have an almost equal, small impact on stopping subsequent IPV ($D = 0.30$ for Duluth programmes; $D = 0.29$ for cognitive-behavioural programmes) (Babcock, Green and Robie, 2004). As researchers, we are obligated to continue to ask the tough questions so that we can improve the interventions designed to stop IPV (Stuart, 2005): Why don't they work better? Which techniques hold promise? How can we improve battering interventions so that they effectively reduce recidivism of IPV?

Transtheoretical Model of Change

One problem with both CBT and Duluth model interventions is that they operate under the assumption that the men are ready to change their violent ways. Few intimate partner abusers enter intervention of their own accord. Most entering battering intervention programmes are mandated to do so by the courts. Yet, we know that court-mandated psychotherapy is less effective than non-mandated therapy (Finney and Moos, 1998). Others may be given an ultimatum by their spouse to attend treatment. When individuals feel coerced rather than self-motivated to change, interventions designed to aid them in doing so are not effective (Daniels and Murphy, 1997). Many batterers react against frequent and intense confrontation with vociferous counterarguments, silence, 'phony' agreement or termination of treatment (Murphy and Baxter, 1997). In addition, teaching batterers to take responsibility for the abuse may have only limited effectiveness on its own because it tends to shame and guilt them and to lead to large dropout rates among already defensive clients (Harway and Evans, 1996).

The transtheoretical model of change posits that the resolution of any problem progresses sequentially through a series of stages: precontemplation, contemplation, preparation, action, maintenance and termination (Prochaska and DiClemente, 1992). Individuals in the precontemplative stage are still unwilling to acknowledge they have a serious problem and are thus more likely to provide justifications or excuses for their aggressive behaviour (Dutton, 1986, 2007). While *precontemplation* entails no wish to change/no recognition of a problem, the *contemplation* stage involves hints of an intention to change problem behaviour, generally within the next six months. Following contemplation is the *preparation* stage that involves an intention to take immediate action, around the next month. Next is the *action* stage that is characterized by readiness to make specific, overt modifications. Once changes have been made, people may move into the *maintenance* stage, which is primarily associated with coping strategies to prevent relapse. The last stage of problem resolution is the *termination* stage, which indicates the completion of relapse prevention, suggesting that maintenance is no longer needed (Velicer *et al.*, 1998).

The stages-of-change model has clear implications for IPV offenders. Most men entering a battering intervention programme are not in the *action* stage, ready to change their behaviour (Babcock *et al.*, 2005; Eckhardt, Babcock and Homack, 2004; Scott and Wolfe, 2003). Rather, they tend to enter in the *precontemplative* stage, still considering whether their behaviour constitutes abuse and, if so, whether it is problematic and worth changing. However, both CBT manuals (e.g., Wexler, 2000) and the Duluth model curriculum (Pence and Paymar, 1993) tend to be geared towards action. Since only a minority of perpetrators come to treatment ready to change in the action stage (Levesque, Gelles and Velicer, 2000), perhaps treatment outcomes can be improved if treatment is targeted towards those in precontemplative and contemplative stages. Curricula could include acknowledgement of the IPV, increased awareness of the negative aspects of the problem and accurate evaluation of self-control (Casey, Day and Howells, 2005; Day *et al.*, 2009). Consciousness-raising strategies such as educating perpetrators about the physical and mental consequences of violence on their victims and strategies such as social comparison, self-monitoring exercises and group feedback during motivating discussions can also facilitate transition to the action stage (Day *et al.*, 2009).

Research suggests that addressing readiness to change can improve the efficacy of batterer interventions. MI is an interviewing technique with an emphasis on autonomy and choice that is used as a pretreatment intervention. By emphasizing autonomy and choice with the client, the therapist is able to build a working relationship and thus work towards using guided confrontation to increase awareness of problems and the need to do something about them. In MI, therapists can help clients gain greater awareness of problem behaviours, articulate motivations and barriers to change, enhance self-efficacy for accomplishing change and facilitate the development of plans and strategies for change, all in a fashion that minimizes the likelihood of client defensiveness (Musser and Murphy, 2009). Importantly, MI can work to evade negative client reactance against being controlled, pressured or forced to change. Through use of consistent demonstration of empathy and affirmation of client autonomy, the therapist is able to help diffuse hostility towards treatment and enhance motivation for self-exploration and change. Although MI has positive influences on the therapeutic process, it is not free of its own complications, and therapists often find themselves walking a thin line between affirming their client's behaviour and condoning abusive behaviour. In a case study conducted by Musser and Murphy (2009), the affirmation of client autonomy was complicated at times by ethical issues in managing risk for future violence, including concerns about explicit or implicit affirmation of free choice to assault and harm others in light of the duty to protect. Researchers also found that affirmation of autonomy was also complicated by the fact that most clients did not perceive themselves as having free choice regarding participation in court-mandated treatment. In one study, IPV offenders were assigned to either cognitive-behavioural or supportive group therapy (Morrel *et al.*, 2003). Both interventions used MI techniques in order to facilitate participant retention (Miller and Rollnick, 1991). Reminder phone calls and handwritten notes of encouragement both after initial consultation and after missed sessions were incorporated. Although the two interventions were markedly different, both produced strong results suggesting that MI techniques may be a powerful addition to existing interventions for IPV.

Recently, two randomized clinical trials tested transtheoretical model interventions for IPV. First, a small study randomly assigned men arrested for partner violence to either receive MI ($n = 16$) or no intervention ($n = 17$). Men in the MI group demonstrated a pre-to-post increase in action, and the control group showed a decrease in action. However, recidivism was not assessed. A larger study ($N = 528$) compared a stages-of-change motivational interviewing (SOCMI) treatment approach with a standard cognitive behavioural therapy gender re-education (CBTGR) approach (Alexander *et al.*, 2010). Partners of men in the SOCMI group were significantly more likely to report a cessation of violence at follow-up. Men in precontemplative or contemplative stages reaped more benefit from the SOCMI group, opposed to men who were more ready to change, who were more successful in the CBTGR approach. These findings are consistent with the notion of tailoring interventions to individuals' initial readiness to change.

Batterer Typologies

Just as battering interventions may be improved by tailoring treatment to readiness to change, tailoring treatments to the type of batterer holds promise. Psychologists have shown that batterers are heterogeneous. The problem is that there are so many typologies of batterers that it is difficult to choose which typology to use. We have batterer typologies based on personality, attachment (Babcock *et al.*, 2004), heart rate (Gottman *et al.*, 1995), empathy (Covell, Huss and Langhinrichsen-Rohling, 2007), risk for future violence (Palmer *et al.*, 2008) or a combination thereof (Holtzworth-Munroe and Stuart, 1994).

Recently, some interventions have begun to follow principles of RNR. The RNR approach is one of the most empirically supported approaches for reducing various forms of criminal recidivism (Andrews and Bonta, 2006, 2010). RNR was originally developed for use by parole boards and, for the most part, was inherent in the development of a tool to assist in the identification of good candidates to return to the community. This principle has since been developed and used in a variety of settings and criminogenic behaviours. *Risk* is defined as historical factors of the offender's involvement in a criminal lifestyle, such as the age of first arrest, number of prior arrests and number of incarcerations. This principle attempts to use an offender's past to determine how heavily his prior criminal activities will weigh on his ability to engage in pro-social activities during and after treatment (Taxman and Thanner, 2006). The risk principle entails matching the intensity of treatment to the risk level of the offender (e.g., high-risk offenders acquire high-intensity services; low-risk offenders receive low-intensity services). This principle maintains that more intense forms of intervention should be reserved for medium- to high-risk offenders because they are more likely to benefit from treatment (Andrews, 2001; McGuire, 2002). *Need* refers to the degree to which deficits that may encourage the offender to continue the criminal behaviour exist (Taxman and Thanner, 2006). The need principle states that targeting aspects of the offender's psychological, social and emotional functioning is most effective in intervention. This principle recognizes that these aspects of functioning are linked to the development and continuation of criminal behaviour, known as criminogenic needs (e.g., attitudes supportive of crime, delinquent peers, substance abuse and unemployment). Essentially, the need principle refers to considering the degree to which the offender has protective factors that can ward against further abusive behaviour. Finally, according to the responsivity principle, offender treatment programmes must be tailored to the learning style, cognitive capabilities, motivation, personality and cultural background of clientele in order to be effective (Babcock *et al.*, 2007). This principle effectively utilizes the information that is obtained using the risk and need principles. The higher the risk and need level, the greater the expectation that resources should be allocated to such offenders. When used, the RNR tenet requires that correctional programmes use a valid risk tool, have the ability to identify dynamic factors to address in treatment and have suitable treatment programmes to bring about the desired changes (Taxman and Thanner, 2006). In other words, the RNR tenet emphasizes the importance of programmes that ensure offenders receive appropriate interventions that are designed to target their criminogenic risk factors, are responsive to their learning styles and are delivered at an appropriate level of dose and intensity.

Interventions that follow the RNR principles are based on the premise that risk, need and treatment factors must match between the offender and the treatment. The most influential batterer typology to date classifies men based on frequency of IPV, personality disorder features and generality of violence (Holtzworth-Munroe and Stuart, 1994). Using these three dimensions, batterers are pegged into one of three groups: family only, borderline/dysphoric or generally violent/antisocial. These hypothesized typologies later withstood empirical testing, thus making this model the most widely accepted batterer typology (Langhinrichsen-Rohling, Huss and Ramsey, 2000).

The *family-only* batterers have relatively low rates of partner violence and do not report symptoms of antisocial or borderline personality disorders. This type of batterer has a better treatment outlook and tends to complete treatment more frequently than members of the other two subtypes (Covell, Huss and Langhinrichsen-Rohling, 2007). Since research has found that treatment attendance and completion are negatively related to recidivism

(Gordon and Moriarty, 2003), it is likely the family-only batterers comprise the success stories of standard batterer intervention groups. On the other hand, because this group is less criminally entrenched and more 'socially bonded', perhaps having been arrested is the causal mechanism in their cessation of violence. Because this group is also likely to participate in bilateral violence, where both partners get physically aggressive when arguments escalate out of control, couples therapy may be beneficial to this group to prevent harmful fights (Babcock *et al.*, 2007).

The *borderline/dysphoric* batterers tend to have moderate to high frequency of partner violence but are not typically violent to others outside the home. They score high on features of borderline personality disorder. It was theorized that their level of alcohol and drug abuse was moderate and their levels of depression and anger were high. In terms of treatment completion, borderline/dysphoric batterers are expected to attend fewer sessions and drop out at higher rates than family-only batterers (Huss, Covell and Langhinrichsen-Rohling, 2006). Borderline/dysphoric batterers have difficulty adopting the viewpoints, or affective experience of others, as well as a poor ability to tolerate the negative emotions of others (Covell, Huss and Langhinrichsen-Rohling, 2007). This group of batterers appear to be preoccupied with their own internal experience, and tend to perceive others only in relation to how they affect them. It is speculated that batterers in this group may be extremely sensitive to criticism and perceived slights from others, and may adopt an arrogant, abrasive interpersonal style to cover deep feelings of inadequacy and isolation and to manage interpersonal conflict (Covell, Huss and Langhinrichsen-Rohling, 2007).

Little research has tested different battering interventions by different types of batterers. However, one study found that borderline/dysphoric batterers fared better in process-oriented psychodynamic groups that address childhood trauma history (Saunders, 1996). Recently, several authors have speculated that dialectical behaviour therapy (DBT; Linehan, 1993), an empirically supported treatment for borderline personality disorder, might be effective with this subtype of batterer (Fruzzetti and Levensky, 2002; Waltz, 2003). First, DBT is typically useful with clinical populations that are difficult to treat, or for whom traditional treatments have shown limited success; often, DBT is used as the last result. Second, the populations for which DBT has been adapted to include people with emotion dysregulation problems. Men who batter their partners experience higher levels of emotion dysregulation than non-violent men. One of the primary goals of DBT is to target emotion dysregulation directly and to help clients increase their ability to modulate intense negative emotions (Waltz, 2003). Finally, these populations tend to have multiple diagnoses and/or life problems and high treatment dropout rates. Indeed, DBT was specifically designed to treat multiproblem/multidiagnostic populations (Linehan, 2000). One crucial dilemma is the dialectic around holding the person accountable for his abusive behaviour and clearly communicating the unacceptability of the behaviour and the need for change, while on the other hand seeing and understanding the client's perspective, his limitations and the factors that have influenced him to be abusive. While clinical trials have yet to test the efficacy of DBT to reduce IPV (Scheel, 2000), an intervention that addresses long-standing emotional dysregulation may be the only responsive way to intervene with batterers with borderline personality features.

The final group of batterers was identified as the *generally violent/antisocial* group. This group persistently engages in moderate to high levels of partner violence and high rates of general violence outside the home and exhibits antisocial features. Antisocial personality disorder (ASPD) is associated with persistent rule-breaking, criminality, substance use,unemployment and relationship difficulties (Gibbon *et al.*, 2010). Like borderline/dysphoric men, generally violent/antisocial batterers evidence low perspective taking and fantasy scores in addition to high personal distress scores (Covell, Huss and Langhinrichsen-Rohling, 2007) and are expected to attend fewer sessions and drop out more from treatment (Holtzworth-Munroe and Stuart, 1994).

Despite the high cost to society for ASPD, there is very little research on how best to intervene with people with antisocial features. In general, MI and substance abuse interventions have been met with some success (Gibbon *et al.*, 2010), as has contingency management, CBT and anticonvulsant medication (Vollm *et al.*, 2010). For IPV offenders, insight-oriented therapies, group treatments conducted with a high proportion of batterers with antisocial or psychopathic traits and the use of couples therapy are thought to be countertherapeutic for this subtype of batterers (Dalton, 2007). One study found that antisocial batterers had greater treatment success in a cognitive-behavioural/feminist-oriented intervention that focused on skill development and attitude change as opposed to one that addressed insight (Saunders, 1996). At any rate, because antisocial men tend not to be psychologically minded, psychological interventions may not be the best course. Alternative sanctions, such as restorative justice (Mills, 2003) or jail, may be more appropriate to batterers who are antisocial, high risk and criminally entrenched. Based on the RNR principles, different types of batterers appear to show differential benefits for each type of treatment available to them. Following a predetermined format, ignoring each individual's personality traits and motivations may hinder treatment efficacy (Levesque, Gelles and Velicer, 2000). Research suggests that the perceived congruence between the abuser's goals and the goals of the treatment inversely correlates with attrition and recidivism in batterer intervention programmes (Cadsky *et al.*, 1996; Jewell and Wormith, 2010).

Family-only batterers may be the ones who benefit the most from participating in group battering intervention programmes, or perhaps arrest is sufficient. An intensive level of treatment may not be needed for IPV men who fit the profile of a 'family-only' type, who typically do not engage in severe or frequent violence and who tend to have minimal psychopathology (Holtzworth-Munroe and Stuart, 1994; Waltz, 1999); rather traditional forms of treatment may be more appropriate for this type of batterer. For borderline/dysphoric batterers, and possibly the generally violent/antisocial batterers, who do not seem to benefit from traditional treatment programmes, DBT is likely to be most appropriate treatment. Generally, violent/antisocial batters are likely the most difficult to have in a group intervention due to their disruptiveness, and are probably the least likely to benefit (Huss, Covell and Langhinrichsen-Rohling, 2006). However, research also shows that this matching (i.e., interaction) accounts for only 5% of variance in recidivism rates (Levesque, Gelles and Velicer, 2000).

Future Directions

In line with the principles of RNR, correctional agencies may be able to identify offenders who are high risk and place those offenders in appropriate multidimensional services to affect the likelihood of desistence and re-offence. The failure of blanket group IPV interventions and the known heterogeneity among batterers point to the need for individualized assessment of each offender's treatment needs. Developing or implementing a new treatment for any problem is justified under the following circumstances: (i) Data shows that existing treatments do not work well; (ii) data demonstrates better outcomes with a new treatment; (iii) a new treatment is more resource efficient than an old one (without diminishing outcomes); or (iv) treatment providers prefer a new treatment (e.g., reduced burnout), as long as outcomes are not diminished and costs do not increase (Fruzzetti and Levensky, 2000). At this stage in IPV research, it is clear that current data supports the idea that existing treatments are less than satisfactory, and there is some data that supports the further development of new treatments. It is expected that further research in IPV will result in more efficient and preferable treatments.

Low-risk men arrested for IPV could be mandated to attend battering intervention programmes, as they exist now. In addition, new, targeted interventions could be developed for the higher-risk offender based on the larger literature of psychological treatments that work. Research on treatment of BPD suggests that DBT may prove helpful in decreasing the frequency of violence of low-risk men. The research on treating ASPD focuses on three common areas of concern: motivation to change, manipulation and deceit (being fooled) and lack of real emotion (Salekin, Worley and Grimes, 2010). People with ASPD tend to remain in the precontemplation stage longer than people without personality disorders because they often do not see anything wrong with their behaviour and blame others for their interpersonal problems. Additionally, antisocial batterers tend to display an absence or reduction in anxiety. Their reduction in anxiety is likely to be a further deterrent to the treatment of their characterological issues (Reid and Gacono, 2000). Motivating non-anxious, antisocial batterers to want to change may be the most difficult part of working with antisocial individuals.

Conclusions

Although criminal justice has a history of using social science information to inform its management of IPV offenders, the research on how best to intervene with IPV is confounded by ideological rifts that outstrip the importance of empirical evidence (Eckhardt *et al.*, 2006). As stated by Echkardt *et al.* (2006), 'The accumulation of largely unremarkable outcomes regarding BIPs [Batterer Intervention Programmes] could potentially signal to those in the criminal justice community that such programmes are simply not worth the effort: Why mandate an intervention that men have little motivation to attend, that at best has a small impact on criminal recidivism, and that doesn't really qualify as a punishment, an educational experience, or a therapeutic intervention?' (p. 379).

Although the research results to date on standard group interventions for batterers are underwhelming, our goal is not to dismantle existing batterer interventions. Rather our goal is to generate new ideas for a new wave of collaborative research designed to develop effective interventions for intimate partner offenders. Clearly, there is a need to develop new and novel programmes and test their efficacy, especially for the difficult-to-treat batterer. Some batterers, embarrassed by their arrest and threatened by the loss of a relationship or social standing, may cease to perpetrate IPV. No additional battering intervention may be needed for these low-level, 'socially bonded' perpetrators. Especially when the violence is bilateral (perpetrated by both partners), couples approaches emphasizing communication skills and ways to keep harmful fights from escalating may be most effective for these perpetrators. For the hardened criminals and psychopathic batterers, we may need to look beyond the narrow literature on interventions for IPV offenders to the broader literature for treatments that work for the criminally entrenched.

References

Alexander, P.C., Morris, E., Tracy, A. and Frye, A. (2010) Stages of change and the group treatment of batterers: a randomized clinical trial. *Violence and Victims*, 25, 571–587.

Andrews, D.A. (2001) Principles of effective correctional programs, in *Compendium 2000 on Effective Correctional Programming* (eds L.L. Motiuk and R.C. Serin), Correctional Service Canada, Ottawa, pp. 9–17.

Andrews, D.A. and Bonta, J. (2006) *The Psychology of Criminal Conduct*, 4th edn, Anderson, Cincinnati.

Andrews, D.A. and Bonta, J. (2010) Rehabilitating criminal justice policy and practice. *Psychology, Public Policy and Law*, 16, 39–55.

Austin, J.B. and Dankwort, J. (1999) Standards for batterer programs: a review and analysis. *Journal of Interpersonal Violence*, 14, 152–168.

Babcock, J.C., Green, C.E. and Robie, C. (2004) Does batterers' treatment work? A metaanalytic review of domestic violence treatment. *Clinical Psychology Review*, 23, 1023–1053.

Babcock, J.C., Green, C.E., Webb, S.A. and Graham, K.H. (2004) A second failure to replicate the Gottman *et al.* (1995) typology of men who abuse intimate partners...and possible reasons why. *Journal of Family Psychology*, 2, 396–400.

Babcock, J.C., Canady, B.E., Senior, A. and Eckhardt, C.I. (2005) Applying the transtheoretical model to female and male perpetrators of intimate partner violence: gender differences in stages and processes of change. *Violence and Victims*, 20 (2), 235–250.

Babcock, J.C., Canady, B., Graham, K.H. and Schart, L. (2007) The evolution of battering interventions: from the Dark Ages into the Scientific Age, in *Family Therapy for Domestic Violence: A Practitioner's Guide to Gender-Inclusive Research and Treatment* (eds J. Hamel and T. Nicholls), Springer, New York, pp. 215–244.

Berk, R.A., Black, H., Lilly, J. and Rikoski, G. (1991) Colorado Springs Spouse Assault Replication Project: Final Report. National Institute of Justice, Washington, DC.

Berk, R.A., Campbell, A., Klap, R. and Western, B. (1992) The deterrent effects of arrest in incidents of domestic violence: a Bayesian analysis of four field experiments. *American Sociological Review*, 57, 698–708.

Browne, A. (1993) Violence against women by male partners: prevalence, outcomes, and policy implications. *American Psychologist*, 10, 1077–1087.

Bruno vs. Codd, 90 Misc.2d 1047, (1977).

Cadsky, O., Hanson, R.K., Crawford, M. and Lalonde, C. (1996) Attrition from a male batterer treatment program: client-treatment congruence and lifestyle instability. *Violence and Victims*, 11, 51–64.

Casey, S., Day, A. and Howells, K. (2005) The application of the transtheoretical model to offender populations: some critical issues. *Legal and Criminological Psychology*, 10, 1–15.

Covell, C.N., Huss, M.T. and Langhinrichsen-Rohling, J. (2007) Empathic deficits among male batterers: a multidimensional approach. *Journal of Family Violence*, 22, 165–174.

Dalton, B. (2007) What's going on out there? A survey of batterer intervention programs. *Journal of Aggression, Maltreatment and Trauma*, 15, 60–62.

Daniels, J.W. and Murphy, C.M. (1997) Stages and processes of change in batterers' treatment. *Cognitive and Behavioral Practice*, 4, 123–145.

Day, A., Chung, D., O'Leary, P. and Carson, E. (2009) Programs for men who perpetrate domestic violence: an examination of the issues underlying the effectiveness of intervention programs. *Journal of Family Violence*, 24, 203–212.

Dunford, F.W., Huizinga, D. and Elliott, D.S. (1990) The role of arrest in domestic assault: the Omaha experiment. *Criminology*, 28, 183–206.

Dutton, D.G. (1986) The outcome of court-mandated treatment for wife assault: a quasi-experimental evaluation. *Violence and Victims*, 1, 163–175.

Dutton, D.G. (2007) The complexities of domestic violence. *American Psychologist*, 62, 708–710.

Dutton, D.G. and Corvo, K. (2006) Transforming a flawed policy: a call to revive psychology and science in domestic violence research and practice. *Aggression and Violent Behavior*, 11, 457–483.

Eckhardt, C.I. and Schram, J. (2000) Cognitive behavioral interventions for partner-abusive men, in *Strength-Based Batterers Interventions* (eds P. Lehmann and C.A. Simmons), Springer, New York, pp. 137–179.

Eckhardt, C.I., Babcock, J. and Homack, S. (2004) Partner assaultive men and the stages and processes of change. *Journal of Family Violence*, 19, 81–93.

Eckhardt, C.I., Murphy, C., Black, D. and Suhr, L. (2006) Intervention programs for perpetrators of intimate partner violence: conclusions from a clinical research perspective. *Public Health Reports*, 121, 369–381.

Edleson, J.L. and Tolman, R.M. (1992) *Intervention for Men Who Batter*, Sage, Thousand Oaks.

Finney, J.W. and Moos, R.H. (1998) Psychosocial treatments for alcohol use disorders, in *A Guide to Treatments That Work* (eds P.E. Nathan and J.M. Gorman), Oxford University Press, New York, pp. 156–166.

Fruzzetti, A.E. and Levensky, E.R. (2000) Dialectical behavior therapy for domestic violence: rationale and procedures. *Cognitive and Behavioral Practice*, 7, 435–447.

Ganley, A. (1981) *Court-Mandated Counseling for Men Who Batter: A Three-Day Workshop*, Center for Women Policy Studies, Washington, DC.

Gibbon, S., Duggan, C., Stoffers, J. *et al.* (2010) Psychological interventions for antisocial personality disorder. *Cochrane Database of Systematic Reviews*, 6, 1–109, Art. no.: CD007668.

Gondolf, E.W. (2007) Cautions About Applying Neuroscience to Batterer Intervention. *Court Review*, 43, 178–192.

Gordon, J.A. and Moriarty, L.J. (2003) The effects of domestic batterer treatment on domestic violence recidivism: the Chesterfield County experience. *Criminal Justice and Behavior*, 30, 118–134.

Gottman, J.M., Jacobson N.S., Rush R.H. *et al.* (1995) The relationship between heart rate reactivity, emotionally aggressive behavior, and general violence in batterers. *Journal of Family Psychology*, 3, 227–248.

Greenfeld, L.A., Rand, M.R., Craven, D. *et al.* (1998). *Violence by Intimates: Analysis of Data on Crimes by Current or Former Spouses, Boyfriends, and Girlfriends*, Bureau of Justice Statistics, Washington, DC.

Harway, M. and Evans, K. (1996) Working in groups with men who batter, in *Men in Groups: Insights, Interventions, and Psychoeducational Work* (ed. M.P. Andronico), American Psychological Association, Washington, DC, pp. 357–375.

Healey, K., Smith, S. and O'Sulivan, C. (1998) *Batterer Intervention: Programme Approaches and Criminal Justice Strategies*, US Department of Justice Office of Justice Programmes, National Institute of Justice, Washington, DC.

Hirschel, D., Buzawa, E., Pattavina A. and Faggiani, D. (2007) Explaining the Prevalence, Context, and Consequences of Dual Arrest in Intimate Partner Cases. Final report submitted to the National Institute of Justice, Washington, DC.

Hirschel, J., Hutchison, I., Dean, C.W., Kelley, J.J., & Pesackis, C.E. (1990). *Charlotte Spouse Assault Replication Project: Final Report*. National Institute of Justice, Washington, DC, unpublished manuscript.

Holtzworth-Munroe, A. and Stuart, G.L. (1994) Typologies of male batterers: three subtypes and the differences among them. *Psychological Bulletin*, 116, 476–497.

Huss, M.T., Covell, C.N. and Langhinrichsen-Rohling, J. (2006) Clinical implications for the assessment and treatment of antisocial and psychopathic domestic violence perpetrators. *Journal of Aggression, Maltreatment & Trauma*, 13, 59–85.

Jewell, L.M. and Wormith, J.S. (2010) Variables associated with attrition from domestic violence treatment programs targeting male batterers: a meta-analysis. *Criminal Justice and Behavior*, 37, 1086–1113.

Jones, A.S. (2000) The cost of batterer intervention programs: how much and who pays? *Journal of Interpersonal Violence*, 15, 566–586.

Labriola, M., Rempel, M. and Davis, R.C. (2008) Do batterer programs reduce recidivism? Results from a randomized trial in the Bronx. *Justice Quarterly*, 25 (2), 252–282.

Langhinrichsen-Rohling, J., Huss, M.T. and Ramsey, S. (2000) The clinical utility of batterer typologies. *Journal of Family Violence*, 15, 37–53.

Lawson, D.M., Brossart, D.F. and Shefferman, L.W. (2010) Assessing gender role of partner violent men using the Minnesota Multiphasic Personality Inventory-2 (MMPI-2): comparing abuser types. *Professional Psychology*, 41, 260–266.

Levesque, D.A., Gelles, R.J. and Velicer, W.F. (2000) Development and validation of a stages of change measure for men in batterer treatment. *Cognitive Therapy and Research*, 24, 175–199.

Linehan, M.M. (1993) *Cognitive Behavioral Therapy of Borderline Personality Disorder*, Guilford, New York.

Linehan, M.M. (2000) Commentary on innovations in dialectical behavior therapy. *Cognitive and Behavioral Practice*, 7, 478–481.

Maxwell, C.D., Garner, J.H. and Fagan, J.A. (2002) Research, policy and theory: the preventive effects of arrest on intimate partner violence. *Criminology and Public Policy*, 2, 51–80.

McGuire, J. (2002) Integrating findings from research reviews, in *Offender Rehabilitation and Treatment: Effective Programmes and Policies to Reduce Re-Offending* (ed. J. McGuire), John Wiley & Sons, Ltd, Chichester, pp. 3–38.

Miller, W.R. and Rollnick, S. (1991) *Motivational Interviewing: Preparing People to Change Addictive Behavior*, Guilford Press, New York.

Mills, L. (2003) *Insult to Injury: Rethinking Our Responses to Intimate Abuse*, Princeton University Press, Princeton.

Morrel, T.M., Elliott, J.D., Murphy, C.M. and Taft, C. (2003) A comparison of cognitive-behavioral and supportive group therapies for male perpetrators of domestic abuse. *Behavior Therapy*, 24, 77–95.

Murphy, C.M. and Baxter, V.A. (1997) Motivating batterers to change in the treatment context. *Journal of Interpersonal Violence*, 12, 607–619.

Musser, P.H. and Murphy, C.M. (2009) Motivational interviewing with perpetrators of intimate partner abuse. *Journal of Clinical Psychology: In Session*, 65, 1218–1231.

Palmer, E.J., McGuire, J., Hatcher R.M. *et al.* (2008) The importance of appropriate allocation to offending behavior programs. *International Journal of Offender Therapy and Comparative Criminology*, 52, 206–221.

Pate, A.M. and Hamilton, E.E. (1992) Formal and informal deterrents to domestic violence: the Dade County spouse assault experiment. *American Sociological Review*, 57, 691–698.

Pence, E. and Paymar, M. (1993) *Education Groups for Men Who Batter: The Duluth Model*, Springer, New York.

Prochaska, J.O. and DiClemente, C.C. (1992) *Stages of Change in the Modification of Problem Behaviors*, Sage, Newbury Park.

Reid, W.H. and Gacono, C. (2000) Treatment of antisocial personality, psychopathy, and other characterological antisocial syndromes. *Behavioral Sciences and the Law*, 18, 647–662.

Rempel, M., Labriola, M. and Davis, R.C. (2008) Does judicial monitoring deter domestic violence recidivism? Results of quasi-experimental comparison in the Bronx. *Violence Against Women*, 14, 185–207.

Salekin, R.T., Worley, C. and Grimes, R.D. (2010) Treatment of psychopathy: a review and brief introduction to the mental model approach for psychopathy. *Behavioral Sciences and the Law*, 28, 235–266.

Saunders, D.G. (1984) Helping husbands who batter. *Social Casework*, 65, 347–356.

Saunders, D.G. (1996) Feminist–cognitive–behavioral and process–psychodynamic treatments for men who batter: interaction of abuse traits and treatment models. *Violence and Victims*, 11, 393–413.

Scheel, K.R. (2000) The empirical basis of dialectical behavior therapy: summary, critique and implications. *Clinical Psychology: Science and Practice*, 7, 68–86.

Scott vs. Hart suit, C-76-2395. N.D. Cal. (1976).

Scott, K.L. and Wolfe, D.A. (2003) Readiness to change as a predictor of outcome in batterer treatment. *Journal of Consulting and Clinical Psychology*, 71, 879–889.

Sherman, L.W. and Berk, R.A. (1984a) *The Minneapolis Domestic Violence Experiment*, vol. 1, Police Foundation Reports, Washington, DC, pp. 1–8.

Sherman, L.W. and Berk, R.A. (1984b) The specific deterrent effects of arrest for domestic assault. *American Sociological Review*, 49, 261.

Sherman, L.W., Schmidt, J. and Rogan, D. (1992a) *Policing Domestic Violence: Experiments and Dilemmas*, Free Press, New York.

Sherman, L.W., Smith, D.A., Schmidt, J.D. and Rogan, D.P. (1992b) Crime, punishment, and stake in conformity: legal and informal control of domestic violence. *American Sociological Review*, 57 (5), 680–690.

Sonkin, D. and Durphy, M. (1989) *Learning to Live Without Violence*, Volcano Press, Volcano.

Stordeur, R.A. and Stille, R. (1989) *Ending Men's Violence Against Their Partners*, Sage, Thousand Oaks.

Straus, M.A. (1985) National Family Violence Survey. Family Research Laboratory, University of New Hampshire.

Straus, M.A. (1990) The conflict tactics scale and its critics: an evaluation and new data on validity and reliability, in *Physical Violence in American Families: Risk Factors and Adaptations in 8145 Families* (eds M. Straus and R.J. Gelles), Transaction Books, New Brunswick.

Straus, M.A. and Gelles, R.J. (1990) *Physical Violence in American Families: Risk Factors and Adaptations to Violence in 8,145 Families*, Transaction, New Brunswick.

Straus, M.A., Gelles, R.J. and Steinmetz, S.K. (1980) *Behind Closed Doors: Violence in the American Family*, Anchor Books, New York.

Stuart, R.B. (2005) Treatment for partner abuse: time for a paradigm shift. *Professional Psychology: Research and Practice*, 36, 254–263.

Taxman, F.S. and Thanner, M. (2006) Risk, need, and responsivity (RNR): it all depends. *Crime & Delinquency*, 52, 28–51.

Thurman vs. City of Torrington, 595 F. Supp. 1521 – Dist. Court, D. Connecticut (1984).

Tjaden, P. and Thoennes, N. (2000) *Extent*, Nature, and Consequences of Intimate Partner Violence: Findings from the National Violence Against Women Survey, Department of Justice (US), Washington, DC, Publication No. NCJ 181867.

Velicer, W.F., Prochaska, J.O., Fava, J.L. *et al.* (1998) Smoking cessation and stress management: applications of the transtheoretical model of behaviour change. *Homeostasis*, 38, 216–233.

Vollm, B., Gibbon, S., Khalifa, N. *et al.* (2010) S08-01 – Cochrane reviews of pharmacological and psychological interventions for antisocial personality disorder (ASPD). *European Psychiatry*, 25 (Suppl. 1), 90.

Waltz, J. (2003) Dialectical behavior therapy in the treatment of abusive behavior. *Journal of Aggression, Maltreatment and Trauma*, 7, 75–103.

Wexler, D.B. (2000) *Domestic Violence 2000: Group Leader's Manual*, W.W. Norton & Company, Inc., New York.

10

What Works in Reducing Sexual Offending

William L. Marshall[1], Liam E. Marshall[1], Geris A. Serran[2] and Matt D. O'Brien[2]

[1]Rockwood Psychological Services, Canada
[2]Correctional Service of Canada, Canada

In this chapter, we will first address the problems with punishment-based strategies with sexual offenders in order to demonstrate the inadequacy of this approach so that we can turn to a consideration of more positively based, and demonstrably effective, ways of dealing with the problems these offenders present. Next, we will consider the relevance of theories for effective treatment, beginning with a brief survey of target-specific theories followed by a similar examination of theories that encompass all aspects of sexual offending. In particular, we identify the limits to the value of the *Relapse Prevention* (RP) model and the essential relevance of Andrews' *Risk–Needs–Responsivity* (RNR) model and Ward's *Good Lives Model* (GLM) as guides to effective treatment. We then note the value of these models for assessment.

Our attention is then directed at treatment evaluation where we consider the value of the random controlled trial (RCT), the so-called incidental design involving a comparison with an incidentally available group of untreated offenders, and finally the use of risk estimates of expected recidivism as the basis upon which to evaluate treatment-induced reductions in reoffending. This is followed by a brief appraisal of the available outcome literature which we interpret as strongly suggesting that treatment for sexual offenders *can* be effective!

On the basis of these results, we suggest that there are certain features of effective treatment that distinguish these programmes from those that are ineffective. Primarily, we propose that a change in our approach to treatment from a deficit model to a positive psychology approach incorporate and integrate two crucial features: the RNR and GLM. We illustrate this approach by describing our own treatment programme and its long-term evaluations.

The primary aim of sexual offender treatment is to reduce subsequent reoffending, and in this sense, treatment is tertiary prevention (Smallbone, Marshall and Wortley, 2008). However, there have been other suggested ways to reduce reoffending which Andrews and Bonta (2006) refer to in a disparaging way as 'getting tough' on crime. They provide clear evidence on the lack of effectiveness and the remarkably increased cost of these approaches. We will briefly review these alternatives.

What Works in Offender Rehabilitation: An Evidence-Based Approach to Assessment and Treatment,
First Edition. Edited by Leam A. Craig, Louise Dixon and Theresa A. Gannon.
© 2013 John Wiley & Sons, Ltd. Published 2013 by John Wiley & Sons, Ltd.

Punitive Alternatives to Treatment

In 1974, Martinson examined the data available at that time on rehabilitation efforts and famously concluded, 'nothing works'. This conclusion led to an abandonment of treatment and the adoption of an increased number and severity of sanctions (see Chapter 2). One startling decision was first made by Washington State which introduced the 'three strikes and you're out' law making life imprisonment mandatory for a third felony. Subsequently, 25 other states adopted this law (Turner *et al.*, 1999). Supporting these increasingly severe responses, Greenwood's (1982) analysis led him to claim that increasing the number of offenders in prison would result in less crime and would be cost effective. However, subsequent analyses, using the same data, resulted in contrary conclusions (Chaiken and Chaiken, 1982; Visher, 1986).

When crime rates began to fall in the 1990s, this was seen by advocates of tough on crime strategies as confirmation of the benefits of increased incarceration. As Andrews and Bonta (2006) point out, however, increases in prison populations began in the early 1970s whereas crime rates did not begin to fall until 20 years later. More telling is the observation that in those states where incarceration rates were highest, the drop in crime was the lowest, while in states with low rates of imprisonment, the reductions in crime were greatest (King, Mauer and Young, 2005).

Gendreau and his colleagues (Gendreau *et al.*, 2001; Smith, Goggin and Gendreau, 2002) have examined the effects of other types of sanctions in large-scale meta-analyses. They compared the relative effects of prison versus community sentences and found no differences (effect size $\emptyset = 0.07$). They also reported a lack of effects for longer as opposed to shorter sentences (effect size $\emptyset = 0.03$). Paparozzi and Gendreau (2005) noted that intensive supervision on its own does not reduce crime; it is only when it is accompanied by treatment that reoffending rates drop. For example, MacKenzie *et al.* (1995) illustrated that 'shock incarceration' and 'boot camps' – both of which represent fiercely punitive responses – did not reduce crime. Consistent with this finding, Jones and Ross (1987) showed that probationers who attended boot camps reoffended at higher rates (50.8%) than did matched offenders given regular probation (32.5%). Similarly, juvenile offenders who participated in 'Scared Straight' programmes (Finckenauer, 1979) had higher reoffence rates (41.3%) than did those who were not involved in these programmes (11.4%).

Finally, electronic, or more recently GPS, monitoring, while touted by law-and-order advocates, is not only very expensive, but its effects appear small and nonsignificant. First, these types of monitoring do not target the most at-risk felons but almost always involve low-risk offenders (Cullen, Wright and Applegate, 1996; Gable and Gable, 2005). More to the point, Bonta, Wallace-Capretta and Rooney (2000a) found that the monitoring system had no effect when risk factors were accounted for. Instead, they found that it was only when monitoring was accompanied by treatment that reductions in recidivism were apparent (Bonta, Wallace-Capretta and Rooney, 2000b).

As is clear from this brief review, harsher penalties do not in themselves reduce reoffending. Instead, when participation in treatment accompanies punitive approaches, it seems that recidivism is reduced. It seems reasonable to assume, on the basis of what we know about general punishment effects (Dinsmoor, 1998; McConville, 2003), that highly punitive responses will reduce the benefits that might otherwise be derived from treatment. These findings, in fact, testify to the resilience of treatment effects, but presumably treatment conducted under less punitive circumstances will be even more effective. Later in this chapter, we will attempt to evaluate this hypothesis.

We will begin the rest of this chapter by considering the relevance of theories about sexual offending for the design and implementation of treatment. We will then comment on their relevance for approaches to assessment. Next, we will review the literature on the effectiveness of treatment including our view on how best to evaluate effectiveness. This will be followed by a description of the latest version of our own programme that attempts to incorporate known effective elements.

Relevance of Theories for Treatment

In this section, we will discuss specific and general theories and examine their relevance for treatment design and implementation. We identify specific theories as those that attempt to explain the role in the aetiology of sexual offending of specific aspects of the behaviour (e.g., deviant interests, empathy), whereas general theories refer to more complex explanations that incorporate a variety of interacting influences.

Specific theories

Conditioning theories exerted the earliest influence on the design of sexual offender programmes. McGuire, Carlisle and Young (1965) outlined an aetiological account of sexual offending in which they proposed that the development of deviant sexual interests underpinned the problematic behaviour. Consequently, it was claimed that changing these preferences would lead to a cessation of offending (Bond and Evans, 1967). The development of deviant interests was framed in conditioning terms, a proposal that others (Abel and Blanchard, 1974; Laws and Marshall, 1990) expanded, although in these latter developments, deviant interests were seen as simply one part of the problem.

The value of these conditioning accounts was that they led to the development of a variety of effective behavioural procedures aimed at modifying deviant sexual preferences (Laws and Marshall, 1991; Marshall, O'Brien and Marshall, 2009), which turned out to be valuable since deviant preferences have been recently shown to predict reoffending (Craig, Browne and Stringer, 2003; Hanson and Bussière, 1998; Hanson and Morton-Bourgon, 2005). Despite these observations, a significant number of sexual offender programmes currently fail to include sexual preferences as a target in treatment. For example, in McGrath, Cumming and Burchard's (2003) survey of 951 programmes for adult sexual offenders, just over 50% targeted deviant sexual preferences, and when they did, the majority employed covert sensitization which does not have resounding empirical support.

Other specific theories have been generated to explain the origin of, and treatment implications for, a variety of targets that have been addressed in sexual offender treatment. There have been theories about the role and nature of empathy deficits (Marshall, Marshall and Serran, 2009; Marshall *et al.*, 1995; Pithers, 1994), self-esteem and shame (Marshall, Anderson and Champagne, 1997; Marshall *et al.*, 2009), self-regulation (Ward, 1999; Ward and Hudson, 2000), offence pathways (Hudson, Ward and McCormack, 1999), attitudes and cognitions (McFall, 1990; Murphy, 1990), schemas (Mann and Shingler, 2006), attachment, intimacy and loneliness (Marshall, 1989; Marshall and Marshall, 2000; Ward *et al.*, 1995) and sexual preoccupation (Marshall and Marshall, 2001, 2006; Marshall and O'Brien, 2009). Each of these specific theories has led to the generation of considerable research which is an important feature in evaluating the utility of a theory (Hooker, 1987; Newton-Smith, 2002).

The results of this research have in some cases justified the issue being targeted in treatment (i.e., self-regulation, attachments and sexual preoccupation), while in other cases (e.g., empathy, and attitudes and cognitions), their status as criminogenic (i.e., predictive of reoffending) appears doubtful.

Overall, specific theories have had more direct relevance to the identification of criminogenic targets and to the development of treatment procedures than have general theories.

General theories

There have been a number of influential general theories concerning the aetiology and maintenance of sexual offending including: Malamuth's *Confluence Model* (Malamuth, 1996; Malamuth, Heavey and Linz, 1993), Hall and Hirschman's (1991, 1992) *Quadripartite Model*, Marshall and Barbaree's (1990) *Integrated Theory* and Finkelhor's *Precondition Model* (Finkelhor, 1984). While these theories have been fruitful in generating research, they all have flaws (see review by Ward, Polaschek and Beech, 2006) and have, for the most part, not provided direct influences on treatment. The exception to this has been Finkelhor's account of the necessary conditions for an offence to occur which has provided some guidance to treatment providers. However, there are three general rehabilitation theories that have exerted a significant influence on both treatment design and on the style of treatment delivery style.

Relapse prevention

The first general theory to exert a very significant and direct influence on treatment design was Marques' (1982) adaptation of Marlatt's (1982) *RP* approach to the treatment of addictions. In North America, in particular, RP rapidly became the framework of all but a few treatment programmes and its influence soon spread beyond the boundaries of the continent. The RP model specified conditions that must be met for the benefits derived from treatment to be maintained after discharge from the programme or release from incarceration. While these notions were sensible, they did unfortunately generate a treatment focus on deficits and represented what others (Marshall *et al.*, 2005, 2011; Yates, 2007; Yates and Ward, 2009) have seen as an excessively and unproductive negative focus in treatment.

Ward and his colleagues (Ward and Hudson, 1996, 1998; Ward, Hudson and Siegert, 1995) offered a series of critical evaluations of the RP approach. They pointed to its many theoretical faults and problematic treatment implications. Most importantly, Marques *et al.* (2005) demonstrated in a carefully designed study that RP did not generate reductions in reoffending.

However, it cannot be denied that the RP approach to treatment, for better or worse, has been one of the most influential models in the history of sexual offender treatment. Fortunately, in recent years, two other rehabilitation theories have exerted a significant influence, and they provide clear frameworks for designing and implementing treatment.

Risk–needs–responsivity   The *RNR* principles of effective offender treatment, enunciated by Andrews and Bonta (2006) and derived from a series of meta-analyses, represent a clearly articulated model to guide treatment. In this sense, it is superior to most of the alternatives because it is entirely empirically based and clearly specifies all the design and implementation features necessary for treatment to be effective. While Andrews' series of studies have focused on treatment effectiveness with a variety of different types of offenders, Hanson *et al.* (2009) have shown that the RNR principles apply equally well to sexual offender programmes.

Both Andrews and Bonta, and Hanson *et al.*, demonstrated that the *Risk* principle exerted the least influence on treatment outcome; in both sets of data, it was the *Needs* and *Responsivity* principles that generated the largest effects. The *Needs* principle simply states that treatment should address established criminogenic features; that is, those characteristics of offenders that have been shown to predict reoffending and that are at least potentially changeable. Hanson (Hanson, 2006; Hanson and Harris, 2000) has identified the criminogenic features relevant to sexual offenders. We should note that while it is clear that addressing too many noncriminogenic features of offenders reduces effectiveness, there are good reasons for targeting some of these needs (see comment by Andrews and Bonta, 2006, p. 281). For example, low self-esteem and shame, which are common characteristics of sexual offenders (Marshall *et al.*, 2009), are both obstacles to effective engagement in change processes (Baumeister, 1993; Tangney and Dearing, 2002). Therefore, it is necessary to address these two noncriminogenic factors in order to win the clients' cooperation with treatment.

Because the effective programmes in Andrews' series of meta-analyses (see Andrews and Bonta, 2006, for details) were all based on cognitive-behavioural therapy (CBT), it was assumed by Hanson *et al.* (2009) that if a programme adopted a CBT approach, then it had met the criteria for the *Responsivity* principle. However, a closer inspection of this principle (Marshall and Marshall, 2011a) reveals that it is only when programmes adhere to what Andrews and Bonta (2006) call the *core correctional practices* (CCP) that they have effective outcomes. However, in Andrews' meta-analyses, the only programmes that met these practices were CBT. This does not mean, however, that non-CBT programmes will be ineffective. Indeed, a report by Kriegman (2006) demonstrated that a psychodynamically oriented programme for high-risk sexual offenders that adhered to both the *Needs* and *Responsivity* principles was remarkably effective (38% recidivism in the untreated group versus 19% in the treated group).

The CCP as outlined by Andrews and Bonta (2006) involve two principles: relationship and structuring. Together these two principles encompass what we have referred to as the effective delivery of treatment. Essentially, they require the careful selection of therapists for specific characteristics, training the therapists in the appropriate application and content of the programme and monitoring their operation of the programme. Therapists should be selected for several qualities (e.g., empathy, warmth, support, respectfulness), and for their behavioural tendencies (e.g., modelling of prosocial attitudes and behaviours). Training should involve not only targeting the specific criminogenic features and implementing appropriate procedures to change them but also emphasizing the important aspects of the delivery of treatments. The latter includes forming an effective alliance as well as rewarding expressions of prosocial attitudes and behaviours and challenging or ignoring inappropriate remarks. Monitoring therapists, once they are running a group, can take various forms, but the best strategy is to hold weekly discussions complemented with periodic *in situ* supervision.

Good Lives Model   The most recent influential rehabilitation theory is Ward's (2002) *GLM*. Ward derived his model from the evidence on human striving which originated in Maslow's (1968) notion that people work towards self-actualization. According to this literature, people, whether they are aware of it or not, attempt to maximize their potential across a variety of domains (see Austin and Vancouver, 1996; Emmons, 1996; Rasmussen, 1999; Schmack and Sheldon, 2001). From this literature, Ward identified nine domains of functioning (or personal goods) within which we all strive to succeed. All people (i) seek optimal mental, physical and sexual health; (ii) pursue knowledge of one type or another; (iii) attempt to gain mastery in work and play; (iv) try to achieve a degree of autonomy; (v) search for inner peace; (vi) strive to be creative; (vii) seek relatedness; (viii) establish some sort of spirituality; and (ix) desire happiness. While people strive towards these goals, and hopefully continually increase their effectiveness, they may never fully self-actualize in any of the domains; it is, rather, the lifelong steady improvement that generates satisfaction. The standard against which individuals should measure their success is themselves so that any improvements can be seen as meaningful achievements.

In their various papers on the GLM, Ward and his colleagues (Ward and Brown, 2003; Ward, Collie and Bourke, 2009; Ward and Gannon, 2006; Ward and Mann, 2004; Ward, Mann and Gannon, 2007; Ward and Marshall, 2004; Ward and Stewart, 2003; Chapter 17, this volume) suggest that this model could provide a framework for treatment that is based on developing offenders' strengths, thereby avoiding the traditional approach of focusing only on clients' deficits and on their problematic past behaviour. The GLM approach declares that sexual offenders have failed to find satisfaction due to a lack of the skills necessary to achieve success in some or all of the nine domains. As a result, they have sought inappropriate ways (i.e., offending) to meet their needs. Thus, training sexual offenders to identify the nine personal goods and equipping them with the skills and attitudes necessary to move towards succeeding in these domains are hypothesized by Ward and colleagues to constitute effective sexual offender treatment (see Chapter 17).

Ward *et al.* (2009) pointed out that treatment framed around the GLM was not only compatible with Andrews and Bonta's (2006) RNR principles, but that attaining the skills necessary to achieve success in the nine domains would reciprocally deal with the deficits identified by the *Needs* principle. Given that the GLM has emerged from the relatively recent 'positive psychology' movement (see Linley and Joseph, 2004; Snyder and Lopez, 2005), with its emphasis on a respectful and hopeful approach to clients, it means that properly adopting the GLM should result in delivering treatment consistent with the *Responsivity* principle.

It is evident that the GLM has clear implications for treatment both in terms of the targets to be addressed and, with its emphasis on a positive approach (Ward and Mann, 2004; Ward and Marshall, 2004), in terms of the delivery of treatment.

Relevance of Theories for Assessment

Again, it is the RNR principles defined by Andrews and Bonta (2006) and Ward's (2002) GLM that are the most relevant theories to designing assessments. Assessments are meant to serve several purposes, the most relevant of which for the purposes of this chapter are to (i) provide an initial basis for individual case formulation and (ii) evaluate treatment gains. The latter can be done by either addressing changes from pre to post treatment, or by conducting a post-treatment estimate of how close to normative functioning the offender is at the end of treatment.

We (Marshall *et al.*, 2011) have expressed reservations about the utility of pre-treatment case formulations. We have suggested that once an offender is effectively engaged in treatment, he is more likely to be honest in his identification of issues that he needs to work on and that, in any event, case formulation is, or should be, a dynamic, continuously modified conceptualization of treatment needs (Persons, 2008). Therefore, we allow case formulations to unfold over the first several treatment sessions within a framework guided by known criminogenic features and the personal goods of the GLM. For these and other reasons (e.g., validity of their self-reports), we have serious reservations about the value of a battery of pre- and post-treatment tests that rely on the offender's self-report. Our solution to the problem of determining the offenders' status at the end of treatment has been to develop a Therapist Rating Scale (Marshall *et al.*, 2011). This scale requires the therapist to rate each offender at the end of treatment on 10 features that represent a combination of criminogenic features and future plans. We (Marshall *et al.*, 2011) have evidence to show that therapist ratings at the end of treatment predict success or failure (i.e., reoffending or not), whereas various other factors (e.g., age, pre-treatment actuarial risk estimates and scores on the PCL-R) do not.

Evaluating Treatment

The first question that is typically asked about this issue is posed as 'Is treatment with sexual offenders effective?' We (Marshall and Marshall, 2011b) suggested that this is an inappropriate way to phrase this critical question. When the issue is framed in this way, it appears to imply that treatment for sexual offenders is uniformly the same across all settings. This is clearly not the case. Surveys of North American programmes (Burton and Smith-Darden, 2001; Marshall and Anderson, 2000; McGrath, Cumming and Burchard, 2003; McGrath *et al.*, 2010), for instance, have consistently shown a remarkable variability in the problems addressed in treatment, the procedures employed to modify these problems, the adherence to a particular model (e.g., cognitive behaviour therapy with or without RP components) and, most particularly, how closely programmes follow the principles of effective treatment delivery.

Given this variability across programmes, it makes little sense to frame the question about effectiveness in such all-encompassing terms. We (Marshall and Marshall, 2011b) rephrased the question as 'Can treatment of sexual offenders be effective?' Framed in this way, we only need to find one report of effectiveness to answer the question positively and then carefully examine the effective programme to determine why it was beneficial. Of course, few reviewers would be satisfied with finding just one programme to be effective, although the remarkable effectiveness of one application of *multi-systemic therapy* with juvenile sexual offenders (Borduin, Schaeffer and Heiblum, 2009) has been lauded by even the most sceptical reviewers (see Hanson, 2010; Rice, 2010; Seto *et al.*, 2008). What, then, does the literature indicate regarding the effectiveness of treatment?

In order to answer this question, we need to consider what would count as a satisfactory evaluation. Almost all reviewers accept that outcome evaluations should rely on official records of reoffences. While official records certainly underestimate the true rate of reoffending, it appears to provide a satisfactory basic upon which to infer the effectiveness, or not, of treatment. For example, we (Marshall and Barbaree, 1988) have shown that when a rich source of unofficial reports of sexual reoffending are accessed and those data are compared with official information, the proportional increase in total reoffending is the same for treated and untreated sexual offenders. Official data alone reflect rather low base rates (i.e., rates of reoffending in untreated offenders) which presents statistical limits to the chance of inferring treatment effects (see Barbaree (1997) for a discussion). However, in most settings the official records are the only available source of information on reoffending.

Once the basis for determining reoffence rates has been established, the next step is to decide what will serve as the comparison against which to compare the outcome of the treated group. There are essentially three possible designs that might allow inferences about effectiveness each with their own advocates.

The RCT requires that volunteers for treatment be randomly assigned to treatment or no treatment, and it has its articulate advocates in the sexual offender field (Quinsey *et al.*, 1993; Rice, 2010; Rice and Harris, 2003; Seto *et al.*, 2008). Two examples of RCT studies were described by Marques (Marques *et al.*, 2005) with adult sexual offenders and by Bourdain *et al.* (2009) with juvenile sexual offenders. Marques' study showed no difference between treated and untreated offenders, while Bourdain's report revealed dramatically positive effects. Actually, Bourdain *et al.* (2009) did not compare those receiving multi-systemic therapy with a nontreatment group, but rather with an alternative treatment that was expected to be, and was, ineffective. Seto (2011) has similarly suggested that within an RCT design, it might be best to compare current versions of treatment that are based on RNR principles and the GLM with earlier forms of treatment such as those commonly employed in the 1980s. This, Seto suggested, would overcome the practical and ethical concerns we (Marshall, 1993; Marshall and Marshall, 2007; Marshall and Pithers, 1994) have expressed about using an RCT design. We certainly find this to be a more acceptable form of this design, but we will have to wait for some years before such a study can be implemented and the evaluation completed.

The second alternative strategy has been described by Hanson *et al.* (2002) as an *incidental* design. In this approach, the treated group is compared with a group of untreated offenders from the same, or a sufficiently similar, setting who have been selected by matching them on the relevant features of the treated men. This design is not without its critics (e.g., the advocates of the RCT approach) and is not always possible to do. For example, in the setting where we operate our programme, we are able to persuade almost all (over 96%) of the available sexual offenders to enter treatment, and all but 4% of those who enter treatment complete the programme. While these data reflect well on our programme since high refusal rates and a large number of dropouts would diminish the value of treatment, they result in the lack of availability of an untreated group. The Correctional Service of Canada, which funds our programmes, expects us to treat all available sexual offenders, and their continued support for our programme would disappear if we did not get close to this goal.

This lack of an available group of untreated offenders led us to search for an alternative way to evaluate our programme. We (Marshall and Marshall, 2007), borrowing from an earlier suggestion by Barbaree, Langton and Peacock (2003), proposed comparing the actual reoffence rates of our treated subjects with their expected rates of reoffending derived from pre-treatment actuarial risk assessment instruments: for sexual reoffences, this was a combination of STATIC-99 and RRASOR estimates; for violent reoffending, it was the VRAG; and for general reoffending, it was the LSI-R. We scored each treated client on each of these measures and then averaged the scores over the whole group to get an estimate of the expected rates of reoffending for the group had they been left untreated. This proposed way of getting around the problem of the lack of availability of an untreated group has not won the acceptance of all researchers, but the specific objections to this design have not yet been clearly presented. In our view, if the results of static, actuarial risk instruments can serve, as they do (see Doren, 2002), to support civilly committing an offender or declaring a convicted man to be a dangerous offender (both of which result in indefinite confinement), then surely they can serve as a basis for estimating treatment effects. The value of accepting this method of evaluating treatment is that it allows many programmes to report their effectiveness or lack thereof. This would markedly increase the number of published treatment outcome studies which would provide a stronger basis for not only examining effectiveness but also for determining what differentiates effective from ineffective treatment.

The available evidence does indeed suggest that treatment can produce beneficial changes with sexual offenders while at the same time demonstrating that a significant number of programmes have been ineffective. A number of meta-analyses have been conducted all showing overall beneficial effects although several of these studies (Alexander, 1999; Gallagher *et al.*, 1999; Hall, 1995) have been criticized for not setting satisfactory standards for the programmes they selected. Two meta-analyses (Hanson *et al.*, 2002; Lösel and Schmucker, 2005), however, have generally been accepted as having adequately established standards for the programmes they chose. Both these large-scale meta-analyses ($K = 43$, $N = 9454$ in Hanson *et al.* and $K = 81$, $N = 22\,181$ in Lösel and Schmucker) demonstrated an overall positive effect for treatment. In Hanson *et al.*'s report, the treated subjects' reoffence rate was 12.3% against a rate of 16.8% for the untreated group. Similar results were evident from Lösel and Schmuckier's analyses (treated = 11.1%; untreated 17.5%). In both studies, CBT programmes generally did better than other programmes. Interestingly, when programmes were effective, they also significantly reduced the sexual offenders' propensities to commit nonsexual offences. This suggests that appropriately designed and implemented treatment is likely to have both specific (reduces sexual reoffending) and general (reduces antisocial behaviour) effects. What then constitutes appropriately designed and implemented treatment?

We believe the sexual offender programmes that are most likely to produce beneficial effects are those that embody the following four features: (i) they target all known criminogenic factors and few, if any, noncriminogenic factors (i.e., adhere to Andrews and Bonta's *Needs* principle); (ii) they deliver treatment in established maximally effective ways (i.e., adhere to Andrews and Bonta's *Responsivity* principle); (iii) they employ procedures to modify criminogenic targets that are known to be effective; and (iv) they frame treatment in a positive, strength-based manner possibly along the lines of the GLM. Consistent with these ideas, Hanson *et al.* (2009) showed that when the RNR principles were appropriately applied, treatment was very effective, but when they were not effectively implemented, treatment had little or no impact. More precisely, the correct application of the *Needs* and *Responsivity* principles explained almost all of the variance in the benefits derived from treatment. Once again, Hanson *et al.* showed that treatment benefits not only reflected reductions in sexual reoffending (10.9% in treated subjects versus 19.2% in untreated offenders) but also in nonsexual reoffending (31.8% in the treated group versus 48.3% in the untreated group).

In 'A positive strength-based approach to treatment', we will describe our own treatment programme which embodies the four features listed in the previous paragraph, and we will then provide outcome data from this programme supporting our claim that these are indeed the critical features of effective treatment.

A Positive Strength-Based Approach to Treatment

Our programme is described in detail in our most recent book (Marshall *et al.*, 2011). While its design principally derives from the RNR principles and is framed to an important degree in terms of the GLM, it is also significantly influenced by the spirit of Miller and Rollnick's (2002) *Motivational Interviewing* and by the recent shift in emphasis in general clinical work away from a deficit model towards a strength-based approach that is exemplified in what has been called *positive psychology* (Aspinwall and Staudinger, 2002; Peterson, 2006; Seligman, 2002; Seligman and Csikszentmihalyi, 2000). Among the many developments in *positive psychology* that have influenced our thinking about treatment, the most important have been *hope theory* (Snyder, 1994, 2000), the development of resilience (Yates and Masten, 2004), the promotion of subjective well-being (Diener, Lucas and Oishi, 2005) and the generation of optimism (Seligman, 1991). The interested reader is referred to the edited books by Linley and Joseph (2004) and Snyder and Lopez (2005) for a broad sampling of this fascinating and relevant literature on *positive psychology*.

Our treatment operates as a rolling (or open-ended) group format with 1 therapist and 10 clients, meeting for two 2.5-hour sessions per week over an average stay of between 4 and 5 months. At any one time, there will be clients who have recently entered the programme, others will be near the end and the rest will be at various points in between. All clients follow approximately the same order of addressing the issues although we flexibly adjust this according to various possible factors. We are especially attentive to each individual's personal characteristics, learning style and capacity, social and cultural background as well as their unique view of human behaviour. More specifically, we emphasize the need for between-sessions practice of their newly acquired skills. In the prison setting, this often requires practice with other inmates as well as prison staff, and in the context of their family visits particularly those involving conjugal visits. When we operated a community programme, we similarly insisted on between-sessions practice, and in both settings there are other homework requirements. Between-sessions practice increases the likelihood of the generalization of skills acquired in the group to the other circumstances of the client's life (Martin and Pear, 1992; Spiegler and Guevremont, 1998). It also provides an opportunity to get feedback to help solve problems with implementation.

In addition to other features of our programme, we attempt to ensure that cognitions, behaviours and emotions are all integrated within every topic and every issue that is addressed (Marshall *et al.*, 2006). Too many so-called cognitive behavioural programmes that we have visited have very few behavioural elements (e.g., little in the way of role-plays, behavioural rehearsals and often no programmed between-sessions practice) and often carefully avoid any more than minimal emotional expressions. As we have pointed out, behavioural elements are essential to effective treatment (Fernandez, Shingler and Marshall, 2006), and treatment that eschews emotional expressiveness is unlikely to be effective (Greenberg, Rice and Elliott, 1993). On this latter point, Beech (Beech and Fordham, 1997; Beech and Hamilton-Giachritsis, 2005) and Pfäfflin *et al.* (2005) have demonstrated the critical importance of emotional expressiveness in achieving the goals of treatment with sexual offenders.

With all these features in mind, we conceptualize our treatment programme as having three phases. Phase 1 is aimed exclusively at engaging each client and winning his trust and confidence in the therapist. Although we target several issues in Phase 1, these targets are specifically chosen because they are nonthreatening and personally enhancing. As a first step, we describe the results of our outcome study (see following text) indicating the likely benefits the clients will derive from treatment. We point out that we will address the issues that led to their offending by providing them with the skills and attitudes necessary to meet their needs in more appropriate ways that will result in them having a better, more satisfying life. It is at this point that we introduce the framework of the GLM and indicate that our treatment will set them on a course that over time, after discharge, they can continue to work to achieve an increasingly greater sense of self-fulfilment.

In Phase 1, we begin to target four specific issues: self-esteem, a sense of shame, coping skills and mood management. On each of these issues, sexual offenders have been shown to be defi-cient and the latter two combine to produce poor emotional regulation which is an identified criminogenic factor and underpins behavioural dysregulation. Low self-esteem and shame, although not shown to be criminogenic, represent obstacles to effective engagement in any programme that aims at producing sought-after changes. These Phase 1 targets are seen by the offenders as beneficial and nonthreatening. Effectively enhancing skills and confidence in these areas increases engagement as well as enhancing trust in the therapist and in the clients' belief that treatment will be helpful to them. Addressing these four issues continues throughout treatment whenever opportunities arise as we target other behaviours.

We also ask offenders to produce an autobiography and to do a disclosure that simply describes the events and emotions that led them to commit an offence. They are told that we do not want them to describe their offence as this is unchangeable. There is no evidence that eliciting offence details, matching what the victim described, enhances treatment effectiveness, and the data from other research areas suggest that this is an unwise strategy (see Marshall, Marshall and Kingston, 2011; Marshall, Marshall and Ware, 2009, for detailed discussions of the relevant evidence).

Phase 2 addresses known criminogenic factors such as deficits in relationship skills including dysfunctional attachment styles that result in deficiencies in intimacy and the experience of chronic loneliness. We address these issues by assisting the clients in developing the skills, attitudes and self-confidence necessary to meet their relationship needs in prosocial and effective ways. Thus, the focus is on developing strengths rather than presenting the issues as deficits to be eliminated. For example, we outline the health and emotional benefits of adequate levels of intimacy rather than the negative consequences of a lack of intimacy. This, we find, is a more motivational way to construe the targets of treatment.

Similarly, when targeting sexual issues (e.g., prudishness and lack of knowledge of effective sexual skills and the behaviours that maximize sexual satisfaction), we emphasize the acquisition of previously absent strengths rather than construing their earlier functioning as indicative of problems. Even when we target deviant sexual interests, the focus is on enhancing their attraction to prosocial sexual activities. For example, our first choice among the various behavioural strategies for changing sexual interests, and the procedure we believe to be most effective, is a combination of orgasmic reconditioning (Marquis, 1970) and satiation therapy (Marshall, 1979; Marshall and Lippins, 1977). These procedures involve shaping appropriate interests during regular masturbatory practices as the first step. Once orgasm occurs and the refractory period onsets, offenders are instructed to associate this period with the rehearsal of their deviant fantasies so as to extinguish their attractiveness (see Marshall, O'Brien and Marshall, 2009, for details of combining these two strategies).

In Phase 2, we continue work on enhancing coping skills and improving mood management during which we emphasize the need to slow down and carefully evaluate the situation before considering the various options open to them. The clients are encouraged to calmly select a course of action that is likely to maximize both the short- and long-term benefits to themselves and others. The skills necessary to deal with life's difficulties can, we emphasize, be readily acquired and, when appropriately implemented, will not only lead to beneficial consequences but will also result in more stable and positive moods.

At the beginning of Phase 3, we reprise the GLM and ask the clients to identify which of the nine personal goods they will choose to put most of their energy into upon release to the community. We suggest they select only two or three to work on most energetically but to keep in mind the remaining goods for future efforts. In terms of the likelihood of relatively immediate benefits, we suggest to most offenders that seeking pleasurable leisure activities might be an important goal. So long as their chosen activities do not place them at risk to reoffend, increasing their level of enjoyable activities will diminish boredom resulting from idle time and thereby reduce their risk. The two other pursuits we encourage upon release involve seeking educational upgrading and enhancing their work skills.

Included in Phase 3 is the requirement to identify a group of people who can support their readjustment back into the community by encouraging their pursuit of the identified GLM goals. Again our emphasis is not on having supports who will directly ensure they avoid reoffending but rather on people who will help facilitate personal development and thereby reciprocally reduce reoffending. While there can be no doubt about the value of personal supports (Wilson, 2007), it is important to have the clients understand that it is they who must take responsibility for achieving their goals. There is clear evidence that a danger of using supports is that clients can readily shift the onus onto these supports for doing the necessary work (Fitzsimons and Finkel, 2011).

Not surprisingly, given our strength-based emphases, we do not require our clients to generate a list of RP strategies. The general psychological literature indicates quite clearly that avoidance goals (which define RP plans) are rarely maintained (Gollwitzer and Bargh, 1996), and in any case RP plans can never be comprehensive enough to cover all possibilities. Approach goals, on the other hand, are readily maintained and are more likely to result in successful outcomes (Emmons, 1996; Gollwitzer and Bargh, 1996). As Mann *et al.* (2004) demonstrated, sexual offender programmes that emphasized approach goals, compared to those that demanded the generation of avoidance strategies, generated higher levels of engagement and motivation, greater completion of between-sessions tasks and an eagerness to disclose valuable information.

This, then, constitutes a brief description of our treatment programme which has emphasized the positive motivational aspects rather than the procedural elements. Readers who want more information on the details of our programme, and particularly the specific procedures we employ, are referred to our series of three books that describe in detail all aspects of our approach (Marshall, Anderson and Fernandez, 1999; Marshall *et al.*, 2006, 2011).

Finally, our outcome evaluations have revealed significant benefits in terms of reduced rates of reoffending. We have followed, and continue to follow, 535 sexual offenders treated in our programme during the period 1991–2001. After release into the community for an average of 5.4 years, 3.2% of our treated clients had reoffended sexually against an expected rate (based on a combination of STATIC-99 and RRASOR scores) of 16.8%. At 8.4 years of follow-up, the sexual reoffence rate slightly increased to 5.6% compared to an increased expected rate of 23.8%. As was the case in both Hanson *et al.*'s (2002) and Lösel and Schmucker's (2005) reports, the additional effects of our programme were to reduce nonsexual and violent reoffending. At 5.4 years of follow-up, the nonsexual reoffending rate among our clients was 13.6% comparing favourably to the expected rate (based on LSI-R scores) of 40.0%, while at 8.4 years of follow-up, violent reoffending was at 8.4% compared to an expected rate (based on VRAG scores) of 34.8%.

Conclusions

The data provided in this chapter not only show that our programme is effective in reducing all indices of reoffending, the effect size related to the reductions in sexual reoffences significantly exceeds the best results reported in all meta-analyses of sexual offender treatment (see Marshall and McGuire, 2003, for a summary of relevant effect sizes). From these findings and the results reported in the meta-analyses earlier in this chapter, we conclude that treatment of sexual offenders can be, and often is, effective. In particular, these findings suggest that our hypothesis stated at the beginning of this chapter was confirmed; that is, treatment conducted in the absence of otherwise punitive circumstances is effective. More specifically, when treatment focuses on building strengths, rather than reducing deficits, and when it addresses known criminogenic features and delivers treatment in a psychotherapeutically appropriate way, the benefits derived from treatment will be maximized. Our results also indicate that treatment conducted in this way will minimize refusers and dropouts.

We believe the future development of programmes should be based on expanding the approach embodied in positive psychology (including the GLM) while attending to the RNR principles and what is known about effective therapeutic delivery style. Continued research devoted to more thoroughly identifying criminogenic features of sexual offenders should lead to an expansion of treatment targets which, in turn, should further enhance the effectiveness of treatment.

References

Abel, G.G. and Blanchard, E.B. (1974) The role of fantasy in the treatment of sexual deviation. *Archives of General Psychiatry*, 30, 467–475.

Alexander, M.A. (1999) Sexual offender treatment efficacy revisited. *Sexual Abuse: A Journal of Research and Treatment*, 11, 101–116.

Andrews, D.A. and Bonta, J. (2006) *The Psychology of Criminal Conduct*, 4th edn, Lexis Nexis, Markham.

Aspinwall, L.G. and Staudingher, U.M. (eds) (2002) *A Psychology of Human Strengths: Fundamental Questions and Future Directions for a Positive Psychology*. American Psychological Association, Washington, DC.

Austin, J.T. and Vancouver, J.B. (1996) Goal constructs in psychology: structure, process, and content. *Psychological Bulletin*, 120, 338–375.

Barbaree, H.E. (1997) Evaluating treatment efficacy with sexual offenders: the insensitivity of recidivism studies to treatment efficacy. *Sexual Abuse: A Journal of Research and Treatment*, 9, 111–128.

Barbaree, H.E., Langton, C. and Peacock, E.J. (2003) The evaluation of sex offender treatment efficacy using samples stratified by levels of actuarial risk. Paper presented at the 22nd Annual Research and Treatment Conference of the Association for the Treatment of Sexual Abusers, St. Louis, October 3.

Baumeister, R.F. (ed.) (1993) *Self-Esteem: The Puzzle of Low Self-Regard*, Plenum Press, New York.

Beech, A.R. and Fordham, A.S. (1997) Therapeutic climate of sexual offender treatment programs. *Sexual Abuse: A Journal of Research and Treatment*, 9, 219–237.

Beech, A.R. and Hamilton-Giachritsis, C.E. (2005) Relationship between therapeutic climate and treatment outcome in group-based sexual offender treatment programs. *Sexual Abuse: A Journal of Research and Treatment*, 17, 127–140.

Bond, I.K. and Evans, D.R. (1967) Avoidance therapy: its use in two cases of underwear fetishism. *Canadian Medical Association Journal*, 96, 1160–1162.

Bonta, J., Wallace-Capretta, S. and Rooney, J. (2000a) A quasi-experimental evaluation of an intensive rehabilitation supervision program. *Criminal Justice and Behavior*, 27, 312–329.

Bonta, J., Wallace-Capretta, S. and Rooney, J. (2000b) Can electronic monitoring make a difference? An evaluation of three Canadian programs. *Crime & Delinquency*, 46, 61–75.

Bourduin, C.M., Schaeffer, C.M. and Heiblum, N. (2009) A randomized clinical trial of Multi-systematic therapy with juvenile sexual offenders: effects on youth social ecology and criminal activity. *Journal of Consulting and Clinical Psychology*, 77, 26–37.

Burton, D.L. and Smith-Darden, J. (2001) *North American Survey of Sexual Abuser Treatment and Models: Summary Data 2000*, Safer Society Press, Brandon.

Chaiken, J.M. and Chaiken, M.R. (1982) *Varieties of Criminal Behavior: Summary and Policy Implications*, Rand, Santa Monica.

Craig, L.A., Browne, K.D. and Stringer, I. (2003) Risk scales and factors predictive of sexual offence recidivism. *Trauma, Violence, and Abuse: A Review Journal*, 4, 45–68.

Cullen, F.T., Wright, J.P. and Applegate, B.K. (1996) Control in the community: the limits of reform? in *Choosing Correctional Options That Work: Defining the Demand and Evaluating the Supply* (ed. A.T. Harland), Sage, Thousand Oaks, pp. 69–116.

Diener, E., Lucas, R.E. and Oishi, S. (2005) Subjective well-being: the science of happiness and life satisfaction, in *Handbook of Positive Psychology* (eds C.R. Snyder and S.J. Lopez), Oxford University Press, New York, pp. 63–73.

Dinsmoor, J.A. (1998) Punishment, in *Learning and Behavior Therapy* (ed. W. O'Donohue), Allyn & Bacon, New York, pp. 188–204.

Doren, D.M. (2002) *Evaluating Sex Offenders: A Manual for Civil Commitments and Beyond*, Sage, Thousand Oaks.

Emmons, R.A. (1996) Striving and feeling: personal goals and subjective well-being, in *The Psychology of Action: Linking Cognition and Motivation to Behavior* (eds P.M. Gollwitzer and J.A. Bargh), Guilford Press, New York, pp. 313–337.

Fernandez, Y.M., Shingler, J. and Marshall, W.L. (2006) Putting "behavior" back into the cognitive-behavioral treatment of sexual offenders, in *Sexual Offender Treatment: Controversial Issues* (eds W.L. Marshall, Y.M. Fernandez, L.E. Marshall and G.A. Serran), John Wiley & Sons, Ltd, Chichester, pp. 211–224.

Finckenauer, J.O. (1979) Juvenile Awareness Project: Evaluation. *Rep. no. 2.* Rutgers' School of Criminal Justice, Newark.

Finkelhor, D. (1984) *Child Sexual Abuse: New Theory and Research*, Free Press, New York.

Fitzsimons, G.M. and Finkel, E.J. (2011) Outsourcing self-regulation. *Psychological Science*, 22, 369–375.

Gable, R.K. and Gable, R.S. (2005) Electronic monitoring: positive intervention strategies. *Federal Probation*, 69, 21–25.

Gallagher, C.A., Wilson, D.B., Hirschfield, P. *et al.* (1999) A quantitative review of the effects of sexual offender treatment on sexual reoffending. *Corrections Management Quarterly*, 3, 19–29.

Gendreau, P., Goggin, C., Cullen, F. and Paparozzi, M. (2001) The effects of community sanctions and incarceration on recidivism, in *Compendium 2000 on Effective Correctional Programming* (eds L.L. Motiuk and R.C. Serin), Correctional Service of Canada, Ottawa.

Gollwitzer, P.M. and Bargh, J.A. (eds) (1996) *The Psychology of Action: Linking Cognition and Motivation to Behavior*, Guilford Press, New York.

Greenberg, L.S., Rice, L.N. and Elliott, R. (1993) *Facilitating Emotional Change: The Moment-by-Moment Process*, Guildford Press, New York.

Greenwood, R.O. (1982) *Selective Incapacitation*, Rand, Santa Monica.

Hall, G.C.N. (1995) Sexual offender recidivism revisited: a meta-analysis of recent treatment studies. *Journal of Consulting and Clinical Psychology*, 63, 802–809.

Hall, G.C.N. and Hirschman, R. (1991) Towards a theory of sexual aggression: a quadripartite model. *Journal of Consulting and Clinical Psychology*, 59, 662–669.

Hall, G.C.N. and Hirschman, R. (1992) Sexual aggression against children: a conceptual perspective of etiology. *Criminal Justice and Behavior*, 19, 8–23.

Hanson, R.K. (2006) Stability and change: dynamic risk factors for sexual offenders, in *Sexual Offender Treatment: Controversial Issues* (eds W.L. Marshall, Y.M. Fernandez, L.E. Marshall and G.A. Serran), John Wiley & Sons, Ltd, Chichester, pp. 17–31.

Hanson, R.K. (2010) Meta-analysis of treatment outcome in sexual offenders. Paper presented at the 11th Conference of the International Association for the Treatment of Sexual Offenders, Oslo, September 5.

Hanson, R.K. and Bussière, M.T. (1998) Predicting relapse: a meta-analysis of sexual offender recidivism studies. *Journal of Consulting and Clinical Psychology*, 66, 348–362.

Hanson, R.K. and Harris, A.J.R. (2000) Where should we intervene? Dynamic predictors of sex offender recidivism. *Criminal Justice and Behavior*, 27, 6–35.

Hanson, R.K., Gordon, A., Harris, A.J.R. *et al.* (2002) First report of the Collaborative Outcome Data Project on the effectiveness of psychological treatment of sex offenders. *Sexual Abuse: A Journal of Research and Treatment*, 14, 169–194.

Hanson, R.K., Bourgon, G., Helmus, L. and Hodgson, S. (2009) The principles of effective correctional treatment also apply to sexual offenders: a meta-analysis. *Criminal Justice Behavior*, 36, 865–891.

Hooker, C.A. (1987) *A Realistic Theory of Science*, State University of New York Press, Albany.

Hudson, S.M., Ward, T. and McCormack, J.C. (1999) Offense pathways in sexual offenders. *Journal of Interpersonal Violence*, 14, 779–798.

Jones, M. and Ross, D.L. (1987) Is less better? Boot camp, regular probation and re-arrest in North Carolina. *American Journal of Criminal Justice*, 21, 145–161.

King, R.S., Mauer, M. and Young, M.C. (2005) *Incarceration and Crime: A Complex Relationship*, Sentencing Project, Washington, DC.

Kriegman, D. (2006) The reduction of sexual offense recidivism following commitment and psychodynamic treatment. *Journal of Sexual Offender Civil Commitment: Science and the Law*, 1, 90–98.

Laws, D.R. and Marshall, W.L. (1990) A conditioning theory of the etiology and maintenance of deviant sexual preference and behavior, in *Handbook of Sexual Assault: Issues, Theories and Treatment of the Offender* (eds W.L. Marshall, D.R. Laws and H.E. Barbaree), Plenum Press, New York, pp. 209–229.

Laws, D.R. and Marshall, W.L. (1991) Masturbatory reconditioning: an evaluative review. *Advances in Behaviour Research and Therapy*, 13, 13–25.

Linley, P.A. and Joseph, S. (eds) (2004) *Positive Psychology in Practice*, John Wiley & Sons, Inc., Hoboken.

Lösel, F. and Schmucker, M. (2005) The effectiveness of treatment for sexual offenders: a comprehensive meta-analysis. *Journal of Experimental Criminology*, 1, 117–146.

MacKenzie, D.L., Brame, R., McDowall, D. and Souryal, C. (1995) Boot camp prisons and recidivism in eight states. *Criminology*, 33, 327–357.

Malamuth, N.M. (1996) The confluence model of sexual aggression: feminist and evolutionary perspectives, in *Sex, Power, Conflict: Evolutionary and Feminist Perspectives* (eds D.M. Buss and N.M. Malamuth), Oxford University Press, New York, pp. 269–295.

Malamuth, N.M., Heavey, C.L. and Linz, D. (1993) Predicting men's antisocial behavior against women: the interaction model of sexual aggression, in *Sexual Aggression: Issues in Etiology, Assessment, and Treatment* (eds G.C.N. Hall, R. Hirschman, J.R. Graham and M.S. Zaragoza), Taylor & Francis, Washington, DC, pp. 63–97.

Mann, R.E. and Shingler, J. (2006) Schema-driven cognition in sexual offenders: theory, assessment and treatment, in *Sexual Offender Treatment: Controversial Issues* (eds W.L. Marshall, Y.M. Fernandez, L.E. Marshall and G.A. Serran), John Wiley & Sons, Ltd, Chichester, pp. 173–185.

Mann, R.E., Webster, S.D., Schofield, C. and Marshall, W.L. (2004) Approach versus avoidance goals in relapse prevention with sexual offenders. *Sexual Abuse: A Journal of Research and Treatment*, 16, 65–75.

Marlatt, G.A. (1982) Relapse prevention: a self-control program for the treatment of addictive behaviors, in *Adherence, Compliance and Generalization in Behavioural Medicine* (ed. R.B. Stuart), Brunner/Mazel, New York, pp. 329–378.

Marques, J.K. (1982) Relapse prevention: a self-control model for the treatment of sex offenders. Paper presented at the 7th annual Forensic Mental Health Conference, Asilomar, March 2.

Marques, J.K., Weideranders, M., Day, D.M. *et al.* (2005) Effects of a relapse prevention program on sexual recidivism: final results from California's Sex Offender Treatment and Evaluation Project (SOTEP). *Sexual Abuse: A Journal of Research and Treatment*, 17, 79–107.

Marquis, J.N. (1970) Orgasmic reconditioning: changing sexual object choice through controlling masturbation fantasies. *Journal of Behavior Therapy and Experimental Psychiatry*, 1, 263–271.

Marshall, L.E. and Marshall, W.L. (2001) Excessive sexual desire disorder among sexual offenders: the development of a research project. *Sexual Addiction & Compulsivity: The Journal of Treatment and Prevention*, 8, 301–307.

Marshall, L.E. and Marshall, W.L. (2006) Sexual addiction in incarcerated sexual offenders. *Sexual Addiction & Compulsivity: The Journal of Treatment and Prevention*, 13, 377–390.

Marshall, L.E. and O'Brien, M.D. (2009) Assessment of sexual addiction, in *Assessment and Treatment of Sex Offenders: A Handbook* (eds A.R. Beech, L.A. Craig and K.D. Browne), John Wiley & Sons, Ltd, Chichester, pp. 163–177.

Marshall, W.L. (1979) Satiation therapy: a procedure for reducing deviant sexual arousal. *Journal of Applied Behavioral Analyses*, 12, 377–389.

Marshall, W.L. (1989) Invited essay: intimacy, loneliness and sexual offenders. *Behaviour Research and Therapy*, 27, 491–503.

Marshall, W.L. (1993) The treatment of sex offenders: what does the outcome data tell us? A reply to Quinsey *et al. Journal of Interpersonal Violence*, 8, 524–530.

Marshall, W.L. and Anderson, D. (2000) Do relapse prevention components enhance treatment effectiveness? in *Remaking Relapse Prevention with Sex Offenders: A Sourcebook* (eds D.R. Laws, S.M. Hudson and T. Ward), Sage Publications, Newbury Park, pp. 39–55.

Marshall, W.L. and Barbaree, H.E. (1988) The long-term evaluation of a behavioural treatment program for child molesters. *Behaviour Research and Therapy*, 26, 499–511.

Marshall, W.L. and Barbaree, H.E. (1990) An integrated theory of sexual offending, in *Handbook of Sexual Assault: Issues, Theories and Treatment of the Offender* (eds W.L. Marshall, D.R. Laws and H.E. Barbaree), Plenum Press, New York, pp. 257–275.

Marshall, W.L. and Lippens, K. (1977) The clinical value of boredom: a procedure for reducing inappropriate sexual interests. *Journal of Nervous and Mental Disease*, 165, 283–287.

Marshall, W.L. and Marshall, L.E. (2000) The origins of sexual offending. *Trauma, Violence, & Abuse: A Review Journal*, 1, 250–263.

Marshall, W.L. and Marshall, L.E. (2007) The utility of the random controlled trial for evaluating sexual offender treatment: the gold standard or an inappropriate strategy? *Sexual Abuse: A Journal of Research and Treatment*, 19, 175–191.

Marshall, W.L. and Marshall, L.E. (2011a) Responsivity: an important but misunderstood principle of effective treatment. *Criminology*, submitted for publication.

Marshall, W.L. and Marshall, L.E. (2011b) Can treatment be effective with sexual offenders or does it do harm? *Sexual Offender Treatment*, 5 (2), article 87. http://www.iatso.org/ejournal (accessed 26 December 2012).

Marshall, W.L. and McGuire, J. (2008) Effect sizes in treatment of sexual offenders. *International Journal of Offender Therapy and Comparative Criminology*, 46, 653–663.

Marshall, W.L. and Pithers, W.D. (1994) A reconsideration of treatment outcome with sex offenders. *Criminal Justice and Behavior*, 21, 10–27.

Marshall, W.L., Hudson, S.M., Jones, R. and Fernandez, Y.M. (1995) Empathy in sex offenders. *Clinical Psychology Review*, 15, 99–113.

Marshall, W.L., Anderson, D. and Champagne, F. (1997) Self-esteem and its relationship to sexual offending. *Psychology, Crime & Law*, 3, 81–106.

Marshall, W.L., Anderson, D. and Fernandez, Y.M. (1999) *Cognitive Behavioural Treatment of Sexual Offenders*, John Wiley & Sons, Ltd, Chichester.

Marshall, W.L., Ward, T., Mann, R.E. *et al.* (2005) Working positively with sexual offenders: maximizing the effectiveness of treatment. *Journal of Interpersonal Violence*, 20, 1096–1114.

Marshall, W.L., Marshall, L.E. Serran, G.A. and Fernandez, Y.M. (2006) *Treating Sexual Offenders: An Integrated Approach*, Routledge, New York.

Marshall, W.L., Marshall, L.E. and Serran, G.A. (2009) Empathy and offending behaviour, in *Personality, Personality Disorder and Violence* (eds M. McMurran and R. Howard), John Wiley & Sons, Ltd, Chichester, pp. 229–240.

Marshall, W.L., Marshall, L.E., Serran, G.A. and O'Brien, M.D. (2009) Self-esteem, shame, cognitive distortions and empathy in sexual offenders: their integration and treatment implications. *Psychology, Crime & Law*, 15, 217–234.

Marshall, W.L., Marshall, L.E. and Ware, J. (2009) Cognitive distortions in sexual offenders: should they all be treatment targets? *Sexual Abuse in Australia and New Zealand*, 2, 70–78.

Marshall, W.L., O'Brien, M.D. and Marshall, L.E. (2009) Modifying sexual preferences, in *Assessment and Treatment of Sexual Offenders: A Handbook* (eds A.R. Beech, L.A. Craig and K.D. Browne), John Wiley & Sons, Ltd, Chichester, pp. 311–327.

Marshall, W.L., Marshall, L.E. and Kingston, D.A. (2011) Are the cognitive distortions of child molesters in need of treatment? *Sexual Aggression*, 17, 118–129.

Marshall, W.L., Marshall, L.E., Serran, G.A. and O'Brien, M.D. (2011) *The Rehabilitation of Sexual Offenders: A Strengths-Based Approach*, American Psychological Association, Washington, DC.

Martin, G. and Pear, J. (1992) *Behavior Modification: What Is It and How to Do It*. Prentice Hall, Englewood Cliffs.

Martinson, R. (1974) What works? – Questions and answers about prison reform. *The Public Interest*, 35, 22–54.

Maslow, A.H. (1968) *Toward a Psychology of Being*, 2nd edn, Van Nostrand Reinhold, New York.

McConville, S. (ed.) (2003) *The Use of Punishment*, Willan Publishing, Devon.

McFall, R.M. (1990) The enhancement of social skills: an information-processing analysis, in *Handbook of Sexual Assault: Issues, Theories, and Treatment of the Offender* (eds W.L. Marshall, D.R. Laws and H.E. Barbaree), Plenum Press, New York, pp. 311–330.

McGrath, R.J., Cumming, G.F. and Burchard, B.L. (2003) *Current Practices and Trends in Sexual Abuser Management: Safer Society 2002 Nationwide Survey*, Safer Society Press, Brandon.

McGrath, R.J., Cumming, G.R., Burchard, B.L. *et al.* (2010) *Current Practices and Emerging Trends in Sexual Abuser Management*, Safer Society Press, Brandon.

McGuire, R.J., Carlisle, J.M. and Young, B.G. (1965) Sexual deviation as conditioned behaviour: a hypothesis. *Behaviour Research and Therapy*, 3, 185–190.

Miller, W.R. and Rollnick, S. (eds) (2002) *Motivational Interviewing: Preparing People for Change*, 2nd edn, Guilford Press, New York.

Murphy, W.D. (1990) Assessment and modification of cognitive distortions in sex offenders, in *Handbook of Sexual Assault: Issues, Theories, and Treatment of the Offender* (eds W.L. Marshall, D.R. Laws and H.E. Barbaree), Plenum Press, New York, pp. 331–342.

Newton-Smith, W. (2002) *A Companion to the Philosophy of Science*, Blackwell, Oxford.

Paparozzi, M.A. and Gendreau, P. (2005) An intensive supervision program that worked: service delivery, professional orientation, and organizational supportiveness. *Prison Journal*, 85, 445–466.

Persons, J.B. (2008) *The Case Formulation Approach to Cognitive Behavior Therapy*, Guilford Press, New York.

Peterson, C. (2006) *A Primer in Positive Psychology*, Oxford University Press, New York.

Pfäfflin, F., Böhmer, M., Cornehl, S. and Mergenthaler, F. (2005) What happens in therapy with sexual offenders? A model of process research. *Sexual Abuse: A Journal of Research and Treatment*, 17, 141–151.

Pithers, W.D. (1994) Process evaluation of a group therapy component designed to enhance sex offenders' empathy for sexual abuse survivors. *Behaviour Research and Therapy*, 32, 565–570.

Quinsey, V.L., Harris, G.T., Rice, M.E. and Lalumière, M.L. (1993) Assessing treatment efficacy in outcome studies of sex offenders. *Journal of Interpersonal Violence*, 8, 512–523.

Rasmussen, D.B. (1999) Human flourishing and the appeal to human nature, in *Human Flourishing* (eds E.F. Paul, F.D. Miller and J. Paul), Cambridge University Press, New York, pp. 1–43.

Rice, M.E. (2010) Treatment of adult sex offenders: may we reject the null hypothesis? Paper presented at the 11th Conference of the International Association for the Treatment of Sexual Offenders, Oslo, September 5.

Rice, M.E. and Harris, G.T. (2003) The size and sign of treatment effects in sex offender therapy. *Annals of the New York Academy of Sciences*, 989, 428–440.

Schmauk, P. and Sheldon, K.M. (eds) (2001) *Life Goals and Well-Being*, Hogrefe & Huber, Toronto.

Seligman, M.E.P. (1991) *Learned Optimism*, Knopf, New York.

Seligman, M.E.P. (2002) *Authentic Happiness: Using the New Positive Psychology to Realize Your Potential for Lasting Fulfillment*, Free Press, New York.

Seligman, M.E.P. and Csikszentmihalyi, M. (2000) Positive psychology: an introduction. *American Psychologist*, 55, 5–14.

Seto, M.C. (2011) Is there a way forward? Paper presented at Advancing Our Understanding of Treatment Change in High-risk Sex Offenders. Carleton University, Ottawa, March 15.

Seto, M.C., Marques, J.K., Harris, G.T. *et al.* (2008) Good science and progress in sex offender treatment are intertwined: a response to Marshall & Marshall (2007). *Sexual Abuse: A Journal of Research and Treatment*, 20, 247–255.

Smallbone, S., Marshall, W.L. and Wortley, R. (2008) *Preventing Child Sexual Abuse: Evidence, Policy and Practice*, Willan Publishing, Devon.

Smith, P., Goggin, C. and Gendreau, P. (2002) The Effects of Prison Sentences and Intermediate Sanctions on Recidivism: General Effects and Individual Differences. *User Rep. no. 2002-01*. Public Safety and Emergency Preparedness Canada, Ottawa.

Snyder, C.R. (1994) *The Psychology of Hope: You Can Get There from Here*, Free Press, New York.

Snyder, C.R. (2000) The past and possible futures of hope. *Journal of Social and Clinical Psychology*, 19, 11–28.

Snyder, C.R. and Lopez, S.J. (eds) (2005) *Handbook of Positive Psychology*, Oxford University Press, New York.

Spiegler, M.D. and Guevremont, D.C. (1998) *Contemporary Behavior Therapy*, 3rd edn, Brooks/Cole, Pacific Grove.

Tamgney, J.P. and Dearing, R.L. (2002) *Shame and Guilt*, Guilford Press, New York.

Turner, S., Greenwood, P.W., Chen, E. and Fain, T. (1999) The impact of truth-in-sentencing and three-strike legislation: prison populations, state budgets and crime rates. *Stanford Law and Policy Review*, 11, 75–91.

Visher, C.A. (1986) The rand inmate survey: a reanalysis, in *Criminal Careers and Career Offenders* (eds A. Blumstein, J. Cohen, J.A. Roth and C.A. Christy), National Academy Press, Washington, DC.

Ward, T. (1999) A self-regulation model of the relapse process in sexual offenders, in *The Sex Offender: Theoretical Advances, Treating Special Populations and Legal Developments*, vol. III (ed. B.K. Schwartz), Civic Research Institute, Kingston, pp. 6.1–6.8.

Ward, T. (2002) Good lives and the rehabilitation of offenders: promises and problems. *Aggression and Violent Behavior*, 7, 513–528.

Ward, T. and Brown, M. (2003) The risk-need model of offender rehabilitation: a critical analysis, in *Sexual Deviance: Issues and Controversies* (eds T. Ward, D.R. Laws and S.M. Hudson), Sage, Thousand Oaks, pp. 338–353.

Ward, T. and Gannon, T.A. (2006) Rehabilitation, etiology, and self-regulation: the Good Lives Model of sexual offender treatment. *Aggression and Violent Behavior*, 11, 77–94.

Ward, T. and Hudson, S.M. (1996) Relapse prevention: a critical analysis. *Sexual Abuse: A Journal of Research and Treatment*, 8, 177–200.

Ward, T. and Hudson, S.M. (1998) A model of the relapse process in sexual offenders. *Journal of Interpersonal Violence*, 13, 700–725.

Ward, T. and Hudson, S.M. (2000) A self-regulation model of relapse prevention, in *Remaking Relapse Prevention with Sex Offenders: A Sourcebook* (eds D.R. Laws, S.M. Hudson and T. Ward), Sage, Thousand Oaks, pp. 79–101.

Ward, T. and Mann, R.E. (2004) Good lives and the rehabilitation of offenders: a positive approach to sex offender treatment, in *Positive Psychology in Practice* (eds P.S. Linley and S. Joseph), John Wiley & Sons, Inc., Hoboken, pp. 598–616.

Ward, T. and Marshall, W.L. (2004) Good lives, aetiology and the rehabilitation of sex offenders: a bridging theory. *Journal of Sexual Aggression*, 10, 153–169.

Ward, T. and Stewart, C. (2003) Good lives and the rehabilitation of sexual offenders, in *Sexual Deviance: Issues and Controversies* (eds T. Ward, D.R. Laws and S.M. Hudson), Sage, Thousand Oaks, pp. 21–44.

Ward, T., Hudson, S.M., Marshall, W.L. and Siegert, R. (1995) Attachment style and intimacy deficits in sex offenders: a theoretical framework. *Sexual Abuse: A Journal of Research and Treatment*, 7, 317–335.

Ward, T., Hudson, S.M. and Siegert, R.J. (1995) A critical comment on Pithers' relapse prevention model. *Sexual Abuse: A Journal of Research and Treatment*, 7, 167–175.

Ward, T., Polaschek, D.L.L. and Beech, A.R. (2006) *Theories of Sexual Offending*. John Wiley & Sons, Ltd, Chichester.

Ward, T., Mann, R.E. and Gannon, T.A. (2007) The Good Lives Model of rehabilitation: clinical implications. *Aggression and Violent Behavior*, 12, 208–228.

Ward, T. Collie, R.M. and Bourke, P. (2009) Models of offender rehabilitation: the good lives model and the risk-need-responsivity model, in *Assessment and Treatment of Sex Offenders* (eds A.R. Beech, L.A. Craig and K.D. Browne), John Wiley & Sons, Ltd, Chichester, pp. 293–310.

Wilson, R.J. (2007) Circles of support and accountability: empowering communities, in *Knowledge & Practice: Challenges in the Treatment and Supervision of Sexual Abusers* (ed. D.S. Prescott), Wood 'N' Barnes, Oklahoma City, pp. 280–309.

Yates, P.M. (2007) Taking the leap: abandoning relapse prevention and applying the self-regulation model to the treatment of sexual offenders, in *Applying Knowledge to Practice: The Treatment and Supervision of Sexual Abusers* (ed. D. Prescott), Wood 'N' Barnes, Oklahoma City, pp. 143–174.

Yates, T.M. and Masten, A.S. (2004) Fostering the future: resilience theory and the practice of positive psychology, in *Positive Psychology in Practice* (eds P.A. Linley and S. Joseph), John Wiley & Sons, Inc., Hoboken, pp. 521–539.

Yates, P.M. and Ward, T. (2009) Yes, relapse prevention should be abandoned: a reply to Carich, Dobkowski, and Delehanty (2008). *ATSA Forum*, 21, 9–21.

11

Evidence-Based Interventions for Serious and Violent Juvenile Offenders

Charles M. Borduin, Alex R. Dopp and Erin K. Taylor

University of Missouri, USA

Introduction

Violent criminal acts and other serious crimes committed by youths present significant problems at several levels of analysis, and these problems argue for the development of effective treatment approaches. On a personal level, youths who commit serious crimes experience numerous psychosocial problems as well as reduced educational and occupational opportunities (Lyons *et al.*, 2001; Odgers *et al.*, 2008). Moreover, serious criminal activity perpetrated by youths has extremely detrimental emotional, physical and economic effects on victims, their families and the larger community (Britt, 2000; Kilpatrick and Acierno, 2003; Miller, Fisher and Cohen, 2001; Robinson and Keithley, 2000). Therefore, effective treatment may not only benefit the youth and his or her family but may also save many persons from victimization.

On an epidemiological level, youths under the age of 18 years account for approximately 28% of all arrests for serious offences, including 30% of robberies and 19% of forcible rapes (Federal Bureau of Investigation, 2009), and such arrests greatly underestimate the prevalence of youth criminal activity (Farrington *et al.*, 2003). In addition, although only about a fourth of youths arrested for delinquent acts could be characterized as serious offenders and even fewer (approximately 10%) as violent offenders, serious and violent juvenile offenders account for more than half of the total number of youth crimes in a community (Farrington *et al.*, 2003; Loeber, Farrington and Waschbusch, 1998). Thus, if one purpose of treating juvenile offenders is to decrease crime, then serious and violent juvenile offenders are a logical target for intervention efforts.

On a social services level, juvenile offenders, especially those who are violent, consume much of the resources of the child mental health, juvenile justice and special education systems and are overrepresented in the 'deep end' of these systems (Shufelt and Cocozza, 2006), with considerable cost to the public treasury and intrusion on family integrity and youth autonomy. Moreover, youths who engage in violence and other serious forms of antisocial behaviour often have continued contact with the mental health and criminal justice systems well into

What Works in Offender Rehabilitation: An Evidence-Based Approach to Assessment and Treatment, First Edition. Edited by Leam A. Craig, Louise Dixon and Theresa A. Gannon.
© 2013 John Wiley & Sons, Ltd. Published 2013 by John Wiley & Sons, Ltd.

adulthood (Farrington, Ttofi and Coid, 2009; Odgers *et al.*, 2008). Therefore, the development of effective treatments for youth violence and criminality may help to free resources to address other important problems of children and their families.

Unfortunately, as numerous reviewers have concluded (e.g., Howell, 2009; Kazdin, 2000; U.S. Public Health Service, 2001), the development of effective interventions for violence and criminality in youths has been an extremely difficult task. Indeed, until the 1990s, the conclusion that 'nothing works' (e.g., Lipton, Martinson and Wilks, 1975) in reducing the criminal behaviour of juvenile offenders was generally accurate, and it continues to be the case that most interventions have not proven effective or have not even been evaluated (Greenwood, 2008). In fact, it has recently been estimated that only 5% of eligible high-risk juvenile offenders are treated with an evidence-based intervention annually (Henggeler and Schoenwald, 2011). Moreover, a number of juvenile justice interventions (e.g., shock incarceration, residential placement) that are intended to reduce the criminal activity of offenders have had the unintended consequence of increasing youth antisocial behaviour (see Drake, Aos and Miller, 2009; Howell, 2009, for reviews). As described subsequently, such findings are not surprising because the interventions do not address well-established risk factors for offending and are delivered in settings (e.g., group home, training school) that bear little relation to the problems being addressed. Clearly, there is a pressing need to develop effective alternatives to the restrictive and narrowly focused practices that currently dominate mental health interventions for serious juvenile offenders.

Although large-scale progress has been slow, several interventions have proven effective over the past 20 years in reducing the criminal activity of serious juvenile offenders, and recent efforts to disseminate these evidence-based interventions have been very promising. This chapter discusses the juvenile justice intervention programmes that have proven most effective and conveys what is known about their effectiveness. This chapter also describes the likely bases of success of these intervention programmes as well as the key limitations of those programmes that have not been successful.

Which Intervention Programmes Are Effective?

Criteria for selection

Our selection of intervention programmes for the present chapter integrates criteria for effectiveness developed by the Office of Juvenile Justice and Delinquency Prevention Blueprints for Violence Prevention (Elliott, 1998; Elliott and Mihalic, 2004) and the American Psychological Association Task Force on the Promotion and Dissemination of Psychological Procedures (Chambless *et al.*, 1998). Specifically, for inclusion in the present review, intervention programmes had to demonstrate (i) decreases in antisocial behaviour among juvenile offenders in randomized clinical trials, (ii) successful replication across at least two research teams at different sites and (iii) sustained favourable outcomes for at least a year. These criteria were met by three intervention programmes: multisystemic therapy (MST; Henggeler and Borduin, 1990), multidimensional treatment foster care (MTFC; Chamberlain, 2003) and functional family therapy (FFT; Alexander and Parsons, 1982). These same programmes have also been cited as effective in sources ranging from journal reviews (e.g., Drake *et al.*, 2009; Eyberg, Nelson and Boggs, 2008; Lipsey, 2009) to volumes published by leaders in the field of delinquency and criminal justice (e.g., Greenwood, 2008; Howell, 2009) to reviews commissioned by the government such as the Surgeon General's report on youth violence (U.S. Public Health Service, 2001). The theoretical and clinical foundations of these programmes and research demonstrating their clinical effectiveness are discussed next.

Multisystemic therapy

MST (Henggeler and Borduin, 1990) is an intensive family- and community-based treatment model that was originally designed for serious and violent juvenile offenders and their families. With 20 published outcome studies (18 randomized trials and 2 quasi-experimental studies), the majority conducted with serious juvenile offenders, and delivery to more than 17 000 youths and families annually in the United States, Canada, Europe and Australia, MST is one of the most extensively validated and widely transported evidence-based psychosocial treatments.

Theoretical foundations Family systems theory (Bateson, 1972; Hoffman, 1981; Minuchin, 1985) and the theory of social ecology (Bronfenbrenner, 1979) fit closely with research findings on the correlates and causes of serious antisocial behaviour in youths and serve as a basis for case conceptualization and treatment planning in MST. Family systems theory views the family as a rule-governed system and assumes that problematic individual behaviours and symptoms are intimately related to patterns of interaction between family members. Although there are differences in how various schools of family therapy interpret systems theory, most attempt to understand how emotional and behavioural problems 'fit' within the context of the individual's family relations and emphasize the reciprocal and circular nature of such relations. Thus, a therapist working from a family systems conceptual framework would consider not only how caregiver discipline strategies influence youth antisocial behaviours but also how the antisocial behaviours of the youth shape the behaviours of the caregivers, and what function the antisocial behaviours might serve in the family.

The theory of social ecology shares some of the basic tenets of family systems theory but encompasses broader and more numerous contextual influences within a youth's life. The youth is viewed as being nested within a complex of interconnected systems that include the individual youth, the youth's family and various extrafamilial (peer, school, neighbourhood, community) contexts. The youth's behaviour is seen as the product of the reciprocal interplay between the youth and these systems and of the relations of the systems with each other. Thus, although the interactions between the youth and family or peers are seen as important, the connections between the systems are viewed as equally important. It is assumed, then, that youth antisocial behaviours can be maintained by problematic transactions within any given system or between some combination of pertinent systems. Importantly, social-ecological theory emphasizes the significance of 'ecological validity' in understanding behaviour, that is, the basic assumption that behaviour can be fully understood only when viewed within its naturally occurring context.

Clinical foundations MST teams usually consist of two to four therapists, each with caseloads of four to six families, and a half-time supervisor. The MST therapist is a generalist who directly provides most mental health services and coordinates access to other important services (e.g., medical, educational, recreational), always monitoring quality control. Although the therapist is available to the family 24 hours a day, 7 days a week, therapeutic intensity is titrated to clinical need; thus, the range of direct contact hours per family can vary considerably. In general, therapists spend more time with families in the initial weeks of therapy (daily, if indicated) and gradually taper off (as infrequently as once a week) during a three- to five-month course of treatment. To remove barriers to service access for challenging clinical populations, therapists have flexible hours (e.g., evenings, weekends) and deliver treatment in settings convenient for the family (e.g., home, school, community). This model of service delivery has been shown to be extremely effective at reducing treatment dropout (e.g., Henggeler *et al.*, 1996).

MST does not follow a rigid protocol in which therapists conduct sets of predetermined tasks in an invariant sequence. Indeed, fully detailing treatment parameters for complex cases that present serious and diverse problems would be an impossible task. Nevertheless, to achieve strong specification, the developers of MST have outlined nine treatment principles to guide therapists' case conceptualizations, prioritization of interventions and implementation of intervention strategies (see Henggeler *et al.*, 2009b). Interventions are designed and implemented using the existing evidence base for the particular problem being addressed (e.g., behavioural therapy interventions for youth oppositional behaviours), and therapists continuously assess the outcomes of the intervention. If not fully successful, the MST team aims to understand the barriers to success and then redesigns and implements new interventions accordingly. This iterative process is followed until treatment goals are achieved or further gains seem unlikely.

Research outcomes MST has been shown to be effective in a number of clinical trials with serious and violent juvenile offenders. In one of the earliest trials, Henggeler, Melton and Smith (1992) found that adolescents who received MST had significantly fewer rearrests (*Ms*=.87 versus 1.52) and weeks incarcerated (M_s=5.8 versus 16.2) at a 59-week post-referral follow-up than did adolescents who received usual services (provided by a state agency). Importantly, results from a 2.4-year follow-up (Henggeler *et al.*, 1993) showed that MST doubled the survival rate (i.e., percentage of adolescents not rearrested) of these offenders when compared with usual services. In a subsequent study that provided the most comprehensive and extensive evaluation of MST to date, Borduin *et al.* (1995) found that MST was more effective than individual therapy (IT) in improving key family correlates of antisocial behaviour and in ameliorating behavioural and emotional problems in individual family members; in addition, results from a four-year follow-up of rearrest data showed that youths treated with MST were significantly less likely to be rearrested (26.1% versus 71.4%) than youths treated with IT. More recently, in a 13.7-year follow-up of the youths who participated in the Borduin *et al.* (1995) clinical trial, Schaeffer and Borduin (2005) found that MST participants evidenced 59% fewer rearrests for violent crimes and 56% fewer arrests for other serious crimes than did IT participants. Furthermore, MST participants were sentenced to 57% fewer days (*Ms*=582.25 versus 1356.53 days) of confinement in adult detention facilities than were comparison counterparts. Several other randomized trials (e.g., Glisson *et al.*, 2010) and quasi-experimental studies (e.g., Henggeler *et al.*, 1986) have also demonstrated the effectiveness of MST in treating juvenile offenders.

In the last decade, several groups of investigators not affiliated with MST developers have independently examined the effectiveness of MST. In each of the independent replications, treatment fidelity and quality assurance were provided by a purveyor organization named MST Services. In a first set of effectiveness studies completed in Norway, Ogden and his colleagues (Ogden and Hagan, 2006; Ogden and Halliday-Boykins, 2004) found that antisocial youth who participated in MST had fewer externalizing and internalizing problems and out-of-home placements than did their counterparts who participated in usual child welfare services.

A second effectiveness study, completed by Timmons-Mitchell *et al.* (2006) in the United States, also found that MST participants had fewer rearrests at a two-year follow-up than did participants in usual services. In contrast, a four-site study of Swedish juvenile offenders found no differences between MST and treatment as usual groups (Sundell *et al.*, 2008) in outcomes; the authors noted that the lack of favourable outcomes for MST was likely due to very low therapist fidelity to the MST model. The results from these independent replications demonstrate the effective transport of MST by purveyor organizations only when high-quality assurance and treatment fidelity can be ensured.

Although MST was originally developed for the treatment of serious juvenile offenders, adaptations of the model have been shown to be effective in treating adolescent sexual offenders (Borduin *et al.*, 1990, 2009; Letourneau *et al.*, 2009), substance abusing adolescents (Henggeler, Pickrel and Brondino, 1999; Henggeler *et al.*, 2006), maltreated children (Brunk, Henggeler and Whelan, 1987; Swenson *et al.*, 2010) and youth with poorly controlled diabetes (Ellis *et al.*, 2004). In some cases (e.g., substance abuse), the adaptations have been relatively circumscribed, while in other cases (e.g., chronic health conditions), the adaptations have been more extensive.

Transport to community settings MST Services (www.mstservices.com) was developed in 1996 to transport MST to real-world clinical settings across the United States. MST Services and its network partners (i.e., purveyor organizations trained by MST Services to carry out programme development and implementation) are the sole transporters of MST and use a well-designed quality assurance and improvement system to support the implementation of MST. Potential MST sites are given assistance with programme development activities (e.g., site readiness, staff recruitment and training) and operations (see Strother, Swenson and Schoenwald, 1998). Training is initially provided during a five-day orientation for MST therapists, on-site supervisors and other relevant treatment personnel within the provider organization (e.g., psychiatrists). Case consultations are provided weekly by MST experts, and follow-up booster training is delivered quarterly via 1.5-day sessions. Furthermore, MST Services conducts regular programme reviews to help teams overcome organizational barriers to implementation. Treatment fidelity is monitored regularly via validated, web-based measures of therapist, supervisor and consultant adherence to the model. Finally, MST Services helps therapy teams to track youth outcomes after the completion of treatment.

Multidimensional treatment foster care

MTFC (Chamberlain, 2003) was developed through the Oregon Social Learning Center in the early 1980s to provide an alternative to incarceration and residential treatment. MTFC targets youths (aged 12–17 years) who have been removed from their homes due to chronic antisocial behaviour and is generally implemented only after other intensive interventions have failed. Seven research studies (based on two randomized clinical trials and two quasi-experimental trials) have supported the effectiveness of MTFC in treating serious and chronic juvenile offenders, and MTFC has now been transported to over 75 sites in the United States, Canada and Europe.

Theoretical foundations MTFC is based on the principles of social learning theory and views antisocial behaviour as the product of both direct (i.e., rewards and punishments) and indirect (i.e., observation and imitation) learning processes. Many of the MTFC intervention techniques are derived from behavioural (e.g., behavioural management plans) and cognitive-behavioural (e.g., problem-solving skills training) approaches and require involvement from the youth, foster family and family of origin. The MTFC model posits that the amelioration of youth anti-social behaviour occurs by intervening in pertinent systems in the youth's natural ecology (e.g., home, school, community). Interventions emphasize foster parent supervision and monitoring of the youth, engagement of the youth with prosocial peers (with simultaneous disengagement from deviant peers) and promotion of positive school performance.

Clinical foundations   The primary goals of MTFC are to decrease youth criminality, promote prosocial behaviour (e.g., through involvement in positive activities and improvement of school performance) and, ultimately, reunite the youth with his or her family of origin. The MTFC team typically has a total caseload of no more than 10 youths, and youth placement in the foster home usually lasts six to nine months. Teams are led by a full-time programme supervisor who maintains daily phone contact with each foster family, provides 24-hour crisis management, monitors treatment implementation, reviews each youth's weekly home and school reports and holds separate weekly meetings with the foster parents, the clinical team and juvenile officers. Foster parents are trained to use behavioural parenting strategies, with emphasis placed on close supervision of the youth's activities, implementation of clear rules and consequences and the development of a supportive relationship with the youth. The youth takes part in weekly meetings with both a skills trainer, who teaches the youth positive behav-ioural and problem-solving skills, and an individual therapist, who serves as an advocate for the youth and helps him or her to adjust to the foster home setting. In addition, a family therapist holds weekly meetings with the youth's caregivers to teach them parenting skills similar to those used by the foster parents so that treatment gains can generalize to the youth's home. The caregivers then practise these skills during the youth's home visits, with on-call supervi-sion and guidance available from the family therapist.

Research outcomes   Several studies have examined the effectiveness of MTFC in treating youths with severe antisocial behaviour. Findings have shown that male juvenile offenders randomized to MTFC versus group care demonstrated greater decreases in running away dur-ing treatment (Chamberlain and Moore, 1998; Chamberlain and Reid, 1998), greater increases in programme completion (Chamberlain and Moore, 1998), fewer days incarcerated one year after baseline (Chamberlain, 1990; Chamberlain and Moore, 1998; Chamberlain and Reid, 1998) and greater decreases in arrests one year following treatment (Chamberlain and Reid, 1998). Furthermore, in a two-year post-baseline follow-up of male juvenile offenders, MTFC resulted in decreased youth incarceration and violent behaviour when compared to group care (Eddy, Whaley and Chamberlain, 2004). Although an early study indicated that female juvenile offenders who participated in MTFC did not achieve the same positive outcomes as did male offenders (Chamberlain and Reid, 1994), subsequent adaptations of the model for girls have been successful. Indeed, recent studies have shown that one year after baseline, female participants in MTFC have greater increases in school attendance and homework compliance, lower rates of parent-reported delinquency and greater decreases in days incarcerated than do their female counterparts in residential care settings (Leve and Chamberlain, 2007; Leve, Chamberlain and Reid, 2005). Moreover, two years after baseline, MTFC has also been successful in reducing rates of pregnancy (Kerr, Leve and Chamberlain, 2009) and decreasing incarceration and violent behaviour in female juvenile offenders (Chamberlain, Leve and DeGarmo, 2007).

The first independent evaluation of the effectiveness of MTFC was recently completed in Sweden (Westermark, Hansson and Olssen, 2011). The results indicated that MTFC was more effective than usual services in reducing youth externalizing behaviours (as reported by parents). Although this was only the first evaluation of MTFC completed without involvement of the treatment developers, the findings suggest that MTFC can be successfully replicated by independent investigators. This replication, coupled with the previously discussed body of MTFC outcome research, provides compelling support for the dissemination of MTFC.

MTFC has also been shown to be effective with several other challenging clinical populations. Randomized trials have provided evidence for the successful use of MTFC with youth returning from psychiatric hospitalization (Chamberlain and Reid, 1991), maltreated children (Chamberlain, Moreland and Reid, 1992; Chamberlain *et al.*, 2008) and preschool-age children with behavioural, emotional and developmental problems (Fisher, Burraston and Pears, 2005; Fisher, Kim and Pears, 2009).

Transport to community settings   Like MST, MTFC has an organized structure for dissemination and monitoring of treatment fidelity. TFC Consultants, Inc. (www.mtfc.com), created in 2002, has well-specified implementation and certification procedures for transporting MTFC into real-world settings. A site visit is first conducted to gain the support of relevant stakeholders, programme administrators, foster parents and other agency representatives (e.g., juvenile officers, mental health providers from the community) for the MTFC model. During the site visit, plans and timelines are established for the recruitment and certification of foster parents and the training of staff (i.e., supervisor, skills trainer, individual therapist, family therapist). Staff receive four days of training at the MTFC development site in Oregon, and foster parents receive two days of training at the treatment site.

After the training is complete, TFC Consultants provide weekly telephone consultations with the programme supervisor. Implementation data (e.g., ratings of staff performance) are examined regularly, and foster parent and clinical treatment team meetings are videotaped and reviewed quarterly for model adherence. Up to six days of on-site booster training for agency staff is provided by TFC Consultants on an as-needed basis during the first year of the treatment team's operation. Most sites apply for MTFC programme certification by the end of the first year. The initial certification is valid for two years, and subsequent recertifications are valid for three years.

Functional family therapy

FFT (Alexander and Parsons, 1982) is a family- and community-based treatment for adolescents presenting with conduct problems, antisocial behaviour and associated family, school and social problems. With its initial efficacy trial published almost 40 years ago, FFT was one of the first evidence-based treatments developed in the field of family therapy. Since then, six FFT outcome studies (based on two randomized trials and two quasi-experimental trials) with antisocial youths have been published. FFT has become one of the most widely transported evidence-based family therapies and is now delivered in over 300 communities worldwide, including four international settings (Sexton, 2011).

Theoretical foundations   FFT has a strong relational focus, with the presenting problem viewed as a symptom of dysfunctional family relations. Proposed mechanisms of change for FFT include improvements in family communication style (Parsons and Alexander, 1973) and decreases in family defensiveness (Barton *et al.*, 1985; Robbins, Alexander and Turner, 2000) and negativity (Robbins *et al.*, 1996), although none of these mechanisms have been formally evaluated. FFT therapists aim to establish and maintain new patterns of family behaviour across individual, family and community levels of experience.

Clinical foundations FFT is most often used to treat less serious juvenile offenders (i.e., status offenders) but is also used with youths exhibiting serious antisocial behaviour. FFT programmes typically include 3–8 therapists, each carrying caseloads of 12–15 families. Treatment averages 12 sessions over approximately three to four months. Services are delivered primarily in clinic and home settings but can also be provided in schools, probation offices and other community locations.

Central to the implementation of FFT are its phase-based treatment protocols. In Phase 1 (i.e., Engagement/Motivation), the therapist aims to engender hope, create positive expectations and define the referral problem within a family focus. In Phase 2 (i.e., Behaviour Change), the therapist attempts to address the referral problem by establishing new patterns of family interaction. The techniques employed are not unique to the FFT model and regularly integrate behavioural (e.g., communication training) and cognitive-behavioural (e.g., assertiveness training, anger management) interventions into the treatment protocol. In Phase 3 (i.e., Generalization), the therapist aims to sustain and extend behaviour change in the broader environment by tapering family contact hours, increasing collaboration with school and juvenile justice authorities and helping the family to anticipate future problems and develop response plans.

Research outcomes Several outcome studies support the effectiveness of FFT. A randomized trial (Alexander and Parsons, 1973) with juvenile status offenders compared FFT to a client-centred family group, a psychodynamic family programme and a no-treatment control condition; results showed that participants in the FFT group had significantly lower recidivism rates for status offences but not criminal offences than did participants in the comparison groups at 18 months following treatment. In addition, a 40-month follow-up revealed that siblings of participants in the FFT group had less court involvement than did siblings in the comparison groups (Klein, Alexander and Parsons, 1977). In a subsequent quasi-experimental study with serious juvenile offenders comparing FFT and group home treatment, Barton *et al.* (1985) found that FFT participants had lower recidivism rates (60% versus 93%) and fewer offences per month among recidivists (0.20 versus 0.47) over a 15-month follow-up period. More recently, an independent quasi-experimental trial with rural offenders found lower recidivism rates for FFT participants compared to their counterparts on probation at 2.5-year (Gordon *et al.*, 1988) and 5-year (Gordon, Graves and Arbuthnot, 1995) follow-ups. Taken together, these early studies support the effectiveness of FFT as a treatment for juvenile offenders.

FFT researchers recently conducted one of the largest effectiveness trials to date ($N=917$) for a family-based treatment: a statewide trial in Washington comparing youth offenders randomized to FFT or usual probation services (Sexton and Turner, 2010). Results showed that the FFT group had significantly lower rates of felony and violent crimes at 12 months following treatment, but only for therapists who received high supervisor ratings of adherence to the FFT model. In addition, two independent evaluations of FFT have been conducted in Sweden and published in Swedish journals (Hansson, Cederblad and Hook, 2000; Hansson *et al.*, 2004). Brief summaries of these studies in English report outcomes favouring the FFT condition, but we were not able to review the manuscripts (e.g., design, measurement methods, treatment fidelity, data analyses) because English translations are not available. These three studies provide preliminary evidence that FFT can be successfully transported into community settings when implemented with fidelity.

Overall, there is promising but limited evidence for the clinical effectiveness of FFT. Early studies suffered from a lack of experimental control, small sample sizes and non-representative samples (e.g., many early trials contained a large proportion of Mormon participants), though the results of the Washington effectiveness trial provide more credible evidence for the model when treatment fidelity is high. Furthermore, although FFT was initially developed for treating low-severity antisocial behaviours, it has demonstrated some success with serious and violent juvenile offenders as a low-intensity treatment option. FFT has also been adapted for youth with substance use disorders (Friedman, 1989; Waldron *et al.*, 2001), although that adaptation has not outperformed alternative treatment groups.

Transport to community settings   The national and international transport of FFT has been led by the purveyor organization FFT Inc. (www.fftinc.com), which oversees a three-phase process for the development and certification of new FFT sites. The goal of the first phase is to train clinicians to high levels of adherence and competence through didactic instruction, weekly consultations and feedback from FFT Inc. personnel. The goal of the second phase is to develop greater site self-sufficiency, primarily by developing a competent on-site supervisor through additional training, monthly phone consultations and other interventions as needed. During the third phase, FFT Inc. personnel focus on maintaining programme standards by monitoring a website database for therapist adherence, service delivery trends and client outcomes and by engaging in continuous quality improvement.

Key Elements of Effective Programmes

Delineation of the common features of effective programmes can provide a useful framework for understanding the bases of success and failure of juvenile justice interventions. The features described here are generally consistent with those identified in various reviews (e.g., Andrews, 2006; Cullen, Myer and Latessa, 2009; Howell, 2009; Lipsey, 2009) and contrast with the features of the vast majority of services provided to juvenile offenders.

Effective programmes address known risk factors for offending

A large number of studies have evaluated the causes and correlates of serious and violent antisocial behaviour in adolescence. Although some differences in risk factors for different populations (e.g., gender, racial and ethnic group, age group) have emerged, findings have been remarkably consistent across these groups throughout the past decades. Antisocial behaviour in adolescents is multidetermined by factors within the youth and across his or her social ecology (i.e., family, peers, school and neighbourhood). Table 11.1 provides a brief overview of the factors that are amenable to treatment (for reviews, see Biglan *et al.*, 2004; Hoge, Guerra and Boxer, 2008; Howell, 2009; Liberman, 2008; Loeber, Burke and Pardini, 2009).

In light of the numerous correlates of violent and other serious antisocial behaviour in adolescents, an increasing number of research groups have developed empirically based multidimensional causal models of antisocial behaviour. These research groups have used path analysis or structural equation modelling to examine the interrelations among variables from several

Table 11.1   Key causes and correlates of serious and violent antisocial behaviour in adolescents

Youth level
- Attention deficit hyperactivity disorder, impulsivity
- Positive attitudes towards delinquency and substance abuse
- Lack of guilt for transgressions
- Negative affect
- Cognitive bias to attribute hostile intentions to others

Family level
- Inconsistent or lax parental discipline
- Poor parental supervision
- Poor affective relations between youth, caregivers and siblings
- High conflict and hostility
- Parental substance abuse, mental health problems and criminality

Peer level
- Association with drug-abusing and/or delinquent peers
- Poor relationship with peers, peer rejection
- Low involvement with pro-social peers

School level
- Negative attitude towards school
- Academic difficulties, low grades, having been retained
- Behavioural problems at school, truancy, suspensions, dropout
- Attending a school that does not flex to youth needs (e.g., zero-tolerance policy)

Neighbourhood level
- Low social support available from church, neighbours and the like
- High environmental and psychosocial stress (e.g., violence)
- Availability of weapons and drugs

of the psychosocial domains (i.e., individual, family, peers, school, neighbourhood) that have been linked with serious antisocial behaviour. Such causal modelling studies allow a determination of which variables have direct versus indirect effects on antisocial behaviour, and which variables are no longer linked with antisocial behaviour when the effects of other correlates are controlled. Findings across studies (e.g., Brown *et al.*, 2005; Fleming *et al.*, 2002; Paschall, Ringwalt and Flewelling, 2003; Tolan, Gorman-Smith and Henry, 2003) are relatively clear and consistent:

1. Involvement with deviant peers is virtually always a powerful direct predictor of violence and other serious antisocial behaviours.
2. Family relations predict serious antisocial behaviours either directly (contributing unique variance) or indirectly by predicting involvement with deviant peers.
3. School difficulties predict involvement with deviant peers.
4. Neighbourhood and community support characteristics add small portions of unique variance or indirectly predict serious antisocial behaviours by, for example, affecting family, peer or school behaviour.

Thus, in spite of substantial variation in research methods and measurement, investigators have shown across studies that youth violence is linked directly or indirectly with key characteristics of youths and of their social systems.

If the primary goal of treatment is to maximally decrease rates of youth violence or other serious antisocial behaviour, then treatment approaches must have the flexibility to address the multiple known determinants of such behaviour. Indeed, there has been a growing consensus among reviewers that the major limitation of most treatments for serious antisocial behaviour is their failure to account for the multidetermined nature of such behaviour, and that effective treatments must have the capacity to intervene comprehensively at individual, family, peer, school and possibly even neighbourhood levels (Borduin, 1994; DeMatteo and Marczyk, 2005; Kashani *et al.*, 1999; Kazdin, 2000). Thus, it is unrealistic to expect even the best conceived office-based treatments to be effective due to their relatively narrow focus. A critical feature of MST, MTFC and FFT is their capacity to address the determinants of violence or serious antisocial behaviour in a comprehensive, intense and individualized fashion. These treatments succeed by focusing their interventions on key aspects of the youth's social ecology, such as building more effective family functioning, disengaging youth from deviant peer networks and enhancing youth school performance.

Effective programmes are rehabilitative in nature

In addition to addressing known risk factors for offending, effective intervention programmes also seek to restore functioning and build protective factors at the individual, family, peer, school and neighbourhood levels. Protective factors are aspects of the youth's social ecology that either reduce antisocial behaviour directly (e.g., negative attitudes towards antisocial behaviour, empathy for others) or mitigate the impact of risk factors (e.g., high parental monitoring of peer relations, social support for caregivers). Recent studies have demonstrated that protective factors account for unique variance when considered together with risk factors in predicting antisocial behaviour (e.g., Carr and Vandiver, 2001; Lodewijks, de Ruiter and Doreleijers, 2010; Turner *et al.*, 2007). These findings suggest that serious and violent antisocial behaviour is best conceptualized within a comprehensive risk and protective factor framework. The MST, MTFC and FFT models all emphasize that protective factors are critical to achieving and sustaining decreased youth antisocial behaviour and improved functioning, and all include interventions designed to build pertinent competencies in family members (e.g., youth social skills, parent behaviour management skills, family communication).

Effective programmes use behavioural interventions within the youths' natural environment

The previously described interventions place important emphasis on the accessibility and ecological validity of services. Traditionally, mental health services for juvenile offenders either have been inaccessible (i.e., office based) or have provided interventions (e.g., residential treatment centres, wilderness programmes, boot camps, incarceration) that have little bearing on the real-world environmental conditions that led to the youth's criminal behaviour and to which the youth will eventually return. In contrast, MST, MTFC and FFT are provided in natural community contexts (e.g., home, school, recreation centre). The delivery of services in youths' natural environments enhances family cooperation, permits more accurate assessment of identified problems and of intervention results and promotes long-term maintenance of therapeutic changes (Henggeler and Borduin, 1990). Indeed, there is a growing consensus that providers of children's mental health services should recognize the natural ecology of the child and diminish barriers to service access (e.g., Burns and Hoagwood, 2002; Cauce *et al.*, 2002; Snell-Johns, Mendez and Smith, 2004).

Effective programmes are well defined and include support for intervention fidelity

In a field where 'nothing works' was a long-standing conclusion, the developers of MST, MTFC and FFT have been determined to sustain the quality and effectiveness of their intervention programmes when transported to community settings. Treatment, training and quality assurance manuals and protocols have been developed and are well specified. The developers have also established purveyor organizations that license service providers to implement their programmes. These organizations employ continuous quality assurance systems to monitor therapist and programme fidelity to the intervention programme and to take corrective actions when necessary.

Future Directions in the Development of Evidence-Based Interventions for Serious and Violent Juvenile Offenders

This chapter provided a review of juvenile justice intervention programmes that have proven most effective in the treatment of serious and violent juvenile offenders and described the likely bases of success of these intervention programmes. The development of MST, MTFC and FFT coincided with emerging family therapy theories that emphasized the reciprocal nature of interpersonal interaction and with social ecological theories that provided highly compatible conceptual frameworks for the development and specification of family-based interventions. Importantly, research outcomes have demonstrated that these family-based interventions, which intensively address the multiple determinants of serious antisocial behaviour in youths' naturally occurring systems, can successfully reduce violent offending and other criminal activity in youths. Of course, extensive validation and replication are needed for even the most effective intervention programmes. Indeed, given the many problems that serious and violent youth offenders present for their communities, as well as the significant costs of providing these youths with interventions that do not produce durable changes, the continued development and refinement of effective intervention programmes such as MST, MTFC and FFT should be a priority for scientists and policymakers alike. Accordingly, in this section, we offer several recommendations related to key areas of research.

Mechanisms of change

Understanding the theories (i.e., mechanisms) of change that underlie the MST, MTFC and FFT intervention models is essential to the efficient use of each model and might ultimately help to improve outcomes. To date, however, there are only a few rigorous tests of the underlying mechanisms of change of these models (for a discussion of criteria for evaluating mechanisms of change, see Kazdin, 2007). In a study of MTFC, in which juvenile offenders received either MTFC or group home care, Eddy and Chamberlain (2000) showed that the positive effects of MTFC on adolescent criminal activity were mediated by improved caregiver behaviour management practices and decreased adolescent association with deviant peers. Similarly, in a randomized effectiveness trial of MST with juvenile sexual offenders, Henggeler *et al.* (2009a) demonstrated that favourable MST effects on youth antisocial behaviour and deviant sexual interest/risk behaviours were mediated by increased caregiver follow-through on discipline practices as well as decreased caregiver disapproval of and concern about the youth's bad friends. Together, these studies suggest that changes in caregiver discipline practices and youth association with deviant peers are critical factors in the attenuation of antisocial behaviour in youths. Given the consistency of results across these studies, the most important goal of future research in this area should be to determine the specific components of treatment (e.g., in-session behaviours, protocols) that lead to improved caregiver discipline and disengagement of youths from deviant peers.

Persistence of change

Clinical trials that have evaluated treatments for youth mental health problems, including antisocial behaviour, have typically included relatively short (i.e., less than one to two years) follow-ups of participant outcomes following treatment completion (see Weisz, Jensen-Doss and Hawley, 2006, for a review). Thus, our understanding of the durability of favourable outcomes achieved in most evidence-based treatments for youths is surprisingly limited. Although Schaeffer and Borduin (2005) provided the longest (i.e., 13.7 years) follow-up to date of an evidence-based intervention (i.e., MST) for serious and violent juvenile offenders, long-term follow-ups of other evidence-based intervention programmes for this population of youths (i.e., MTFC and FFT) are sorely needed. Indeed, it is critical to determine whether evidence-based interventions are effective in preventing longer-term criminal activity among serious juvenile offenders because such youths are, by far, at greatest risk for committing additional serious crimes. Information regarding the lasting benefits of empirically supported treatments could greatly assist policymakers and programme administrators in selecting and implementing mental health programmes for serious juvenile offenders. However, if treatment effects similar to those observed at shorter-term follow-ups were not maintained over a longer period of time, then such findings could suggest a need for refinements in treatment, such as providing post-treatment booster sessions or ongoing support services in early adulthood.

Economic analysis

Given the evidence of clinical effectiveness of MST, MTFC and FFT, it seems logical to evaluate the economics of these interventions, as treatments that are clinically effective are also likely to be cost-beneficial. Indeed, for evidence-based interventions to compete in the mental health treatment marketplace with other types of interventions for serious and violent juvenile offenders (e.g., individual counselling, group therapy, pharmacotherapy), it is important to determine the potential cost advantages of evidence-based interventions. Information regarding the economics of empirically supported interventions, and especially widely disseminated ones such as those discussed in this chapter, could greatly assist government funding agencies in selecting and administering clinically effective mental health programmes for serious juvenile offenders (Mihalopoulos *et al.*, 2011). Furthermore, if the benefits of evidence-based interventions to society do not exceed the costs of providing the interventions, such findings might provide an impetus to examine whether the interventions could be further refined and improved.

   Although methodologies for conducting economic analyses of mental health interventions have been well articulated (e.g., Fals-Stewart, Yates and Klostermann, 2005; Singh, Hawthorne and Vos, 2001), such work has clearly lagged behind tests of effectiveness of these interventions. Indeed, only a few studies have examined the costs and benefits of intervention programmes designed for juvenile offenders, and the majority of those studies have included relatively serious methodological limitations. An exception to this overall dearth of studies is a series of cost–benefit analyses of programmes for juvenile offenders, including MST, MTFC and FFT, conducted by the Washington State Institute for Public Policy (WSIPP; Aos *et al.*, 2001, 2004; Drake *et al.*, 2009). WSIPP researchers reported benefit–cost ratios of $2.64–28.21 for MST, $10.88–43.70 for MTFC and $13.25–28.34 for FFT. Although encouraging, these findings were based on estimates of criminal justice system expenditures and treatment effect sizes and should be replicated using more accurate data (e.g., Klietz, Borduin and Schaeffer, 2010). Moreover, future studies should expand the scope of costs beyond the criminal justice system and include other service sectors (e.g., social welfare, mental health, primary care) to explore the possibility of cost shifting during treatment or follow-up.

Validation of quality assurance systems and intervention transport

The quality assurance and training systems used by the MST, MTFC and FFT purveyor organizations have been designed to support programme development and enhance intervention fidelity, which, in turn, are intended to promote favourable youth and family outcomes. However, research is needed to demonstrate that the respective quality assurance systems actually enhance treatment fidelity and lead to improved outcomes. Numerous aspects of the MST quality assurance system have been validated (Schoenwald, 2008), especially the link between therapist adherence to MST treatment principles and positive youth outcomes (e.g., Henggeler *et al.*, 1997). However, continued research is needed to demonstrate the value of the training and quality assurance protocols for each of the intervention programmes discussed in this chapter. In addition, more work is needed by researchers, especially independent groups of investigators, to demonstrate the viability of efforts to transport these intervention programmes to community settings using community therapists and purveyor organizations. This research could be designed as a randomized clinical trial (e.g., Timmons-Mitchell *et al.*, 2006) or a benchmarking study that replicates findings from an efficacy trial (e.g., Curtis *et al.*, 2009).

References

Alexander, J.F. and Parsons, B.V. (1973) Short-term behavioral intervention with delinquent families: impact on family process and recidivism. *Journal of Abnormal Psychology*, 81, 219–225.

Alexander, J.F. and Parsons, B.V. (1982) *Functional Family Therapy*, Brooks/Cole, Pacific Grove.

Andrews, D.A. (2006) Enhancing adherence to risk-need responsivity. *Criminology and Public Policy*, 5, 595–602.

Aos, S., Phipps, P., Barnoski, R. and Lieb, R. (2001) *The Comparative Costs of and Benefits of Programs to Reduce Crime*, Washington State Policy Institute, Olympia, http://www.wsipp.wa.gov/pub.asp (accessed 13 December 2012).

Aos, S., Lieb, R., Mayfield, J. *et al.* (2004) Benefits and Costs of Prevention and Early Intervention Programs for Youth. *Document no. 04-07-3901*. Washington State Policy Institute, Olympia, http://www.wsipp.wa.gov/pub.asp (accessed 13 December 2012).

Barton, C., Alexander, J.F., Waldron, H. *et al.* (1985) Generalizing treatment effects of functional family therapy: three replications. *American Journal of Family Therapy*, 13, 16–26.

Bateson, G. (1972) *Steps to an Ecology of the Mind*, Ballentine, New York.

Biglan, A., Brennan, P.A., Foster, S.L. and Holder, H.D. (2004) *Helping Adolescents at Risk: Prevention of Multiple Problem Behaviors*, Guilford Press, New York.

Borduin, C.M. (1994) Innovative models of treatment and service delivery in the juvenile justice system. *Journal of Clinical Child Psychology*, 23 (Suppl.), 19–25.

Borduin, C.M., Henggeler, S.W., Blaske, D.M. and Stein, R. (1990) Multisystemic treatment of adolescent sexual offenders. *International Journal of Offender Therapy and Comparative Criminology*, 34, 105–113.

Borduin, C.M., Mann, B.J., Cone, L.T. *et al.* (1995) Multisystemic treatment of serious juvenile offenders: long-term prevention of criminality and violence. *Journal of Consulting and Clinical Psychology*, 63, 569–578.

Borduin, C.M., Schaeffer, C.M. and Heiblum, N. (2009) A randomized clinical trial of multisystemic therapy with juvenile sexual offenders: effects on youth social ecology and criminal activity. *Journal of Consulting and Clinical Psychology*, 77, 26–37.

Britt, C.L. (2000) Health consequences of criminal victimization. *International Review of Victimology*, 8, 63–73.

Bronfenbrenner, U. (1979) *The Ecology of Human Development: Experiments by Nature and Design*, Harvard University Press, Cambridge.

Brown, E.C., Catalano, R.F., Fleming, C.B. *et al.* (2005) Mediator effects in the social development model: an examination of constituent theories. *Criminal Behaviour and Mental Health*, 15, 221–235.

Brunk, M., Henggeler, S.W. and Whelan, J.P. (1987) Comparison of multisystemic therapy and parent training in the brief treatment of child abuse and neglect. *Journal of Consulting and Clinical Psychology*, 55, 171–178.

Burns, B.J. and Hoagwood, K. (eds) (2002) *Community Treatment for Youth: Evidenced-Based Interventions for Severe Emotional and Behavioral Disorders*, Oxford University Press, New York.

Carr, M.B. and Vandiver, T.A. (2001) Risk and protective factors among youth offenders. *Adolescence*, 36, 409–426.

Cauce, A.M., Domenech-Rodriguez, M., Paradise, M. *et al.* (2002) Cultural and contextual influences in mental health help seeking: a focus on ethnic minority youth. *Journal of Consulting and Clinical Psychology*, 70, 44–55.

Chamberlain, P. (1990) Comparative evaluation of specialized foster care for seriously delinquent youths: a first step. *Community Alternatives: International Journal of Family Care*, 2, 21–36.

Chamberlain, P. (2003) *Treating Chronic Juvenile Offenders: Advances Made Through the Oregon Multidimensional Treatment Foster Care Model*, American Psychological Association, Washington, DC.

Chamberlain, P. and Moore, K. (1998) A clinical model for parenting juvenile offenders: a comparison of group care versus family care. *Clinical Child Psychology and Psychiatry*, 3, 375–386.

Chamberlain, P. and Reid, J. (1991) Using a specialized foster care community treatment model for children and adolescents leaving the state mental hospital. *Journal of Community Psychology*, 19, 266–276.

Chamberlain, P. and Reid, J. (1994) Differences in risk factors and adjustment for male and female delinquents in treatment foster care. *Journal of Child and Family Studies*, 3, 23–39.

Chamberlain, P. and Reid, J. (1998) Comparison of two community alternatives to incarceration for chronic juvenile offenders. *Journal of Consulting and Clinical Psychology*, 6, 624–633.

Chamberlain, P., Moreland, S. and Reid, K. (1992) Enhanced services and stipends for foster parents: effects on retention rates and outcomes for children. *Child Welfare*, 71, 387–401.

Chamberlain, P., Leve, L.D. and DeGarmo, D.S. (2007) Multidimensional treatment foster care for girls in the juvenile justice system: 2-year follow-up of a randomized clinical trial. *Journal of Consulting and Clinical Psychology*, 75, 187–193.

Chamberlain, P., Price, J., Leve, L.D. *et al.* (2008) Prevention of behavior problems for children in foster care: outcomes and mediation effects. *Prevention Science*, 9, 17–27.

Chambless, D.L., Baker, M.J., Baucom, D.H. *et al.* (1998) Update on empirically validated therapies, II. *Clinical Psychologist*, 51, 3–16.

Cullen, F.T., Myer, A.J. and Latessa, E.J. (2009) Eight lessons from *Moneyball*: the high cost of ignoring evidence-based corrections. *Victims and Offenders*, 4, 197–213.

Curtis, N.M., Ronan, K.R., Heiblum, N. and Crellin, K. (2009) Dissemination and effectiveness of multisystemic treatment in New Zealand: a benchmarking study. *Journal of Family Psychology*, 23, 119–129.

DeMatteo, D. and Marczyk, G. (2005) Risk factors, protective factors, and the prevention of antisocial behavior among juveniles, in *Juvenile Delinquency: Prevention, Assessment, and Intervention* (eds K. Heilbrun, N.E.S. Goldstein and R.E. Redding), Oxford University Press, New York, pp. 19–44.

Drake, E.K., Aos, S. and Miller, M.G. (2009) Evidence-based public policy options to reduce crime and criminal justice costs: implications in Washington state. *Victims and Offenders*, 4, 170–196.

Eddy, J.M. and Chamberlain, P. (2000) Family management and deviant peer association as mediators of the impact of treatment condition on youth antisocial behavior. *Journal of Consulting and Clinical Psychology*, 68, 857–863.

Eddy, M.J., Whaley, R.B. and Chamberlain, P. (2004) The prevention of violent behavior by chronic and serious male juvenile offenders: a 2-year follow-up of a randomized clinical trial. *Journal of Emotional and Behavioral Disorders*, 12, 2–8.

Elliott, D.S. (1998) *Blueprints for Violence Prevention* (Series Ed.). University of Colorado, Center for the Study and Prevention of Violence, Blueprints Publications, Boulder.

Elliott, D.S. and Mihalic, S. (2004) Issues in disseminating and replicating effective prevention programmes. *Prevention Science*, 5, 47–52.

Ellis, D.A., Naar-King, S., Frey, M.A. *et al.* (2004) Use of multisystemic therapy to improve regimen adherence among adolescents with type 1 diabetes in poor metabolic control: a pilot study. *Journal of Clinical Psychology in Medical Settings*, 11, 315–324.

Eyberg, S.M., Nelson, M.M. and Boggs, S.R. (2008) Evidence-based psychosocial treatments for children and adolescents with disruptive behavior. *Journal of Clinical Child and Adolescent Psychology*, 37, 215–237.

Fals-Stewart, W., Yates, B.T. and Klostermann, K. (2005) Assessing the costs, benefits, cost-benefit ratio, and cost-effectiveness of marital and family treatments: why we should and how we can. *Journal of Family Psychology*, 19, 28–39.

Farrington, D.P., Jolliffe, D., Hawkins, J.D. *et al.* (2003) Comparing delinquency careers in court records and self-reports. *Criminology*, 41, 933–958.

Farrington, D.P., Ttofi, M.M. and Coid, J.W. (2009) Development of adolescence-limited, late onset, and persistent offenders from age 8 to age 48. *Aggressive Behavior*, 35, 150–163.

Federal Bureau of Investigation, U. S. Department of Justice (2009) *Uniform Crime Reports*, Federal Bureau of Investigation, Washington, DC.

Fisher, P.A., Burraston, B. and Pears, K. (2005) The early intervention foster care program: permanent placement outcomes from a randomized trial. *Child Maltreatment*, 10, 61–71.

Fisher, P.A., Kim, H.K. and Pears, K.C. (2009) Effects of Multidimensional Treatment Foster Care for Preschoolers (MTFC-P) on reducing permanent placement failures among children with placement instability. *Children and Youth Services Review*, 31, 541–546.

Fleming, C.B., Catalano, R.F., Oxford, M.L. *et al.* (2002) A test of generalizability of the social development model across gender and income groups with longitudinal data from the elementary school developmental period. *Journal of Quantitative Criminology*, 18, 423–439.

Friedman, A.S. (1989) Family therapy vs. parent groups: effects on adolescent drug abusers. *American Journal of Family Therapy*, 17, 335–347.

Glisson, C., Schoenwald, S.K., Hemmelgarn, A. *et al.* (2010) Randomized trial of MST and ARC in a two-level EBT implementation strategy. *Journal of Consulting and Clinical Psychology*, 78, 537–550.

Gordon, D.A., Arbuthnot, J., Gustafson, K.E. and McGreen, P. (1988) Home-based behavioral-systems family therapy with disadvantaged juvenile delinquents. *American Journal of Family Therapy*, 16, 243–255.

Gordon, D.A., Graves, K. and Arbuthnot, J. (1995) The effect of functional family therapy for delinquents on adult criminal behavior. *Criminal Justice and Behavior*, 22, 60–73.

Greenwood, P. (2008) Prevention and intervention programs for juvenile offenders: the benefits of evidence-based practice. *Future of Children*, 18, 11–36.

Hansson, K., Cederblad, M. and Hook, B. (2000) Functional family therapy: a method for treating juvenile delinquents. *Socialvetenskaplig Tidskrift*, 3, 231–243.

Hansson, K., Johansson, P., Drott-Englen, G. and Benderix, Y. (2004) Functional family therapy in child psychiatric practice. *Nordisk Psykologi*, 56, 304–320.

Henggeler, S.W. and Borduin, C.M. (1990) *Family Therapy and Beyond: A Multisystemic Approach to Treating the Behavior Problems of Children and Adolescents*, Brooks/Cole, Pacific Grove.

Henggeler, S.W. and Schoenwald, S.K. (2011) Evidence-based interventions for juvenile offenders and juvenile justice policies that support them. *Society for Research in Child Development: Social Policy Report*, 25, 1–20.

Henggeler, S.W., Rodick, J.D., Borduin, C.M. *et al.* (1986) Multisystemic treatment of juvenile offenders: effects on adolescent behavior and family interaction. *Developmental Psychology*, 22, 132–141.

Henggeler, S.W., Melton, G.B. and Smith, L.A. (1992) Family preservation using multisystemic therapy: an effective alternative to incarcerating serious juvenile offenders. *Journal of Consulting and Clinical Psychology*, 60, 953–961.

Henggeler, S.W., Melton, G.B., Smith, L.A. *et al.* (1993) Family preservation using multisystemic treatment: long-term follow-up to a clinical trial with serious juvenile offenders. *Journal of Child and Family Studies*, 2, 283–293.

Henggeler, S.W., Pickrel, S.G., Brondino, M.J. and Crouch, J.L. (1996) Eliminating (almost) treatment dropout of substance abusing or dependent delinquents through home-based multisystemic therapy. *American Journal of Psychiatry*, 153, 427–428.

Henggeler, S.W., Melton, G.B., Brondino, M.J. *et al.* (1997) Multisystemic therapy with violent and chronic juvenile offenders and their families: the role of treatment fidelity in successful dissemination. *Journal of Consulting and Clinical Psychology*, 65, 821–833.

Henggeler, S.W., Pickrel, S.G. and Brondino, M.J. (1999) Multisystemic treatment of substance abusing and dependent delinquents: outcomes, treatment fidelity, and transportability. *Mental Health Services Research*, 1, 171–184.

Henggeler, S.W., Halliday-Boykins, C.A., Cunningham, P.B. *et al.* (2006) Juvenile drug court: enhancing outcomes by integrating evidence-based treatments. *Journal of Consulting and Clinical Psychology*, 74, 42–54.

Henggeler, S.W., Letourneau, E.J., Chapman, J.E. *et al.* (2009a) Mediators of change for multisystemic therapy with juvenile sexual offenders. *Journal of Consulting and Clinical Psychology*, 77, 451–462.

Henggeler, S.W., Schoenwald, S.K., Borduin, C.M. *et al.* (2009b) *Multisystemic Therapy for Antisocial Behavior in Children and Adolescents*, 2nd edn, Guilford Press, New York.

Hoffman, L. (1981) *Foundations of Family Therapy*, Basic Books, New York.

Hoge, R.D., Guerra, N.D. and Boxer, P. (eds) (2008) *Treating the Juvenile Offender*, Guilford Press, New York.

Howell, J.C. (2009) *Preventing and Reducing Juvenile Delinquency: A Comprehensive Framework*, 2nd edn, Sage, Thousand Oaks.

Kashani, J.H., Jones, M.R., Bumby, K.M. and Thomas, L.A. (1999) Youth violence: psychosocial risk factors, treatment, prevention, and recommendations. *Journal of Emotional and Behavioral Disorders*, 7, 200–210.

Kazdin, A.E. (2000) Treatments for aggressive and antisocial children. *Child and Adolescent Psychiatric Clinics of North America*, 9, 841–858.

Kazdin, A.E. (2007) Mediators and mechanisms of change in psychotherapy research. *Annual Review of Clinical Psychology*, 3, 1–27.

Kerr, D.C.R., Leve, L.D. and Chamberlain, P. (2009) Pregnancy rates among juvenile justice girls in two randomized controlled trials of MTFC. *Journal of Consulting and Clinical Psychology*, 77, 588–593.

Kilpatrick, D.G. and Acierno, A. (2003) Mental health needs of crime victims: epidemiology and outcomes. *Journal of Traumatic Stress*, 16, 119–132.

Klein, N.C., Alexander, J.F. and Parsons, B.V. (1977) Impact of family systems intervention on recidivism and sibling delinquency: a model of primary prevention and program evaluation. *Journal of Consulting and Clinical Psychology*, 45, 469–474.

Klietz, S.J., Borduin, C.M. and Schaeffer, C.M. (2010) Cost-benefit analysis of multisystemic therapy with serious and violent juvenile offenders. *Journal of Family Psychology*, 24, 657–666.

Letourneau, E.J., Henggeler, S.W., Borduin, C.M. *et al.* (2009) Multisystemic therapy for juvenile sexual offenders: 1-year results from a randomized effectiveness trial. *Journal of Family Psychology*, 23, 89–102.

Leve, L.D. and Chamberlain, P. (2007) A randomized evaluation of multidimensional treatment foster care: effects on school attendance and homework completion in juvenile justice girls. *Research on Social Work Practice*, 17, 657–663.

Leve, L.D., Chamberlain, P. and Reid, J.B. (2005) Intervention outcomes for girls referred from juvenile justice: effects on delinquency. *Journal of Consulting and Clinical Psychology*, 73, 1181–1185.

Liberman, A.M. (ed) (2008) *The Long View of Crime: A Synthesis of Longitudinal Research*, Springer, New York.

Lipsey, M.W. (2009) The primary factors that characterize effective interventions with juvenile offenders: a meta-analytic overview. *Victims and Offenders*, 4, 124–147.

Lipton, D., Martinson, R. and Wilks, J. (1975) *The Effectiveness of Correctional Treatment: A Survey of Treatment Evaluation Studies*, Praeger, New York.

Lodewijks, H.P.B., de Ruiter, C. and Doreleijers, T.A.H. (2010) The impact of protective factors in desistance from violent reoffending: a study in three samples of adolescent offenders. *Journal of Interpersonal Violence*, 25, 568–587.

Loeber, R., Farrington, D.P. and Waschbusch, D.A. (1998) Serious and violent juvenile offenders, in *Serious and Violent Juvenile Offenders: Risk Factors and Successful Interventions* (eds R. Loeber and D.P. Farrington), Sage, Thousand Oaks, pp. 13–29.

Loeber, R., Burke, J.D. and Pardini, D.A. (2009) Development and etiology of disruptive and delinquent behavior. *Annual Review of Clinical Psychology*, 5, 291–310.

Lyons, J.S., Baerger, D.R., Quigley, P. *et al.* (2001) Mental health service needs of juvenile offenders: a comparison of detention, incarceration, and treatment settings. *Children's Services: Social Policy, Research, and Practice*, 4, 69–85.

Mihalopoulos, C., Vos, T., Pirkis, J. and Carter, R. (2011) The economic analysis of prevention in mental health programs. *Annual Review of Clinical Psychology*, 7, 169–201.

Minuchin, P.P. (1985) Families and individual development: provocations from the field of family therapy. *Child Development*, 56, 289–302.

Miller, T.R., Fisher, D.A. and Cohen, M.A. (2001) Costs of juvenile violence: policy implications. *Pediatrics*, 107, e3. http://www.pediatrics.org/cgi/content/full/107/1/e3 (accessed 13 December 2012).

Odgers, C.L., Moffitt, T.E., Broadbent, J.M. *et al.* (2008) Female and male antisocial trajectories: from childhood origins to adult outcomes. *Development and Psychopathology*, 20, 673–716.

Ogden, T. and Hagen, K.A. (2006) Multisystemic therapy of serious behaviour problems in youth: sustainability of therapy effectiveness two years after intake. *Journal of Child and Adolescent Mental Health*, 11, 142–149.

Ogden, T. and Halliday-Boykins, C.A. (2004) Multisystemic treatment of antisocial adolescents in Norway: replication of clinical outcomes outside of the US. *Child and Adolescent Mental Health*, 9, 77–83.

Parsons, B.V. and Alexander, J.F. (1973) Short-term family intervention: a therapy outcome study. *Journal of Consulting and Clinical Psychology*, 41, 195–201.

Paschall, M.J., Ringwalt, C.L. and Flewelling, R.L. (2003) Effects of parenting, father absence, and affiliation with delinquent peers on delinquent behavior among African-American male adolescents. *Adolescence*, 38, 15–34.

Robbins, M.S., Alexander, J.F., Newell, R.M. and Turner, C.W. (1996) The immediate effect of reframing on client attitude in family therapy. *Journal of Family Psychology*, 10, 28–34.

Robbins, M.S., Alexander, J.F. and Turner, C.W. (2000) Disrupting defensive family interactions in family therapy with delinquent adolescents. *Journal of Family Psychology*, 14, 638–701.

Robinson, F. and Keithley, J. (2000) The impacts of crime on health and health services: a literature review. *Health, Risk, and Society*, 2, 253–266.

Schaeffer, C.M. and Borduin, C.M. (2005) Long-term follow-up to a randomized clinical trial of multisystemic therapy with serious and violent juvenile offenders. *Journal of Consulting and Clinical Psychology*, 73, 445–453.

Schoenwald, S.K. (2008) Toward evidence-based transport of evidence-based treatments: MST as an example. *Journal of Child and Adolescent Substance Abuse*, 17, 69–91.

Sexton, T.L. (2011) *Functional Family Therapy in Clinical Practice: An Evidence-Based Treatment Model for Working with Troubled Adolescents*, Taylor & Francis, New York.

Sexton, T. and Turner, C.W. (2010) The effectiveness of functional family therapy for youth with behavioral problems in a community practice setting. *Journal of Family Psychology*, 24, 339–348.

Shufelt, J.S. and Cocozza, J.C. (2006) *Youth with Mental Health Disorders in the Juvenile Justice System: Results from a Multi-State, Multi-System Prevalence Study*, National Center for Mental Health and Juvenile Justice, Delmar.

Singh, B., Hawthorne, G. and Vos, T. (2001) The role of economic evaluation in mental health care. *Australian and New Zealand Journal of Psychiatry*, 35, 104–117.

Snell-Johns, J., Mendez, J.L. and Smith, B.L. (2004) Evidence-based solutions for overcoming access barriers, decreasing attrition, and promoting change with underserved families. *Journal of Family Psychology*, 18, 19–35.

Strother, K.B., Swenson, M.E. and Schoenwald, S.K. (1998) *Multisystemic Therapy Organizational Manual*, MST Institute, Charleston.

Sundell, K., Hansson, K., Lofholm, C.A. *et al.* (2008) The transportability of MST to Sweden: short-term results from a randomized trial of conduct disordered youth. *Journal of Family Psychology*, 22, 550–560.

Swenson, C.C., Schaeffer, C., Henggeler, S.W. *et al.* (2010) Multisystemic therapy for child abuse and neglect: a randomized effectiveness trial. *Journal of Family Psychology*, 24, 497–507.

Timmons-Mitchell, J., Bender, M.B., Kishna, M.A. and Mitchell, C.C. (2006) An independent effectiveness trial of multisystemic therapy with juvenile justice youth. *Journal of Clinical Child and Adolescent Psychology*, 35, 227–236.

Tolan, P.H., Gorman-Smith, D. and Henry, D.B. (2003) The developmental ecology of urban males' youth violence. *Developmental Psychology*, 39, 274–291.

Turner, M.G., Hartman, J.L., Exum, M.N. and Cullen, F.T. (2007) Examining the cumulative effects of protective factors: resiliency among a national sample of high-risk youths. *Journal of Offender Rehabilitation*, 46, 81–111.

U.S. Public Health Service (2001) *Youth Violence: A Report of the Surgeon General*, U.S. Public Health Service, Washington, DC.

Waldron, H.B., Slesnick, N., Turner, C.W. *et al.* (2001) Treatment outcomes for adolescent substance abuse at 4- and 7-month assessments. *Journal of Consulting and Clinical Psychology*, 69, 802–813.

Weisz, J.R., Jensen-Doss, A. and Hawley, K.M. (2006) Evidence-based youth psychotherapies versus usual clinical care: a meta-analysis of direct comparisons. *American Psychologist*, 61, 671–689.

Westermark, P.K., Hansson, K. and Olsson, M. (2011) Multidimensional Treatment Foster Care (MTFC): results from an independent replication. *Journal of Family Therapy*, 33, 20–41.

12

Reducing Anger-Related Offending
What Works

Raymond W. Novaco
University of California, USA

Introduction

Violence imposes a major burden on the well-being of populations, and as we seek to attenuate violence, that ambition naturally reaches for anger control. Violence is a public health problem for which the international scope is clear, as reflected in reports by the World Health Organization (Krug *et al.*, 2002) and by the US Centers for Disease Control and Prevention (CDC) (Center for Disease Control and Prevention, 2006). A national population study in the United Kingdom (Coid *et al.*, 2006) involving 8397 households found that 12% affirm violent behaviour in the previous five years. In addition to the human tragic consequences of violence, there is also the financial burden. A US CDC study that examined violence as a public health problem (Corso *et al.*, 2007) reported that the costs associated with non-fatal injuries and deaths due to violence in the year 2000 were more than $70 billion. More broadly, the implicit costs of violent crime in the United States, in terms of value of lost life and value of injuries, were estimated by Anderson (1999) to be over $574 billion annually, and that is separate from his calculations of crime-induced production costs (e.g., police, corrections, security systems), opportunity costs (lost production) and economic transfers. Soares (2006) estimated the welfare cost of violence across 73 countries and put the yearly costs in the United States at 2.9% of GDP (for comparison, it was 5.7% for Latin America). To take another perspective, for UK National Health Service staff, the National Audit Office (2003) estimate of the direct cost of violence was £69 million or more per year, not counting costs associated with psychological distress, staff morale or staff retention.

While anger is neither necessary nor sufficient for violence, we know intuitively and empirically that violent behaviour is often activated by anger (Novaco, 2011). Social gatekeepers prudently look for ways of reducing violence risk, and anger management programmes have proliferated. The societal call for anger control fits with a quotidian conflict resolution agenda and broadly based quests for interpersonal harmony, including the Nobel Peace

What Works in Offender Rehabilitation: An Evidence-Based Approach to Assessment and Treatment,
First Edition. Edited by Leam A. Craig, Louise Dixon and Theresa A. Gannon.
© 2013 John Wiley & Sons, Ltd. Published 2013 by John Wiley & Sons, Ltd.

prize, which sometimes goes astray. Anger management programmes abound in correctional settings, both institutional and community, but it is not clearly evident that such programmes are effective interventions for violent offenders. In the reviews by Blackburn (2004) and McGuire (2008), anger management programmes are promissory, and some authors, such as Polaschek (2004, 2006), have questioned their appropriateness as a primary intervention for many violent offenders. Some time ago, Howells (1989) cogently observed that not all violent offenders are candidates for anger therapy and discussed the congruities and incongruities. Indeed, from the origination of anger management as a therapeutic intervention (Novaco, 1975) to its initial implementaion with high security forensic patients (Renwick *et al.*, 1997), it was thought to be an adjunctive therapy. It was not meant to supplant either psychotherapy for a client's larger mental health needs or the multifaceted interventions needed to rehabilitate violent offenders, such as that implemented by Polaschek and her colleagues in New Zealand (e.g., Polaschek *et al.*, 2005). Nevertheless, meta-analytic reviews of interventions for offenders by Landenberger and Lipsey (2005) and by Dowden and Andrews (2000) were sanguine about recidivism reduction associated with programmes that included anger control.

Anger control is a vexing issue, precisely because anger is a normal emotion having survival value. For aggression-disposed individuals and subcultures, it's a hard sell to dislodge attachment to anger. Humans are hard-wired for anger, and there can be no sensible thoughts to erase it, much as the Stoics and the Victorians tried. Yet, the violence-linked interpersonal and societal harm-doing capacity of anger is unmistakable, as are its manifestations in self-harm. Beyond anger's violence-engendering faculty, it also can adversely affect prudent thought, core relationships, work performance and physical well-being. Hence, community caretakers, social scientists, clinical professionals and great thinkers seek remedies for it. The problem conditions, however, are not derivative of anger per se, but instead result from 'anger dysregulation' – that is, its activation, expression and ongoing experience occur without appropriate controls.

Many violent offenders become attached to their anger routines, which can be oddly satisfying. The psychosocial symbolism of anger (Novaco, 2000) casts it, in one of its Janus-faced forms, as energizing, empowering, signalling, justifying, rectifying and relieving. Hence, interventions aimed at anger reduction might be disparagingly viewed as totalitarian ploys to stifle individuality and the human spirit. Like the coerced cures imposed on fictionalized anti-heroes, such as those in Anthony Burgess' *A Clockwork Orange* or Michael Crichton's *The Terminal Man*, the term 'anger management' might, in an Orwellian sense, connote invasive control over the will to determine one's own destiny. Social gatekeepers (parents, school principals, employers, police and magistrates), though, are not charmed by the mastery-toned elements of anger, but rather are sensitized to and unsettled by the Janus opposing face social metaphors of anger as eruptive, unbridled, savage, venous, burning and consuming. Thus, a UK public information campaign on problem anger was launched by the Mental Health Foundation (2008). Until recent decades, the turbulent emotions underpinning harm-doing behaviour had eluded clinical focus, having been long ignored in the privileging of other antecedents, such as criminal history, mental illness and psychopathic personality. Anger and its vicissitudes – rage, hate and revenge – have come to the fore, and court-referred 'anger management' treatments, as well as prison programmes for it, are now commonplace for many varieties of offending behaviour.

The efficacy of intervention programmes for anger with violent offenders is the core topic of this chapter, but before addressing that, some contextual background is in order. The forensic relevance of anger in its ties to violence and to madness has a long history.

Historical Backdrop

Systematic attention to anger as a dynamic risk factor for violence has been remarkably slow in coming. In the forensic field, anger eruptions are often cast as symptoms of the person's 'illness'. Yet, anger has long been known to be an activator of violent behaviour. Anger is the prototype of the classical and medieval view of emotions as 'passions' that seize the personality, disturb judgement, alter bodily conditions and imperil behaviour. Plato and Aristotle, seeking perfection of character and temperament, viewed moderation in anger as desirable. Seneca (44/1817), arguably the first anger scholar, understood it as a pernicious and vicious force that makes us destroy one another. Perhaps inspired by Horace, he saw anger as a 'short madness'. Anger's association with mental disorder was also noted by Galen, the physician of Marcus Aurelius, who saw anger episodes as marked by madness (Galen, 1963). Although the involvement of anger in psychopathology is complex (Novaco, 2010a), its relevance for violence and mental disorder has long been known, as has its enlargement as 'wrath' or 'rage'.

Wrath, as linked with loss of rationality and vengeful destructiveness, is an ancient tale with reverberating forensic relevance. The Iliad, the first composition of Western civilization, opens with the anger of Achilles: 'Anger be now your song, immortal one, Akhilleus' anger, doomed and ruinous,...leaving so many dead men – carrion...' (Homer, 2004, p. 5). Achilles was enraged at Agamemnon the Athenian king but followed (obeyed) Athena's advice to stay his sword – divinity inspired anger control; but he remained stewing in his tent while thousands of his soldiers perished in battle. Among those fallen was his close friend Patroclus, the news of which engulfed Achilles in a 'black stormcloud of pain...tore his hair with both hands' (p. 430), and he became 'mad with rage for his friend's death' (p. 468). In an intensity of anger (*mēnis*) thought to be reserved for the gods, Achilles viciously kills Hector and defiles his body.

Another tragic hero in the Iliad, Ajax (Achilles' cousin), is driven to madness by Athena in his rage against Odysseus. Simon (1978) gives an engaging account of Sophocles' portrayal of the cold wrath of Athena and Ajax's psychotic breakdown, which culminates in suicide. Lansky (1996) highlighted the role of shame in Ajax's psychopathology and views his madness as dissociated narcissistic rage. In Euripides' play, the *Madness of Heracles* (Hercules Furens in Latin), that tragic hero is driven mad by the goddesses Iris and Lyssa (the latter being madness personified), and in a frenzy, he kills his wife and children (cf. Mikalson, 1986; Simon, 1978). Such rage-without-reason portrayals were not restricted to men, as Euripides and Seneca composed plays of Medea, whose paroxysm of rage at being betrayed by Jason leads her, in vengeance, to kill her children whom Jason fathered. *Medea* is another shame–rage cycle tale.

Those are just a few classical examples of anger's ties to violence, mental disorder and self-harm that reverberate in the contemporary forensic field. In drafting criminal statutes, Plato differentiated intentional homicide as having greater culpability when driven by angry revenge than by angry impulse (Woozley, 1972). Literary illustrations are Shakespeare's hot-tempered, impulsively violent Tybalt in *Romeo and Juliet*, and his *King Lear*, whose easily activated rage accompanied his progressive insanity; there is also Dostoyevsky's Dmitri Fyodorovitch, in *Brothers Karamazov*, who resorts to irrational, violent solutions in mad rages, and his 'underground man' protagonist in *Notes from Underground*, who ruminates about revenge. Dysregulated anger features in temporary insanity 'heat of passion' defences (Novaco, 2010a).

Anger's generic link to psychopathology is also semantic. Becoming 'enraged' suggests being 'rabid', connoting a diseased state of mind. *Being* angry, *becoming* mad and *creating* Bedlam (echoing the historic asylum) are semantically and metaphorically linked. The classical notion of anger 'passion' posing danger carried through to the eighteenth century, as reflected in Hutcheson's (1742) essay, where he characterized anger as 'a Propensity to occasion Evil to another, arising upon apprehension of an Injury done by him' (p. 75). Early texts in psychiatry (Von Krafft-Ebing, 1905; Tuke, 1892) designated 'excandescentia furibunda' to pertain to the insanity of anger – that is, the loss of mental control or inhibitory central control that was seen to occur during rage episodes. Von Krafft-Ebing saw the condition as indicative of brain abnormalities caused by biological conditions, trauma or structural defects ('idiocy') and stated that 'In such conditions the slightest cause leads to the explosive affect of anger, which, owning to continued reproduction of painful thoughts, is maintained at its height' (p. 56).

A thematic account of anger as portrayed historically and culturally can be found in Potegal and Novaco (2010), and contemporary relevance is easy to track. In preliterate societies, angry malevolent spirits caused misfortune and physical discomfort. Angry gods presented more grave danger, bringing calamities and instilling abject fear. Wrathful gods, and monotheistic deities, become angry about disobedience, disloyalty, disrespect and imperfections. Transposed to the human arena, anger is associated with manhood in warrior cultures, such as the Assyrians, Hittites, Norse/Viking berserkers, Aztecs and Maori. Anger makes for fearsomeness. In psychopathological forms, it erupts in cases of 'wild man' and 'amok' syndromes, the latter involving frenzied violence, as observed by anthropologists in Micronesia and other Pacific Island societies (e.g., Carr and Tan, 1976; Gaw and Bernstein, 1992). Spree murder is, of course, the Western cultural parallel of amok.

Noteworthy in leaving this historical backdrop is a fundamental symbolic structure for understanding anger and aggression, evident since the classical period, which is 'justification'. It is rooted in ancient religious texts, such as the Bible and the Koran, as well as classical mythologies about deities and historical accounts of the behaviour of ancient rulers. Anger, as well, is very much infused with themes of justification, and even righteousness – perhaps prototypical exemplified by God's anger in the *Dies Ire* (Days of Rage) segment of the Requiem mass (the Latin Mass of the Dead, *Missa de Profundis*). Grasping the centrality of the justification theme is important for anger assessment and treatment for offender and non-offender populations. What is judged to be a transgression, affront or wickedness is shaped by schema or macro knowledge structures. Threat perception is intrinsic to anger activation. The threat schema of a social group can heighten attention to transgressions or signals of malicious intent. Violations or encroachments might be exacerbated or excused by status variables that mark the action as especially onerous or, alternatively, as forgivable. Retaliatory aggression recruits anger as an energizer. In contemporary pleas of temporary insanity, the 'heat of passion' defence or the 'provocation doctrine' (cf. Horder, 1992, 2005; Novaco, 2010a) is rooted in principles of justified moral outrage, whereby severe provocation provides a moral warrant for retailing in anger, which operates as a passion that overrides reason and defeats self-control. The anger is viewed as an uncontrolled reaction to wrongdoing or perceived injustice.

Because anger is too easily transformed into destructive aggression, it beckons for self-regulation. However, many of those who have anger regulatory difficulties and offend violently are otherwise beset with adversities that attenuate control capacity. High-anger people often lead lives with multiple sources of anger/aggression instigation. While they are architects as well as recipients of their misfortunes, their anger troubles can be reflective of trauma, hardship, chaotic social relationships and mental disorder. When high in avenues of friction, impoverished in support structures and short in countervailing resources for inhibitory controls, anger easily becomes a default response. The provision of treatment and its evaluation for high-anger persons hinges, importantly, on proficient assessment of the anger problem.

Anger Assessment

Referrals for anger treatment or 'anger management' often run afoul of the elementary point that, when someone's violent behaviour is not driven by anger dysregulation, providing therapy for anger is mis-targeted. Some studies of 'anger management' programmes conducted in prison settings have tempered their findings of limited efficacy by noting that high-anger level inclusion criteria were lacking (e.g., Eamon, Munchua and Reddon, 2001; McMurran *et al.*, 2001; Smith and Beckner, 1993). Not all violent offenders are candidates for anger therapy, and Howells *et al.* (1997) articulated the importance of individual formulation, needs assessment and attention to cultural factors.

At the outset, it must be understood that people who are in forensic or other custodial settings should be expected to 'mask' their anger, as they are unlikely to perceive gain in disclosing it. Instead, they are inclined to respond on a 'need to know' basis – telling you what they think they need for you to know. Anger assessment in forensic settings is subject to measurement reactivity. Reactivity pertains to responses obtained in an assessment procedure that are reactions by the person to his or her inferences about the test situation, rather than to the explicit elements of the testing – that is, the person is inclined to produce anger reports in anticipation of what those test responses will mean to some audience. Measurement reactivity is a form of response distortion and constitutes a threat to internal validity, which some anger assessment procedures (Novaco, 2003) try to address. An example of such reactivity occurs in the study by Loza and Loza-Fanous (1999a), who sought to examine anger as a predictor of violent recidivism among Canadian criminal offenders but did not notice that their anger score means approached the lowest possible scores for one of their main anger instruments.

There are multiple sources of reactivity bias in anger assessment. People who have long-standing anger difficulties are characteristically suspicious and distrustful, and anger testers may be viewed as representative of a threatening system deserving guarded responses. Importantly, the psychosocial symbolism associated with anger (particularly its boiling/eruptive and savage/non-rational aspects) deters respondents from disclosing anger and the actions to which anger might dispose them. Moreover, anger can be a protected part of the person, centrally involving matters of self-worth. Thus, it is not readily revealed or surrendered. As Goffman (1961) helped us to understand, the 'identity stripping' features of custodial institutions take away the customary affirmations of the self – a patient once commented in reflecting about life in an institution, 'All you've got is your anger'. Disclosing anger may be perceived to carry the psychological cost of losing power and, what may be for that person, the last remaining symbol of personal freedom and self-worth.

Many instruments have been constructed for the assessment of anger, hostility and aggression. Two reviews provide valuable coverage. Eckhardt, Norlander and Deffenbacher's (2004) give attention to the range of anger and hostility self-report scales, and Suris *et al.* (2004) deal with aggressive behaviour measures. The latter article has overlapping coverage of anger and hostility scales; its content is more overview than analytical but does provide a catalogue of measures and their psychometric properties. Additional coverage is provided in Taylor and Novaco (2005), particularly with regard to persons with intellectual disabilities (IDs).

Self-report measures

The three main self-report measures of anger in contemporary forensic studies are the Spielberger State-Trait Anger Expression Inventory (STAXI; Spielberger, 1996), the Buss–Perry Aggression Questionnaire (AQ; Buss and Perry, 1992) and the Novaco Anger Scale and Provocation Inventory (NAS-PI; Novaco, 1994, 2003). The NAS-PI was developed for use with mentally disordered respondents, and it was implemented in the landmark MacArthur project on violence and mental disorder (Monahan *et al.*, 2001). Both the NAS-PI and the STAXI have been validated for use with forensic patients with IDs (Novaco and Taylor, 2004).

Anger psychometric scales are generally 'nomothetic' in nature, suited to detecting mean differences with reference to normative data and changes within or between groups following intervention. An alternative and more 'idiographic' procedure is the Imaginal Provocation Test (IPT), first developed by Novaco (1975) and more recently extended to hospitalized forensic patients (Taylor *et al.*, 2004). The IPT involves presentation of provocation scenes that the person is asked to imagine actually happening and then to provide ratings on the anger experience and on prospective behavioural reactions to the provocation. The measurement indices are sensitive to change associated with anger treatment (e.g., Chemtob *et al.*, 1997; Novaco, 1975; Taylor *et al.* 2004). The imaginal provocation procedure is exportable for use in a variety of settings, has minimal logistical requirements and the content of the imaginal scenes can be tailored to the modal types of anger-inducing events for a client group or ultimately to the particular circumstances of an individual client's anger control problem.

Observation procedures

Anger also can be assessed by staff observation procedures. There are a number of staff-rated measures of behaviour for use in residential settings, which are catalogued in Suris *et al.* (2004). For the most part, these measures attend to aggression, typically excluding anger. In contrast, the Ward Anger Rating Scale (WARS; Novaco and Renwick, 2003) is a two-part scale (anger attributes are rated on Part B) completed by a staff member who knows the patient and has observed his or her behaviour over the previous week. Novaco and Taylor (2004) and Doyle and Dolan (2006a) demonstrated its validity for anger assessment and the prediction of violence among hospitalized forensic patients, and Cornell, Peterson and Richards (1999) used its anger attributes index (Novaco, 1994) with incarcerated adolescents. A noteworthy perspective on inpatient aggression is the functional analysis approach of Daffern, Howells and Ogloff (2007), whereby anger-driven aggression can be differentiated from other functional types, such as demand avoidance, forcing compliance, obtain tangibles and enhance status.

Staff observation procedures and use of archival records make for a multimethod approach to anger assessment, which is an important principle, not only from a research standpoint but also with regard to case formulation. Nevertheless, client self-report is a central measurement procedure. Anger is a subjective emotion, and the factors that bear on anger reactions and anger control must be uncovered from the person's cognitive processing and symbolic structures, so as to understand how people construe their anger experiences. Proficient anger assessment, though, is not about tallying numbers on a rating scale. It involves integration of multiple channels of information and is geared towards understanding the psychological deficits associated with the anger dysregulation and problematic behaviour.

Pertinent to anger intervention programmes with offenders, Williamson *et al.* (2003) have developed an 'Anger Readiness to Change Questionnaire'. Knowing a person's 'readiness for anger treatment' and responsivity to provided programmes, as Howells and Day (2003) have cogently explained, requires understanding the clinical complexity of cases (e.g., co-morbid disorders), clients' inferences about their problems, clients' personal goals, mandatory treatment issues, institutional/agency factors and cultural and gender differences. To be sure, anger assessment is made more difficult by severe mental disorder and by ID; however, reliable and valid psychometric assessments can be obtained with such clinical populations (cf. Novaco, 1994, 2003; Taylor and Novaco, 2005). The admixture of client and setting conditions bears on client responsivity to provided programmes.

Anger as a Viable Treatment Target in Forensic Settings

Forensic settings are efficient anger factories. In jails, prisons and forensic hospitals, the person is subjected to various 'mortifying' conditions (Goffman, 1961), and the social and physical environments of custodial settings are conducive to anger activation (cf. Levey and Howells, 1991; Novaco, 1994). Environmental design, privacy restrictions, limited affordances, resident attributes, staffing levels and unit social climate so often entail aversive elements that could trigger anger in normal, well-adjusted people. Overcrowding alone is an anger-generating adversity, and while the United States leads the world in its rate of incarceration, being five to eight times higher than that of Canada and Western Europe (Walmsley, 2006), concerns about prison overcrowding and failed prisons policy are not unique to the United States. Imprisonment in the United Kingdom between 1997 and 2007 increased by one-third (Ministry of Justice, 2007), and the UK prison system was said to be in crisis by the country's own Chief Inspector of Prisons (Owens, 2007). Since then, the population in custody in England and Wales has continued to grow from 80067 at the end of 2007 to 87531 at the end of March 2012 (Ministry of Justice, 2012).

Prison environments are replete with aggression-engendering elements and are all too thin on prosocial antidotes (Ireland, 2000; Maghan, 1999). Miller (1973) stated that, in adjustment to life in a Florida prison, anger was 'a ubiquitous feeling state, the expression of which itself becomes a method of dealing with depression' (p. 24). Nurse, Woodcock and Ornsby (2003) reported on how environmental factors in a prison in England lead to 'extreme stress, anger, and frustration' (p. 481). Incisive accounts of the short-term and long-term effects of solitary confinement are given by Haney (2003) and by Arrigo and Bullock (2008), which feature intense anger and hostility. Haney found that both irrational anger and ruminations were present among 88% of the prisoners at a California maximum security prison. In Michie and Cooke's (2006) study with Scottish prisoners, anger, in rigorous multivariate analyses, was the strongest predictor of violence without a weapon. Among over 800 incarcerated juveniles in California, DeLisi *et al.* (2010) found anger to be predictive of institutional misconduct, including assaults, controlling for a host of background and psychological variables. Similar findings were obtained by Cornell *et al.* (1999) elsewhere.

Psychiatric hospitals have been known for decades to have long-standing problems with assaultive behaviour by patients against other patients and against staff (e.g., Depp, 1976; Foster, Bowers and Nijman, 2007; Fottrell, 1980; Haller and Deluty, 1988; Nijman *et al.*, 2005; Whittington and Richter, 2005). Assaultive behaviour by patients seriously impairs treatment milieu, results in restrictions and diminished chances for discharge, constitutes risk for harm among staff and has considerable financial cost in workers' compensation claims and employee turnover. A number of studies have now shown anger, a dynamic variable amenable to treatment, to be predictive of assaultive behaviour by forensic patients during hospitalization (Doyle and Dolan, 2006a; Linaker and Busch-Iversen, 1995; Novaco, 1994; Novaco and Taylor, 2004; Wang and Diamond, 1999) and in the community after discharge (Doyle and Dolan, 2006b; Doyle et al., 2012; Monahan et al., 2001; Skeem et al. 2006; Swogger et al., 2012). Taken together with the findings for anger activating assaultiveness among prisoners, there is a solid rationale for anger therapeutic intervention.

Challenges for Anger Treatment with Offenders

The survival functions of anger and aggression thwart efforts to change offending behaviour. People with severe anger problems are often reluctant to change routines that have 'worked' for them, which, from a system's theory perspective (cf. Novaco, 2007), can be seen as exhibiting *inertia*. However, many people with anger/aggression problems are too readily viewed as 'treatment-resistant' cases. When faced with a 'Formula One anger case, it is easy to be unsettled by the person's volatility and history of so much having been tried with so little result. However, Howells and Day (2003) scuttled the 'treatment resistance' notion by asserting instead that the treatment engagement problem be understood as a matter of client 'readiness'. In their discussion of impediments that are prevalent in forensic and correctional contexts, it can be seen that low readiness is not only about the client's disposition but also about characteristics of the treatment situation that can impede engagement in therapy. Among the issues that Howells and Day (2003) discuss in this regard are the complexities of cases (e.g., multiple co-morbidities), goals and expectations of the institutional setting, clients' inferences about their anger problem, treatment being mandated and ethnic/cultural/gender differences. Monahan and Steadman (2012) turned the 'treatment resistance' characterization completely on its head by arguing that, for the vast majority of people in the criminal justice system who have serious mental disorder, the situation is one of 'client-resistant services'.

Treatment of anger proceeds successfully when two thresholds are met: (i) when the client recognizes that costs of anger outweigh the benefits of anger/aggression habits, and (ii) when the client commits to engage with the therapist. Treatment engagement, of course, may be followed by disengagement, necessitating re-engagement efforts. Many scientist-practitioners working in the criminal justice and forensic psychology fields have called attention to the value of motivational interviewing (Miller and Rollnick, 2002) to facilitate treatment engagement, and parallel procedures have been part of a 'preparatory phase' of cognitive-behavioural anger treatment (Novaco, 1997; Renwick et al., 1997; Taylor and Novaco, 2005).

Many offenders who have anger regulatory difficulties have long been beset with adversities that attenuate control capacity. While they have been architects of many of their misfortunes, their anger troubles can be reflective of trauma, economic hardship, chaotic social relationships as well as mental disorder and substance abuse. The prevalence of trauma and post-traumatic stress disorder (PTSD) among prisoners has been insufficiently studied (Goff et al., 2007); yet, it is clear that such conditions are higher than normal among incarcerated populations and are especially problematic for females (Cauffman et al., 1998; Huang et al., 2006; Komarovskaya et al., 2011; Pollack et al., 2006; Zlotnick, 1999). Given the relationship between, PTSD and anger (Orth and Wieland, 2006), high levels of trauma may account for the higher levels of anger found among female prisoners and forensic hospital patients (e.g., Archer and Haigh, 1997; Novaco, 1997; Sutter et al., 2002). Among female prisoners, anger is substantially related to self-harm and suicide attempts (e.g., Chapman and Dixon-Gordon, 2007; Milligan and Andrews, 2005).

The embeddedness of anger in an admixture of adversities sharply distinguishes this emotion in offender populations from the anger reactions observed in the subject pools of university laboratories in analogue studies. Achieving change in clinically problematic anger dysregulation is a bit more complicated than offering distraction, supplying a cool drink, hitting a bop bag, being a 'fly on the wall' or providing mitigating information about a perceived slight from an experimental confederate – all of which far too many psychology lab researchers wax on about clinical relevance. Garden-variety anger reactions, whether laboratory grown or real life based, are qualitatively different from those rooted in long-standing distress. For those high in avenues of friction, impoverished in support structures, beset with delusions and depression and short in countervailing resources for inhibitory controls, anger easily becomes a default response that catalyzes an overdetermined act of aggression. It carries the aura of repelling threat and provides fortification of self-worth. With seriously angry people, simply engaging them in the process of treatment is fraught with many obstacles, and their readiness for anger treatment often must be fostered therapeutically.

Anger Treatment with Offenders: Background and Empirical Challenges

Injunctions for 'anger management' have taken many forms in recent decades, from the judicial proscriptive to the satirical. Yet, anger control has been a societal agenda since classical philosophers grappled with the regulation of inner life and the enhancement of virtue. The military strategy writings attributed to Sun Tzu saw anger as a fault upon which military commanders could capitalize. The Stoics precluded the viability of anger, as readily seen in the writings of Seneca and Epictetus. Roman and Greek philosopher/historians, such as Cicero and Plutarch, also sought eradication of anger in the quest for tranquillity of mind. Roman poets Horace and Juvenal saw anger as marked by madness and foolishness. Pre-dating the Greek and Roman Stoics were Buddhist teachings about the path to enlightenment, seeking to train the mind to gain inner strength. Original cognitive-behavioural therapies (CBTs) were influenced by Stoic proscriptions, and new wave CBT approaches, such as 'Mindfulness' or 'Acceptance and Commitment Therapy', have forerunners in Buddhist ideas – if drawn to seeing remedies for anger in acceptance and compassion, there is much of value to be gleaned from Hanh (2001).

Since the origination of 'anger management', as it was then called (Novaco, 1975), nine meta-analyses on the effectiveness of psychotherapy for anger have been published (Beck and Fernandez, 1998; Del Vecchio and O'Leary, 2004; DiGuiseppe and Tafrate, 2003; Edmondson and Conger, 1996; Gansle, 2005; Ho, Carter and Stephenson, 2010; Saini, 2009; Sukhodolsky, Kassinove and Gorman, 2004; Tafrate, 1995), which overall have found medium to strong effect sizes, indicating that approximately 75% of those receiving anger treatment improved compared to controls. When various therapies are examined, CBT approaches have greatest efficacy. However, many of the studies that qualify for meta-analytic review (by virtue of control group conditions) have not concerned patients with serious clinical problems or violent behaviour. Thus, the strictures of meta-analyses allow for the inclusion of studies with normal functioning college student volunteers, minimally screened for anger problems, while excluding clinical case series studies with clients having demonstrable psychopathology and violence histories. Pertinent to the forensic field, there are a number of case series studies that bolster confidence in anger treatment efficacy with offenders (e.g., Bornstein, Weisser and Balleweg, 1985; Burns *et al.*, 2003; Haddock *et al.*, 2004; Lindsay *et al.*, 2003; McMurran *et al.*, 2001; Nomellini and Katz, 1983; Renwick *et al.*, 1997).

Landenberger and Lipsey's (2005) meta-analysis of 58 studies of the effects of CBT programmes on recidivism of adult and juvenile offenders found that 20 of those studies incorporated anger control as a treatment element. After controlling for method variables, participant characteristics, quality of implementation and CBT emphasis, their regression model found that having an anger control component in the intervention was significantly related to the effect size for reduced recidivism. Landenberger and Lipsey defined 'anger control' as 'training in techniques for identifying triggers and cues that arouse anger and maintaining self-control' (p. 466). Similarly, the meta-analysis by Dowden and Andrews (2000) of 35 primary studies of correctional treatment programmes had found those that targeted 'negative affect/anger' were positively and significantly associated with effect size in reducing violent recidivism. To be sure, the incorporation of an anger control component in a broader intervention programme (such as 'Reasoning and Rehabilitation' or 'Aggression Replacement Training') is of course different from a focused anger therapeutic intervention which then receives focused evaluation of its efficacy; yet, those two meta-analytic reviews certainly provide a boost for the value of delivering anger treatment to violent offenders. However, despite these meta-analytic results concerning studies with offenders, plus the supportive findings from the nine meta-analytic studies including non-offenders, there remain reasons for doubt about the efficacy of treating anger with forensic populations. There are several challenges in this regard.

Anger may be 'irrelevant'

One challenge came from the Canadian prison study by Loza and Loza-Fanous (1999b), who, in effect, asserted that anger was irrelevant to the criminal behaviour and treatment needs of violent offenders. They obtained a random sample of 271 males incarcerated in Ontario institutions and compared violent with non-violent offenders, and then rapists with non-rapists, using four anger instruments. While showing that violent offenders and rapists were much more likely to be recommended for an anger programme by case managers, they found no significant differences in assessed anger between their offender categories, with the exception that the violent offenders had lower anger on one of the measures (NAS Total). Loza and Loza-Fanous thereby concluded that it is fallacious to treat anger. Their claim of the irrelevancy of anger was, unfortunately, picked up by others (e.g., Serin, Gobeil and Preston, 2009; Walker and Bright, 2009b), but insufficient attention was given to the actual data. In the Loza and Loza-Fanous (1999b) study, as with their other study published that year (Loza and Loza-Fanous, 1999a) with virtually the same sample, the Mean scores on the anger measures are suppressed, showing signs of anger measurement reactivity (cf. Novaco, 2010b). For example, the Mean score on STAXI Trait Anger for the violent prisoners is 14.45 – yet, the possible score range on that scale is 10–40. That Mean score for Trait Anger is nearly one standard deviation below the STAXI norms for males. Similarly, the Loza and Loza-Fanous (1999b) Mean NAS Total score for the violent prisoners is 68.52 – yet, the possible score range is 48–144. So, their prisoner-reported anger (like that in another Ontario prison study, Mills and Kroner, 2003) is also quite low in that instrument's score range and in comparison to its standardization norms for offenders (cf. Novaco, 2003) and to other studies with prisoners using the same measures in three other countries (Baker, Van Hasselt and Sellers, 2008; Lindqvist, Daderman and

Hellstrom, 2005; Sutter *et al.*, 2002) as well as in another study in Canada (Ford, 1991). It is then dubious to deem anger to be irrelevant to the criminogenic needs of violent prisoners, when the prisoners' anger reports are plausibly suppressed or 'masked'.

Indeed, one must establish whether anger treatment is relevant. Low anger scores on psychometric measures may be a product of masking, or they may be due to the absence of anger, as discussed earlier in conjunction with violent offending and as can be seen in McMurran *et al.* (2001) in their discussion of one of their cases.

Anger treatment is 'weak'

A more formidable challenge to the value of anger treatment with prisoners comes from studies by Kevin Howells and his colleagues with male prisoners in Australia. Straightaway, it should be noted that their prisoner study participants indeed had high anger scores and violent offence histories, that they attended to treatment programme fidelity and that programme recipients showed gains in anger control knowledge. Their news for the efficacy of the programmes, though, was not reassuring. When Watt and Howells (1999) conducted two small sample studies evaluating a prison anger management programme in Western Australia, they found no effect for the treatment condition compared to the control condition in either study and no change in anger. The treatment programme was ten 2-hour sessions over five weeks. Howells *et al.* (2005) then followed with a study of 285 prisoners in South and Western Australia, again evaluating the same type of programme and involving follow-up assessments. Although they found declines in anger over time and the treatment group showed more improvement than the control group, the between-group effects were not significant. They did, however, find that 'treatment readiness' significantly moderated change in anger. Greater readiness for treatment was associated with significant declines in anger in the anger treatment condition and significant increases in anger in the control condition.

Heseltine, Howells and Day (2010), in another study with Australian prisoners, concluded that the anger management programme did not have a significant impact on experience of anger or behaviour, except for gain in knowledge; but they did find that *high-anger* prisoners in the treatment condition improved in social functioning, clinical problem level and self-harm risk. In that latter study, the authors noted that there were lower levels of anger overall than in previous studies, and there was a 30% attrition rate. Howells *et al.* (2005) speculated that the poor showing for the efficacy of the treatment may have been due to poor motivation of participants – which can be found noted in other failed treatment studies with offenders (e.g., Valliant, Jensen and Raven-Brook, 1995). Beyond the motivation issue, Howells *et al.* questioned whether the treatment was sufficiently intensive, noting that the length of their programme (20 hours) stands in contrast to the 50-hour programme of Dowden, Blancette and Serin (1999) in Canada. They conjectured that the complexity of problems that characterize high-risk offenders, as Howells and Day (2003) and Novaco (1997) have highlighted, interferes with establishing a working therapeutic alliance. Dealing with multilayered clinical problems does require more treatment time than brief anger management programmes provide.

Anger treatment does not 'reach'

Walker and Bright (2009b) put forward a view that, for violent people in clinical and forensic settings, anger management falls short of client treatment needs. That article sprung from one just prior (Walker and Bright, 2009a) that centrally implicated the arrogant/aggression ('macho') protection of low self-esteem in the activation of violence. Their central argument is that the cognitive models underpinning 'anger management', which rely on information-processing frameworks for understanding anger, citing those of Beck (1999) and Novaco (Novaco, 1994; Novaco and Welsh, 1989), have omitted the importance of the deeper concepts of shame, humiliation and damaged pride or low self-esteem. They assert that CBT approaches to anger have missed 'working at the level of personal meaning' (Walker and Bright, 2009a, p. 7). Their formulation stresses core beliefs of vulnerability and negative self-schemas. Fundamentally low self-esteem is covered up by machismo, which spurs violence and falsely inflated self-esteem. As non-violent behavioural alternatives are viewed as weakness, the situational threat and the threat of embarrassment are averted by violent attack. For Walker and Bright (2009a) and Walker and Bright (2009b), the central focus of therapy is to build self-esteem, and the goal of therapy is to help patients relinquish violence to protect self-esteem and to build a more enduring sense of personal respect. They have done well in calling attention to the importance of shame and perceived vulnerability in the activation of anger and violent behaviour, and they give a fair account of the informational processing frameworks; however, they are too quick to characterize CBT anger treatment as being entailed by information processing (i.e., ignoring CBT arousal reduction and behavioural components), and they have missed seeing that cognitive restructuring is certainly about working on the personal meaning of anger episodes and their sequelae.

We have known about the interrelationships between shame, anger and violence since Sophocles wrote Ajax. Medea's violent rage is also about shame, as noted earlier, along with Dostoevsky's *Brothers Karamazov*, which features rage and violence that spring from shame and humiliation (cf. Moran, 2009). Yet, shame has indeed been neglected as a salient theme in the study of anger among offenders, and it is crucially important with regard to trauma populations, such as victims of domestic violence and sexual assault, as well as combat veterans. Thomas Scheff, who has been broadly influential in advancing the sociological perspective of mental illness, has otherwise written about shame–rage spirals or shame–anger loops (Scheff, 1988) and, collaborating with Retzinger, has extended the shame–rage connection to understanding violence (Retzinger, 1991; Scheff and Retzinger, 1991). In the forensic domain, Morrison and Gilbert's (2001) study of male Special Hospital patients found that shame in both primary and secondary psychopaths was related to anger in provoking situations of humiliation and rejection and to acting out aggression. They suggest that secondary psychopaths, who are unable to project a confident, dominant image, 'suffer attendant feeling of shame, anger, and seething resentment' (p. 345). In exploring shame, self-blame and anger, Gilbert and Miles (2000) developed a 'sensitivity to put-down scale', which is highly populated by the type of items that appear on anger provocation inventory measures. Shanahan, Jones and Thomas-Peter (2011) found that violent offenders categorized by cluster analysis as 'anger disordered' had higher shame and lower self-worth. They concluded that anger can serve as a protective reaction against shame and low self-worth. That assertion, however, has long been part of the functionalist contextual perspective on anger and its treatment (cf. Novaco, 2007) that guides CBT anger treatment.

Are there clinical problems or psychological deficits that CBT anger treatment does not reach? That is most certainly the case, and this author's treatment manuals have long badged the therapeutic procedure as 'an adjunctive treatment for a targeted clinical problem'. That has most certainly been the case in representing its application to combat veterans (Novaco and Chemtob, 1998) where anger dyscontrol occurs in conjunction with trauma and to its use with offenders (Novaco, Ramm and Black, 2001). Regarding offenders, Novaco, Ramm and

Black (2001) differentiated general clinical care for anger, anger management and anger treatment. We stated that 'this anger treatment approach views anger dyscontrol as relating to the historically constituted core needs of the person, to ingrained psychological deficits in self-regulation, and to bio-medical factors' (p. 292) and highlighted themes of self-worth. The designated importance of self-esteem can be traced back to being the second of nine core propositions for 'anger management' (Novaco, 1975). What one reaches, though, is certainly in part dependent on how far and long one stretches, and many anger control interventions have been insufficiently intensive, as discussed earlier. To be sure, anger will surface in various forensic populations in forms that require more than CBT anger treatment. For example, Milligan and Andrews' (2005) study of women prisoners found anger to strongly differentiate those who self-harm, to be significantly related to shame and to be significantly associated with self-harming behaviour, controlling for childhood abuse. Anger treatment will not reach many of the needs of such clients.

Illustrative Anger Treatment Programmes with Offender Populations

In lieu of a comprehensive review of focused anger treatment studies with offender populations, a chronological narrative of illustrative studies with control groups is presented here, giving attention to important issues, topical content, types of intervention, populations and settings. Although the anger treatment interventions vary across studies, those selected are CBT based, which is in accord with the Andrews (1995) and Andrews (2012) general responsivity principle.

The first three controlled studies of anger treatment with offenders were conducted by Schlichter and Horan (1981), involving male adolescents in a correctional facility, by Feindler *et al.* (1986), with institutionalized adolescent males in a psychiatric treatment facility, and by Stermac (1986), involving court-referred male adult forensic inpatients on remand for psychiatric assessment. The treatment used by Schlichter and Horan (1981) was the CBT stress inoculation (SI) approach (Novaco, 1977, 1980) implemented in twice-weekly individual sessions over five weeks. Their research design compared SI to relaxation treatment and to a no-treatment control. Both treatments produced significant reductions on anger measures compared to the no-treatment condition, but only the SI treatment resulted in significant reductions in verbal aggressive behaviour in provocation tests. Stermac (1986) also followed the SI approach to anger treatment, implemented in a six-session individual format. The patients who received the anger treatment were compared to control patients who received an eight-session psycho-educational group treatment. She found significant declines in anger, reduced self-denigration and improved stress-coping strategies to be associated with the anger treatment, compared to the control condition, but there were no aggressive behaviour criteria in her study. Feindler and her colleagues delivered the treatment in a group format, which is fully elaborated in Feindler and Ecton (1986) and has had independent demonstration of effectiveness (e.g., Nugent, Champlin and Wiinimaki, 1997). In the Feindler *et al.* (1986) study, half of the adolescents at the psychiatric treatment facility had voluntary status and were not court remands. Their anger treatment augmented the early Novaco anger control approach with elaborated self-monitoring, social problem-solving, assertion techniques and self-evaluation procedures. They found anger treatment group effects for increased reflective thinking and self-control, decreased aggressive behaviours in role-play tests and lower rates of rule violations and restrictions.

Each of these three studies showed that anger treatment reduced anger, two found behavioural change in role-play testing, but only one demonstrated behavioural change on non-analogue criteria, and the rule violations in the Feindler *et al.* study were not exclusively due to aggressive behaviours (stealing and elopement were also rule violations). Therefore, it was not established that anger treatment reduced violent behaviour.[1]

In the next decade, there were a number of anger management studies in prison settings, most without satisfactory research methodology, such as having a comparison condition or a robust assessment battery. Descriptive accounts of anger management programmes with female prisoners also appeared (e.g., Fitzharding, 1997). The empirical projects were primarily conducted with males. One such study (Serin and Kuriychuk, 1994) reported reduction in aggressiveness, but the measure and analysis were unclear. Hughes (1995), for a group-based programme with maximum security prisoners, had a partial control condition and reported encouraging results for post-release four-year follow-up data. Compared to those who did not complete or receive the anger management, the programme participants had significantly higher coping skills ratings by case management officers and longer latency to re-arrest; their percent convicted for violent crimes was marginally ($p=0.07$) lower. Hughes also found significant pre- to post-programme reductions on many anger and anger-related measures.

A substantial programme for anger management was implemented in Canadian prisons in the 1990s that had effects on recidivism. Dowden, Blancett and Serin (1999) compared a sample of 110 male federal inmates who were treated in the programme (delivered in 25 two-hour sessions) to a matched untreated group and obtained significant differences in non-violent and violent recidivism, but only for the ($N=56$) higher-risk cases. Dowden and Serin (2001) did more extensive analyses, including a programme dropout comparison group and an array of risk predictor control variables (viz., an overall prison programme performance index, age, time at risk in the community, offence history variables and institutional incidents). Logistic regression analyses on post-release outcome (success/failure) found that anger management programme completion was associated with success, controlling for the array of control variables. They also examined whether programme participation was associated with reduction in institutional incidents, but no significant gains resulted on that criterion.

Three studies that did find reductions on institutional behaviour measures are Ireland (2004), Jones and Hollin (2004) and Bus, Stefan and Visu-Petra (2009). Each of these studies involved a group-based therapy programme. Ireland's (2004) intervention was 12 one-hour sessions, delivered by two staff facilitators over a 3-day period to young male prisoners. She evaluated this brief programme, which is conspicuously psycho-educational in nature, by comparing 50 participants to 37 wait-list control subjects on self-report and staff-rated outcomes. Treatment effects were obtained on self-reported reduced angry thoughts, feelings and behaviour and on reduced angry behaviour as rated by staff. Isolating the 22 participants who improved the most, she found that they had the highest proportion of violent offences, which, like the findings of Dowden *et al.* (1999), is consistent with Andrews's (2012) risk principle. Bus, Stefan and Visu-Petra (2009) implemented a programme said to be similar to Ireland's (2004), but in 12 weekly 2-hour sessions. Conducted in a maximum-security prison, those who received the anger management programme, compared to a control group, had significant reductions in anger (STAXI), decreased aggressive behaviours as rated by staff and a reduced number of disciplinary incidents, although statistical tests were not reported on the latter two criteria.

---

[1] Three other early studies, albeit with aggressive youths in non-forensic facilities, Saylor, Benson and Einhaus (1985), Dangel, Deshner and Rasp (1989) and Wilcox and Dowrick (1992) obtained modest-to-strong anger treatment gains. Each used a modified SI treatment, and they were small sample studies.

In contrast to the brevity of Ireland's intervention and the Bus, Stefan and Visu-Petra's extension of it, Jones and Hollin (2004), with eight males at a high-security forensic hospital, implemented a 36-week, 2-hour group programme that was supplemented by a 1-hour individual CBT. That group-plus-individual hybrid approach had been disseminated from the State Hospital Scotland, where it was initiated by the present author and his colleagues.[2] Although the Jones and Hollin (2004) study did not have a control group, its involvement of personality-disordered violent offenders is noteworthy. They reported clinical-level reductions on STAXI, NAS and AQ anger measures, plus much reduced verbal and physical aggression incidents, the latter being recorded and coded by nursing staff on a daily basis from pre treatment to eight weeks post treatment. Thus, there is some indication, with this study and that of Bus, Stefan and Visu-Petra (2009), that anger treatment can reduce aggressive behaviour in long-term care facilities, but the evidence here is not robust.

While there have been a few uncontrolled studies of anger management with female offenders (e.g., Fitzharding, 1997; Robertson, 2005; Wilfley, Rodon and Anderson, 1986), as well as programme descriptions by other writers, there have been two studies with control conditions. Eamon, Munchua and Reddon (2001) implemented a 12-week, CBT group intervention with women in a Canadian federal prison. Compared to a treatment-as-usual control group, those who received anger management had significant gains in anger regulation (NAS), and marginally significant reductions on multiple anger disposition measures (NAS and AQ). For the treatment recipients, there were many significant pre-post reductions on various anger scores. Also, the number of disciplinary charges decreased significantly for the treatment group, but not for the control group. The second controlled study was done by Goldstein *et al.* (2007), which concerned female juvenile offenders, compared a nine-week, two sessions per week, group-based anger management to treatment-as-usual, with random assignment to conditions. Medium-to-large effect size reductions were observed in anger and aggression measures (AQ), but there were no behavioural criteria.

The most fully assessed anger treatment study with offenders is that of Taylor *et al.* (2005), which was conducted with male forensic hospital patients having IDs. The intervention was an individually based, modified SI anger treatment, the full 18-session protocol for which is given in Taylor and Novaco (2005). It was delivered in twice-weekly sessions by qualified, chartered psychologists. The protocol included a six-session preparatory/motivational phase for fostering treatment engagement and building basic skills, such as emotion awareness, self-monitoring, relaxation strategies and goal setting. The treatment condition was compared to an anonymously assigned, matched waiting-list control condition where treatment-as-usual was received. Assessments on multiple anger self-report instruments (NAS, PI and STAXI) and a staff-rated measure were obtained at screening, pre-treatment, post-treatment and four-month follow-up. In the mixed-model repeated measures analysis, significant differences in favour of the anger treatment were obtained on NAS and PI measures, and marginal effects were obtained for STAXI measures. Staff-rated anger declined more strongly through follow-up in the treatment condition but not at a statistically significant level. Further evidence of anger treatment gains with these patients were reported by Taylor *et al.* (2004) for an IPT, including parallel gains for the control group occurring following their completion of treatment.

Hospital assaultive behavioural measures were not incorporated in those studies (Taylor *et al.* 2002, 2004, 2005), but we have now found, for a cohort of 50 patients, significant

[2] A detailed protocol for anger treatment at the State Hospital Scotland is given in Walker, Novaco, O'Hanlon and Ramm (2009), along with supplementary resources for patients and treatment staff.

reductions in physical assaults, comparing the 12-month interval prior to anger treatment with the 12 months after it. Generalized estimating equations controlled for age, gender, IQ, length of stay and violent offence. Further, we have found that those reductions in physical assaults were associated with reductions in anger and increases in anger regulation that occurred in anger treatment (Novaco and Taylor, 2013). Evidence for anger treatment lowering incidents of aggressive behaviour in the community for ID clients is provided by Lindsay *et al.* (2004).

Two additional anger treatment studies are noteworthy, one because of its innovative approach (drama therapy), and the other because its client population (combat veterans), while not forensic, is nevertheless highly relevant. Blacker, Watson and Beech (2008) implemented a combined CBT and drama-based treatment with adult male violent offenders in six UK prisons. The treatment was given in a nine-day course, delivered in three 3-day blocks with two sessions per day. Their single group pre-post design found significant reductions across the subscales of the STAXI, which was the only instrument used. Previously, a related but not CBT-structured drama therapy programme was evaluated by Reiss *et al.* (1998). Conducted at Broadmoor Hospital with 12 male patients having violent histories, they found post-treatment reductions in anger on the STAXI and on another anger inventory. Theatre has been relevant to the psychology of anger and anger dyscontrol since the plays of Seneca and Shakespeare noted earlier. John Osborne's *Look Back in Anger* in 1956 famously initiated a movement in British theatre and sparked the expression of 'angry young men'. The psychological aspects of anger and violence on the stage, including what derives from the Stanislavski system, are elucidated by Konecni (1991). From a clinical standpoint in working with offenders, one value of involving clients in stage plays is that it provides them the opportunity to examine, express and learn about anger in a mode that is less likely to activate their threat-protective defences.

The combat veterans study by Marshall *et al.* (2010) concerned veterans (not from contemporary wars) with PTSD and antisocial personality characteristics, who received care through US Department of Veterans Affairs clinics. Anger is prevalent among combat veterans, for whom it is a violence risk factor (Novaco and Chemtob 2002; Novaco *et al.*, 2012). The efficacy of individual SI anger treatment with combat veterans with severe PTSD and severe anger had previously been established (Chemtob *et al.*, 1997). The Marshall *et al.* (2010) treatment was a CBT group intervention delivered in 90-minute weekly sessions for 12 weeks. They obtained, in multilevel modelling analyses, reductions in anger (STAXI) and in physical aggression, the latter evaluated by self-report, comparing a three-month interval prior to treatment with the three-month treatment interval. Antisocial personality characteristics were associated with smaller decreases in trait anger and physical aggression. While this latter study did not have a control group, it does provide support for the value of anger treatment with clients having serious psychological disorder and histories of aggressive behaviour.

Treatment Gains with Offenders: Does Anger Treatment Reduce Aggressive Behaviour?

Although some studies with *prisoners* have not found anger reductions to follow anger control interventions, the illustrative studies reviewed here, as well as many others, have demonstrated that self-reported anger does decline following intervention programmes. Anger reductions were not obtained in the prison-based studies of Howells and his colleagues, nor in one by

Serin, Gobeil and Preston (2009), but numerous studies with incarcerated men and women have reported reduced-anger treatment gains. Programme evaluative research with forensic hospital patients and with adolescents in residential treatment facilities, illustrated by studies reviewed in this chapter, typically has found reduced anger following treatment. Also in the forensic domain, significant anger treatment gains have been obtained with child abusing parents (Nomellini and Katz, 1983; Sanders *et al.*, 2004) and with aggressive drivers (Deffenbacher *et al.*, 2002; Sanders *et al.*, 2004). One can say with reasonable confidence that anger management or anger treatment interventions are successful in reducing anger levels in offender populations, provided that the treatment recipients have certified anger regulatory problems. When anger treatment is applied to persons for whom the treatment target is absent, the outcome evaluation enterprise is dubious.

Regarding whether therapeutic interventions for anger have been successful in reducing aggressive behaviour, the evidence is less clear. One first must be mindful that a *behavioural* criterion is something independent of the subject's self-report, for example, 'physical aggression' scales on self-report instruments, such as the AQ, are not *behaviour*. Further, while verbal aggression is behaviour and is antagonistic, it is qualitatively different from physical aggression, which is targeted harm-doing. Physical aggression is the prime criterion for offender populations. Most anger intervention studies have simply not included measures of physical aggression or violence, much less re-offending. Of the studies reviewed in this chapter, reductions in aggressive behaviour were obtained in Feindler *et al.* (1986) (lowered rule violations), Hughes (1995) (lowered re-arrest and violent crime), Dowden *et al.* (1999) (lowered violent recidivism), Ireland (2004) (reduced angry behaviour rated by staff), Bus, Stefan and Visu-Petra (2009) (reduced aggressive behaviour and disciplinary incidents), Jones and Hollin (2004) (reduced verbal and physical aggression incidents), Lindsay *et al.* (2004) (reduction in role-play angry behaviour and assaultive incidents in the community) and Novaco and Taylor (2013) (reduction of physical assaults in hospital). Anger intervention studies aimed at female offenders have not had physical aggression criteria. While the evidence for anger treatment lowering physical aggression is relatively sparse, it is reassuring that, in considering multifaceted offender programmes, the meta-analyses by Landenberger and Lipsey (2005) and Dowden and Andrews (2000) did find reduced recidivism to be associated with the programmes having an anger control component.

Major Methodological Issue

Many issues concerning research methodology surface in this literature, which cannot be elaborated here. Various methodological shortcomings can be gleaned from what has been presented, such as inadequate specification of study sample inclusion criteria, small sample sizes, substantial variation in treatment programmes, insufficient articulation of treatment protocols, inadequacy of control group conditions, high drop-out rates and absence of follow-up assessment. The major problem, though, that merits imminent attention is the all too common deficiency in the anger/aggression measurement protocol.

Treatment outcome evaluation designs will often be driven by the exigencies of the service provision context, which can limit possibilities for study samples, treatment comparison conditions, assessment opportunities and can affect attrition (e.g., when patients are discharged from hospital before treatment or follow-up are completed). However, what is too prevalent in the literature on anger control interventions, both with offenders and non-offenders, is an impoverished anger assessment set. Many studies exclusively assess anger by self-report instruments, and, of those, few studies have a measurement set that provides a look at whether there is convergence in multiple validated self-report instruments. Anger is a construct having cognitive, somatic and behavioural referents (Novaco, 2000). No set of operations will exhaust the meaning of that construct; but if we wish to infer that treatment has produced a beneficent change in anger disposition, we must do better in capturing the referent criteria, in scrutinizing our observation base and in establishing assessment standards for treatment evaluation.

Concluding Perspective

Anger is neither necessary nor sufficient for violence, but it is part of the confluence of multilevel risk factors affecting violent behaviour, and its relevance has been insufficiently prioritized. Anger and its vicissitudes – rage, hate and revenge – are drivers of violent offending, as established empirically in forensic contexts. Studies conducted with violent offenders in institutions (prisoners and hospital patients) and in the community (discharged patients and offenders on probation) have implicated anger as an activator of aggressive behaviour, as has been found with other forensic populations (e.g., perpetrators of domestic violence and road driving violations). Anger dysregulation is prevalent among those in forensic settings; for example, for all adult patients ($N=4246$) in California's five State Hospitals, 35% were rated by their primary clinician as someone who 'gets angry and annoyed easily' (Novaco, 1997). To the extent that anger operates as a relevant antecedent variable in assaults by those who are institutionally detained, whether in a hospital or a correctional facility, it serves as a focus for intervention.

Importantly, anger treatment interventions are congruent with the well-known Risk–Need–Responsivity (RNR) principles articulated by Andrews (1995) and Andrews (2012). According to the *Risk* principle, higher-risk offenders should receive more intensive correctional programming than lower-risk offenders. The *Need* principle holds that risk reduction efforts must focus on criminogenic needs, or changeable factors that predict crime and violence. The *Responsivity* principle holds that correctional programming should be delivered in a format that matches, or is responsive to, the learning styles of offenders. Anger dysregulation raises violence risk, anger is a dynamic variable that is responsive to treatment, and cognitive behavioural anger treatment has a structured social learning format that is readily adaptable to client populations, including those with IDs and psychoses.

Because anger is a common precursor of aggressive behaviour, it can be unsettling for mental health professionals to engage as a treatment focus, regardless of its salience as a clinical need. Moreover, the anger dysregulation problems of offender populations are complex, having been shaped by the conjunction of impoverished family backgrounds, developmental disabilities, early conduct problems, substance use, institutionalization, amalgamative emotional distress, recurrent offending and prior disconnects with mental health care staff. Their anger is often intermingled or entangled with fear, sadness, shame and disappointment. When seeking to access their anger, the probe hits upon the admixture of distressed emotions and negativistic schemas within which the anger is nested. Clinical research has brought forward advances in anger assessment that should be better utilized by service providers and study teams.

The provision of anger control treatment is an adjunctive therapy. Especially with forensic populations, it is best done as part of a multifaceted treatment programme. The rewards for anger and aggression are in the present. The rewards for their control are in the future. Without a stake in the future, there is little reason for someone to control violent behaviour or to adopt prosocial values. Anger treatment requires a centered and supportive therapist and a sufficiently resourced and cohesive therapeutic environment. Beyond anger control, if the aim is to reduce violent offending, an elaborated account of the complexities and the prospects is provided by Dvoskin *et al.* (2012).

The cognitive-behavioural treatment of anger has been shown to have applicability to a wide range of client populations and many clinical disorders. Prisoners and hospitalized patients with long-standing aggression histories, mental disorder and even IDs can be engaged in CBT anger treatment and have been shown to benefit. While the therapeutic mechanisms underlying treatment gains are not clear, nor their sustainability or generalizability, we are fortified in seeking further advances in providing remedies for anger dyscontrol.

References

Anderson, D.A. (1999) The aggregate burden of crime. *Journal of Law and Economics*, 42, 611–642.

Andrews, D.A. (1995) The psychology of criminal conduct and effective treatment, in *What Works: Reducing Reoffending. Guidelines from Research and Practice* (ed. J. McGuire), John Wiley & Sons, Ltd, Chichester.

Andrews, D.A. (2012) The Risk-Needs-Responsivity (RNR) model of correctional assessment and treatment, in *Applying Social Science to Reduce Violent Offending* (eds J. Dvoskin, J.L. Skeem, R.W. Novaco and K.S. Douglas), Oxford University Press, New York, pp. 127–156.

Archer, J. and Haigh, A. (1997) Beliefs about aggression among male and female prisoners. *Aggressive Behavior*, 23, 405–415.

Arrigo, B.A. and Bullock, J.L. (2008) The psychological effects of solitary confinement on prisoners in supermax units: reviewing what we know and recommending what should change. *International Journal of Offender Therapy and Comparative Criminology*, 52, 622–640.

Baker, M.T., Van Hasselt, V.B. and Sellers, A.H. (2008) Validation of the Novaco Anger Scale in an incarcerated offender population. *Criminal Justice and Behavior*, 35, 741–754.

Beck, A.T. (1999). *Prisoners of Hate: The Cognitive Basis of Anger, Hostility, and Violence.* Harper Collins, New York.

Beck, R. and Fernandez, E. (1998) Cognitive-behavioral therapy in the treatment of anger: a meta-analysis. *Cognitive Therapy and Research*, 22, 63–74.

Blackburn, R. (2004) "What works" with mentally disordered offenders. *Psychology, Crime & Law*, 10, 297–308.

Blacker, J., Watson, A. and Beech, A.R. (2008) A combined drama-based and CBT approach to working with self-reported anger aggression. *Criminal Behaviour and Mental Health*, 18, 129–137.

Bornstein, P.H., Weisser, C.E. and Balleweg, B.J. (1985) Anger and violent behaviour, in *Handbook of Clinical Behavior Therapy with Adults* (eds M. Hersen and A. S. Bellack), Plenum Press, New York, pp. 603–629.

Burns, M, Bird, D., Leach, C. and Higgins, K. (2003) Anger management training: the effects of a structured programme on the self-reported anger experience of forensic inpatients with learning disability. *Journal of Psychiatric and Mental Health Nursing*, 10, 569–577.

Bus, I., Stefan, E.-C. and Visu-Petra, G. (2009) Anger management in the penitentiary: an intervention study. *Cognition, Brain, & Behavior: An Interdisciplinary Journal*, 13, 329–340.

Buss, A.H. and Perry, M. (1992) The Aggression Questionnaire. *Journal of Personality and Social Psychology*, 63, 452–459.

Carr, J.E. and Tan, E.K. (1976) In search of the true amok: Amok as viewed within the Malay culture. *American Journal of Psychiatry*, 133, 1295–1299.

Cauffman, E., Feldman, S., Waterman, J. and Steiner, H. (1998) Posttraumatic stress disorder among female juvenile offenders. *Journal of the American Academy of Child and Adolescent Psychiatry*, 37, 1209–1216.

Center for Disease Control and Prevention. (2006) Homicides and Suicides – National Violent Death Reporting System, United States, 2003–2004. *Journal of the American Medical Association*, 296, 506–510.

Chapman, A.L. and Dixon-Gordon K.L. (2007) Emotional antecedents and consequences of deliberate self-harm and suicide attempts. *Suicide and Life-Threatening Behavior*, 37, 543–552.

Chemtob, C.M., Novaco, R.W., Hamada, R. and Gross, D. (1997) Cognitive-behavioral treatment for severe anger in posttraumatic stress disorder. *Journal of Consulting and Clinical Psychology*, 65, 184–189.

Coid, J., Yang, M., Roberts, A. *et al.* (2006) Violence and psychiatric morbidity in the national household population of Britain: public health implications. *British Journal of Psychiatry*, 189, 12–19.

Cornell, D.G., Peterson, C.S. and Richards, H. (1999) Anger as a predictor of aggression among incarcerated adolescents. *Journal of Consulting and Clinical Psychology*, 67, 108–115.

Corso, P.S., Mercy, J.A., Simon, T.R. *et al.* (2007) Medical costs and productivity losses due to interpersonal and self-directed violence in the United States. *American Journal of Preventive Medicine*, 32, 474–482.

Daffern, M., Howells, K. and Ogloff, J. (2007) What's the point? Toward a methodology for assessing the function of psychiatric inpatient aggression. *Behaviour Research and Therapy*, 45, 101–111.

Dangell, R.F., Deschner, J.P. and Rasp, R.R. (1989) Anger control training for adolescents in residential treatment. *Behavior Modification*, 13, 447–458.

Deffenbacher, J.L., Filetti, L.B., Lynch, R.S. *et al.* (2002) Cognitive-behavioral treatment of high anger drivers. *Behaviour Research and Therapy*, 40, 895–910.

DeLisi, M., Caudill, J.W., Trulson, C.R. *et al.* (2010) Angry inmates are violent inmates: a Poisson regression approach to youthful offenders. *Journal of Forensic Psychology Practice*, 10, 419–439.

Del Vecchio, T. and O'Leary, K.D. (2004) Effectiveness of anger treatments for specific anger problems: a meta-analytic review. *Clinical Psychology Review*, 24, 15–34.

Depp, F.C. (1976) Violent behavior on psychiatric wards. *Aggressive Behavior*, 2, 295–306.

DiGuiseppe, R. and Tafrate, R.C. (2003) Anger treatment for adults: a meta-analytic review. *Clinical Psychology: Science and Practice*, 10, 7084.

Dowden, C. and Andrews, D.A. (2000) Effective correction treatment and violent reoffending: a meta-analysis. *Canadian Journal of Criminology*, 42, 449–467.

Dowden, C. and Serin, R. (2001) Anger management programming for offenders: the impact of program performance measures. *Research Report (R-106)*. Correction Service Canada, Ottowa.

Dowden, C., Blancette, K. and Serin, R. (1999) Anger management programming for federal male inmates: an effective intervention. *Research Rep.no. R-82*. Correction Service Canada, Ottawa.

Doyle, M. and Dolan, M. (2006a) Evaluating the validity of anger regulation problems, interpersonal style, and disturbed mental state for predicting inpatient violence. *Behavioral Sciences and the Law*, 24, 783–798.

Doyle, M. and Dolan, M. (2006b) Predicting community violence from patients discharged from mental health services. *British Journal of Psychiatry*, 189, 520–526.

Doyle, M., Carter, S., Shaw, J., and Dolan, M. (2012) Predicting community violence from patients discharged from acute mental health units in England. *Social Psychiatry and Psychiatric Epidemiology*, 47, 627–637.

Dvoskin, J., Skeem, J.L, Novaco, R.W. and Douglas, K.S. (2012) *Applying Social Science to Reduce Violent Offending*, Oxford University Press, New York.

Eamon, K.C., Munchua, M.M. and Reddon, J.R. (2001) Effectiveness of an anger management program for women inmates. *Journal of Offender Rehabilitation*, 34, 45–60.

Eckhardt, C., Norlander, B. and Deffenbacher, J. (2004) The assessment of anger and hostility: a critical review. *Aggression and Violent Behavior*, 9, 17–43.

Edmondson, C.B. and Conger, J.C. (1996) A review of treatment efficacy for individuals with anger problems: conceptual, assessment, and methodological issues. *Clinical Psychology Review*, 16, 251–275.

Feindler, E.L. and Ecton, R.B. (1986) *Adolescent Anger Control: Cognitive-Behavioral Techniques*, Pergamon Press, New York.

Feindler, E.L., Ecton, R.B., Kingsley, D. and Dubey, D.R. (1986) Group anger-control training for institutionalized psychiatric male adolescents. *Behavior Therapy*, 17, 109–123.

Fitzharding, S. (1997) Anger management groupwork with women prisoners. *Forensic Update*, 48, 3–7.

Ford, B.D. (1991) Anger and irrational beliefs in violent inmates. *Personality and Individual Differences*, 12, 211–215.

Foster, C., Bowers, L. and Nijman, H. (2007) Aggressive behaviour on acute psychiatric wards: prevalence, severity and management. *Journal of Advanced Nursing*, 58, 140–149.

Fottrell, E. (1980) A study of violent behaviour among patients in psychiatric hospitals. *British Journal of Psychiatry*, 136, 216–221.

Galen, C. (1963) *On the Passions and Errors of the Soul* (trans. P.W. Harkins), Ohio State University Press, Columbus.

Gansle, K.A. (2005) The effectiveness of school-based anger interventions and programs: a meta-analysis. *Journal of School Psychology*, 43, 321–341.

Gaw, A.C. and Bernstein, R.L. (1992) Classification of amok in DSM-IV. *Hospital and Community Psychiatry*, 43, 789–793.

Gilbert, P. and Miles, J.N.V. (2000) Sensitivity to social put-down: it's relationship to perceptions of social rank, shame, social anxiety, depression, anger and self-other blame. *Personality and Individual Differences*, 29, 757–774.

Goff, A., Rose, E., Rose, S. and Purves, D. (2007) Does PTSD occur in sentenced prison populations? A systematic literature review. *Criminal Behaviour and Mental Health*, 17, 152–162.

Goffman, E. (1961) *Asylums: Essays on the Social Situation of Mental Patients and Other Inmates*, Anchor Books, New York.

Goldstein, N.E.S., Dovidio, A., Kalbeitzer, R. *et al.* (2007) Anger management for female juvenile offenders: results of a pilot study. *Journal of Forensic Psychology Practice*, 7, 1–28.

Haddock, G., Lowens, I., Brosnan, N. *et al.* (2004) Cognitive-behavioural therapy for inpatients with psychosis and anger problems within a low secure environment. *Behavioural and Cognitive Psychotherapy*, 32, 77–98.

Haller, R.M. and Deluty, R.H. (1988) Assaults on staff by psychiatric in-patients. *British Journal of Psychiatry*, 152, 174–179.

Hanh, T.N. (2001) *Anger: Wisdom for Cooling the Flames*, Riverhead Books, New York.

Haney, C. (2003) Mental health issues in long-term, solitary and "supermax" confinement. *Crime & Delinquency*, 49, 124–156.

Heseltine, K., Howells, K. and Day, A. (2010) Brief anger interventions with offenders may be ineffective: a replication and extension. *Behaviour Research and Therapy*, 48, 246–250.

Ho, B.P.V., Carter, M. and Stephenson, J. (2010) Anger management using a cognitive-behavioural approach for children with special education needs: a literature review and meta-analysis. *International Journal of Disability, Development and Education*, 57, 245–265.

Homer (2004) *The Iliad* (trans. R. Fitzgerald), Farrar, Straus and Giroux, New York.

Horder, J. (1992) *Provocation and Responsibility*, Clarendon Press, Oxford.

Horder, J. (2005) Reshaping the subjective element in the provocation defence. *Oxford Journal of Legal Studies*, 25, 123–140.

Howells, K. (1989) Anger management methods in relation to the prevention of violent behaviour, in *Human Aggression: Naturalistic Accounts* (eds J. Archer and K. Browne), Routledge, London, pp. 153–181.

Howells, K. and Day, A. (2003) Readiness for anger management: clinical and theoretical issues. *Clinical Psychology Review*, 23, 319–337.

Howells, K., Watt, B., Hall, G. and Baldwin, S. (1997) Developing programmes for violent offenders. *Legal and Criminological Psychology*, 2, 117–128.

Howells, K., Day, A., Williamson, P. *et al.* (2005) Brief anger management programs with offenders: outcomes and predictors of change. *Journal of Forensic Psychology & Psychology*, 16, 296–311.

Huang, G., Zhang, Y., Momartin, S. *et al.* (2006) Prevalence and characteristics of trauma and posttraumatic stress disorder in female prisoners in China. *Comprehensive Psychiatry*, 47, 20–29.

Hughes, G.V. (1995) Short and long-term outcomes for a cognitive-behavioral anger management program, in *Psychology, Law, and Criminal Justice: International Developments in Research and Practice* (eds G. Davies, S. Lloyd-Bostock, M. McMurran and C. Wilson), Walter de Gruyter & Co., Berlin, pp. 485–494.

Hutcheson, F. (1742) *An Essay on the Nature and Conduct of the Passions and Affections*, Printed for Ward *et al.*, London.

Ireland, J.L. (2000) "Bullying" among prisoners: a review of research. *Aggression and Violent Behavior*, 5, 201–215.

Ireland, J.L. (2004) Anger management therapy with young male offenders: an evaluation of treatment outcome. *Aggressive Behavior*, 30, 174–185.

Jones, D. and Hollin, C. (2004) Managing problematic anger: the development of a treatment program for personality disordered patients in high security. *International Journal of Forensic Mental Health*, 3, 197–210.

Konecni, V.J. (1991) Psychological aspects of the expression of anger and violence on the stage. *Comparative Drama*, 25, 215–241.

Komarovskaya, I.A., Loper, A.B., Warren, J. and Jackson, S. (2011) Exploring gender differences in trauma exposure and the emergence of symptoms of PTSD among incarcerated men and women. *Journal of Forensic Psychiatry and Psychology*, 22, 395–410.

Krug, E.G., Dalhberg, L.L., Mercy, J.A. *et al.* (2002) *World Report on Violence and Health*, World Health Organization, Geneva.

Landenberger, N.A. and Lipsey, M.W. (2005) The positive effects of cognitive-behavioral programs for offenders: a meta-analysis of factors associated with effective treatment. *Journal of Experimental Criminology*, 1, 451–476.

Lansky, M.R. (1996) Shame and suicide in Sophocles' Ajax. *PsychoanalyticQuarterly*, LXV, 761–786.

Levey, S. and Howells, K. (1991) Anger and its management. *Journal of Forensic Psychiatry*, 1, 305–327.

Linaker, O.M. and Busch-Iversen, H. (1995) Predictors of imminent violence in psychiatric inpatients. *Acta Psychiatrica Scandinavia*, 92, 250–254.

Lindqvist, J.K., Daderman, A.M. and Hellstrom, A. (2005) Internal reliability and construct validity of the Novaco Anger Scale-1998-S in a sample of violent prison inmates in Sweden. *Psychology, Crime & Law*, 11, 223–237.

Lindsay, W.R., Allan, R., Macleod, F. *et al.* (2003) Long-term treatment and management of violent tendencies of men with intellectual disabilities convicted of assault. *Mental Retardation*, 41, 47–56.

Lindsay, W.R., Allan, R., Parry, C. *et al.* (2004) Anger and aggression in people with intellectual disabilities: treatment and follow-up of consecutive referrals and a waiting list comparison. *Clinical Psychology and Psychotherapy*, 11, 255–264.

Loza, W. and Loza-Fanous, A. (1999a) Anger and prediction of violent and non-violent offenders' recidivism. *Journal of Interpersonal Violence*, 14, 1014–1029.

Loza, W. and Loza-Fanous, A. (1999b) The fallacy of reducing rape and recidivism by treating anger. *International Journal of Offender Therapy and Comparative Criminology*, 43, 492–502.

Maghan, J. (1999) Dangerous inmates: maximum security incarceration in the State Prison Systems of the United States. *Aggression and Violent Behavior*, 4, 1–2.

Marshall, A.D., Martin, E.K., Warfield, G.A. *et al.* (2010) The impact of antisocial personality characteristics on anger management treatment for veterans with PTSD. *Psychological Trauma: Theory, Research, Practice, and Policy*, 2, 224–231.

McGuire, J. (2008) A review of effective interventions for reducing aggression and violence. *Philosophical Transaction of the Royal Society, B*, 363, 2577–2597.

Mental Health Foundation (2008) *Boiling Point: Problem Anger and What We Can Do About It*, Mental Health Foundation, London.

Michie, C. and Cooke, D.J. (2006) The structure of violent behavior: a hierarchical model. *Criminal Justice and Behavior*, 33, 706–737.

Mikalson, J.D. (1986) Zeus the father and Heracles the son in tragedy. *Transactions of the American Philological Association*, 116, 89–98.

McMurran, M., Charlesworth, P., Duggan, C. and McCarty, L. (2001) Controlling angry aggression: a pilot group intervention with personality disordered offenders. *Behavioural and Cognitive Psychotherapy*, 29, 473–483.

Miller, W.B. (1973) Adaptation of young men to prison. *Corrective and Social Psychiatry and Journal of Applied Behavior Therapy*, 19, 15–26.

Miller, W.R. and Rollnick, S. (2002) *Motivational Interviewing: Preparing People for Change*, 2nd edn, Guilford, New York.

Milligan, R.-J. and Andrews, B. (2005) Suicidal and other self-harming behaviour in offender women: the role of shame, anger and childhood abuse. *Legal and Criminological Psychology*, 10, 13–25.

Mills, J.F. and Kroner, D.G. (2003) Anger as a predictor of institutional misconduct and recidivism in a sample of violent offenders. *Journal of Interpersonal Violence*, 18, 282–294.

Ministry of Justice (2007) *Penal Policy – A Background Paper (National Offender Management Service)*, Ministry of Justice, London.

Ministry of Justice (2012) *Offender Management Statistics Quarterly Bulletin: October to December 2011, England and Wales*, Ministry of Justice, London, http://www.justice.gov.uk/downloads/statistics/mojstats/omsq-q4/omsq-q4-2011-bulletin.pdf (accessed 26 December 2012).

Monahan, J. and Steadman, H. (2012) Extending violence reduction principles to justice-involved persons with mental illness, in *Applying Social Science to Reduce Violent Offending* (eds J. Dvoskin, J. Skeem, R. Novaco and K. Douglas), Oxford University Press, New York, pp. 245–261.

Monahan, J., Steadman, H.J., Silver, E. *et al.* (2001) *Rethinking Risk Assessment: The MacArthur Study of Mental Disorder and Violence*, Oxford University Press, Oxford.

Moran, J.P. (2009) The roots of terrorist motivation: shame, rage, and violence in The Brothers Karamazov. *Perspectives on Political Science*, 38, 187–196.

Morrison, D. and Gilber, P. (2001) Social rank, shame and anger in primary and secondary psychopaths. *Journal of Forensic Psychiatry*, 12, 330–356.

National Audit Office (2003) *A Safer Place to Work: Protecting NHS Hospital and Ambulance Staff from Violence and Aggression* Comptroller & Auditory General, London, March 27.

Nijman, H., Bowers, L., Oud, N. and Jansen, G. (2005) Psychiatric nurses' experiences with inpatient aggression. *Aggressive Behavior*, 31, 217–227.

Nomellini, S. and Katz, R.C. (1983) Effects of anger control training on abusive parents. *Cognitive Therapy and Research*, 7, 57–68.

Novaco, R.W. (1975) *Anger Control: The Development and Evaluation of an Experimental Treatment*, D.C. Heath, Lexington.

Novaco, R.W. (1977) Stress inoculation: a cognitive therapy for anger and its applicability to a case of depression. *Journal of Consulting and Clinical Psychology*, 45, 600–608.

Novaco, R.W. (1980) Training of probation counselors for anger problems. *Journal of Counseling Psychology*, 27, 385–390.

Novaco, R.W. (1994) Anger as a risk factor for violence among the mentally disordered, in *Violence and Mental Disorder: Developments in Risk Assessment. The John D. and Catherine T. MacArthur Foundation Series on Mental Health and Development* (eds J. Monahan and H.J. Steadman), University of Chicago Press, Chicago, pp. 21–59.

Novaco, R.W. (1997) Remediating anger and aggression with violent offenders. *Legal and Criminological Psychology*, 2, 77–88.

Novaco, R.W. (2000) Anger, in *Encyclopedia of Psychology*, vol. 1 (ed. A.E. Kasdin), American Psychological Association, Washington, DC, pp. 170–174.

Novaco, R.W. (2003) *The Novaco Anger Scale and Provocation Inventory (NAS-PI)*, Western Psychological Services, Los Angeles.

Novaco, R.W. (2007) Anger dysregulation: its assessment and treatment, in *Anger, Aggression, and Interventions for Interpersonal Violence* (eds T.A. Cavell and K.T. Malcolm), Erlbaum, Mahwah, pp. 3–54.

Novaco, R.W. (2010a). Anger and psychopathology, in *Handbook of Anger* (eds M. Potegal, G. Stemmler and C. Spielberger), Springer, New York, pp. 465–498.

Novaco, R.W. (2010b) Anger assessment in forensic settings. *Forensic Update*, 100, 42–47.

Novaco, R.W. (2011) Anger dysregulation: driver of violent offending. *Journal of Forensic Psychiatry and Psychology*, 22, 650–668.

Novaco, R.W. and Chemtob, C.M. (1998) Anger and trauma: conceptualization, assessment, and treatment, in *Cognitive-Behavioral Therapies for Trauma* (eds V.M. Follette, J.I. Ruzek and F. Abueg), Guilford, New York, pp. 162–190.

Novaco, R.W. and Chemtob, C.M. (2002) Anger and combat-related posttraumatic stress disorder. *Journal of Traumatic Stress*, 15, 123–132.

Novaco, R.W. and Renwick, S.J. (2003) Anger predictors of assaultiveness and the validation of a ward behavior scale for anger and aggression. Unpublished manuscript.

Novaco, R.W. and Taylor, J.L. (2004) Assessment of anger and aggression in offenders with developmental disabilities. *Psychological Assessment*, 16, 42–50.

Novaco, R.W. and Taylor, J.L. (2013) Reduction of hospital assaultive behavior following anger treatment of forensic patients having intellectual disabilities. (unpublished manuscript)

Novaco, R.W. and Welsh, W. (1989) Anger disturbances: cognitive mediation and clinical prescriptions, in *Clinical Approaches to Violence* (eds K. Howells and C. Hollin), John Wiley & Sons, Ltd, Chichester, pp. 39–60.

Novaco, R.W., Ramm, M. and Black, L. (2001) Anger treatment with offenders, in *Handbook of Offender Assessment and Treatment* (ed. C.R. Hollin), John Wiley & Sons, Ltd, Chichester, pp. 281–296.

Novaco, R.W., Swanson, R.D., Gonzalez, O., Gahm, G.A. and Reger, M.D. (2012) Anger and postcombat mental health: validation of a brief anger measure with U.S. soldiers postdeployed from Iraq and Afghanistan. *Psychological Assessment*, 24, 661–675.

Nugent, W.R., Champlin, D. and Wiinimaki, L. (1997) The effects of anger control training on adolescent antisocial behavior. *Research on Social Work Practice*, 7, 446–462.

Nurse, J., Woodcock, P. and Ornsby, J. (2003) Influence of environmental factors on mental health within prisons: focus group study. *BMJ*, 327, 480–483.

Orth, U. and Wieland, E. (2006) Anger, hostility, and posttraumatic stress disorder in trauma-exposed adults: a meta-analysis. *Journal of Consulting and Clinical Psychology*, 74, 698–706.

Owens, A. (2007) Sentenced to filth, chaos and mayhem in our jails. *Sunday Times*, June 24. http://www.thesundaytimes.co.uk/sto/news/uk_news/article66889.ece (accessed on 21 January 2013).

Polaschek, D. (2004) Rehabilitating serious violent adult offenders: an empirical and theoretical stocktake. *Psychology, Crime & Law*, 10, 321–334.

Polaschek, D. (2006) Violent offender programmes: concept, theory, and practice, in *Offending Behaviour Programmes: Development, Application, and Controversies* (eds C.R. Hollin and E.J. Palmer), John Wiley & Sons, Ltd, Chichester, pp. 113–154.

Polaschek, D.L.L., Wilson, N.J., Townsend, M.R. and Daly, L.R. (2005) Cognitive-behavioral rehabilitation for high-risk violent offenders. *Journal of Interpersonal Violence*, 20, 1611–1627.

Pollack, J.M., Mullings, J.L. and Crouch, B.M. (2006) Violent women: findings from the Texas women inmates study. *Journal of Interpersonal Violence*, 21, 485–502.

Potegal, M. and Novaco, R.W. (2010) A brief history of anger, in *Handbook of Anger* (eds M. Potegal, G. Stemmler and C. Spielberger), Springer, New York, pp. 9–24.

Reiss, D., Quayle, M., Brett, T. and Meux, C. (1998) Dramatherapy for mentally disordered offenders: changes in levels of anger. *Criminal Behaviour and Mental Health*, 8, 139–153.

Renwick, S., Black, L., Ramm, M. and Novaco, R.W. (1997) Anger treatment with forensic hospital patients. *Legal and Criminological Psychology*, 2, 103–116.

Retzinger, S.M. (1991) Shame, anger, and conflict: case study of emotional violence. *Journal of Family Violence*, 6, 37–59.

Robertson, A. (2005) Anger treatment for women with developmental disabilities, in *Anger Treatment for People with Developmental Disabilities* (eds J.L. Taylor and R.W. Novaco), John Wiley & Sons, Ltd, Chichester, pp. 167–180.

Saini, M. (2009) A meta-analysis of the psychological treatment of anger: developing guidelines for evidence-based practice. *Journal of the American Academy of Psychiatry and the Law*, 34, 473–488.

Sanders, M.R., Pidgeon, A.M., Gravestock, F. *et al.* (2004) Does parental attributional retraining and anger management enhance the effects of the triple p – positive parenting program with parents at risk of child maltreatment? *Behavior Therapy*, 35, 513–535.

Saylor, C.F., Benson, B. and Einhaus, L. (1985) Evaluation of an anger management program for aggressive boys in inpatient treatment. *Journal of Child and Adolescent Psychotherapy*, 2, 5–15.

Scheff, T.J. (1988) Shame and conformity: the deference-emotion system. *American Sociological Review*, 53, 395–406.

Scheff, T.J. and Retzinger, S.M. (1991) *Emotions and Violence: Shame and Rage in Destructive Conflicts*, Lexington Books, Lexington.

Schlichter, K.J. and Horan, J.J. (1981) Effects of stress inoculation on the anger and aggression management skills of institutionalized juvenile delinquents. *Cognitive Therapy and Research*, 5, 359–365.

Seneca, L. (44/1817) *Seneca's Morals*, Harper & Brothers, New York.

Serin, R.C. and Kuriychuk, M. (1994) Social and cognitive processing deficits in violent offenders: implications for treatment. *International Journal of Law and Psychiatry*, 17, 431–441.

Serin, R.C., Gobeil, R. and Preston, D.L. (2009) Evaluation of the persistently violent offender treatment program. *International Journal of Offender Therapy and Comparative Criminology*, 53, 57–73.

Shanahan, S., Jones, J. and Thomas-Peter, B. (2011) Are you looking at me, or am I? Anger aggression, shame and self-worth in violent individuals. *Journal of Rational-Emotive Cognitive Behavior Therapy*, 29, 77–91.

Simon, B. (1978) *Mind and Madness in Ancient Greece: The Classical Roots of Modern Psychiatry*, Cornell University Press, Ithaca.

Skeem, J.L., Schubert, C., Odgers, C. *et al.* (2006) Psychiatric symptoms and community violence among high risk patients: a test of the relationship at the weekly level. *Journal of Consulting and Clinical Psychology*, 74, 967–979.

Smith, L.L. and Beckner, B.M. (1993) An anger management workshop for inmates in a medium security facility. *Journal of Offender Rehabilitation*, 19, 103–111.

Soares, R.R. (2006) The welfare costs of violence across countries. *Journal of Health Economics*, 25, 821–846.

Spielberger, C.D. (1996) *State–Trait Anger Expression Inventory Professional Manual*, Psychological Assessment Resources, Inc., Odessa.

Stermac, L. (1986) Anger control treatment for forensic patients. *Journal of Interpersonal Violence*, 1, 446–457.

Sukhodolsky, D.G., Kassinove, H. and Gorman, B.S. (2004) Cognitive-behavior therapy for anger in children and adolescents: a meta-analysis. *Aggression and Violent Behavior*, 9, 247–269.

Suris, A., Lind, L., Emmett, G. *et al.* (2004) Measures of aggressive behavior: overview of clinical and research instruments. *Aggression and Violent Behavior*, 9, 165–227.

Sutter, J.M., Byrne, M.K., Byrne, S. *et al.* (2002) Anger in prisoners: women and different from men. *Personality and Individual Differences*, 32, 1087–1100.

Swogger, M.T., Walsh, Z., Homaifar, B.Y. *et al.* (2012) Predicting self- and other-directed violence among discharged psychiatric patients: the roles of anger and psychopathic traits. *Psychological Medicine*, 42, 371–379.

Tafrate, R.C. (1995) Evaluation of treatment strategies for adult anger disorders, in *Anger Disorders: Definition, Diagnosis, and Treatment* (ed. H. Kassinove), Taylor & Francis, Washington, DC, pp. 109–129.

Taylor, J.L. and Novaco, R.W. (2005) *Anger Treatment for People with Developmental Disabilities*, John Wiley & Sons, Ltd, Chichester.

Taylor, J.L., Novaco, R.W., Gillmer, B. and Thorne, I. (2002) Cognitive-behavioural treatment of anger intensity among offenders with intellectual disabilities. *Journal of Applied Research in Intellectual Disabilities*, 15, 151–165.

Taylor, J.L., Novaco, R.W., Guinan, C. and Street, N. (2004) Development of an imaginal provocation test to evaluate treatment for anger problems in people with intellectual disabilities. *Clinical Psychology and Psychotherapy*, 11, 233–246.

Taylor, J.L., Novaco, R.W. Gillmer, B. *et al.* (2005) A controlled trial of individual cognitive-behavioural anger treatment for people with mild-borderline intellectual disabilities and histories of aggression. *British Journal of Clinical Psychology*, 44, 367–382.

Tuke, D.H. (1892) *A Dictionary of Psychological Medicine*, J. & A. Churchill, London.

Valliant, P.M., Jensen, B. and Raven-Brook, L. (1995) Brief cognitive behavioural therapy with male adolescent offenders in open custody or on probation: an evaluation of management of anger. *Psychological Reports*, 76, 1056–1058.

Von Krafft-Ebing, R. (1905) *Textbook of Insanity* (trans. C.G. Chaddock), F.A. Davis, Philadelphia.

Walker, J.S. and Bright, J.A. (2009a) Inflated self-esteem and violence: a systematic review and cognitive model. *Journal of Forensic Psychiatry & Psychology*, 20, 1–32.

Walker, J.S. and Bright, J.A. (2009b) Cognitive therapy for violence: reaching the parts that anger management doesn't reach. *Journal of Forensic Psychiatry & Psychology*, 20, 174–201.

Walker, C., Novaco, R.W., O'Hanlon, M. and Ramm, M. (2009) *Anger Treatment Protocol*, State Hospital, Carstairs.

Walmsley, R (2006) *World Prison Population List*, 6th edn, King's College, International Centre for Prison Studies, London.

Wang, E.W. and Diamond, P.M. (1999) Empirically identifying factors related to violence risk in corrections. *Behavioral Sciences and the Law*, 17, 377–389.

Watt, B.C. and Howells, K. (1999) Skills training for aggression control: evaluation of an anger management programme for violent offenders. *Legal and Criminological Psychology*, 4, 285–300.

Whittington, R. and Richter, D. (2005) Interactional aspects of violent behaviour on acute psychiatric wards. *Psychology, Crime & Law*, 11, 377–388.

Wilcox, D. and Dowrick, P.W. (1992) Anger management with adolescents. *Residential Treatment for Children and Youth*, 9, 29–39.

Wilfley, D.E., Rodon, C.J. and Anderson, W.P. (1986) Angry women offenders: a case study of a group. *International Journal of Offender Therapy and Comparative Criminology*, 30, 41–51.

Williamson, P., Day, A., Howells, K. *et al.* (2003) Assessing offenders readiness to change problems with anger. *Psychology, Crime & Law*, 9, 295–307.

Woozley, A.D. (1972) Plato on killing in anger. *Philosophical Quarterly*, 22, 303–317.

World Health Organization (2004) *The Economic Dimensions of Interpersonal Violence*, World Health Organization, Geneva, http://whqlibdoc.who.int/publications/2004/9241591609.pdf (accessed on 13 December 2012).

Zlotnick, C. (1999) Antisocial personality disorder, affect dysregulation and childhood abuse among incarcerated women. *Journal of Personality Disorders*, 13, 90–95.

13

What Works in Reducing Substance-Related Offending?

John R. Weekes,[1,2] Andrea E. Moser,[1] Michael Wheatley[3] and Flora I. Matheson[4,5,6]

[1]Correctional Service of Canada, Ottawa, ON, Canada
[2]Carleton University, Ottawa, ON, Canada
[3]National Offender Management Services, London, UK
[4]St. Michael's Hospital, Toronto, ON, Canada
[5]Dalla Lana School of Public Health, Toronto, ON, Canada
[6]Institute for Clinical Evaluative Sciences, Toronto, ON, Canada

It is well-established that the use and abuse of alcohol and other substances has been, and continues to be, a serious problem for individuals who become involved in the criminal justice system. Indeed, alcohol and other drug use is strongly related to criminal behaviour, either directly (e.g., alcohol-related violence) or indirectly (e.g., engagement in 'acquisitive' criminal activity such as theft and robbery to obtain funds to purchase drugs) (Weekes, Moser and Langevin, 1999). In this chapter, we present data to support the argument that substance abuse represents one of the most serious 'criminogenic' factors that contribute to criminal behaviour, and therefore, the need for effective, evidence-based intervention, support and aftercare for offenders with substance abuse problems is paramount to reduce the likelihood of future substance abuse and related crime and improve public safety.

We begin the discussion of what works in reducing substance-related offending by briefly reviewing research on the prevalence and dynamics of substance abuse problems in incarcerated populations, and the relationship between substance abuse and criminal offending. Next we explore the role of assessment with a view towards identifying specific client characteristics that are fundamental to the development of a relatively individualized treatment plan, before describing theoretically based, evidence-informed, intervention models. Finally, we briefly present evidence from treatment outcome research which demonstrates that some treatment models and approaches are effective in reducing the likelihood of future problematic use of alcohol and other drugs.

What Works in Offender Rehabilitation: An Evidence-Based Approach to Assessment and Treatment,
First Edition. Edited by Leam A. Craig, Louise Dixon and Theresa A. Gannon.
© 2013 John Wiley & Sons, Ltd. Published 2013 by John Wiley & Sons, Ltd.

Substance Abuse and Criminal Behaviour

There is a sizeable body of evidence that links substance abuse and criminal behaviour. Data from the federal correctional system in Canada indicate that almost all offenders consume either alcohol or other drugs, between 70% and 80% of offenders engage in problematic use at a level that suggests the need for intervention (e.g., Kunic and Grant, 2006; Weekes, Moser and Langevin, 1999). Other correctional agencies and jurisdictions have found similar prevalence rates in diverse regions and correctional populations from around the world, including the United Kingdom (HMP, 2003), the United States (Graves and Bell, 2004) and New Zealand (Morris, 2001). Amongst federal offenders in Canada, just over half self-report that substance use and abuse was somehow related to the offence(s) on their most recent criminal involvements (Kunic and Grant, 2006; Weekes, Moser and Langevin, 1999). Research indicates that alcohol is consistently linked with violent crimes (e.g., murder/manslaughter, aggravated assault, sexual assault, forcible confinement, etc.), and drug use is typically associated with 'acquisitive' crimes such as robbery, theft and fraud offences (Kunic and Grant, 2006; Weekes, Moser and Langevin, 1999).

However, substance abuse is not a binary, or an all-or-none phenomenon; indeed, offenders vary widely on the seriousness or *severity* of their substance abuse problem. This is an important dimension for conceptualizing the person and his or her problem as well as for treatment planning. About one third of offenders do not show signs of problematic use just prior to incarceration. A second third evidence low severity problems, and a final third have much more serious problems including extremely serious, chronic and problematic use (e.g., Weekes, Moser and Langevin, 1999). As Figure 13.1 illustrates, the severity of offender substance abuse problems form a clearly positively skewed distribution. There is distinct kurtosis at the lower end of the severity continuum, and fewer individuals at the extreme tail of severity (i.e., 'severe' problems).

Exploration of the dynamics of offenders' substance abuse problems shows that offenders are more likely to understand they have a problem as the severity of the problem increases, if they started using and abusing alcohol and other drugs at younger ages, if they indicate that substance use and abuse was more likely to be involved in their present and past criminal offending, if they recognize the need for treatment, if they have previous treatment experiences and involvements and if they are more likely to have failed to complete previous treatment (Weekes, Moser and Langevin, 1999).

The important 'take-home' message from these results is that offenders, like others in society, are a diverse group of individuals, and the severity and dynamics of their substance

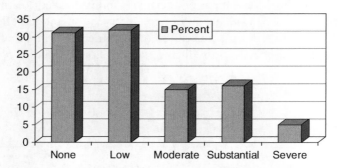

Figure 13.1   Distribution of combined alcohol and other drug severity scores

abuse problems lie on a continuum ranging from non-problematic use (of both legal and illegal substances) to highly problematic use. As we discuss later, treatment and other support services need to be conceptualized and made available in ways that respond to the individual treatment needs of the offender. Assessment is a critical ingredient to the development of an intervention plan for the individual. Treatment is not a 'one-size-fits-all' model. All too often, we have found in our work that this is not the case. In practice, substance-abusing clients (offenders or otherwise) are often tracked to the one and only treatment programme offered by the service provider. This appears to occur even after an elaborate assessment protocol has been administered.

Substance-abusing women offenders

The proportion of female offenders who are assessed with substance abuse problems at intake to prison is very high, reaching close to 90% (Matheson, Doherty and Grant, 2009). A history of drug use prior to incarceration is also significantly associated with institutional misconduct for women offenders (Flanagan, 1983). Evidence suggests that segregation from the general female prison population for administrative reasons is frequently associated with substance use histories. Moreover, substance abuse affects women offenders' chances for success in the community after release. In a recent study of female offenders under federal supervision in Canada, approximately 60% returned to custody within two years of release because of drug use (Matheson, Doherty and Grant, 2009). Substance abuse treatment in the correctional system is known to reduce the probability of revocation and re-arrest (Pelissier and Jones, 2005). Such programmes are also beneficial in reducing relapse into substance abuse in the community. Moreover, these treatment programmes have a positive impact on employment rates, especially for women (Pelissier and Jones, 2005), and may be instrumental in reducing drug-related deaths amongst newly released offenders (Bird and Hutchinson, 2003; Sattar, 2003; Sattar and Killias, 2005; Singleton, Pendry and Taylor, 2003). Taken together, these data suggest that the prevalence of substance abuse amongst offenders is significant. Further, a history of substance abuse is strongly associated with impaired institutional adjustment, programme participation and re-admission.

Assessment

The Center for Substance Abuse Treatment (2005) describes assessment as the process of defining the nature of a problem and developing specific treatment recommendations for addressing the problem. Why is assessment necessary?

All clients are different even when similar global diagnostic labels such as 'alcoholic', problem drug user, offender, criminal or 'addict' are applied. Clients present with a variety of issues and problematic behaviours as a result of a unique set of determinants. Together, the practitioner and client must identify the relevant issues and negotiate the means to address them explicitly. A quality assessment is the foundation of this process.

While custom and practice vary, practitioners usually conduct assessments over one or two sessions depending on the complexity of the assessment which is being undertaken, the seriousness of the case and the range of treatment options open to the client. A client's active participation, coupled with an honest disclosure during the assessment process, is critical.

The purpose of an assessment

Structured approaches to assessment are relatively new and are evolving as diagnostic criteria develop. Experts have described various rationales to inform the purpose of assessment. The essence of these descriptions is to identify individuals' needs and risks in order to develop an appropriate treatment plan that promotes non-problematic desirable behaviours.

To begin the process, it is useful to deliver what the Institute of Medicine (1990) described as the 'sequential' aspects of assessment. This involves the process of screening for the presence of a particular problem (problem existence), finding what problems are associated with substance misuse (problem areas) and what other problems not specific to, but reinforcing of, substance misuse are present (personal issues). In summary, the first stage in assessment is to identify if a problem exists, is present and if further assessment is necessary (Connors, 1995).

In addition, in order to determine the seriousness or *severity* of an individual's alcohol or other drug problem, a number of screening instruments are available – all of which have been used extensively in criminal justice settings. These include the Alcohol Dependency Scale (Skinner and Horn, 1984), Alcohol Use Disorder Identification Test (Babor *et al.*, 2001), the Drug Abuse Screening Test (Skinner, 1982) and the Severity of Dependency Scale (Gossop *et al.*, 1995). These screening tools are very inexpensive (or free), and they are quick and easy to administer and score. However, these screening instruments are limited to a single administration at the pre-treatment initial assessment. This is due to the fact that these measures are typically used to target historical, pre-incarceration substance abuse and are unlikely to yield dynamic change as a result of the delivery of treatment services. Each of these instruments have adequate test–retest reliability (the extent to which the scores are the same on two administrations of the instrument with the same people), although the validity of the instruments can vary depending on the individuals being screened.

If no problem is suggested during the initial stage, administering further lengthy and potentially expensive assessments to qualify the problem is not necessary. However, Miller, Westerberg and Waldron (1995) encouraged practitioners who use screening instruments to be cautious in drawing conclusions as they may over-simplify the multi-dimensional nature of problematic substance misuse and dependence. Accordingly, where collateral evidence suggests the existence of problems, which have not been identified or minimized by the screening instruments, the practitioner should use their clinical judgement to override the findings and proceed to a further, more detailed, assessment of needs to ensure nothing is being overlooked.

The initial pre-treatment assessment can provide a brief intervention in itself (advice and guidance) or promote further, more detailed, assessment leading to specialized treatment (Heather and Stockwell, 2004; Miller, Westerberg and Waldron, 1995).

If required, a more comprehensive assessment is advisably kept to the second, plus any subsequent sessions, once the rapport and a therapeutic alliance have been established and the client expresses a desire to change. The Institute of Medicine (1990) advocates using this 'multi-dimensional' assessment process to further explore a number of domains related to client's problems and personal matters. Sundel and Sundel (1993) broke this down into detailed identification of problem areas, problem selection, target behaviour, response strength (magnitude and frequency) and controlling conditions (antecedents and consequences). A problem area is a broad concern such as offending behaviour, alcohol or drug misuse, unemployment or unstable housing. The practitioner should assist the client in ranking problem areas and helping prioritize the ones that are of most concern (problem selection). To assist the problem selection process, the practitioner and the client should review what is of immediate concern to the client or significant others, what has severe aversive or negative consequences if not handled immediately and what can be sequenced to be addressed later in treatment. Once problem areas have been selected and prioritized, specific target behaviours need to be identified and explored. Target behaviours are specific observable actions (e.g., going to a dealer's house, injecting heroin, criminal conduct) usually driven by unobservable responses (thoughts, feelings and attitudes) that contribute to the presenting issue. To measure the strength of the behaviour being targeted, practitioners and clients should together identify its magnitude (intensity) and frequency (rate and duration). If the magnitude or frequency is high, the greater the challenge to change the target behaviour and potentially the greater the treatment dose will have to be. While gathering all this information, the practitioner and the client are working to improve their understanding of the antecedents (preceding warning signs or trigger factors that elicit a specific behaviour) and consequences (reinforcing events following the behaviour either positive or negative) of the problematic behaviour in order to understand why certain behaviours developed and how they are maintained. This is essential information in helping establish a comprehensive treatment plan that supports the development of new non-problematic behaviours. Completing a multi-dimensional comprehensive assessment can therefore be challenging as it reaches across a complex set of biological, psychological and social determinants (Gossop, 2000).

Thus far, assessment has largely been described and associated with a model that identifies and addresses needs related to dependency, health and well-being. Advances in the criminology and forensic psychology literature have also seen the rise in the concept of 'risk' that has become a significant organizing principle within criminal justice organizations and an increasing priority for inclusion in assessments. Risk is understood as the probability that a dangerous, harmful or undesirable event will occur. Often bolstered by the media, public alarm over risk, and in particular a violent offender's risk of re-offending, has transformed assessment approaches in criminal justice settings.

The creation of risk and need profiles on offenders signalled the widespread introduction and use of mechanical or actuarial assessments within criminal justice organizations to identify levels of risk and need as opposed to subjective or clinical judgements. These assessments of offending behaviour are equal or superior to clinical prediction for a wide range of circumstances (Grove *et al.*, 2000). A preference for mechanical prediction (where an algorithm is followed) has led to the development of numerous actuarial assessment instruments to facilitate a more comprehensive understanding of presenting risks and needs to work on.

There are numerous examples of actuarial assessment instruments available for practitioners and clients to use. The Centre for Substance Abuse Treatment (2005) cites the Addiction Severity Index (*ASI*; McLellan *et al.*, 1980, 1992) as the most commonly used instrument for screening, assessment and treatment planning with individuals with substance abuse problems. The *ASI* was supported by the National Institute on Drug Abuse and is reproduced in TIP 7, *Screening and Assessment for Alcohol and Other Drug Abuse among Adults in the Criminal Justice System* (Center for Substance Abuse Treatment, 1994), and TIP 38, *Integrating Substance Abuse Treatment and Vocational Services* (Center for Substance Abuse Treatment, 2000). The instrument provides a structured interview format to examine seven areas of functioning that are commonly affected by substance misuse, including drug/alcohol use, family/social relationships, employment/support status and mental health status. Many agencies, including those in criminal justice settings, have adapted modified versions of the *ASI* for use as a substance misuse screening instrument. A positive feature of the ASI is that it has been validated for use in criminal justice populations (McLellan *et al.* 1985, 1992; Peters *et al.*,

2000). A self-report version of the ASI was developed that has been shown to be a reliable and accurate alternative to the counsellor-administered instrument (Butler *et al.*, 2001).

Another example of an actuarial assessment instrument is the Offender Assessment System (OASys) that was introduced into England and Wales prison and probation services in 2001. OASys combines the best of actuarial methods of prediction with structured professional judgement to provide standardized assessments of offenders' risk of re-offending and risk of serious harm. *OASys* is designed to fulfil the following purposes: to assess how likely an offender is to re-offend; to identify and classify offending-related needs; to assess risk of serious harm, risks to the individual and other risks; to assist with management of risk of serious harm; to link the assessment to the sentence plan; to indicate the need for further specialist assessments to inform treatment; and to measure change during the offenders sentence. (For a review of the main components of OASys and current evidence base for offending-related risk factors included in OASys, see Debidin, 2009.)

To establish a clear understanding of an offender's situation and issues frequently requires the administration of a number or battery of assessment instruments to examine how substance use has affected all the domains of their life. There are a variety of screening and assessment instruments available to assess specific and non-specific problems associated with substance misuse. Further commentary on the range of screening and assessment instruments available to use is beyond the scope of this chapter. However, online databases are available such as the Alcohol and Drug Abuse Institute's Substance Use Screening and Assessment Instruments Database at the University of Washington (http://lib.adai.washington.edu/instruments/). These resources are intended to help clinicians and researchers find instruments used for screening and assessment of substance use and substance use disorders. Some instruments are in the public domain and can be freely downloaded from the web; others can only be obtained from the copyright holder. Links to contact and availability of information are often included if known.

Practitioners must be mindful that the effectiveness of substance misuse screening and assessment instruments can vary according to the criminal justice setting and the goals of information gathering in the organization. Research shows significant variability in the reliability and validity of different instruments with different populations. For example, in a study by Peters *et al.* (2000), eight different substance abuse screening instruments were examined for use among male prisoners. Each of the instruments had adequate test–retest reliability (the extent to which the scores are the same on two administrations of the instrument with the same people), but the validity of the instruments varied considerably in sensitivity, specificity and positive predictive value with different subpopulations. Practitioners should therefore select an assessment instrument based on test reliability and validity, and acceptability to clients and service providers that is relevant to their particular population.

In summary, the art of assessment involves the creation of a coherent picture of the client's situation. To achieve this, practitioners would be wise to ask broad, open questions during the assessment, allowing the client to speak freely. The client is not likely to present their problems in medical or psychological terms. Astute observation and active listening are therefore needed to recognize problem indicators. Remember client's lives are rarely as neat as our assessment forms (Harris, 2007). The complexity of a client's situation means that many of their problems are inter-related across many domains. For example, a client may reveal serious health concerns, mental health issues, marital problems and employment difficulties.

Understanding how one domain may link to other areas is vital for understanding the interlocked forces that may drive consumption. Especially relevant are screening and assessment for all forms of abuse for both male and female offenders because it is now recognized that the effects of trauma contribute to many disorders including substance misuse. Treatment outcomes may be compromised if the abuse and trauma issues are not explored or integrated into treatment plans. Essentially, a practitioner should therefore have a good working knowledge of each domain they are assessing and the typical issues that individuals with substance abuse problems experience in their areas.

Assessment – feedback and reporting

Assessment is not just a test of the practitioner's information gathering and diagnostic talents; its function goes well beyond this. Providing personalized feedback is a vital component of the assessment process and helps promote behavioural change (Heather and Stockwell, 2004). Practitioners should provide assessment feedback in supportive ways to help build readiness and motivation to change, using principles of motivational interviewing (MI; see Miller and Rollnick, 1991). Developments in MI and objective feedback from assessment results have shown promise in secondary prevention of further problem development (Miller and Rollnick, 1991) and enhancing treatment readiness (Ginsberg *et al.*, 2002). Using standard measures that have available non-clinical or sub-clinical norms can be a powerful strategy for providing objective feedback to clients who may not be aware of how they compare with others in their level of substance use and related problems. Feedback can help promote cognitive dissonance, create ambivalence and tip clients towards wanting to change. This can help engage the client in treatment (Heather and Stockwell, 2004).

The practitioner should also remember that the assessment record is often a legal document, the outcomes of which may be shared with others and in some circumstances may be read in a courtroom or shared at a parole hearing. A practitioner should always ensure that the record of the assessment could stand up to this scrutiny and that recommendations made or conclusions drawn are defensible.

Integrity

Restrictions of liberty and treatment opportunity are usually determined by assessment. Good assessment therefore demands a very wide range of experience and knowledge in the assessors, to evaluate all the potential problems that can emerge explicitly or implicitly in the interview. Although some instruments can be administered and scored without significant training, treatment decisions can be greatly improved when they are made by professionally trained and supervised staff. Assessors can make mistakes particularly if they do not follow the instructions for completing the instruments or fail to interpret the information correctly. Bonta *et al.*, (2001) described two general findings of importance with regard to the integrity of offender assessment. First, even after highly structured training in the use of an assessment system, high rates of error often remain. Errors such as simple addition mistakes or misunderstandings of how some of the items were to be scored may be found. To negate this, organizations need to ensure that robust process monitoring is in place and action is taken quickly when errors are found. Second, staff may not fully utilize new and better assessment instruments due to reluctance to change what they have done for years. When Schneider, Ervin and Snyder-Joy (1996) surveyed staff about their views of a newly introduced assessment system, less than one-half of probation officers found it was helpful and only 27% thought the instrument was more accurate than their professional judgement. Other authors cite similar findings (Maung and

Hammond, 2000). To address this, organizations that impose expectations for the completion of assessments often achieve the improvements they desire. Bonta, Wallace-Capretta and Rooney (2000) argued that staff need to be helped to recognize the benefits of an empirically based assessment or it can lead to errors and resistance in using the results in treatment plans/case management. As Andrews and Bonta (2003) point out, 'This points to the need for a high degree of training, personal professionalism and managerial supervision. Staff who administer offender assessments must conduct the assessments conscientiously and manager's must actively assist and supervise' (p. 265).

The need to keep assessment quality high and relevant to treatment planning is essential. Gossop (2003) encouraged practitioners to remember that overly complex assessment procedures simply increase dropout rates. In addition, assessment should not be about filling in endless forms. Acquiring a large amount of data that is unlikely to be useful in treatment is a waste of time. Practitioners should focus on gathering information that is most likely to help tailor treatment to meet clients needs (Jarvis, Tebbutt and Mattick, 1995). Using information from an objective assessment can result in treatment that is better matched to a client's need, resulting in better outcomes.

The best assessments focus on the relationship between offenders' needs and risk factors. Whilst static risk factors (such as the number of previous criminal convictions) cannot be changed, many dynamic risk factors and 'criminogenic' needs can be addressed and are changeable via treatment interventions. This risk/need assessment therefore provides an indication of the level or intensity of intervention required, as well as their treatment needs, thereby allowing often scarce resources to be targeted to specific levels of risk and need. It enables practitioners and clients to formulate an individualized care plan that describes the appropriate treatment required to modify problematic behaviours and controlling conditions. Assessment is therefore both relevant and essential to ensure appropriate matching of treatment interventions with client need. Assessment provides the basis for matching (Institute of Medicine, 1990), with the central aim of the intervention being to 'help the client find the means to achieve what otherwise feels unobtainable' (Harris, 2007).

The Center for Substance Abuse Treatment (2005) found that in criminal justice settings, 'screening' and 'assessment' are often equated with 'eligibility' and 'suitability', respectively. 'Eligibility' is determined by screening offenders to see if substance misuse treatment is needed and essentially answers whether the offender meets the system's criteria for receiving treatment services and warrants further assessment to determine problematic issues. 'Suitability' for placement in one of several different levels of treatment services is determined by an assessment to help identify key bio-psychosocial problems related to referral to treatment and/or supervision, and whether the offender is capable of benefiting from treatment or responding to a particular intervention.

Once a screen alerts the clinician to the presence of a problem, further assessment is needed. The initial assessment gathers the minimal level of relevant information necessary to:

- Identify and verify the existence of a drug and or alcohol problem warranting intervention.
- Provide detail and shed light on the nature and seriousness of the clients' drug misuse.
- Recognize related or coexisting issues such as withdrawal symptoms or mental health problems.
- Evaluate any immediate risks including self-harm or suicide.
- Discover links with criminal behaviour and potential risks upon release.

- Explore levels of motivation to engage in treatment.
- Guide decision making in the development of an appropriate individualized care or treatment plan for the client.

Treatment

Decades of dedicated research into 'what works' with respect to correctional interventions for offenders (Lipsey and Cullen, 2007; Smith, Gendreau and Swartz, 2009) and substance abuse programmes (McMurran, 2007; Moos, 2003) has resulted in a wealth of accumulated research knowledge that informs contemporary substance abuse intervention models. A combined review of this literature suggests that there are seven key components of effective substance abuse programmes for a correctional clientele. These are described individually as follows.

Component 1: Programmes should be based on a social learning/ cognitive-behavioural approach

According to social learning and cognitive-behavioural models of psychology, addiction is a learned, maladaptive behaviour that can be addressed by teaching and modelling pro-social behaviour (Pearce and Holbrook, 2002). From this perspective, offenders initially develop antisocial thoughts and behaviours (including substance abuse) as coping mechanisms, which are subsequently maintained by immediate, internal reinforcers such as feelings of pleasure. These, in turn, are more powerful than delayed negative consequences that may derive from the behaviour such as arrest and incarceration. Treatment approaches based on these interrelated theories attempt to modify the individual's behavioural coping skills and cognitive processes to change the target behaviour (Parks and Marlatt, 1999). Specifically, if substance abuse behaviour is initiated and maintained by past learning experiences, including peer modelling, reinforcement contingencies and cognitive beliefs (Donovan and Marlatt, 2005), then these same processes can be used to assist the individual to learn more adaptive cognitive, behavioural and interpersonal coping responses (Andrews and Bonta, 2010; Parks and Marlatt, 1999). This approach typically places a heavy emphasis on skill acquisition through techniques such as role-play, cognitive restructuring (i.e., identifying and correcting thinking patterns that support the maladaptive behaviour) and behavioural rehearsal (Smith, Gendreau and Swartz, 2009).

Research has strongly and consistently supported the effectiveness of interventions based on social learning and cognitive-behavioural interventions over other treatment modalities for offenders for target behaviours including substance abuse (Antonowicz and Ross, 1994; Smith, Gendreau and Swartz, 2009).

Component 2: Programmes should adhere to the 'Risk–Needs–Responsivity' model of correctional intervention

This model, originally articulated by Andrews and Bonta (2010), postulates that three conditions must be met for effective intervention with offenders. First, programme priorities should be managed so that treatment is delivered to the highest risk offenders (the *Risk Principle*) as they typically represent a higher risk to re-offend and also have more room for change in comparison to those of lower risk (Smith, Gendreau and Swartz, 2009). The *Need Principle* states that dynamic or changeable risk factors, such as alcohol and drug use, should be the targets of change in order to reduce recidivism. Finally, the *Responsivity Principle* can be divided into two elements – general and specific responsivity. General responsivity supports the point noted earlier that the most effective interventions for offenders are those based on cognitive, behavioural and social learning theories (Gendreau, 1996). Specific responsivity, on the other hand, refers to the need for treatment providers to match offenders to interventions according to key offender characteristics, including factors such as motivation and cognitive functioning (Gendreau, 1996), as well as gender and ethnicity (Hubbard, 2007). Reviews of the literature since the early 1990s have provided clear empirical support for the efficacy of programmes based on the risk, need and responsivity model in reducing recidivism among offenders (Smith, Gendreau and Swartz, 2009). This includes programmes that target substance abuse.

Component 3: The intensity of the programme should match problem severity

A key component to consider when assessing an individual's substance abuse history is problem severity. In the past, there have been critiques of the 'one-size-fits-all' approach, in the area of substance abuse treatment. According to this perspective, which is often associated with the disease model of addictions, an individual either has a substance abuse problem or not. Therefore, if the client is deemed to have a problem, he or she is put through a standardized programme, which likely includes a residential component of several weeks, regardless of the severity of abuse (Weekes, Moser and Langevin, 1999). The rationale is that, even if the problem is not yet severe, addiction is a progressive illness which will eventually result in a substantial problem if the individual continues to engage in the behaviour. Aside from the inefficiencies in terms of cost and access to treatment posed by such an approach, research on correctional populations has demonstrated that putting low-risk and low-need offenders in high-intensity programmes may result in negative effects. Some have hypothesized that this may be the result of intensive programmes interfering with other existing positive factors for those with low needs, such as good family relationships, positive supports, pro-social attitudes and the ability to gain steady employment (Lowenkamp and Latessa, 2005).

Based on such research, certain correctional jurisdictions, including the Correctional Service of Canada, have adopted an approach of providing correctional programmes based on an assessment of offender risk for re-offending and problem severity. Therefore, a range of interventions are available, from community-based low-intensity interventions (if required) for those assessed as having a low-intensity problem, to intensive prison-based programmes for those with substantial and severe substance abuse histories. Research on these programmes has demonstrated their effectiveness, particularly in reducing recidivism (Grant *et al.*, 2003; Kunic and Varis, 2010).

Component 4: The programme should incorporate the use of motivational enhancement techniques

While research clearly demonstrates that appropriate treatment interventions with offenders who have substance abuse problems can have a significant impact on outcomes, research has also found that the best results are evident for those who complete a programme and remain engaged in aftercare following the intensive phase of intervention. For example, McMurran and

Theodosi (2007) conducted a review of cognitive-behavioural treatment outcome studies that reported recidivism rates for treatment completers, non-completers and untreated offenders. Overall, they found the non-completion rate was 24%, and that completers had lower rates of recidivism than non-completers. McMurran and Theodosi (2007) noted that, aside from the cost-efficiency implications of these non-completion rates, the findings on recidivism rates indicate the importance of addressing both recruitment and retention in treatment.

One important intervention that aims to encourage people to commit to goals for change and therefore engage in the treatment process is 'motivational interviewing'. This approach was originally developed by Miller and Rollnick (2002) as a technique for motivating substance abusers to change. The key element of the approach is to elicit 'change statements' by using several techniques such as expressing empathy and working on ambivalence to strengthen the commitment to change (Miller, 2011). In addition, motivational enhancement techniques such as allowing clients to establish their own treatment goals and completing exercises such as a 'decisional balance' can be incorporated into group treatments.

Research evidence has demonstrated the effectiveness of MI, with studies supporting its use as both a stand-alone intervention and a prelude to more intensive interventions (Burke, Arkowitz and Menchola, 2003; Vasilaki, Hosier and Cox, 2006). It should therefore be viewed as an important element of any substance abuse treatment approach to address issues of engagement and retention in treatment.

Component 5: The programme should have therapeutic integrity

Beyond the importance of correctional programmes having a research-based theoretical framework, studies have also demonstrated the key role of 'therapeutic integrity' for programme success (Gendreau, 1996; Gendreau *et al.*, 2006). Therapeutic integrity refers to factors such as therapists being adequately selected, trained and supervised and the programme being delivered in a consistent and standardized way. Studies using an assessment tool developed to evaluate eight domains of therapeutic integrity with respect to correctional programmes (Correctional Programme Assessment Inventory – *CPAI-2000* – Gendreau and Andrews, 2001) have demonstrated a positive correlation between principles of therapeutic integrity and treatment effectiveness (Lowenkamp, Latessa and Smith, 2006).

Component 6: Adjunctive interventions such as Opioid Substitution Therapy should be available

Opioid Substitution Therapy (OST) is one of the most widely used and effective interventions for heroin and other opiate addictions. As reported in the Health Canada (2002) document *Best Practices in Methadone Maintenance Treatment*, research demonstrates that there are multiple benefits to individuals with an opiate addiction receiving OST. These include, but are not limited to, reducing the risk of acquiring HIV/AIDS, Hepatitis C or other blood-borne pathogens; improving their physical and mental health; improving their likelihood for full-time employment and their overall quality of life; reducing their use of illicitly obtained opioids; reducing their use of other substances; spending less time involved in criminal activities; spending less time incarcerated; having much lower death rates than individuals not receiving treatment; and reducing injection drug use behaviour. As a result of the effectiveness of OST in reducing risk behaviours, it positively benefits society by decreasing criminal activity and improving public health (Health Canada, 2002; Stallwitz and Stöver, 2007).

Component 7: The programme should have a maintenance or aftercare component

In many substance abuse treatment settings, the focus of programme resources is often on the 'intensive' phase of the programme. This typically consists of frequent sessions over a specified period of time in either an inpatient or outpatient treatment setting. However, research has demonstrated the critical role of ongoing, longer-term treatment engagement beyond the intensive phase of treatment, which is often referred to as treatment maintenance or continuing care. In fact, several studies have demonstrated that the duration of care is more important than the amount of care (Crits-Christoph and Sidqueland, 1996; Moos *et al.*, 2000). As Moos (2003) states, 'the finding that duration of treatment for alcohol and drug use disorders is more closely related to outcome than is the sheer amount of treatment is consistent with the fact that the enduring aspects of individuals' life contexts are associated with the recurrent course of remission and relapse' (p. 4).

Conclusion: Effective Approaches to Offender Substance Abuse Assessment and Treatment

In this chapter, we have presented a comprehensive and integrated model for the assessment and treatment of offenders' substance abuse problems that is driven by theory and guided by empirical research. While recognizing that biological and possibly genetic factors may interact with social, situational, experiential and individual difference or personality factors, the clinical approach discussed stems from a social-learning perspective (Miller and Dollard, 1941) on substance abuse. Accordingly, it employs cognitive-behavioural (Bandura, 1989), clinical intervention techniques and modalities such as coping skill development and structured relapse prevention (Lightfoot, 1999; Marlatt and Gordon, 1985; Parks and Marlatt, 1999) that clearly 'fit' and extend from a social-learning perspective.

We have chosen to deliberately and explicitly describe this approach in this chapter because it has been our experience that many of the treatment approaches and services available to people involved in the criminal justice system (and elsewhere) are founded more on 'beliefs' about what works to address substance abuse than the 'science' of what works and represent a serious shortcoming in the field. Indeed, this chapter highlights that with notable exceptions, many, perhaps most, of the intervention services available to offenders with substance abuse problems lack a solid theoretical base and supporting evidence from research to demonstrate their efficacy. Surprisingly, some lack any form of empirical evaluation whatsoever. As clinicians and researchers ourselves, we believe it is fundamental that ethical practice involves the delivery of evidence-based intervention to clients that is founded on comprehensive theory.

Research demonstrates that there are a number of treatment techniques and intervention modalities that are effective in changing substance use behaviour (summarized by Weekes, Thomas and Graves, 2004). These include social skills training, problem-solving, coping skills training, high-risk identification, structured relapse prevention, goal-setting, motivational interviewing/enhancement, employment skills training, stress management, community rein-forcement techniques and post-treatment maintenance, monitoring and aftercare (Weekes, Thomas and Graves, 2004).

Over the years, a number of treatment programme evaluations and systematic reviews have demonstrated the effectiveness of substance abuse treatment for individuals involved in the criminal justice system (e.g., Bahr, Masters and Taylor, 2012; Inciardi, 1999; Love, 2002; Martin *et al.*, 1999; Mullen *et al.*, 2001; Pelissier *et al.*, 2001; Porporino *et al.*, 2002; Wexler, Falkin and Lipton, 1990; Wexler *et al.*, 1999a,b). A number of these studies examined the effectiveness of the therapeutic community model and yielded significant reductions in outcome (e.g., Bahr, Masters and Taylor, 2012; Wexler, Falkin and Lipton, 1990; Wexler *et al.*, 1999a,b) and other types of prison-based residential (e.g., Pelisier *et al.*, 2001) and non-residential (Porporino *et al.*, 2002) programmes.

Pelisier *et al.* (2001) found that six-months post-release, a positive urinalysis rate of 20% for programme participants compared with 36% for programme participants. Further, 3.1% of treatment participants were re-arrested with a new criminal charge compared with 15% for offenders who did not participate in the residential programme during their incarceration. A Canadian research team (Porporino *et al.*, 2002) followed offenders for one full year after their release from prison and found reconviction rates of 16% for programme participants (including programme non-completers) versus 23% for a comparison group who were matched on key characteristics such as substance abuse severity, age, offence, length of sentence and so on.

A meta-analytic review undertaken by Holloway, Bennett and Farrington (2008) for the Swedish National Council for Crime Prevention confirms the efficacy of the model and approach discussed in this report. It also lends support for the conclusion that intervention models have the potential to not only reduce or eliminate substance abuse, but to also significantly reduce offenders' risk for future involvement in a range of criminal activity.

Over the years, both the British and Canadian federal prison systems have developed criteria to evaluate the likely effectiveness of substance abuse programmes for offenders under their supervision (Weekes, Thomas and Graves, 2004). This framework is used to review and accredit programmes. Existing treatment programmes, as well as those under consideration, are systematically assessed against these criteria before a decision to implement is rendered.

Although the criteria vary slightly between the English and Canadian prison systems, they generally include:

1. A programme founded on theory that is comprehensive and evidence-based.
2. The intervention uses effective methods, techniques and modalities.
3. Programmes are 'multi-faceted' – they incorporate multiple treatment modalities.
4. Intensity and duration of treatment are designed to respond to participants' needs (low to high problem severity).
5. Treatment services are delivered consistently and according to design and established principles.
6. Programme staff are recruited using established selection criteria that assess treatment-relevant strengths and abilities.
7. Programme staff are well-trained and they are monitored, supported and certified.
8. Prison administrators and management support rehabilitative priorities and goals.
9. There is proper assessment and selection of programme participants.
10. There is an identifiable and comprehensive monitoring and quantitative evaluation framework surrounding the programme.

Similar accreditation schemes are now being used by non-governmental organizations (e.g., European Association for the Treatment of Addictions) to assess the likely effectiveness of treatment services to non-criminal justice clients. The goal of these approaches is to attempt to foster the use of evidence-informed practice with the long-term goal of facilitating significant positive behaviour change on the part of programme participants to reduce their risk of future substance abuse and criminal behaviour and to enhance public safety.

Acknowledgements

The authors would like to thank Chad Dubeau, Information Specialist with the Canadian Centre on Substance Abuse (www.ccsa.ca), for his assistance with the background research for this chapter. The Centre for Research on Inner City Health (CRICH) is part of the Keenan Research Centre in the Li Ka Shing Knowledge Institute of St. Michael's Hospital. CRICH receives annual core funding from the Government of Ontario.

Disclaimer

The views and opinions expressed in this chapter are those of the authors and do not necessarily reflect the policies and perspectives of the Correctional Service of Canada; Public Safety Canada; St. Michael's Hospital, Toronto, Ontario; the Government of Ontario; or the National Offender Management Service, United Kingdom.

References

Andrews, D.A. and Bonta, J. (2003) *The Psychology of Criminal Conduct*, Anderson Publishing, Cincinnati.

Andrews, D.A. and Bonta, J. (2010) *The Psychology of Criminal Conduct*, 5th edn, Lexis Nexis, New Providence.

Antonowicz, D.H. and Ross, R.R. (1994) Essential components of successful rehabilitation programs for offenders. *International Journal of Offender and Comparative Criminology*, 38, 97–194.

Babor, T.F., Higgins-Biddle, J.C., Saunders, J.B. and Monteiro, M.G. (2001) *The Alcohol Use Disorders Identification Test: Guidelines for Use in Primary Care*, 2nd edn, World Health Organisation, Geneva.

Bahr, S.J., Masters, A.L. and Taylor, B.M. (2012) What works in substance abuse treatment programs for offenders? *Prison Journal*, 92, 155–174.

Bandura, A. (1989) Human agency in social cognitive theory. *American Psychologist*, 44, 1175–1184.

Bird, S.M. and Hutchinson, S.J. (2003) Male drugs-related deaths in the fortnight after release from prison: Scotland, 1996–99. *Addiction*, 98, 185–190.

Bonta, J., Wallace-Capretta, S. and Rooney, J. (2000) A quasi-experimental evaluation of an intensive rehabilitation supervision program. *Criminal Justice and Behavior*, 27, 312–329.

Bonta, J., Bogue, B., Crowley, M. and Motiuk, L. (2001) Implementing offender classification systems: lessons learned, in *Offender Rehabilitation in Practice: Implementing and Evaluating Effective Programs* (eds G.A. Bernfeld, D.P. Farrington and A.W. Leschied), John Wiley & Sons, Ltd, Chichester, pp. 227–245.

Burke, B.L., Arkowitz, H. and Menchola, M. (2003) The efficacy of motivational interviewing: a meta-analysis of controlled clinical trials. *Journal of Consulting and Clinical Psychology*, 71, 843–861.

Butler, S.F., Budman, S., Goldman, R. *et al.* (2001) Initial validation of a computer-administered Addiction Severity Index: The ASI-MV. *Psychology of Addictive Behavior*, 15, 4–12.

Center for Substance Abuse Treatment (1994) Screening and Assessment for Alcohol and Other Drug Abuse Among Adults in Criminal Justice System. Treatment Improvement Protocol Series 7, DHHS Publication no (SMA) 00-3477. Substance Abuse and Mental Health Services Administration, Rockville.

Center for Substance Abuse Treatment (2000) Integrating Substance Abuse Treatment and Vocational Service. Treatment Improvement Protocol Series 38, DHHS Publication no. (SMA) 00-3470. Substance Abuse and Mental Health Services Administration, Rockville.

Center for Substance Abuse Treatment (2005) Substance Abuse Treatment for Adults in the Criminal Justice System. Treatment Improvement Protocol (TIP) Series no. 44. Substance Abuse and Mental Health Services Administration (US), Rockville. http://www.ncbi.nlm.nih.gov/books/NBK64137/ (accessed 17 January 2013).

Connors, G.J. (1995) Screening for alcohol problems, in *Assessing Alcohol Problems: A Guide for Clinicians and Researchers*. National Institute on Alcohol Abuse and Alcoholism Treatment Handbook Series 4 (eds J.P. Allen and M. Columbus), US Department of Health and Human Services, Public Health Service, National Institutes of Health, National Institute on Alcohol Abuse and Alcoholism, Bethesda, pp. 17–29.

Crits-Christoph, P. and Sidiqueland, L. (1996) Psychosocial treatment for drug abuse: selected review and recommendations for national health care. *Archives of General Psychiatry*, 53, 749–756.

Debidin, M. (2009) *A Compendium of Research and Analysis on the Offender Assessment System (OASys) 2006–2009*. Ministry of Justice Research Series 16/09. Ministry of Justice, London.

Donovan, D.M. and Marlatt, G.A. (eds) (2005) *Assessment of Addictive Behaviors*, 2nd edn, Guilford Press, New York.

Flanagan, T. (1983) Correlates of institutional misconduct among state prisoners. *Criminology*, 21, 29–40.

Gendreau, P. (1996) The principles of effective intervention with offenders, in *Choosing Correctional Options that Work: Defining the Demand and Evaluating the Supply* (ed. A.T. Harland), Sage Publications, Thousand Oaks, pp. 117–130.

Gendreau, P. and Andrews, D.A. (2001) *Correctional Programs Assessment Inventory (CPAI-2000)*, University of New Brunswick, Saint John.

Gendreau, P., Goggin, C., French, S. and Smith, P. (2006) Practicing psychology in correctional settings: "What works" in reducing criminal behavior, in *The Handbook of Forensic Psychology*, 3rd edn) (eds A.K. Hess and I.B. Weiner), John Wiley & Sons, Inc., New York, pp. 722–750.

Ginsberg, J.I.D., Mann, R.E., Rotgers, F. and Weekes, J.R. (2002) Motivational interviewing with criminal justice populations, in *Motivational Interviewing: Preparing People for Change*, 2nd edn (eds W.R. Miller and S. Rollnick), Guilford, New York.

Gossop, M. (2000) *Living with Drugs*, Ashgate Publishing Ltd, Aldershot.

Gossop, M. (2003) *Drug Addiction and Its Treatment*, Oxford University Press, Oxford.

Gossop, M., Darke, S., Griffiths, P. *et al.* (1995) The severity of dependence scale (SDS): psychometric properties of the SDS in English and Australian samples of heroin, cocaine and amphetamine users. *Addiction*, 90, 607–614.

Grant, B.A., Kunic, D., MacPherson, P. *et al.* (2003) *The High Intensity Substance Abuse Program (HISAP): Results from the Pilot*, Correctional Service of Canada, Ottawa.

Graves, G. and Bell, R. (2004) *Computerized Screening Assessment: Data Analysis Report*, State of Maine, Office of Substance Abuse, Augusta.

Grove, W.M., Zald, D.H., Lebow, B.S. *et al.* (2000) Clinical versus mechanical prediction: a meta-analysis. *Psychological Assessment*, 12, 19–30.

Harris, P. (2007) *Empathy for the Devil: How to Help People Overcome Drugs and Alcohol Problems*, Russell House Publishing Ltd, Dorset.

Health Canada. (2002) *Best Practices – Methadone Maintenance Treatment*, Health Canada, Ottawa.

Heather, N. and Stockwell, T. (2004) *The Essential Handbook of Treatment and Prevention of Alcohol Problems*, John Wiley & Sons, Ltd, Chichester.

Her Majesty's Prison Service (HMP) (2003) *The Prison Service Drug Strategy*, Her Majesty's Prison Service, London.

Holloway, K., Bennett, T.H. and Farrington, D.P. (2008) *Effectiveness of Treatment in Reducing Drug-Related Crime*, Swedish National Council for Crime Prevention, Stockholm.

Hubbard, D. (2007) Getting the most out of correctional treatment: testing the responsivity principle on male and female offenders. *Federal Probation*, 71 (1), 2–8.

Inciardi, J.A. (1999) Prison-based therapeutic communities: an effective modality for treating drug-involved offenders, in *The Dilemmas of Punishment* (eds K.C. Haas and G.P. Alpert), Waveland, Prospect Heights.

Institute of Medicine (1990) Broadening the base of treatment for alcohol problems. Report of a study by a Committee of the Institute of Medicine, Division of Mental Health and Behavioural Medicine, in *Case Needs Review: Substance Misuse Domain* (eds F.J. Boland, K. Henderson and J. Baker), National Academy Press, Washington, DC.

Jarvis, T.J., Tebbutt, J. and Mattick, R.P. (1995) *Treatment Approaches for Alcohol and Drug Dependence: An Introductory Guide*, John Wiley & Sons, Ltd, Chichester.

Kunic, D. and Grant, B.A. (2006) *The Computerized Assessment of Substance Abuse (CASA): Results from the Demonstration Project (R-173)*, Correctional Service of Canada, Ottawa.

Kunic, D. and Varis, D.D. (2010) *The Aboriginal Offender Substance Abuse Program (AOSAP): Examining the Effects of Successful Completion on Post-release Outcomes*, Report No R-217, Correctional Service of Canada, Ottawa.

Lightfoot, L.O. (1999) Treating substance abuse and dependence in offenders: a review of methods and outcomes, in *Strategic Solutions: The International Community Corrections Association Examines Substance Abuse* (ed. E.J. Latessa), American Correctional Association Press, Lanham, pp. 43–80.

Lipsey, M.W. and Cullen, F.T. (2007) The effectiveness of correctional rehabilitation: a review of systematic reviews. *Annual Review of Law and Social Science*, 3, 297–320.

Love, C.T. (2002) Substance abuse treatment and corrections, in *Changing Substance Abuse Through Health and Social Systems* (eds W.R. Miller and C.M. Weisner), Plenum, New York, pp. 183–196.

Lowenkamp, C.T. and Latessa, E.J. (2005) Increasing the effectiveness of correctional programming through the risk principle: identifying offenders for residential placement. *Criminology and Public Policy*, 4, 263–289.

Lowenkamp, C.T., Latessa, E.J. and Smith, P. (2006) Does correctional program quality really matter? The importance of adhering to the principles of effective intervention. *Criminology and Public Policy*, 5, 210–220.

Marlatt, G.A. and Gordon, J.R. (1985) *Relapse Prevention: Maintenance Strategies in the Treatment of Addictive Behaviours*, Guilford, New York.

Martin, S.S., Butzin, C.A., Saum, C.A. and Inciardi, J.A. (1999) Three-year outcomes of therapeutic community treatment for drug-involved offenders in Delaware: from prison to work release to aftercare. *Prison Journal*, 79, 294–320.

Matheson, F.I., Doherty, S. and Grant, B. (2009) *Women Offender Substance Abuse Programming & Community Reintegration (R-202)*, Correctional Service of Canada, Ottawa.

Maung, N.A. and Hammond, N. (2000) Risk of Re-Offending and Needs Assessment: The User's Perspective. *Home Office Research Study no. 216.* Home Office, London.

McLellan, A.T., Luborsky, L., Woody, G.E. and O'Brien, C.P. (1980) An improved diagnostic evaluation instrument for substance abuse patients: the Addiction Severity Index. *Journal of Nervous and Mental Disease*, 168, 26–33.

McLellan, A.T., Luborsky, L., Cacciola, J. *et al.* (1985) New data from the Addiction Severity Index: reliability and validity in three centers. *Journal of Nervous and Mental Disease*, 173, 412–423.

McLellan, A.T., Kushner, H., Metzger, D. *et al.* (1992) The fifth edition of the Addiction Severity Index. *Journal of Substance Abuse Treatment*, 9, 199–213.

McMurran, M. (2007) What works in substance misuse treatment for offenders? *Criminal Behaviour and Mental Health*, 17, 225–233.

McMurran, M. and Theodosi, E. (2007) Is offender treatment non-completion associated with increased reconviction over no treatment? *Psychology, Crime and Law*, 13, 333–343.

Miller, W.R. (2011) Motivational interviewing: research, practice, and puzzles. *Addictive Behaviors*, 21, 835–842.

Miller, N.E. and Dollard, J. (1941) *Social Learning and Imitation*, Yale University Press, New Haven.

Miller, W.R. and Rollnick, S. (1991) *Motivational Interviewing: Preparing People to Change Addictive Behaviour*, Guilford, New York.

Miller, W.R. and Rollnick, S. (2002) *Motivational Interviewing: Preparing People for Change*, 2nd edn, Guilford, New York.

Miller, W.R., Westerberg, V.S. and Waldron, H.B. (1995) Evaluating alcohol problems in adults and adolescents, in *Handbook of Alcoholism Treatment Approaches: Effective Alternatives*, 2nd edn (eds R.K. Hester and W.R. Miller), Allyn and Bacon, Boston, pp. 61–88.

Moos, R.H. (2003) Addictive disorders in context: principles and puzzles of effective treatment and recovery. *Psychology of Addictive Behaviors*, 17, 3–12.

Moos, R., Finney, J.W., Federman, B. and Suchinsky, R. (2000) Specialty mental health care improves patients' outcomes: findings from a nationwide program to monitor the quality of care for patients with substance use disorders. *Journal of Studies on Alcohol*, 61, 704–713.

Morris, R. (2001) Alcohol and drugs: a perspective from New Zealand. *Forum on Corrections Research*, 13, 18–19.

Mullen, R., Rowland, J., Arbiter, N. *et al.* (2001) California's first prison therapeutic community: aa10-year review. *Offender Substance Abuse Report*, 1, 17–32.

Parks, G.A. and Marlatt, G.A. (1999) Keeping "what works" working: cognitive-behavioral relapse prevention with substance-abusing offenders, in *Strategic Solutions: The International Community Corrections Association Examines Substance Abuse* (ed. E.J. Latessa), American Correctional Association Press, Lanham.

Pearce, S.C. and Holbrook, D. (2002) Research Findings and Best Practices in Substance Abuse Treatment of Offenders. Report prepared for the North Carolina Department of Corrections Substance Abuse Advisory Council.

Pelissier, B. and Jones, N. (2005) A review of gender differences among substance abusers. *Crime & Delinquency*, 51, 343–372.

Pelisier, B., Wallace, S., O'eil, J.A. *et al.* (2001) Federal prison residential drug treatment reduces substance use and arrests after release. *American Journal of Drug and Alcohol Abuse*, 27, 315–339.

Peters, R.H., Greenbaum, P.E., Steinberg, M.L. and Carter, C.R. (2000) Effectiveness of screening instruments in detecting substance use disorders among prisoners. *Journal of Substance Abuse Treatment*, 18, 349–358.

Porporino, F.J., Robinson, D., Millson, W.A. and Weekes, J.R. (2002) Outcome evaluation of prison-based treatment programming for substance users. *Substance Use and Misuse*, 37, 1047–1077.

Sattar, G. (2003) The death of offenders in England and Wales. *Crisis: The Journal of Crisis Intervention and Suicide Prevention*, 24, 17–23.

Sattar, G. and Killias, M. (2005) The death of offenders in Switzerland. *European Journal of Criminology*, 2, 317–340.

Schneider, A.L., Ervin, L. and Snyder-Joy, Z. (1996) Further exploration of the flight from discretion: the role of risk/need instruments in probation supervision decisions. *Journal of Criminal Justice*, 24, 109–121.

Singleton, N., Pendry, E. and Taylor, C. (2003) *Drug-Related Mortality Among Newly-Released Offenders*, Home Office, London.

Skinner, H.A. (1982) The drug abuse screening test. *Addictive Behaviors*, 7, 363–371.

Skinner, H.A. and Horn, J.L. (1984) *Alcohol Dependence Scale (ADS) User's Guide*, Addiction Research Foundation, Toronto.

Smith, P., Gendreau, P. and Swartz, K. (2009) Validating the principles of effective intervention: a systematic review of the contributions of meta-analysis in the field of corrections. *Victims and Offenders*, 4, 148–169.

Stallwitz, A. and Stover, H. (2007) Impact of substitution treatment in prisons: a literature review. *International Journal or Drug Policy*, 18, 464–474.

Sundel, S.S. and Sundel, M. (1993) *Behaviour Modification in the Human Services: A Systematic Introduction to Concepts and Applications*, Sage, Newbury Park.

Vasilaki, E., Hosier, S.G. and Cox, W.M. (2006) The efficacy of motivational interviewing as a brief intervention for excessive drinking: a meta-analytic review. *Alcohol and Alcoholism*, 41, 328–335.

Weekes, J.R., Moser, A.E. and Langevin, C.M. (1999) Assessing substance-abusing offenders for treatment, in *Strategic Solutions: The International Community Correctional Association Examines Substance Abuse* (ed. E.J. Latessa), American Correctional Association Press, Lanham.

Weekes, J.R., Thomas, G. and Graves, G. (2004) *Substance Abuse in Corrections – Frequently Asked Questions*, Canadian Centre on Substance Abuse, Ottawa.

Wexler, H.K., Falkin, G.P. and Lipton, D.S. (1990) Outcome evaluation of a prison therapeutic community for substance abuse treatment. *Criminal Justice and Behavior*, 17, 71–92.

Wexler, H.K., De Leon, G., Thomas, G. *et al.* (1999a) The amity prison TC evaluation reincarceration outcomes. *Criminal Justice and Behavior*, 26, 147–167.

Wexler, H.K., Melnick, G., Lowe, L. and Peters, J. (1999b) 3-year reincarceration outcomes for amity in-prison therapeutic community and aftercare in California. *Prison Journal*, 79, 321–336.

14

What Works in Reducing Arson-Related Offending

Katarina Fritzon[1], Rebekah Doley[1] and Fiona Clark[2]

[1]Bond University, Australia
[2]West London Mental Health Trust, UK

Introduction

The crime of arson is the only offence to have a higher prevalence among juvenile offenders than adults (Kolko, 2004). Consequently, the literature on clinical and forensic assessment and treatment of fire-setters has tended to focus on interventions aimed at children and adolescents (Hollin and Epps, 1996; Kolko, Watson and Faust, 1991). Compared to other topics of interest in the 'What Works' literature, most notably sexual and violent offenders, arson and fire-setting have been curiously under-examined. It is important to distinguish the term arson from that of fire-setting, in that the former concerns a legal definition, with varying criteria across jurisdictions, whereas fire-setting is a purely behavioural description (Doley, 2009). Although both terms may be used interchangeably in this chapter, we do not wish to imply that findings are restricted to those people who are charged and convicted as it is important to recognize that international conviction figures for arson are very low. In the past two years, there has been a growth of interest in this population with the publication of a number of recent reviews (Dolan et al., 2011; Doley et al., 2011; Ducat and Ogloff, 2011; Fritzon, Lewis and Doley, 2011; Fritzon et al., 2011; Gannon and Pina, 2010; Horley and Bowlby, 2011; Lowenstein, 2003; McEwan and Freckelton, 2011) as well as the development of a new comprehensive theoretical model for understanding arson (Gannon et al., 2011). However, there is much work to be done in building an evidence base to inform our knowledge of 'What Works' with fire-setters.

Over the years, a number of clinical approaches to the treatment of fire-setting have been developed, not all of which have been solidly grounded in the theoretical framework of modern offender behaviour programmes. In reviewing these contributions to our knowledge of fire-setting intervention, what is apparent is the diversity of potential aetiological sequences that may lead to fire-setting behaviour, and thus numerous treatment orientations may provide promising avenues for reducing that behaviour. A model has been proposed recently that draws together a number of key features from existing theoretical and empirical work on

What Works in Offender Rehabilitation: An Evidence-Based Approach to Assessment and Treatment,
First Edition. Edited by Leam A. Craig, Louise Dixon and Theresa A. Gannon.
© 2013 John Wiley & Sons, Ltd. Published 2013 by John Wiley & Sons, Ltd.

arson, and hypothesizes that four primary pathways exist (with a fifth 'mixed' type), each of which emphasizes a different core clinical treatment need. The Multi-Trajectory Theory of Adult Fire-setting (M-TTAF; Gannon *et al.*, 2011) provides a summary of key developmental, social, biological and contextual factors that give rise to fire-setting behaviour (Tier 1), and also provides a basis for differentiating subgroups of fire-setters (Tier 2). This second level of the theory describes the four primary pathways as: (i) inappropriate fire interest/scripts (concerning the use of and interest in fire); (ii) offence-supportive cognitions (antisocial beliefs including entitlement and other justifications for setting fires); (iii) self/emotional regulation concerns (recognition of, monitoring and defusing affective states); and (iv) communication problems (social and intimacy skills). Gannon *et al.* (2011) also draw attention to the links between these four pathways and existing work from other offence types, specifically Ward and Siegert's (2002) sexual offender pathways model. This aspect of the model is useful given that theoretically similar work has received some empirical validation (e.g., Fritzon, 2001; Fritzon, Canter and Wilton, 2001), and thus offers the possibility for evidence-based practice in terms of the development of clinical interventions targeting these main problem areas.

The following section provides a review of the existing literature describing treatment approaches derived from particular theoretical standpoints on fire-setting. The discussion reflects the four M-TTAF pathways to the extent that the inherent components have been recognized in existing clinical approaches to fire-setting. To some extent, this is also a historical review, beginning with the psychoanalytic theory of fire-setting, and concluding with the most recent cognitive behavioural programmes.

Theoretical and Treatment Approaches Associated with Fire-Setting

Inappropriate fire-interest/scripts

The earliest psychological studies of arson stemmed from the psychoanalytic tradition and emphasized pathological sexual motivation (Freud, 1932). However, both descriptive clinical studies and attempts to investigate the sexual arousal hypothesis experimentally have found limited support. For example, 8.3% of the 38 arsonists studied by Hill *et al.* (1982) reported having a sexual motivation for their fire-setting, while 11.1% reported experiencing sexual arousal at the time of their fire-setting. These findings suggest that only a small proportion of arsonists are likely to be sexually motivated. In an experimental study, Quinsey, Chaplin and Upfold (1989) compared the penile plethysmograph responses of 26 fire-setters (defined as individuals with at least one documented episode of fire-setting) with 15 non-fire-setters. No significant differences were reported in responses between the two groups, with both showing significantly greater responses to heterosexual and sexually motivated arson than neutral stories. These results were taken to support the view that arsonists are not specifically sexually aroused by fire-related stimuli. However, the authors acknowledged several possible methodological limitations of the study, including the small sample size, and the fact that the stimulus material used was auditory rather than visual, and thus may not have captured the most relevant cues.

In terms of treatment of this element of fire-setting, Lande (1980) described the case of a 20-year-old man known to have set fires in association with masturbation in order to obtain sexual gratification. This client consented to a treatment programme consisting of a combination of orgasmic reconditioning to increase arousal to heterosexual fantasies and covert sensitization to decrease arousal to fire-related stimuli. The intervention was evaluated using PPG and self-reported measures of arousal to imagined heterosexual activity whilst viewing slides of nude females and to imagined masturbation whilst viewing fire-related slides. Before treatment, there was a greater response to fire-related stimuli on both measures but the pattern was reversed post-treatment and the change was maintained at four- and nine-month follow-up. In addition, the man reported that prior to treatment he had five or more fire-related fantasies per day, some of which were associated with masturbation and he was reported to have set two fires in his parents' home with subsequent fire-setting episodes in prison. After treatment, he reported masturbating about five times per week to heterosexual stimuli and no further episodes of fire-setting were reported by prison officers (four months post-treatment) or by his parents (nine months post-treatment). However, after the four-month assessment, the client began attending a social skills training programme. This raises the possibility that the additional intervention contributed to the maintenance of the described improvement at nine months.

In summary, although small, this body of literature would seem to indicate that a sexual response to fire-related stimuli is not a common finding amongst male arsonists. In those cases where abnormal arousal is identified, specific behavioural interventions may be of benefit. It is also important to note that the hypothesized existence of deviant fire scripts in some fire-setters refers to a broader domain of excitement, of which sexual arousal is just one component. Excitation transfer theory (Zillman, Katcher and Milavksy, 1972) provides a possible theoretical bridge that links the small number of fire-setters who experience sexual arousal specifically, with a larger group who may feel more generally aroused, or excited by their fire-setting activity. According to this theory, originally proposed to account for acts of aggression that occur in the context of stressful arousal, fire-setters who experience excitement during their fire-setting behaviour may 'mis-label' their heightened physiological arousal as sexual arousal. Lande (1980) posits the development over time of a repeated association between fire, arousal and sexual excitement until a predominant or exclusive fire–sexual arousal pattern has formed. Reinhardt (1957) described sexually motivated arsonists as excitement offenders in that they receive pleasure in the power and control provided by the destruction of the fire. For arsonists whose fire excitement is not sexual, it may be that interventions that focus on cognitive restructuring, emphasizing the dangerous consequences of fire-setting, will assist the offender in increasing inhibition towards seeking excitement in this way.

Offence-supportive cognitions

It is widely accepted that some offenders hold offence-supportive schemas (e.g., Polaschek and Gannon, 2004; Ward, 2000), and while this has not been directly investigated in fire-setters, it is proposed that a variety of beliefs may be held that contribute to a lack of inhibition towards, or actively encourage, setting fires. Drawing on the previous literature on implicit theories of other offender types (including violent and sexual offenders) as well as clinical experience with fire-setters, Ó Ciardha and Gannon (2012) have recently proposed a set of implicit beliefs that they believe may be relevant for understanding fire-setting. These include: *Dangerous World* (beliefs that the world is a hostile place and people cannot be trusted); *Normalization of Violence* (beliefs that violence is a relatively normal means for communicating discontent); *Fire as a Powerful Tool* (beliefs that fire sends a clear message [linked to Jackson's (1994) Only Viable Option and Geller's (1992) Communication Arson theories]); *Fire is Fascinating* (beliefs that fire is inherently interesting); and *Fire is Controllable* (beliefs that fire can be controlled and so will not harm unintended targets/parties).

In an early investigation of cognitive factors in fire-setting, Fransella and Adams (1966) described an individualized assessment method using a repertory grid technique (derived from Kelly's (1955) personal construct theory) in an attempt to address the question of the meaning of fire to the arsonist. The main focus of their paper was on the utility of the technique in exploring a complex clinical problem. They described a series of six grids that were used to test various hypotheses about the client's behaviour. In this way, they illustrated the potential of the method for elucidating important aspects of the fire-setting per se and the element of the behaviour that was most important to the individual, such as the act of putting the match to the fire, the moment before the blaze got under way, or the blaze itself. The authors also commented on the fact that the client saw himself as dispensing appropriate justice rather than committing 'arson'. Some of the themes identified in this single case study appear similar to some of the implicit theories hypothesized by Ó Ciardha and Gannon (2012), especially *Fire as a Powerful Tool*, and *Dangerous World*. Consistent with the idea of dispensing justice, Doley (2009) drew attention to the high prevalence of revenge as a reported motive for fire-setting. In addition to postulating the central role of power as an underlying theme in fire-setting, Doley hypothesized that arsonists may be particularly prone to experiencing maladaptive vengeance, with revenge-based acts of fire-setting arising from feelings of injustice.

The theme of entitlement and justification for fire-setting was also identified in a recent paper by Fritzon, Lewis and Doley (2011) which drew on Narrative theory (McAdams, 1988, 2001) to explain the meaning assigned to fire and fire-setting within the life stories of perpetrators. McAdams proposes that adults create meaning and purpose in their lives through the construction of an internalized and evolving life story, and Canter (1994) has suggested that it may be the inability to achieve that purpose or meaning through legitimate means which is responsible for the individual resorting to criminal behaviour. In their analysis of four case studies of arsonists, Fritzon, Lewis and Doley (2011) highlighted themes that represented justifications for fire-setting, including need for recognition, escaping responsibility, enjoyment and empowerment from mastering the environment, and victimization and powerlessness to deal with situations. The authors also provide treatment suggestions for each of these cognitive justifications.

A recent approach to the analysis and working through of cognitive processes involved in dysfunctional behaviour is that of Cognitive Analytic Therapy (CAT; Ryle, 2003), which is based on both Kelly's (1955) personal construct theory and psychoanalysis. The focus is on identifying implicit cognitive associations between current behaviour and past interpersonal experiences in order to highlight ongoing patterns that are ultimately self-defeating. This approach has been taken in the treatment of individuals with repetitive fire-setting behaviour in two published case studies. In the first of these, Hall, Clayton and Johnson (2005) reported on the treatment of an individual with intellectual impairment who had set only one significant fire. Following treatment, they report that this individual was able to interact and communicate with staff on the ward, and approach problems in a far more positive and complex manner than previously.

In a second case study, Pollock (2006) described an arson offender with borderline personality disorder, with a complex history including 11 arson offences, and 13 hospitalizations since the age of 17 years. Following 24 sessions of CAT treatment, this individual was able to cease self-injury, reported less unpredictable and intensely felt subjective experiences, and at two-year follow-up post release from prison, had committed no further crimes. While the outcomes of these two cases are certainly promising, the technique of CAT has been criticized on the grounds of its theoretical basis, as well as lack of empirical evidence (McGuire, 2006). As an alternative to the more evidence-based cognitive-behavioural approach to working with antisocial justifications for arson offending, models such as Narrative Therapy and CAT would certainly need to be subjected to further empirical validation before being incorporated as a mainstream approach to working with these offenders. Unfortunately, as will be discussed later in this chapter, however, there is also a lack of strong empirical evidence for the efficacy of cognitive behavioural therapy programmes with this offender group (Gannon and Pina, 2010; Horley and Bowlby, 2011).

Communication problems

Noting the link between de-institutionalization and fire-setting by former psychiatric patients, Geller (1984) proposed the concept of 'communicative arson' to account for a proportion of the fires set by this population. In reviewing all admissions to a State Hospital over a 200-day period, he noted that several of the 17 cases precipitated by a fire-setting episode (3% of total admissions) could be understood as a means of communicating a wish to be transferred to a different hostel/institution or more frequently back to the original hospital. Such a finding is said to be consistent with previous suggestions that arson is an effective way of redressing grievances or of achieving some control over the environment which is perceived to be unobtainable in other ways (Vreeland and Levin, 1980). This has also been described as a 'pathetic attempt to produce a solution to a problem', occurring as a panic reaction in a situation that otherwise appears insoluble (Soothill and Pope, 1973, p. 137) – although one might question the extent to which a solution is 'pathetic' if it is also effective.

Geller (1992) later described fire-setting as a non-confrontational behaviour, requiring no verbal exchange, easy to commit and leading to a significant event: 'Firesetting has a high success rate for persons whose histories are rife with failures and the activity is reinforced by its nature and results' (p. 76). This subsequent study broadened the definition of communicative arson to include any fire-setting that expresses 'a desire, wish or need'. In this way, arson is conceptualized as a functional behaviour for individuals who may lack the psychological resources to achieve their communication needs through more socially appropriate means.

Jackson (1994) developed a complex formulation of repeat arson utilizing functional analysis and viewed arsonists as a psychosocially disadvantaged group, as a result of personal inadequacies and/or adverse social experiences (e.g., intellectual impairment, physical abnormality, disrupted family history and poor interpersonal skills). As a result of these difficulties, fire-setters are considered to believe themselves to be ineffective and unable to bring about desired changes in their world. Faced with a perceived negative event in their external environment, the fire-setter is confronted by their generalized sense of helplessness and ineffectual past attempts to exert influence over their environment. The resulting emotional tension provides the impetus for their — by now — learned response of fire-setting using an inherently powerful tool to make a statement against the world. In the short-term, setting the fire is reinforced either positively through a greater sense of personal effectiveness, an increase in social attention or engagement or a heightened sense of arousal and an intensified interest in fire, or negatively through avoidance or escape from undesirable situations, mood states or cognitions. However, particularly if apprehended, the likely consequences are transfer to a more restricted social environment with reduced social contact and, as a result, greater interpersonal problems and an increased sense of their own inadequacies. Thus, in the longer term, the fire-setting conditions are reinforced and future fire-setting remains a possibility. For any individual, there may be a combination of internal and external factors contributing to the behaviour and arson may serve multiple functions for the individual.

In summary, within this approach arson is viewed as an adaptive response since it provides a highly effective means of escaping from or changing difficult-to-tolerate circumstances when other means have proved impossible, excessively difficult, have been inhibited or ineffective or have been perceived as ineffective. It occurs when lack of confidence, skill or opportunity prevent problem solving by socially acceptable means.

As evidence supporting this theory, social skills deficits in arsonists were noted as early as 1969 (Hurley and Monahan, 1969) and corroborated by later work. Harris and Rice (1984) reported a study in which 13 fire-setters and a matched control sample were assessed using staff behavioural ratings, self-report questionnaires and behavioural measures. The results were considered to support the hypothesis that arsonists are generally less assertive than other hospitalized offenders and believe they have less control over their own lives. Similarly, Jackson, Hope and Glass (1987) compared 18 arsonists with 18 violent offenders and 18 controls (nurses) and found that they rated themselves as less assertive, as well as showing less interpersonal aggression both prior to and during their hospital admission.

In terms of treatment focusing on these social skills deficits, Rice and Chaplin (1979) described an evaluation of a social skills training programme with 10 male fire-setters detained in a maximum security hospital. The social skills training consisted of behavioural rehearsal, modelling, coaching, instruction and feedback based on situations identified by the group as difficult or devised by the therapist. The control treatment, consisting of the same pattern of sessions, was described as non-directive psychotherapy. Half of the identified group received social skills training first and half the control treatment. Assessment was conducted pre-, mid- and post-treatment and consisted of videotaped role plays, which were blind rated on four scales, and a written questionnaire assessment was made of knowledge of appropriately assertive responses. The results for the behavioural role-play assessment revealed significant improvements in both groups as a result of social skills training but not as a result of the control treatment. Results for the written test, while not significant, were in the same direction. With regard to follow-up data, it was reported that eight of the patients (who had been responsible for 19 fires in the 6 months prior to hospital admission) were released and had been living in the community an average of 12 months. During that time, none was known to have set or been suspected of setting a fire. While it is not possible to attribute this directly to the social skills training (not least because all the participants also received non-directive psychotherapy), it is at least an encouraging finding, particularly in a field where follow-up data of any kind is rare.

Also drawing on the functional analysis model, a comprehensive individualized approach to assessment and treatment was described by Clare *et al.* (1992). They presented a cognitive behavioural analysis and treatment – over an extended period – of a 23-year-old man with two serious arson convictions. As an illustration of the communicative nature of arson, on assessment by the authors, the patient identified anxiety as the most important precipitant of his fire-setting, followed by not being listened to or paid attention to, anger, sadness and boredom. The patient (detained in hospital) had a harelip and a cleft palate, a history of developmental delay, and attendance at a special school. His full scale IQ (WAIS-R) was 65 and his mother described him as socially isolated. In his early teenage years, he made a series of hoax calls to the fire brigade and then set a number of small fires, all linked to a wish to see and talk to firemen. This individual reported that the fire-setting did not seem to reduce his anxiety, but helped him to gain attention, feel less sad and possibly less angry.

A variety of treatment approaches were adopted. These included behavioural training in social and coping skills and a programme of daily activities in conjunction with specific interventions in relation to his attitude to fires (i.e., graded exposure and 'assisted' covert sensitization). After an 18 month treatment programme, including two facial operations, the patient was followed up for a further 30 months. At this time, there was no evidence that he made hoax calls to the fire services or set any fires either during his admission or on subsequent discharge to a staffed house. On two occasions during follow-up, he reported feeling tempted to set fires when he felt he was having difficulty in making his feelings understood. On both occasions, he used a combination of coping strategies and the 'assisted' covert sensitization tape.

In commenting on their work Clare *et al.* (1992) highlighted the apparent importance of the aversive covert sensitization procedure. However, they also noted that the client reflected that the procedure helped him desist from fire-setting due to the sound of the familiar calming voice on the tape. This highlights the difficulty in identifying the mechanism of therapeutic agency, in that there appeared to be in this case crossover from one behavioural modality (covert sensitization) to another (relaxation).

In view of these and other similar findings, treatment packages developed at secure hospitals in the United Kingdom have incorporated modules designed to develop inter- and intrapersonal skills with the aim of providing fire-setters with more appropriate and successful methods of controlling and influencing their environment (Jackson 1994; Swaffer, Haggett and Oxley, 2001). These treatment models will be reviewed in more detail later in the chapter. Unfortunately, very limited evaluation data, consisting of a handful of small case reports, has been reported to date.

Moving Towards Evidence-Based Practice in Treatment

Many treatment programmes for adult arsonists are primarily based on Jackson's (1994) functional analysis model. For example, Hall (1995) described a programme that consisted of four main components: education and information, coping strategies, self-awareness and self-esteem and family and related issues. Education and Information includes issues such as the dangers of fire, fire prevention, reactions of others to fire and fire-setters and personal beliefs in relation to these issues. Alternative Skills Training includes training in assertiveness, social problem solving, anxiety management, negotiation skills, conflict resolution and coping with insoluble situations. Self-Awareness and Self-Esteem addresses human rights; expectations of self and others; ideal, current and acceptable self; sources of self-esteem; and trust. Finally, Family and Related Issues is concerned with the function of fire-setting to the family and the institutional system, realistic appraisal of family members, family life cycle, drugs, alcohol and unemployment, abuse and abusing and sexuality. The delivery of this programme was described by Hall, who referred to evaluation by discussion, questionnaires and post-group assessments, but no data on these evaluations was made available.

Similar group interventions have also been run in UK prisons and special hospitals, which emphasize education about the consequences of fire-setting (Lynch, 2000). The model reported by Swaffer, Haggett and Oxley (2001) as conducted with mentally disordered fire-setters in a special hospital, involves a combination of group and individual work, delivered by a team (usually a nurse and psychologist). The group work component consists of four modules based on the structure suggested by Jackson, Hope and Glass (1987): (i) Dangers of fire – assessing and developing insight (12 sessions); (ii) Skills development – coping without fire-setting (24 sessions); (iii) Insight and self-awareness – assessing and developing (12 sessions); and (iv) Relapse prevention – practical strategies to help break offence cycles (14 sessions).

A series of papers by Taylor and colleagues (Taylor, Thorne, and Slavkin, 2004; Taylor *et al.*, 2002; Taylor *et al.*, 2006) report on a group intervention format similar to that reported by Swaffer, Haggett and Oxley (2001) with 14 mixed-gender patients with intellectual disabilities. For example, the latest paper by Taylor *et al.* (2006) reported on a two-year follow-up with six of the female patients from this group. None of the six had set a further fire, although it was noted that these individuals were either still living in the hospital, or in intensive support community placements.

In order to assess the extent to which group programmes such as those described earlier follow the principles for effective intervention outlined in the 'What Works' literature (Risk, Need, Responsivity; Andrews and Bonta, 2003), what is required is an evaluation of the extent to which the programmes address the criminogenic risk needs of fire-setters. Unfortunately, although previous theoretical models of arson have generated hypotheses about the possible biopsychosocial mechanisms that lead to fire-setting, these hypotheses have yet to be tested empirically. Furthermore, models such as Jackson's (1994) and Fineman's (1995) fail to account for the possibility of unique biopsychosocial trajectories leading to variations in arson that have been identified in empirical research (e.g., Fritzon, Canter, and Wilton, 2001).

Gannon *et al.*'s (2011) previously mentioned M-TTAF brings together existing theory and empirical contributions from the fire-setting literature to highlight four key pathways or trajectories (with a fifth, *mixed* type) that seem to predominate in arson. These are: (i) *Inappropriate fire interest/scripts*; (ii) *Offence-supportive attitudes*; (iii) *Self/emotional regulation issues; and* (iv) *Communication problems*. As Gannon *et al.* (2011) highlight, these four trajectories are very similar to Ward and Siegert's (2002) Pathways Model, which proposes that sexual offending is the result of (i) *distorted sexual scripts;* (ii) *anti-social cognitions*; (iii) *emotional dysregulation*; and (iv) *intimacy deficits.* Although Gannon *et al.*'s fourth pathway is labelled Communication problems, arguably such difficulties are likely to be linked to problems with intimacy. As Gannon *et al.* also highlight, it is the broader aspect of communication that is of critical importance as a risk factor for arson since this skill has the potential to cause difficulties across wide areas of social functioning, and not just intimate relationships. Compared to earlier models, the M-TTAF explains a broader range of fire-setting behaviour and incorporates the concept of fire-setting desistence and typological knowledge to distinguish between different trajectories of fire-setting. While the model is premised on the most recent research literature concerning fire-setters, it remains largely untested empirically. However, drawing the same corollary to the Ward and Siegert (2002) pathways model, Fritzon (2001) drew attention to the links between the four pathways (or trajectories) and the four forms of fire-setting observed in multivariate models utilizing the Faceted Action Systems Theory framework (Almond *et al.*, 2005; Canter and Fritzon, 1998; Doley, R., Fritzon, K. and Hollows, K. (2012) Empirical validation of the M-TTAF model: an analysis of pathways to offending in arsonist background characteristics and crime-scene actions. Manuscript in preparation; Fritzon, Canter and Wilton, 2001; Miller and Fritzon, 2007), thus providing some empirical support for these hypothesized four pathways that the M-TTAF model outlines.

The various treatment programmes described previously appear to cover only three of the four main M-TTAF pathways; there are no reported cases utilizing emotional regulation techniques with arsonists. However, in an adaptation of the Swaffer, Haggett and Oxley (2001) model by one of the present authors (Easton and Fritzon, 2004), a treatment package was delivered to three groups of eight women detained in a medium secure unit in England during 2004–2006. This adapted package incorporated emotional regulation skills including affect naming and recognition, as well as the use of self-soothing techniques to manage difficult emotions. This treatment programme also incorporated elements of both group work and individual work, and although no formal outcome data has been published, it was noted by ward staff that the women participants had reduced or ceased their self-harming behaviours as well as other expressions of emotional regulation difficulties, such as impulsive aggression towards others.

We are aware of one treatment programme that examines all four main M-TTAF pathways (see Gannon, Lockerbie and Tyler, 2012) which is currently undergoing evaluation with fire-setters in secure hospitals across numerous hospital sites in the United Kingdom. This treatment programme – named the *Firesetting Intervention Programme for Mentally Disordered Offenders (FIP-MO;* Gannon and Lockerbie, 2011) – is a semi-structured cognitive behavioural treatment programme for all-male or all-female patient groups and incorporates work examining fire interest and fire-related issues, offence-supportive cognition, communications problems, emotional regulation, the offence process and family/developmental factors. The results of this treatment programme evaluation are not due until sometime early 2013 (T. A. Gannon, personal communication, September 21, 2011). Presumably, however, the results will provide at least some empirical evidence regarding the effectiveness of treatment for mentally disordered fire-setters.

The M-TTAF model contains a number of hypotheses concerning risk pathways that contribute to fire-setting offending as well as a number of theories concerning the treatment needs of fire-setters. Further testing and validation of the M-TTAF is essential in order to integrate these hypotheses into a treatment approach. Some empirical evidence for the robustness of the four factors exists in the form of the conceptual links between this model and the Action Systems framework which has been found to reliably distinguish four themes in the actions and characteristics of fire-setters (Almond *et al.*, 2005; Fritzon, Canter and Wilton, 2001; Miller and Fritzon, 2007). Furthermore, a recent study (Doley, R., Fritzon, K. and Hollows, K. (2012) Empirical validation of the M-TTAF model: an analysis of pathways to offending in arsonist background characteristics and crime-scene actions. Manuscript in preparation.) has found further evidence for the four M-TTAF factors within the developmental and psychosocial characteristics of a sample of Australian fire-setters.

Future Directions: Risk Assessment

Risk assessment specific to fire-setters is evolving as our understanding of the risk and protective factors driving the behaviour broadens. Factors traditionally associated with the likelihood of repeat fire-setting in adult offenders include criminal history, mental illness and sociodemographic variables (Doley *et al.*, 2011). Doley *et al.* note that there is a lack of evidence comparing serial with one-time fire-setters, which limits the substantiation of these general factors as important in determining risk for repeat fire-setting. Doley *et al.* argue for the use of a general recidivism tool such as the LSI-R or LS/CMI (Andrews and Bonta, 1995; Andrews, Bonta and Wormwith, 2004) as a useful tool in structuring an individual risk assessment with an arson offender, given many have a lengthy criminal history encompassing offences other than fire-related crimes (Dickens *et al.*, 2009; Doley, 2009; Rice and Harris, 1991).

Another important aspect of aligning arson treatment development with 'What Works' Risk, Need, Responsivity principles is the establishment of dynamic criminogenic risk factors that both inform treatment as well as allow for the possibility of assessing risk for future offending.

Unlike other areas of offending behaviour, there is little evidence to support assertions that particular personality, behavioural or environmental factors actually relate to higher levels of risk for fire-setting than others. One study which used multiple regression to derive predictive equations for three forms of recidivism identified 10 variables associated with future fire-setting (Rice and Harris, 1996). Using data from a sample of 208 offenders with an index offence for arson, the research found that 16% went on to set a further fire within the follow-up period of 7.8 years, whilst 57% committed a non-violent offence and 31% committed a violent offence. The variables that had a positive association with fire-setting recidivism were (in decreasing order of strength): total number of fire-setting offences, whether there was a childhood fire-setting problem, whether the offender had acted alone. Additionally, the following variables had a negative association with recidivism: age, IQ, whether there were other criminal charges concurrent with the index fire and the participant's aggression score. This last variable implies that assertiveness and aggression lie on a continuum with previous research supporting the contention that individuals at the lower end of this scale (under-assertive) are those most likely to set fires.

It must be noted that this study employed predominantly historical (static) variables to predict risk. An important future aim for developing risk assessment tools for fire-setters is to include more dynamic factors, including motivational aspects involved in the acts themselves. The recognition that different fire-setting episodes by the same individual might involve various emotional and cognitive antecedents, as highlighted by the M-TTAF model (Gannon *et al.*, 2011) emphasizes the need to understand how the behaviour changes over time. Thus, risk prediction must take account of these dynamic fluctuations and the M-TTAF model appears to provide a sound theoretical framework for the identification of relevant dynamic risk factors within each of the four areas described.

In terms of the *Inappropriate fire interest/scripts* pathway, Doley and Watt (2012) note it is important for assessors to examine not only those factors likely to explain antisocial behaviour tendencies, but also the elements likely to lead a person to use fire as a means of stimulating change in their environment. One suggestion these authors highlight is the potential use of a modified Stroop task, developed by Gallagher-Duffy *et al.* (2009) for measuring fire interest. Presenting 49 images on a computer, of which 15 were fire-related stimuli (e.g., campfire, matchbook with smoking matches, fire truck), Gallagher-Duffy *et al.* hypothesized that emotionally relevant stimuli would require a longer response time, as well as decreased accuracy, thereby reflecting an information processing bias. Results demonstrated adolescents referred for fire-setting behaviours were less accurate and required more time for responses to fire-related stimuli, compared to two control groups of adolescents (healthy controls and clinic controls). Interestingly, it was noted in this study that self-reported interest in fire and fire-related materials did not significantly differentiate adolescent fire-setters from the two control groups. This is in contrast to the findings of Doley (2009) in which more arsonists than non-arsonists reported playing with fire as children, and more serial than one-time arsonists reported making hoax calls to emergency services and being obsessed with fire. Therefore, while both groups of adolescents may appear to have a similar interest in fire, on self-report measures, the possibility of an implicit measure that identifies a higher level of fire interest and is consistent with behavioural evidence (actually playing with fire) is potentially useful as a dynamic risk measure. Clearly, further research would be needed to determine whether differences on a Stroop task would actually lead to greater risk for future re-offending.

In terms of the M-TTAF pathway concerning *Offence-supportive cognition*, while there has been work suggesting attitudes supporting offending have been found to differentiate violent offenders and sex offenders from non-offenders (Bumby, 1996; Kelty, Hall and Watt, 2011), little attention has been given to this area in arson research, with a lack of standardized assessment tools for appraising cognitive content supportive of fire-setting behaviours (Doley *et al.*, 2011). Cognitive distortions arising from anger, interpersonal skills deficits and distortions in information processing have been highlighted as noteworthy areas for future development (Doley and Watt, 2012). Future research might also focus on examining core beliefs and empathy, given the relevance of these factors in risk assessment of violent and sex offenders (i.e., Andrews and Bonta, 2006; Blake and Gannon, 2008; Polaschek, Collie and Walkey, 2004).

The third pathway indicated in the M-TTAF model concerns *Self/emotional regulation issues*. Once again, this is a direction of research which has yet to be developed in the arson field. In their review, Doley and Watt (2012) focus on impulsivity and anger as potential factors of interest. In terms of impulsivity, for instance, the Barratt Impulsiveness Scale (BIS; Patton, Stanford, and Barratt, 1995) has been utilized with offenders, including arsonists (e.g., Smith and Waterman, 2006), and reveals moderate to high effect sizes in differentiating offender from non-offender samples (Patton, Stanford and Barratt, 1995; Smith and Waterman, 2006). The role of anger as a precursor of fire-setting behaviours (Kolko and Kazdin, 1991; Stewart, 1993) and as a predictor of arson recidivism (Root *et al.*, 2008) has been noted in the literature. Yet this factor has rarely been investigated using well-standardized and validated measures (Doley and Watt, 2012). The field is limited by a lack of standardized assessment tools with norms appropriate for a fire-setter assessment. Moreover, research is required to determine the role of these factors in recidivistic arson, as hypothesized by current theories such as the M-TTAF. Without an understanding of the relevance of the feature to serial fire-setting, it is not possible to determine accurately the utility of the construct as a risk assessment variable.

Recent research has highlighted the strong emotive component of fire-setting as a distinguishing feature between one-time and serial fire-setters (Doley, 2009). However, in a longitudinal study exploring differences between one-time and repeat fire-setters over a 24-year period, other authors have reported that while feelings of excitement and tension were evident more frequently in the repeat fire-setter group, overall it was not a common feature for this sample (Dickens *et al.*, 2009). The discrepant results may speak to differences in the source of data. Doley used file information as well as self-report through interviews with convicted offenders, whereas Dickens *et al.* based their results on data from file reviews. Potentially, some of the elevated emotional elements may have not been routinely recorded throughout the duration of the lengthy study period, leading to an underestimation of the prevalence of this component in fire-setters in the sample (Doley *et al.*, 2011). Clearly, future research needs to focus on establishing the role of emotional issues in fire-setting in order to clarify the relevance of this factor as a component for the assessment of risk of repeat arson offending.

Finally, the M-TAFF suggests a fourth pathway involving *Communication problems*. The limited interpersonal skills of arsonists have been frequently commented on, as discussed previously within this chapter. As with many offenders, arsonists exhibit limited social skills and difficulties in interpersonal relations, as well as maladjustment across a range of life domains such as education, employment and peer and personal relations (Barker, 1994; Bradford, 1982; O'sullivan and Kelleher, 1987; Puri, Baxter and Cordess, 1995; Sapsford, Banks and Smith, 1978; Vreeland and Levin, 1980). Arsonists are also typically described as less self-confident and assertive than other offenders (Geller, 1987; Hurley and Monahan, 1969; Inciardi, 1970; McKerracher and Dacre, 1966; Rice and Harris, 1991) with problems of shyness, social isolation, occupational maladjustment and difficulty in expressing anger verbally (Bradford, 1982; Inciardi, 1970; Leong, 1992; Lewis and Yarnell, 1951; O'sullivan and Kelleher, 1987; Puri, Baxter and Cordess, 1995; Rix, 1994; Tennent *et al.*, 1971). However, the role of communication issues in distinguishing serial from one-time arsonists has yet to be substantiated in the empirical literature. Accordingly, while it is a high-frequency feature in many arsonist samples, the utility of this factor in risk assessment for repeat fire-setting is yet to be established empirically.

Conclusions

The current chapter has outlined existing treatment approaches to arson, and reviewed evidence for their efficacy. In addition, we have examined how the hypothesized areas of criminogenic risk needs could be assessed, using already existing self-report and implicit assessment technologies. Unfortunately, the literature is sparse and a number of potentially promising treatment models have only been evaluated through small or single case study designs, so their applicability to larger samples of fire-setters remains untested.

Nevertheless, the success of individualized approaches to treatment with fire-setters (as with other offenders) highlights the potential for a combined approach to treatment, consisting of a unified package of treatment addressing the criminogenic needs as outlined in the M-TTAF model, supplemented by an individual treatment plan targeting the assessed areas of deficit. For example, an individual whose primary identified area of risk need is emotional regulation, and whose fire-setting is always directed at people with whom a conflict has occurred, may demonstrate a long-standing and recurring pattern of interactions that lend themselves to conceptualization and formulation within a Cognitive Analytic Therapy frame. Thus, individual therapy may be offered to supplement the generic group fire-setting programme. Alternatively, an individual who has a pattern of fire-setting, which is formulated as representing a deviant fire interest that appears to be associated in some way with his/her concept of self, such as indicated by *hero* fire-setters, may benefit from an individualized case formulation and treatment plan adopting a Narrative perspective (McAdams, 2001). Of course, within a corrections framework, it may not be practical from a resource perspective to deliver both group and individual treatment, even though this type of delivery model exists in other areas of clinical practice (e.g., Dialectical Behaviour Therapy, Linehan, 1993).

The M-TTAF (Gannon *et al.*, 2011) model indicating four primary trajectories for arson is conceptually well supported by existing theory for other crime types (e.g., Ward and Siegert, 2002), builds on previous theories of fire-setting (Fineman, 1995; Jackson, 1994) and empirical classifications from the profiling literature (Doley, R., Fritzon, K. and Hollows, K. (2012) Empirical validation of the M-TTAF model: an analysis of pathways to offending in arsonist background characteristics and crime-scene actions. Manuscript in preparation; Fritzon, Canter and Wilton, 2001). It is important that treatment models deriving from this (or indeed other) theoretical frameworks be subjected to rigorous evaluation so that a body of literature demonstrating 'What Works' with arsonists can be amassed. Given the small numbers of arsonists that may be found within individual prisons and forensic mental health institutions, it is important for professionals to be aware of this emerging literature so that a consolidated and consistent approach can be taken to case conceptualization, treatment planning and treatment outcome reporting. In some countries such as Australia, a national forum for the prevention of bushfire arson has led to widespread recognition, collaboration and networking of professionals. Similarly, in the United Kingdom, the government has provided large-scale funding for research and development of a treatment programme for arsonists (T. A. Gannon, personal communication, September 21, 2011). International developments such as these provide an opportunity for targeted efforts at building a body of literature to support and validate the models summarized in this chapter.

References

Almond, L., Duggan, L., Shine, J. and Canter, D. (2005) Test of the arson action system model in an incarcerated population. *Psychology, Crime & Law*, 11 (1), 1–15.

Andrews, D.A. and Bonta, J. (1995) *Level of Service Inventory – Revised*, Multi-Health Systems, Toronto.

Andrews, D.A. and Bonta, J. (2003) *The Psychology of Criminal Conduct*, 3rd edn, Anderson, Cincinnati.

Andrews, D.A. and Bonta, J. (2006) *The Psychology of Cirminal Conduct*, 4th edn, Lexis Nexis Matthew Bender, New York.

Andrews, D.A., Bonta, J. and Wormwith, S. (2004) *The Level of Service/Case Management Inventory (LS/CMI)*, Multi-Health Systems, Toronto.

Barker, A. (1994) *Arson: A Review of the Psychiatric Literature*. Maudsley Monographs no. 35, Oxford University Press, New York, p. 110.

Blake, E. and Gannon, T. (2008) Social perception deficits, cognitive distortions, and empathy deficits in sex offenders: a brief review. *Trauma, Violence, and Abuse*, 9 (1), 34–55.

Bradford, J. (1982) Arson: a clinical study. *Canadian Journal of Psychiatry*, 27 (3), 188–193.

Bumby, K.M. (1996) Assessing the cognitive distortions of child molesters and rapists: development and validation of the MOLEST and RAPE scales. *Sexual Abuse: A Journal of Research and Treatment*, 8, 37–54.

Canter, D. (1994) *Criminal Shadows*, HarperCollins, London.

Canter, D. and Fritzon, K. (1998) Differentiating arsonists: a model of firesetting actions and characteristics. *Legal and Criminological Psychology*, 3, 73–96.

Clare, I., Murphy, G., Cox, D. and Chaplin, E. (1992) Assessment and treatment of firesetting: a single-case investigation using a cognitive-behavioural model. *Criminal Behaviour and Mental Health*, 2, 253–268.

Dickens, G., Sugarman, P., Edgar, S. *et al.* (2009) Recidivism and dangerousness in arsonists: characteristics of repeat firesetters referred for psychiatric assessment. *Journal of Forensic Psychiatry & Psychology*, 20, 621–639.

Dolan, M., McEwan, T., Doley, R. and Fritzon, K. (2011) Risk factors and risk assessment in juvenile firesetting. *Psychology, Psychiatry and Law*, 18 (3), 378–394.

Doley, R. (2009) *A Snapshot of Serial Arson in Australia*, Lambert Academic Publishing, Saarbrücken.

Doley, R. and Watt, B. (2012) Assessment of firesetters, in *Arson and Mental Health: Theory, Research and Practice* (eds G. Dickens, P. Sugarman and T. Gannon), RCPsych Pubs, London, pp. 184–205.

Doley, R., Fineman, K., Fritzon, K. *et al.* (2011) Risk factors for recidivistic arson in adult arson offenders. *Psychology, Psychiatry and Law*, 18 (3), 409–423.

Ducat, L. and Ogloff, J. (2011) Understanding and preventing bushfire-setting: a psychological perspective. *Psychology, Psychiatry and Law*, 18 (3), 341–356.

Easton, D. and Fritzon, K. (2004) Unpublished treatment manual. The Dene hospital, East Sussex.

Fineman, K.R. (1995) A model for the qualitative analysis of child and adult fire deviant behavior. *American Journal of Forensic Psychology*, 13 (1), 31–60.

Fransella, F. and Adams, B. (1966) An illustration of the use of repertory grid technique in a clinical setting. *British Journal of Social and Clinical Psychology*, 5, 51–62.

Freud, S. (1932) The acquisition of power over fire. *International Journal of Psychoanalysis*, 13 (Part 4), 405–410.

Fritzon, K. (2001) An examination of the relationship between distance travelled and motivational aspects of firesetting behaviour. *Journal of Environmental Psychology*, 21, 45–60.

Fritzon, K., Canter, D. and Wilton, Z. (2001) The application of an action systems model to destructive behaviour: the examples of arson and terrorism. *Behavioral Sciences and the Law*, 19, 657–690.

Fritzon, K., Dolan, M., Doley, R. and McEwan, T. (2011) Juvenile fire-setting: a review of treatment programs. *Psychology, Psychiatry and Law*, 18 (3), 395–408.

Fritzon, K., Lewis, H. and Doley, R. (2011) Looking at the characteristics of adult arsonists from a narrative perspective. *Psychology, Psychiatry and Law*, 18 (3), 424–438.

Gallagher-Duffy, J., MacKay, S., Duffy, J. *et al.* (2009) The pictorial fire stroop: a measure of processing bias for fire-related stimuli. *Journal of Abnormal Child Psychology*, 37, 1165–1176.

Gannon, T.A. and Pina, A. (2010) Firesetting: psychopathology, theory and treatment. *Aggression and Violent Behavior*, 15, 224–238.

Gannon, T.A. and Lockerbie, L. (2011) Firesetting Intervention Programme for Mentally Disordered Offenders (FIP-MO). CORE-FP, University of Kent and Kent Forensic Psychiatry Services, NHS.

Gannon, T.A., Ó Ciardha, C., Doley, R.M. and Alleyne, E. (2011) The Multi-Trajectory Theory of Adult Firesetting (M-TTAF). *Aggression and Violent Behavior*, 17 (2), 107–121.

Gannon, T.A., Lockerbie, L. and Tyler, N. (2012) A long time coming? The Firesetting Intervention Programme for Mentally Disordered Offenders (FIP-MO). *Forensic Update*, 102, 6–10.

Geller, J. (1984) Arson: an unforeseen sequela of deinstitutionalization. *American Journal of Psychiatry*, 141, 504–508.

Geller, J. (1987) Firesetting in the adult psychiatric population. *Hospital and Community Psychiatry*, 38 (5), 501–506.

Geller, J. (1992) Communicative arson. *Hospital and Community Psychiatry*, 43, 76–77.

Hall, G. (1995) Using group work to understand arsonists. *Nursing Standard*, 9 (23), 25–28.

Hall, I., Clayton, P. and Johnson, P. (2005) Arson and learning disability, in *Handbook of Forensic Learning Disabilities* (eds T. Riding, C. Swann and B. Swann), Radcliffe Publishing, Abingdon, pp. 51–72.

Harris, G. and Rice, M. (1984) Mentally disordered firesetters: psychodynamic versus empirical approaches. *International Journal of Law and Psychiatry*, 7, 19–34.

Hill, R., Langevin, R., Paitich, D. *et al.* (1982) Is arson an aggressive act or a property offence? A controlled study of psychiatric referrals. *Canadian Journal of Psychiatry*, 27 (8), 648–654.

Hollin, C.R. and Epps, K.J. (1996) Adolescent firesetters, in *Clinical Approaches to Working with Young Offenders* (eds C.J. Hollin and K. Howells), John Wiley & Sons, Ltd, Chichester, pp. 197–207.

Horley, J. and Bowlby, D. (2011) Theory, research, and intervention with arsonists. *Aggression and Violent behaviour*, 16, 241–249.

Hurley, W. and Monahan, T. (1969) Arson: the criminal and the crime. *British Journal of Criminology*, 9, 4–21.

Inciardi, J. (1970) The adult firesetter: a typology. *Criminology*, 8 (2), 145–155.

Jackson, H. (1994) Assessment of fire-setters, in *The Assessment of Criminal Behaviours of Clients in Secure Settings* (eds M. McMurran and J. Hodge), Jessica Kingsley Publishers, London, pp. 94–126.

Jackson, H., Hope, S. and Glass, C. (1987) Why are arsonists not violent offenders? *International Journal of Offender Therapy and Comparative Criminology*, 31 (2), 143–151.

Kelly, G.A. (1955) *The Psychology of Personal Constructs*, 2 vols, Norton, New York.

Kelty, S.F., Hall, G. and Watt, B.D. (2011) You have to hit some people! Endorsing violent sentiments (Part 2: The measurement and criminogenic nature of justifications for violence). *Psychiatry, Psychology and Law*, 18 (1), 15–32.

Kolko, D.J. (2004) Firesetters, in *The Essential Handbook of Offender Assessment and Treatment* (ed. C.R. Hollin), John Wiley & Sons, Inc., Chichester, pp. 177–200.

Kolko, D. and Kazdin, A. (1991) Aggression and psychopathology in matchplaying and firesetting children: a replication and extension. *Journal of Clinical Child Psychology*, 20 (2), 191–201.

Kolko, D.J., Watson, S. and Faust, J. (1991) Fire safety/prevention skills training to reduce involvement with fire in young psychiatric inpatients: preliminary findings. *Behaviour Therapy*, 22, 269–284.

Lande, S. (1980) A combination of orgasmic reconditioning and covert sensitisation in the treatment of a fire fetish. *Journal of Behaviour Therapy and Experimental Psychiatry*, 11, 291–296.

Leong, G. (1992) A psychiatric study of persons charged with arson. *Journal of Forensic Sciences*, 37 (5), 1319–1326.

Lewis, N. and Yarnell, H. (1951) *Pathological Firesetting (Pyromania)*. Nervous and Mental Disease Monographs, No. 82, Nervous and Mental Disease Publishing Company, New York, p. 437.

Linehan, M.M. (1993) *Cognitive-Behavioral Treatment of Borderline Personality Disorder*, Guilford, New York.

Lowenstein, L.F. (2003) Recent research into arson (1992–2000): incidence, causes and associated features, predictions, comparative studies and prevention and treatment. *Psychiatry, Psychology and Law*, 10 (1), 192–198.

Lynch, A. (2000) Convicted arsonists talk about fire-setting. *Fire*, 92, 16–18.

McAdams, D.P. (1988) Biography, narrative, and lives: an introduction, in *Psychobiography and Life Narratives* (eds D.P. McAdams and L.R. Ochberg), Duke University Press, Durham, pp. 1–18).

McAdams, D.P. (2001) The psychology of life stories. *Review of General Psychology*, 5, 100–122.

McEwan, T. and Freckelton, I. (2011) Assessment, treatment and sentencing of arson offenders: an overview. *Psychiatry, Psychology and Law*, 18 (3), 318–328.

McGuire, J. (2006) An invited critique of cognitive analytic therapy for offenders, in *Cognitive Analytic Therapy for Offenders: A New Approach to Forensic Psychotherapy* (eds P.H. Pollock, M. Stowell-Smith and M. Gopfert), Routledge, East Sussex, pp. 327–330.

McKerracher, D. and Dacre, A. (1966) A study of arsonists in a special security hospital. *British Journal of Psychiatry*, 112, 1151–1154.

Miller, S. and Fritzon, K. (2007) Functional consistency across two behavioural modalities: firesetting and self harm in female special hospital patients. *Criminal Behaviour and Mental Health*, 17, 31–44.

Ó Ciardha, C. and Gannon, T.A. (2012) The implicit theories of firesetters: a preliminary conceptualization. *Aggression and Violent Behaviour*, 17 (2), 122–128.

O'Sullivan, G. and Kelleher, M. (1987) A study of firesetters in the South-West of Ireland. *British Journal of Psychiatry*, 151, 818–823.

Patton, J.H., Stanford, M.S. and Barratt, E.S. (1995) Factor structure of the Barratt Impulsiveness Scale. *Journal of Clinical Psychology*, 51, 768–774.

Polaschek, D.L.L. and Gannon, T.A. (2004) The implicit theories of rapists: what convicted offenders tell us. *Sexual Abuse: Journal of Research and Treatment*, 16 (4), 299–314.

Polaschek, D.L.L., Collie, R.M. and Walkey, F.H. (2004) Criminal attitudes to violence: development and preliminary validation of a scale for male prisoners. *Aggressive Behavior*, 30, 484–503.

Pollock, P. (2006) Cognitive analytic therapy for an arsonist with borderline personality disorder, in *Cognitive Analytic Therapy for Offenders: A New Approach to Forensic Psychotherapy* (eds P.H. Pollock, M. Stowell-Smith and M. Gopfert), Routledge, East Sussex, pp. 43–65.

Puri, B., Baxter, R. and Cordess, C. (1995) Characteristics of firesetters: a study and proposed multiaxial psychiatric classification. *British Journal of Psychiatry*, 166, 393–396.

Quinsey, V., Chaplin, T. and Upfold, D. (1989) Arsonists and sexual arousal to firesetting: correlation unsupported. *Journal of Behavior Therapy and Experimental Psychology*, 20 (3), 203–209.

Reinhardt, J.M. (1957) *Sex Perversions and Sex Crimes*, Charles C Thomas, Springfield.

Rice, M.E. and Chaplin, T.C. (1979) Social skills training for hospitalized male arsonists. *Journal of Behavior Research and Experimental Psychiatry*, 10, 105–108.

Rice, M.E. and Harris, G. (1991) Firesetters admitted to a maximum security psychiatric institution. *Journal of Interpersonal Violence*, 6 (4), 461–475.

Rice, M.E. and Harris, G. (1996) Predicting the recidivism of mentally disordered firesetters. *Journal of Interpersonal Violence*, 11 (3), 364–375.

Rix, K. (1994) A psychiatric study of adult arsonists. *Medicine Science and Law*, 34 (1), 21–34.

Root, C., MacKay, S., Henderson, J. *et al.* (2008) The link between maltreatment and juvenile fireset-ting: correlates and underlying mechanisms. *Child Abuse and Neglect*, 32, 161–176.

Ryle, A. (2003) *Cognitive Analytic Therapy: Active Participation in Change*, John Wiley & Sons, Ltd, Chichester.

Sapsford, R., Banks, C. and Smith, D. (1978) Arsonists in prison. *Journal of Medicine, Science and Law*, 18 (4), 247–254.

Smith, P. and Waterman, M. (2006) Self-reported aggression and impulsivity in forensic and non-forensic populations: the role of gender and experience. *Journal of Family Violence*, 21, 425–437.

Soothill, K. and Pope, P. (1973) Arson: a twenty-year cohort study. *Medicine, Science, and the Law*, 13 (2), 127–138.

Stewart, L. (1993) Profile of female firesetters: implications for treatment. *British Journal of Psychiatry*, 163, 248–256.

Swaffer, T., Haggett, M. and Oxley, T. (2001) Mentally disordered firesetters: a structured intervention programme. *Clinical Psychology and Psychtherapy*, 8, 468–475.

Taylor, J., Thorne, I., Robertson, A. and Avery, G. (2002) Evaluation of a group intervention for con-victed arsonists with mild and borderline intellectual disabilities. *Criminal Behaviour and Mental Health*, 12, 282–293.

Taylor, J., Thorne, I. and Slavkin, M. (2004) Treatment of fire setting behaviour, in *Offenders with Developmental Disabilities* (eds W.L. Lindsey, J.L. Taylor and P. Sturmey), John Wiley & Sons, Ltd, Chichester, pp. 221–240.

Taylor, J., Robertson, A., Thorne, I. *et al.* (2006) Responses of female fire-setters with mild and bor-derline intellectual disabilities to a group intervention. *Journal of Applied Research in Intellectual Disabilities*, 19 (2), 179–190.

Tennent, T., McQuaid, A., Loughnane, T. and Hands, A. (1971) Female arsonists. *British Journal of Psychiatry*, 119, 497–502.

Vreeland, R. and Levin, B. (1980) Psychological aspects of firesetting, in *Fires and Human Behaviour*, 1st edn (ed. D. Canter), David Fulton, London, pp. 31–46.

Ward, T. (2000) Sexual offenders' cognitive distortions as implicit theories. *Aggression and Violent Behaviour*, 5 (5), 491–507.

Ward, T. and Siegert, R. J. (2002) Toward a comprehensive theory of child sexual abuse: a theory knitting perspective. *Psychology, Crime & Law*, 9, 319–351.

Zillman, D., Katcher, A.H. and Milavsky, B. (1972) Excitation transfer from physical exercise to subsequent aggressive behaviour. *Journal of Experimental Social Psychology*, 8 (3), 247–259.

15

What Works with Female Sexual Offenders

Franca Cortoni[1] and Theresa A. Gannon[2]

[1]University of Montreal, Canada
[2]University of Kent, UK

It is estimated that female sexual offenders constitute approximately 5% of all sexual offenders (Cortoni, Hanson and Coache, 2009). Among general female offenders, approaches to treatment based on the 'What works' literature have been shown to be effective in reducing criminal recidivism (see Blanchette and Brown, 2006 for a review of that literature). Among female sexual offenders, however, systematic empirically validated knowledge about the factors related to sexual offending among females has only recently emerged (see Gannon and Cortoni, 2010). Nevertheless, there is now sufficient information to permit the elaboration of gender-informed empirically based assessment and treatment practices with female sexual offenders. This chapter reviews this information and provides guidelines on what the research evidence suggests *would* work with female sexual offenders.

What Works with the Female Sexual Offender Population?

The following discussion on effective treatment for female sexual offenders is based on the basic premises of Andrews and Bonta's (2010) rehabilitation model. Starting from a social-psychological theory of criminal behaviour, over the last two decades, Andrews and Bonta (2010) have developed and refined the principles of effective correctional interventions. While technically, Andrews (2001) discusses 18 specific principles, there are 3 overriding principles, the risk-need-responsivity principles, containing a number of more specific principles, that directly speak to the 'who, what, and how' of treatment with offenders. The other principles are related to the overall process of developing and implementing interventions, issues which are not discussed in this chapter.

The risk principle

The risk principle guides the selection of participants for treatment. In this context, treatment does not imply a medical model of offending in which offending behaviour is

What Works in Offender Rehabilitation: An Evidence-Based Approach to Assessment and Treatment,
First Edition. Edited by Leam A. Craig, Louise Dixon and Theresa A. Gannon.
© 2013 John Wiley & Sons, Ltd. Published 2013 by John Wiley & Sons, Ltd.

viewed as a psychopathology. Rather, treatment refers to psychosocial interventions designed to reduce the likelihood of recidivism (Hollin, 2006). The risk principle determines how much treatment an offender should receive, with higher-risk offenders needing more intense levels of interventions and follow-up. There are two aspects to the risk principle: the assessment of risk and the matching of treatment intensity to that risk level (Andrews, Bonta and Hoge, 1990; Andrews, Bonta and Wormith, 2006). In order to assess risk among female sexual offenders, an understanding of the factors specifically associated with their offending behaviour is necessary. Research has shown that there are two types of risk factors: static and dynamic (Andrews and Bonta, 2010). Static risk factors are aspects in the offender's history that are related to recidivism and cannot be changed through interventions. Examples of static factors include past criminal history and age. Dynamic factors are those aspects of the offender that are amenable to change and, when modified, are related to changes in recidivism. Examples of dynamic factors are antisocial attitudes, antisocial associates and low self-control.

Female sexual offenders, like all offenders, and indeed all human beings, demonstrate individual differences that will impact on their chances of engaging in a wide range of behaviours. They will consequently also vary on their chances/risk of engaging in future criminal behaviour. This is why a valid assessment of risk is necessary to differentiate among these women in order to match them with the most appropriate level of treatment. Of course, this is easier said than done: contrary to the well-developed state of knowledge regarding risk among male sexual offenders, knowledge of the risk factors of female sexual offenders is still in its infancy. There are currently no validated tools designed to assess risk of sexual recidivism among female sexual offenders. Hence, their assessment of risk of recidivism is a task that necessarily requires the use of a structured professional judgement approach.

Recidivism rates of female sexual offenders   As a first step, any evaluation of risk requires knowledge of the base rates of recidivism for the population of interest. For example, the base rates of recidivism among male sexual offenders are, over a follow-up period of five years, 13.5% for new sexual offences, 25.5% for new violent (including sexual) offences, and 36% for any new type of recidivism (Hanson and Morton-Bourgon, 2005). These base rates demonstrate that male sexual offenders are more likely to commit a new non-sexual, rather than a new sexual, offence once they have been detected and sanctioned by the criminal justice system. In addition, the sexual recidivism rates of males have also been found to vary according to the age and gender of the victim (Harris and Hanson, 2004), indicating that not all sexual offenders present with the same risk of reoffending. This is also the case for female sexual offenders. As we will see later, women's varying recidivism rates, however, do not appear based on victim's age and gender, but rather on offending *type*.

First, research shows that women who commit sexual offences have very different base rates of recidivism from their male counterparts. In an initial review of the recidivism rates of 380 convicted female sexual offenders, Cortoni and Hanson (2005) found a sexual recidivism rate of 1% with a five-year follow-up period. The number of female offenders included in that review, however, was small and a number of large sample studies have appeared since that review was completed. Consequently, Cortoni, Hanson and Coache (2010) conducted an updated meta-analytic review of the recidivism rates of female sexual offenders.

Cortoni, Hanson and Coache (2010) analysed the results from a total of 10 recidivism studies with an aggregated total number of 2490 convicted female sexual offenders and an average follow-up time of 6.5 years. Cumulative sexual, violent and any recidivism were examined separately, thereby permitting comparison with the recidivism base rates of male sexual offenders. The analyses showed that the recidivism rates among female sexual offenders are much lower than those of males. Specifically, the weighted average recidivism rates were 1.5% for new sexual offences, 6% for new violent (including sexual) offences, and 20% for any new type of recidivism. These results establish that, like male sexual offenders, female sexual offenders also engage in various types of criminal activities beside their sexually offending behaviour. Further, and more importantly, these results confirm that the base rate of sexual recidivism among women is extremely low.

One of the studies included in the Cortoni, Hanson and Coache (2010) meta-analysis was that of Sandler and Freeman (2009). Sandler and Freeman (2009) examined the recidivism rates and the factors associated with recidivism among 1400 female sexual offenders convicted in the State of New York. Their study indicates that two different types of female offending patterns are associated with different recidivism rates: (i) females convicted of contact (hands-on) or pornography sexual offences (i.e., behaviours typically considered sexual offences in the male sexual offender recidivism studies) and (ii) women engaged only in prostitution-related offences (e.g., promoting prostitution of a child or patronizing prostitution of a child). The distinction between women who only engage in prostitution-related offences and those with contact offences is important: the prostitution-only females actually had much higher 'sexual' recidivism rates than those with hands-on (including child-related pornography) offences. The hands-on offenders had a 1.2% sexual recidivism rate (22 out of 1387) while the prostitution-only group had a 12.66% rate of recidivism (10 out of the 79 women). Perhaps more importantly, these women were all rearrested for new prostitution-related offences; none had engaged in hands-on offending. Consequently, and although this evidence is of course preliminary, it suggests that evaluators (and researchers) should distinguish between women who only commit prostitution types of offences from those with hands-on or pornography offences, as their risk of recidivism and accompanying risk factors appear very different.

Assessing risk among females   Besides understanding base rates, an assessment of risk entails an evaluation of the static and dynamic factors established by research as being related to recidivism. Over the last 20 years, great strides have been made in our understanding of these issues in male sexual offenders (see Chapter 5 for a review). In contrast, research into the risk factors of female sexual offenders is still in its infancy but emerging results suggest promising areas of investigation.

Before examining the risk factors of female sexual offenders, a discussion of the term 'high risk' within the context of these women's risk for future recidivism is warranted. Compared to men, women have not only shown a lower involvement in criminal activity but also lower recidivism rates (Blanchette and Brown, 2006). For example, among offenders released from the Correctional Service of Canada (CSC) during the 1990s, the two-year reconviction rate for new violent offences in female offenders was half the rate of the male offenders (6.7% versus 13.2%; Bonta, Rugge and Dauvergne, 2003). Consequently, while some women may present with a *higher* risk of recidivism, the comparison is in relation to other female sexual offenders, and not necessarily indicative of an absolute *high* risk of recidivism. In fact, in comparison to males, given their much lower base rates of recidivism, female sexual offenders would virtually never be considered to pose a *high risk* for sexual recidivism. This issue indicates the difference between relative versus absolute rates of recidivism; evaluators need to carefully frame the evaluation of risk of recidivism of female sexual offenders within that context (Vess, 2011).

In terms of factors related to the commission of new offences, as with males, it appears that the presence of a prior criminal history and being at a younger age is indicative of a *higher* risk of recidivism among female sexual offenders – but only for new non-sexual offences. Specifically, in her follow-up of 471 women, Vandiver (2007) found that the number of prior convictions for any type of offence predicted rearrest for new general and violent offences. Similarly, in their study of 1466 women, Sandler and Freeman (2009) found that prior misdemeanours, prior drug offences, and prior violent offences were related to non-sexual recidivism. In addition, a younger age (less than 30) was related to non-sexual recidivism. The finding that prior criminal history and younger age are related to future general recidivism among female sexual offenders is not surprising. This finding is gender-neutral in that it holds true for both male and female offenders (Andrews and Bonta, 2010; Blanchette and Brown, 2006).

In terms of factors related to sexual recidivism, different results have emerged. Despite having a large sample ($N = 471$) and a high base rate of sexual recidivism among women (10.8%), Vandiver (2007) could not establish any static factor specifically related to the commission of a new sexual offence. Sandler and Freeman (2009) did find a relationship between age and sexual recidivism. In contrast to males though, these authors found that being *older* was linearly related to sexual recidivism among females, but *only* for those women convicted of promoting/patronizing prostitution. For females convicted of contact (hands-on) or pornography sexual offences (i.e., behaviours typically considered sexual offences in the male sexual offender recidivism studies), age was not related to sexual recidivism.

The different patterns of age in relation to sexual recidivism established by Sandler and Freeman (2009) was based on the type of 'sexual offence' committed by the women, raising an important issue related to the definition of sexual offending by women. While sustained efforts have led to consistent definitions of what constitutes a sexual crime in the male research (e.g., Hanson and Morton-Bourgon, 2005; Harris *et al.*, 2003; Quinsey *et al.*, 1995), the story is not so clear among females. Results from Sandler and Freeman (2009) indicate that there are actually two distinct subgroups of women that are considered 'sexual offenders' in their study: those with actual hands-on or other sexually related offences such as child pornography (this group would be equivalent to standard definitions for male sexual offenders) and those with prostitution types of offences (males only convicted of prostitution-related offences would not be considered sexual offenders).

Finally, despite the low base rates of sexual recidivism, Sandler and Freeman (2009) found that the presence of a prior child abuse offence *of any type* was specifically and only related to sexual recidivism – but only for hands-on offenders. This finding is certainly gender-specific in that research has never identified a general pattern of child abuse as being related to sexual recidivism among male sexual offenders. The significance of this factor is as of yet unclear. Perhaps because women tend to be the primary caregivers, they are more likely than men to come to the attention of the criminal justice system for non-sexual abuse of children. Alternatively, and perhaps more likely, it may be that the sexual abuse of children, for these women, is part of a broader generalized pattern of abuse against children. Of course, these postulations are still hypothetical and await empirical verification.

There is currently no validated actuarial risk assessment tool to assess the risk of sexual recidivism among women. As a result, many evaluators turn to risk tools for male sexual offenders (e.g., STATIC-99, Hanson and Thornton, 2000) in the mistaken belief that such tools are better than nothing. There are two reasons why male-based tools are inappropriate to assess risk of recidivism among female sexual offenders. First, these risk assessment instruments provide estimates of risk of recidivism that are predicated on the base rate of recidivism among adult male sexual offenders. Consequently, given the significantly lower rates of sexual recidivism of female sexual offenders, these assessment instruments would grossly overestimate risk among these women. Second, the items in male-based risk assessment tools were selected based on their established empirical relationship with recidivism among *male* sexual offenders. For example, having male, stranger, and/or unrelated victims all have a well-established relationship to sexual recidivism of male offenders (Hanson and Thornton, 2000). However, no research to date has established a relationship between those factors and sexual recidivism among females. For example, in their examination of the recidivism patterns of 61 female sexual offenders incarcerated in Canada between 1972 and 1998, Williams and Nicholaichuk (2001) found two women who had committed a new sexual offence. The distinguishing feature was that both were the only ones who had exclusively engaged in solo sexual offending – a factor not present in male-based tools. Williams and Nicholaichuk found no relationship between the various items of the RRASOR (Rapid Risk Assessment Sexual Offender Recidivism – Hanson, 1997) and sexual recidivism for these women nor did they find any evidence that having a particular type of victim was related to sexual recidivism. Hence, risk assessment tools for males not only overestimate risk in female sexual offenders, but they provide these overestimates on the basis of items that have no demonstrated links to female sexual recidivism.

Like in men, general (i.e., non-sexual) recidivism is much more common than sexual recidivism among female sexual offenders. Evaluators tasked with the assessment of these women should therefore select a risk assessment tool that has been validated to assess risk of recidivism among female offenders in general (e.g., LSI-R, Andrews and Bonta, 1995). The use of general risk assessment tools, however, still requires an understanding of the research on risk factors and recidivism among general female offenders as these issues differ according to the gender of the offender (e.g., Blanchette and Brown, 2006; Folsom and Atkinson, 2007; Holtfreter and Cupp, 2007; Manchak *et al.*, 2009).

Given the lack of validated tools to assess risk of sexual recidivism, an empirically guided clinical judgement of risk should be used. This approach to risk assessment normally entails that the prediction of risk for sexual recidivism is based on a structured judgement of the extent and combination of *established* (i.e., empirically validated) risk factors in a given case. While risk factors for sexual recidivism among females have not been validated, they could plausibly include the dynamic elements that have been established in clinical samples. The ways in which these factors manifest themselves in female sexual offenders, however, are likely to be different from the typical patterns found in male sexual offenders (e.g., Gannon, Rose and Ward, 2008). Ultimately, however, when conducting an assessment of female sexual offenders, it must be remembered that the base rate of sexual recidivism among women is extremely low. Consequently, conclusions on the likely risk of sexual recidivism in a given case must be framed within that context.

The need principle

The need principle suggests that *criminogenic needs*, as opposed to general psychological needs, are the appropriate targets of treatment. Criminogenic needs are those elements that are directly related to the offending behaviour and that are changeable. There is a rich and extensive theoretical literature, backed by empirical evidence, on the factors related to criminal behaviour in general as well as for subtypes of offending such as violent and sexual crimes (e.g., Andrews and Bonta, 2010; Hanson and Morton-Bourgon, 2005; Ward, Polaschek and Beech, 2006). This literature recognizes that criminal behaviour is learned rather than inherent to the person, and that there are many factors related to criminality that are amenable to change through therapeutic intervention.

Criminogenic needs are also called *criminogenic factors* or *dynamic risk factors*. They are in fact those same dynamic risk factors that form part of a comprehensive risk assessment. Research shows that it is those criminogenic factors that have clinical relevance for intervention when the aim is to manage and reduce the risk of further involvement in criminal behaviour (Andrews and Bonta, 2010). Targeting general psychological or other factors unrelated to the offending behaviour, typically an attractive proposition for most mental health clinicians (Ogloff and Davis, 2004), does not lead to a reduction of recidivism (Andrews and Bonta, 2010; Andrews, Bonta and Hoge, 1990). In fact, when criminogenic factors are appropriately targeted, there is a significant improvement in outcome (i.e., reduced recidivism; McGuire, 2001), while the inclusion of inappropriate targets in treatment could actually reduce its efficacy (Andrews and Bonta, 2010).

Targeting criminogenic factors does not mean, however, a blanket application of identical interventions for all women. Criminogenic factors, while globally applicable to all offenders, will be manifested differently when individual cases are considered. Consequently, treatment should be based on individual case formulations of criminogenic factors (Hollin, 2006). This is particularly relevant for female sexual offenders given that our knowledge about the elements related to their offending behaviour is still embryonic.

The offence process   Until recently, knowledge about the characteristics of the offence process among female sexual offenders was based on typological work that established subcategories of female sexual offenders based either on the woman and offending characteristics (Mathews, Matthews and Speltz, 1989) or a classification of the relationship, the gender, and the age differential between the offender and the victim (Sandler and Freeman, 2007; Vandiver and Kercher, 2004). While the Matthews *et al.* typology has provided psychologically based information, it was based on a very small sample size ($n = 16$) that does not account for all types of female offenders. Attempts to replicate their typology have also failed (e.g., Atkinson, 1996). In contrast, Vandiver and Kercher's (2004) and Sandler and Freeman's (2007) typologies were based on large sample sizes and provide a greater variety in types of female sexual offenders. However, those typologies provided no information regarding the offending   patterns of these women.

In efforts to provide a richer theoretical framework to understand female sexual offending, Gannon and colleagues (Gannon, Rose and Ward, 2008, 2010) developed the *Descriptive Model of the Offence Process for Female Sexual Offenders* (DMFSO) from the offence narratives of 22 UK female sexual offenders who had either child or adult victims. The authors identified how the offending process of female offenders unfolded and established patterns of sexual offending that help identify elements relevant for clinical intervention.

The DMFSO describes the sequence of contextual, behavioural, cognitive and affective events in the women's lives that facilitated and maintained their sexually offending behaviour. Overall, Gannon, Rose and Ward (2008) found that female sexual offenders tend to follow one of two main pathways. In the *Directed-Avoidant* pathway, the women were typically child sexual abusers who were characterized by negative affect and by attempts to avoid the sexual offence. These women offended either out of extreme fear for their lives or because they wanted to obtain intimacy with their male co-offender. Women in the second pathway, the *Explicit-Approach* pathway, offended against either child or adult victims and appeared to explicitly plan their offence. Within this context, these women attempted to achieve various goals such as sexual gratification, intimacy with victim or financial reward. These women reported experiencing positive affect such as excitement in anticipation of their offence. Gannon and her colleagues also noted the potential presence of a third pathway, the *Implicit-Disorganized* pathway, but the evidence for this pathway was weak. Women in this group offended against either children or adults and appeared to be characterized by little organized planning, and sudden and disorganized offending associated with either negative or positive affect.

In an extension of their research, Gannon *et al.* (2012b) analysed the offence pathways of an additional sample of 36 women incarcerated for sexual offences in North America. Gannon *et al.* found evidence for each of the three pathways described in the original DMFSO model – including the *Implicit-Disorganized* pathway – and were unable to find evidence of any other additional characteristic pathways. Alongside this research, Gannon *et al.* also describe the development of an Offence Pathway Checklist which can be used by professionals to guide decision-making regarding the offence styles of female sexual offender clients engaged in assessment and/or therapy.

Despite being restricted in terms of empirical validation, the DMFSO provides a gender-specific model of offending that does not assume a presence of the dynamic risk factors typically found in males. In fact, the accumulating evidence indicates that the elements present in a woman's life that likely contributed to her offending behaviour are either unique to women or tend to manifest themselves in ways that are specific to them. As such, a blanket application of male-based knowledge to female sexual offenders is now considered outdated.

Dynamic risk factors As a reminder, dynamic risk factors are elements associated with the potential of recidivism that can be modified through interventions. No research to date has established the dynamic factors specifically related to sexual recidivism among women. This is not surprising given the very low rates of female sexual recidivism. As such, and although much has been written to date on the treatment needs of female sexual offenders, it is still unclear whether this treatment would indeed impact on future sexual recidivism – after all, it is rather difficult to examine the effectiveness of treatment to reduce a behaviour (i.e., sexual recidivism) that is already near 0.

Of course, it could be argued that, given their low sexual recidivism rates, there is no need to provide sexual offender-specific treatment to women. This argument, however, neglects to consider two important issues. First, it assumes that the sexually offending behaviour is the sole problematic criminal behaviour in the woman's life, thereby neglecting the fact that these women are much more likely to engage in other criminal behaviour. Interventions should aim to reduce all likelihood of future recidivism, not just some specific types of reoffending. Consequently, female sexual offenders should be provided with the opportunity to engage in a comprehensive treatment approach that targets all areas of their functioning to address their general likelihood of criminal recidivism. Second, and perhaps more importantly, the argument ignores the fact that among female sexual offenders, their sexual abuse of children tends to co-occur with other types of child maltreatment (Grayston and De Luca, 1999; Sandler and Freeman, 2009; Wijkman and Bijleveld, 2008). Within this context, there should be a focus on their general propensity for child abuse since it is likely that this type of behaviour involves some (if not most) of the factors that led to the sexually offending behaviour. This is particularly relevant when we consider that women tend to be the primary caregivers of children; family reunification issues are therefore more at play for women than men. Treatment of the woman's attitudes and behaviours that are likely to result in significant harm to a child is required before reunification can be contemplated – and this should occur even if the woman is at low risk of sexual recidivism (Saradjian and Hanks, 1996).

Treatment needs of female sexual offenders   Cortoni and her colleagues have written extensively on the treatment needs of female sexual offenders (see Cortoni, 2010; Cortoni and Gannon, 2011; Denov and Cortoni, 2006; Ford, 2010; Ford and Cortoni, 2008). Briefly, based on the available clinical and research literature, it is suggested that offence-supportive cognitions (e.g., Beech *et al.*, 2009; Gannon *et al.*, 2012a), relationship issues including intimacy deficits and male dependency – particularly when a co-offender is present (Eldridge and Saradjian, 2000; Gannon, Rose and Ward, 2008; Vandiver, 2006; Wijkman and Bijleveld, 2008), and emotional regulation and coping deficits (Denov and Cortoni, 2006; Eldridge and Saradjian, 2000; Ford and Cortoni, 2008; Gannon, Rose and Ward, 2008; Grayston and De Luca, 1999; Nathan and Ward, 2002) would all merit therapeutic attention. Instrumental goals such as financial gains, revenge or humiliation are also associated with female sexual offending and require interventions (Gannon, Rose and Ward, 2008; Sandler and Freeman, 2009).

For some women, deviant sexual fantasies and the search for sexual gratification are also part of the dynamics of the offending behaviour (Eldridge and Saradjian, 2000; Gannon, Rose and Ward, 2008; Grayston and De Luca, 1999; Mathews, Matthews and Speltz, 1989; Nathan and Ward, 2002). Here though, it must be remembered that it is as of yet unclear whether deviant arousal and fantasies among females play the same role in the offending as they do for males (Rousseau and Cortoni, 2010). General sexuality research indicates that women's sexual arousal patterns are very different than those of males: while men's physiological sexual arousal actually reflects their sexual preferences, women's arousal patterns are much more fluid and tend not to demonstrate such specificity (Basson, 2002; Chivers *et al.*, 2004; Suschinsky, Lalumière and Chivers, 2009). Therefore, caution is warranted during treatment not to interpret female sexual issues in the same manner as those of males.

Finally, for at least those female sexual offenders who also engage in other criminal behaviour, more gender-neutral factors such as the presence of antisocial attitudes and associates, substance abuse problems and egocentric or antisocial personality traits are also likely to play a role in their offending behaviour. As such, treatment also needs to address these features as they are integral to the overall criminogenic patterns of female sexual offenders.

These findings outlined here indicate a variety of motivations for the sexual offending behaviour among women that would require elucidation during treatment in order to help her develop appropriate alternatives to manage her life. Within this context, treatment should focus on five broad areas: (i) cognitive processes, (ii) emotional processes, (iii) intimacy and relationship issues, (iv) sexual dynamics and (v) psychosocial functioning. Treatment should address the interrelationships among these factors as well as help the woman develop a self-management plan that includes goals for a healthier life. This approach recognises that the sexual offending behaviour cannot be treated in isolation from the rest of the woman's life, ensures that all areas of functioning are targeted and allows for flexibility to tailor the treatment according to each woman's individual treatment needs (Ford and Cortoni, 2008).

The responsivity principle

The responsivity principle states that the selected modes and styles of treatment for offenders should be based on findings about which type of treatment generally works with offenders. The types of treatment that have been empirically demonstrated to be effective with all types of offenders, including female offenders, are cognitive and behaviourally based structured interventions (Hollin, 2006). Unstructured, non-directive and insight-oriented psychodynamic therapies have been found ineffective in reducing offending behaviour (Andrews, Bonta and Hoge, 1990). In fact, such treatment modes are generally contra-indicated for offenders as they demonstrate characteristics that preclude them from engaging meaningfully in non-directive, insight-oriented interventions (e.g., impulsivity problems, ineffective problem-solving skills, antisocial attitudes; low motivation for change; see Andrews and Bonta, 2010; Andrews, Bonta and Hoge, 1990; Day *et al.*, 2006). Generally, effective interventions include cognitive-behavioural approaches such as cognitive restructuring; modelling and reinforcement of anticriminal attitudes, provision for graduated acquisition of skills, reinforcement and role playing to consolidate new skills, providing resources and providing concrete verbal suggestions (e.g., giving reasons for the need to change; prompting).

The responsivity principle also specifies that the intervention must take into consideration the clients' individual characteristics that may impact on their ability to benefit from treatment (Andrews and Bonta, 2010). Individual characteristics of female offenders tend to be particularly neglected in correctional treatment. Indeed, the traditional practice of applying male-based treatment models to women is based on the assumption that the factors that lead to criminal behaviour offending are gender-neutral; hence, validated male-based interventions are viewed as valid for all offenders regardless of gender (Blanchette and Brown, 2006). Yet, beside the gender-specific nature of the offending process of female sexual offenders, the cognitive, personality, and learning styles and abilities of these women and additional responsivity factors such as the presence of anxiety or low self-esteem, past victimization issues (see Johansson-Love and Fremouw, 2006) and general psychological discomfort would impact on their ability to benefit from treatment. Consequently, these issues would also need to be addressed within a sexual offender–specific treatment programme (Ashfield *et al.*, 2010). It is important to note, however, that treatment that addresses those responsivity issues cannot replace treatment targeted at the criminogenic factors (Andrews and Dowden, 2007).

Beside recognizing and addressing gender-specific issues that may create impediments in treatment, positive aspects of the women should also be identified and strengthened. Regardless of their level of criminogenic factors, female sexual offenders, like all human beings, invariably have strengths that should be capitalized upon during treatment. Enhancing existing strengths while concurrently addressing criminogenic factors promotes a more comprehensive picture of the offender and provides avenues to establish positive future-oriented goals incompatible with offending (Andrews and Dowden, 2007; Ward and Maruna, 2007).

The characteristics of therapeutic staff are also important elements of positive rehabilitative efforts with female sexual offenders. Professionals should ensure they have a clear understanding of the gender-specific nature of their clients' offending. The effectiveness of treatment is enhanced when the services are delivered by professionals who are well-trained in the relevant treatment model and adhere to the treatment objectives and strategies, and who concurrently serve as anti-criminal models and reinforce the women's pro-social efforts and attitudes (Andrews, 1980; Dowden and Andrews, 2004). Within this context, therapeutic staff should relate to their client in clear, open, caring, enthusiastic and respectful ways; help them distinguish between rules and requests; demonstrate and reinforce vivid alternatives to pro-offending styles of thinking, feeling and acting; provide a structured positive therapeutic environment; and help the woman identify and resolve psychosocial obstacles to her desired pro-social life.

Not surprisingly, genuineness, the ability to remain non-judgemental, respect, warmth and empathy, all elements that contribute to a positive therapeutic relationship with other non-criminal populations, are equally important when working with female sexual offenders. It is vital, however, that treatment providers not confuse acceptance of and empathy for the woman, with unconditional acceptance of the woman's potentially distorted views of herself, others and her offending. The latter is actually counterproductive when working with female sexual offenders as it would only reinforce, rather than reduce, the problematic issues that likely contributed to her offending behaviour. Behaviours in treatment include adopting a Socratic rather than a didactic approach, asking open-ended questions, being flexible, encouraging and rewarding participation, instilling hope and confidence and being emotionally responsive to the woman (Ashfield *et al.*, 2010).

Because of the low number of female sexual offenders, some jurisdictions treat female sexual offenders alongside male sexual offenders. While this approach may sometimes be based on pure logistical reasons (e.g., not enough resources to treat these women separately), there still exists an assumption that females have the same dynamic risk factors and, by extension, the same treatment needs as males (see Blanchette and Taylor, 2010 for a review). There are a number of reasons why using a male-based model for the treatment of female sexual offenders is inappropriate – even if additional resources for women-only services are not readily available. First, gender matters. Men and women differ in the paths that led them to the offending behaviour, in the risk they pose to society and in the nature and extent of their needs (Blanchette and Brown, 2006; Cortoni, Hanson and Coache, 2010; Gannon, Rose and Ward, 2008). Consequently, while there are some commonalities among female and male sexual offenders on the issues related to their sexually offending behaviour (e.g., cognitive distortions, relationship issues), they manifest themselves in very different ways according to gender. As a result, a gendered approach to their treatment is required.

Second, female sexual offenders tend to have important victimization histories, often at the hands of males (Gannon, Rose and Ward, 2008; Johansson-Love and Fremouw, 2006; Wijkman and Bijleveld, 2008). Victimization issues are likely to affect not only how these women will respond to treatment in general, but also to males in particular. Requiring these women to then share their innermost thoughts with male offenders, particularly in relation to victimization or relationship issues, could actually be counter-therapeutic and quite possibly add to their victimization issues.

Third, it is now recognized that the treatment of female offenders needs to take into account women's specific communication and relational styles (Blanchette and Brown, 2006; Young, 1993). This includes understanding how men and women differently behave within group contexts. Specifically, men and women do not use similar communication patterns. Rather, they tend to listen for different things and express themselves in different ways (DeLange, 1995). In addition, and contrary to popular beliefs, men do talk more and interrupt more than women within a group environment (DeLange, 1995). Given that many female sexual offenders already have views that males are dangerous (Gannon *et al.*, 2012a), and given that males will tend to dominate group discussions, these women will have little opportunities to fully express their innermost thoughts to a group of male offenders.

Finally, in comparison to men, women tend to have greater needs for healthy connections to significant others including children and family, as well as the broader community (Blanchette and Brown, 2006). In addition, women's ability to deal with stress is greatly improved when extensive supportive social networks are available (Rumgay, 2004) – a feature typically lacking for female sexual offenders (Gannon, Rose and Ward, 2008). Consequently, women typically require much more extensive support than men to improve their general functioning, particularly when the focus is on their ability to develop and maintain a more stable life with less dependence on others. This important relationship feature will require additional treatment efforts that will not easily reconcile with the treatment needs of males – who will typically take precedence due to their greater presence in mixed-gender sexual offender treatment groups. Taken together, these issues indicate that the treatment needs of female sexual offenders are unlikely to be satisfactorily met if they were to be mixed with males in the same treatment programme.

Conclusion

In this chapter, we have reviewed and discussed contemporary research evidence suggesting what is likely to 'work' in the assessment and treatment of female sexual offenders. However, we have also noted that empirically validated knowledge about the factors relating to female-perpetrated sexual offending has only recently started to emerge (see Gannon and Cortoni, 2010). Thus, the general guidelines that we have provided for professionals working with female sexual offenders are necessarily preliminary in nature. In terms of *risk*, the research literature shows clearly that the base rates of recidivism for female sexual offenders are extremely low relative to male sexual offenders. Consequently, male-based risk assessment tools should not be used to assess risk of recidivism amongst female sexual offenders since they are highly likely to overestimate risk. Instead, professionals should consider using tools that have been validated on females more generally (e.g., the LSI-R, Andrews and Bonta, 1995) and/or consider conducting an empirically guided clinical judgement of risk. In terms of *need*, our knowledge of female sexual offenders' criminogenic needs or dynamic risk factors is still very preliminary. No research yet exists which has established the dynamic factors related to sexual recidivism in women. However, various factors have been highlighted as probable treatment needs based on the clinical and research literature. These factors include, but are not limited to, offence-supportive cognitions, relationship factors (e.g., dependency, intimacy issues), emotional regulation and coping deficits and deviant sexual interest/fantasies. Particular goals underlying the sexual offence (e.g., to gain revenge or to humiliate others) are also likely to represent pertinent treatment needs. What appears most important, however, is that professionals take heed of research suggesting that the treatment needs of women – although seemingly similar to male sexual offenders' needs – appear to manifest quite differently. Relatedly, in terms of *responsivity*, it is important that professionals remain cognizant of gender differences that are highly likely to affect engagement and ability to reflect and learn in therapy. In particular, for example, we do not advocate treating women alongside males in sexual offender therapy since women often hold extensive victimization histories at the hands of males. Under such circumstances, women are likely to feel reluctant or fearful of exploring such issues in male company. To summarize, we believe that professionals working with females who have sexually abused are now in the unique position of having preliminary research evidence to guide their practice. Thus, we urge professionals to use this knowledge in every aspect of their assessment and treatment work with female sexual offenders until further evidence of 'what works' with female sexual offenders becomes available.

References

Andrews, D.A. (1980) Some experimental investigations of the principles of differential association through deliberate manipulations of the structure of service systems. *American Sociological Review*, 45, 448–462.

Andrews, D.A. (2001) Principles of effective correctional programs, in *Compendium 2000 on Effective Corrections*, vol. I (eds L.L. Motiuk and R.C. Serin), Correctional Service Canada, Ottawa, pp. 9–17.

Andrews, D.A. and Bonta, J. (1995) *Level of Service Inventory – Revised*, Multi-Health Systems, Toronto.

Andrews, D.A. and Bonta, J. (2010) *The Psychology of Criminal Conduct*, 5th edn, Anderson, Cincinnati.

Andrews, D.A. and Dowden, C. (2007) The Risk-Need-Responsivity model of assessment and human service in prevention and corrections: crime-prevention jurisprudence. *Canadian Journal of Criminology and Criminal Justice*, 49, 439–464.

Andrews, D.A., Bonta, J. and Hoge, R.D. (1990) Classification for effective rehabilitation. *Criminal Justice and Behavior*, 17, 19–52.

Andrews, D.A., Bonta, J. and Wormith, J.S. (2006) The recent past and near future of risk and/or need assessment. *Crime & Delinquency*, 52, 7–27.

Ashfield, S., Brotherston, S., Eldridge, H. and Elliot, I. (2010) Working with female sexual offenders: therapeutic process issues, in *Female Sexual Offenders: Theory, Assessment, and Treatment* (eds T.A. Gannon and F. Cortoni), Wiley-Blackwell, Chichester, pp. 161–180.

Atkinson, J.L. (1996) Female sex offenders in the Correctional Service Canada: case studies. Correctional Service Canada, Ottawa. http://www.csc-scc.gc.ca/text/pblct/so/female/toc-eng.shtml (accessed 9 December 2012).

Basson, R. (2002) A model of women's sexual arousal. *Journal of Sex and Marital Therapy*, 28, 1–10.

Beech, A.R., Parrett, N., Ward, T. and Fisher, D. (2009) Assessing female sexual offenders' motivations and cognitions: an exploratory study. *Psychology, Crime, and Law*, 15, 201–216.

Blanchette, K. and Brown, S.L. (2006) *The Assessment and Treatment of Women Offenders: An Integrated Perspective*, John Wiley & Sons, Ltd, Chichester.

Blanchette, K. and Taylor, K.N. (2010) A review of treatment initiatives for female sexual offenders, in *Female Sexual Offenders: Theory, Assessment, and Treatment* (eds T.A. Gannon and F. Cortoni),Wiley-Blackwell, Chichester, pp. 119–141.

Bonta, J., Rugge, T. and Dauvergne, M. (2003) The Reconviction Rate of Federal Offenders. *User Rep. no. 2003-03.* Public Safety Canada, Ottawa. http://www.publicsafety.gc.ca/res/cor/rep/_fl/2003-02-rec-rte-eng.pdf (accessed on 26 December 2012).

Chivers, M.L., Rieger, G., Latty, E. and Bailey, J.M. (2004) A sex difference in the specificity of sexual arousal. *Psychological Science*, 15, 736–744.

Cortoni, F. (2010) The assessment of female sexual offenders, in *Female Sexual Offenders: Theory, Assessment, and Treatment* (eds T.A. Gannon and F. Cortoni), Wiley-Blackwell, Chichester, pp. 87–100.

Cortoni, F. and Gannon, T.A. (2011) Female sexual offenders, in *International Perspectives on the Assessment and Treatment of Sex Offenders: Theory, Practice and Research* (eds D.P. Boer, R. Eher, L.A. Craig *et al.*), Wiley-Blackwell, Chichester, pp. 35–54.

Cortoni, F. and Hanson, R.K. (2005) A Review of the Recidivism Rates of Adult Female Sexual Offenders. *Research Report no. R-169.* Correctional Service Canada, Ottawa.

Cortoni, F., Hanson, R.K. and Coache, M.E. (2009) Les délinquantes sexuelles: Prévalence et récidive. *Revue internationale de criminologie et de police technique et scientifique*, LXII, 319–336.

Cortoni, F., Hanson, R.K. and Coache, M.E. (2010) The recidivism rates of female sexual offenders are low: a meta-analysis. *Sexual Abuse: A Journal of Research and Treatment*, 22, 387–401.

Craig, L.A., Beech, A.R. and Cortoni, F. (2013) What works in assessing risk in sexual and violent offenders, in *What Works in Offender Rehabilitation: An Evidenced Based Approach to Assessment and Treatment* (eds L.A. Craig, L. Dixon and T.A. Gannon). Wiley-Blackwell, Chichester, pp. 94–114.

Day, A., Bryan, J., Davey, L. and Casey, S. (2006) The process of change in offender rehabilitation programmes. *Psychology, Crime & Law*, 12, 473–487.

DeLange, J. (1995) Gender and communication in social work education: a cross-cultural perspective. *Journal of Social Work Education*, 311, 75–81.

Denov, M.S. and Cortoni, F. (2006) Adult female sexual offenders, in *Comprehensive Mental Health Practices with Sex Offenders and Their Families* (eds C. Hilarski and J. Wodarski), Haworth Press, New York, pp. 71–99.

Dowden, C. and Andrews, D.A. (2004) The importance of staff practice in delivering effective correctional treatment: a meta-analytic review of core correctional practice. *International Journal of Offender Therapy and Comparative Criminology*, 48, 203–214.

Eldridge, H. and Saradjian, J. (2000) Replacing the function of abusive behaviors for the offender: remaking relapse prevention in working with women who sexually abuse children, in *Remaking Relapse Prevention with Sex Offenders: A Sourcebook* (eds D.R. Laws, S.M. Hudson and T. Ward), Sage Publications, Thousand Oaks, pp. 402–426.

Folsom, J. and Atkinson, J.L. (2007) The generalizability of the LSI-R and the CAT to the prediction of recidivism in female offenders. *Criminal Justice and Behavior*, 34, 1044–1056.

Ford, H. (2010) The treatment needs of female sexual offenders, in *Female Sexual Offenders: Theory, Assessment, and Treatment* (eds T.A. Gannon and F. Cortoni), Wiley-Blackwell, Chichester, pp. 101–117.

Ford, H. and Cortoni, F. (2008) Sexual deviance in females: assessment and treatment, in *Sexual Deviance*, 2nd edn (eds D.R. Laws and W. O'onohue), Guilford Press, New York, pp. 508–526.

Gannon, T.A. and Cortoni, F. (eds) (2010) *Female Sexual Offenders: Theory, Assessment, and Treatment*, Wiley-Blackwell, Chichester.

Gannon, T.A., Rose, M.R. and Ward, T. (2008) A descriptive model of the offense process for female sexual offenders. *Sexual Abuse: A Journal of Research and Treatment*, 20, 352–374.

Gannon, T.A., Rose, M.R. and Ward, T. (2010) Pathways to female sexual offending: a preliminary study. *Psychology, Crime & Law*, 16, 359–380.

Gannon, T.A., Hoare, J., Rose, M.R. and Parrett, N. (2012) A re-examination of female child molesters' implicit theories: evidence of female specificity? *Psychology, Crime & Law*, 18, 209–224.

Gannon, T.A., Waugh, G., Taylor, K. *et al.* (2012b) *Women Who Sexually Offend Display Three Main Offense Styles: A Re-examination of the Descriptive Model of Female Sexual Offending*. Manuscript under review.

Grayston, A.D. and De Luca, R.V. (1999) Female perpetrators of child sexual abuse: a review of the clinical and empirical literature. *Aggression and Violent Behavior*, 4, 93–106.

Hanson, R.K. (1997) The Development of a Brief Actuarial Risk Scale for Sexual Offense Recidivism. *User Rep. no. 1997-04*. Department of the Solicitor General of Canada, Ottawa.

Hanson, R.K. and Morton-Bourgon, K.E. (2005) The characteristics of persistent sexual offenders: a meta-analysis of recidivism studies. *Journal of Consulting and Clinical Psychology*, 73, 1154–1163.

Hanson, R.K. and Thornton, D. (2000) Improving risk assessments for sex offenders: a comparison of three actuarial scales. *Law and Human Behavior*, 24, 119–136.

Harris, A.J.R. and Hanson, R.K. (2004) Sex Offender Recidivism: A Simple Question. *User Rep. no. 2004-03*. Public Safety Canada, Ottawa. http://www.publicsafety.gc.ca/res/cor/rep/2004-03-se-off-eng.aspx (accessed 9 December 2012).

Harris, A.J.R., Phoenix, A., Hanson, R.K. and Thornton, D. (2003) STATIC-99 Coding Rules: Revised-2003. *User Rep. no. 2003-03*. Corrections Research, Public Safety Canada, Ottawa. www.static99.org (accessed on 9 December 2012).

Hollin, C.R. (2006) Offending behaviour programmes and contention: evidence-based practice, manuals, and programme evaluation, in *Offending Behaviour Programmes: Development, Application, and Controversies* (eds C.R. Hollin and E.J. Palmer), John Wiley & Sons, Ltd, Chichester, pp. 33–67.

Holtfreter, K. and Cupp, R. (2007) Gender and risk assessment: the empirical status of the LSI-R for women. *Journal of Contemporary Criminal Justice*, 23, 363–382.

Johansson-Love, J. and Fremouw, W. (2006) A critique of the female sexual perpetrator research. *Aggression and Violent Behavior*, 11, 12–26.

Manchak, M.A., Skeem, J.L., Douglas, K.S. and Siranosian, M. (2009) Does gender moderate the predictive utility of the Level of Service Inventory—Revised (LSI-R) for serious violent offenders? *Criminal Justice and Behavior*, 36, 425–442.

Mathews, R., Matthews, J.K. and Speltz, K. (1989) *Female Sexual Offenders: An Exploratory Study*, Safer Society Press, Orwell.

McGuire, J. (2001) What works in correctional intervention? Evidence and practical implications, in *Offender Rehabilitation in Practice: Implementing and Evaluating Effective Programs* (eds G.A. Bernfeld, D.P. Farrington and A.W. Leschied), John Wiley & Sons, Ltd, Chichester, pp. 25–43.

Nathan, P. and Ward, T. (2002) Female sex offenders: clinical and demographic features. *Journal of Sexual Aggression*, 8, 5–21.

Ogloff, J.R.P. and Davis, M.R. (2004) Advances in offender assessment and rehabilitation: contributions of the risk-needs-responsivity approach. *Psychology, Crime & Law*, 10, 229–242.

Quinsey, V.L., Lalumière, M.L., Rice, M.E. and Harris, G.T. (1995) Predicting sexual offenses, in *Assessing Dangerousness: Violence by Sexual Offenders, Batterers, and Child Abusers* (ed. J.C. Campbell), Sage, Thousand Oaks, pp. 114–137.

Rousseau, M.M. and Cortoni, R. (2010) The mental health needs of female sexual offenders, in *Female Sexual Offenders: Theory, Assessment, and Treatment* (eds T.A. Gannon and F. Cortoni), Wiley-Blackwell, Chichester, pp. 73–86.

Rumgay, J. (2004) Living with paradox: community supervision of women offenders, in *Women Who Offend* (ed. G. McIvor), Jessica Kingsley Publishers, London, pp. 99–125.

Sandler, J.C. and Freeman, N.J. (2007) Typology of female sex offenders: a test of Vandiver and Kercher. *Sexual Abuse: A Journal of Research and Treatment*, 19, 73–89.

Sandler, J.C. and Freeman, N.J. (2009) Female sex offender recidivism: a large-scale empirical analysis. *Sexual Abuse: A Journal of Research and Treatment*, 21, 455–473.

Saradjian, J. and Hanks, H. (1996) *Women Who Sexually Abuse Children: From Research to Clinical Practice*, John Wiley & Sons, Inc., New York.

Suschinsky, K.D., Lalumière, M.L. and Chivers, M.L. (2009) Sex differences in patterns of genital sexual arousal: measurement artifacts or true phenomena? *Archives of Sexual Behavior*, 38, 559–573.

Vandiver, D.M. (2006) Female sex offenders: a comparison of solo offenders and co-offenders. *Violence and Victims*, 21, 339–354.

Vandiver, D.M. (2007) *An Examination of Re-arrest Rates of 942 Male and 471 Female Registered Sex Offenders*, Academy of the Criminal Justice Sciences, Feature Panel on Sex Offenders, Seattle.

Vandiver, D.M. and Kercher, G. (2004) Offender and victim characteristics of registered female sexual offenders in Texas: a proposed typology of female sexual offenders. *Sexual Abuse: A Journal of Research and Treatment*, 16, 121–137.

Vess, J. (2011) Risk assessment with female sex offenders: can women meet the criteria of community protection laws? *Journal of Sexual Aggression*, 17, 77–91.

Ward, T. and Maruna, S. (2007) *Rehabilitation: Beyond the Risk Paradigm*, Routledge, London.

Ward, T., Polaschek, D.L. and Beech, A.R. (2006) *Theories of Sexual Offending*, John Wiley & Sons, Ltd, Chichester.

Wijkman, M. and Bijleveld, C. (2008) Female sex offenders: recidivism and criminal careers. Paper presented at the 8th Annual Conference of the European Society of Criminology, Edinburgh, September.

Williams, S.M. and Nicholaichuk, T. (2001) Assessing static risk factors in adult female sex offenders under federal jurisdiction. Paper presented at the 20th Research and Treatment Conference of the Association for the Treatment of Sexual Abusers, San Antonio, November.

Young, V. (1993) Women abusers: a feminist perspective, in *Female Sexual Abuse of Children: The Ultimate Taboo* (ed. M. Elliot), Guilford Press, New York, pp. 93–99.

16

What Works for Offenders with Intellectual Disabilities

William R. Lindsay[1,2] and Amanda M. Michie[3]

[1]University of Abertay, UK
[2]Bangor University, UK
[3]NHS Lothian, UK

Introduction

Some 15 years ago, a number of systems were developed for evaluating the quality of evidence supporting interventions in a range of settings. The three most important of these were the Cochrane review system, the American Psychological Association system for categorizing Empirically Supported Psychological Interventions and the 'What Works' system for evaluating evidence-based interventions in Criminal Justice Settings. The Cochrane review system has been influential in the United Kingdom in categorizing evidence on the effectiveness of psychological and pharmaceutical interventions from different studies. The highest quality of evidence from clinical research includes randomized controlled trials (RCTs) and high-quality meta-analyses that include controlled trials. The next quality of evidence includes cohort studies and waiting list controlled trials and the quality below that includes case studies and expert opinion.

The system developed through the American Psychological Association (APA) had a similar aim to review the quality of evidence from outcome studies on the effectiveness of psychological therapy. Chambless and colleagues (Chambless and Hollon, 1998; Chambless and Ollendick, 2001; Chambless *et al.*, 1998) have described the way in which treatments for specific diagnostic groups can be categorized into well-established treatments, possibly efficacious treatments, experimental treatments and treatments for which there is no evidence of efficacy. Similar to the Cochrane system, 'well-established treatments' are characterized as those that have at least two good between-group design experiments that would usually be RCTs. In contrast to the Cochrane system, if an intervention has two supporting, well-controlled case series, with at least three participants in each study, this will serve as persuasive supportive evidence. One feature of the APA criteria is that treatment should be supported by a manual or its equivalent in order to standardize presentation in clinical settings. Probably, efficacious treatments have a lower standard of verification with two experiments that should show the treatment to

What Works in Offender Rehabilitation: An Evidence-Based Approach to Assessment and Treatment,
First Edition. Edited by Leam A. Craig, Louise Dixon and Theresa A. Gannon.
© 2013 John Wiley & Sons, Ltd. Published 2013 by John Wiley & Sons, Ltd.

be superior to waiting list control. Alternatively, one RCT should show the treatment to be superior to a pill placebo or psychotherapy placebo. Experimental treatments are those which are not yet tested and do not meet the criteria for either well-established treatments or probably efficacious treatments.

The third influential system was developed in response to a request by the US Congress for an evaluation of the effectiveness of annual grants from the Department of justice of more than $3 billion. Sherman *et al.* (1997) developed a technique for reviewing the evidence that has since cumulated into the 'What Works' literature in mainstream criminal research. The system considers five levels relating to the quality of the evidence supporting any given intervention in the field of criminal behaviour. Level I (the lowest level) studies indicate some correlation between the programme and measures of recidivism. Interventions lack a comparison group and the evidence is not sufficiently robust to help assess the effectiveness. Level II studies indicate some association between the program and recidivism. However, at this level, the poor research design could not rule out alternative explanations for the outcome. Level III studies compare two or more groups, one with the programme and one without the programme. The study design will allow a reasonable similarity between the two groups. Level IV studies include comparisons between a program group and one or more control groups controlling for extraneous factors. Level V studies represent the highest quality of evidence with randomized assignment to conditions with comparable programs and comparable/ matched participants. This level of evidence would also control for attrition, a common problem in offender studies.

The system developed by Sherman *et al.* (1997) has paved the way for a developing literature on Evidence-based Corrections that has published guidelines on 'What Works', 'What Does Not Work' and 'What Is Promising'. The findings from this body of work have set out broad requirements for effective programs including a focus on clearly defined overt behaviour as opposed to non-directive counselling, a focus on developing skills including behavioural and cognitive skills, programs that are structured and focused and programs that use multiple treatment components. There should be meaningful contact between the treatment personnel and the participants, and crucially, interventions should focus on characteristics of the offenders that are associated with criminal activities and can be changed (criminogenic needs).

There have been criticisms of these systems that are particularly important from the point of view of the current chapter. The APA requirements included a condition that reliable and valid methods should be employed to determine outcome. Any review of outcome methods in psychological therapy for emotional disorders will reveal that these are largely self-report measures such as self-reported anxiety, self-reported depression, self-esteem, confidence and so on. In work on offenders, self-reported measures can only be considered proximal and the mean evidence of interest from a social policy point of view is whether or not another offence has been committed. It is of little value to society to know that an offender reports lower levels of anger if he or she continues to commit an equivalent number of violent offences following treatment. Therefore, the most valid measure for offender treatment is the number of future incidents in comparison to the number of incidents prior to the commencement of treatment. Similarly, for an assessment study, the data of interest is whether or not the assessment (e.g., a risk assessment) is related to future offending in the predictive manner. It is a more exacting standard than is the case for other psychological interventions, pharmaceutical interventions or management systems but it is the case.

Another relevant criticism is related to the conditions created during follow-up periods. For the APA task force, the follow-up period should be as uncontaminated as possible so that the effects of the treatment can be evaluated in the absence of other variables or conditions that may be affecting the problem that has been treated. This can be extremely difficult in learning disability services where a number of agencies may be involved with individuals in order to help them maintain community placements and a presence in society. For example, a housing agency may be involved to help establish residency, or criminal justice agencies may continue to monitor the individual as part of their disposal from court. As we shall see, some of the evaluations of treatments have been made within the context of forensic intellectual disability services that apply a holistic approach to individuals. This is clearly important from the point of view of evaluating particular treatment components since the maintenance of treatment effects may be due to these other conditions rather than the intervention itself. Paradoxically, it is probably less important from the point of view of social validity. Social validity demands that the intervention, irrespective of the potency of its individual components, be effective in reducing recidivism. If it works in making a safer society and less crime in the community, then it is socially valid. As scientists and therapists, we wish to understand the nature of the effective components both to see whether or not they can be developed into even more effective aspects and to understand whether or not ineffective components are reducing the potency of the intervention.

'What Works' in the Treatment of Anger

The most common treatment designed to help individuals with problems in the emotion of anger is Anger Management Treatment (AMT). Like many other treatment programmes in the field of offending, this is a composite treatment with a number of components, each designed to address the emotion of anger in different ways. We will deal with AMT in some detail as an exemplar of the way that treatment aimed to address criminal behaviour is constructed. One of the essential aspects of AMT is to stress that anger is a normal emotion and that it can be dealt with in ways that will not place the individual in difficult situations. Most people with intellectual disabilities (ID) who have problems with the emotion of anger will have found themselves in extremely difficult situations from time to time. Typically, the way in which they express their anger will have got them into trouble with the criminal justice system, may have resulted in exclusion from day placements, or may even have caused them to jeopardize their tenancy or living arrangements. Therefore, in these cases, the expression of the emotion of anger has been considerable.

AMT relies on a number of components all of which are built towards the control of anger in real situations or in situations that approximate to these real situations as closely as possible. One of the first essential components is to rehearse ways in which the individual can control their arousal. This is generally done through the use of relaxation exercises. There are a number of different forms of relaxation exercises but the main one is abbreviated progressive relaxation in which the participant tenses and relaxes major muscle groups including arms, torso, head, neck and shoulders, buttocks and thighs, and legs and feet. Abbreviated progressive relaxation techniques also focus on breathing as a way of both regulating respiration and focusing attention. This method of arousal reduction is common in AMT but other ways of controlling arousal are quite acceptable. For example, simple relaxation through breathing exercises or other relaxation methods such as behavioural relaxation (Sturmey *et al.*, forthcoming) are quite acceptable. The important aspect is that the person is able to reduce his or her own arousal. Most AMT approaches will use arousal reduction methods at an early stage (e.g., Willner *et al.*, 2002).

A second component in AMT is to develop a better understanding of the person's own and others' emotion. Here, there are likely to be exercises on understanding a range of emotions including anger. This section will also foster an understanding of different aspects of emotion including the behavioural, physiological, cognitive and affective components of emotion. Typically, treatment should promote an understanding of these various aspects in relation to emotions such as happiness, sadness, jealousy, anxiety, anger and so on. The therapist can also encourage an understanding of the difference between emotions such as anxiety and anger. Another component of AMT is to encourage the participant to maintain a diary of situations that may have caused them to be angry during the week. This diary helps the person to reflect on their anger, on the way in which kind affects their life and also provides information to the therapist on situations that provoke such difficulties for the client that will be used later on in treatment to construct an anger hierarchy.

The next component is the construction of the anger hierarchy itself. This is made up of a series of idiomatic situations that make the individual angry. Some aspects of this anger hierarchy may have emerged from the weekly diaries and review of incidents in the week prior to the therapeutic session. A further component of AMT is cognitive restructuring. This is based on the relationship between arousal and cognitions. Some authors have demonstrated that individuals with ID who have a propensity to anger may have a tendency to construe threat in situations where they feel arousal (Jahoda, Pert and Trower, 2006). This perception of threat may lead to an interpretation of the arousal as one of anger with corresponding behavioural consequences to deal with the perceived threat, that is, aggression. The importance of the cognitive restructuring is to help the person make realistic appraisals of the situation. The next component involves a series of problem-solving exercises to deal with situations of perceived threat. The problem-solving exercises are likely to involve accurate self-perception, arousal reduction, effective communication and action alternative to aggression. These problem-solving exercises are likely to involve role-play and discussion about understanding the other person's point of view in situations. This may impinge directly on the perception of threat in that perspective taking is likely to involve some understanding that the other person is not presenting a threat from their point of view.

The final, crucial component is that of stress inoculation. Stress inoculation was first developed by Meichenbaum (1985) and involves the introduction of personalized stress-inducing stimuli to the individual under conditions where they are supported to control their arousal and stress reactions. It is usually done in a graded manner, in the case of AMT, using the anger hierarchy. It can be done in imagination, through role-play and in actual situations while encouraging and supporting the client to use coping skills they have learned during other parts of the AMT process. Therefore, AMT is a series of components including arousal reduction, understanding emotion, cognitive restructuring, keeping a record of anger situations, developing an anger hierarchy, problem-solving exercises and stress inoculation. This, typically in the field of offender treatment, is a complex amalgamation of methods and it has to be acknowledged that these methods have not been evaluated separately. It is the case in this field that these complex interventions are evaluated as a whole and there have been a number of studies of AMT as a treatment programme to the extent that it is probably the best evaluated treatment in the field of offenders with ID.

Research evaluating anger treatment began with a number of publications reviewing successful case studies. Black and Novaco (1993) described the successful treatment of a man with mild ID who presented repeated episodes of physical and verbal aggression. They adapted the AMT approach for people with ID including a cognitive preparation phase that involved understanding emotion and an introduction to relaxation, a skill acquisition phase (including additional sessions on arousal reduction and the development of coping strategies) and the final phase including stress inoculation to individually tailored situations. Treatment lasted over 28 sessions and improvements were monitored through observations of aggressive incidents, observations of pro-social behaviour and an individualized anger diary. There were improvements on all behavioural measurements with reductions in the frequency of recorded aggressive behaviour and increases in pro-social behaviour. Improvements were maintained during a 21-week follow-up period.

Subsequent to this case report, there were number of case studies on group and individual AMT on people with ID. Rose (1996) reported on three men and two women who were treated using a group therapy format that included self-monitoring of feelings of anger, arousal reduction through relaxation, identification of personal triggers for anger, emotional recognition, the development of coping skills and self-instructional training. Treatment lasted for 16 sessions and effectiveness was assessed using an anger diary and records of incidents. Reports from carers suggested that all participants had fewer aggressive incidents per month following treatment. Moore *et al.* (1997) used a variant of AMT in a group therapy format to treat two men and four women with mild to moderate ID. Treatment methods were similar to those reported in Rose (1996) but on this occasion, treatment lasted only eight weeks. Similar to the study by Rose (1996), evaluation was conducted using an anger diary and a record of incidents. By the end of treatment, there was a 39% reduction in aggressive incidents, and an informal six month follow-up suggested that these improvements were maintained. Further case studies (King *et al.*, 1999; Rose and West, 1999; Rossiter, Hunniset and Pulsford, 1998; Walker and Cheseldine, 1997) have all reported similar improvements following some form of AMT.

While these case evaluations have all demonstrated positive outcomes from a treatment using AMT principles, none of them have been conducted according to the controlled design recommended by Chambless and Hollon (1998). If the case studies are well-controlled, Chambless and Hollon (1998) suggest that two reports of three case studies each are sufficient to establish efficacy. Unfortunately, none of the case studies contain the required experimental control. Another pertinent criticism in the context of the current chapter is that these case studies were not confined to offenders with ID. Indeed, in only one case it was identified that the individual was in a forensic establishment and had presumably been involved with the criminal justice system (Black and Novaco, 1993). While it is valuable to establish the effectiveness of treatment under relatively controlled conditions, it is crucial to go on to verify effectiveness in the target population (in this case, offenders with ID).

A well-controlled study on three cases has been conducted recently by Travis and Sturmey (forthcoming). Three participants, selected because of the high frequency of their aggressive responses, were treated using a behavioural approach that focused on the identification of anger-provoking situations and using repeated trials to support these individuals in using 'socially acceptable replacement responses' rather than aggression. Essentially, this controlled treatment study focused on the stress inoculation aspect, using situations that, in AMT terms, emerged from the anger hierarchy. For these authors, the preparation phase consisted of teaching on replacement responses. They used a *multiple baseline across participants* design with the treatment approaches being introduced in a staggered fashion, to control for the passage of time. All participants demonstrated a huge reduction in aggressive responses from 54–79% at baseline to 9–12% following the introduction of treatment with a corresponding increase in replacement responses. These improvements only occurred when the treatment procedures were implemented.

While these case studies have been important in the establishment of the feasibility of AMT for people with anger problems, they have not been conducted on forensic cases, which, from the point of view of the present chapter, is an essential focus.

Case Interventions on Offenders with ID

Following Black and Novaco (1993), the first study reported on participants who had been involved with the criminal justice system was conducted by Allan *et al.* (2001). They reported on five women with mild ID, and AMT was conducted in a group format including the usual aspects of psycho-education, arousal reduction, role-play of anger provocation incidents, problem-solving exercises, exercises on emotional recognition and stress inoculation through imagination of anger-provoking situations. Treatment lasted around 40 sessions and was assessed using self-report measures, reports of aggressive incidents and an anger diary. Participants were also assessed using videotaped role-plays in anger-provoking situations. Improvements were reported on all measures for all the women and these improvements maintained to 15-month follow-up. Only one of the women had another incident of violence.

In a follow-up study, Lindsay *et al.* (2003) reported on six men with mild ID, all of whom had been involved with the criminal justice system for reasons of aggression and violence. Treatment was similar to that described by Allan *et al.* (2001) and there were improvements on all measures which were maintained at 15-month follow-up. None of the men had been violent at four year follow-up. Novaco and Taylor (2006) describe a single case study of AMT for a man who was referred for violent behaviour in a medium secure setting (suggesting criminal justice involvement). Following treatment, self-reported anger reduced and care staff reported reductions in its violence at one month and four months follow-up.

These studies suffer from some of the same criticisms that have been mentioned previously in that they have not been controlled case studies. Neither have they had measures taken after the introduction of each of the many methods used in the AMT. Therefore, the effectiveness of these methods has not been verified either by staggering the baseline for each of the participants (thereby introducing methods for each individual at a different point in the programme), or by a return to baseline conditions. Indeed, it is impossible to come to baseline conditions for these participants once they have been taught cognitive and behavioural skills to control their anger. Once learned and used, these skills cannot then be unlearned. While this presents experimental difficulties for the validation of treatment, from the point of view of society it is less problematic. Indeed, from the point of view of the criminal justice system, the fact that people reduce their violence across a number of settings is a strength, whether or not specific potent elements have been identified. These case studies have strengths that previous case studies lacked. The first is that participants were clearly drawn from populations of offenders. A second strength is that follow-up periods in these case studies were significant. Allan *et al.* (2001) and Lindsay *et al.* (2003) had follow-up periods of 15 months and 4 years, respectively.

Controlled Studies of AMT

Interestingly, one of the first studies to evaluate the effects of AMT was an RCT. Benson, Johnson Rice and Miranti (1986) used modifications of the Novaco treatment components in a group application across four conditions (self-instruction, relaxation training, problem solving and a combined condition) with community-based clients. They obtained significant effects on self- and staff-rated outcome measures and role-play ratings but found no significant differences between the groups and conditions. It should be noted that in this controlled trial, all the conditions involved active treatments.

A second RCT was conducted by Willner *et al.* (2002) when they invited community support teams to refer individuals who would benefit from attendance at an AMT group. Sixteen participants with ID were then randomly allocated to treatment group and waiting list control condition. Two participants dropped out leaving seven in each group. This study was built on the work of Benson, Johnson Rice and Miranti (1986) by using the Anger Inventory (Benson and Ivins, 1992) and a provocation index. Both participants and carers were asked to fill out the inventories. Treatment consisted of nine weekly 2-hour sessions and participants could attend alone or with their carer. Methods described were the normal AMT procedures. The participants in the treated group showed substantial improvements in anger ratings which further improved relative to their own pre-treatment scores at three month follow-up. There were no equivalent improvements in the control group, and at post-treatment, there was a large effect size for the difference between groups. These authors also found that the degree of improvement during treatment was strongly correlated with IQ. The intervention was significantly shorter than that reported in previous studies (e.g., Allan *et al.*, 2001; Benson, Johnson Rice and Miranti, 1986) was no loss of efficacy.

The field of AMT has seen several other controlled group studies although none of the others employs a randomized control design. In one study with greater social validity, Lindsay *et al.* (2004) included participants referred from the courts and criminal justice agencies to a community forensic ID service. This was a waiting list control study with several outcome measures, including a provocation inventory (the Dundee Provocation Inventory; Alder and Lindsay, 2007), provocation role-plays and self-report diaries, that were repeated before treatment and at several points in a follow-up period of 15 months. They compared 33 participants who received AMT with 14 who made up a waiting list control condition. Treatment lasted 40 sessions and control participants were on the waiting list for around six months. Control participants were seen by community nursing staff but did not receive any form of anger treatment until after the cessation of the study period. For the AMT group, there were significant within-group improvements on all measures. In post-treatment comparisons between the two groups, there were no differences on the Dundee Provocation Inventory while the self-report diaries and the anger provocation role-plays showed significant differences between groups. These improvements were maintained at follow-up. The study also reported on the number of aggressive incidents and re-offences recorded for both groups. At the post-waiting-list assessment point (six month follow-up), 45% of the control group had committed another assault while at the post-treatment assessment point (nine months), 14% at the treatment group had committed a further incident of assault. A chi square analysis on this data revealed a significant difference between groups. Therefore, although the follow-up period was relatively short, there was some evidence that AMT had a significant impact on the number of aggressive incidents recorded in these participants.

Taylor and colleagues have conducted a series of waiting list control studies on AMT (Taylor *et al.*, 2002a, 2004a, 2005a). All participants had been detained under sections of the England and Wales Mental Health Act (1983) for reasons of cognitive impairment (ID) and abnormally aggressive or seriously irresponsible behaviour. Taylor *et al.* (2002a) compared 10 men allocated to the AMT condition with 10 on the waiting list. Treatment was guided by a manual (Taylor and Novaco, 2005) and delivered individually to participants over the 18 session program.

The program involved a preparatory phase of six sessions designed to present information on the nature and purpose of anger treatment, encourage motivation to change and develop basic skills including self-disclosure, emotional awareness and self-monitoring. Participants then proceeded to the 12-session treatment phase that included core competencies of cognitive restructuring, arousal reduction, skills training and stress inoculation. Participants in the treatment group reported significantly lower anger intensity and key nurse ratings supported these improvements showing modest gains for the treatment group. Taylor *et al.* (2005a) employed the same detailed protocol with 20 participants allocated to the AMT condition and 20 to the waiting list control. Scores on self-reported anger disposition and reactivity indices were significantly reduced following intervention in the treatment group compared with scores for the control group and these differences were maintained to a four month follow-up. Start ratings of study participants' anger disposition converged with self-report ratings but did not reach statistical significance. Although this study did not randomize participants, it did have the strength of using a treatment manual with a waiting list control condition and a four month follow-up.

In the final waiting list control comparison, Rose *et al.* (2005) compared 50 participants who received a form of AMT with 36 controls. Outcome was measured using the provocation inventory administered at pre-treatment, post-treatment and three to six month follow-up. Between-group comparisons showed a statistically significant treatment effect but examination of clinical significance was more equivocal with only 11 of the 50 participants in the intervention group showing reliable clinical change. A reduction in provocation inventory scores was more likely to occur if a participant was accompanied by a member of staff who knew them. The results on reliable clinical change suggested that although improvement was statistically significant, the approach may not be as effective as seems apparent from the initial statistical analysis.

Analysis of the Evidence on AMT

Although there has been a considerable amount of work on the effectiveness of AMT, evaluations have been completed on AMT as a complex conglomerate of treatment approaches. This is of interest because some of these methods may contribute nothing to the effectiveness of the approach as a whole while others may indeed reduce the effectiveness or work against the effectiveness of the more potent procedures. As an example, one carefully controlled study (Travis and Sturmey, 2013) that seems to focus on the stress inoculation aspects of AMT demonstrated considerable effectiveness for this truncated anger treatment. This section has considered a series of case studies on the effectiveness of AMT. Three of these case studies have been conducted on forensic cases and two of them have had long follow-up periods of 15 months to 4 years (Allan *et al.*, 2001; Lindsay *et al.*, 2003). The section has also considered a number of controlled treatment trials, two of which have been randomized with the rest waiting list control trials.

One of the RCTs (Benson, Johnson Rice and Miranti, 1986) did not employ a 'no treatment' control condition and while all four treatment conditions improved, there were no significant differences between groups. The other controlled trial (Willner *et al.*, 2002) did show significant differences between groups but was not conducted on forensic cases. Studies which have been conducted on forensic cases (Lindsay *et al.*, 2004; Taylor *et al.*, 2002a, 2004a, 2005a) have shown significant improvements following the AMT and one study (Lindsay *et al.*, 2004) found a significant reduction in aggressive incidents for the treated group. The studies by Taylor *et al.* (2002a, 2004a, 2005a) and Travis and Sturmey (2013) have used manualized treatment, a condition recommended by Chambless and Ollendick (2001). For these reasons, AMT and other anger treatments that employ stress inoculation procedures fulfil the requirements for 'well-established treatment' and certainly fulfil the requirements for Levels IV and V in the Sherman *et al.* (1997) system underpinning the 'What Works' literature for the following reasons:

- One RCT has demonstrated treatment effectiveness.
- One well-controlled case series has demonstrated treatment effectiveness.
- The characteristics of samples have been specified clearly in studies.
- Treatment manual has been used in four of the reports.
- Several of the case studies and one of the controlled trials has recorded violent incidents over six months to four years, demonstrating social validity.
- Treatment effectiveness has been demonstrated by five different investigating teams.
- Treatment has been shown to be more effective than a waiting list control in five group-controlled comparisons.

However, if we were to address a different question, 'what works in AMT', we would reach a different conclusion. Relaxation treatments have been assessed separately in relation to both the reduction of anxiety and the reduction of aggression. McPhail and Chamov (1989) conducted an RCT which compared a group of six participants with ID who received 12 sessions of abbreviated progressive relaxation with a control group who had a storytelling condition (an equivalent amount of active interaction). Participants' intellectual disability ranged from profound to mild and they were selected because they regularly displayed destructive behaviour in activity groups. All participants were assessed for relaxation effects on 17 categories of disruptive behaviour. The results demonstrated significant and substantial reductions in disruptive behaviour for their participants receiving relaxation with no changes in the control condition. Unfortunately, at 12-week follow-up, disruptive behaviour had returned to baseline levels. Therefore, in this small RCT, there was evidence of the short-term effectiveness of relaxation in relation to aggression.

There have been no equivalent studies on most other aspects of AMT including emotional recognition, cognitive restructuring, the establishment of an anger hierarchy, or presenting information concerning the purpose of anger. As has been indicated, there has been one study focusing predominantly on the stress inoculation aspect of AMT. The carefully controlled case studies by Travis and Sturmey (2013) demonstrated the effectiveness of training replacement responses in critical situations where individuals have previously become angry and violent. Therefore, there is evidence that relaxation coupled with stress inoculation and a focus on adaptive responses to these situations are effective components of AMT.

'What Works' in the Treatment for Inappropriate Sexual Behaviour

Throughout the 1970s and 1980s, sexual reorientation and behavioural management approaches have been the most common psychological treatments for the management of sexual offending (Plaud *et al.*, 2000). Kelly (1982) wrote that in the treatment of sexual offenders, especially those who offended against children, 78% of studies employed aversion therapy to change deviant sexual preference. For example, Rosenthal (1973) described the treatment of a 21-year-old man with mild ID who had committed offences against children.

He was referred for aversion therapy following his third arrest. The painful nature of aversion therapy was explained to him and he discussed it with his lawyer and probation officer. The description of treatment in the paper is disturbing with electric shocks being administered after the presentation of images of girls. The duration and intensity of shocks increased over the treatment period and did result in rapid increases in response latencies until the client spontaneously reported an inability to obtain deviant sexual images or sexual arousal while being presented with the stimulus items. Periodic follow-ups in the next 32 months suggested that treatment effects maintained with the absence of paedophilic images and sexual arousal to children. While this case study suggested that it is indeed possible to suppress paedophilic images and sexual arousal to them, the disturbing nature of the treatment would, understandably, discourage any consideration in contemporary programmes.

In a less aversive study, Luiselli *et al.* (1977) treated persistent masturbation in an eight-year-old male with ID. They found that social praise, positive feedback and token reinforcement for resisting failed to reduce the frequency. The addition of over-correction procedure consisting of arm movements completely suppressed masturbation after nine days. This was maintained to a 12-month follow-up period. Several other studies (e.g., Cook *et al.*, 1978; Hingsburger, Griffiths and Quinsey, 1991) have demonstrated the effectiveness of these behavioural approaches using case illustrations. However, the case studies have not been conducted to a standard that would be considered acceptable according to criteria suggested by Chambless and Hollon (1998). In addition, the goals of such treatment were essentially restrictive rather than rehabilitative in contrast to subsequent behavioural approaches.

Two influential developments were published around the same time in the treatment of sex offenders with ID using a comprehensive programme aimed at improving social functioning, improving sexual awareness and sexual knowledge, extending relationships, promoting coping skills and reducing inappropriate sexuality (Griffiths, Quinsey and Hingsburger, 1989; Haaven, Little and Petre-Miller, 1990). Both sets of authors addressed the fact that individuals with ID may have restricted social and sexual opportunities. Both developed a multifactorial treatment plan designed to increase personal and social skills as well as addressing issues of sexuality. Griffiths, Quinsey and Hingsburger (1989) in particular included protective relapse prevention methods. Both sets of authors presented up to 30 cases with no reoffending but the cases presented by Haaven, Little and Petre-Miller (1990) were all contained in a secure setting and clients had little opportunity to engage in inappropriate sexual behaviour. This illustrates a significant problem in the evaluation of sex offender treatment for men with ID. In many studies, participants have been monitored 24 hours a day and have little opportunity to offend (e.g., Craig, Stringer and Moss, 2006). In the absence of measures of sexual behaviour taken in uncontrolled settings, no conclusion can be drawn on the effectiveness of treatment.

Case studies using cognitive behaviour therapy

Cognitive behaviour therapy (CBT) techniques have become the predominant approach for the treatment of sex offenders in the last 20 years. In the meta-analysis on the effectiveness of sex offender treatment, Hanson *et al.* (2002) reported that 'current treatments (any treatment currently offered and cognitive therapy treatment offered since 1980) were associated with significant reductions in both sexual and a general recidivism whereas older treatments were not' (p. 187). 'Older treatments' were predominantly behavioural, employing aversion therapy, reorientation of sexual preference through masturbatory reconditioning and teaching social skills. Current treatments generally employed CBT methods in addressing sexual offending and inappropriate sexual behaviour.

The first report on a cognitive approach for sex offenders with ID was that of O'Connor (1996) in a problem-solving intervention for 13 adult males. This involved consideration of a range of risk situations in which participants had to develop safe solutions for both themselves and potential victims. She reported positive results from the intervention with most participants achieving increased community access, but the extent to which this increased community access was supervised is not mentioned in the report.

In a series of case studies, Lindsay *et al.* (1998a, b, c, 1999) reported on the treatment of men with ID who had offended against children, exhibitionists and stalkers. CBT treatment was developed to challenge cognitions supporting denial and mitigation of the offence. After each session, client's attitudes were assessed in relation to that specific topic using an earlier version of the Questionnaire on Attitudes Consistent with Sexual Offences (QACSO; Lindsay, Whitefield and Carson, 2007). The QACSO reviews the extent to which participants endorse a range of cognitive distortions consistent with rape and attitudes to women, exhibitionism, voyeurism, dating abuse, offences against men, stalking and offences against children. Therefore, it was possible to link the content of each session to the impact on specific cognitive distortions. The second distinctive aspect was that all participants lived in the community and had unsupervised access to community facilities. These reports, therefore, did not have the drawback of continued close supervision. Finally, there was extensive follow-up and the authors did not publish any of the outcomes until they had data for at least four years after referral with several participants followed up for up to seven years. They found that cognitions based on factual information, such as age of consent, changed much more readily than those based on more entrenched opinions such as the view that victims share some of the responsibility. At the time of writing, despite participants having free access to the community, there was only one instance of significant recidivism in one of the 17 stalking cases. In three carefully controlled case studies, Singh *et al.* (2011) evaluated the use of mindfulness-based procedures to control deviant sexual arousal to children. Using a multiple baseline design, they demonstrated the effectiveness of mindfulness meditation and observation in controlling sexual urges when compared to participants' own self-control strategies. This was an unusual intervention study since it impacted directly on deviant sexual arousal and was carefully controlled.

These cases, addressing cognitive distortions and sexual arousal through CBT methods, provide some basis for optimism in treatment. The Lindsay *et al.* (1998a, b, c, 1999, 2003, 2004, 2006, 2011a, b) cases did not suffer from the drawback of continued supervision and the Singh *et al.* (2011) cases measured sexual arousal. Therefore, some of the requirements noted by Chambless and Ollendick (2001) such as a relatively unpolluted follow-up period and a reasonable follow-up period length were fulfilled. However, the cases of Lindsay *et al.* (1998a, b, c, 1999, 2003, 2004, 2006, 2011a, b) did not contain adequate experimental control.

Rose and colleagues (Rose *et al.*, 2002, 2012) have evaluated uncontrolled group treatments. Rose *et al.* (2002) reported on a 16-week group treatment for five men with ID who had perpetrated sexual abuse. Treatment employed self-control procedures, victim empathy procedures, sex education, assertiveness training and training to avoid risk. Therefore, as with other treatments for offenders with ID it was a complex multifactorial procedure assessed as an entity. They reported no reoffending at one year but the follow-up was contaminated by the fact that participants were generally escorted and monitored. Rose *et al.* (2012) reported on a similar treatment with 12 individuals all of whom had been referred from the criminal justice system for at least one sexual offence. Participants showed significant improvements on a range of cognitive assessments including the QACSO, a victim empathy scale and a measure of locus of control. In the follow-up period of 12–16 months, only one individual reoffended despite the fact that all had unescorted access to the community. Given the lengthy follow-up in their study and participants' access to the community, these findings are of crucial social significance and validity.

The evaluation of sex offender treatment through group comparison

There had been no evaluations of sex offender treatment in this client group using an RCT or waiting list controlled trial. One of the main difficulties is that referring agencies such as the courts or criminal justice services are reluctant to allow any delay of treatment for reasons of public protection. A number of researchers have taken advantage of existing control comparison groups. For example, Keeling, Rose and Beech (2007) compare that 11 special-needs offenders with 11 mainstream offenders matched on level of risk, sex of the victim, offence type and age. All participants were treated in prison; all were released from prison into the community and the average time from release was 16 months. There were no significant differences between groups on any proximal measures (victim empathy scale, the social intimacy scale, the relationships questionnaire, the emotional loneliness scale) but at 16-month follow-up, there were no reconviction for sex offending for any of the special-needs participants. Lindsay *et al.* (2011a) compared 15 men with ID who had committed offences against adults with another 15 who had offended against children. All treated for 36 months using a manualized approach (Lindsay, 2009). Both groups improved on the QACSO, significantly reducing the level of cognitive distortions, and reoffending at six year follow-up was between 20% and 25% for both groups with no significant differences.

Perhaps the clearest comparison of convenience was conducted by Lindsay and Smith (1998) when they compared seven men who had been on treatment for two or more years with seven men being treated for less than one year. The comparisons were predicated on probation sentences delivered by the court. Those individuals who had been in treatment for less than a year showed significantly poorer progress, retained a higher level of cognitive distortions and were more likely to reoffend than those in treatment for two or more years.

Three large-scale reports on the outcome of treatment for sex offenders have been published. Again, the main drawback of these reports is that they either have no comparison group or the comparison is one of convenience. McGrath, Livingstone and Falk (2007) reviewed the treatment and management of 103 adult sex offenders with ID who had moved from institutions to staffed private houses with 24 hour support. Treatment programmes consisted of the promotion of social and community living skills and the promotion of risk management strategies. Therefore, treatment was focused on skill promotion rather than CBT. In an 11-year follow-up period with an average of 5.8 years, they reported 10.7% reoffending. The 11 individuals who reoffended committed 20 new sexual offences. As a comparison, they reported on 195 treated and untreated male sexual offenders without ID who had been followed up for an average period of 5.72 years. These individuals had a prison sentence and 23.1% were charged with a new sexual offence at some point in the follow-up period. In a further comparison, they reported on 122 treated and untreated male sex offenders who received probation orders followed up for 5.24 years, of whom 6.5% were charged with a new sexual offence. As with other studies, one of the difficulties in sex offenders with ID cohort was that 62.1% received 24 hour supervision which, presumably, limited access to potential victims. However, McGrath, Livingstone and Falk (2007) also considered that this level of supervision resulted in a more comprehensive reporting of incidents compared to the other two cohorts. They also reported a considerable amount of harm reduction in that 83% of participants were classified as contact sexual offenders while only 45% of the new offences were non-contact offences, typified by exhibitionism and public masturbation.

Lindsay *et al.* (2006) compared 121 sexual offenders with 105 non-sexual offenders (all with ID) followed up for periods of up to 13 years. The sex offender cohort had a lower rate of reoffending at 23% when compared to the other offenders at 59%. All sex offenders had been treated using CBT and relapse prevention methods. The 23% reoffending rate in the sex offender cohorts is considerably higher than the 10.7% reoffending reported by McGrath, Livingstone and Falk (2007) but in the Lindsay *et al.* (2006) study, all participants had unsupervised access to the community. Lindsay *et al.* (2006) also recorded the number of incidents perpetrated by the reoffenders over the follow-up period. They found a significant reduction in the number of incidents committed when comparing figures from 2 years prior to referral and up to 12 years after referral. There was around a 70% reduction in the number of incidents in those individuals who did commit further offences.

In a study reporting the outcome for sex offenders only, Murphy *et al.* (2010) conducted a treatment study on 46 sex offenders with ID living in community settings. Treatment was manualized, conducted across a number of different settings and services and run over a period of one year. They found that sexual knowledge, victim empathy and cognitive distortions improved significantly following treatment and that sexual knowledge and reduced cognitive distortions maintained at six month follow-up. They also reported that 8.7% of their sample reoffended after the treatment programme. Separately, Murphy and Sinclair (2006) had reported that although their study was designed as a treatment control trial, it proved difficult to recruit and retain control participants.

The evaluation of 'What Works' in sex offender treatment

As has been indicated, proximal measures of improvement such as greater sexual knowledge, reductions in cognitive distortions and improved victim empathy may be of interest to researchers and therapists but from the point of view of social policy, the data of interest and the extent to which treatment services have produced a reduction in the number of offending incidents. All of the three major evaluations of sex offender ID treatment services (Lindsay *et al.*, 2006; McGrath, Livingstone and Falk, 2007; Murphy *et al.*, 2010) have shown reductions in reoffending in comparison to rates recorded prior to treatment or in comparison to other groups of sex offenders. A further strength of these reports (Lindsay *et al.*, 2006; Murphy *et al.*, 2010) is that therapists have followed detailed manualized treatment. In addition, follow-up periods have been lengthy and these major evaluations have been conducted by three different research groups. Therefore, sex offender treatment fulfils some of the criteria for Empirically Supported Therapies. However, other conditions have not been met: there is no random allocation to treatment conditions and control conditions; the follow-up periods have been polluted by contact with other services such as criminal justice; 24 hour supervision has continued in one report and there has been no untreated comparison. Therefore, while these large-scale studies have social validity, they lack experimental rigour.

The specific treatment comparisons have all been comparisons of convenience. Lindsay and Smith (1998) compared sex offenders with ID treated for one versus two years, Keeling, Rose and Beech (2007) compared special needs offenders to mainstream offenders and Lindsay *et al.* (2011a) compared two types of sex offenders with ID. While all of these reports recorded treatment effectiveness, only Lindsay and Smith (1998) made a realistic comparison of alternative approaches. The criteria that have been met are as follows:

- Studies have been completed by six different research groups.
- Follow-up has been conducted over lengthy periods.
- One study has been reported using an alternative treatment comparison (Lindsay and Smith, 1998).
- Reoffending has been recorded in addition to proximal measures.
- In these reports, therapists have followed a detailed treatment manual (Lindsay *et al.*, 2006, 2011a; Murphy *et al.*, 2010; Singh *et al.*, 2011).

Criteria that have not been met are as follows:

- All studies lack a no-treatment control comparison.
- All comparisons are comparisons of convenience.
- There is no random allocation to treatment conditions.
- Only one study addressing sexual deviance is an adequate case-control study (Singh *et al.*, 2011).
- In several studies, the follow-up period is contaminated by 24 hour supervision.

Because so many criteria have not been met, treatment for sex offenders with ID can only be considered to fulfil the criteria for Level V interventions. Level IV requires group comparison controlling for extraneous factors. The Lindsay and Smith (1998) study fulfils this requirement but is only on a small number of participants. The Singh *et al.* (2011) study is well-controlled, fulfilling the criteria of experimental treatments required by Chambless and Ollendick (2001). None of the other studies meet those criteria for Empirically Supported Therapies. Therefore, according to APA criteria, and despite a wealth of data showing reductions in reoffending and harm reduction, CBT for sex offenders with ID fulfils only criteria for experimental treatment. According to the 'What Works' criteria, these studies conform to Levels II–V criteria with the weight of evidence fulfilling only Level V.

What Works for Other Forensic Problems in Offenders with ID

In a review of the literature on mainstream offender programmes, Gendreau and Andrews (1990) concluded that those intervention programs for the rehabilitation of criminals which employ cognitive behavioural techniques in order to change and improve thinking styles were the most effective interventions. Ten years later, Layton Mackenzie (2000) came to similar conclusions writing that CBT programmes, addressing criminogenic needs such as criminal thinking, were more effective than non-directive methods. One of the main developments in mainstream criminal work has been in the area of criminal thinking and social problem-solving programs. The purpose of these cognitive skills programmes is to equip offenders with thinking skills that will promote alternative, pro-social means of approaching social situations including high-risk situations in which the person is at risk of offending.

There have been a number of interventions for mainstream offenders. Wilson, Bouffard and MacKenzie (2005) evaluated a range of cognitive behavioural programmes noting two dominant approaches: Moral Reconation Therapy (MRT) and Reasoning and Rehabilitation (R&R). They employed meta-analytic techniques computing effect sizes across 20 studies. Wilson, Bouffard and MacKenzie (2005) concluded that all of the higher-quality studies, including those on MRT and R&R, found significant reductions in offending in programme participants (around 16%) which translated into a moderate effect size. Others, (Joy Tong and Farrington, 2006; Pearson *et al.*, 2002), in reviews of published treatment studies, have also found reductions in recidivism for offenders who have completed cognitive skills programmes.

Given the fact that offenders with ID have, by definition, deficits in cognitive and reasoning skills, it is surprising that these developments have not spread their application to this field. The first such treatment report was by O'Connor (1996), already discussed as a cognitive therapy for sex offenders. She implemented a problem-solving program for high-risk situations that might be encountered by participants in her study. She reported successful outcomes although there was no information on the development of thinking skills. Lindsay *et al.* (2011b) have developed the Social Problem-Solving and Offence-Related Thinking (SPORT) programme. This has been specifically designed for offenders with ID to improve problem identification, problem specification, goal setting and solution generation in a range of settings. Particular focus was given to analysing situations, enhancing appraisal of the important features and considering the consequences of both adaptive and maladaptive solutions. The SPORT programme employs problem-solving exercises and role-plays extensively, and an emphasis is placed on practical exercises rather than discussion or written work. Lindsay *et al.* (2011b) reported on the successful implementation of the SPORT programme with five sex offenders with ID and five violent offenders with ID. All participants were assessed at baseline, post-treatment and four month follow-up using the Social Problem-Solving Inventory – Revised. Across the 10 participants, there were significant improvements with large effect sizes in positive problem orientation, impulsive problem-solving style and avoidant style.

On its own, this study fulfils a number of APA criteria. The treatment was supported by a manual with details on how to deliver the programme, assessment was conducted using an adapted version of a recognized psychometric test, improvements were seen in a reasonable sized series of case studies, the characteristics of the sample were specified and statistical improvements were supported by calculation of effect sizes. Therefore, this one study achieves the same classification, for this treatment field (experimental treatment) has the many significant treatment and service outcome studies for the treatment of sex offenders with ID. The study by Lindsay *et al.* (2011b) does not evidence the control of conditions required in single case studies, it has no comparison condition and, importantly, there are no reports on the effects of the programme on reoffending. Because a single study provides an evidence base equivalent to the whole field on treatment of sex offenders with ID (according to APA criteria), it points out the limitations of this classification system. Against 'What Works' criteria, it does not meet even Level I criteria, since there is no indication of a correlation between the programme and measures of recidivism.

A number of case studies have been reported in the treatment of arson on people with ID. In an early report, Rice and Chaplin (1979) conducted a study that involved the delivery of social skills training programme on two groups of fire setters, one of which consisted of individuals with mild ID. Following treatment, both groups improved significantly on a reliable observations scale of role-play behaviour and 8 of the 10 patients treated had been discharged for around 12 months with no recidivism. Clare *et al.* (1992) reported on another case study of a man with ID with two convictions of arson. They implemented a very comprehensive treatment package which resulted in improvements, but because of the complexity of the treatment it was impossible to evaluate the impact of its components. However, the client was discharged to a community setting and had not engaged in any fire-related offending behaviour at 30-month follow-up.

Taylor, Thorne and Slavkin (2004b) reported a successful case series of four detained men with histories of fire setting. They developed a 40-session cognitive behavioural treatment and demonstrated improvements on a range of proximal measures. Taylor *et al.* (2005b) extended this work to a further case series of six women. All completed the programme, and scores on measures related to fire treatment targets generally improved following the intervention. All but one of the treatment group had been discharged to community placements at two year follow-up and there had been no reports of participants setting any fires or engaging in fire-risk-related behaviour. The results of these small and methodologically weak pilot studies do provide some limited encouragement and guidance to practitioners concerning utility of group-based, cognitive behavioural interventions for fire-setting behaviour in people with ID. However, the quality of the data would fulfil only Level II criteria.

Conclusions

Research on the treatment of offenders with ID has increased considerably over the last 15 years. There are, however, constraints on research studies using cognitive behavioural methods. One of the main requirements from our criminal justice and social validity perspective is that participants will learn skills that will not be lost. Given that these cognitive skills are relatively permanent, there can be no return to baseline conditions, which is one of the requirements of experimental control in case studies. Therefore, a return to baseline conditions cannot be part of a realistic treatment intervention for offenders. As an example, self-regulation skills for the emotion of anger should be taught in such a way that the offender can internalize them and employ them in different situations. This is a strength for social validity but an experimental weakness.

The results of AMT are the strongest in the field of offenders with ID. However, this treatment is complex and multifactorial and it is unclear which of the treatment components generates effectiveness. One study (Travis and Sturmey, 2013) developed behavioural approach which seemed to focus on the stress inoculation, in vivo, and anger-provoking situations rather than all the other aspects of AMT. This was a well-controlled case study and suggested that the stress inoculation component of AMT may be one of the most successful. The evidence for anger treatment fulfils criteria for Levels IV and V.

Although there has been a great deal of work on sex offender treatment, none of the case studies or group comparison studies fulfil the criteria of randomized allocation or single case control. One study is a realistic alternative treatment comparison (Lindsay and Smith, 1998) and all studies are comparisons of convenience. Many of the studies suggest that treatment is effective in reducing recidivism, but for some, the follow-up period is contaminated by the fact that participants have been maintained on 24 hour supervision. Despite a wealth of research reports, the evidence fulfils only Level II criteria.

Research on offenders with ID has a number of strengths that may not be evident in the fields with data that may suggest stronger support. Treatments for AMT, sex offender treatment, fire setting and criminal thinking have all been conducted with manuals allowing for a standardized approach. In addition, the outcome data is of a quality that is more relevant to social policy than in many other fields, that is, it is data on reoffending rather than proximal measures such as level of anxiety or self-reported depression. However, there is clearly a need for better controlled research in this field. For reasons mentioned, it will remain difficult. Ethical committees may be reluctant to allow a no-treatment control group for sex offenders in the way that has been possible for violent offenders. For the treatment areas of fire setting and criminal thinking, it may indeed be possible to gather waiting list control information more readily. These treatment and research developments should be considered with some priority.

References

Alder, L. and Lindsay, W.R. (2007) Exploratory factor analysis and convergent validity of the Dundee Provocation Inventory. *Journal of Intellectual & Developmental Disabilities*, 32, 179–188.

Allan, R., Lindsay, W.R., Macleod, F. and Smith, A.H.W. (2001) Treatment of women with intellectual disabilities who have been involved with the criminal justice system for reasons of aggression. *Journal of Applied Research in Intellectual Disabilities*, 14, 340–347.

Benson, B.A. and Ivins, J. (1992) Anger, depression and self-concept in adults with mental retardation. *Journal of Intellectual Disability Research*, 36, 169–175.

Benson, B.A., Johnson Rice, C. and Miranti, S.V. (1986) Effects of anger management training with mentally retarded adults in group treatment. *Journal of Consulting and Clinical Psychology*, 54, 728–729.

Black, L. and Novaco, R.W. (1993) Treatment of anger with a developmentally disabled man, in *Casebook of the Brief Psychotherapies* (eds R.A. Wells and V.J. Giannetti), Plenum Press, New York.

Chambless, D.L. and Hollon, S.D. (1998) Defining empirically supported therapies. *Journal of Consulting and Clinical Psychology*, 66, 7–18.

Chambless, D. and Ollendick, T. (2001) Empirically supported psychological interventions: controversies and evidence. *Annual Review of Psychology*, 52, 685–716.

Chambless, D.L., Baker, M., Baucom, D.H. *et al.* (1998) Update on empirically validated therapies, II. *Clinical Psychologist*, 51 (1), 3–16.

Clare, I.C.H., Murphy, G.H., Cox, D. and Chaplain, E.H. (1992) Assessment and treatment of fire setting: a single case investigation using a cognitive behavioural model. *Criminal Behaviour and Mental Health*, 2, 253–268.

Cook, J.W., Altman, K., Shaw, J. and Blaylock, M. (1978) Use of contingent lemon juice to eliminate public masturbation by a severely retarded boy. *Behaviour Research and Therapy*, 18, 131–134.

Craig, L.A., Stringer, I. and Moss, T. (2006) Treating sexual offenders with learning disabilities in the community. *International Journal of Offender Therapy and Comparative Criminology*, 50, 111–122.

Gendreau, P. and Andrews, D.A. (1990) Tertiary prevention: what the meta-analyses of the offender treatment literature tells about "what works." *Canadian Journal of Criminology*, 32, 173–184.

Griffiths, D.M., Quinsey, V.L. and Hingsburger, D. (1989) *Changing Inappropriate Sexual Behaviour: A Community Based Approach for Persons with Developmental Disabilities*, Paul Brooks Publishing, Baltimore.

Haaven, J., Little, R. and Petre-Miller, D. (1990) *Treating Intellectually Disabled Sex Offenders: A Model Residential Programme*, Safer Society Press, Orwell.

Hanson, R.K., Gordon, A., Harris, A.J.R. *et al.* (2002) First report of the collaborative outcome data project on the effectiveness of psychological treatment for sex offenders. *Sexual Abuse: A Journal of Research & Treatment*, 14, 169–194.

Hingsburger, D., Griffiths, D. and Quinsey, V. (1991) Detecting counterfeit deviance: differentiating sexual deviance from sexual inappropriateness. *Habilitation Mental Health Care Newsletter*, 10, 51–54.

Jahoda, A., Pert, C. and Trower, P. (2006) Frequent aggression and attribution of hostile intent in people with mild to moderate intellectual disabilities: an empirical investigation. *American Journal on Mental Retardation*, 111, 90–99.

Joy Tong, L.S. and Farrington, D.P. (2006) How effective is the "Reasoning and Rehabilitation" Programme in reducing offending? A meta-analysis of evaluations in four countries. *Psychology, Crime & Law*, 12, 3–24.

Keeling, J.A., Rose, J.L. and Beech, A.R. (2007) Comparing sexual offender treatment efficacy: mainstream sexual offenders and sexual offenders with special needs. *Journal of Intellectual & Developmental Disability*, 32 (2), 117–124.

Kelly, R.J. (1982) Behavioural reorientation of paedophiliacs: can it be done? *Clinical Psychology Review*, 2, 387–408.

King, N., Lancaster, N., Wynne, G. *et al.* (1999) Cognitive behavioural anger management training for adults with mild intellectual disability. *Scandinavian Journal of Behaviour Therapy*, 28, 19–22.

Layton MacKenzie, D. (2000) Evidence based corrections: Identifying what works. *Crime & Delinquency*, 46 (4), 457–471.

Lindsay, W.R. (2009) *The Treatment of Sex Offenders with Developmental Disabilities: A Practice Workbook*, Wiley-Blackwell, Chichester.

Lindsay, W.R. and Smith, A.H.W. (1998) Responses to treatment for sex offenders with intellectual disability: a comparison of men with 1 and 2 year probation sentences. *Journal of Intellectual Disability Research*, 42, 346–353.

Lindsay, W.R., Marshall, I., Neilson, C.Q. *et al.* (1998a) The treatment of men with a learning disability convicted of exhibitionism. *Research on Developmental Disabilities*, 19, 295–316.

Lindsay, W.R., Neilson, C.Q., Morrison, F. and Smith, A.H.W. (1998b) The treatment of six men with a learning disability convicted of sex offences with children. *British Journal of Clinical Psychology*, 37, 83–98.

Lindsay, W.R., Olley, S., Jack, C. *et al.* (1998c) The treatment of two stalkers with intellectual disabilities using a cognitive approach. *Journal of Applied Research in Intellectual Disabilities*, 11, 333–344.

Lindsay, W.R., Olley, S., Baillie, N. and Smith, A.H.W. (1999) The treatment of adolescent sex offenders with intellectual disability. *Mental Retardation*, 37, 320–333.

Lindsay, W.R., Allan, R., Macleod, F. *et al.* (2003) Long term treatment and management of violent tendencies of men with intellectual disabilities convicted of assault. *Mental Retardation*, 41, 47–56.

Lindsay, W.R., Allan, R., Parry, C. *et al.* (2004) Anger and aggression in people with intellectual disabilities: treatment and follow-up of consecutive referrals and a waiting list comparison. *Clinical Psychology and Psychotherapy*, 11, 255–264.

Lindsay, W.R., Steele, L., Smith, A.H.W. *et al.* (2006) A community forensic intellectual disability service: twelve year follow-up of referrals, analysis of referral patterns and assessment of harm reduction. *Legal and Criminological Psychology*, 11, 113–130.

Lindsay, W.R., Whitefield, E. and Carson, D. (2007) An assessment for attitudes consistent with sexual offending for use with offenders with intellectual disability. *Legal and Criminological Psychology*, 12, 55–68.

Lindsay, W.R., Michie, A.M., Haut, F. *et al.* (2011a) Comparing offenders against women and offenders against children on treatment outcome for offenders with intellectual disability. *Journal of Applied Research in Intellectual Disability*, 24 (4), 361–369.

Lindsay, W.R., Hamilton, C., Moulton, S. *et al.* (2011b) Assessment and treatment of social problem solving in offenders with intellectual disability. *Psychology, Crime & Law*, 17, 181–197.

Luiselli, J.K., Helfen, C.S., Pemberton, B.W., and Reisman, J. (1977). The elimination of a child's in class masturbation by over correction and reinforcement. *Journal of Behaviour Therapy and Experimental Psychiatry*, 8, 201–204.

McGrath, R.J., Livingston, J.A. and Falk, G. (2007) Community management of sex offenders with intellectual disability: characteristics, services and outcome of a statewide programme. *Intellectual and Developmental Disabilities*, 45, 391–398.

McPhail, C.H. and Chamov, A.S. (1989) Relaxation reduces disruption in mentally handicapped adults. *Journal of Mental Deficiency Research*, 33, 399–406.

Meichenbaum, D. (1985) *Stress Inoculation Training*, Pergamon Press, Oxford.

Moore, E., Adams, R., Elsworth, J. and Lewis, J. (1997) An anger management group for people with a learning disability. *British Journal of Learning Disabilities*, 25, 53–57.

Murphy, G. and Sinclair, N. (2006) Group cognitive behaviour treatment for men with sexually abusive behaviour. Paper presented to 6th Seattle Club Conference on Research and People with Intellectual Disabilities, Kendal, December.

Murphy, G.H., Sinclair, N., Hays, S.J. *et al.* (2010) Effectiveness of group cognitive behavioural treatment for men with intellectual disabilities at risk of sexual offending. *Journal of Applied Research in Intellectual Disabilities*, 23, 537–551.

Novaco, R.W. and Taylor, J.L. (2006) Cognitive-behavioural anger treatment, in *Handbook of Adult Clinical Psychology: An Evidence Based Practice Approach* (eds M. McNulty and A. Carr), Routledge, London, pp. 978–1009.

O'Connor, W. (1996) A problem solving intervention for sex offenders with intellectual disability. *Journal of Intellectual & Developmental Disability*, 21, 219–235.

Pearson, F.S., Lipton, D.S., Cleland, C.M. and Yee, D.S. (2002) The effects of behavioural/cognitive behavioural programmes on recidivism. *Crime & Delinquency*, 48, 476–496.

Plaud, J.J., Plaud, D.M., Colstoe, P.D. and Orvedal, L. (2000) Behavioural treatment of sexually offending behaviour. *Mental Health Aspects of Developmental Disabilities*, 3, 54–61.

Rice, M.E. and Chaplin, T.C. (1979) Social skills training for hospitalised male arsonists. *Journal of Behaviour Therapy & Experimental Psychiatry*, 10, 105–108.

Rose, J. (1996) Anger management: a group treatment programme for people with mental retardation. *Journal of Physical & Developmental Disabilities*, 8, 133–150.

Rose, J. and West, C. (1999) Assessment of anger in people with intellectual disabilities. *Journal of Applied Research in Intellectual Disabilities*, 12, 211–224.

Rose, J., Jenkins, R., O'Conner, C. *et al.* (2002) A group treatment for men with intellectual disabilities who sexually offend or abuse. *Journal of Applied Research in Intellectual Disabilities*, 15, 138–150.

Rose, J., Loftus, M., Flint, B. and Carey, L. (2005) Factors associated with the efficacy of a group intervention for anger in people with intellectual disabilities. *British Journal of Clinical Psychology*, 44, 305–317.

Rose, J., Rose, D., Hawkins, C. and Anderson, C. (2012) Sex offender treatment group for men with intellectual disabilities in community settings. *Journal of Forensic Practice*, 14, 21–28.

Rosenthal, T.L. (1973) Response contingent versus fixed punishment in aversion conditioning of paedophilia: a case study. *Journal of Nervous and Mental Diseases*, 156, 440–443.

Rossiter, R., Hunniset, E. and Pulsford, M. (1998) Anger management training and people with moderate learning disabilities. *British Journal of Learning Disabilities*, 26, 67–74.

Sherman, L.W., Gottfredson, D., MacKenzie, D.L. *et al.* (1997) *Preventing Crime: What Works, What Doesn't, What's Promising*, National Institute of Justice, Washington, DC.

Singh, N.N., Lancioni, G., Winton, A.S.W. *et al.* (2011) Can adult offenders with intellectual disabilities use mindfulness-based procedures to control and deviant sexual arousal? *Psychology, Crime & Law*, 17, 165–180.

Sturmey, P., Lindsay, W., Yause, T. and Neil, N. Anxiety disorders, in *Evidence Based Practice for People with Intellectual and Developmental Disabilities* (eds P. Sturmey and R. Didden), Wiley-Blackwell, Chichester, forthcoming.

Taylor, J.L. and Novaco, R.W. (2005). *Anger Treatment for People with Developmental Disabilities: A Theory, Evidence and Manual Based Approach*. John Wiley & Sons, Ltd, Chichester.

Taylor, J.L., Novaco, R.W., Gillmer, B. and Thorne, I. (2002a) Cognitive behavioural treatment of anger intensity among offenders with intellectual disabilities. *Journal of Applied Research in Intellectual Disabilities*, 15, 151–165.

Taylor, J.L., Thorne, I., Robertson, A. and Avery, G. (2002b) Evaluation of a group intervention for convicted arsonists with mild and borderline intellectual disabilities. *Criminal Behaviour and Mental Health*, 12, 282–293.

Taylor, J.L., Novaco, R.W., Gillmer, B.T. and Robertson, A. (2004a) Treatment of anger and aggression, in *Offenders with Developmental Disabilites* (eds W.R. Lindsay, J.L. Taylor and P. Sturmey), John Wiley & Sons, Ltd, Chichester, pp. 201–220.

Taylor, J.L., Thorne, I. and Slavkin, M.L. (2004b) Treatment of fire setting behaviour, in *Offenders with Developmental Disabilities* (eds W.R. Lindsay, J.L. Taylor and P. Sturmey), John Wiley & Sons, Ltd, Chichester, pp. 221–240.

Taylor, J.L., Novaco, R.W., Gillmer, B.T. *et al.* (2005a) Individual cognitive behavioural anger treatment for people with mild-borderline intellectual disabilities and histories of aggression: a controlled trial. *British Journal of Clinical Psychology*, 44, 367–382.

Taylor, J.L., Robertson, A., Thorne, I. *et al.* (2005b) Responses of female fire-setters with mild and borderline intellectual disabilities to a group based intervention. *Journal of Applied Research in Intellectual Disabilities*, 19, 179–190.

Travis, R. and Sturmey, P. Using behavioral skills training to teach anger management skills to adults with mild intellectual disability. *Journal of Applied Research in Intellectual Disabilities*, forthcoming.

Walker, T. and Cheseldine, S. (1997) Towards outcome measurements: monitoring effectiveness of anger management and assertiveness training in a group setting. *British Journal of Learning Disabilities*, 25, 134–137.

Willner, P., Jones, J., Tams, R. and Green, G. (2002) A randomised controlled trial of the efficacy of a cognitive behavioural anger management group for clients with learning disabilities. *Journal of Applied Research in Intellectual Disabilities*, 15, 224–253.

Wilson, D.B., Bouffard, L.A. and MacKenzie, D.L. (2005) A quantitative review of structured group orientated cognitive behavioural programmes for offenders. *Criminal Justice and Behaviour*, 32, 172–204.

17

The Good Lives Model
Does It Work? Preliminary Evidence

Gwenda M. Willis and Tony Ward

Deakin University, Australia

Introduction

Offender rehabilitation endeavours are unlikely to live up to their aim without actively engaging their participants in the rehabilitation process and promoting desistance from crime. The traditional and predominant approach of identifying risk factors associated with recidivism and delivering interventions designed to reduce, or at the very least manage such risk, constitutes a key ingredient of rehabilitation endeavours. It is fair to say that great strides have been made in identifying changeable (i.e., dynamic) risk factors associated with reoffending (e.g., Andrews and Bonta, 2006; Hanson *et al.*, 2007), and the efficacy of rehabilitation programmes that target these risk factors (i.e., criminogenic needs) and conform to other principles of effective rehabilitation (see Andrews and Bonta, 2006) has been demonstrated in meta-analyses (e.g., Hanson *et al.*, 2009; Landenberger and Lipsey, 2005). However, a major problem associated with an emphasis on risk reduction is the difficulty motivating and engaging participants in the rehabilitation process (e.g., Ward and Maruna, 2007). The Good Lives Model (GLM) was developed as an alternative overarching theoretical framework that seeks to preserve the merits of traditional approaches whilst actively engaging participants in the rehabilitation process and promoting desistance from crime. The aims of strength-oriented frameworks such as the GLM are to utilize offenders' core commitments and capabilities in the process of behaviour change and, by doing so, reduce risk and also increase their chances of achieving better lives.

The Risk, Need, and Responsivity model (RNR; Andrews and Bonta, 2006; Bonta and Andrews, 2010) provides the backbone of effective offender rehabilitation and is, as the name suggests, comprised of three major principles. Arguably, inherent in the RNR model is the supposition that offenders are bearers of risk for recidivism, and the primary aim of offender rehabilitation is to reduce this recidivism risk through adherence to the RNR principles. The inference that offenders are the primary source of recidivism risk has its origins in the related theoretical assumption of the RNR that individuals vary in their predisposition to commit crimes and that this predisposition is largely constituted by psychological and behavioural variables.

What Works in Offender Rehabilitation: An Evidence-Based Approach to Assessment and Treatment,
First Edition. Edited by Leam A. Craig, Louise Dixon and Theresa A. Gannon.
© 2013 John Wiley & Sons, Ltd. Published 2013 by John Wiley & Sons, Ltd.

Thus, the RNR principles are firmly rooted in a psychology of criminal conduct. The *risk principle* states that the dosage or intensity of interventions should match an offender' risk level, such that intensive interventions are directed at high-risk offenders and less intense (or no) interventions are aimed at lower-risk offenders. The *need principle* informs intervention targets, specifically stating that interventions should target criminogenic needs, also known as *dynamic risk factors*, which are those factors causally related to offending that, for a given individual, are changeable – for example, antisocial attitudes and antisocial associates (Andrews and Bonta, 2006). The overall aim of treatment is to reduce dynamic risk factors. Thus, according to the needs principle, directing intervention efforts at non-criminogenic needs such as low self-esteem and a history of victimization will prove ineffective, given they have not been linked with recidivism (e.g., Andrews and Bonta, 2006; Hanson and Morton-Bourgon, 2005). The explicit targeting of non-criminogenic needs is viewed as discretionary, and essentially, a waste of resources. Finally, the *responsivity principle* informs the actual delivery of interventions in order to maximize their efficacy. Consideration is given to cognitive ability, learning style, culture, and other characteristics of individual offenders, and delivering treatment accordingly. Meta-analyses have consistently shown that rehabilitation programmes conforming to each of the RNR principles are effective in reducing reoffending (e.g., Hanson *et al.*, 2009; Landenberger and Lipsey, 2005).

Notwithstanding the effectiveness of RNR-based rehabilitation programmes, treatment attrition rates are often high – up 30–50% in sex offender treatment programmes (e.g., Browne, Foreman and Middleton, 1998; Moore, Bergman and Knox, 1999; Ware and Bright, 2008). We argue that the narrow focus of pure RNR-based programmes, which translates to to an almost exclusive focus on individual deficits (e.g., poor emotional regulation, poor problem-solving skills), offers minimal appeal to the population they intend to engage (see Porporino, 2010). Indeed, research shows that participants often complete rehabilitation programmes for external reasons such as parole eligibility (e.g., Jones, Pelissier and Klein-Saffran, 2006) rather than any internal desire to change patterns of behaviour that contribute to their risk of reoffence. Thus, the RNR represents a necessary, but not sufficient, model for effective offender rehabilitation.

Owing to greater awareness of limitations with an overemphasis on client deficits and risk factors, researchers and clinicians have documented a range of techniques designed to increase client motivation for, and engagement in, offender rehabilitation programmes. Many of these techniques have been adopted from the general psychotherapy literature and include Motivational Interviewing (Miller and Rollnick, 1991, 2002), greater attention to positive therapist characteristics, and the use of approach (versus avoidant) treatment goals. As we will review later in this chapter, research supports the incorporation of these techniques into offender rehabilitation initiatives. The GLM capitalizes on this research by providing a practice framework in which each of these techniques can be naturally intertwined rather than grafted on to core treatment by the use of additional modules such as motivational interviewing. In this chapter, we provide an overview of the GLM and then review the growing body of empirical research investigating its utility and effectiveness in offender rehabilitation endeavours.

The Good Lives Model

The GLM was developed and advanced by Ward and colleagues (Laws and Ward, 2011; Ward, 2002; Ward and Maruna, 2007) and represents a strengths-based rehabilitation theory that aims to equip clients with internal and external resources to live a *good or better life* – a life that is socially acceptable and personally meaningful. Criminogenic needs (i.e., dynamic risk factors) are conceptualized as internal or external barriers towards living a good life, and are thus addressed within the broader strengths-based framework. One of the advantages of the GLM is that it outlines the relationship between criminogenic needs and human needs, by specifying their relationship to the pursuit of primary human goods (Ward and Maruna, 2007). Drawing from psychological, social, biological and anthropological research, the GLM posits that like all human beings, individuals with a history of offending are goal-directed and predisposed to seek a number of *primary human goods*. Primary goods are certain states of mind, personal characteristics, and experiences that are intrinsically beneficial and sought for their own sake and represent an individual's core values and life priorities. Ward and colleagues have proposed 11 classes of primary goods[1]: (i) life (including healthy living and functioning); (ii) knowledge; (iii) excellence in play; (iv) excellence in work (including mastery experiences); (v) excellence in agency (i.e., autonomy and self-directedness); (vi) inner peace (i.e., freedom from emotional turmoil and stress); (vii) friendship (including intimate, romantic and family relationships); (viii) community; (ix) spirituality (in the broad sense of finding meaning and purpose in life); (x) happiness; and (xi) creativity (e.g., Purvis, 2010; Ward and Gannon, 2006). Whilst it is assumed that all humans seek out all the primary goods to some degree, the weightings or priorities given to specific primary goods reflect an individual's values and life priorities. In a sense, primary goods sit at the centre of the individual's sense of who they are and what is really worth having in life. Thus, when thinking about how to help offenders to desist from further criminal actions, pro-social ways of achieving these primary goods should be made available. Cutting off access to the primary goods without pointing to alternative means of achieving them is likely to result in frustration, lack of meaning or purpose and, ultimately, increase the chances of further offending (Laws and Ward, 2011).

Instrumental or *secondary goods* provide concrete means of securing primary goods and take the form of approach goals. A useful way to understand the relationship between primary and secondary goods is to view the latter as comprised of the specific roles, practices and actions that provide routes to primary goods. For example, the primary good of relatedness might be satisfied through spending time with friends and family, meeting new people, or being in an intimate relationship; and the primary good of excellence in play might be achieved through involvement in sport or other hobbies. Importantly, appropriate secondary goods represent socially acceptable means of securing primary goods, such that they are incompatible with offending. It is important to grasp that criminogenic needs always exert their influence on, or through, secondary goods – for example, relying on the criminogenic need of antisocial peers as a means to achieve the primary good of relatedness.

The GLM assumes that all humans fashion their lives around their core values, meaning we all follow some sort of (often implicit) good life plan, however rudimentary. According to the GLM, offending results from flaws in an individual's life plan, and relates either directly and/ or indirectly to the pursuit of primary goods (Ward and Gannon, 2006; Ward and Maruna, 2007). The direct route is evident when primary good(s) are explicitly sought through offence-related actions. A central flaw in the direct route is the use of harmful secondary goods (i.e., means) to achieve primary goods. For example, an individual lacking the competencies to satisfy the good of intimacy with an adult might instead attempt to meet this good through sexual offending against a child. To reinforce the point concerning the link between secondary goods and criminogenic needs, in this example the criminogenic need of intimacy deficits is associated with seeking intimacy through sex with a child. The indirect route is implicated when an individual does not have the direct intention to offend, but has problems in the

---

[1] Note that this is a recent change from the initial 10 classes of primary goods identified by Ward and Stewart (2003).

pursuit of other goods which eventually culminate in an offence. Such problems might include a *lack of scope*, in that a number of goods are omitted from a good life plan, *conflict and/or lack of coherence* in the secondary goods (i.e., means) used to secure primary goods, and lack of *internal and external capabilities* to satisfy primary goods in the environment and individual lives. Consider the example of an individual prioritizing the primary goods of relatedness (more specifically an intimate relationship with his wife) and excellence in work. Increased hours at work might eventually lead to a breakdown in his intimate relationship (i.e., the means, or secondary goods, used to satisfy the primary good of excellence in work conflicts with satisfying the good of relatedness). The use of pornography to cope with his emotional distress following a potential end to the relationship (i.e., problems with internal capability-mood regulation) might lead a person who did not initially set out to offend, to lose control in certain situations, and commit an offence. Thus, a lack of adequate mood management skills led to his relying on sexual arousal as a distraction, and this in turn, resulted in the entrenchment of deviant sexual feelings and, ultimately, to his sexually assaulting a woman.

In the direct and indirect examples provided, problems with internal capabilities were evident, many of which reflect criminogenic needs/dynamic risk factors. Internal capabilities include knowledge and skill sets, while external capabilities include environmental opportunities, resources and supports. Thus, criminogenic needs are conceptualized in the GLM as obstacles blocking goods attainment. For example, antisocial orientation, a dynamic risk factor for general, violent and sexual recidivism (e.g., Andrews and Bonta, 2006; Hanson and Morton-Bourgon, 2005) might represent a barrier towards fulfilling the primary good of autonomy through frequent sentences of incarceration. Similarly, poor emotional regulation – again a dynamic risk factor for all types of recidivism (Bonta and Andrews, 2010) – might block attainment of inner peace.

Considering clinical implications of the GLM, in addition to a comprehensive assessment of static and dynamic risk factors, a key task of assessment involves mapping out an individual's good lives conceptualization by identifying the weightings given to the various primary goods. This is achieved through: (i) asking increasingly detailed questions about an offender's core commitments in life and his or her valued day-to-day activities and experiences, and (ii) identifying the goals and underlying values that were evident (either directly or indirectly) in an offender's offence-related actions. Once an individual's conceptualization of what constitutes a good life is understood, future-oriented secondary goods aimed at satisfying primary goods in socially acceptable ways are formulated collaboratively with the client and translated into a Good Lives (GL) treatment/intervention plan. Interventions aim to add to a client's repertoire of functioning through strengthening their capacity to achieve valued goods in socially acceptable ways. Traditional treatment targets (i.e., criminogenic needs) are conceptualized within GL plans as obstacles blocking goods fulfilment, and are targeted within the broader focus of goods fulfilment.

Ward, Mann and Gannon (2007) outlined a group-based application of the GLM based on seven modules typical of best-practice sex offender treatment programmes: establishing therapy norms, understanding offending and cognitive restructuring, dealing with deviant arousal, victim impact and empathy training, affect regulation, social skills training, and relapse prevention. They highlighted that most modules were associated with an overarching primary good. For example, an overarching good contained within the understanding offending and cognitive restructuring module is that of knowledge, attained through providing offenders with an understanding of how their thoughts, feelings and actions led them to offend. The social skills training module is associated with the overarching goods of friendship, community and agency. The overarching good(s) addressed through each module ought to be clarified and linked explicitly to individual clients' GL plans. Thus, each group member's unique GL plan should inform the nature of interventions received, meaning that certain interventions – and sometimes entire modules – might not be relevant for some clients. Tailoring intervention content and intensity to match individual clients' GL plans is best facilitated using rolling groups (i.e., a new member joins the group when another is discharged, resulting in group members being at different stages of treatment/rehabilitation) rather than closed groups. It is beyond the scope of this chapter to describe applications of the GLM in any detail; however, we refer interested readers to the following resources: Willis *et al.* (forthcoming), Yates and Prescott (2011), and Yates, Prescott and Ward (2010).

The GLM has undergone extensive theoretical evaluation (see Laws and Ward, 2011; Ward and Maruna, 2007), and several empirical studies have offered support for the GLM's underlying assumptions (e.g., Barnett and Wood, 2008; Bouman, de Ruiter and Schene, 2008; Purvis, 2010; Willis and Grace, 2008; Willis and Ward, 2011; Yates *et al.*, 2009). We now turn out attention to reviewing empirical support for the GLM as an overarching framework for offender rehabilitation programmes.

Empirical Support for the Effectiveness of GLM-Informed Interventions

Integrated appropriately, the GLM incorporates each of the RNR principles, thus it can be argued that the large body of empirical literature supporting the RNR also supports the main basis comprising the GLM (see Willis *et al.*, 2011). In short, the GLM retains the merits of the RNR while addressing its limitations – especially its failure to motivate and engage offenders in the rehabilitation process (Mann, 2000; Ward and Maruna, 2007; Yates, 2009). It does so through promoting those goods or goals that individuals value in life using pro-social means, which requires that criminogenic needs be addressed because the two are simply incompatible. To illustrate, like most of us, many of our clients value satisfying interpersonal relationships. It is arguably impossible to promote satisfying pro-social relationships when clients lack the skills required to develop respectful, appropriate and mutually satisfying adult relationships and/or have high levels of emotional identification with children. Accordingly, interventions designed to develop relationship skills would comprise one component of a client's GL plan. In this way, the GLM incorporates the RNR need principle (i.e., needs are conceptualized as internal or external obstacles towards pro-social goods fulfilment). Along with the need principle, the GLM also accommodates the RNR principles of risk and responsivity. The risk principle is incorporated by virtue of the fact that high-risk individuals typically experience greater problems of internal and external capacity to achieve pro-social personal goals than low-risk individuals and, therefore, require greater levels of therapeutic intervention (Ward and Gannon, 2008; Yates, Prescott and Ward, 2010). Consistent with the risk principle, low-risk individuals typically require minimal or no therapeutic intervention – and might reap greater benefits through practical support (provided, for example, by a case manager, probation officer or support network) which ensures external conditions are in place to effectively implement GL plans. The GLM can be delivered within the framework of the risk principle, simply by varying the intensity of intervention according to the risk posed by individual clients (Yates, forthcoming) and, in fact, this is the recommended approach (Yates, Prescott and Ward, 2010).

Lastly, the responsivity principle is addressed within the GLM through its central focus on fulfilment of goods that are prioritized by individual clients, as well as its capacity to increase engagement with treatment and motivation to participate in treatment (e.g., Yates, 2009). In other words, interventions are delivered in ways that maximize their relevance to the individual, a common and well-established practice in effective treatment more generally (Yates, 2003; Yates, Prescott and Ward, 2010). Thus, it is clearly a mistake to claim that the GLM ignores the RNR principles. 'It simply reconceptualises and integrates them within a different theoretical framework' (Ward and Gannon, 2008, p. 4).

Accordingly, any programme appropriately implementing the GLM should have at least equal efficacy as a strictly RNR-based programme. It is important to stress that the GLM is a rehabilitation framework that is intended to supply practitioners with an overview of the aims and values underpinning practice rather than a specific treatment model (Ward and Maruna, 2007). It is intended to provide a more comprehensive framework for offender practice than currently exists. In essence, it functions as a broad *map* which needs to be supplemented by specific theories concerning concrete interventions such as cognitive behavioural treatment techniques (Ward and Maruna, 2007). Programmes can be, and are, constructed that reflect GLM assumptions and, as we will outline, evaluations of these programmes are in progress. Such programmes are best understood as GLM-consistent programmes, and are not the GLM itself (Laws and Ward, 2011; Ward and Maruna, 2007).

In this section, we (i) review empirical research that has investigated the added effectiveness of integrating GLM-related concepts (e.g., approach goals, attention to well-being as well as risk reduction) into rehabilitation endeavours, and (ii) describe those studies reporting findings from GLM-consistent programmes/interventions that have explicitly integrated the GLM as an overarching framework. Much of this research appears in the sexual offending literature, since the GLM was first developed within this context (e.g., Ward and Stewart, 2003).

Empirical research investigating the integration of GLM-related concepts

Several studies have examined the utility of integrating GLM-related concepts or ideas into offender rehabilitation programmes. In one of the first such studies, Mann *et al.* (2004) compared two orientations to a relapse prevention intervention: a traditional, avoidant-goal-focused intervention (e.g., including identifying high-risk situations and outlining ways to avoid such situations), and an adapted approach-goal-focused intervention. In the approach-goal-focused intervention, Haaven, Little and Petre-Miller's (1990) New Me/Old Me strategy was used and clients developed approach-oriented goals focused on achieving their 'New Me' conceptualization, similar to a good lives conceptualization. Forty-seven sexual offenders were randomly assigned to either condition. Results indicated that participants in the approach-goal-oriented intervention engaged better in treatment (as measured by between-session task completion and participants' willingness to disclose problem areas) and were more genuinely motivated to live an offence-free life after treatment (as rated by therapists) compared to participants in the avoidant-goal-oriented intervention.

Ware and Bright (2008) reported preliminary findings following changes made to a prison-based sex offender treatment programme in response to a high attrition rate. These changes included switching from closed to rolling groups, greater use of approach (versus avoidant) goals, greater emphasis on positive therapist characteristics, and 'structuring treatment to reflect the good lives model, whereby it is strength based and concerned with promoting offenders' goals alongside the management of their recidivism risk' (p. 347). Since the implementation of these changes, the treatment attrition rate has reduced, staff have reported feeling more effective and positive in their work likely benefiting their therapeutic relationship (which itself is related to treatment change, e.g., Marshall *et al.*, 2003; Serran *et al.*, 2003), and clients have been able to exercise greater autonomy in the rehabilitation process through working towards treatment targets at their own pace – for example, high functioning and highly motivated clients are able to complete the programme in a shorter time period (6 months) than they could previously (8–10 months).

The GLM's focus on goods fulfilment necessitates a much broader focus than what is typical of RNR-based programmes. In addition to addressing internal capacity for change, external resources and opportunities require consideration. Finding employment represents a common re-entry concern, and depending on the individual, employment might help satisfy several primary goods, including excellence in work, autonomy, happiness and creativity. Martin *et al.* (2010) investigated whether inclusion of an intervention directly assisting clients to attain and maintain employment was more efficacious than social cognitive training (a programme targeting criminogenic needs) alone, using a quasi-experimental design. Their sample comprised 117 repeat offenders, mostly convicted for property/drug offences. A social worker facilitated the employment intervention, which involved securing jobs through liaising with external agencies and assisting participants maintain their jobs. The authors reported no significant between-group differences based on age, educational level, type of offence, sentence duration and stages of correctional classification. After a six-year follow-up, survival analyses showed that the social cognitive skills programme produced a statistically significant delay in time to reoffence compared to the control group (offenders eligible to receive either intervention but for reasons not described by Martin *et al.* (2010) did not). Although not significant (perhaps due to low statistical power – only 12 participants received the employment intervention), participants receiving both social cognitive training and the employment intervention displayed a lengthier time to reoffence (and lower percentage of reoffences) than participants receiving social cognitive training alone. Thus, the employment intervention appeared to strengthen the effects of the social cognitive training programme. As suggested by Martin *et al.* (2010) preparing participants to attain and maintain a job might increase motivation to engage in rehabilitation programmes, and therefore indirectly contribute to reductions in recidivism. Findings support the importance of working towards pro-social approach goals that relate to the GLM primary goods – in this case, excellence in work.

In their recent book, Marshall *et al.* (2011) described their strength-based approach to sex offender treatment, which incorporates many GLM-related concepts. In addition to an emphasis on the use of approach goals, attention to positive therapist characteristics, and an overview of the GLM at the beginning of treatment, the GLM is used towards the end of the programme to integrate learning from previous phases and prepare clients for discharge. Marshall *et al.* (2011) write that 'the final phase of the programme aims at integrating what has been learned so far into plans for release and for the continued development of a more fulfilling life. The first step involves identifying the goals and plans to achieve these goals, within the framework of our version of the GLM' (p. 156). In their modified version of the GLM, the 11 primary goods are condensed into 6 areas: 'health (good diet and exercise), mastery (in work and play), autonomy (self-directiveness), relatedness (intimate/sexual relationship, family friends, kinship, and community), inner peace (freedom from turmoil and stress, a sense of purpose and meaning in life), knowledge and creativity (satisfaction from knowing and creating things – job- or hobby-related knowledge, playing music, writing)' (Exhibit 7.2, p. 127). Clients are assisted to generate goals relating to these life domains and construct plans for achieving their various goals. In an evaluation of the Rockwood Primary Programme, independent research assistants collected recidivism data for 535 clients and found a 3.2% sexual recidivism rate over 5.4 years and a 5.6% rate at 8.4 years, clearly below expected rates based on their sample's mean scores on actuarial risk assessment tools[2] (16.8% and 23.8%, respectively), and below average reoffending rates for treated sexual offenders reported in meta-analyses (e.g., 12%, Hanson *et al.*, 2002). Importantly, a broad definition of recidivism was used such that actual convictions, withdrawn charges and parole revocations/suspensions were all included. These findings provide further support for strengths-based approaches such as the GLM over and above deficits-based approaches.

Thus far, we have reviewed a selection of empirical studies that have described offender rehabilitation interventions that have incorporated GLM-related concepts to varying degrees. Findings from these studies highlight that attention to the therapeutic relationship, use of approach goals and consideration for life concerns not directly related to recidivism (i.e., non-criminogenic needs) appear to address key problems evident with a pure risk management approach – especially client engagement. Next, we consider those studies that have reported findings from interventions and programmes that have explicitly integrated the GLM as an overarching framework.

Empirical research investigating GLM-consistent interventions

In the first report of a GLM-consistent intervention, Simons, McCullar and Tyler (2006) evaluated a GLM approach to treatment planning at a prison-based sex offender treatment programme. Prior to the adoption of GLM-informed treatment planning, a Relapse Prevention (RP; Laws, 1989) framework was used in which treatment goals were assigned by the therapist based solely on criminogenic needs, and framed as avoidance goals (e.g., abstain from masturbation). Using a GLM approach, treatment goals were collaboratively arrived at and formulated as personally meaningful approach goals. Clients receiving the GLM approach to treatment planning (*n*=96) were more likely to complete treatment, remain in treatment longer and be rated by therapists as more motivated to participate in treatment compared to clients who received RP-based treatment planning (*n*=100). Pre/post-treatment comparisons on a range of measures revealed that clients who received either RP- or GLM-based treatment planning improved similarly on social skills and victim empathy, and while both groups improved in problem-solving ability, clients receiving GLM-based treatment planning demonstrated significantly greater improvements compared to clients receiving RP-based treatment planning. Moreover, clients in the GLM approach demonstrated significantly better coping skills post-treatment, and no such gains were observed for participants in the RP approach. Lastly, clients receiving GL treatment planning were more likely to have a social support system post-treatment compared to clients who received RP.

A number of case study applications of GLM-consistent approaches to offender rehabilitation have also been reported. Lindsay *et al.* (2007) designed GLM-based interventions for two men with histories of sexual offending. Both men were initially reluctant to engage in sex offender treatment, however, utilizing a GLM approach, both men engaged. Lindsay *et al.* (2007) reported that the dual focus on improving quality of life as well as managing risk enhanced treatment engagement and provided both men with a pro-social and personally meaningful life focus. Both offenders remained offence-free five years following their referrals for treatment. In another case study application, Whitehead, Ward and Collie (2007) applied the GLM with a high-risk violent offender. Whitehead, Ward and Collie (2007) reported that

[2]   Static-99 (Hanson and Thornton, 1999) and the Rapid Risk Assessment for Sexual Offence Recidivism (Hanson, 2007).

the implementation of GLM principles facilitated treatment readiness, and promoted long-term reintegration goals, including engaging in university study and developing pro-social leisure pursuits. Both activities fostered moving away from associating with an antisocial peer group (itself a dynamic risk factor for violent recidivism, e.g., Andrews and Bonta, 2006) and increased association with a pro-social peer group. Official statistics reveal that the individual concerned has not been convicted of a new crime after an approximate six-year period.

More recently, Gannon *et al.* (2011) detailed a group-based application of the GLM with sex offenders residing in an inpatient mental health unit in the United Kingdom. The GLM was integrated into assessment and treatment planning, and GLM content was incorporated into the modular structure of the programme. More specifically, treatment modules included: general group formation, understanding good lives and risk factors, understanding offending, sexual arousal and fantasy, coping skills, offence-supportive thinking, victim awareness and empathy, intimacy and relationships, and recognizing risk and leading a good life. In addition, nursing staff and a therapeutic activities team were recruited to support clients obtain valued goods outside of treatment sessions. Treatment progress for five of the six clients who participated in the programme was described (the remaining client did not consent to his data being used for publication). Notwithstanding the complex mental health needs represented in this particular group, all clients engaged successfully with the programme and completed the programme in its entirety – including one client who was discharged before the programme ended and voluntarily returned to the unit to complete the programme. Gannon *et al.* (2011) reported that all clients understood the concept of primary human goods and the importance of pro-social goods attainment. However, they noted that clients with lower intelligence levels and/or indirect pathways to offending (i.e., offending not the *direct* result of attempting to satisfy one or more primary goods) struggled to understand the links between the GLM and their risk factors for sexual offending; and that some of the more intelligent clients 'focussed so much on the Good Lives aspect of the group that they failed to fully appreciate the importance of their own risk and treatment factors' (p. 164). Such findings provide valuable guidance for future GLM-based programmes, specifically that treatment providers should take care to ensure that clients recognize the relationship between the GLM and their offending and appreciate the importance of addressing criminogenic needs in the broader pursuit of goods fulfilment.

Finally, Harkins *et al.* (2012) recently conducted an evaluation of the Better Lives module, introduced as a replacement to an RP-oriented module for community-based sex offenders in the United Kingdom. The Better Lives module was developed using a GLM approach and involved promoting pro-social attainment of each of the GLM primary goods. Several comparisons were made between clients who participated in the RP-oriented module ($n=701$) and the Better Lives module ($n=76$). Although there were no differences in attrition rates or treatment change (as measured using a psychometric battery), both facilitators and programme participants described the Better Lives module more positively. Of note, most of the facilitators interviewed reported that the Better Lives module did not pay sufficient (if any) attention to criminogenic needs. Accordingly, the programme was amended to better reflect the GLM twin focus of risk reduction and well-being enhancement. Preliminary findings from an evaluation of the amended programme suggest that participants in the GLM-based programme were more likely to attain a treated profile (i.e., indistinguishable from a sample of non-offenders) on a battery of psychometric tests assessing criminogenic needs compared to participants receiving the RP module (Barnett, Manderville-Norden and Rakestrow, under review).

In sum, the available evidence offers support that the GLM addresses limitations of pure risk-based approaches to offender rehabilitation. Together, research findings reviewed in this chapter suggest that appropriate integration of the GLM has the potential to enhance treatment engagement, and better its outcomes. We acknowledge that findings reported in this review are preliminary, and that it is too early to know whether GLM-consistent programmes will provide significant reductions in recidivism compared to pure RNR-based programmes. Several treatment programmes in the United States and Canada purport to have adopted the GLM (McGrath *et al.*, 2010), and evaluations of these programmes are in progress (Willis, Ward and Levenson, in press). Accordingly, intermediate and longer-term outcomes of GLM-consistent programmes will become available in due course.

Conclusion

While it is apparent that offenders respond positively to interventions that focus on reducing dynamic risk factors, there are significant limitations with this method. The most striking problems are the difficulty in engaging people in the process of change and the failure to integrate programmes targeting psychological variables with the rich and impressive criminological literature on desistance (e.g., Laub and Sampson, 2003). According to researchers such as Porporino (2010) and Laws and Ward (2011), desistance research underlines the necessity of incorporating community-based factors such as employment or education within rehabilitation programmes and spells out some of the ways to achieve this. Psychological interventions are conceptualized as ways of providing the skills and motivation required to ensure offenders capitalize on desistance moments, or 'turning points', and by doing so, embed themselves into local social networks. Strength-oriented rehabilitation frameworks such as the GLM, and intervention programmes derived from them, are ideally placed to reinforce desistance processes because of their sensitivity to offender commitments and social ecology. The GLM provides a systematic, comprehensive framework for designing offender treatment and management. It is anchored in sound psychological theory and has a strong ethical base. In addition, as we have outlined, evidence is accumulating that specific programmes derived from the GLM address limitations of pure risk management or deficits-based approaches. Simply addressing risk factors is unlikely to encourage individuals who have committed crime to adopt new, socially adaptive, ways of thinking about themselves and their lives. As one of us stated many years ago, offenders need the possibility of better lives not merely the promise of less harmful ones.

References

Andrews, D.A. and Bonta, J. (2006) *The Psychology of Criminal Conduct*, 4th edn, Anderson Publishing, Cincinnati.

Barnett, G. and Wood, J.L. (2008) Agency, relatedness, inner peace, and problem solving in sexual offending: how sexual offenders prioritize and operationalize their good lives conceptions. *Sexual Abuse: Journal of Research and Treatment*, 20, 444–465.

Barnett, G., Manderville-Norden, R. and Rakestrow, J. (under review) The Good Lives Model or relapse prevention: what works better in facilitating and maintaining change?

Bonta, J. and Andrews, D.A. (2010) Viewing offender assessment and rehabilitation through the lens of the risk-need-responsivity model, in *Offender Supervision: New Directions in Theory, Research and Practice* (eds F. McNeill, P. Raynor and C. Trotter), Willan Publishing, Oxon, pp. 19–40.

Bouman, Y.H.A., de Ruiter, C. and Schene, A.H. (2008) Quality of life of violent and sexual offenders in community-based forensic psychiatric treatment. *Journal of Forensic Psychiatry & Psychology*, 19, 484–501.

Browne, K.D., Foreman, L. and Middleton, D. (1998) Predicting treatment drop-out in sex offenders. *Child Abuse Review*, 7, 402–419.

Gannon, T.A., King, T., Miles, H. *et al.* (2011) Good lives sexual offender treatment for mentally disordered offenders. *British Journal of Forensic Practice*, 13, 153–168.

Haaven, J., Little, R. and Petre-Miller, D. (1990) *Treating Intellectually Disabled Sex Offenders: A Model Residential Program*, Safer Society Press, Orwell.

Hanson, R.K. and Morton-Bourgon, K.E. (2005) The characteristics of persistent sexual offenders: a meta-analysis of recidivism studies. *Journal of Consulting and Clinical Psychology*, 73, 1154–1163.

Hanson, R.K. and Thornton, D. (1999) Static-99: Improving Actuarial Risk Assessments for Sex Offenders. *User Rep. no. 1999-02*. Department of the Solicitor General of Canada, Ottawa.

Hanson, R.K., Gordon, A., Harris, A.J.R. *et al.* (2002) First report of the collaborative outcome data project on the effectiveness of psychological treatment for sex offenders. *Sexual Abuse: A Journal of Research and Treatment*, 14, 169–194.

Hanson, R.K., Harris, A.J.R., Scott, T. and Helmus, L. (2007) Assessing the Risk of Sexual Offenders on Community Supervision: The Dynamic Supervision Project no. 2007-05. Public Safety Canada, Ottawa.

Hanson, R.K., Bourgon, G., Helmus, L. and Hodgson, S. (2009) The principles of effective correctional treatment also apply to sexual offenders: a meta-analysis. *Criminal Justice and Behavior*, 36, 865–891.

Harkins, L., Flak, V.E., Beech, A. and Woodhams, J. (2012) Evaluation of a community-based sex offender treatment program using a Good Lives Model approach. *Sexual Abuse: A Journal of Research and Treatment*, 24, 519–543.

Jones, N., Pelissier, B. and Klein-Saffran, J. (2006) Predicting sex offender treatment entry among individuals convicted of sexual offense crimes. *Sexual Abuse: A Journal of Research and Treatment*, 18, 83–98.

Landenberger, N.A. and Lipsey, M.W. (2005) The positive effects of cognitive-behavioral programs for offenders: a meta-analysis of factors associated with effective treatment. *Journal of Experimental Criminology*, 1, 451–476.

Laub, J.H. and Sampson, R.J. (2003) *Shared Beginnings, Divergent Lives: Delinquent Boys to Age 70*, Harvard University Press, Cambridge.

Laws, D.R. (1989) *Relapse Prevention with Sex Offenders*, Guilford Press, New York.

Laws, D.R. and Ward, T. (2011) *Desistance and Sexual Offending: Alternatives to Throwing Away the Keys*, Guildford Press, New York.

Lindsay, W.R., Ward, T., Morgan, T. and Wilson, I. (2007) Self-regulation of sex offending, future pathways and the Good Lives Model: applications and problems. *Journal of Sexual Aggression*, 13, 37–50.

Mann, R.E. (2000) Managing resistance and rebellion in relapse prevention intervention, in *Remaking Relapse Prevention with Sex Offenders: A Sourcebook* (eds D.R. Laws, S.M. Hudson and T. Ward), Sage Publications, Thousand Oaks, pp. 187–200.

Mann, R.E., Webster, S.D., Schofield, C. and Marshall, W.L. (2004) Approach versus avoidance goals in relapse prevention with sexual offenders. *Sexual Abuse: A Journal of Research and Treatment*, 16, 65–75.

Marshall, W.L., Serran, G.A., Fernandez, Y.M. *et al.* (2003) Therapist characteristics in the treatment of sexual offenders: tentative data on their relationship with indices of behaviour change. *Journal of Sexual Aggression*, 9, 25–30.

Marshall, W.L., Marshall, L.E., Serran, G.A. and O'rien, M.D. (2011) *Rehabilitating Sexual Offenders: A Strength-Based Approach*, American Psychological Association, Washington, DC.

Martin, A.M., Hernandez, B., Hernandez-Fernaud, E. *et al.* (2010) The enhancement effect of social and employment integration on the delay of recidivism of released offenders trained with the R & R programme. *Psychology, Crime & Law*, 16, 401–413.

McGrath, R., Cumming, G., Burchard, B. *et al.* (2010) *Current Practices and Emerging Trends in Sexual Abuser Management: The Safer Society 2009 North American Curvey*, Safer Society Press, Brandon.

Miller, W.R. and Rollnick, S. (1991) *Motivational Interviewing: Preparing People to Change Addictive Behavior*, The Guilford Press, New York.

Miller, W.R. and Rollnick, S. (eds) (2002) *Motivational Interviewing: Preparing People for Change*, 2nd edn, Guildford Press, New York.

Moore, D.L., Bergman, B.A. and Knox, P.L. (1999) Predictors of sex offender treatment completion. *Journal of Child Sexual Abuse*, 7, 73–88.

Porporino, F.J. (2010) Bringing sense and sensitivity to corrections: from programmes to 'fix' offenders to services to support desistance, in *What Else Works? Creative Work with Offenders* (eds J. Brayford, F. Cowe and J. Deering), Willan Publishing, Portland.

Purvis, M. (2010) *Seeking a Good Life: Human Goods and Sexual Offending*, Lambert Academic Press, Saarbrücken.

Serran, G., Fernandez, Y., Marshall, W.L. and Mann, R.E. (2003) Process issues in treatment: application to sexual offender programs. *Professional Psychology: Research and Practice*, 34, 368–374.

Simons, D.A., McCullar, B. and Tyler, C. (2006) Evaluation of the Good Lives Model approach to treatment planning. Paper presented at the 25th Annual Association for the Treatment of Sexual Abusers Research and Treatment Conference, September, Chicago.

Ward, T. (2002) Good lives and the rehabilitation of offenders: promises and problems. *Aggression and Violent Behavior*, 7, 513–528.

Ward, T. and Gannon, T.A. (2006) Rehabilitation, etiology, and self-regulation: the comprehensive Good Lives Model of treatment for sexual offenders. *Aggression and Violent Behavior*, 11, 77–94.

Ward, T. and Gannon, T.A. (2008) Goods and risks: misconceptions about the Good Lives Model. *Correctional Psychologist*, 40, 1–7.

Ward, T. and Maruna, S. (2007) *Rehabilitation: Beyond the Risk Assessment Paradigm*, Routledge, London.

Ward, T. and Stewart, C.A. (2003) The treatment of sex offenders: risk management and good lives. *Professional Psychology: Research and Practice*, 34, 353–360.

Ware, J. and Bright, D.A. (2008) Evolution of a treatment programme for sex offenders: changes to the NSW Custody-Based Intensive Treatment (CUBIT). *Psychiatry, Psychology and Law*, 15, 340–349.

Ward, T., Mann, R.E. and Gannon, T.A. (2007) The good lives model of offender rehabilitation: clinical implications. *Aggression and Violent Behavior*, 12, 87–107.

Whitehead, P.R., Ward, T. and Collie, R.M. (2007) Time for a change: applying the Good Lives Model of rehabilitation to a high-risk violent offender. *International Journal of Offender Therapy and Comparative Criminology*, 51, 578–598.

Willis, G.M. and Grace, R.C. (2008) The quality of community reintegration planning for child molesters: effects on sexual recidivism. *Sexual Abuse: A Journal of Research and Treatment*, 20, 218–240.

Willis, G.M. and Ward, T. (2011) Striving for a good life: the Good Lives Model applied to released child molesters. *Journal of Sexual Aggression*, 17, 290–303.

Willis, G.M., Ward, T. and Levenson, J.S. The Good Lives Model (GLM): an evaluation of GLM operationalization in North American Treatment Programs. *Sexual Abuse: A Journal of Research and Treatment*, forthcoming.

Willis, G.M., Gannon, T.A., Yates, P.M. *et al.* (2011) "In style" or evolving through research? Misperceptions about the Good Lives Model. *ATSA Forum*, 23, 16–21.

Willis, G.M., Yates, P.M., Gannon, T.A. and Ward, T. (2013) How to integrate the Good Lives Model into treatment programs for sexual offending: an introduction and overview. *Sexual Abuse: A Journal of Research and Treatment*, 25, 123–142.

Yates, P.M. (2003) Treatment of adult sexual offenders: a therapeutic cognitive-behavioral model of intervention. *Journal of Child Sexual Abuse*, 12, 195–232.

Yates, P.M. (2009) Using the Good Lives Model to motivate sexual offenders to participate in treatment, in *Building Motivation to Change in Sexual Offenders* (ed. D.S. Prescott), Safer Society Press, Brandon.

Yates, P.M. Models of sexual offender treatment, in *Sexual Offenders: Classification, Assessment, and Management* (eds A. Phenix and H. Hoberman).

Yates, P.M. and Prescott, D.S. (2011) *Building a Better Life: A Good Lives and Self-Regulation Workbook*, Safer Society Press, Brandon.

Yates, P.M., Goguen, B.C., Nicholaichuk, T.P. *et al.* (2000) *National Sex Offender Programs (Moderate, Low, and Maintenance Intensity Levels)*, Correctional Service of Canada, Ottawa.

Yates, P.M., Kingston, D.A., Simons, D.A. and Tyler, C. (2009) The Good Lives Model of rehabilitation applied to treatment: assessment and relationship to treatment progress and compliance. Paper presented at the 28th Annual Convention of the Association for the Treatment of Sexual Abusers (ATSA), October 2009, Dallas.

Yates, P.M., Prescott, D.S. and Ward, T. (2010) *Applying the Good Lives and Self Regulation Models to Sex Offender Treatment: A Practical Guide for Clinicians*, Safer Society Press, Brandon.

Part IV
What Works in Secure Settings

18

Treatment of People with Schizophrenia Who Behave Violently Towards Others

A Review of the Empirical Literature on Treatment Effectiveness

Nathan Kolla[1] and Sheilagh Hodgins[2,3]

[1]University of Toronto, Canada
[2]Université de Montréal, Canada
[3]King's College, London, UK

Criminal Offending among Persons with Schizophrenia

Schizophrenia limits cognitive, emotional and behavioural functioning in most cases from onset in late adolescence or early adulthood through the subsequent decades of adult life (Mueser and McGurk, 2004; Patel *et al.*, 2007). Consequently, the costs of caring for adults with schizophrenia represent a significant part of mental health budgets (Mangalore and Knapp, 2007) even though schizophrenia affects less than 1% of men and women (Perälä *et al.*, 2007). In addition, some people with schizophrenia repeatedly engage in aggressive behaviour towards others, some of which leads to criminal prosecutions for violent crimes, and some also engage in other types of antisocial behaviour, some of which leads to prosecutions for non-violent criminal offending. There is now robust evidence demonstrating that both men and women with schizophrenia[1] are at elevated risk, as compared to the general population, to be convicted of non-violent criminal offences, at higher risk to be convicted of violent criminal offences and at even higher risk to be convicted of homicide. For example, Hodgins and colleagues examined a birth cohort composed of all the 358 180 persons born in Denmark from 1944 through 1947 followed until participants were in their mid-40s. Individuals who had died or emigrated before the end of the follow-up period were excluded from the analyses.

---

[1] Throughout this chapter, the term 'schizophrenia' is used to refer to schizophrenia and schizoaffective disorder.

What Works in Offender Rehabilitation: An Evidence-Based Approach to Assessment and Treatment,
First Edition. Edited by Leam A. Craig, Louise Dixon and Theresa A. Gannon.
© 2013 John Wiley & Sons, Ltd. Published 2013 by John Wiley & Sons, Ltd.

The official criminal records of cohort members who had been admitted to a psychiatric ward at least once with a discharge diagnosis of schizophrenia were compared to those with no psychiatric admissions. The risk of a violent crime was elevated 4.6 (3.8–5.6) times among the men and 23.2 (14.4–37.4) times among the women with schizophrenia as compared to those with no admissions to a psychiatric ward (Brennan, Mednick and Hodgins, 2000). Similar elevations in risk have been documented among persons with schizophrenia identified in other birth and population cohorts (Arseneault *et al.*, 2000; Hodgins, 1992; Tiihonen *et al.*, 1997; Van Dorn, Volavka and Johnson, 2011; Wallace, Mullen and Burgess, 2004).

Most persons with schizophrenia who commit crimes acquire their first conviction prior to the onset of their illness (Wallace, Mullen and Burgess, 2004). A study from Denmark, where the age of criminal responsibility is 15 years, used national registers to document criminality among all persons born in 1963 or later and diagnosed with schizophrenia by 1999. Thirty-seven percent of the men and 7% of the women were found to have a criminal conviction prior to contact with mental health services (Munkner *et al.*, 2003). In studies of clinical samples of patients with schizophrenia, the proportion with a criminal conviction prior to first contact with services is lower, for example, 20% in Berne, Switzerland, between 1985 and 1987 (Modestin and Ammann, 1996) and 16% in the Edinburgh High Risk Study (Humphreys, Johnstone and Macmillan, 1994). Hodgins and co-authors examined a representative sample of individuals within one geographic area in the United Kingdom who received treatment for a first episode of psychosis. One-third of the men and 10% of the women had a conviction for a criminal offence, and 20% of the men and 5% of the women had at least one conviction for a violent offence (Hodgins *et al.*, 2011a). In one review, the proportions of patients experiencing their first episode of psychosis who had previously committed a homicide ranged from 13% to 76% (Large and Nielssen, 2008), while in another systematic review and meta-analysis of persons seeking treatment for a first episode of psychosis, 34.5% were reported to have engaged in violent behaviour, 16.6% in serious violence and 0.6% in severe violence. The studies of clinical samples likely underestimate the proportions of patients with criminal records as those with a history of antisocial behaviour and/or crime are more likely than others to refuse to participate in research studies (Munkner *et al.*, 2009).

The studies reviewed thus far describe crimes committed in the community by persons with schizophrenia. During an acute episode on an inpatient psychiatric ward, many patients with schizophrenia engage in aggressive behaviour that usually does not lead to prosecution. Such behaviour often remits within days after initiation of antipsychotic medication (Steinert, Sippach and Gebhardt, 2000). Once the acute phase is resolved, antipsychotic medication continues to be necessary to control psychotic symptoms, but it no longer is sufficient to prevent aggressive behaviour (Hodgins and Riaz, 2011). At this stage of illness when patients are discharged to the community, factors such as male gender, young age, a history of conduct problems, co-morbid antisocial personality disorder and substance misuse are associated with aggressive behaviour. The present chapter provides a review of the empirical literature that considers the effectiveness of services and treatments that aim to prevent antisocial and aggressive behaviour among persons with schizophrenia living in the community. We begin by summarizing the pathways through which individuals with schizophrenia and a history of criminal offending come to receive psychiatric care, highlighting differences between general and forensic psychiatric services. Next, we discuss what is known about the different subtypes of offenders with schizophrenia. Finally, we consider specific interventions for palliating aggressive behaviour in schizophrenia, including psychopharmacological strategies, community-based psychosocial interventions and psychological treatments.

Current Services and Treatments for Persons with Schizophrenia Who Have a History of Criminal Offending

General considerations

Most patients with a history of violence towards others and/or criminal convictions are treated within general adult psychiatric services. While many countries have now established specialized clinics for persons experiencing their first episode of psychosis, we know of no studies evaluating treatments that target aggressive and antisocial behaviour at first episode. Unfortunately, current practice is to wait, often many years, before addressing these problems. For example, Hodgins and collaborators assessed a sample of 205 inpatients with severe mental illness (SMI) from a UK inner city mental health trust, most of whom suffered from schizophrenia. The patients were, on average, in their late 30s, and more than 80% had previously required inpatient care. Official criminal records indicated that 46.7% of the men and 16.5% of the women had at least one conviction for a violent crime, and, on average, the violent offenders had each been convicted of more than two crimes. The 82 men with criminal records had acquired convictions for 1792 crimes and the 23 female offenders for 458 crimes (Hodgins *et al.*, 2007a). In the two years following this admission, many patients continued to engage in antisocial behaviour, substance misuse and criminality, but these behaviours were not targeted by specific services or treatments (Hodgins *et al.*, 2009).

Admission to forensic services occurs, in most cases, many years after first admission to general adult services during which time patients continue to engage in antisocial and aggressive behaviours (Hodgins and Müller-Isberner, 2004). Yet, general adult services do not typically provide treatments aimed at reducing these behaviours. By contrast, forensic services are mandated to provide treatments that address both the illness and the aggressive and antisocial behaviours. Outcomes from forensic services for this population can be positive. In the only study to directly compare matched samples of men with schizophrenia treated within forensic and general adult services, Hodgins and colleagues found that during the two years in the community after discharge, the patients from the forensic hospitals had fewer psychotic symptoms, and proportionately fewer of them had used alcohol and/or drugs or had engaged in aggressive behaviour (Hodgins *et al.*, 2007b).[2] This study clearly shows that when services assess and treat both the illness and the related antisocial and aggressive behaviours, good outcomes can be achieved. Forensic hospitals in different countries detain offenders with schizophrenia for periods varying from less than a year to life. In most European countries, stays are approximately four years, with patients gradually spending more and more time in the

---

[2] Another study compared outcomes of patients with SMI who were treated in either general adult or forensic after-care services after being discharged from forensic hospitals (Coid, Hickey and Yang, 2007). This study differs from the one described earlier in that all patients were treated in a forensic hospital and the comparison focuses only on care provided after discharge. No difference in the rate of criminal convictions was observed among the ex-forensic patients who were cared for by general or forensic after-care services during six years. Since most treatments that directly target antisocial and aggressive behaviours are provided within forensic hospitals, as well as social skills and work training, the findings from this study of after-care do not contradict the comparison of forensic and general adult services that observed better outcomes in the forensic group. Further, this latter study included only men with schizophrenia.

community for leisure activities and/or work after about a year (Hodgins *et al.*, 2007b). Follow-up studies of patients discharged from forensic hospitals document relatively low rates of re-conviction (Coid *et al.*, 2007; Maden *et al.*, 2004). It is difficult to draw conclusions about the treatment of offenders with schizophrenia from these latter studies as samples included large proportions of patients with other diagnoses. Moreover, patients who were never discharged or had spent time in general adult wards were not taken into account, while the effect of court orders on appointment attendance in the community was also not considered.

As we noted at the beginning of the chapter, schizophrenia is a devastating illness that affects most aspects of adult functioning. Consequently, almost all persons with schizophrenia require antipsychotic medications to reduce psychotic symptoms and psychosocial interventions aimed at encouraging compliance with medications and treatments that target problems commonly associated with schizophrenia. Presently, there is evidence of effective treatments for people with schizophrenia that increase social skills (Kopelowicz, Liberman and Zarate, 2006); improve psychosocial functioning, such as Integrated Psychological Therapy (Roder *et al.*, 2006); remediate cognitive skills (McGurk *et al.*, 2007; Wykes *et al.*, 2007); provide education about the illness (Lincoln, Wilhelm and Nestoriuc, 2007); and support the development of employment skills (Burns *et al.*, 2007; Cook *et al.*, 2005). In addition, evidence suggests that patients benefit from a case manager who organizes the different treatments needed. Many persons with schizophrenia misuse alcohol and drugs, even some who do not engage in other antisocial or aggressive behaviours. Several programmes designed specifically for persons with schizophrenia have been shown to effectively reduce substance misuse (Bellack *et al.*, 2006; Haddock *et al.*, 2003; Kavanagh and Mueser, 2007). In addition to all of these interventions, offenders with schizophrenia require treatments designed specifically to reduce antisocial and aggressive behaviours. However, offenders with schizophrenia do not constitute a homogeneous group.

Subtypes of offenders with schizophrenia

Early-start offenders The early-starters display a pattern of antisocial behaviour that onsets in childhood or early adolescence and remains stable across the life span. These individuals are usually convicted of crimes prior to illness onset and commit more crimes and a greater diversity of crimes than other offenders with schizophrenia (Crocker *et al.*, 2005; Fulwiler and Ruthazer, 1999; Hodgins, 2004, 2008; Mueser *et al.*, 2006). They have criminal histories similar to those of non-mentally-ill offenders who also have a childhood history of conduct problems (Hodgins and Côté, 1993; Schug, Raine and Wilcox, 2007). In addition, almost all display a pattern of substance misuse going back to early adolescence (Fulwiler *et al.*, 1997; Moran and Hodgins, 2004; Mueser *et al.*, 1999; Tengström, Hodgins and Kullgren, 2001).

In clinical samples of adults with schizophrenia, the prevalence of conduct disorder prior to age 15 years varies from 22% in samples recruited in general adult services to 75% in samples recruited in forensic hospitals or prisons (Hodgins, Côté and Toupin, 1998; Hodgins *et al.*, 2008). Notably, among persons with schizophrenia, the prevalence of conduct disorder is much higher than among sex- and age-matched samples of the general population, and it is similar among men and women. Several studies have shown that the number of conduct disorder symptoms present prior to age 15 years is positively and linearly related to the number of convictions for non-violent and violent offences and to aggressive behaviour after controlling for current and past substance misuse (Hodgins, Tiihonen and Ross, 2005; Hodgins *et al.*, 2008; Swanson *et al.*, 2006). Thus, the evidence strongly suggests that this subtype of patient with schizophrenia requires interventions to reduce antisocial and/or aggressive behaviours and accompanying problems such as substance misuse and a lack of pro-social skills as soon as the acute symptoms of the first episode of psychosis resolve.

No antisocial behaviour prior to illness onset   A group of violent offenders with schizophrenia show no antisocial behaviour prior to the onset of the prodrome or illness and then repeatedly engage in aggressive behaviour towards others. There are very few studies of these persons. In a Danish study of a cohort of 4619 persons with schizophrenia, within seven years of first contact with services, 19% of the patients (with no prior criminal convictions) acquired a conviction, and 9% a conviction for a violent offence. Male sex and substance misuse were associated with criminal convictions (Munkner *et al.*, 2005). In the sample of 248 men with schizophrenia that we recruited from forensic and general psychiatric hospitals, offenders without antisocial behaviour prior to illness onset, compared to those with prior conduct disorder, included similar proportions with at least one conviction for a violent crime, but, on average, they had acquired fewer convictions for violent crimes and many fewer convictions for non-violent crimes. Importantly, however, a greater proportion of patients with no antisocial behaviour prior to illness onset had been convicted of a homicide (Hodgins, 2004). Some evidence (Mueser *et al.*, 1999, 2006) suggests that such persons with schizophrenia may be particularly vulnerable to illicit drug use, and that drug use may be directly associated with their violent behaviour. While two studies showed a similar prevalence of substance misuse disorders among early-starters and after-illness starters (Hodgins, Tiihonen and Ross, 2005; Hodgins *et al.*, 2008), it may be that these latter individuals behave aggressively only when intoxicated. Despite the lack of research, the available evidence suggests that reducing substance misuse while promoting compliance with antipsychotic medications might positively impact aggressive behaviour in this subtype of patient with schizophrenia.

Violent, late starters   A small group of individuals who display a chronic course of schizophrenia show no aggressive behaviour prior to their late 30s or early 40s and then engage in serious violence, often killing a carer. Homicides are often committed by patients with schizophrenia who have no history of violence or antisocial behaviour (Beaudoin, Hodgins and Lavoie, 1993; Erb *et al.*, 2001). Little is known about these individuals, but some evidence suggests that they become more callous with age, possibly due to changes in the brain associated with the progressing illness (Hodgins, 2008).

Conclusion   Despite this robust evidence of the heterogeneity among offenders with schizophrenia, services rarely provide treatments that address the needs of each subtype of offender (Müller-Isberner and Hodgins, 2000; Volavka and Citrome, 2008). In the sections that follow, we review the evidence of effectiveness of interventions aimed at reducing offending and antisocial and aggressive behaviours among persons with schizophrenia.

Evaluating the Efficacy of Specific Treatments for Aggressive Behaviour in Schizophrenia

Antipsychotic medication

As mentioned earlier, the mainstay of treatment for schizophrenia is antipsychotic medications. Medication non-compliance is a risk factor for violence in schizophrenia (Fazel *et al.*, 2010).

Numerous studies have investigated the salutatory effects of antipsychotic medications on aggressive behaviour, hostility and violence in schizophrenia, primarily among inpatients. While a comprehensive review of these medication trials is beyond the scope of this chapter, we present an overview of the most important findings. By far, the psychopharmacological agent with the strongest evidence base for reducing aggressive behaviour among persons with schizophrenia is the second-generation antipsychotic clozapine. The positive effects of clozapine on reducing aggressive behaviour necessitating the use of physical restraints were first identified in several retrospective studies (Chiles, Davidson and McBride, 1994; Ebrahim *et al.*, 1994; Maier, 1992; Mallya, Roos and Roebuck-Colgan, 1992; Ratey *et al.*, 1993; Wilson and Claussen, 1995). Two randomized controlled trials (RCTs) subsequently demonstrated the superiority of clozapine over other antipsychotic medications in decreasing hostility (Citrome *et al.*, 2001) and the number and severity of physical assaults (Krakowski *et al.*, 2006) among hospitalized patients with schizophrenia. These studies and others provide evidence of an antiaggressive effect of clozapine independent of its antipsychotic properties (Buckley *et al.*, 1995; Volvaka *et al.*, 1993). While medication trials of other second-generation antipsychotics have reported beneficial effects on hostility and aggression, the results from these investigations are much less robust (Aleman and Khan, 2001; Swanson *et al.*, 2004). Swanson *et al.* (2008) examined data from the National Institute of Mental Health Clinical Antipsychotic Trials of Intervention Effectiveness (CATIE) to determine whether antipsychotic medications were associated with a reduction in aggressive behaviour among patients with schizophrenia who were living in the community. Participants were randomized to one of five antipsychotic medications (four second-generation or 'newer' antipsychotics and one first-generation or 'older' antipsychotic). Notably, clozapine was *not* tested in this study. Contrary to previous research documenting a relative advantage of the newer antipsychotics over the older medications in reducing violent behaviour (Swanson, Swartz and Elbogen, 2004), results from the CATIE trial showed no difference between first- and second-generation antipsychotics on violent behaviour. Finally, an open investigation of combined treatment with the second-generation antipsychotic risperidone and electroconvulsive therapy reported a reduction in aggressive behaviour in patients with schizophrenia and aggression who received both treatments concurrently (Hirose, Ashby and Mills, 2001). Readers are referred to two excellent reviews (Citrome and Volavka, 2011; Volavka and Citrome, 2008) for further information on pharmacological interventions aimed at reducing aggressive behaviour among persons with schizophrenia. These medication trials, however, do not address the problem that many persons with schizophrenia, especially those who display antisocial behaviour, often fail to take their medications and/or combine antipsychotic medications with alcohol and illicit drugs. Without antipsychotic medication, the risk of developing an acute episode increases dramatically, and with it, the risk of aggressive behaviour. In addition, without antipsychotic medication, participation in other treatments is greatly hindered.

Community interventions

Assertive community treatment and intensive case management The best-studied community interventions are assertive community treatment (ACT) and intensive case management (ICM). ACT programmes provide comprehensive services to consumers in the community, including direct clinical care, housing and vocational assistance and 24-hour crisis overage. They are run by a multidisciplinary team – psychiatrist, nurses and case managers – with patient-to-staff ratios on the order of 10:1 (Stein and Test, 1980). ICM programmes share many features in common with ACT but do not necessarily have direct access to a psychiatrist and nurse or residential services. In contrast to ACT, case-loads tend not to be shared in ICM models and are typically larger (Surles *et al.*, 1992). There is a large body of research on clinical and social outcomes of persons with schizo-phrenia participating in ACT and ICM programmes. Some studies have also examined the influence of ACT and ICM on criminal recidivism. Mueser *et al.* (1998) reviewed con-trolled studies of ACT and ICM and found only 2 of 10 investigations (the proportion of study participants with a diagnosis of schizophrenia or schizoaffective disorder in each study ranged from 48% to 100%) that reported reductions in jail time served by ACT and ICM participants compared with those receiving less intensive, standard models of care. While the authors of the review speculated that low base rates of incarceration in some studies may have made it difficult to detect a change, they also suggested that the more intensive models of case management studied were not adequately resourced to address the needs of consumers at risk of engaging in illegal behaviours. Other studies, including an RCT that followed more than 700 patients with psychotic disorder over a two-year period, found no difference in the prevalence of violence among those assigned to ICM or standard case management (Walsh *et al.*, 2001). Another RCT compared the effectiveness of ACT, standard care and an integrated treatment model and similarly reported no significant effect of the type or intensity of mental health treatment on a variety of criminal justice system outcome measures in a homeless population with schizophrenia and substance misuse disorders (Calsyn *et al.*, 2005).

Forensic assertive community treatment (FACT)   This programme is an outgrowth of ACT tailored to the needs of mentally ill offenders. It differs from conventional ACT in several respects. First, FACT targets individuals with arrest histories. Second, prevention of re-arrest is the principal goal, and court sanctions can be imposed to encourage participation. Third, probation officers are members of the treatment team, and programme referrals are accepted from criminal justice agencies (Lamberti, Weisman and Faden, 2004). While there are few empirical studies of FACT, the available evidence links FACT programmes to improved criminal justice outcome measures. For example, two, small, pre-post study designs reported reduced arrests and days spent in jail among FACT consumers (Lamberti *et al.*, 2001; McCoy *et al.*, 2004). A recent RCT comparing FACT with usual treatment (65% of the sample had a psy-chotic disorder) similarly found that FACT participants had significantly fewer stays in jail (Cusack *et al.*, 2010).

Jail diversion and re-entry programmes   These interventions aim to reduce or circumvent jail time served by people with SMI by offering them treatment in the community as an alternative. Diversion programmes that span the criminal justice system continuum, from pre-booking strategies by law enforcement officials that avoid arrest to post-booking, jail- and court-based interventions, which become active once charges are filed, have been piloted. Although several retrospective and quasi-experimental investigations have reported lower rates of arrests, vio-lence and length of incarceration among participants of various diversion programmes (Broner, Maryl and Landsberg, 2005; Cimino and Jennings, 2002; Frisman *et al.*, 2006; Godley *et al.*, 2000; Hoff *et al.*, 1999; Lamb, Weinberger and Reston-Parham, 1996; Lurigio, Fallon and Dincin, 2000; McCoy *et al.*, 2004; Ventura *et al.*, 1998; Weisman, Lamberti and Price, 2004; Wilson, Tien and Eaves, 1995), two RCTs failed to detect a difference in incarceration rates between patients randomized to ICM and diversion or usual care (Cosden *et al.*, 2003; Solomon and Draine, 1995). As most of these studies involved participants with heterogeneous psychiatric diagnoses, the generalizability of these findings to patients with schizophrenia is limited.

Mental health court   These specialized courts have been the focus of a number of empirical investigations. Several features distinguish mental health courts from the traditional court system, including a separate docket for defendants with SMI, a non-adversarial and collaborative approach to problem solving adopted jointly by criminal justice and mental health professionals, monitoring by the court with penalties for non-compliance and the availability of appropriate treatment services prior to a ruling by a mental health court judge (Steadman *et al.*, 2001). Initial results of studies of such courts were equivocal. For instance, a study of Seattle's two mental health courts (Trupin and Richards, 2003) found that offenders with SMI who were referred to the programme and opted to participate had significantly fewer jail admissions after a nine-month period than programme refusals. Another pre-post design (Herinckz *et al.*, 2005) and controlled study (Moore and Hiday, 2006) similarly reported significant reductions in arrests among offenders with SMI participating in a mental health court. Conversely, a different investigation showed that offenders with SMI tried in mental health courts showed similar times to re-arrest and numbers of aggressive incidents as those who were tried in traditional courts (Christy *et al.*, 2005). An RCT compared outcomes among offenders with SMI tried in mental health courts who then received ACT and those who received treatment as usual (e.g., adversarial criminal processing and less ICM). While the majority of participants spent fewer days in jail during the follow-up period, no differences were detected in outcomes of the two groups (Cosden *et al.*, 2005). Notably, individuals with schizophrenia accounted for less than 40% of the sample in this investigation. McNiel and Binder (2007) compared criminal justice outcomes of individuals participating in a San Francisco mental health court during the first 22 months of its operation with those who were eligible for the programme but entered jail instead. They determined that trials in mental health courts were associated with a longer time to re-arrest. Because the MHC group included a significantly greater proportion of individuals with SMI (schizophrenia was diagnosed in 66% and 9% of persons in the experimental and control groups, respectively), the results may have been an underestimate of the benefits provided by mental health courts, given the higher base rates of violence among persons with SMI. The limitations of generalizing research results from single-site studies were overcome by a recent prospective investigation that pooled data from four different mental health courts involving 447 clients (40.3% with schizophrenia) and 600 jail detainees with SMI (19.8% with schizophrenia) (Steadman *et al.*, 2011). Compared with offenders who received treatment as usual, those tried in mental health courts had significantly fewer subsequent arrests and days of incarceration. However, a diagnosis of schizophrenia or depression predicted longer periods of incarceration in the follow-up period.

Involuntary outpatient commitment (OPC)   This is court-mandated, community-based treatment available to persons meeting certain statutorily defined criteria with SMI who require ongoing mental health care. OPC statutes exist in many jurisdictions, including the United Kingdom, Australia, Canada, New Zealand, Israel and the United States (Kisely, Campbell and Preston, 2011). Compliance with outpatient appointments and prescribed medications comprise typical OPC orders. In certain jurisdictions, OPC consumers are mandated to receive treatment through designated ICM or ACT programmes. Swanson *et al.* (1997) outlined several mechanisms through which OPC could potentially reduce arrest rates among mentally ill persons in the community. These include increased compliance with medications, improved access to substance abuse treatment, intensification of clinical surveillance during crises and the ability of treatment teams to leverage community-based resources. A recent systematic review that considered two RCTs of OPC concluded that OPC provided no significant benefit in social functioning compared with standard care (Kisely, Campbell and Preston, 2011). The authors calculated that 238 OPC orders would be necessary to prevent one new arrest among court-mandated patients. Nonetheless, secondary analyses of data from one RCT – which admittedly garnered their own criticism (Hotopf *et al.*, 2007) – in addition to evidence from other investigations point towards possible benefits of OPC in improving criminal justice outcomes.

The first RCT to investigate the effectiveness of OPC coupled with community-based management followed 262 participants for one year who had been involuntarily hospitalized in North Carolina and received a court order for treatment in the community following discharge (Swanson *et al.*, 2001). This study was also one of the first to examine the impact of OPC on violent behaviour and arrest frequency. Thirty-eight percent of the study sample had schizophrenia, while another psychotic disorder was diagnosed in an additional 30%. While all participants were initially given outpatient commitment orders, those randomized to the control group were subsequently released from OPC and followed by case management alone. Patients with a history of physically assaultive behaviour in the preceding year were excluded from the randomization process for ethical reasons; they were required to remain on outpatient commitment for at least the first 90 days of their order after which renewals of the commitment order were at the discretion of the clinical team and court. Arrest frequency was determined by inspection of electronic records archived in two North Carolina public agency databases for a period beginning one year prior to the enrolment hospital admission and ending one year after discharge. Reports from case managers supplemented official records. During the 12-month, post-enrolment period, 52 study participants (19.8%) were arrested. The majority of arrests (40%) were for nuisance offences, while approximately one third were due to substance-related crimes and fewer than 15% were the result of violent offending. Among participants who adhered to their medications, refrained from substance abuse, and did not engage in violent behaviour during the follow-up period, the likelihood of arrest was significantly reduced. However, a comparison of the two randomized groups (OPC and case management versus case management alone) revealed no difference in rates of arrest. Alternatively, six months or more of OPC was associated with a significantly decreased probability of arrests for participants with a history of multiple hospitalizations and previous arrests and/or violence.

Incidence of violence during the year of follow-up was assessed by self-report and collateral information supplied by case managers and family members (Swanson *et al.*, 2000). Violence was defined as police apprehension or arrest for a physical assault on another individual, participation in a fight involving physical contact or threats with a weapon. No difference in violent outcomes was observed between the two randomized groups. However, periods of court-ordered treatment greater than six months were associated with a significantly lower incidence of violence. Moreover, when the non-randomized participants with a history of violence were included in the analysis, the incidence of violence among the court-ordered group receiving at least six months of OPC (26.7%) was significantly less than in the control group (41.6%). Although multivariate analyses determined that neither extended OPC nor frequent services alone significantly reduced violent behaviour, the combination of a minimum six months of OPC and three or more outpatient visits per month was associated with a significant decrease in violence. As court-mandated treatment in this study was also associated with improved medication adherence and less substance abuse, the authors concluded that these outcomes could have mediated the relationship between OPC and reduced incidence of arrests and violent behaviour.

A second RCT assessed the effectiveness of an OPC pilot programme in New York City (Steadman *et al.*, 2001). One hundred and forty-two participants were randomized to either court-ordered, enhanced services or enhanced services in the absence of a court order. After 11 months of follow-up, no difference emerged between groups on all major outcome measures, including the proportion of patients arrested. The investigators were hesitant in drawing firm conclusions from their data, given the infancy of the programme and the fact that removal orders were never implemented for non-compliant, court-ordered participants during the study period. The impact of New York State's eventual OPC statute or "Assisted Outpatient Treatment" on reducing patients' involvement with the criminal justice system was considered in a subsequent study that examined arrest data among participants currently receiving "Assisted Outpatient Treatment" (Gilbert *et al.*, 2010). This study compared 181 individuals with SMI (70.7% with a diagnosis of schizophrenia) who received "Assisted Outpatient Treatment" or who had signed a voluntary service agreement or who were awaiting entry to the programme. Group comparisons revealed that participants currently receiving compulsory services were less likely to be arrested than the others who received the same clinical services but on voluntary basis. Apart from a single retrospective, pre-post investigation conducted in Australia that reported significantly fewer violent incidents among patients with schizophrenia mandated to OPC (Ingram, Muirhead and Harvey, 2009), studies on the relationship between OPC and criminal justice outcomes in persons with schizophrenia carried out in jurisdictions outside the United States are scarce.

Psychosocial interventions

Group psychoeducation This treatment, commonly offered in forensic settings, involves teaching individuals about their illness in order to increase coping skills and prevent relapse. One small uncontrolled study found that group psychoeducation improved illness knowledge and had a positive impact on attitudes towards taking medication among patients with schizophrenia in a high-security forensic hospital (Jennings *et al.*, 2002), while another investigation with a similar patient population failed to detect any significant improvement in self-reported functioning (Vallentine *et al.*, 2010). Aho-Mustonen *et al.* (2008) reported that forensic and non-forensic, hard-to-treat, dangerous patients with schizophrenia who participated in an eight-session psychoeducational group were significantly more knowledgeable about schizophrenia and showed a greater awareness of their illness than matched patients who did not receive the intervention. A subsequent RCT conducted by the same research group revealed comparable results: a significantly greater benefit on illness knowledge, self-esteem and insight into illness was observed among high-security patients with schizophrenia randomized to group psychotherapy compared with those randomized to usual care (Aho-Mustonen *et al.*, 2011). A small study of interventions aimed at increasing feelings of well-being reported improved levels of subjective well-being among patients with schizophrenia in a forensic hospital (Ferguson *et al.*, 2009).

Cognitive-behavioural interventions Cognitive-behavioural therapy (CBT) aims to help patients understand the connections between their thoughts, feelings and behaviours and enables them to develop strategies that challenge the negative or unreasonable thoughts fuelling maladaptive behaviours. CBT has been shown to reduce psychotic symptoms among persons with schizophrenia (Wykes *et al.*, 2008). Haddock *et al.* (2009) conducted an RCT that tested the effectiveness of CBT in reducing aggression and violence among patients with schizophrenia with a history of violent behaviour. In addition to receiving usual care, 77 inpatients and outpatients were randomized to either CBT or social activity therapy, a programme designed to promote patients' involvement in activities they enjoy. Results revealed that CBT was superior to social activity therapy in reducing aggressive incidents during the 6- and 12-month treatment and follow-up periods. Two empirical studies of treatment programmes incorporating CBT interventions for forensic inpatients with treatment-resistant schizophrenia or chronic psychosis have also reported modest improvement in participants' cognitive skills (Hodel and West, 2003; Hornsveld and Nijman, 2005).

Reasoning and rehabilitation   This skills-focused treatment programme adapts CBT principles to address underdeveloped problem-solving skills, values and attitudes connected with pro-criminal thinking and behaviour (Ross and Fabiano, 1985). Compared with empirical studies involving non-mentally disordered offenders, there are comparatively fewer investigations of reasoning and rehabilitation (R&R) with offenders with SMI. Donnelly and Scott (1999) first reported that hospitalized mentally disordered offenders participating in R&R showed more improvement on social and problem-solving skills than their peers who did not receive the intervention. Another study evaluated a token economy programme incorporating elements of R&R that was specifically developed for state hospital patients with SMI and repeated aggression and/or criminal behaviour (Kunz *et al.*, 2004). Among the 85 participants who completed the programme (80% with a psychotic illness), 39% remained stable in community during follow-up, 35% were re-hospitalized and 20% were arrested. As this study lacked a comparison group, the investigators acknowledged that this was not a rigorous evaluation of their programme. A prospective investigation that evaluated a modified R&R programme for forensic outpatients with SMI (70% of the sample had schizophrenia) found that participants who completed the entire intervention had significantly fewer arrests than comparison participants who were ineligible for the programme (Ashford, Wong and Sternbach, 2008). Two recent studies from the United Kingdom evaluated the impact of R&R on violent patients with SMI detained in medium- and high-security forensic hospitals. Among participants receiving the intervention, improvements were noted in attitudes towards violence (Young, Chick and Gudjonsson, 2010) and problem-solving abilities (Clarke *et al.*, 2010). Finally, preliminary results from the first RCT of R&R for violent male patients with psychotic illness (81% with schizophrenia) in forensic hospitals observed that the patients randomized to R&R showed significant improvements in measures of social problem solving, some of which were maintained at 12 months post treatment. Programme completers showed improvements in social problem solving and criminal attitudes at 12 months post treatment (Cullen *et al.*, 2012). Importantly, however, only half of those allocated to receive R&R completed the programme. Co-morbid antisocial personality disorder, high levels of psychopathic traits and recent violence were associated with failure to complete the R&R programme (Cullen *et al.*, 2011). By contrast to these studies conducted in forensic hospitals, the only study of R&R with violent men with schizophrenia living in the community found that these men would not participate in R&R. Completion of motivational interviewing did not increase participation. Refusal was specific to R&R as these men kept regular appointments with their case workers who primarily looked after their social benefits, and they also participated in research interviews documenting symptoms, aggressive behaviour, crime and substance misuse for which they earned £5.50 (Hodgins *et al.*, 2011b).

Consequences of treatment that reduced aggressive and antisocial behaviours

Effective treatment that reduced aggressive and antisocial behaviours among persons with schizophrenia would have several positive consequences. One, it would limit suffering on the part of the perpetrators resulting from loss of liberty, limit their own victimization that is strongly associated with their own aggressive behaviour (Hodgins *et al.*, 2007a; Silver *et al.*, 2005; Teplin *et al.*, 2005; Walsh *et al.*, 2003) and promote engagement in treatments aimed at reducing symptoms of psychosis and improving cognitive and psychosocial functioning. Two, injuries to victims, usually family members or carers, would be reduced. Three, stigma against all persons with SMI would be reduced (Link and Pelhan, 2006; Thornicroft, 2006). Four, the financial burden of prosecuting and incarcerating offenders with schizophrenia would be reduced, as would lengthy stays in expensive forensic psychiatric hospitals. Five, effective treatment has the potential to reduce crime. For example, depending on the country, effective treatment of persons with schizophrenia would reduce the rate of homicide by anywhere from 6% to 28% (Erb *et al.*, 2001) and the rate of sexual offending by approximately 8% (Alden *et al.*, 2007).

Conclusions

All persons with schizophrenia, from first episode onwards, require evidence-based interventions to reduce psychotic and depressive symptoms, enhance cognitive functioning and develop skills allowing them to have meaningful interpersonal relationships, to live autonomously and to be financially independent. In addition, treatments are required to reduce and prevent antisocial and aggressive behaviours. Most persons with schizophrenia who will commit criminal offences will already have a conviction or a history of antisocial and aggressive behaviour at the onset of their first episode of psychosis. These persons require interventions that directly target their antisocial and aggressive behaviours. Attempts to treat such individuals outside of forensic hospitals suggest that some form of compulsion, such as court orders for community treatment that include consequences for non-participation, may be required to achieve engagement. Presently, however, most general psychiatric services lack the financial and human resources necessary to implement these treatments. A small group of patients with schizophrenia, who have no history of antisocial or aggressive behaviour prior to illness onset, will commit violent crimes. Presently, these individuals are difficult to identify as risk prediction instruments rely heavily on past violence to predict future violence. There are few studies of such patients, but the evidence suggests that from first episode onwards, in addition to treating schizophrenia, evidence-based interventions to reduce substance misuse may reduce the risk of violence. Finally, among chronic male patients, increases in callousness and insensitivity towards carers may signal increased risk of violence.

As shown by this review, there is a very small evidence base on effective treatments for persons with schizophrenia who engage in criminal behaviours. RCTs of overall forensic programmes and of specific treatment components of these programmes (e.g., programmes aiming to reduce aggressive behaviour or substance misuse or to increase compliance with medication and relapse prevention) are urgently needed. Evidence is also needed about the optimal time (e.g., at first contact with mental health services for psychosis or after multiple offences) and the optimal place (e.g., clinics for first episode psychosis, general psychiatric inpatient wards, forensic psychiatric hospitals, general psychiatric or forensic community treatment programmes) for services. Thus, presently, policy and practice regarding the treatment of offenders with schizophrenia is not based on empirical evidence.

References

Aho-Mustonen, K., Miettinen, R., Koivisto, H. *et al.* (2008) Group psychoeducation for forensic and dangerous non-forensic long-term patients with schizophrenia. A pilot study. *European Journal of Psychiatry*, 22, 84–92.

Aho-Mustonen, K., Tiihonen, J., Repo-Tiihonen, E. *et al.* (2011) Group psychoeducation for long-term offender patients with schizophrenia: an exploratory randomised controlled trial. *Criminal Behaviour and Mental Health*, 21, 163–176.

Alden, A., Brennan, P., Hodgins, S. and Mednick, S. (2007) Psychotic disorders and sex offending in a Danish birth cohort. *Archives of General Psychiatry*, 64, 1251–1258.

Aleman, A. and Kahn, R.S. (2001) Effects of the atypical antipsychotic risperidone on hostility and aggression in schizophrenia: a meta-analysis of controlled trials. *European Neuropsychopharmacology*, 11, 289–293.

Arseneault, L., Moffitt, T.E., Caspi, A. *et al.* (2000) Mental disorders and violence in a total birth cohort: results from the Dunedin Study. *Archives of General Psychiatry*, 57, 979–986.

Ashford, J.B., Wong, K.W. and Sternbach, K.O. (2008) Generic correctional programming for mentally ill offenders. *A pilot study. Criminal Justice and Behavior*, 35, 457–473.

Beaudoin, M.N., Hodgins, S. and Lavoie, F. (1993) Homicide, schizophrenia and substance abuse or dependency. *Canadian Journal of Psychiatry. Revue canadienne de psychiatrie*, 38, 541–546.

Bellack, A.S., Bennett, M.E., Gearon, J.S. *et al.* (2006) A randomized clinical trial of a new behavioral treatment for drug abuse in people with severe and persistent mental illness. *Archives of General Psychiatry*, 63, 426–432.

Brennan, P.A., Mednick, S.A. and Hodgins, S. (2000) Major mental disorders and criminal violence in a Danish birth cohort. *Archives of General Psychiatry*, 57, 494–500.

Broner, N., Maryl, D.M. and Landsberg, G. (2005) Outcomes of mandated and nonmandated New York City jail diversion for offenders with alcohol, drug, and mental disorders. *Prison Journal*, 85, 18–49.

Buckley, P., Bartell, J., Donenwirth, K. *et al.* (1995) Violence and schizophrenia: clozapine as a specific antiaggressive agent. *The Bulletin of the American Academy of Psychiatry and the Law*, 23, 607–611.

Burns, T., Catty, J., Becker, T. *et al.* (2007) The effectiveness of supported employment for people with severe mental illness: a randomised controlled trial. *Lancet*, 370, 1146–1152.

Calsyn, R.J., Yonker, R.D., Lemming, M.R. *et al.* (2005) Impact of assertive community treatment and client characteristics on criminal justice outcomes in dual disorder homeless individuals. *Criminal Behaviour and Mental Health*, 15, 236–248.

Chiles, J.A., Davidson, P. and McBride, D. (1994) Effects of clozapine on use of seclusion and restraint at a state hospital. *Hospital and Community Psychiatry*, 45, 269–271.

Christy, A., Poythress, N.G., Boothroyd, R.A. *et al.* (2005) Evaluating the efficiency and community safety goals of the Broward County Mental Health Court. *Behavioral Sciences and the Law*, 23, 227–243.

Cimino, T. and Jennings, J.L. (2002) Arkansas partnership program: an innovative continuum of care program for dually diagnosed forensic patients. *Psychiatric Rehabilitation Skills*, 6, 104–114.

Citrome, L. and Volavka, J. (2011) Pharmacological management of acute and persistent aggression in forensic psychiatry settings. *CNS Drugs*, 25, 1009–1021.

Citrome, L., Volavka, J., Czobor, P. *et al.* (2001) Effects of clozapine, olanzapine, risperidone, and haloperidol on hostility among patients with schizophrenia. *Psychiatric Services*, 52, 1510–1514.

Clarke, A.Y., Cullen, A.E., Walwyn, R. and Fahy, T. (2010) A quasi-experimental pilot study of the Reasoning and Rehabilitation programme with mentally disordered offenders. *The Journal of Forensic Psychiatry & Psychology*, 21, 490–500.

Coid, J., Hickey, N., Kahtan, N. *et al.* (2007) Patients discharged from medium secure forensic psychiatry services: reconvictions and risk factors. *British Journal of Psychiatry: The Journal of Mental Science*, 190, 223–229.

Coid, J., Hickey, N. and Yang, M. (2007) Comparisons of outcomes following after-care from forensic and general adult psychiatric services. *British Journal of Psychiatry: The Journal of Mental Science*, 190, 509–514.

Cook, J.A., Leff, H.S., Blyler, C.R. *et al.* (2005) Results of a multisite randomized trial of supported employment interventions for individuals with severe mental illness. *Archives of General Psychiatry*, 62, 505–512.

Cosden, M., Ellens, J.K., Schnell, J.L. *et al.* (2003) Evaluation of a mental health treatment court with assertive community treatment. *Behavioral Sciences and the Law*, 21, 415–427.

Cosden, M., Ellens, J.K., Schnell, J.L. and Yamini-Diouf, Y. (2005) Efficacy of a mental health treatment court with assertive community treatment. *Behavioral Sciences and the Law*, 2, 199–214.

Crocker, A.G., Mueser, K.T., Drake, R.E. *et al.* (2005) Antisocial personality, psychopathy, and violence in persons with dual disorders: a longitudinal analysis. *Criminal Justice and Behavior*, 32, 452–476.

Cullen, A.E., Soria, C., Clarke, A.Y. *et al.* (2011) Factors predicting dropout from the Reasoning and Rehabilitation Program with mentally disordered offenders. *Criminal Justice and Behavior*, 38, 217–230.

Cullen, A.E., Clarke, A.Y., Kuipers, E. *et al.* (2012) A multi-site randomized controlled trial of a cognitive skills programme for male mentally disordered offenders: social-cognitive outcomes. *Psychological Medicine*, 42, 557–569.

Cusack, K.J., Morrissey, J.P., Cuddeback, G.S. *et al.* (2010) Criminal justice involvement, behavioral health service use, and costs of forensic assertive community treatment: a randomized trial. *Community Mental Health Journal*, 46, 356–363.

Donnelly, J.P. and Scott, M. (1999) Evaluation of an offending behaviour programme with a mentally disordered offender population. *British Journal of Forensic Practice*, 1, 25–32.

Ebrahim, G.M., Gibler, B., Gacono, C.B. and Hayes, G. (1994) Patient response to clozapine in a forensic psychiatric hospital. *Hospital and Community Psychiatry*, 45, 271–273.

Erb, M., Hodgins, S., Freese, R. *et al.* (2001) Homicide and schizophrenia: maybe treatment does have a preventive effect. *Criminal Behaviour and Mental Health*, 11, 6–26.

Fazel, S., Buxrud, P., Ruchkin, V. and Grann, M. (2010) Homicide in discharged patients with schizophrenia and other psychoses: a national case-control study. *Schizophrenia Research*, 123, 263–269.

Ferguson, G., Conway, C., Endersby, L. and MacLeod, A. (2009) Increasing subjective well-being in long-term forensic rehabilitation: evaluation of well-being therapy. *The Journal of Forensic Psychiatry & Psychology*, 20, 906–918.

Frisman, L.K., Lin, H., Sturges, G.E. *et al.* (2006) Outcomes of court-based jail diversion programs for people with co-occurring disorders. *Journal of Dual Diagnosis*, 2, 5–26.

Fulwiler, C. and Ruthazer, R. (1999) Premorbid risk factors for violence in adult mental illness. *Comprehensive Psychiatry*, 40, 96–100.

Fulwiler, C., Grossman, H., Forbes, C. and Ruthazer, R. (1997) Early onset substance abuse and community violence by outpatients with chronic mental illness. *Psychiatric Services*, 48, 1181–1185.

Gilbert, A.R., Moser, L.L., Van Dorn, R.A *et al.* (2010) Reductions in arrest under assisted outpatient treatment in New York. *Psychiatric Services*, 61, 996–999.

Godley, S.H., Finch, M., Dougan, L. *et al.* (2000) Case management for dually diagnosed individuals involved in the criminal justice system. *Journal of Substance Abuse Treatment*, 18, 137–148.

Haddock, G., Barrowclough, C., Tarrier, N. *et al.* (2003) Cognitive-behavioural therapy and motivational intervention for schizophrenia and substance misuse. 18-month outcomes of a randomised controlled trial. *British Journal of Psychiatry: The Journal of Mental Science*, 183, 418–426.

Haddock, G., Barrowclough, C., Shaw, J.J. *et al.* (2009) Cognitive-behavioural therapy v. social activity therapy for people with psychosis and a history of violence: randomised controlled trial. *British Journal of Psychiatry: The Journal of Mental Science*, 194, 152–157.

Herinckx, H.A., Swart, S.C., Ama, S.M. *et al.* (2005) Rearrest and linkage to mental health services among clients of the Clark County mental health court program. *Psychiatric Services*, 56, 853–857.

Hirose, S., Ashby, C.R., Jr. and Mills, M.J. (2001) Effectiveness of ECT combined with risperidone against aggression in schizophrenia. *Journal of ECT*, 17, 22–26.

Hodel, B. and West, A. (2003) A cognitive training for mentally ill offenders with treatment-resistant schizophrenia. *Journal of Forensic Psychiatry & Psychology*, 14, 554–568.

Hodgins, S. (1992) Mental disorder, intellectual deficiency, and crime. Evidence from a birth cohort. *Archives of General Psychiatry*, 49, 476–483.

Hodgins, S. (2004) Criminal and antisocial behaviours and schizophrenia: a neglected topic, in *Search for the Causes of Schizophrenia*, vol. 5 (eds W.F. Gattaz and H. Häfner), Steinkopff Verlag, Darmstadt, pp. 315–341.

Hodgins, S. (2008) Violent behaviour among people with schizophrenia: a framework for investigations of causes, and effective treatment, and prevention. *Philosophical Transactions of the Royal Society of London. Series B, Biological Sciences*, 363, 2505–2518.

Hodgins, S. and Côté, G. (1993) Major mental disorder and antisocial personality disorder: a criminal combination. *Bulletin of the American Academy of Psychiatry and the Law*, 21, 155–160.

Hodgins, S. and Müller-Isberner, R. (2004) Preventing crime by people with schizophrenic disorders: the role of psychiatric services. *British Journal of Psychiatry*, 185, 245–250.

Hodgins, S. and Riaz, M. (2011) Violence and phases of illness: differential risk and predictors. *European Psychiatry*, 26, 518–524.

Hodgins, S., Côté, G. and Toupin, J. (1998) Major mental disorders and crime: an etiological hypothesis, in *Psychopathy: Theory, Research and Implications for Society* (eds D.J. Cooke, A.D. Forth and R.D. Hare). Kluwer Academic Publishers, Dordrecht, pp. 231–256.

Hodgins, S., Tiihonen, J. and Ross, D. (2005) The consequences of conduct disorder for males who develop schizophrenia: associations with criminality, aggressive behavior, substance use, and psychiatric services. *Schizophrenia Research*, 78, 323–335.

Hodgins, S., Alderton, J., Cree, A. *et al.* (2007a) Aggressive behaviour, victimization and crime among severely mentally ill patients requiring hospitalisation. *British Journal of Psychiatry*, 191, 343–350.

Hodgins, S., Muller-Isberner, R., Tiihonen, J. *et al.* (2007b) A comparison of general and forensic patients with schizophrenia living in the community. *International Journal of Forensic Mental Health*, 6, 63–75.

Hodgins, S., Cree, A., Alderton, J. and Mak, T. (2008) From conduct disorder to severe mental illness: associations with aggressive behaviour, crime and victimization. *Psychological Medicine*, 38, 975–987.

Hodgins, S., Cree, A., Khalid, F. *et al.* (2009) Do community mental health teams caring for severely mentally ill patients adjust treatments and services based on patients' antisocial or criminal behaviours? *European Psychiatry*, 24, 373–379.

Hodgins, S., Calem, M., Shimel, R. *et al.* (2011a) Criminal offending and distinguishing features of offenders among persons experiencing a first episode of psychosis. *Early Intervention in Psychiatry*, 5, 15–23.

Hodgins, S., Carlin, P., Moorhouse, R. *et al.* (2011b) Reducing antisocial behaviour among patients with severe mental illness living in the community: a feasibility study of the Reasoning and Rehabilitation Programme. *Criminal Behaviour and Mental Health*, 21, 75–76.

Hoff, R.A., Baranosky, M.V., Buchanan, J. *et al.* (1999) The effects of a jail diversion program on incarceration: a retrospective cohort study. *Journal of the American Academy of Psychiatry and the Law*, 27, 377–386.

Hornsveld, R.H. and Nijman, H.L. (2005) Evaluation of a cognitive-behavioral program for chronically psychotic forensic inpatients. *International Journal of Law and Psychiatry*, 28, 246–254.

Hotopf, M., Dunn, G., Owen, G. and Churchill, R. (2007) Involuntary community treatment. *British Journal of Psychiatry: The Journal of Mental Science*, 191, 358–359.

Humphreys, M., Johnstone, E. and Macmillan, F. (1994) Offending among first episode schizophrenics. *Journal of Forensic Psychiatry*, 5, 51–61.

Ingram, G., Muirhead, D. and Harvey, C. (2009) Effectiveness of community treatment orders for treatment of schizophrenia with oral or depot antipsychotic medication: changes in problem behaviours and social functioning. *Australian and New Zealand Journal of Psychiatry*, 43, 1077–1083.

Jennings, L., Harris, B., Gregoire, J. *et al.* (2002) The effect of a psycho-educational programme on knowledge of illness, insight and attitudes towards medication. *British Journal of Forensic Practice*, 4, 3–10.

Kavanagh, D.J. and Mueser, K.T. (2007) Current evidence on integrated treatment for serious mental disorder and substance misuse. *Journal of the Norwegian Psychological Association*, 44, 618–637.

Kisely, S.R., Campbell, L.A. and Preston, N.J. (2011) Compulsory community and involuntary outpatient treatment for people with severe mental disorders. *Cochrane Database of Systematic Reviews (Online)*, 2, Art. no.: CD004408.

Kopelowicz, A., Liberman, R.P. and Zarate, R. (2006) Recent advances in social skills training for schizophrenia. *Schizophrenia Bulletin*, 32 (Suppl. 1), S12–S23.

Krakowski, M.I., Czobor, P., Citrome, L. *et al.* (2006) Atypical antipsychotic agents in the treatment of violent patients with schizophrenia and schizoaffective disorder. *Archives of General Psychiatry*, 63, 622–629.

Kunz, M., Yates, K.F., Czobor, P. *et al.* (2004) Course of patients with histories of aggression and crime after discharge from a cognitive-behavioral program. *Psychiatric Services*, 55, 654–659.

Lamb, H.R., Weinberger, L.E. and Reston-Parham, C. (1996) Court intervention to address the mental health needs of mentally ill offenders. *Psychiatric Services*, 47, 275–281.

Lamberti, J.S., Weisman, R.L., Schwarzkopf, S.B. *et al.* (2001) The mentally ill in jails and prisons: towards an integrated model of prevention. *Psychiatric Quarterly*, 72, 63–77.

Lamberti, J.S., Weisman, R. and Faden, D.I. (2004) Forensic assertive community treatment: preventing incarceration of adults with severe mental illness. *Psychiatric Services*, 55, 1285–1293.

Large, M. and Nielssen, O. (2008) Evidence for a relationship between the duration of untreated psychosis and the proportion of psychotic homicides prior to treatment. *Social Psychiatry and Psychiatric Epidemiology*, 43, 37–44.

Lincoln, T.M., Wilhelm, K. and Nestoriuc, Y. (2007) Effectiveness of psychoeducation for relapse, symptoms, knowledge, adherence and functioning in psychotic disorders: a meta-analysis. *Schizophrenia Research*, 96, 232–245.

Link, B.G. and Phelan, J.C. (2006) Stigma and its public health implications. *Lancet*, 367 (9509), 528–529.

Lurigio, A.J., Fallon, J.R. and Dincin, J. (2000) Helping the mentally ill in jails adjust to community life: a description of a post release ACT program and its clients. *International Journal of Offender Therapy and Comparative Criminology*, 44, 532–548.

Maden, A., Scott, F., Burnett, R. *et al.* (2004) Offending in psychiatric patients after discharge from medium secure units: prospective national cohort study. *BMJ (Clinical Research Ed.)*, 328, 1534.

Maier, G.J. (1992) The impact of clozapine on 25 forensic patients. *Bulletin of the American Academy of Psychiatry and the Law*, 20, 297–307.

Mallya, A.R., Roos, P.D. and Roebuck-Colgan, K. (1992) Restraint, seclusion, and clozapine. *Journal of Clinical Psychiatry*, 53, 395–397.

Mangalore, R. and Knapp, M. (2007) Cost of schizophrenia in England. *Journal of Mental Health Policy and Economics*, 10, 23–41.

McCoy, M.L., Roberts, D.L., Hanrahan, P. *et al.* (2004) Jail linkage assertive community treatment services for individuals with mental illnesses. *Psychiatric Rehabilitation Journal*, 27, 243–250.

McGurk, S.R., Mueser, K.T., Feldman, K. *et al.* (2007) Cognitive training for supported employment: 2–3 year outcomes of a randomized controlled trial. *American Journal of Psychiatry*, 164, 437–441.

McNiel, D.E. and Binder, R.L. (2007) Effectiveness of a mental health court in reducing criminal recidivism and violence. *American Journal of Psychiatry*, 164, 1395–1403.

Modestin, J. and Ammann, R. (1996) Mental disorder and criminality: male schizophrenia. *Schizophrenia Bulletin*, 22, 69–82.

Moore, M.E. and Hiday, V.A. (2006) Mental health court outcomes: a comparison of re-arrest and re-arrest severity between mental health court and traditional court participants. *Law and Human Behavior*, 30, 659–674.

Moran, P. and Hodgins, S. (2004) The correlates of comorbid antisocial personality disorder in schizophrenia. *Schizophrenia Bulletin*, 30, 791–802.

Mueser, K.T. and McGurk, S.R. (2004) Schizophrenia. *Lancet*, 363, 2063–2072.

Mueser, K.T., Bond, G.R., Drake, R.E. and Resnick, S.G. (1998) Models of community care for severe mental illness: a review of research on case management. *Schizophrenia Bulletin*, 24, 37–74.

Mueser, K.T., Rosenberg, S.D., Drake, R.E. *et al.* (1999) Conduct disorder, antisocial personality disorder and substance use disorders in schizophrenia and major affective disorders. *Journal of Studies on Alcohol*, 60, 278–284.

Mueser, K.T., Crocker, A.G., Frisman, L.B. *et al.* (2006) Conduct disorder and antisocial personality disorder in persons with severe psychiatric and substance use disorders. *Schizophrenia Bulletin*, 32, 626–636.

Müller-Isberner, R. and Hodgins, S. (2000) Evidence-based treatment for mentally disordered offenders, in *Violence, Crime and Mentally Disordered Offenders* (eds S. Hodgins and R. Müller-Isberner), John Wiley & Sons, Ltd, Chichester, pp. 7–38.

Munkner, R., Haastrup, S., Joergensen, T. and Kramp, P. (2003) The temporal relationship between schizophrenia and crime. *Social Psychiatry and Psychiatric Epidemiology*, 38, 347–353.

Munkner, R., Haastrup, S., Joergensen, T. and Kramp, P. (2005) Incipient offending among schizophrenia patients after first contact to the psychiatric hospital system. *European Psychiatry*, 20, 321–326.

Munkner, R., Haastrup, S., Joergensen, T. and Kramp, P. (2009) The association between psychopathology of first-episode psychosis patients within the schizophrenia spectrum and previous offending. *Nordic Journal of Psychiatry*, 63, 124–131.

Patel, V., Flisher, A.J., Hetrick, S. and McGorry, P. (2007) Mental health of young people: a global public-health challenge. *Lancet*, 369, 1302–1313.

Perälä, J., Suvisaari, J., Saarni, S.I. *et al.* (2007) Lifetime prevalence of psychotic and bipolar I disorders in a general population. *Archives of General Psychiatry*, 64, 19–28.

Ratey, J.J., Leveroni, C., Kilmer, D. *et al.* (1993) The effects of clozapine on severely aggressive psychiatric inpatients in a state hospital. *Journal of Clinical Psychiatry*, 54, 219–223.

Roder, V., Mueller, D.R., Mueser, K.T. and Brenner, H.D. (2006) Integrated psychological therapy (IPT) for schizophrenia: is it effective? *Schizophrenia Bulletin*, 32 (Suppl. 1), S81–S93.

Ross, R.R. and Fabiano, E.A. (1985) *Time to Think: A Cognitive Model of Delinquency Prevention and Offender Rehabilitation*, Institute of Social Science and Arts, Johnson City, TN.

Schug, R.A., Raine, A. and Wilcox, R.R. (2007) Psychophysiological and behavioural characteristics of individuals comorbid for antisocial personality disorder and schizophrenia-spectrum personality disorder. *British Journal of Psychiatry*, 191, 408–414.

Silver, E., Arseneault, L., Langley, J. *et al.* (2005) Mental disorder and violent victimization in a total birth cohort. *American Journal of Public Health*, 95, 2015–2021.

Solomon, P. and Draine, J. (1995) One-year outcomes of a randomized trial of case management with seriously mentally ill clients leaving jail. *Evaluation Review*, 19, 256–273.

Steadman, H.J., Gounis, K., Dennis, D. *et al.* (2001) Assessing the New York City involuntary outpatient commitment pilot program. *Psychiatric Services*, 52 (3), 330–336.

Steadman, H.J., Redlich, A., Callahan, L. *et al.* (2011) Effect of mental health courts on arrests and jail days: a multisite study. *Archives of General Psychiatry*, 68, 167–172.

Stein, L.I. and Test, M.A. (1980) Alternative to mental hospital treatment. I. Conceptual model, treatment program, and clinical evaluation. *Archives of General Psychiatry*, 37, 392–397.

Steinert, T., Sippach, T. and Gebhardt, R.P. (2000) How common is violence in schizophrenia despite neuroleptic treatment? *Pharmacopsychiatry*, 33, 98–102.

Surles, R.C., Blanch, A.K., Shern, D.L. and Donahue, S.A. (1992) Case management as a strategy for systems change. *Health Affairs*, 11, 151–163.

Swanson, J.W., Swartz, M.S., George, L.K. *et al.* (1997) Interpreting the effectiveness of involuntary outpatient commitment: a conceptual model. *Journal of the American Academy of Psychiatry and the Law*, 25, 5–16.

Swanson, J.W., Swartz, M.S., Borum, R. *et al.* (2000) Involuntary out-patient commitment and reduction of violent behaviour in persons with severe mental illness. *British Journal of Psychiatry: The Journal of Mental Science*, 176, 324–331.

Swanson, J.W., Borum, R., Swartz, M.S. *et al.* (2001) Can involuntary outpatient commitment reduce arrests among persons with severe mental illness? *Criminal Justice and Human Behavior*, 28, 156–189.

Swanson, J.W., Swartz, M.S. and Elbogen, E.B. (2004) Effectiveness of atypical antipsychotic medications in reducing violent behavior among persons with schizophrenia in community-based treatment. *Schizophrenia Bulletin*, 30, 3–20.

Swanson, J.W., Swartz, M.S., Elbogen, E.B. and Van Dorn, R.A. (2004) Reducing violence risk in persons with schizophrenia: olanzapine versus risperidone. *Journal of Clinical Psychiatry*, 65, 1666–1673.

Swanson, J.W., Swartz, M.S., Van Dorn, R.A. *et al.* (2006) A national study of violent behavior in persons with schizophrenia. *Archives of General Psychiatry*, 63, 490–499.

Swanson, J.W., Swartz, M.S., Van Dorn, R.A. *et al.* (2008) Comparison of antipsychotic medication effects on reducing violence in people with schizophrenia. *British Journal of Psychiatry: The Journal of Mental Science*, 193, 37–43.

Tengström, A., Hodgins, S. and Kullgren, G. (2001) Men with schizophrenia who behave violently: the usefulness of an early- versus late-start offender typology. *Schizophrenia Bulletin*, 27, 205–218.

Teplin, L.A., McClelland, G.M., Abram, K.M. and Weiner, D.A. (2005) Crime victimization in adults with severe mental illness: comparison with the National Crime Victimization Survey. *Archives of General Psychiatry*, 62, 911–921.

Thornicroft, G. (2006) *Shunned: Discrimination Against People with Mental Illness*, Oxford University Press, Oxford.

Tiihonen, J., Isohanni, M., Räsänen, P. *et al.* (1997) Specific major mental disorders and criminality: a 26-year prospective study of the 1966 northern Finland birth cohort. *American Journal of Psychiatry*, 154, 840–845.

Trupin, E. and Richards, H. (2003) Seattle's mental health courts: early indicators of effectiveness. *International Journal of Law and Psychiatry*, 26, 33–53.

Vallentine, V., Tapp, J., Dudley, A. *et al.* (2010) Psycho-educational groupwork for detained patients: understanding mental illness. *Journal of Forensic Psychiatry & Psychology*, 21, 393–406.

Van Dorn, R., Volavka, J. and Johnson, N. (2011) Mental disorder and violence: is there a relationship beyond substance use? *Social Psychiatry and Psychiatric Epidemiology*, 47 (3), 487–503.

Ventura, L.A., Cassel, C.A., Jacoby, J.E. and Huang, B. (1998) Case management and recidivism of mentally ill persons released from jail. *Psychiatric Services*, 49, 1330–1337.

Volavka, J. and Citrome, L. (2008) Heterogeneity of violence in schizophrenia and implications for long-term treatment. *International Journal of Clinical Practice*, 62, 1237–1245.

Volavka, J., Zito, J.M., Vitrai, J. and Czobar, P. (1993) Clozapine effects on hostility and aggression in schizophrenia. *Journal of Clinical Psychopharmacology*, 13, 287–289.

Wallace, C., Mullen, P.E. and Burgess, P. (2004) Criminal offending in schizophrenia over a 25-year period marked by deinstitutionalization and increasing prevalence of comorbid substance use disorders. *American Journal of Psychiatry*, 161, 716–727.

Walsh, E., Gilvarry, C., Samele, C. *et al.* (2001) Reducing violence in severe mental illness: randomised controlled trial of intensive case management compared with standard care. *BMJ (Clinical Research Ed.)*, 323, 1093–1096.

Walsh, E., Moran, P., Scott, C. *et al.* (2003) Prevalence of violent victimisation in severe mental illness. *British Journal of Psychiatry*, 183, 233–238.

Weisman, R.L., Lamberti, J.S. and Price, N. (2004) Integrating criminal justice, community healthcare, and support services for adults with severe mental disorders. *Psychiatric Quarterly*, 75, 71–85.

Wilson, W.H. and Claussen, A.M. (1995) 18-month outcome of clozapine treatment for 100 patients in a state psychiatric hospital. *Psychiatric Services*, 46, 386–389.

Wilson, D., Tien, G. and Eaves, D. (1995) Increasing the community tenure of mentally disordered offenders: an assertive case management program. *International Journal of Law and Psychiatry*, 18, 61–69.

Wykes, T., Reeder, C., Landau, S. *et al.* (2007) Cognitive remediation therapy in schizophrenia: randomised controlled trial. *British Journal of Psychiatry: The Journal of Mental Science*, 190, 421–427.

Wykes, T., Steel, C., Everitt, B. and Tarrier, N. (2008) Cognitive behavior therapy for schizophrenia: effect sizes, clinical models, and methodological rigor. *Schizophrenia Bulletin*, 34, 523–537.

Young, S., Chick, K. and Gudjonsson, G.H. (2010) A preliminary evaluation of reasoning and rehabilitation 2 in mentally disordered offenders (R&R2M) across two forensic settings in the United Kingdom. *Journal of Forensic Psychiatry & Psychology*, 21, 336–349.

19

Treating Offenders in a Therapeutic Community

Richard Shuker

HMP Grendon, UK

Therapeutic Communities (TCs) have provided an intervention for offenders in the United Kingdom for over half a century. In doing so, they have formed one of the most long-standing approaches to offender rehabilitation within the Criminal Justice System, maintaining their role during times when interest in offender rehabilitation has been declining. Despite this achievement and the sustained position as an intervention for offenders, TCs have only recently emerged into the mainstream of forensic interventions. This chapter aims to provide a discussion of the role and efficacy of TCs in treating UK offenders. It will first outline the origins, recent developments and contribution of TCs to forensic practice. It will provide clarity about their treatment approaches and methods and address the value of TCs as a model of risk reduction. It will go on to explore the opportunities that TCs provide for risk assessment and how they engage offenders in a treatment process which is safe, collaborative and enabling. Finally, this chapter will shed light on why TCs have sometimes been met with professional scepticism and provide an analysis of their evidence base.

Origins and Background

TCs for offenders have their roots within a social psychiatric tradition (Kennard, 1998) which emphasizes the importance of the organization in rehabilitative outcomes. Social psychiatry questioned the belief that responsibility for the patient's recovery should automatically lie with the treating professional and advocated two key principles:

- An organization that could foster therapeutic relationships where safety, collaboration and open communication are ingrained within its structures would enhance patient recovery.
- Treatment was likely to be more effective in an organization where genuine and appropriate responsibility and ownership for personal recovery could be given to the patient.

What Works in Offender Rehabilitation: An Evidence-Based Approach to Assessment and Treatment,
First Edition. Edited by Leam A. Craig, Louise Dixon and Theresa A. Gannon.
© 2013 John Wiley & Sons, Ltd. Published 2013 by John Wiley & Sons, Ltd.

Early TCs adopted values originating from the Quaker movement, which emphasized the importance of social expectation and humane relationships. Initially pioneered in the 'York Retreat' in the 1800s (Tuke, 1813), these principles became established in the treatment of traumatized servicemen after World War II. TCs for offenders were implemented in the Prison Service in the early 1960s and were given the remit of providing an 'experimental' approach, offering psychological treatment to prisoners not qualifying for incarceration under the Mental Health Act (East and Hubert, 1939). These were based more on a set of underlying principles, emphasizing responsibility, community participation and personal accountability, rather than being based on a clear psychological model of offender rehabilitation. It was not until the 1990s that TCs articulated an empirically based psychological 'model of change' (Cullen, 1997; Shine and Morris, 2000).

The democratic and hierarchical distinction

The TCs that emerged in the United Kingdom during the last 50 years had as their focus the treatment of psychological disturbance, emotional distress and personality disorder (see Campling and Haigh, 1999). These integrated group therapy with community democracy and are recognizable by the role that residents have in managing one another's behaviour and became referred to as 'democratic' TCs. This approach regards the rehabilitative effect as stemming from the interpersonal and social learning processes occurring within a structured community setting, as much as it does from the 'psychotherapeutic' experience.

At the same time, parallel developments seen in North America witnessed TCs emerge which had rather different influences. This treatment model focused primarily on addictive behaviours and viewed drug misuse as 'a symptom of the essence of the disorder' (Lipton, 2010). The TC movement emphasized a recovery-orientated approach for those with chronic substance misuse problems, rather than having the social psychiatric underpinnings of those in the United Kingdom. Within these settings, addictive behaviours were seen to reflect a disorder of the whole person, and the treatment framework was centred on the belief that patterns of drug use are less important than behavioural and psychological disorders (Lipton, 2010). Whilst incorporating the principles of patient involvement, responsibility and community living, a central emphasis of this approach concerned patient recovery and abstinence. Conforming to certain moral and social values was considered essential in the process of change. The idea of 'right living' recognized a moral code concerning right or wrong behaviour and the need for participants to commit themselves to values such as honesty, integrity, social responsibility and productivity (DeLeon, 1995). These were known as 'hierarchical' or 'concept' TCs with a set of formal structures differentiating those who were beginning the process of recovery from those who had progressed through certain defined stages. The stratified nature of the community and its social relationships is central to its therapeutic model with participants being able to achieve greater responsibilities and privileges, and move up the strata as they demonstrate competency, maturity and growth.

Whilst there are distinctive differences between these two types of TCs, there are also many areas of common ground. Many of the key ideas emphasizing participation, support, collaboration and personal responsibility see the two approaches having more similarities than differences. An important defining feature which has distinguished them from other interventions is considered to be the 'purposive use of the community as a primary method for facilitating social and psychological change in individuals' (De Leon, 1995) and the notion of their providing a 'living learning' experience.

The Challenges of the 'What Works' Ideas

The growth in treatment programmes witnessed in the last 20 years can be put down to a number of core factors. Widespread dissatisfaction with the 'just deserts' approach to incarceration (Bottoms, 1998) occurred simultaneously with a growing evidence base providing convincing evidence for the efficacy of interventions with offenders. At the same time, developments in research methods enabled meta-analytic techniques to draw conclusions through combining the results from the large number of studies which were becoming available. This provided seemingly incontrovertible evidence that Cognitive Behavioural Therapy (CBT) methods were effective in reducing rates of offender recidivism. They were also those which had most direct relevance to targeting the attitudinal, cognitive and interpersonal deficits related to offender risk (Andrews, 1995; Andrews and Bonta, 2003). These cognitive behavioural methods and procedures also had their attractiveness to service providers and practitioners. Compared with other psychotherapeutic approaches, CBT could be delivered on a relatively short-term basis and adopted methods which enabled treatment to be delivered without requiring extensive and costly training. Furthermore, it was considered that offenders were most likely to engage and respond to CBT methods. With the subsequent widespread development of offending behaviour programmes, psychoanalytic therapeutic approaches and those derived from traditional person-centred counselling approaches became marginalized as irrelevant to offender risk and need and were seen as using outdated methods to which many offenders would be unlikely to engage with (Lösel, 1993).

Controversies and developments

The emerging evidence base and developments in CBT practice presented TCs with a significant challenge, as their treatment model appeared discrepant with these new approaches. A major obstacle was the lack of an articulated and empirically derived 'model of change' which could demonstrate that their approach was sufficiently inclusive to address psychological disturbance and offence-specific treatment needs.

The 'what works' developments placed TCs outside of mainstream practice for other reasons. The emphasis given to the therapeutic relationships as both a prerequisite for treatment and as a clinical priority appeared inconsistent with the established 'what works' principles of effective practice. These considered an emphasis on alliance building and relationships being of relatively low importance in programme design and delivery (McGuire and Priestly, 1995). With the CBT framework becoming widely viewed as the only credible approach in offender treatment, TCs needed to demonstrate the effectiveness of their regime and long-term outcomes of relevance to recidivism.

A further obstacle to the wider recognition of TCs within the psychology of criminal conduct was their association with clinically unorthodox practice. Controversy and scepticism became associated with TC practice following the Oak Ridge study (Rice, Harris and Cormier, 1992). This concluded that interventions based on TC ideas made psychopathic offenders 'worse', in terms of their risk of future recidivism. Whilst clinical practices at Oak Ridge were associated with an environment of rather unfettered patient autonomy, their associations with TC practice remained (Hare, 2003), and the Oak Ridge study led to an overgeneralized conclusion that 'treatment made psychopaths worse'. Of greater concern, TCs were regarded as an irrelevant and perhaps harmful form of intervention. Despite radical differences between the practices at Oak Ridge and those within UK TCs, the terms 'therapeutic community' and 'Oak Ridge' continued, until fairly recently, to be used interchangeably.

TCs have been consistently challenged to frame their work in terms of an empirically based model. Standards for accreditation within the UK Prison Service have demanded that a cognitive behavioural model be adopted. However, fitting this requirement with the clinical programme of a TC proved difficult (Joint Accreditation Panel Report, 1998). It was not until consistent evidence demonstrated the effectiveness of alternative empirically based approaches delivered in TCs and the revision of clinical guidelines (Joint Accreditation Panel Report, 2000) that TCs became acknowledged as a legitimate intervention relevant to addressing offender risk (HM Prison Service, 2004).

Treatment Model of Therapeutic Communities

Treatment readiness and the therapeutic relationship

The importance of the therapeutic relationship in clinical change and the impact which TCs have on their development has been recognized by many authors (Kennard, 1998). Haigh (2002) viewed TCs as having an almost innate capacity to establish therapeutic alliances, create a 'culture of belonging' and an ability to instil a therapeutic climate defined by the reciprocal exploration of the relationships between its members. This, he argued, was necessary for developing the safety and collaboration required for engaging offenders in treatment, and essential when working with high need, high risk and complex disturbance. He suggests that 'when disturbance is…fundamental, the first task of treatment is to reconstruct a secure attachment, and then use that to bring about changes in the deeply ingrained expectations of relationships and patterns of behaviour' (Haigh, 2002, p. 247).

TCs explore core beliefs relating to self and other, often through analysis of early experiences with key caregivers. An initial aim of group work is to address the mistrust, hostility, suspicion and dependency which often typifies these relationships by identifying how early patterns of relating may have subsequently emerged in later experiences. The exploration of relationships remains a continued focus of the TC clinical model for two reasons. First, establishing trust and safety is a core component of a therapeutic environment associated with enhancing treatment readiness (Ward *et al.*, 2004). Second, by utilizing the interpersonal processes operating within TCs, positive attachments are able to disconfirm dysfunctional beliefs about self and others.

Therapeutic communities, attachment theory and offending

An issue that TCs have faced in achieving recognition as a mainstream intervention is in demonstrating the effective use of psychodynamic ideas and practice with offender populations. There was the need to respond to the perception that therapeutic work was unduly informed by outdated clinical ideas derived from analytic approaches, ideas which were regarded as lacking relevance to the needs of offenders (Andrews, 1995). The task which faced TCs was to define, adapt and, if necessary, refine practice in a way which demonstrated that coherent and clinically informed methods informed their work. Whilst orthodox psychoanalytical approaches are not representative of practice in TCs (Shine and Morris, 2000), the association of TCs with analytically based group therapy and insight-orientated programmes has presented a challenge for TCs (Hare, 2003).

As indicated previously, the treatment framework of offender programmes derived from the 'what works' ideas was not readily applicable to TC approaches. Based on principles of group work and community living, TCs followed a conceptually different approach. Group work did not follow a prescribed and formalized session plan but focused instead on the observation and exploration of behaviour and relationships which inevitably emerged in this setting, an approach that did not easily lend itself to easy clinical definition or that could be readily subsumed within pre-existing theoretical models.

One clinical model which has informed an understanding of the TC model is that of attachment theory (Haigh, 2002). Attachment theory regards people as having an innate tendency to make attachments to others and particularly focuses on the enduring attachments that are formed in early life (Bowlby, 1988). These relationships are fundamental to the beliefs, expectations and ideas which people come to have about the world, themselves and others. Bowlby referred to these ideas as an 'internal working map'. Where infants experience difficulties in early relationships, did not have their basic needs met or experienced erratic or inconsistent parenting, later problems in relating and dysfunctional residual beliefs and unhelpful predictions about others become apparent. As adults, relating styles become harmed by a sense of 'internal fragmentation' (Klein, 1946). Maladaptive attachment styles, referred to by Ainsworth (1991) as 'insecure-avoidant and insecure-ambivalent', come to dominate later patterns of relating.

Whilst attachment theory has been the subject of ongoing interest (Adhead and ven Velson, 1996) since it first featured in offender research (Bowlby, 1944), mainstream interventions for offenders have not generally been informed by this work. More recent research, however, has identified there are a disproportionate number of violent offenders who have disorganized or disorientated attachment styles (Frodi *et al.*, 2001; Fonagy, 2004), and a consistent evidence base seems to suggest that attachment-related deficits present as significant predisposing factors to later risk of violent behaviour (Smallbone, 2005; Rich, 2006). The extensive growth of CBT interventions and programmes for offenders emerging in the 1990s was little informed by attachment-based research and practice. Whilst the need to establish a therapeutic alliance was seen as good practice, approaches to offender treatment largely steered away from a focus on attachment deficits or developmental traumas such as abusive experiences. Similarly, interventions were not adapted to respond to the treatment needs and engagement deficits presented by offenders with attachment disorders.

More recently, however, trauma research and the implications this presents for offender engagement and treatment need have informed treatment design. Developments in interventions (Saradjian, Murphy and McVey, 2010) have responded to some of the issues by focusing explicitly on areas such as trauma, abuse and attachment deficits.

Core therapeutic factors and the role of staff

When working with personality-disordered offenders, the importance of 'core therapeutic factors' as an essential component of therapeutic change has been widely recognized. Livesley (2007) suggests that certain conditions are necessary for therapeutic work. These include collaborative treatment alliances, the presence of a safe and supportive environment and a range of opportunities being present to acquire and generalize alternative behaviours.

The therapeutic culture of a TC rests on the principle that where certain conditions prevail (see Figure 19.1), opportunities for therapeutic exploration, learning and change will follow. This culture is further enhanced by a framework which establishes therapeutic boundaries and

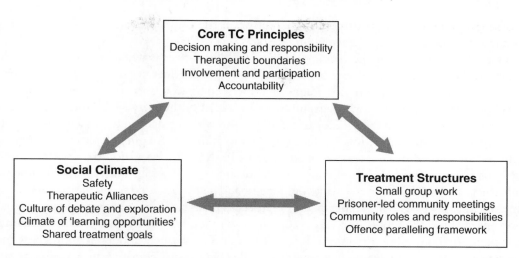

Figure 19.1 The relationship between TC core principles, social climate and treatment structures

provides a structure which defines the extent of prisoner decision making; furthermore, a mutually shared 'constitution', which governs expectations of behaviour and participation, is balanced by a culture which tolerates the expression of offence paralleling behaviours (OPBs). Two additional factors are essential to the therapeutic culture: the engagement of the staff group and involvement of the wider regime. Promoting staff involvement and engagement in the intervention needs to be a core goal of any treatment programme (Murphy, 2010; Sheldon and Tennant, 2011), especially when working with offenders with personality disorder. This can often present personal and professional challenges with attempts to rupture or undermine the therapeutic alliance (Lewis and Appelby, 1988). Undermined professional confidence, interdisciplinary rivalry and an oscillation between the 'condemnatory and collusion roles' have been identified as sometimes inevitable features of working with this client group (Craissati *et al.*, 2011). TCs directly address some of these challenges by offering a structure for team working which adopts 'democratized' practices, where the ownership of decision making is shared by the staff team. Staff involvement includes treatment planning and deselection, a central role in the delivery of group work and ongoing involvement in the assessment of risk and treatment progress. In parallel with this, the organization defines itself as one which not only supports treatment but provides significant opportunities for learning, change and skill development. Therapeutic work is enhanced by the opportunities presented by a regime where all its various components (therapy, work, regime activities) are recognized as having an interlinked role in treatment.

A Model of Risk Reduction

The means by which TCs address risk has been considered by various authors (e.g., Cullen, 1997; Jones, 1997; Shine and Morris 2000; Brookes, 2010). The clinical environment provides the arena for the exploration of attitudes and behaviour. This process has been referred to by some authors as 'social analysis' (Genders and Player, 1995). At its core is the exploration of interpersonal beliefs and the reciprocal feedback given between members. Therapy constitutes the learning which occurs within this dynamic social environment.

These therapeutic processes become apparent when the OPBs activated within this setting become the routine focus of therapeutic work.

One of the features of the TC approach which has differentiated it from interventions adopting a CBT framework is that the core small group work does not follow a predetermined session content. Sessions do not follow a prescribed session format but instead offer a psychotherapeutic approach which explores the inter-relationship between its members' recent or current behaviour and the parallels of this behaviour with offence sequences and early developmental experiences. A criticism levied at this model is that where offender interventions lack a clearly established structure and content, they are likely to lack relevance to offender risk and need (Andrews, 1995). This is of course an important consideration. The risk that traditional 'unstructured' modes of group work could fail to adequately respond to offence-related need could well apply to TCs if the therapeutic approaches practiced were not anchored in the core principles which allow both the expression and exploration of OPB. Figure 19.1 highlights this point, demonstrating the interrelated features of the treatment model. It shows how the core principles help to establish a treatment enhancing social climate where prisoners are accountable to each other and where a culture of collaboration, openness and leaning is present. This enables specific therapeutic structures to be introduced, such as therapeutic group work, community meetings, feedback sessions and prisoner responsibility and participation.

Therapeutic communities and offence paralleling behaviour

One of the most clinically potent features of a TC is the creation of a therapeutic climate which allows OPBs to emerge, to be identified and to be addressed. Emerging from the work of Clark, Fisher and Thomas (1991), who developed a framework for risk assessment that identified links between offending and institutional behaviours, OPB has a crucial role in risk assessment, case formulation and treatment (Jones, 2004). The central concept of OPB is the notion that consistency in behaviour, or at least the function of behaviour, will be evident across different situations. This provides clinicians with a critical source of information relevant to ongoing assessments of risk and an assessment of the impact of treatment programmes.

Daffern, Jones and Shine (2010) define OPB as '...a behavioural sequence incorporating overt behaviours (that may be muted by environmental factors) appraisals, expectations, beliefs, affect, goals and behavioural scripts all of which may be influenced by the patient's mental disorder, that is functionally similar to behavioural sequences involved in previous offending acts' (p. 267). Although interest in the OPB framework is expanding (Daffern, Jones and Shine, 2010), Shine (2010) considers there are a number of problems that need to be addressed when adopting an offence paralleling framework. Many forensic environments such as prisons can limit the extent to which identifying and working with the OPBs may be possible. Shine argues, however, that two of the main issues which place limitations on the OPB framework in forensic settings can be largely overcome when adopted in the framework of TCs. These are the influence of the inmate subculture and an overemphasis on 'within session' therapy behaviour. Within TCs, the inmates subculture, identified as a powerful determinate of behaviour and attitude (Harris, Rice and Cormier, 1991), can be harnessed to a positive effect to help recognize offence-specific patterns of behaviour and reinforce pro-social alternative behaviours. This environment also provides a context for treatment which focuses on the interactions that occur out of formal therapy sessions as much as it does on in-session behaviour. In doing so, it highlights clinically relevant behaviours which may not always emerge within the treatment session itself (Shine, 2010).

The emphasis on the use of the regime as providing opportunities for learning invariably leads to a rich climate for OPB to be observed. The relationships, roles and responsibilities which form the basis of TCs lead almost inevitably to offence-related chains and sequences becoming re-enacted. Whether evident in hostile interpersonal appraisals, dysfunctional emotional responses, self-management or coping deficits, the environment within a TC offers considerable opportunity for behavioural consistency to become evident. The major therapeutic strength of this approach is seen in its culture of exploration and debate where the offence-related patterns of behaviour form the basis of therapeutic exploration, instilling a rigorous 'culture of enquiry'.

Shine and Morris (2000) describe a 'mutlifactorial' TC model based on three domains of therapeutic work. This model explores the inter-relation between attachments (belief systems and relationship styles originating from early developmental experiences), offending behaviour (sequences observed in their offending history) and behaviours occurring within the TC itself (relationships, interactions, attitudes, beliefs and appraisal). Incorporating concepts from analytic, interpersonal and cognitive behavioural psychology, the TC model focuses on clinically relevant behaviours observed both in and out of the immediate treatment setting. Developments in practice for personality-disordered offenders have made it apparent that efforts to respond to a complex range of needs that can be resistant to treatment require a range of interventions that can be provided as part of an integrative approach (Livesley, 2007). This requires an approach where different therapeutic methods can be adopted within one overarching model. A number of authors (e.g., Shine and Morris, 2000; Brookes, 2010; Shuker, 2010) have described how the climate of a TC allows the integration of therapeutic approaches to address antisocial patterns of behaviour and establish 'positive alternative behaviours' (Jones, 2004).

Community reinforcement, feedback and skill generalization

As highlighted, one of the difficulties when applying offending behaviour programmes within settings such as prisons is the challenge this presents to participants when attempting to practice the skills they have learnt in the treatment setting, within the wider context of prison life. Treatment components regarded as essential to skill acquisition and attitudinal change emphasize the importance of a supportive environment. This reinforces newly learned behaviours and provides opportunities for positive reinforcement of alternative behaviours when released. The impact of a wider social context on programme outcome, where antisocial beliefs are a heavily ingrained part of its culture, is unlikely to support the gains made in treatment groups (Zamble and Porporino, 1988).

A component which has an important influence on programme effectiveness is the beliefs and attitudes held not only by those delivering treatment but also by those involved in the routine supervision and management of the offenders in treatment. Attitudes and values of staff have been recognized as an important variable in creating positive regimes which promote decency, collaboration and regime quality (Thornton *et al.*, 1984; Liebling and Price, 2001; James 2006). These have an important value, not only in their 'pro-social modelling' function, but also in reinforcing the attitudes, beliefs and skills addressed within session content. Evidence suggests that the TCs' ability to effectively engage staff promotes staff identification with the aims and ethos of treatment and promotes beliefs congruent with rehabilitation and attitudes which support, reinforce and enhance the treatment process (Shefer, 2010).

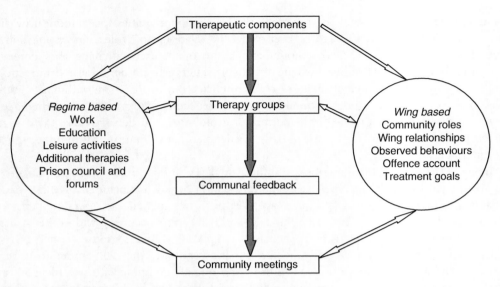

Figure 19.2 Organizational structure facilitating OPBs in a TC

The TC model provides other important organizational and clinical features which have a direct bearing on learning and skill consolidation. Figure 19.2 demonstrates the inter-relationship between the core therapy sessions (treatment groups and wing meetings) and the wider organization. This highlights a key operating principle of TCs that is making 'lateral linkages' (Morris, 2004), whereby behaviours observed in one setting (e.g., gym, work, informal social activities) are routinely explored in the therapy groups and parallels or links between these and the offence sequences identified. The reinforcement of positive alternative behaviours occurs where community members recognize how observed patterns of behaviour are in conflict with a fellow prisoner's treatment objectives and personal goals, and can help in identifying and exploring these. The shared therapeutic process of supporting individual members in their attempts to test out beliefs and to attempt alternative means of resolving interpersonal and emotional problems, while observing therapeutic change and progress, is a powerful and reinforcing activity. Whilst the concept that group members can provide a valuable role in challenging each other's beliefs and behaviour is well established in forensic interventions, what TCs provide in addition is the opportunity to identify relevant behaviours observed outside of the therapy group. This process of engaging participants in each other's therapeutic work becomes a potent therapeutic tool, which is further enhanced by another process, shared community 'feedbacks'. This process, where members openly disclose or 'feed back' the content of the therapy sessions to the whole community, ensures that all participants become mutually involved in each other's treatment.

Therapeutic openness where individual areas of risk and need are readily known (an individual's treatment targets and progress are also discussed in detail in the wing meetings) provides an additional mechanism to address a further aspect of offender need, 'detection evasion skills'. Development of detection evasion skills (Jones, 2004) is an important concept, providing one possible explanation for the discrepancy between high rates of offending and low rates of reconviction. These can also be evident in the discrepancy frequently observed between offender behaviour shown during the treatment session and that demonstrated outside of that setting (Shine, 2010). A transparent treatment culture is established where collective knowledge about risk, treatment goals, detection evasion strategies and OPBs is established by everything being 'out in the open' and open to scrutiny. This is supported further by the open community feedbacks which provide a powerful mechanism which challenges the 'no grassing' (or informing) code within prison subculture.

TCs and the structures and clinical practices outlined earlier are linked very intrinsically to the setting in which they operate. Establishing and sustaining an environment that is not merely 'treatment supportive', but is also an integral element of the intervention, creates a mutually dependent relationship where 'treatment' and 'organization' do not become disconnected but serve to enhance and support each other's role. The contribution of TCs where related principles have been adopted to utilize the host organization in the design and delivery of treatment will now be discussed.

Therapeutic Communities and Enabling Environments

Whilst TCs have appeared attractive as a means of establishing a safe and humane environment (Rhodes, 2010), distilling the factors which would allow a TC to be translated to other forensic settings is difficult. Therapeutic principles cannot be translated on a piecemeal basis because, to a considerable extent, they are mutually dependent. For example, decision making and involvement cannot be given to its members without the principles of personal responsibility and accountability. Neither can the principles of behavioural 'tolerance' be practised without clearly understood boundaries and systems for conflict management. Attempts to provide a democratized environment, investing responsibility to its members, is fraught with risks and challenges (Rhodes, 2010). Bennett and Shuker (2010) note that '...importing wholesale a TC regime rests upon certain conditions being in place, conditions which are not readily achieved... it is notoriously difficult to set up...which raises questions about whether it is an appropriate intervention within a custodial setting' (p. 493). It also says something about how fragile the TC culture can be. This is evident from recent history, which shows that while some attempts to establish TCs have been successful (Cullen and Miller, 2010), others have encountered significant difficulties (see Stevens, 2010). Furthermore, research suggests that the risk, need and responsivity principles need to be carefully adhered to when assessing suitability for treatment (Shine, 2001; Shuker, Falshaw and Newton, 2007) with assessment and selection procedures aimed at identifying those most likely to respond. The risks of erosion of treatment integrity are as much, if not more, of a concern for TCs as they are for other forensic interventions (Genders and Player, 2010). To address this, an ongoing initiative for TCs has been to embark on the process of identifying an agreed set of standards by which TCs operate (The Royal College of Psychiatrists, 2010). Together with the development of clinical audit procedures, TCs now have a set of 'core standards' which provide the clarity and consistency to protect against drift. Whilst TCs are not an intervention to which all offenders will respond, initiatives aimed at promoting 'decent' regimes are now core to the majority of forensic services, with TC principles being acknowledged as having an influence on practice. This relevance of TC ideas has also been seen in recent developments in defining what a psychologically 'enabling environment' should look like. Johnson and Haigh (2011, pp. 19–20) consider that those aspects of the TC which could provide the forum for positive, enabling environments outside of the formal TC settings should be based on a set of principles and values derived to a considerable extent from TCs. For example, they describe the following features of enabling environments as important:

- The nature and quality of relationships between its members is recognized and highly valued.
- Participants share some measure of responsibility for the environment as a whole.
- Participants are equally valued and supported.
- Engagement and purposeful activity are encouraged.
- Opportunities for creativity and initiative are emphasized.
- There is transparent leadership.
- Formal and informal roles are acknowledged.
- Power and authority is accountable and open for discussion.
- Formal rules and expectations of behaviour are clear.
- Behaviour which is potentially disruptive is seen as meaningful and as a communication to be understood.

Within forensic practice, these developments have been extended to include the formation of Psychologically Informed Planned Environments as part of a progression pathway for personality-disordered offenders who have received high-intensity intervention (Joseph and Benefield, 2011). These are underpinned by some of the values and practices emerging from TCs focusing on the use of everyday situations as opportunities for learning. They also emphasize the importance of relationships being established within a safe and supportive environment, demonstrating the wider applicability of TC principles.

What Works: The Effectiveness of Therapeutic Communities?

Whilst a considerable knowledge base about the effectiveness of Democratic TCs has developed (Lees, Manning and Rawlings, 2004), questions have remained about how far this research provides clear and robust evidence of their efficacy. A systematic review of TC research concluded that 'therapeutic communities have not produced the amount or quality of research literature that we might have expected, given the length of time they have been in existence' (Lees, Manning and Rawlings, 1999, p. 9). More recently Smith, Gates and Foxcroft (2006), in reviewing the research into the efficacy of concept TCs, considered that methodological weaknesses have limited the extent to which conclusions can be confidently drawn. Methodological problems such as inadequate definitions about what constitutes a TC, inherent problems in defining what treatment 'completion' means, studies which have often failed to recognize the distinction between TC 'completers' and 'non-completers', the heterogeneous nature of TC participants and the broad range of outcome measures adopted, have all impacted upon the quality of TC research. It has been argued by some that these issues can only be effectively addressed by adopting randomized control trial methodology (Rutter and Tyrer, 2003).

Despite problems identified in the extent and quality of the research evidence available, there is a growing evidence base. Haigh, Pearce and Diamond (2010) refer to there being a 'great deal of good quality evidence for TC practice…Much of this has remained "under the radar"' (p. 319). Likewise Warren *et al.* (2003), in a review of treatments for severe personality disorder, cite therapeutic communities as having the 'most promising evidence'. They conclude that 'the therapeutic community ethos could be used as the dominant approach and structure…of new regimes…and could include other treatments targeting specific aspects of psychopathology' (p. 5.). Furthermore, Lees, Manning and Rawlings (1999), whilst conscious of the lack of high-quality studies in their systematic review, concluded that TCs did appear to demonstrate a range of positive outcomes. These included improvements in institutional adjustment, positive impact on mental health and psychological adjustment, lower rates of self-harm and drug misuse, and more adaptive pro-social attitudes and beliefs.

Mental health outcomes

TCs have traditionally attracted and targeted those with personality disorder and related mental health and psychological problems (Shine and Newton, 2000). A substantial amount of research has addressed the question of whether TCs are effective in the treatment of personality disorder and psychological disturbance. Research findings have persistently supported the use of TCs as an intervention which is effective in reducing symptoms of personality disorder and psychological and emotional distress (Chiesa and Fonagy, 2000; Bateman and Fonagy, 2001; Norton and Warren, 2004). Research has consistently suggested that treatment in a TC routinely sees improvements in symptoms of mental disorder including self-esteem, anxiety, impulsivity and emotional instability. Rates of attempted suicide and self-harm (another useful indicator of emotional stability and psychological health) also show significant post-treatment improvement. Whilst those accepted for a TC tend to have a disproportionately high level of previous self-harm and attempted suicide (Newbury, 2009), research has consistently indicated that extremely low rates of self-injurious behaviour are evident within these settings (Newton, 2006; Rivelin, 2010).

Individuals with personality disorders often present with significant interpersonal deficits (Blackburn, 1998) and dysfunctional patterns of relating frequently present as primary treatment needs in those referred to TCs. Birchnell *et al.* (2009) demonstrated that significant improvements in interpersonal relating were demonstrated during the course of treatment in a TC with prisoners developing improved interpersonal 'competence' and the ability to respond effectively to a range of interpersonal demands.

Attitudinal and behavioural change

Research examining the extent to which TCs are effective in targeting offence-specific attitudinal and behavioural factors, alongside improvements in mental health, supports their efficacy as an intervention able to address criminogenic factors. Newton (1998) demonstrated that those prisoners who had participated in treatment for over 18 months showed reductions in antisocial traits, including lower rates of hostility, impulsivity and 'tough-minded' personality characteristics. In a more recent study, Shuker and Newton (2008) found that offenders demonstrated reliable and clinically significant reductions in offence-related attitudes where they had been in treatment for over 18 months (these occurred simultaneously with improvement in psychological well-being).

Research has also explored the extent to which TCs have an impact on institutional behaviour. Levels of institutional misconduct are important as they provide useful indices of an unsafe and antisocial environment. Furthermore, institutional misconduct has been seen as an important predictor of reconviction (Newton, 2010). Research within prison settings has shown that TCs lead to significant reductions in rates of institutional misconduct, both for violent and non-violent offences, with adjudication rates identified at approximately one-sixth of those seen in comparable prisons (Cullen, 1994; Newton, 2010). These improvements in institutional behaviour are of interest as TCs typically attract men with high levels of risk, need and disturbance (Shine and Newton, 2000). Furthermore, Newton (2010) found that the improved rates of behaviour observed during treatment were unlikely to be attributed solely to differences in adjudication policies within these settings, and improvements in behaviour were sustained to a statistically significant level upon transfer to different prisons.

Reconviction

Addressing the question of whether or not TCs have an impact on reconviction has presented a challenge. Whilst researchers from North America (De Leon, 2004, Lipton, 2010) argue that there is a sufficiently strong evidence base to point to the effectiveness of hierarchical TCs in reducing rates of reconviction for substance misusers, less confidence seems to accompany UK findings. Debates about the need for and appropriateness of conducting a randomized control trial continue (Hinshelwood, 2010; Pearce and Autrique, 2010), which may be partly due to the sensitivities that TCs continue to have in response to the charge that they may not be effective (Lees, Manning and Rawlings, 2004). However, from the growing number of reconviction studies which have taken place, whilst some inconsistent and mixed findings have emerged, there is also a sufficiently consistent picture to suggest that TCs do, for some groups of offenders, impact upon reconviction (Miller and Brown 2010).

Evidence from studies of European TCs also suggests that Democratic TCs are effective in reducing reoffending for those with severe personality disorders (Lösel, Koferl and Weber, 1987; De Boer-van Schaik and Derks, 2010) with reoffending rates reported at between 11% and 16% lower than those serving standard prison sentences. Although a review of the TC data based on UK research has presented some inconclusive findings (Gunn and Robertson, 1982), studies have demonstrated a treatment effect. Marshall (1997), in a four-year post-treatment follow-up, found significant reductions in risk of reconviction for prisoners who had remained in treatment for over 18 months. He estimated this group demonstrated a reduction in reconviction rates of between one-fifth and a quarter. Following the same sample, Taylor (2000) found that reductions in reconviction rates were sustained at the seven-year stage (although these were no longer significant at the 0.05% level). In a more recent study, Newton and Erikson (2007) found a reconviction rate of 39% for those who remained in treatment for over 18 months (completing treatment). This group was significantly less likely to be reconvicted than those who left prematurely. These findings still held even after the risk level of the two groups was taken into account. Whilst methodological weaknesses limit the extent to which claims about their effectiveness on reconviction can be made (Rutter and Tyrer, 2003), evidence points to TCs as having promise and potential in risk reduction. However, an important observation by Lipton (2002) when assessing the impact of North American TCs on recidivism was the more limited treatment effect where an aftercare component was not included. Only where a substantial follow-up component was a routine part of the intervention was a significant treatment effect observed.

What the research appears to be highlighting is that certain types of offenders appear to engage and to reduce risk in a TC. Whilst some indications point to the efficacy of TCs with the most complex and high-risk groups, there is limited evidence to support this (McMurran, 2002). Challenging and disturbed prisoners appear to be safely and effectively managed within these settings (Shine and Newton, 2000). However, research has suggested that in terms of engagement and length of stay in treatment, or in reductions in risk, those with the most complex needs (or highest risk of recidivism) do less well than their lower-risk counterparts. Research has highlighted that those who are most likely to engage, remain in and benefit from treatment are the more intelligent, introvert and less hostile and 'tough-minded' prisoners (Shine, 2001). Those demonstrating greater psychological insight, problem recognition and behavioural stability are also more likely to complete or remain longer in treatment (Shuker, Falshaw and Newton, 2007). This indicates that initiatives to enhance 'treatment readiness' for the higher-risk groups may be of value (e.g., by participating in motivational or skills-based group work prior to referral), whilst those with the most complex and severe needs should be referred to other specialist, higher-intensity services.

Social climate and quality of life

Given their emphasis on providing a positive, enabling and treatment-enhancing environment, research has also examined the social climate and 'quality of life' within TCs. Research measuring quality of life in prisons has become increasingly important, reflecting the growing emphasis on the 'decency' agenda. Based on research identifying those factors associated with quality of life in custodial settings (Liebling and Arnold, 2002), the extent to which prisons are effective in achieving a positive quality of life is now routinely assessed. Areas identified as being important in providing a high quality of life include features such as safety, humanity, fairness, trust and resettlement. In all dimensions measured, TCs have routinely been found to have the highest quality of life out of all secure prisons (Ministry of Justice Report, 2009; Shefer, 2010).

Assessments of social climate in secure settings have also been undertaken. The dimensions of the therapeutic supportive environment, cohesion and trust, and safety were assessed using the ESSEN Climate Evaluation Schema (Schalast *et al.*, 2008) with prisoners and staff within a TC perceiving social climate more favourably than those within high secure hospitals and European mental health settings (Tonkin and Howells, 2009). Shefer (2010) found that although staff within TCs experienced high levels of stress, they have more positive beliefs about prisoners and rated the overall quality of prison life as very high. Lower rates of bullying have also consistently been identified with prisoners reporting that the level of bullying experienced within TCs is extremely low compared with that in other establishments (Evans *et al.*, 2009).

Conclusions

This chapter has described the role which TCs have had in offender rehabilitation in the United Kingdom. It has explored how their work has come to occupy a key position in the treatment of offenders and highlighted how TCs have come to be of increased relevance as an intervention for offenders. TCs have also seen their model adopted and adapted for clinical services for mentally disordered offenders. They have evident utility in addressing risk and promoting psychological adjustment. TCs are in a unique position because they provide a custodial model that cultivates decency and mutual respect. Their role in the management and incarceration of offenders has been to provide a safe and collaborative environment for those who work and reside in them, and they present an important contribution to offender rehabilitation.

References

Adhead, G. and van Velsen, C. (1996) Psychotherapeutic work with victims of trauma, in *Forensic Psychotherapy: Crime, Psychodynamics and Offender Patient* (eds C. Cordess and M. Cox), Jessica Kingsley Publishers, London, pp. 359–365.

Ainsworth, M. (1991) Attachments and other affectional bonds across the life cycle, in *Attachment Across the Life Cycle* (eds C.M. Parkes, J. Stevenson-Hindle and P. Marris), Routledge, London, pp. 33–51.

Andrews, D.A. (1995) The psychology of criminal conduct and effective treatment, in *What Works: Reducing Offending: Guidelines from Research and Practice* (ed. J. McGuire), John Wiley & Sons, Ltd, Chichester.

Andrews, D.A. and Bonta, J. (2003) *The Psychology of Criminal Conduct*, Anderson Publishing, Cincinnati.

Bateman, A. and Fonagy, P. (2001) Treatment of borderline personality disorder with psychoanalytically oriented partial hospitalization: an 18-month follow-up. *American Journal of Psychiatry*, 158, 36–42.

Bennett, P. and Shuker, R. (2010) Improving prisoner-staff relationships: exporting Grendon's good practice. *Howard Journal of Criminal Justice*, 49, 491–502.

Birtchnell, J., Shuker, R., Newberry, M. and Duggan, C. (2009) The assessment of change in negative relating in two male forensic therapy samples using the Person's Relating to Others Questionnaire. *Journal of Forensic Psychiatry & Psychology*, 20, 387–407.

Bottoms, A. (1998) Five puzzles in von Hirsch's theory of punishment, in *Fundamentals of Sentencing Theory: Essays in the Honour of Andrew von Hirsch* (eds A.J. Ashworth and M. Wasik), Oxford University Press, Oxford, pp. 53–100.

Bowlby, J. (1944) Forty-four juvenile thieves: their characters and their home lives. *International Journal of Psychoanalysis*, 25, 19–52.

Bowlby, J. (1988) *A Secure Base*, Basic Books, New York.

Blackburn, R. (1998) Psychopathy and personality disorder: implications of interpersonal theory, in *Psychopathy: Theory, Research and Implications for Society* (eds D.J. Cooke, S.J. Hart and A.E. Forth), Kluwer, Amsterdam.

Brookes, M. (2010) Putting principles into practice: the therapeutic community regime at HMP Grendon and its relationship with the Good Lives Model, in *Grendon and the Emergence of Forensic Therapeutic Communities: Developments in Research and Practice* (eds R. Shuker and E. Sullivan), Wiley-Blackwell, Chichester, pp. 99–113.

Campling, P. and Haigh, R. (1999) *Therapeutic Communities: Past, Present and Future*, Jessica Kingsley, London.

Chiesa, M. and Fonagy, P. (2000) Cassell personality disorder study: methodology and treatment effects. *British Journal of Psychiatry*, 176, 485–491.

Clark, M.A., Fisher, M. and Thomas, M.E. (1991) *The assessment of Risk: A Guide*. HMP Wakefield. Unpublished manuscript.

Craissati, J., Minoudis, P., Shaw, J. *et al.* (2011) *Working with Personality Disordered Offenders: A Practitioners' Guide*, Ministry of Justice, London.

Cullen, E. (1994) Grendon: the therapeutic community that works. *Therapeutic Communities for Offenders*, 15, 301–311.

Cullen, E. (1997) Can a prison be therapeutic? The Grendon template, in *Therapeutic Communities for Offenders* (eds E. Cullen, L. Jones and R. Woodward), John Wiley & Sons, Ltd, Chichester.

Cullen, E. and Miller, A. (2010) Dovegate therapeutic community: bid, birth, growth and survival, in *Grendon and the Emergence of Forensic Therapeutic Communities: Developments in Research and Practice* (eds R. Shuker and E. Sullivan), Wiley-Blackwell, Chichester, pp. 25–44.

Daffern, M., Jones, L. and Shine, J. (2010) *Offence Paralleling Behaviour: A Case Formulation Approach to Offender Assessment and Intervention*, Wiley-Blackwell, Chichester.

De Boer-van Schaik, J. and Derks, F. (2010) The Van der Hoeven clinic: a flexible and innovative forensic psychiatric hospital based on therapeutic community principles, in *Grendon and the Emergence of Forensic Therapeutic Communities: Developments in Research and Practice* (eds R. Shuker and E. Sullivan), Wiley-Blackwell, Chichester, pp. 45–60.

De Leon, G. (1995) Therapeutic communities – is there an essential model? in *As Community as Method. Therapeutic Communities for Special Populations and Special Settings* (ed. G. De Leon), Greenwood Publishing Group, Westport.

De Leon, G. (2004) Therapeutic communities, in *The American Psychiatric Publishing Textbook of Substance Abuse*, 3rd edn (eds M. Galanter and H.D. Kleber), American Psychiatric Publishing, Inc., Washington, DC, pp. 485–501.

East, W.N. and Hubert, W. (1939) *The Psychological Treatment of Crime*, His Majesty's Stationery Office, London.

Evans, R., Roberts, J., Jacobs, L. and Shuker, R. (2009) Survey of Bullying at HMP Grendon, *Internal Report*, HMP Grendon.

Fonagy, P. (2004) The developmental roots of violence in the failure to mentalize, in *A Matter of Security: The Application of Attachment Theory to Forensic Psychiatry and Psychotherapy* (eds G. Adshead and F. Pfafflin), Jessica Kingsley Publishers, London, pp. 13–56.

Frodi, A., Dernevik, M., Sepa, A. *et al.* (2001) Current attachment representations of incarcerated offenders varying in degree of psychopathy. *Attachment and Human Development*, 3, 269–283.

Genders, E. and Player, E. (1995) *Grendon: A Study of a Therapeutic Prison*, Clarendon Press, Oxford.

Genders, E. and Player, E. (2010) Therapy in prison: revisiting Grendon 20 years on. *Howard Journal of Criminal Justice*, 49, 431–450.

Gunn, J. and Robertson, G. (1982) An evaluation of Grendon prison, in *Abnormal Offenders, Delinquency and the Criminal Justice System* (eds J. Gunn and D. Farrington), John Wiley & Sons, Ltd, Chichester.

Haigh, R. (eds) (2002) The quintessence of a therapeutic environment: five universal qualities, in *Therapeutic Communities: Past, Present and Future*, Jessica Kingsley, London, pp. 246–257.

Haigh, R., Pearce, S. and Diamond, J. (2010) Evidence of evidence (editorial). *Therapeutic Communities*, 31, 317–320.

Hare, R.D. (2003) Psychopathy and risk for recidivism and violence, in *Criminal Justice, Mental Health, and the Politics of Risk* (eds N. Gray, J. Laing and L. Noaks), Cavendish, London.

Harris, G.T., Rice, M.E. and Cormier, C.A. (1991) Psychopathy and violent recidivism. *Law and Human Behaviour*, 15, 625–637.

Hinshelwood, R.D. (2010) Manual or matrix: how can we know our outcomes? *Therapeutic Communities*, 31, 328–337.

HM Prison Service. (2004) *Theory Manual for Democratic Therapeutic Communities*. Home Office Publications, London.

James, E. (2006) Life inside, in *Humane Prisons* (ed. D. Jones), Radcliffe Publishing Ltd, Oxford, pp. 19–28.

Johnson, R. and Haigh, R. (2011) Social psychiatry and social policy for the 21st century: new concepts for new needs – the "Enabling Environments" initiative. *Mental Health and Social Inclusion*, 15, 17–23.

Joint Accreditation Panel Report. (1998) Home Office, London.

Joint Accreditation Panel Report. (2000) Home Office, London.

Jones, L. (1997) Developing models for managing treatment integrity and efficacy in a prison-based TC: the Max Glatt Centre, in *Therapeutic Communities for Offenders* (eds E. Cullen, L. Jones and R. Woodward), John Wiley & Sons, Ltd, Chichester, pp. 121–160.

Jones, L. (2004) Offence paralleling behaviour as a framework for assessment and intervention with offenders, in *Applying Psychology to Forensic Practice* (eds A. Needs and G. Towl), Blackwell, Oxford, pp. 34–63.

Joseph, N. and Benefield, N. (2011) The development of an offender personality disorder strategy. *Mental Health Review Journal*, 15, 10–15.

Kennard, D. (1998) *An Introduction to Therapeutic Communities*, Jessica Kingsley Publishers, London.

Klein, M. (1946) *The Writings of Melanie Klein*, vol. 3, Hogarth Press, London.

Lees, J., Manning, N. and Rawlings, B. (1999) Therapeutic Community Effectiveness: A Systematic International Review of Therapeutic Community Treatment for People with Personality Disorders and Mentally Disordered Offenders. *CRD Rep. no. 17*. NHS Centre for Reviews and Dissemination, York.

Lees, J., Manning, N. and Rawlings, B. (2004) A culture of enquiry: research evidence and the therapeutic community. *Psychiatric Quarterly*, 75, 279–294.

Lewis, G. and Appleby, L. (1988) Personality disorder: the patients psychiatrists dislike. *British Journal of Psychiatry*, 153, 44–59.

Liebling, A. and Arnold, H. (2002) Measuring the Quality of Prison Life. *Home Office Research Findings 174*. Home Office Research, Development and Statistics Directorate, London.

Liebling, A. and Price, D. (2001) *The Prison Officer*. Prison Service Journal, HMP Leyhill.

Lipton, D.S. (2002) Therapeutic community treatment programming in corrections, in *Handbook of Offender Assessment and Treatment* (ed. C.R. Hollin), John Wiley & Sons, Ltd, Chichester.

Lipton, D.S. (2010) A therapeutic distinction with a difference: comparing American concept-based therapeutic communities and British democratic therapeutic community treatment for prison inmates, in *Grendon and the Emergence of Forensic Therapeutic Communities: Developments in Research and Practice* (eds R. Shuker and E. Sullivan), Wiley-Blackwell, Chichester, pp. 61–77.

Livesley, J. (2007) The relevance of an integrated approach to the treatment of personality disordered offenders, in *Handbook of Personality Disorders: Theory, Research, and Treatment* (eds C. Hollin, P. Koppen, S. Penrod and K. Howells), Guilford Press, New York.

Lösel, F. (1993) Evaluating psychosocial interventions in prisons and other penal contexts. Paper presented to the 20th Criminological Research Conference, Council of Europe, Strasbourg, November.

Lösel, F., Koferl, P. and Weber, F. (1987) *Meta evaluation der Socialtherapie*, Enke, Stuttgart. Cited in Lösel, F. and Egg, R. (1997) Social therapeutic institutions in Germany, in *Therapeutic Communities for Offenders* (eds E. Cullen, L. Jones and R. Woodward), John Wiley & Sons, Ltd, Chichester, pp. 181–203.

Marshall, P. (1997) A reconviction study of HMP Grendon Therapeutic Community. *Home Office Research Findings 53*. Home Office, London.

McGuire, J. and Priestly, P. (1995) *Offending Behaviour: Skills and Stratagems for Going Straight*, Batsford, London.

McMurran, M. (2002) Offenders with personality disorders, in *Handbook of Offender Assessment and Treatment* (ed. C.R. Hollin), John Wiley & Sons, Ltd, Chichester, pp. 467–480.

Miller, S. and Brown, J. (2010) HMP Dovegate's therapeutic community: an analysis of reconviction data. *Therapeutic Communities*, 31, 62–76.

Morris, M. (2004) *Dangerous and Severe – Process, Programme and Person: Process, Programme and Person – Grendon's Work*, Jessica Kingsley, London/Philadelphia.

Ministry of Justice Report (2009) MQPL Survey carried out at HMP Grendon, June 2009, supplementary report illustrating a comparison of dimension scores to those from 15 other training prisons.

Murphy, N. (2010) Effective transdisciplinary teamworking, in *Treating Personality Disorder* (eds N. Murphy and D. McVey), Routledge, London/New York.

Newberry, M. (2009) Changes in the Profile of Prisoners at HMP Grendon, Unpublished report. HMP Grendon, Oxford.

Newton, M. (1998) Changes in measures of personality, hostility and locus of control during residence in a prison therapeutic community. *Legal and Criminological Psychology*, 3, 209–223.

Newton, M. (2006) Evaluating Grendon as a prison: research into quality of life at Grendon. *Prison Service Journal*, 165, 18–22.

Newton, M. (2010) Changes in prison offending among residents of a prison-based therapeutic community, in *Grendon and the Emergence of Forensic Therapeutic Communities: Developments in Research and Practice* (eds R. Shuker and E. Sullivan), Wiley-Blackwell, Chichester, pp. 281–291.

Newton, M. and Erikson, M. (2007) *Reconviction After Treatment in a Prison Based Therapeutic Community*. Unpublished manuscript.

Norton, K. and Warren, F. (2004) Assessing outcome at Henderson Hospital: challenges and achievements, in *A Culture of Enquiry: Research Evidence and the Therapeutic Community* (eds J. Lees, N. Manning, D. Menzies and N. Morant), Jessica Kingsley, London.

Pearce, S. and Autrique, M. (2010) On the need for randomised trials of therapeutic community approaches. *Therapeutic Communities*, 31, 338–355.

Rhodes, L. (2010) This can't be real: continuity at HMP Grendon, in *Grendon and the Emergence of Forensic Therapeutic Communities: Developments in Research and Practice* (eds R. Shuker and E. Sullivan), Wiley-Blackwell, Chichester, pp. 203–216.

Rice, M.E., Harris, G.T. and Cormier, C.A. (1992) An evaluation of a maximum security therapeutic community for psychopaths and other mentally disordered offenders. *Law and Human Behaviour*, 16, 399–412.

Rich, P. (2006) *Attachment and Sexual Offending*, John Wiley & Sons, Ltd, Chichester.

Rivelin, A. (2010) Suicide and self-injurious behaviours at HMP Grendon, in *Grendon and the Emergence of Forensic Therapeutic Communities: Developments in Research and Practice* (eds R. Shuker and E. Sullivan), Wiley-Blackwell, Chichester, pp. 265–280.

Royal College of Psychiatrists. (2010) *The Community of Communities*. http://www.rcpsych.ac.uk/quality/quality,accreditationaudit/communityofcommunities.aspx (accessed 26 December 2012).

Rutter, D. and Tyrer, P. (2003) The value of therapeutic communities in the treatment of personality disorder: a suitable place for treatment? *Journal of Psychiatric Practice*, 9, 291–302.

Saradjian, J., Murphy, N. and McVey, D. (2010) Delivering integrated treatment to people with personality disorder, in *Treating Personality Disorder* (eds N. Murphy and D. McVey), Routledge, London/New York.

Schalast, N., Redies, M., Collins, M. *et al.* (2008) EssenCES, a short questionnaire for assessing the social climate of forensic psychiatric wards. *Criminal Behaviour and Mental Health*, 18, 49–58.

Shefer, G. (2010) The quality of life of prisoners and staff at HMP Grendon, in *Grendon and the Emergence of Forensic Therapeutic Communities: Developments in Research and Practice* (eds R. Shuker and E. Sullivan), Wiley-Blackwell, Chichester, pp. 247–263.

Sheldon, K. and Tennant, A. (2011) Considerations for working with personality-disordered patients. *British Journal of Forensic Practice*, 3, 44–52.

Shine, J. (2001) Characteristics of inmates admitted to Grendon therapeutic prison and their relationships to length of stay. *International Journal of Offender Therapy and Comparative Criminology*, 45, 252–263.

Shine, J. (2010) Working with offence paralleling behaviour in a therapeutic community setting, in *Offence Paralleling Behaviour: A Case Formulation Approach to Offender Assessment and Intervention* (eds M. Daffern, L. Jones and J. Shine), Wiley-Blackwell, Oxford, pp. 203–214.

Shine, J. and Morris, M. (2000) Addressing criminogenic needs in a prison therapeutic community. *Therapeutic Communities*, 21, 197–219.

Shine, J. and Newton, M. (2000) Damaged, disturbed and dangerous: a profile of receptions to Grendon therapeutic prison 1995–2000, in *A Compilation of Grendon Research* (ed. J. Shine), Leyhill Press, HMP Grendon.

Shuker, R. (2010) Personality disorder: using therapeutic communities as an integrative approach to address risk, in *Grendon and the Emergence of Forensic Therapeutic Communities: Developments in Research and Practice* (eds R. Shuker and E. Sullivan), Wiley-Blackwell, Chichester, pp. 113–136.

Shuker, R. and Newton, M. (2008) Treatment outcome following intervention in a prison-based therapeutic community: a study of the relationship between reduction in criminogenic risk and improved psychological well-being. *British Journal of Forensic Practice*, 10, 33–44.

Shuker, R., Falshaw, L. and Newton, M. (2007) Risk and treatment readiness: the impact of historical and psychosocial variables on treatment completion, in *Readiness for Treatment* (eds R. Shuker and E. Sullivan). Issues in Forensic Psychology No. 7 vol. 7, British Psychological Society, Leicester, pp. 87–97.

Smallbone, S.W. (2005) Attachment insecurity as a predisposing and precipitating factor for young people who sexual abuse, in *Attachment Issues in Psychopathology and Intervention* (ed. M.C. Calder), Erlbaum, Mahwah, pp. 181–206.

Smith, L.A., Gates, S. and Foxcroft, D.R. (2006) Therapeutic communities for substance related disorder. *Cochrane Database of Systematic Reviews*, 1, Art. no.: CD005338.

Stevens, A. (2010) Introducing forensic democratic therapeutic communities, in *Grendon and the Emergence of Forensic Therapeutic Communities: Developments in Research and Practice* (eds R. Shuker and E. Sullivan), Wiley-Blackwell, Chichester, pp. 7–24.

Taylor, R. (2000) A Seven-Year Reconviction Study of HMP Grendon Therapeutic Community. *Home Office Research Findings 115*. Home Office, London.

Thornton, D., Curran, L., Grayson, D. and Holloway, V. (1984) *Tougher Regimes in Detention Centres: Report of an Evaluation of the Young Offender Psychology Unit*. HMSO, London.

Tonkin, M. and Howells, K. (2009) Social Climate in Secure Settings: A Report for HMP Grendon. Peaks Academic and Research Unit, Rampton Hospital: Institute of Mental Health.

Tuke, S. (1813) *Description of the Retreat* (reprinted in 1996 with an introduction by K. Jones), Process Press, London.

Ward, T., Day, A., Howells, K. and Birgden, A. (2004) The multifactor offender readiness model. *Aggression and Violent Behavior*, 9, 645–673.

Warren, F., McGauley, G., Norton, K. *et al.* (2003) Review of treatments for severe personality disorder. *Home Office Online Rep. no 30/03*. http://www.cjp.org.uk/publications/archive/review-of-treatments-for-severe-personality-disorder-10-07-2003/ (accessed 17 January 2013).

Zamble, E. and Porporino, F.J. (1988) *Coping Behavior and Adaptation in Prison Inmates*, Springer, Syracuse.

20

Best Practice in SVP Treatment Programmes

David Thornton[1] and Deirdre D'Orazio[2]

[1]University of Bergen, Norway
[2]Central Coast Clinical & Forensic Psychological Services, USA

Introduction

Arguably the most stringent of criminal justice system responses to sexual offending, less severe only to death penalty and lifetime incarceration sentencing, is involuntary civil commitment legislation. Sexual offender civil commitment laws are commonly referred to as 'SVP laws' reflecting the common statutory phraseology – 'sexually violent predator'. SVP laws are a criminal justice policy option constrained to the United States. These laws began to emerge in the early 1990s, as the continued momentum of the United States' Women's Movement, which for the first time in national history focused societal attention on the severity and prevalence of the problem of abuse against women and children (U.S. Dept. of Justice, retr. 1 June 2012). The US Women's Movement illuminated that the extant socio-political culture had been suppressing the reporting, arrest and conviction of crimes of abuse upon women and children perpetrated by men (D'Orazio et al., 2009).

Perhaps equally as galvanizing as the US Women's Movement upon the genesis of SVP laws were advances in media technology and increased media coverage and sensationalism of extreme cases of violent repeat sexual offending. The confluence of these events served to elicit strong emotional reaction to the problem of sexual abuse from the public, which in turn motivated legislators to increase criminal justice sanctions for sexual offence perpetrators. The final years of the twentieth century and the early years of the twenty-first century were a season of blossoming SVP laws across the United States. No politician aspired to look more lenient on the problem of sexual offending than the other. For example, in California, the growing SVP population quickly came to dominate the patient census of Atascadero State Hospital forcing the construction of a new facility designed for the sole purpose of detaining and treating the SVP population. Opening in 2005, at a cost of almost 400 million dollars, 1500 bed facility, Coalinga State Hospital is one of the largest maximum-security psychiatric hospitals in the world (D'Orazio et al., 2009).

The topic of SVP laws continues to rouse more controversy and debate among mental health and criminal justice professionals than most other American criminal justice policies.

What Works in Offender Rehabilitation: An Evidence-Based Approach to Assessment and Treatment,
First Edition. Edited by Leam A. Craig, Louise Dixon and Theresa A. Gannon.
© 2013 John Wiley & Sons, Ltd. Published 2013 by John Wiley & Sons, Ltd.

The complexity and affective charge of the socio-political matrix out of which these laws exist confounds the objective appraisal of the best practices in the treatment of SVPs.

SVP Programmes: Summary Description

Since 1990, when the first SVP statute was implemented in the state of Washington, 20 of the country's 50 states plus the federal government have enacted laws that allow courts to civilly commit sexual offenders. The 20 states legislating SVP laws are as follows: Arizona, California, Florida, Illinois, Iowa, Kansas, Massachusetts, Minnesota, Missouri, Nebraska, New Hampshire, New Jersey, New York, North Dakota, Pennsylvania, South Carolina, Texas, Virginia, Washington and Wisconsin (Schlank, 2010). This list includes two atypical SVP states. Pennsylvania allows only for the civil commitment of sexual offenders who perpetrated as juveniles and are 'aging out' of the juvenile justice system at age 21 (42 PA, C.S.A., Subchapter H). The Texas SVP law is atypical because it does not involve confinement; it is implemented entirely in an outpatient setting (Health and Safety Code 11, Chapter 841, Texas).

While the cost of individual SVP programmes ranges significantly, in total such programmes cost $500 million yearly to detain and treat SVP individuals (Lohn, 2010). California, Florida and Minnesota have the largest number of individuals detained or committed pursuant to SVP laws, while Minnesota, North Dakota and Wisconsin have the highest per capita rates (Jackson, Schneider and Travia, 2011). In 2010, there were 5200 offenders detained or committed pursuant to SVP laws. Table 20.1 provides summary data on the numbers of sexual offender individuals detained pursuant to SVP laws and the associated costs.

The total number of individuals detained pursuant to SVP laws and the percent involved in treatment varies widely across states. SVP programme census numbers usually make a distinction between the number of fully committed SVP individuals and the number of individuals who are detained having legally met a probable cause threshold for commitment. These probable cause level SVP individuals, also called pre-commitments or detainees, have not been formally civilly committed but have been determined to meet a lesser threshold of proof that commitment criteria are met. In some states, the percent of detainees is very sizeable and the length of pre-commitment lasts several years. For example, in California, 37% of the total SVP population are detainees (Jackson, Schneider and Travia, 2011), and some are in

Table 20.1 Sexual offender detained under SVP laws and the associated costs

Average SVP programme size, cost and treatment participation	*United States*
Number of individuals committed or detained pursuant to SVP laws[a]	5 200
Average rate of committed participating in treatment[b]	82%
Average rate of detainees participating in treatment[b]	34%
Number of individuals detained or committed who have been discharged[b]	1 275
Average annual SVP programme cost per SVP[a]	$96 000
Average annual Department of Correction cost per inmate[c]	$25 994

[a]Lohn (2010). Costs listed do not include the legal and judicial expenses of commitment proceedings.
[b]Jackson, Schneider and Travia (2011). Note: does not include data on 6–7 of 21 programmes.
[c]Gookin (2007).

detainee status for more than 10 years before commitment trials are held (D'Orazio *et al.*, 2009). The issue of the number of detainees is highly important in relation to treatment participation and resultant programme cost analysis as detainees are very much less likely to volunteer for treatment than committed SVPs. A survey of 17 of the 21 programmes revealed an 82% rate of treatment participation among committed SVPs and a rate of 34% for detainees (Jackson, Schneider and Travia, 2011).

There are several reasons why the yearly cost of an SVP programme is almost four times greater than the yearly cost of incarceration. The primary of these involve that SVP commitment is a civil rather than criminal matter, which means it falls under the state's obligation to care for its dangerously mentally ill. SVP individuals are determined to be mentally ill and highly sexually dangerous such that they require inpatient involuntary detainment and treatment. As such, SVP programmes are built in keeping with a high-security treatment model, which necessitates the employment of much greater numbers of staff compared to prison settings. In addition, they require intensive mental health services including sexual-offender-specific treatment involving a larger number of mental health professionals than prison settings. Further, the physical layout of residential units is often smaller in SVP facilities than prison, requiring more physical space and much higher staff to resident ratios to allow the kind of 24-hour observations required in a high-security mental health facility. Lastly, compared to prison environments, SVP facilities are built with more attention to therapeutic goals (e.g., including treatment rooms, recreational areas and leisure spaces with relevant equipment).

Regardless of the components of cost, it is undisputed that SVP programmes are costly and represent a significant portion of state's criminal justice programme funding. Some posit that the costs are much greater than anticipated and are draining states' economic reserves especially during the current period of national and global economic crisis, 'They've (SVP programs) created a political quandary for lawmakers who need to cut spending but don't want to be seen as soft on rapists and child molesters' (Lohn, 2010). Given the current state of financial downturn, it is likely that states will take measures that reduce the cost of the implementation of SVP statutes. This has already occurred in at least one state; in 2011, California passed legislation that greatly reduces the proportion of sexual offenders assessed for potential SVP commitment, thereby reducing the cost of SVP evaluation services (AB109, 29 March 2011).

The very large majority of SVP individuals are adult males. There are, however, a small number of female SVP individuals. There are also a small number of juvenile SVP individuals arising from the handful of states that allow such. Because of the very small numbers of female and juvenile SVP individuals, the topic of the current chapter is constrained to best treatment practices of adult male SVP individuals.

Common Features of SVP Commitment Statutes

Civil commitment is a mechanism designed for individuals who suffer from such significant mental illness that they pose a serious threat to the safety of others. Commitment to a mental health facility provides for treatment and other rehabilitative services until the person is safe to return to the community. Civil commitment involves a mechanism to potentially indefinitely commit the subgroup of the most dangerous sexual offenders, those who are mentally ill and present the greatest threat to communities, thereby warranting their placement in a secure facility for treatment and detainment.

SVP laws generally include four commitment requirements:

1. At least one sexual offence conviction involving either violence or hands-on sexual offending against a child;
2. The current presence of a mental disorder;
3. The determination of a certain degree of risk for sexually violent acts in the future;
4. A relationship between the mental disorder and the likelihood of future sexually violent acts (Doren, 2006).

In order to be discharged from SVP commitment, most states require that the sexual offender no longer have the mental disorder that predisposed them to sexual offending or to no longer present with the statutorily defined level of risk for re-offence (Doren, 2006). Several states allow conditional release in which SVP individuals are supervised and treated in the community under strict conditions. Although conditional release is not available in every state's civil commitment process, the majority of those that do allow for conditional release require that the sexual offender continue to meet criteria for SVP legal commitment, but their condition has changed sufficiently such that they can now be safely treated and reintegrated into the community.

Legal Support for SVP Statutes

Two widely noted US Supreme Court cases solidified the legitimacy of SVP laws. They eliminated arguments under substantive due process, double jeopardy and *ex-post-facto* theories. On 23 June 1997, the US Supreme Court reversed the Kansas Supreme Court's decision to invalidate the SVP act in the trial of Hendricks (*Kansas vs. Hendricks*, 1997). In a five to four decision, the Supreme Court's ruling upheld the constitutionality of Kansas' SVP statute. Judge Clarence Thomas in his majority opinion highlighted the indispensable nexus between mental illness and dangerousness. Justice Kennedy wrote a brief concurring opinion in which he decreed that civil confinement should not be used to achieve retribution or general deterrence. The dissenting minority opinion, written by Justice Breyer, focused on an *ex-post-facto* claim. In 2002, *Kansas vs. Crane* further affirmed the constitutionality of the SVP laws, and allowed a broader interpretation of volitional control than Hendricks, by clarifying that complete inability to control behaviour is not required (*Kansas vs. Crane*, 534 US 407 2002).

Early history of SVP treatment

The advent of SVP commitment posed serious difficulties for those charged with working with this new type of commitment. In general, forensic mental health facilities and the clinicians who worked with them were used to dealing with offenders with psychotic mental illnesses. Such individuals pose very different treatment and management needs from the high-risk sexual offenders committed under SVP laws who in general have personality disorders or paraphilias but who were not disabled by these disorders in the way that someone with schizophrenia would be.

Early SVP programmes drew on Marques' (1982) adaptation of the Relapse Prevention (RP) model from the substance abuse field. However, the assumption that all sexual offenders volunteering for treatment are motivated to avoid re-offending, which is inherent in the RP model, had been proven incorrect, partially by the Sexual Offender Treatment and Evaluation

Project (SOTEP: Marques *et al.*, 2005) results but also by other research (Ward and Hudson, 1998; Ward, Hudson and Keenan, 1998).

In recent years, SVP programmes have moved away from crude RP models. Rather than one-size-fits-all approach, features of the RP model of sexual offender treatment are considered useful adjuncts to a more comprehensive treatment programme.

A social policy model

A social policy perspective considers what best serves the public good. Considered from such a perspective, SVP systems are intended to concentrate exceptional resources on managing those offenders who present an exceptional risk.

The whole package, including legal costs, commonly amounts to more than $100 000 a year per detained or committed offender. Therefore, a million dollars of public money is spent for each 10 years someone is incarcerated under these laws. The mere detention of sexual offenders under SVP laws reduces their ability to re-offend, and this is further reduced by intensive treatment. But the dollar amount spent to avoid further potential offending by one individual is clearly very high. The cost-effectiveness of SVP civil commitment might be thought of as the SVP dollars that have to be spent in order to (on average) prevent one additional person being sexually victimized. SVP programmes make more social policy sense when they prevent more offences for fewer dollars spent. The number of offences prevented depends on how risky the average person committed under SVP laws actually is and on how effectively the programme prevents their offending. The dollars spent depends substantially on the duration of commitment.

This kind of consideration of the costs of preventing offences can seem somewhat cold-blooded, and if you are attuned to the social harm that can be caused by sexual offences, it is easy to insist that no cost is too high to prevent a single sexual offence being committed.

A social policy analysis also considers the justice costs of the system. Involuntarily committing someone based on what they might do in the future infringes upon the liberty rights of those committed, and the precedent involved indirectly threatens the civil liberties of others. This justice cost will be less (or more justifiable) when those committed present higher risks, when the number committed is small and the duration of commitment is short. With these important social policy considerations in mind, the ideal SVP system should adhere to the following principles:

1. SVP systems should be part of an integrated response to sexual offending that includes primary prevention programmes, reducing the opportunity to offend through community supervision and imprisonment, as well as reducing the inclination to offend through treatment programmes of different intensities. SVP commitment should only be applied when other less extreme and less costly interventions have failed. This means that every state with an SVP programme should have a prison-based sex offender treatment programme that allows potential SVPs the opportunity for treatment while serving their sexual offence sentence.
2. SVP systems should be very selective in who gets committed. Only those who truly pose an exceptional risk should be committed.
3. The legal steps involved in initial commitment as well as decisions regarding release under supervision and discharge should proceed efficiently and without preventable delays or costs.

4. SVP programmes should provide treatment services that efficiently reduce risk below the 'exceptional' threshold. This has three aspects: meaningfully engaging a high proportion of those who have been committed in treatment, providing treatment that effectively addresses the factors that underlie their offending and providing sufficient treatment to reduce risk over as short a period of time as possible.
5. SVP programmes should provide effective community reintegration services that gradually allow those who have been committed to develop a healthy and safe lifestyle in which they contribute to the community through engaging in productive work.
6. Throughout the SVP system, the restrictions placed on persons who have been committed should be no more than is practically required for their safe management and treatment. This means that these restrictions need to be adjusted in response to reductions in risk.
7. SVP programmes should include active research programmes designed to develop the knowledge on which following the earlier principles depends.

In the following sections, best practices in SVP treatment will be discussed in relation to these principles.

Evidence base

Trying to form opinions about best practice, the authors have drawn on the wider research literature, notably meta-analyses of both the general correctional treatment outcome literature (see Andrews and Bonta, 2006; McGuire, 2002) and the much more limited set of meta-analyses of sexual offender treatment outcome studies (notably Lösel and Schmucker, 2005, and Hanson *et al.*, 2009). Meta-analyses are of particular importance here both because their findings are always more reliable than those of individual studies and because at present they are the only kind of analysis which allows the relative effect of different kinds of treatment to be compared.

Meta-analyses consistently establish the potential effectiveness of cognitive and behavioural methods in treating offenders (McGuire, 2002). The most compelling demonstration of this is Lipton *et al.*'s (2002a) meta-analysis of an extraordinarily comprehensive international collection of data sets. Lipton's findings specifically support the efficacy of both cognitive-behavioural methods and structured development of relevant interpersonal skills in treating offenders. The results also provide some support for the effectiveness of behavioural incentive programmes. A separate set of meta-analyses have found that structured therapeutic communities demonstrate moderate effectiveness in reducing the recidivism of adults while effects for other kinds of milieu therapy were less clear (Lipton *et al.*, 2002b).

The programme of research carried out by Andrews and his colleagues and summarized in Andrews and Bonta (2006) has been particularly helpful in developing general principles distinguishing effective correctional programmes. These are the Risk–Need–Responsivity (RNR) principles (see Chapter 4).

Risk principle The level of treatment resources assigned to working with an offender should be proportionate to their statistical risk for recidivism.

Need principle Treatment efforts should be concentrated on addressing psychological and social factors that predispose towards offending, often called criminogenic needs.

Responsivity principle Treatment should use methods that have generally been shown to work with offenders. It should be adapted to maximize participants' responsiveness and attend to their individual learning style, abilities and culture.

Of particular interest as well is their finding that when you hold constant the three RNR principles, demonstration projects get substantially better results than routine treatment practice. A plausible interpretation of this finding is that in demonstration projects, greater care is taken to implement treatment in the way it was intended to be run, while in routine practice, there tends to be corner cutting and a drift away from therapeutic models.

Evaluation of different forms of sexual offender treatment is in its infancy. The number of studies is much more limited than in the field of general offender treatment. Many studies are severely methodologically flawed, and there are too few well-controlled studies to allow strong conclusions. Two meta-analyses have made laudable attempts to take into account methodological limitations while comparing different treatment methods.

Lösel and Schmucker (2005) sought to statistically control the effect of methodological limitations and then examine the relative effect of different kinds of therapeutic intervention. Their findings supported the greater effectiveness of treatment that included cognitive therapy, of treatment that is specialized for sexual offenders and of treatment that did not solely rely on group therapy. They also found that smaller-scale studies, those supervised by researchers, and those in which the treatment concept was better documented tended to get better results. These latter two findings are consistent with Andrews and Bonta's finding regarding the superiority of demonstration projects.

Hanson *et al.* (2009) tested the application of RNR principles to sexual offender treatment. They classified studies according to methodological criteria that had been consensually developed among highly regarded evaluation researchers (Collaborative Outcome Data Committee (2007a, b) and retained for analysis the limited number of studies they found to be minimally adequate. Like Andrews and Bonta, they found that the more studies complied with each of the RNR principles, the greater the reduction in recidivism associated with treatment.

Finally, there are two other principles of effective sexual offender treatment that are sufficiently supported by research to provide general guidance. First, persisting in showing risk-related functioning late in treatment (or after it is completed) is associated with elevated recidivism rates. This principle is supported by findings indicating that raised recidivism rates are associated with (i) beginning treatment but failing to complete it (Hanson *et al.*, 2002; Lösel and Schmucker, 2005), (ii) failure to demonstrate treatment gains (Marques *et al.*, 2005; McGrath, Lasher and Cumming, 2012) and (iii) continuing to show behavioural evidence of psychological risk factors at the end of treatment (Beggs and Grace, 2010; Olver *et al.*, 2007). This pattern of findings suggests that participation in treatment only implies reduced risk when there is change in the underlying factors being targeted in treatment.

Second, sexual offending often reflects offenders having a positive attitude to offending and actively seeking (or taking advantage of) opportunities to offend. Evidence for this comes from studies of the prevalence of what Ward and Hudson call the 'Approach' pathway to offending (Ward and Hudson, 1998; Ward, Hudson and Keenan, 1998) and from studies indicating that recidivism after treatment reflects a failure to attempt to use self-management strategies rather than poor self-management skills (Marques *et al.*, 2005; Webster, 2005).

This pattern of findings implies that effectively recruiting motivation to change is particularly important among high-risk offenders. The recommendations that follow for best practice in SVP treatment reflect the authors' experience of trying to develop treatment for SVP populations that is consistent with the aforementioned research findings.

The Inpatient Treatment Component of SVP Programmes

Treatment philosophy

Purpose of treatment The legal mandates under which SVP programmes typically require them to provide prompt and adequate treatment designed to address the conditions that led to persons being committed under SVP laws. This implies that treatment should address the exceptional risk that they have been deemed to present, and the factors underlying this risk, including but not limited to the mental disorders, deemed predisposing.

One interpretation of this view is that treatment activities assigned to any other purpose than to directly target known risk factors will compete for scarce resources with those that contribute directly to the SVP treatment mission and should therefore be avoided. Any dilution of the direct treatment of risk factors can only lengthen the time required to reduce risk sufficiently to justify release.

This is, however, an overly narrow view. SVP programmes have a duty of care towards those in their charge, which is often for many years. This means that they need to address the whole person, not just the aspects of them directly related to sexual offending. In addition, there are likely important risk factors for sexual offending that have yet to be discovered. In particular, current research methods are unlikely to detect risk factors that only apply in individual cases or in a small minority of sexual offenders. Therefore, when careful case formulation identifies factors as individually related to risk, it is important to target these factors even if they are not associated with recidivism in sex offenders in general. Significantly, motivation to change and responsivity factors greatly impact how treatment of known risk factors is internalized and must be addressed. Also related is a duty to ensure the safety of their staff, which is increased when resident's overall well-being is prioritized. Thus, SVP treatment programmes need to address a broader range of goals than directly targeting known risk factors.

Making decisions from a whole person or wellness perspective creates an overall healthier environment and can be an antidote to the human misery that can otherwise pervade these facilities. The provision of a positive, engaging regime that provides therapeutic services that residents see as responsive to their needs can also enhance security and build therapeutic relationships, leading to a greater willingness to engage with treatment activities that are more directly designed to reduce risk of sexual offending.

Autonomy An important influence on the effectiveness of psychotherapy is the formation of a therapeutic alliance involving some degree of shared goals and mutual trust developing between the person participating in treatment and the treatment provider (e.g., Martin, Garske and David, 2000). Further, a meta-analysis that looked specifically at treatment of offenders found that in both institutional and community settings, the more treatment participants were forced into treatment, the less effective it was in reducing recidivism (Parhar *et al.*, 2008). Both of these meta-analytic findings speak to the importance of respecting the autonomous choices of treatment participants.

This poses a dilemma for SVP programmes since, by their very nature, they involve the coercive power of the state infringing on the autonomy of the persons. A major reason that people are committed under SVP laws is that they have demonstrated through their behaviour an inability or unwillingness to voluntarily refrain from sexual offending. Thus, there is a sense in which there is an inherent conflict between the people committed under SVP laws who wish to continue offending and SVP systems that are intended to prevent them from doing so. SVP regimes need to provide a safe environment in which residents are prevented from victimizing each other, staff or people in the outside community. Such an environment will involve restrictions on behaviour and sometimes direct physical coercion.

One arena in which the issue of autonomy is foremost is the question of treatment participation. Within voluntary healthcare settings, a typical standard is that free and informed consent is a precondition for treatment participation. In the SVP arena, the contingencies around treatment can be complex. In some facilities, non-participants may put significant pressure on peers not to participate. Some residents may feel (or may be advised by their attorneys) that treatment will require them to disclose facts that may be used against them in court. Residents may also fear that some parts of treatment, such as analysis of past offending, will be personally distressing. On the other hand, there may be organizational privileges (such as placement on a better living unit, more money-making work hours or a higher degree of freedom) associated with treatment participation. Further, sufficient progress in treatment may be seen as reducing risk in a way that can lead to release, and fellow treatment participants allied with the same may provide better company and more supportive friends when residential units for treatment participants only are an option. Obviously, the most necessary criterion for increased volunteerism of those committed SVP is evidence that those who participate get released from the programme. In several SVP programmes to date, no treatment participants have been released (Jackson, Schneider and Travia, 2011).

A wise treatment philosophy seeks to manage this mix of treatment participation pressures so that they are favourable to treatment participation but under the condition that residents feel encouraged and motivated to participate but not coerced. This is achieved in part by reducing pressures against participation, for example, by enabling treatment participants to live on different units than non-participants and providing wellness-related activities that give residents positive experiences of clinical staff and increased exposure to pro-social models.

Special features of the SVP population

Risk-related demographic features   Unsurprisingly, given how they are selected, SVP populations tend to have high mean scores on actuarial risk assessment instruments (Elwood, Doren and Thornton, 2008). For example, Elwood's survey found mean Static-99 scores of around 6 in the SVP populations, more than twice the mean commonly found in less selected populations. Elevated scores relative to non-SVP sexual offender groups are apparent both on instruments that predominantly reflect sexual deviance like RRASOR (Hanson, 1997) and on instruments that weight antisociality more heavily (MnSOST-R: Epperson, Kaul and Hesselton, 1998; and PCL-R: Hare, 2003). This means that sexual offenders who are committed under SVP laws tend to have demonstrated more persistence in sexual offending and greater general antisociality as compared to less exceptional sexual offenders. One might speculate that they would also tend to be younger as youth is a risk indicator in these actuarial instruments. However, since SVP proceedings can only occur at the end of other commitments or sentences, and sexual offender sentences have become longer over the past decade, the bulk of those committed under these laws tend to fall in the age range of 35 and 60. Difficulties in getting those committed under SVP laws released come on top of long American prison sentences, making it not uncommon for committed SVPs to have last been in the community 20 or more years.

Diagnoses   Elwood, Doren and Thornton (2008) compared rates of different diagnoses in SVP populations from four states (Wisconsin, Washington, Arizona and Florida). Paedophilia was diagnosed in about half of those committed, paraphilia not otherwise specified in about half, between half and four-fifths were diagnosed with some personality disorder (mainly anti-social personality disorder) and about half with some substance abuse disorder. Diagnoses listed are often co-morbid with each other.

Responsivity issues   In jurisdictions where the prison system provides treatment programmes for higher-risk sexual offenders, those who go on to become SVPs will also typically be those who failed to respond to treatment (refusing, dropping out, being kicked out or re-offending after treatment). These factors underscore the importance of responsivity issues in designing treatment programmes.

Treatment-interfering factors are aspects of psychological functioning that make it harder to benefit from standard treatment methods, compromising participants' response to treatment. A variety of treatment-interfering factors are commonly found in an SVP population. A non-exhaustive list based on those commonly identified within SVP programmes includes the following:

1. *Reluctance to give up the gratifications of sexual offending* Many high-risk sexual offenders have lived miserable lives, devoid of joy or happiness, in which they feel pushed around by forces that are at best indifferent to them and often perceived as victimizing. Offending, and rehearsing fantasies of offending, may be the part of their lives where they feel powerful, excited and that their needs are being met. Treatment asks them to give up the one part of their lives that has reliably brought them pleasure, to disavow what they may regard as an essential part of themselves.
2. *Hopelessness* High-risk sexual offenders may be acutely aware of how persistently they have offended, how they have kept offending despite the state seeking to deter them in different ways and how they have sometimes wanted to change and then always fallen back into offending. Seeing what causes their offending as some internal and unchangeable aspect of who they are makes treatment seem hopeless or as something that they could only succeed in by destroying themselves.
3. *Distrust* Men recently committed under SVP laws commonly feel that the SVP system is hostile to them, and that mental health professionals are untrustworthy. Treatment may be seen as a trick to get them to give away things that will be used against them in court.
4. *The secret self* A common feature of high-risk sexual offenders is that they have had to hide an important aspect of who they are from those around them. Treatment asks them to disclose their secret self, to become transparent and so to become vulnerable and powerless.
5. *Poor regulation of emotions* A significant feature of many high-risk sexual offenders is that they experience negative emotional reactions that are too intense, too prolonged and which they are unable to voluntarily let go of. Indeed, sitting in some negative emotions (e.g., anger) may leave them feeling more powerful and so be something they do not want to let go of. Commonly, these emotional reactions are associated with highly biased ways of seeing other people that make it hard for them to take in veridical information about what is happening.
6. *Acute sensitivity to control and respect issues* High-risk sexual offenders commonly experience others as disrespecting them and as trying to control them. In part, this reflects how they are really treated (after all, they are widely despised and society does seek to control their behaviour), but they are also hypersensitive to cues

indicating that others might be disrespecting them or trying to control them and respond strongly and negatively to these cues.

7. *Falling back into old patterns* High-risk sexual offenders have over-learnt dysfunctional ways of coping with the world. Treatment may persuade them to try out new ways of coping, but if these do not immediately give them what they want or are in any way frustrating, there will be a great temptation to fall back into their familiar (dysfunctional) ways of coping.

8. *Elevated levels of psychopathy* SVPs tend to have higher levels of psychopathy than other groups of sexual offenders (Elwood, Doren and Thornton, 2008). Harkins, Beech and Thornton (2012) found that among participants in SVP treatment, psychopathy was associated with less group cohesion. Thornton and Blud (2007) identified a range of treatment-interfering factors theoretically liable to be associated with specific aspects of psychopathy. They concluded that pathological lying, playing power games in group or a grandiose feeling that no personal change is desired are expected to result from elevations in PCL-R facet one (the interpersonal features of psychopathy) while callousness and difficulty bonding with a therapeutic relationship are expected to result from facet two elevations (the affective features of psychopathy). They concluded that difficulty complying with treatment rules, impulsiveness and difficulty persisting with new patterns of behaviour emerge from PCL-R factor two (Social Deviance). Thornton and Blud make recommendations for principles to be followed to work around these treatment-interfering factors.

9. *Level of cognitive functioning* This can have a profound effect on participants' ability to benefit from particular forms of treatment. This is not simply a matter of overall IQ level since there can be far more specific cognitive deficits. Common patterns include a (i) relatively normal overall IQ but suppressed working memory and executive functioning (sometimes associated with schizophrenia or sustained alcohol abuse), (ii) marked reading difficulties accompanied by impaired verbal intelligence but with normal non-verbal intelligence, (iii) intact verbal functioning but with markedly impaired non-verbal functioning and (iv) generalized deficits with functioning impaired in verbal intelligence, non-verbal intelligence, executive functioning and working memory.

10. *Other mental disorders that are not routinely related to risk* Serious and persistent mental illness, for example, schizophrenia or bipolar disorders, need to be managed to allow engagement with normal treatment.

Patterns of criminogenic needs The Need principle from the RNR model holds that treatment should target the main factors (criminogenic needs) deemed to push the offender towards further offending. Structured risk assessment (Beech, Fisher and Thornton, 2003; Knight and Thornton, 2007; Thornton, 2002) provides a framework for the main empirically identified criminogenic needs for sexual offenders, organizing them into four domains. Table 20.2 outlines a summary of this framework.

Commonly, persons committed under SVP laws have significant problems in each of the four domains. This means that in general they will have unusual sexual interests related to their offending, an intense interest in sex, belief systems that rationalize their offending, impaired ways of relating to other adults and difficulty managing their behaviour so that it serves their longer-term self-interests.

This is not to say that they have identical patterns of criminogenic needs. Thornton and Sachsenmaier (2012) found four Need profiles in men committed under Wisconsin's SVP

Table 20.2   Deviancy domains

Domain	Subdomain
Sexual interests	Offence-related sexual interests
	Sexual preoccupation
Distorted attitudes	Victim schema
	Rights schema
	Means schema
Relational style	Inadequate relational style
	Lack of emotionally intimate relationships with adults
	Aggressive relational style
Self-management	Social deviance
	Dysfunctional coping

laws using cluster analysis. There were two rapist profiles: agonistic and antisocial rapists. Agonistic rapists were characterized by power and conflict issues pervading a different aspect of their functioning. They had sexualized both violence and dominance, had suspicious angry relationships with peers and oppositional reactions to authority figures. Antisocial rapists, on the other hand, had normal sexual interests, and their rapes seemed more an expression of general antisociality. Similarly, there were two paedophilic profiles. Romantic paedophiles sought to meet their needs for sex and for emotional closeness with children. They were sexually preoccupied, but outside the sexual arena were in better control of themselves. Aggressive paedophiles, in contrast, used children to satisfy sexual needs but were not emotionally connected to children, and had a more generally callous approach to other people.

These profiles are, of course, prototypes; individuals might approximate them more or less closely. These prototypes give an idea of the diversity of the criminogenic needs found in this population.

Therapeutic optimism   It is easy to see persons who have been committed under SVP laws as irretrievably doomed to engage in further offending. Such a thought arises naturally from reviewing the sheer persistence of their past offending and the pervasiveness of the psychological factors pushing them towards offending. Nevertheless, this degree of therapeutic pessimism is unhelpful for both treatment providers and persons committed under SVP laws.

Fortunately, a closer look at recidivism statistics suggests a more optimistic view. Reviewing the 10-year sexual recidivism rates for the Static-99R High Risk/High Need reference group indicates that, even in a group selected to have a higher base rate, the 2% with the highest Static-99R scores have a sexual recidivism rate that is around 50% (see www.static99.org). This means that about half of these apparently 'hopeless cases' avoid known re-offending for 10 years after release. Furthermore, for any group of sexual offenders who avoid known sexual offending for 10 years, we know that the proportion who offend subsequently is very small (Harris *et al.*, 2003).

This suggests that rather than seeing high-risk sexually offenders as doomed to re-offend, we should see them as delicately poised between re-offending and desistance, with either outcome a real possibility. Like someone walking along a thin mountain ridge able to walk down either slope. In such a circumstance, surely it is not unreasonable to hope that a determined nudge from treatment might lead many of them towards desistance.

Treatment design

Engagement Quality of treatment engagement is intricately tied to treatment Responsivity. It is a critical issue throughout treatment participation. Meaningful engagement may be considered as involving six components. Strengthening them should be a central goal from the beginning of treatment.

Components of Engagement

1. *Complying with minimum conditions for participation* Group therapy depends on all participants complying with certain minimum conditions (group rules). They are required for the group to proceed in a safe and effective way. Someone who is not prepared to agree to these things, or repeatedly violates them, is effectively declining to participate in treatment.
2. *Motivation* To what extent are people motivated to use treatment to make the sort of changes that would reduce their risk of offending? Developing such motivation is perhaps the key ingredient in determining response to treatment. It is liable to depend on their seeing it as possible to make that kind of change through treatment, on their coming to hope that their lives will be better if they do make such a change, on their believing that respected others will support and approve their making this change and on their feeling some urgency to start making these changes now (see Miller and Rollnick, forthcoming). Motivation to change tends to be unstable, and full commitment to such changes is generally something that develops through treatment rather than being there at the outset. Effective treatment will be easier if they have or can develop a growth mindset (Dweck, 2006) – a way of understanding their personal characteristics that depicts them as resulting from learning, effort and choices. Without such a mindset, it is hard for people to be motivated to work towards real change since within their implicit theory, such change is impossible.
3. *Being open to other points of view* Treatment, and especially treatment through group therapy, provides participants with an opportunity to learn from the perspectives of other group members. Listening in a non-defensive, open way to others (rather than, e.g., not listening or listening while preparing refutations of what you are hearing) greatly facilitates taking advantage of this opportunity.
4. *Developing self-awareness* Like motivation, self-awareness is something that develops during the treatment process. Nevertheless, learning from the group process is greatly facilitated by at least some degree of self-awareness, and learning will proceed more quickly as the person learns to accurately attend to their internal states, to patterns in their internal functioning and external behaviour.
5. *Maintaining an open channel of communication* This refers to communicating openly and honestly with treatment providers about significant events, choices and issues that are being struggled with and listening with an open mind to communications from treatment providers.
6. *Willingness to experiment with new behaviour* Talking in the treatment group is one thing, changing your behaviour outside group is something else. Learning will be much easier if treatment participants are willing to try out new ways of behaving outside group and bring back what they learn from this experience to process in group.

Ways Staff Can Contribute to Engagement. Preparatory programmes, use of motivational interviewing (MI) and features of therapist style have been found to contribute to the development of these features of engagement.

Preparatory programmes have been shown to help with engagement with other kinds of treatment (e.g., Davidson, 1998; Larson *et al.*, 1983; Mayerson, 1984). They have also more specifically been found to enhance self-disclosure and self-exploration (Annis and Perry, 1977; Garrison, 1978) as well as motivation during treatment (Curran, 1978; Strupp and Bloxom, 1973). An apparently effective preparatory programme for sexual offender treatment was reported by Marshall *et al.* (2008). Some central features of this programme included rehearsal of miniature forms of later treatment activities, allowing participants to proceed at their own pace, rewarding any movement in direction of greater engagement, empathizing with participants, accepting participants as persons with strengths as well as areas for development and providing information about potential benefits of treatment.

MI is a style of engaging with treatment participants that has been found to be beneficial in itself as well as adding to the effectiveness of other treatment programmes (Miller and Rollnick, forthcoming). The spirit of MI includes the treatment provider respecting the participants' autonomy, engaging with participants in a collaborative way that is respectful and attentive to participants' points of view and seeking to evoke the wisdom/insights that the participant already has. The MI approach assumes that participants already have motives for change but that these are either insufficiently attended to or blocked by motives they have for maintaining the status quo.

Therapist style is generally thought of as one of the potent non-specific factors in psychotherapy. Marshall (2005) reports that progress in treatment was facilitated by therapist use of open questions, therapist empathy, warmth, rewardingness (use of praise and attention to encourage desired behaviours or attitudes) and directiveness (maintaining control of the agenda of the session, raising possibilities when the treatment participant is stuck, directing attention through focused questions along with an absence of aggressive disrespectful confrontation) and asking patients to engage in tasks from which they can learn. A notable implication of this research is that authoritarian and aggressive techniques (i.e., harsh confrontation, shock, anger, revenge on behalf of victims, demand for change) will be ineffective with abusive individuals. Such techniques tend to elicit treatment resistance including argumentativeness, placations, shame and treatment dropout.

Effective therapeutic process facilitates emotion processing (Pfafflin *et al.*, 2005) and takes advantage of the 'here and now' environment of therapy to evoke change in the affective precursors of offending. Maladaptive interpersonal schemas can be changed through the therapist–client and client–group processes. Sexual offender clients often have personal histories of being abused or otherwise betrayed by someone in a position of trust which renders them particularly responsive to therapy process variables.

Strategies for tailoring treatment services to the individual Given the diversity of the SVP population, it is clear that a one-size-fits-all approach is not effective. Treatment services should be tailored to the individual. There are, however, practical constraints on this. Treatment can only be tailored to the individual to the extent that the relevant features of the individual are identified. Quality assessment processes are critical to individualizing treatment. Even if an optimum form of treatment has been identified for the individual, it may not be within the therapeutic repertoire of the facility. Further, where treatment is delivered through the medium of group therapy, the diversity of the needs or learning styles of members of the same group may limit the extent to which the overall group process can be tailored towards any specific individual.

One strategy for addressing some of these challenges to individualization is to use structured assessment at the front end of treatment to divide treatment participants into groups that are broadly homogeneous with regard to some important characteristics. As an example of one possible model, the Wisconsin SVP programme takes into account the degree of psychopathic traits along with a fairly comprehensive cognitive assessment battery to assign treatment participants between four treatment tracks. Each track is a self-contained treatment programme specialized for the more common treatment needs and learning styles of those assigned to the track. This then allows treatment services to be developed differently for higher functioning individuals with more psychopathic traits as compared to lower functioning individuals with less psychopathic traits.

Strategies like this are only viable where the overall number of treatment participants is relatively large, at least 100 people in treatment at any one time.

Specializing treatment for broad groups of patients can be helpful, but even when this has been done, there is a requirement for further individualization. Treatment plans are normally the medium through which this individualization is accomplished. There are many ways in which these can be structured. Arguably, SVP treatment plans should include the following elements:

1. A characterization of learning style that includes main treatment strengths and treatment-interfering factors.
2. Longer-term goals for the phase of the programme that the person is currently in.
3. Measurable short-term goals and action plans defining the focus of treatment activity over the next 90 days.

In such a system, short-term goals and action plans should be formulated in a way that takes into account the treatment participant's learning style. They should have a fast enough cycle time that they direct treatment activity in a meaningful way, and their completion should move the person towards completion of the goals of their current phase and so towards making sufficient progress to justify release.

A model for SVP treatment programme progress   A key requirement for any SVP programme is that there is a coherent map of the gains treatment participants need to make in order to justify some form of release. This can be complicated since there may be different legal criteria for different kinds of release, and decisions about release are commonly made by the courts rather than by the treatment programme. Many SVP programmes use a phase model of treatment. A simple phase model is illustrated in the following text.

Phase 1

Focus Treatment engagement, improving general self-management skills, addressing personality disorder issues.

Criterion for moving to the next phase Generally committing to the goal of non-abusive behaviour; behaving as a 'good citizen' within the facility; sufficient progress in Phase 1 goals to allow effective participation in Phase 2.

Phase 2

Focus Developing an agreed and comprehensive identification of the main factors driving past sexual offending; addressing distorted attitudes; developing motivation to manage factors that drove past sexual offending. In a sense, Phase 2 prepares all the ingredients for change.

Criterion for moving to the next phase Maintaining the achievements made in Phase 1; identification of main factors driving past offending agreed between the treatment team and participant; verbal and behavioural demonstration of motivation to work on managing these factors; able to credibly rebut attitudes that in the past supported offending.

Phase 3

Focus Managing the main factors that drove past sexual offending; developing intrinsically motivating healthy alternative behaviour that is used in circumstances that previously triggered risk factors.

Criterion for moving to the next phase Risk factors reliably managed within the inpatient facility; healthy alternative behaviour generally displayed within the inpatient facility.

Phase 4 (outpatient)

Focus Applying the skills and attitudes developed during treatment to the challenges presented by living under supervision in the community. Building and meaningfully engaging with social networks that support pro-social community adjustment. Supervision and support are intensive to start with and are then changed in response to treatment participant behaviour.

Criterion for moving to the next phase Continuing to apply and maintain skills and attitudes developed during treatment with reduced levels of supervision and support.

Phase systems can be defined in a number of ways and can work better or worse. There are several ways that they can malfunction. For example, treatment services in a particular phase may not be sufficient to effectively assist treatment participants in meeting the criteria for moving to the next phase. This results in large numbers of participants getting stuck in the earlier phase. Another kind of issue concerns the criteria for moving to the next phase. These should be transparent, understood by participants and staff, and judgement about whether they have been met should, so far as is possible, be made based on objective criteria. At the same time, judgements need to be made in a way that validly reflects whether the criteria have really been met. This can be difficult to achieve when treatment participants are motivated to conceal behaviours that might indicate that they were failing to meet criteria. Finally, the phase system must link to the legal decision-making process in a way that connects to forensic criteria so that release decisions follow from progress through the phases.

Decisions about movement from one phase to the next can be taken by the treatment programme. Decisions regarding release on the other hand are normally rendered by the courts and may involve forensic evaluations done independently of the treatment. This is a desirable arrangement from the point of view of objectivity and so of community safety. Nevertheless, it opens the possibility of releases happening before the treatment team would see a treatment participant as ready or release being delayed long after the person has 'completed treatment'. Another factor that can contribute to this latter possibility is the difficulty of finding acceptable community placements. Persons committed under SVP laws arouse extraordinary public anxiety, even more so than the moral panic triggered by the category of sexual offenders. This can make it very difficult to find placements, and in some jurisdictions lack of viable community placements is a severe deterrent to treatment participation (Arkowitz, Shale and Carabello, 2008). It must be emphasized that while this level of public concern is natural, it does not actually serve the public good. If it effectively closes off all possibility of release, then it brings the constitutionality of SVP laws into question while also greatly increasing the cost of SVP programmes as no releases means the number in programmes increases. Alternatively, if placement under supervision is made too hard, then it may be easier to obtain absolute discharges. Absolute discharges direct from a secure facility put the community in much more peril than discharge to supervised conditions.

Preparation for release   Preparation from the start. From the first point that someone becomes a resident within the inpatient programme, there is an obligation to offer services that would assist with return to the community.

For those who are detained but whose commitment has not yet been decided, there is a real possibility of imminent release to the community so the programme needs to be ready to complete a discharge checklist (see the section 'When discharge is imminent'). When residents are committed under SVP law, the timescale changes since potential release will generally be years in the future. At this stage, the focus should be on skills that enable independent living (e.g., managing finances, shopping, healthy meal preparation, etc.) in a wide range of settings.

Many offenders, not just those committed under SVP laws, have deficits in what are broadly called cognitive skills (problem-solving, communication and interpersonal skills). These skills contribute to many aspects of life including the practical issues involved in community reintegration. They are also the most generalizable aspect of employability skills (Kitagawa, 2005), contributing to being a good employee under most circumstances. This kind of generic employability skills can be developed through a therapeutic work programme if staff are taught to specifically look for and encourage these skills. They are also often targeted as part of Phase 1 of the SVP programme.

When Someone Is Close to Release Under Supervision. When someone is potentially close to release under supervision, the person's treatment plan will need to be adjusted in a number of ways.

The first step is preparation for the current realities of life under SVP supervision. This can be done by providing factual information about life under supervision, by using role play and other experiential exercises to simulate some of the challenges they will face and help them address some of the challenges to their skills and attitudes and by adjusting the supervised world. 'Adjusting their supervised world' may involve changes in living circumstances, supervision and daily routine within the secure perimeter or supervised outings in which they sleep within the secure facility but go to supervised work or other supervised activities outside it.

Second, the community team that is going to take over the treatment, support and supervision of the treatment participant needs to become included as a key member of the person's treatment team. They will need to be thoroughly briefed about the treatment participant including understanding the treatment participant's criminogenic needs, learning style, course of treatment and how well the treatment participant is managing these needs. The community team should meet with the treatment participant and begin working to form a therapeutic relationship with him. A community management and treatment plan is then developed.

When Discharge Is Imminent

If someone committed under SVP laws is released under supervision, the community team will have continuing responsibility for their care. Even if the individual is about to be discharged straight from the secure facility, there are still a lot of practical issues that have to be addressed. Since there may be comparatively little warning of such a situation developing, the inpatient team will be well advised to work through a pre-discharge checklist whenever there is a hearing that might order discharge. These checklists should be detailed and comprehensive. This should include internal communication within the facility; review of urgent needs in the community, medications and the possibilities for continuing health care, resources where residence may be possible; referrals to County Human Services, Social Services and so on; completing requirements for GPS and for registration if these are mandated by law; preparation of notification information for relevant authorities and for community notification; notification of past victims where this is appropriate; arrangements of the patient's money and property to be released and arrangements for transport on the day of release.

SVP programme staff issues

Environmental pulls for counter-therapeutic dynamics　The therapeutic attitudes and efficacy of SVP programme staff are susceptible to being undermined by three inter-related features endemic to SVP treatment environments. These are repeated exposure to trauma material, treatment participants' ongoing abusive tendencies and the attitudes and values of the prevailing socio-cultural system. A common underlying feature of all three is that they tempt programme staff to get pulled in to the cycle of abuse. These counter-therapeutic environmental pulls contribute to staffing problems and negatively impact SVP clients' response to treatment, a cornerstone principle of effective treatment (Andrews and Bonta, 2006).

The cycle of abuse refers to the phenomenon that one incident of abuse can potentially trigger ongoing rippling abuse patterns that increase the number of victims and perpetrators, and with shifting roles such that a victim becomes a perpetrator and vice versa (D'Orazio, 2005). This has to do with the link between the receptivity of fear and the reactivity of aggression. Abuse is often accompanied by potent negative affective charge, for example, anger, callousness, rejection in perpetrators and fear, pain and confusion in victims. The abuse passes from perpetrator to recipient when the recipient cannot assimilate and manage the abuse. Out of self-preservation, the recipient transforms their fear into abusive tendencies, which are directed towards themselves or others. Being pulled in to the cycle of abuse happens in SVP programmes when the abuse perpetrated by the offender continues to thrive in a psychological way, negatively impacting SVP system, such that staff within the system react as one being victimized, such as with overt or passive expressions of retaliation, defeat, defensiveness, a desire for power or identification as the aggressor (D'Orazio, 2005). In a sense, this is a legitimate job hazard that naturally arises out of immersing oneself daily into the depths, complexities and pain of interpersonal trauma.

The following three counter-therapeutic dynamics of SVP environments greatly impact participants' response to treatment. As described previously in this chapter, research indicates that the criminogenic needs of sexual offenders are ameliorated within environments that facilitate treatment engagement (Marshall, 2005). Effective programmes strive to nurture the kind of therapist qualities that increase treatment response, empathy, warmth, genuineness and directiveness (Marshall, 2005; Rogers, 1957). It can be argued that at the core of these effective therapist qualities is developing empathy for sexual offender clients (D'Orazio, 2005, 2006). Carl Rogers eloquently described empathy and its relationship to client change as follows:

> To sense the client's private world as if it were your own, but without ever losing the 'as if' quality— this is empathy, and this seems essential to therapy. To sense the client's anger, fear, or confusion as if it were your own, yet without your own anger, fear, or confusion getting bound up in it, (is empathy). When the client's world is this clear to the therapist, and he moves about in it freely, then he can both communicate his understanding of what is clearly known to the client and can also voice meanings in the client's experience of which the client is scarcely aware (Rogers, 1957, p. 99).

SVP programme mental health staff are tasked with seeing the best and worst of SVP individuals, at times reliving the abuse perpetrated and at other times understanding such abuse as coming from a real place of pain within the offender. One way that staff attitudes and efficacy are undermined is through repeated exposure to detailed accounts of abuse and predation. Mental health staff must be keenly attentive and aware cognitively, emotionally and physiologically in their work with treatment participants. Treatment providers' ability to be fully present and unencumbered by their own distress allows an opportunity for the treatment participant to enact and work through in the therapeutic relationship the ongoing maladaptive ways of relating that put them in the position of sexually abusing others.

The challenge is that being fully attentive and psychologically present has its cost. In typical human functioning, psychological defences such as avoidance and distraction typically protect the self from being overwhelmed by distressing material, whereas mental health clinicians must over-ride natural defences, moving towards trauma material in their work with abusive individuals. They must continually overcome personal fears, ever narrowly vigilant for their own safety and ever broadly vigilant for the future safety of the community. This puts mental health staff in the unique position of playing a role in the recreation of often horrifically detailed past abusive incidents, the explicit and implicit ongoing abusive tendencies common among abusive individuals, with the potential for real physical or psychological harm.

A second environmental pull for counter-therapeutic dynamics present in SVP systems involves exposure to treatment participants' ongoing pathology. This is manifested in the inter-actions between staff and SVP individuals, and quite significantly as a group phenomenon. This is evident in SVP programmes when the overall pathology of the SVP population dominates the treatment milieu in a seemingly contagion of pro-criminal and abusive attitudes, grievance thinking, hostility and treatment resistance. This route leads those that work with individuals and groups possessing strong and persistent pathological features to become vulnerable to behaving like them. It also leads to diminished therapeutic optimism. Some insight into how this can happen is provided by recent research into priming. For example, it has been demonstrated that stereotypical social behaviour can be unconsciously elicited through priming by similar stimuli (Bargh, Chen and Burrows, 1996), and that automatic attitudes are quite malleable in response to exposure to others' attitudes (Dasgupta and Greenwald, 2001).

A third significant environmental pull for counter-therapeutic dynamics in SVP systems is the tide of implicit pressure exerted on programmes by the prevailing socio-cultural system that ensconces the SVP system. Such is replete with myths and exaggerations about monstrous features of sexual offenders. The larger socio-cultural climate in which SVP programmes exist is not supportive of a healing approach towards violent offenders. The tiers of programmatic authority concentrically extending from the SVP individuals throughout the SVP programme are likewise at times pulled in to the cycle of abuse. This interactional matrix includes the mental health staff, their clinical supervisors, department chiefs, programme administrative directors and security personnel. Conceptually, this continues on to the judicial personnel, the legislators, the state governor's office and the community at large. One or more parts exert, in a psychological sense, an abuse reaction upon other parts that can lead to system-wide psychological process involving hostile stereotyping that parallels those involved in offending themselves. This can manifest in overly punitive stances towards SVP individuals, power struggles between treatment participants and staff, conflict between staff disciplines or staff categories (i.e., psychologists–psychiatrists, clinicians–administrators and staff–supervisors), over-identification as a patient advocate and boundary violations between staff and residents.

The concepts themselves can be traced back to some of the grandfathers of psychotherapy: Sigmund Freud in his ideas about transference and counter-transference (Freud, 1910) and Carl Jung in his ideas about the collective unconscious and archetypes (Jung, 1968).

Left unchecked, these kinds of counter-therapeutic pulls can lead to SVP programme staff to experience a variety of trauma reactions themselves. These range from job dissatisfaction, diminished work quality, 'burnout', physical complaints, staff turnover and vicarious traumatization.

What is a programme to do? A tiered approach to targeting counter-therapeutic pulls   As a whole and at each tier of administration, effective SVP programmes function with an explicit awareness that these kinds of psychological challenges are endemic to SVP systems. They continually assess and ameliorate counter-therapeutic pulls at each level of programme structure. In a general sense, effective SVP programmes strive to mirror the kind of value system it desires to instil in offenders. The treatment mission, flowing from the treatment process model, is communicated clearly, consistently and credibly.

Programme Administrators: The Structural and Attitudinal Foundation

1. At the highest level, the SVP programme must embrace a mission that mental health needs are a priority and amenable to change. They must believe in the treatability of severe and mentally ill sexual offenders.
2. Programme administrators prioritize creating a programme milieu that is engaging, flexible, communicative and treatment oriented.
3. Administrators understand staff well-being is a necessary requirement for the provision of quality services and to prevent staff turnover. They prioritize the self-care of staff. They are aware that an unseen psychological toll is invoked upon SVP programme staff by the nature of doing effective work.
4. In building layout and physical security features, administrators ensure a physically safe environment for staff and patients to work together that is free from encumbrance by fear of personal harm. Programme security officers are viewed as having an essential role in the treatment milieu, as opposed to a separate police body.
5. Administrators and managers avoid overly authoritative ways of engaging with underlinks in the system, in a sense mirroring their expectation of staff–resident interactions.
6. Effective SVP programme administrators are invested in the goal of providing state-of-the-art, high-quality treatment services. They are knowledgeable about the mental health programming of the institution and prioritize programme pride and fidelity. They support the professional development of staff. They allow lower ranks of staff opportunities to be involved in programme development.

Clinical Staff: The Heart of the Treatment Programme

Clinical Staff Selection

1. Ideally prospective clinical staff should have some familiarity with the SVP arena and specifically working with abusive individuals. While newer professionals are often drawn to the experience afforded by SVP programmes, this requires a higher number of experienced clinical supervisors with a more extensive clinical training programme.
2. Clinical staff should be selected based not only on experience and knowledge but also on the skills and traits that are responsive to participants' unique learning styles and abilities. Such traits and skills often reflect a personal commitment to self-awareness, growth, compassion and a desire to ally with others to evoke change. Staff that are empathic, genuine, direct and possess general positive regard for others are most effective in evoking change in offender clients. Respect for the professional boundary between staff and client is unwavering.
3. Programmes seek diversity and heterogeneity (i.e., gender, ethnicity, cultural background, gender identity and preference, special needs) among clinical staff. This assures that the

broad range of offender clients can associate meaningful features of themselves with their caretakers. Diversity awareness promotes empathy, respect and treatment generalizability.

Clinical Staff Retention

1. Staff may find working with abusive individuals too difficult or the emotional and psychological toll too great. The goal of staff retention is served by promoting awareness of counter-therapeutic pulls and its effects, signs and symptoms of burnout, vicarious traumatization and boundary violation.
2. Promote strategies to avoid getting pulled in to the cycle of abuse. These include: expecting counter-transference negative reactions to the work, continually assessing personal signs of burnout, practising mindfulness techniques, striving to incorporate their best qualities in their work, prioritizing their personal life, developing a passion in their professional life, allowing themselves personal therapy and utilizing debriefing, supervision, consultation and foster connections with other professionals in the field.
3. SVP programmes implement strategies to enhance the self-care of staff. Some examples of this are: allowing flexible work schedules (i.e., a 4-day, 10-hour workweek), on-ground staff exercise facility and break areas, in-service trainings involving staff care and staff celebratory events.
4. Staff retention, work satisfaction and work quality are enhanced by encouraging professional development. This includes providing ample time for off-site professional development and allowing staff time to pursue and develop niches of expertise within the SVP programme.
5. Creating opportunities for position advancements and shifts in lateral level duties helps keep staff freshly motivated and well balanced in their skill sets.

Clinical Supervisors: Guardians of Clinician Well-Being and Efficacy

1. Clinical supervisors play a vital role in the efficacy of the treatment programme. They are seen as the primary role models of the therapeutic process. Supervisors must possess well-developed self-awareness and judgement.
2. Supervisors safeguard time for clinical supervision and treatment debriefing.
3. They continually assess for counter-therapeutic attitudes and behaviours of clinical staff.
4. They assure that clinicians adhere to best practice standards.
5. They are aware of parallel process issues wherein the supervisory relationship can at times parallel the therapeutic relationship. They strive to be aware of the multi-level patterns of interactions and relational complexities involved in therapy, supervision and system functioning.
6. They provide a safe, supportive, continual and reliable environment for which supervisors can sincerely utilize clinical supervision, at times disclosing uncomfortable material.
7. They strive to increase clinician resilience by facilitating therapist's competency and by encouraging more effective coping styles (Clarke, 2008).

Community Reintegration

If someone who has been committed under SVP laws is placed in the community under supervision, a new range of programmatic issues arise.

The community team has at least three distinguishable functions: support, supervision and treatment. This typically involves multiple players including a supervisor (like a parole agent), a polygraph examiner and a case manager in addition to one or more treatment providers. There may also be someone charged with providing overall supervision for multiple community teams.

The community team's support responsibilities include placement in a suitable residence, assisting the supervisee in finding suitable work and other positive structured activities. While this can be challenging when the community is hostile, a well-functioning community team should find suitable accommodation, and suitable work should be found within the first year of placement.

Treatment providers in community reintegration teams (also often called containment teams) have three key requirements:

1. To facilitate a smooth transition, the outpatient treatment provider must be familiar with and respectful of the inpatient treatment programme, the specifics of the inpatient treatment received and of the institutional life the person would have experienced.
2. The outpatient treatment provider must be a skilled team player, able to take into account the roles and perspectives of other members of the community team. They will need to understand and respect the roles played by others but also be alert to the possibility that others may not be fulfilling their roles properly and respond appropriately.
3. The outpatient treatment provider must have a broad clinical repertoire, being skilled in sexual offender treatment but also able to address anxiety, depression, loneliness, substance abuse, family reintegration issues and unemployment. They should also have experience of working with mental illness or developmental or physical disabilities.

There are two fundamental decisions that have to be made about the role and operation of the community team: Are they intended to provide primary treatment or only maintenance treatment? Is their purpose reintegration or is it containment?

Some SVP programmes seek to retain treatment participants in the inpatient programme until all major treatment needs are met. The role of the outpatient programme then is maintenance and generalization of treatment gains. There are two problems with this strategy. First, it encourages a form of perfectionism that may lead to overly conservative decisions about release based on requiring a superhuman level of attainment. Second, it is likely that some treatment issues are easier to treat effectively in the community. Indeed, when differences between community and institutional treatment emerge, they have generally suggested that community treatment is more effective (Lösel and Schmucker, 2005). An alternative strategy is to provide sufficient inpatient treatment that the individual can reside with reasonable safety in the community under supervision and is able to benefit from community treatment. The problem with too early a release is that supervision problems in the community may lead to many recalls, and that a concern with sustaining community safety that excessively weights containment.

The second fundamental decision is regarding the balance between reintegration and containment. Is the purpose of the programme to contain the person safely or is it to reintegrate the person with the surrounding community in preparation for discharge? Of course, all programmes have to address both these goals, but the question is one of emphasis. If what amounts to house arrest with supervised outings is maintained indefinitely, then no real preparation for reintegration or discharge can take place. Indeed, this kind of containment will likely either perpetuate a form of dependent institutionalization or lead to a level of loneliness and frustration that actually increases the inclination to re-offend. On the other hand, too quick relaxation into full community access will create too many opportunities to re-offend.

This brings to attention an essential feature of an efficient community. The team must be able to vary the intensity of supervision, support and treatment in response to changes in the person's response to these services. Non-compliance, risky behaviour or other forms of deterioration may require making all these services more intense.

Varying the intensity of community services in this way depends on effective ongoing monitoring. Monitoring involves two aspects: maintaining multiple sources of information about the person being monitored and integrating this information in a way that gives it meaning. Potential sources of information include monitors, searches of the person's residence, electronic monitoring, polygraph examinations, reports from collateral contacts including the supervisee's employer and routine contacts with supervising agents, case managers and treatment providers.

Monitors may be used to escort or may make unannounced visits to the residence and carry out searches. Early in supervision, movements outside the residence may always be with a monitor, including with the monitor being present at the supervisee's place of work, and unannounced visits may be at any time and occur several times a day. Although this frequency of monitoring may seem intrusive, it also provides the supervisee with regular social contact in what otherwise may be a very lonely existence.

Electronic monitoring systems include place-based systems that determine whether the supervisee is within a certain distance of the home system (commonly linked to a telephone within the residence) and GPS that can track the supervisee's movements. Early in supervision, a common practice is for a weekly schedule of approved movements to be authorized by the supervising agent and then tracked by a monitoring centre. If the supervisee moves outside the schedule, he becomes liable to be arrested. Common problems with these systems include GPS inaccurately determining location and difficulty moving in buildings that block the signal.

Polygraph examinations may either focus on compliance issues or on re-offence. For technical reasons, it is ill advised to mix issues of different seriousness in the same examination. Research into the accuracy of polygraph examinations indicates predictive accuracy coefficients close to 0.9 when techniques approved by the American Polygraph Association are used (Gougler *et al.*, 2011). Level of accuracy greatly exceeds unaided human judgement of veracity (and represents a greater degree of test validity than that shown by most psychological tests) but still involves a significant degree of error. This means that polygraph examinations can appropriately be used to generate disclosures from supervisees and as grounds for tightening or loosening supervision. Ideally, results from polygraph examinations are integrated with information from other sources in informing decision-making. The problem arises when the only source of concern is someone testing deceptive on a polygraph examination. In such cases, the relatively high accuracy of polygraph examinations should mean that this is taken seriously and may appropriately lead to tighter supervision. It should not, however, be taken as absolute proof regarding what the supervisee did.

To be useful, however, this information has to be pooled and interpreted, and guidance needs to be given to those who provide the information on what to attend to. Probably the most useful focusing device would be something akin to ACUTE-2007 (Hanson *et al.*, 2007; see Chapter 23, this volume).

A limitation of existing technologies of this kind is that they are too risk-focused. Someone who does little by putting out little behaviour may achieve a score indicating little risk. However, this kind of passivity is a poor preparation for discharge. A potentially fruitful

Table 20.3   SAPROF protective factors

Internal factors	Motivational factors	External factors
Intelligence	Work	Social network
Secure attachment in childhood	Leisure activities	Intimate relationships
Empathy	Financial management	Professional care
Coping	Motivation for treatment	Living circumstances
Self-control	Attitudes towards authority	Supervision
	Life goals	
	Medication	

development then would be to focus on the development of strengths and protective factors. There is at present only a very limited empirical foundation for this. In recent years, the desistance literature has highlighted the central role of the active development and use of pro-social networks of friends and associates (Giordano *et al.*, 2002). This is consistent with the Circles of Accountability and Support models that have been developed in recent years in the sexual offender field. This uses trained volunteers to a pro-social network. This kind of initiative appears to be effective in reducing the risk presented by high-risk sexual offenders (Wilson, Cortoni and McWhinnie, 2009).

A more general approach to protective factors has been developed in Holland. Structured Assessment of PROtective Factors (SAPROF) for violence risk is intended for high-risk offenders, though its focus has been more on violence in general rather than sexual offending in particular. Some of the SAPROF factors are the positive pole of familiar risk factors, though assessed in a more dynamic way. Others, while positive in their focus, go beyond traditional risk factors. Despite the apparent overlap with risk factors, the protective factors defined by SAPROF have been shown to have incremental predictive validity relative to standard risk assessment (de Vries Robbe and de Vogel, 2010). SAPROF protective factors have been divided into three categories: Internal, Motivational and External (Table 20.3). The SAPROF manual provides detailed guidance on what is relevant under each category.

Conclusion

The SVP arena is a difficult one to operate in, and there is no doubt that in practice even the better SVP programmes fall short of at least some of the best practice standards advocated here. Our hope is that we have sketched the direction in which SVP programmes ought to progress. Viewing some of the less-developed programmes, those from which there have been few or no releases for example, it is easy to be pessimistic. Nevertheless it is important to recognize that progress has been made. Programmes tend to be more soundly based now, and a significant number of persons committed under SVP laws have been returned to the community. This is a reflection both of the professional intelligence and dedication of those who work in those programmes and of the periodic legal pressures that have sometimes energized steps to improve the functioning of SVP programmes. The financial crises currently afflicting many states in the United States potentially provide opportunities to further improve SVP programmes since they may motivate changes in policy and practice in the direction of improved quality and efficiency that may reduce both the financial and justice costs. We anticipate that the next decade will see further improvements in the development and operation of SVP programmes. It is hoped that the practices detailed in this chapter will help pave the way for these improvements.

References

Andrews, D.A. and Bonta, J. (2006) *The Psychology of Criminal Conduct*, 4th edn, Lexis Nexis, Newark.

Annis, L.V. and Perry, D.F. (1977) Self-disclosure modeling in same-sex and mixed-sex unsupervised groups. *Journal of Counseling Psychology*, 24, 370–372.

Arkowitz, S., Shale, J. and Carabello, K. (2008) Conditional release programs for civilly committed sex offenders. *Journal of Psychiatry and Law*, 36, 485–511.

Bargh, J., Chen, M. and Burrows, L. (1996) Automaticity of social behaviour: direct effects of trait construct and stereotype activation on action. *Journal of Personality and Social Psychology*, 71, 230–244.

Beech, A.R., Fisher, D.D. and Thornton, D. (2003) Risk assessment of sex offenders. *Professional Psychology: Research and Practice*, 34, 339–352.

Beggs, S.M. and Grace, R.C. (2010) Assessment of dynamic risk factors: an independent validation study of the violence risk scale: sexual offender version. *Sexual Abuse: A Journal of Research and Treatment*, 22, 234–251.

Clarke, J.M. (2008) Promoting professional resilience, in *Contemporary Risk Assessment in Safeguarding Children* (ed. M. Calder), Russell House Publishing, Dorset, pp. 164–180. http://www.russellhouse.co.uk/pdfs/Contriskass.pdf (accessed 28 January 2013).

Collaborative Outcome Data Committee. (2007a) Sexual Offender Treatment Outcome Research: CODC Guidelines for Evaluation Part 1: Introduction and Overview. *Corrections Research User Rep. no. 2007-02*. Public Safety Canada, Ottawa.

Collaborative Outcome Data Committee. (2007b) The Collaborative Outcome Data Committee's Guidelines for the Evaluation of Sexual Offender Treatment Outcome Research Part 2: CODC Guidelines. *Corrections Research User Rep. no. 2007-03*. Public Safety Canada, Ottawa.

Curran, T. (1978) Increasing motivation to change in group treatment. *Small Group Behaviour*, 9, 337–348.

Dasgupta, N. and Greenwald, A. (2001) On the malleability of automatic attitudes: combating automatic prejudice with images of admired and disliked individuals. *Journal of Personality and Social Psychology*, 81, 800–814.

Davidson, M.A. (1998) The effects of pre-therapy information audiotape on client satisfaction, anxiety level, expectations, and symptom reduction. *Dissertation Abstracts International*, 58 (8-B), 4441.

De Vries Robbe, M. and de Vogel, V. (2010) Protective factors for violence. Paper presented at the International Association of Forensic Mental Health Services Conference, Vancouver, May 27.

D'Orazio, D. (2005) Addressing the pitfalls of the relapse prevention model: empathy, trauma, & affective factors in sexual offender treatment and assessment. Workshop presented at the California Coalition on Sexual Offending, 8th Annual Conference, San Diego, May 6.

D'Orazio, D. (2006) Empathy: the gift of pain. *Perspectives*, the CCOSO Newsletter (Spring), 5.

D'Orazio, D., Arkowitz, S., Adams, J. and Maram, W. (2009) The California Sexually Violent Predator Statute: History, Description, and Areas of Improvement. California Coalition on Sexual Offending, San Jose.

Doren, D. (2006) The model for considering release of civilly committed sexual offenders, in *The Sexual Predator*, vol. III (ed. A. Schlank), Civic Research Institute, Kingston, pp. 61–67.

Dweck, C.S. (2006) *Mindset: The New Psychology of Success*. Random House, New York.

Elwood, R.W., Doren, D.M. and Thornton, D. (2008) Diagnostic and risk profiles of men detained under Wisconsin's sexually violent person law. *International Journal of Offender Therapy and Comparative Criminology*, 54 (2), 187–196.

Epperson, D.L., Kaul, J.D. and Hesselton, D. (1998) Final report on the development of the Minnesota Sex Offender Screening Tool-Revised (MnSOST-R). Unpublished manuscript.

Freud, S. (1910) The future prospects of psycho-analytic therapy, in *The Standard Edition of the Complete Psychological Works of Sigmund Freud*, vol. 11 (ed. and trans. J. Strachey): Five Lectures on Psycho-Analysis, Leonardo da Vinci and Other Works, Hogarth, London, pp. 139–152.

Garrison, J. (1978) Written vs. verbal preparation of patients for group psychotherapy. *Psychotherapy: Theory, Research, and Practice*, 15, 130–134.

Giordano, P.C., Cernkovich, S.A. and Rudolph, J.L. (2002) Gender, crime, and desistance: toward a theory of cognitive transformation. *American Journal of Sociology*, 107, 990–1064.

Gookin, K. (2007) Comparison of state laws authorizing involuntary commitment of sexually violent predators: 2006 update, revised (electronic version). Washington Institute for Public Policy, Olympia, Document no. 07-08-1101.

Gougler, M., Nelson, R., Handler, M. *et al.* (2011) Report of the ad hoc committee on validated techniques. *Polygraph*, 40, 203–305.

Hanson, R.K. (1997) *The Development of a Brief Actuarial Risk Scale for Sexual Offense Recidivism*, Ministry of the Solicitor General of Canada, Ottawa.

Hanson, R.K., Gordon, A., Harris, A.J.R. *et al.* (2002) First report of the Collaborative Outcome Data Project on the effectiveness of psychological treatment of sex offenders. *Sex Abuse: A Journal of Research and Treatment*, 14, 169–195.

Hanson, R.K., Harris, A.J.R., Scott, T. and Helmus, L. (2007) Assessing the Risk of Sexual Offenders on Community Supervision: The Dynamic Supervision Project. *Corrections Research User Rep. no. 2007-05.* Public Safety Canada, Ottawa.

Hanson, R.K., Bourgon, G., Helmus, L. and Hodgson, S. (2009) The principles of effective correctional treatment also apply to sexual offenders: a meta-analysis. *Criminal Justice and Behaviour*, 36, 865–891.

Hare, R.D. (2003) *The Hare Psychopathy Checklist-Revised*, 2nd edn, Multi-Health Systems, Toronto.

Harkins, L., Beech, A.R. and Thornton, D. (2012) The influence of risk and psychopathy on the therapeutic climate in sex offender treatment. *Sexual Abuse*, 24, 519–543, first published on January 30, doi:10.1177/1079063211429469.

Harris, A., Phenix, A., Hanson, R.K. and Thornton, D. (2003) STATIC-99 coding rules: revised 2003. Public Safety Canada. www.publicsafety.gc.ca (accessed 21 January 2013).

Jackson, R., Schneider, J. and Travia, T. (2011) SOCCPN Annual Survey of Sex Offender Civil Commitment Programs, 2011. http://www.soccpn.org/images/SOCCPN_Annual_Survey_2011_revised_1_.pdf (accessed 24 December 2012).

Jung, C. (1968) *Collected Works of C.G. Jung: The Archetypes and the Collective Unconscious*, vol. 9 part 1, 2nd edn, Princeton University Press, Princeton.

Kansas vs. Crane, 534 US 407, (2002).

Kansas vs. Hendricks, 521 US 346, (1997).

Kitagawa, K. (2005) Skills Canadian employers are looking for – a national program. *Forum on Corrections Research*, 17 (1), 6–9.

Knight, R.A. and Thornton, D. (2007) Evaluating and improving risk assessment schemes for sexual recidivism: a long term follow up of convicted sexual offenders. *Final Report*. US Department of Justice. *Award Number 2003-WG-BX-1002*. http://www.ncjrs.gov/pdffiles1/nij/grants/217618.pdf (accessed 24 December 2012).

Larsen, D.L., Nguyen, T.D., Green, R.S. and Attkinson, C.C. (1983) Enhancing the utilization of outpatient mental health services. *Community Mental Health Journal*, 19, 305–320.

Lipton, D., Pearson, F.S., Cleland, C.M. and Yee, D. (2002a) The effectiveness of cognitive-behavioural treatment methods on recidivism, in *Offender Rehabilitation and Treatment* (ed. J. McGuire), John Wiley & Sons, Ltd, Chichester.

Lipton, D., Pearson, F.S., Cleland, C.M. and Yee, D. (2002b) The effects of therapeutic communities on recidivism, in *Offender Rehabilitation and Treatment* (ed. J. McGuire), John Wiley & Sons, Ltd, Chichester.

Lohn, M. (2010) Sexual predator treatment squeezes budget. http://www.msnbc.msn.com/id/37819608/ns/us_news-crime_and_courts (accessed 24 December 2012).

Lösel, F. and Schmucker, M. (2005) The effectiveness of treatment for sexual offenders: a comprehensive meta-analysis. *Journal of Experimental Criminology*, 1, 117–146.

Marques, J.K., Wiederanders, M., Day, D.M. *et al.* (2005) Effects of a relapse prevention program on sexual recidivism: final results from California's Sex Offender Treatment and Evaluation Project (SOTEP). *Sexual Abuse: A Journal of Research of Research and Treatment*, 17, 79–107.

Marshall, W.L. (2005) Therapist style in sexual offender treatment: influence on indices of change. *Sexual Abuse: A Journal of Research and Treatment*, 17, 109–116.

Marshall, L.E., Marshall, W.L., Fernandez, Y.M. *et al.* (2008) The Rockwood Preparatory Program for sexual offenders: description and preliminary appraisal. *Sexual Abuse*, 20, 25–42.

Martin, D.J., Garske, J.P. and David, M.K. (2000) Relation of the therapeutic alliance with outcome and other variables: a meta-analytic review. *Journal of Consulting and Clinical Psychology*, 68, 438–450.

Mayerson, N.G. (1984) Preparing clients for group therapy: a critical review and theoretical formulation. *Clinical Psychology Review*, 4, 191–213.

McGrath, R.J., Lasher, M.P. and Cumming, G.F. (2012) The Sex Offender Treatment Intervention and Progress Scale (SOTIPS): psychometric properties and incremental predictive validity with Static-99R. *Sexual Abuse*, 24, 431–458, first published on February 24, 2012 doi:10.1177/1079063211432475.

McGuire, J. (2002) *Offender Rehabilitation and Treatment*. John Wiley & Sons, Ltd, Chichester.

Miller, W.R. and Rollnick, S. (2013) *Motivational Interviewing: Preparing People for Change*, 3rd edn, Guilford Press, New York.

Olver, M.E., Wong, S.C.P., Nicholaichuk, T. and Gordon, A. (2007) The validity and reliability of the Violence Risk Scale – sexual offender version: assessing sex offender risk and evaluating therapeutic change. *Psychological Assessment*, 19, 318–329.

Parhar, K.K., Wormith, J.S., Derkzen, D.M. and Beauregard, A.M. (2008) Offender coercion in treatment: a meta-analysis of effectiveness. *Criminal Justice and Behaviour*, 35, 1109–1135.

Pfafflin, F., Bohmer, M., Cornehl, S. and Mergenthaler, E. (2005) What happens in therapy with sexual offenders: a model of process research. *Sexual Abuse*, 17, 141–152.

Rogers, C. (1957) The necessary and sufficient conditions of therapeutic personality change. *Journal of Consulting Psychology*, 21, 95–103.

Schlank, A. (ed.) (2010) *The Sexual Predator*, vol. 4, *Legal Issues, Assessment, Treatment*, Civic Research Institute, Kingston.

Strupp, J. and Bloxom, A.L. (1973) Preparing lower class patients for group psychotherapy: development and evaluation of a role-induction film. *Journal of Consulting and Clinical Psychology*, 41, 373–384.

Thornton, D. (2002) Constructing and testing a framework for dynamic risk assessment. *Sexual Abuse: A Journal of Research and Treatment*, 14, 137–151.

Thornton, D. and Blud, L. (2007) The influence of psychopathic traits on response to treatment, in *The Psychopath: Theory, Research, and Practice* (eds H.F. Hervé and J. Yuille), Lawrence Erlbaum Associates, Mahwah.

Thornton, D. and Sachsenmaier, S. (2012) Need profiles in an SVP population: implications for treatment. Paper to be presented at the 31st ATSA Annual Research and Treatment Conference, Denver, October 18.

U.S. Dept of Justice. (n.d.) The history of the Violence Against Women Act. http://www.ovw.usdoj.gov/docs/history-vawa.pdf (accessed 26 December 2012).

Ward, T. and Hudson, S.M. (1998) A model of the relapse process in sexual offenders. *Journal of Interpersonal Violence*, 13, 700–725.

Ward, T., Hudson, S.M. and Keenan, T. (1998) A self-regulation model of the sexual offence process. *Sexual Abuse*, 10, 141–157.

Webster, S.D. (2005) Pathways to sexual offence recidivism following treatment: an examination of the Ward and Hudson self-regulation model of relapse. *Journal of Interpersonal Violence*, 20, 1175–1196.

Wilson, R.J., Cortoni, F. and McWhinnie, A.J. (2009) Circles of support & accountability: a Canadian national replication of outcome findings. *Sexual Abuse*, 21, 412–430.

Part V
Cultural Factors and Individualized Approaches to Offender Rehabilitation

21

The Role of Cultural Factors in Treatment

Jo Thakker

University of Waikato, New Zealand

Introduction

The association of cultural factors with various aspects of offender treatment is complex and multifaceted. Conceivably, an individual's cultural background may impact on the process of rehabilitation in many different ways. For example, an offender's world view, including his or her religious beliefs, is likely to be shaped by his or her cultural background, and this in turn is likely to have implications for the relevance and impact of treatment. Also, on a more practical level, the language (or languages) that an offender speaks will impact on his or her ability to understand the content of the treatment programme, and of course language is steeped in cultural understandings. Perhaps less obvious is the impact of the cultural background of the therapist which may also impact on the client–therapist relationship.

Given the title of this book, with its focus on 'what works', this chapter will examine some of the culture-based and culture-sensitive treatment programmes that have been developed around the world and will provide some discussion of their efficacy. As will be evident throughout, the research in this area is limited and frequently preliminary in nature. In other words, the findings are generally tentative and the conclusions somewhat speculative, due to a range of factors, such as small sample size and the low base rates for recidivism in some offender groups. Also, the large majority of studies have been conducted 'in-house' by various government departments and have not been disseminated beyond their own web sites and internal publications. This, of course, means that many of the evaluations have not been scrutinized via a formal peer-review process. However, despite these limitations, some significant trends seem to be emerging in the growing body of data and these allow for some tentative conclusions to be drawn.

The chapter begins by defining the concept of culture. It then focuses on two key treatment models, which provide a theoretical foundation and framework for the ensuing discussion. Following this, the approaches of three different countries are examined, namely, Canada, New Zealand and Australia. Canada and New Zealand were chosen because, arguably, they have the highest number of culture-inclusive programmes. On the other hand, Australia was chosen to provide an example of a country that has recently begun to introduce and develop such programmes. A thorough search of the literature revealed that there are very few

What Works in Offender Rehabilitation: An Evidence-Based Approach to Assessment and Treatment,
First Edition. Edited by Leam A. Craig, Louise Dixon and Theresa A. Gannon.
© 2013 John Wiley & Sons, Ltd. Published 2013 by John Wiley & Sons, Ltd.

culture-focused programmes available for women, thus only programmes for males are included. The programmes that are included herein are all of the programmes that have been subjected to some sort of evaluation (even if the evaluation was limited and preliminary) and that have been made available via an in-house web site or peer-reviewed publication. Unfortunately, the majority of the evaluations were published in-house and not peer-reviewed. Also, many were not especially robust; for example, they often did not include a control group. The evidence available at the time of writing this chapter suggested that all of the programmes discussed are currently still in use. The chapter concludes with a summary of the key findings and a discussion of key implications relating to these findings.

Defining Culture

The term 'culture' is broad and complex. The complexity of the term lies in the fact that it has many different definitions and that it bears some similarity to other terms. Given this complexity, it is necessary to provide a definition of the term. Out of the array of definitions provided by the online Merriam-Webster Dictionary (2011), one is most pertinent to this discussion. It is 5b: 'the customary beliefs, social forms and material traits of a racial, religious, or social group; *also*: the characteristic features of everyday existence (as diversions or a way of life) shared by people in a place or time'. The relevant definition (number 2) from the online Oxford Dictionary (2011) mirrors this definition in a more succinct manner. It defines culture as: 'the ideas, customs, and social behaviour of a particular people or society'.

Thus, central to the concept of culture are the beliefs and behaviours of a particular group of people. Also, related to this, is the suggestion that specific groups of people will have specific beliefs and behaviours that may differ from other groups. As explained by Durrant and Thakker (2003, p. 121): 'a cultural group is one that *shares* a set of norms, values, concepts, beliefs, and practices, which, in part, *differentiates* them from other cultural groups'. Further, as stated by Durrant and Thakker, 'culture' is often associated with 'ethnicity' and the largely outdated term 'race'. While the latter term has, in the past, been used to classify people according to physiological characteristics, the term 'ethnicity' is generally seen as broader, insofar as it is typically used to refer to the 'shared cultural history' of individuals from a particular lineage (Durrant and Thakker, 2003).

With regard to the various culture-sensitive therapeutic programmes that are discussed in this chapter, it appears that most participants are recruited via a combination of both ethnic and cultural identification. Most prison databases around the world include information pertaining to ethnic identity. For example, in New Zealand, offenders are requested to document their ethnicity when they enter the prison system as this is when basic demographic information is collected (S. Nicholls, personal communication, January 27, 2012). Further, in terms of criminogenic treatment programmes, typically an in-depth interview conducted prior to recruitment will include the collection of demographic information as well as a discussion of cultural issues. Treatment options are usually discussed with offenders so that they can weigh up the costs and benefits of various programmes. It is at this point that cultural factors would usually be considered, including, asking the offender whether he would like to be involved in a culture-focused programme and/or a culture-focused therapeutic community. In this way, both ethnicity and culture are relevant in deciding on the most appropriate form of treatment for an offender. It should be noted, however, that there are currently no standardized formal risk assessment tools designed for use with indigenous offender populations (see also Chapter 22).

Relevant Rehabilitation Models

This section examines two key contemporary treatment models in order to provide a theoretical touchstone for the discussion of cultural factors in treatment. As illustrated later, both models suggest that the inclusion of cultural factors in treatment is likely to be valuable.

Risk need rehabilitation

One of the most influential models is the Risk-Need-Responsivity (RNR) approach (Andrews and Bonta, 1998, 2003). The risk aspect of the RNR model refers to the nature and level of risk that an offender poses and Andrews and Bonta propose that this risk level should determine the intensity of treatment. In other words, if an offender is considered to have a low risk for further offending, then he or she should engage in a less intensive treatment programme (if any). The need aspect of the model refers to an offender's rehabilitative needs (which are sometimes termed criminogenic needs or dynamic risk factors). According to the model, treatment should address the specific dynamic risk factors that are empirically related to offending that – when targeted – will lead to reductions in reoffending. Some common examples of such factors or needs include: substance abuse, impulsivity, relationship problems and emotional regulation deficits.

The final component of the RNR theory is the responsivity principle which refers to an offender's likely response to treatment and the factors that might affect this response. According to the model, the chosen treatment approach should be appropriate for the individual offender insofar as it should match his or her motivation level, learning style and other personal characteristics. Furthermore, the responsivity principle suggests that it is essential that the treatment approach that is selected for a particular offender is based on sound research which supports its use with the specific needs of that offender. Thus, it may be extrapolated that treatment should be culturally responsive; in other words, that it should be sensitive to the offender's cultural needs.

The RNR model has had a significant impact on the development and delivery of offender treatment and has 'constituted a revolution in the way that criminal conduct is managed in Canada, Britain, Europe, Australia, and New Zealand' (Ward, Gannon and Yates, 2008, p. 180). Arguably, the key strength of the model is its practical utility; it provides a comprehensive theoretical framework which has clear implications for the development of rehabilitative programmes. For instance, the model assists in identifying and prioritizing treatment needs and in selecting the most appropriate treatment options for offenders.

However, some researchers have criticized the RNR model. For example, it has been argued that while a focus on rehabilitative needs is useful in treatment, it should not be the sole focus (Ward, Melser and Yates, 2007; Wilson and Yates, 2009). The point that these researchers make is that the RNR model seems to be applied in such a way that other important aspects of treatment are overlooked. For instance, Wilson and Yates propose that therapist qualities, such as respect for clients and an ability to empathize are also important in bringing out positive change. Furthermore, Ward and colleagues argue that the tendency to categorize offenders in relation to the level of risk they pose may lead to a lack of attention to the unique needs of the offender. Another criticism that Ward has made of the RNR model is that the emphasis on risk can result in a generally negative treatment approach in which the offender is encouraged to avoid certain risk-related activities or situations (e.g., Ward and Stewart, 2003). The upshot of this is that the focus is on avoidance rather than the identification of future goals and positive pro-social activities.

Implications of RNR for culture-focused treatment approaches   As explained already, according to the RNR model, treatment intensity should match the level of recidivism risk that the offender poses. In other words, a high-risk offender should complete a more intensive rehabilitation programme. As illustrated later, it appears that most of the culture-focused programmes are designed according to this principle. For example, Saili Matagi (a Pacific Island Violence Prevention Programme in New Zealand) is a high-intensity programme which has high risk as one of its key eligibility criteria (New Zealand Department of Corrections, 2005). With regard to the needs principle, there are a number of ways in which cultural variables may impact on an offender's criminogenic needs. One particularly important aspect is an offender's sense of cultural identity. It has been theorized that the process of colonization may lead to suppression of the indigenous culture, which in turn can lead to a diminished sense of cultural identity in indigenous people (e.g., Kirmayer, Brass and Tait, 2000). Furthermore, research suggests that the suppression of indigenous culture is associated with offending (Monchalin, 2010). For example, research in New Zealand indicates that the cultural disenfranchisement of Māori has been associated with an increase in vulnerability to criminal behaviour (Maynard *et al.*, 1999). Therefore, a culture-focused rehabilitative approach which aims to assist in strengthening the offender's cultural identity may be especially beneficial. Another important criminogenic need which may be addressed by the inclusion of a focus on culture is social support. As illustrated later, many of the culture-based programmes include a strong focus on relationships with family and community.

More generally, many of the cultural programmes that are discussed herein use cultural values, norms, and traditions as a way of challenging an offender's tendency to engage in certain problematic behaviours. For instance, an offender may have antisocial attitudes and beliefs which contribute to domestic violence. Therefore, one common approach to modify such beliefs is to show how such beliefs are inconsistent with traditional beliefs which encourage the respect and protection of one's family members. In this way, culture may be used to address a particular criminogenic need. Furthermore, placing an emphasis on cultural values and traditions can enable an offender to create a new and more positive moral code which they can use to make changes to their behaviour.

The final part of the RNR model, the responsivity principle, is especially relevant to cultural approaches as it has probably been a key driver in the development of such approaches. Specifically, one of the main aims of culture-centred programmes is to provide treatment that specific cultural groups are likely to respond to. For example, the Saili Matagi programme 'aims to increase responsivity of Pacific offenders through the inclusion of Pacific values, beliefs and concepts' (New Zealand Department of Corrections, 2005, p. 6). Thus, the underlying theory is that an individual from a particular cultural background will respond better in treatment if the treatment itself is consistent with (or perhaps embodies) the language, values and traditions of their particular cultural group.

The Good Lives Model

Another relevant and increasingly influential rehabilitation theory is the Good Lives Model (GLM) by Ward and colleagues (e.g., Ward and Gannon, 2006; Ward and Stewart, 2003). As explained earlier, over the last decade or so, Ward and various colleagues have criticized the RNR approach, and in relation to this criticism they have presented a new approach to rehabilitation (the Good Lives Model; GLM) which they suggest obviates some of the problems with the RNR model. The GLM has a very different focus to that of the RNR model; rather than examining risk level, the GLM begins by asking the question of what the offender is trying to achieve through his or her offending. Specifically, the question is: What gap or need is the offending filling? Ward and colleagues (e.g., Ward, Mann and Gannon, 2007) propose that in order to produce long-term change in an offender's pattern of behaviour, therapy must uncover and respond to the underlying motivation for the behaviour. The GLM is founded on the idea that all human activity is associated with the desire to fulfil basic needs or 'goods'. For example, regular exercise and eating healthy food may fulfil the basic good of maintaining excellent physical health, while painting a picture may fulfil the basic good of experiencing creativity. When these sorts of goods are met in an individual pro-socially, then it can be said that he or she has a 'good' life.

In explaining the GLM, Ward distinguishes between primary and secondary goods: while the former refer to actions or conditions that are ends in themselves, the latter refer to ways and means of attaining primary goods. For instance, if intimacy is a primary good then anything that is instrumental in bringing about or enhancing intimacy would be a secondary good. Drawing on work from a range of research areas, including evolutionary theory, self-regulation, quality of life, well-being, ethics and anthropology, Ward and Stewart (2003) propose that there are at least 10 primary human goods, namely: 'Life (including healthy living and functioning), knowledge, excellence in play and work (including mastery experiences), excellence in agency (i.e., autonomy and self-directedness), inner peace (i.e., freedom from emotional turmoil and stress), friendship (including intimate, romantic and family relationships), community, spirituality (in the broad sense of finding meaning and purpose in life), happiness, and creativity' (p. 356).

As outlined by Ward (2002), offenders, like all human beings, need and value these goods and seek to realize them in their daily lives. Ward is careful to stress, that for most offenders, and indeed many non-offenders, there is often no conscious awareness of this tendency. In other words, while most people will have an underlying drive to attain these basic human goods they may not be aware of these drives. Ward suggests that while offenders attempt to attain the same goods as non-offenders, they go about this in a problematic way, and he outlines four basic types of problems: the use of *inappropriate means* (i.e., goods are sought in ways that are inappropriate and counterproductive), a *lack of scope* (i.e., only some goods are sought); *conflict or lack of coherence* (i.e., the ways some goods are sought directly reduces the chances of others being secured); and *a lack of capacity* (i.e., individuals lack the skills, opportunities, and resources to achieve a certain good in specific ways).

A GLM approach to offender rehabilitation would include an assessment of the relationship between the offending and the goods which the individual is attempting to attain via the offending. Then a Good Lives Plan would be developed which would allow the offender to set goals for the future which would seek to bring about the attainment of various identified goods in a pro-social manner. Thus, basic human needs are acknowledged and offenders are encouraged to continue to strive to attain these needs, but to do so in a manner that is consistent with societal norms and personal interests and which does not cause harm to others. According to the GLM, when such needs are met, risks are mitigated because offenders are less likely to choose a pathway that leads to offending.

The GLM is consistent with the work of Maruna (e.g., Maruna, 2001; Maruna and Roy, 2007), which emphasizes the importance of taking a positive approach to treatment. It also fits within the increasingly favoured strengths-based conceptualization which has gained a firm foothold in the mental health treatment (Rudolph and Epstein, 2000; Wong, 2006). However, there is as yet insufficient empirical research showing that applying the GLM in rehabilitation leads to effective treatment (Whitehead, Ward and Collie, 2007; Chapter 17 , this volume; Willis *et al.*, 2012). Also, it has been argued Ward and colleagues' proposition that the more traditional RNR model was not at all strengths-based is somewhat unfair because many treatment programmes that use the RNR framework include positive and supportive treatment components (New Zealand Department of Corrections, 2009a).

Implications of the GLM for culture-focused treatment approaches

There are numerous aspects of the GLM that are relevant to the discussion of culture. Perhaps most pertinent are the primary goods of community and spirituality as these are central to an individual's sense of self and cultural identity. Thus, according to the GLM, any treatment should include a focus on these aspects. As will be illustrated later, most of the culture-sensitive treatment approaches that have been developed around the globe include components that cover community and spirituality. This is especially true in regard to the Canadian programmes for indigenous offenders which pay particular attention to connecting the offender with his or her community and learning about indigenous beliefs and traditions.

More broadly, it could be argued that culture is relevant to all aspects of the GLM. For example, for an individual to have a healthy life and lifestyle he or she needs to uphold particular values about the importance of healthy living. For an indigenous offender, learning about traditional understandings of health and well-being may facilitate the development of attitudes and beliefs that support healthy living. The 'good' of friendship would also have important implications for culture. Friendship, according to the GLM, refers to all close relationships and arguably cultural factors play an important role in the nature and quality of such relationships. For example, beliefs about male dominance may contribute to family violence (Val r-Segura, Exposito and Moya, 2011) and arguably such beliefs may have a cultural origin. Also, in terms of rehabilitation, teaching offenders about cultural traditions which encourage the respect of women and of their elders may play an important role in improving relationships with immediate and extended family.

So, according to the GLM, culture is important in terms of an individual's rehabilitation and thus any programme that attempts to cater for minority cultural groups would be seen as advantageous. Essentially, the GLM would probably view culture as providing a context in which each of the 'goods' could be addressed. However, more importantly, to ignore that context would be seen as unacceptable, especially if it was seen as integral to the individual. Thus, it may be concluded that the GLM would be consistent and compatible with the development of culture-centred rehabilitation programmes.

The Canadian Approach

In Canada, Aboriginal people are over-represented in all areas of the justice system (Correctional Service Canada, 2011). As noted by the Correctional Service, while Aboriginal people comprise 2.7% of the general adult population, they make up 17% of the total number of offenders who are sentenced by the federal system. Thus, it is not surprising that the Canadian Justice System has attempted to develop treatment approaches that are specifically designed to cater for the needs of Aboriginal offenders. Such developments are probably also associated with the Canadian Multiculturalism Act which was passed in 1988. Some of the key goals of this Act were to preserve the language and practices of diverse cultural groups (including indigenous people), to make sure that all people were treated equally by the law, and to ensure that cultural diversity would be respected (Wayland, 1997).

It is commonly understood that many, if not most, of the problems faced by Canadian Aboriginal people today can be traced to the impact of colonization (Martel, Brassard and Jaccoud, 2011). As argued by Martel *et al.*, traditional ways of life, including cultural, economic and political traditions and structures were all adversely affected by the influx of colonists and colonial ways of life. In turn, these losses contributed to the emergence of a range of serious social problems such as violence, substance abuse problems and suicide. Furthermore, Martel suggests that until quite recently (about the last two decades) the Criminal Justice System was experienced by many Aboriginal people as oppressive because it was founded on a strongly Western world view and was not sensitive to Aboriginal beliefs and practices. For example, treatment programmes available to Aboriginal offenders in the past have used Western concepts and philosophies of human behaviour and have not included Aboriginal understandings. Similar points have also been made in relation to health services in Canada. For example, it has been suggested that using traditional Western models of health and ill-health in the provision of health care for Aboriginal people is a '…form of oppression and continued colonization…' (Green, 2010, p. 29).

According to Kunic and Varis (2009), the move towards a more culture-sensitive approach to offender rehabilitation within Canada is – in part – associated with the acknowledgement that Aboriginal people have a unique understanding of the world which sees the process of healing as complex and multifaceted. This process which has an overarching holistic aspect is understood to include mind, body, community, ceremony and spirituality. Kunic and Varis state: 'It is generally accepted that for Western therapies and models to be most effective with Aboriginal peoples, they must examine Aboriginal spirituality, incorporate traditional Aboriginal thinking and practice and understand the Aboriginal worldview' (p. 6). In Canada, culture-sensitive programmes have been designed for a variety of offender types and offence-related problems, including programmes for sexual offenders, violent offenders, female offenders, and for offenders with substance abuse problems. Several of these programs are discussed later.

Programs for Indigenous Offenders

In Search of Your Warrior Program

The In Search of Your Warrior (ISOYW) program is a prison-based treatment programme for male Aboriginal offenders, which combines Western treatment methods with Aboriginal concepts and practices (Trevethan, Moore and Allegri, 2005). As outlined by Trevethan, Moore and Allegri (2005), the program, which targets violence, is a 'high intensity' group-based programme that involves eight components delivered over 75 sessions. The eight components include the development of awareness in five key areas (self, anger, violence, family of origin and culture) along with the development of general and group skills and a focus on cognition (Trevethan, Moore and Allegri, 2005). As explained by Trevethan and colleagues, an Aboriginal Elder is involved in programme delivery, in particular, in covering the key cultural elements, namely, traditional Aboriginal beliefs and rituals. The goal of the ISOYW programme is to instruct the participants in traditional ways of living so that they can take pride in their cultural identity and use their cultural understandings to live without violence. Note that there is some degree of flexibility in the delivery of the programme. For example, in some instances the programme includes six weeks of delivery in a bush setting, whereas in other cases the entire programme is delivered within a correctional institution.

Trevethan, Moore and Allegri (2005) completed an evaluation of the ISOYW programme which examined the involvement of 218 participants who were compared to a control group who were matched on a range of criteria, including: age, ethnicity, violent offence and risk of reoffending. Unfortunately, the evaluation did not provide any information on what, if any, alternative treatment the individuals in the control group completed. It simply stated that these individuals did not complete the ISOYW programme. Trevethan *et al.* found that the programme appeared to have a positive effect on a number of criminogenic needs (including, substance abuse, antisocial attitudes and beliefs, and antisocial associates), which were assessed before and after treatment (by unidentified measures). However, they found that the matched controls also showed similar improvements in these criminogenic areas; thus, they concluded that these positive changes were probably not a result of specific involvement in the ISOYW programme. Nonetheless, the researchers found that all of those who were involved in the program – both the participants and those involved in the delivery of the program – described their experiences in the program in very positive terms. Another interesting finding was that the cultural and self-awareness components were identified by the participants as being the most effective aspects of the programme. Furthermore, while the rates of readmission to correctional facilities was similar at 12 months post-release, significantly fewer ISOYW graduates than untreated controls were readmitted for a further violent offence (7% compared to 57%).

The Tupiq Program for Inuit Sexual Offenders

The Tupiq Program for Inuit Sexual Offenders is designed to provide culture-focused treatment for imprisoned Inuit sexual offenders (Trevethan, Moore and Naqitarvik, 2004). As detailed by Trevethan and colleagues, the programme, which uses Inuit facilitators to deliver 75 two and half hour group-based sessions, also includes 20 hours of individual counselling. The programme, which is founded on a social learning approach, has three key elements: 'self, responsibility, and community' (p. 14) and uses a process of 'Inuit healing', which involves a focus on cultural values to highlight the individual's sense of responsibility to himself and his community.

In 2004, Trevethan, Moore and Naqitarvik conducted an evaluation of the Tupiq Program. The evaluation assessed the involvement of 24 program participants who were compared to matched controls (Inuit sexual offenders who had not completed the programme) and it reported that 93% of participants completed the programme. Again, as with the aforementioned evaluation, this study did not provide any information on what, if any, treatment the individuals in the control group engaged in. The researchers note the high rate of completion, stating that typically high numbers of Inuit offenders drop out of programmes. The researchers found that the programme brought about positive changes in offenders' attitudes, as measured by the Denial/Minimization Checklist (Barbaree, 1991) and the Sex Offender Need Assessment Rating (Hanson, 2001), and they reported that both participants and facilitators expressed satisfaction with the programme. Further, the results showed that the programme appeared to reduce the risk for further sexual offending but not general offending (as measured by re-incarceration rates).

More recently, Stewart and colleagues (Stewart *et al.*, 2009a) examined the efficacy of the Tupiq Program via an analysis of 71 individuals who were involved in the programme across a seven year period up until 2008. Like the aforementioned study, this one also compared the participants to a group of matched controls. Stewart *et al.* reported that there was a very high completion rate (97%, $N = 69$) which was significantly higher than the completion rate for matched controls (73%, $N = 33$). Note that the matched controls were a group of 146 Inuit sexual offenders; of which 45 had completed a mainstream sexual offender programme. The researchers found that men who had completed the Tupiq Program were significantly less likely (than matched controls) to commit further general offences, or further violent offences. However, while the sexual recidivism rate for the Tupiq Program participants was less than half the recidivism rate of the comparison group, the difference was not statistically significant. In relation to this, the authors point out that it is difficult to find a statistically significant difference when both the participant numbers and the base rates for recidivism are low. Stewart and colleagues (Stewart *et al.*, 2009b, p. 1) conclude that the study provided evidence that 'the Tupiq Programme reduces general and violent recidivism among moderate to high-risk Inuit sex offenders and that it may also reduce sexual reoffending'.

Aboriginal Offender Substance Abuse Program

The Aboriginal Offender Substance Abuse Program (AOSAP) was designed to cater for the high number of Aboriginal offenders in Canada who have substance abuse problems (more than 90% in federal prisons) (Kunic and Varis, 2009). The AOSAP is a group-based program delivered in prisons, which involves 75 two and a quarter hour sessions and a maximum of four individual sessions. While the programme has a strong cultural aspect, it recognizes the diversity within the Aboriginal people and it is therefore adapted to meet the needs of specific Aboriginal groups, such as First Nations, Metis and Inuit (Kunic and Varis, 2009).

As explained by Brazil (2009), the AOSOP combines traditional Western psychological models (such as cognitive behavioural therapy and social learning theory) with Aboriginal concepts and understandings. Further, Brazil states that the programme is divided into several modules, which cover a range of areas including: cultural foundations, Aboriginal spirituality, the after-effects of trauma, using substances to cope with trauma, triggers for substance use, the impact of substance abuse on communities, the restoration of well-being and the links between substance abuse and offending.

Kunic and Varis (2009) carried out an evaluation of the AOSAP which compared 94 Aboriginal men who completed the AOSAP to 423 Aboriginal men who completed the National Substance Abuse Program (NSAP), which is the mainstream equivalent. The evaluation included a number of versions of each of these programmes; an earlier and later version of the AOSAP and a lower and higher intensity version of the NSAP. According to the Correctional Service Canada web site, the NSAP is based on the *Transtheoretical Model of Change* as espoused by Prochaska, DiClemente and Norcross (1992). Kunic and Varis reported that Aboriginal offenders who completed the AOSAP were significantly less likely to be re-imprisoned compared to those who completed the NSAP (5–6% compared to 16–20%, depending on the version of the programme that was delivered). Similarly, Brazil's (2009) preliminary evaluation of the programme found that offenders who completed the AOSAP were significantly less likely to be re-imprisoned compared to those who completed mainstream programmes or no programme. Also, Brazil suggested that Aboriginal offenders who completed the AOSAP developed a stronger sense of their Aboriginal origins, a greater understanding of how to manage their substance use difficulties, and displayed more motivation to change. Note that as this was a brief report, no further details about this evaluation were available.

Healing lodges

Another type of therapeutic approach for Aboriginal offenders is the healing lodge, which is essentially a therapeutic community. While there appears that there is limited research available on the efficacy of therapeutic communities, one recent study (Ware, Frost and Hoy, 2009) concluded that there is some evidence that they are effective. The healing lodge, of which there are several throughout Canada, provides Aboriginal offenders with an opportunity to reside in a culture-focused community which is structured around Aboriginal values and practices (Corectional Service Canada, 2011). The healing lodge also encourages offenders to have contact with children and with Elders and to interact with the natural environment (Nielson, 2003). Thus, consistent with many Aboriginal treatment programmes, the approach of the healing lodge is holistic insofar as it attempts to meet the diverse and complex needs of each individual. There is also a focus on re-integrating offenders with their families and communities. It is important to note that healing lodges typically also offer a wide variety of programmes, including, substance abuse treatment, employment skills, and budgeting, and some also offer individual psychological therapy.

There appears to be little research available that has evaluated the efficacy of healing lodges. However, Nielson (2003) reported that a study conducted by the Correctional Service of Canada found that some individuals who had participated in healing lodges had a reasonably low rate of recidivism. Obviously, this is a rather underwhelming conclusion and it is perhaps surprising that no other research is available that gives a clearer picture of the efficacy of this rehabilitative approach. However, one recent study (Ware, Frost and Hoy, 2009) examined the use of therapeutic communities with sexual offenders and included a brief review of their use with general offenders. The researchers assert that '...there is now an emerging foundation of evidence attesting to their efficacy' (p. 727). Furthermore, Ware *et al.* report that evidence indicates that there is a strong positive correlation between the length of time spent in a therapeutic community and the extent of reduction in reoffending. However, it is important to note that the studies that they cite looked only at mainstream (i.e., not culture-specific) therapeutic communities.

New Zealand Approaches

The indigenous people of New Zealand, the Māori, are over-represented in offender populations. They make up about 15% of the general population; however, they comprise about 52% of those who are in prison and about 30% of individuals who are serving community-based sentences (Huriwai *et al.*, 2001; see also Chapter 22, this volume). Thus, there is an obvious need for rehabilitative approaches that are effective for Māori offenders. The New Zealand Department of Corrections has attempted to respond to this need through the development of a number of treatment programmes that are specifically designed for Māori. Arguably, New Zealand has been a world leader in the development of such programmes.

During the 1980s, within the mental health field, there was an emerging interest in various aspects of Māori culture and a growing awareness of the limitations of Western treatment models in addressing the mental health needs of Māori (Huriwai *et al.*, 2001).

This awareness and understanding contributed to the development of a number of Māori models of mental health, such as Te Pounamu (e.g., Manna, 2001), which literally means 'the greenstone', and Te Whare Tapa Wha (e.g., Glover, 2005), which translates as 'the four sided house'. The development of the Te Whare Tapa Wha model has been seen as particularly significant, as explained by Glover (2005) who stated that the emergence of the model represented a paradigm shift according to Kuhn's (1962) definition of paradigmatic changes. Similarly, Marie and colleagues (Marie, Forsyth and Miles, 2004) state that the model '…has now been canonised within New Zealand public and social policy as the received view of Māori health' (p. 228).

The Te Whare Tapa Wha model uses the image of a house to depict the four key elements of well-being, namely: te taha tinana (the physical body), te taha hinengaro (the psychological aspect), te taha wairua (the spiritual realm) and te taha whanau (the family and community). The image of the house is used to demonstrate the interaction and interdependence of all of these elements; for example, if one aspect is weak then the house itself is weakened. This is a particularly significant metaphor for Māori, as traditionally, the house, or 'whare', is seen as the spiritual centre of the community. Furthermore, the model highlights the importance of taking a holistic and integrated approach to health and well-being. While this model was initially utilized mainly in the mental health field, it is now widely used within correctional settings in New Zealand. For example, it has been integrated into treatment programmes for non-indigenous offenders (such as group-based interventions for sexual offenders) and programmes which are designed more specifically for Māori offenders (such as the Māori Therapeutic Programme or MTP) (New Zealand Department of Corrections, 2008).

Over the last decade, there has been a general move towards a more culture-inclusive approach to programme delivery within correctional settings in New Zealand (New Zealand Department of Corrections, 2009a). Along with the inclusion of Māori models of well-being, attempts have been made to tailor Western-based treatment approaches, such as cognitive behaviour therapy, to the needs of Māori offenders. For example, The Department states '… these programmes encourage participants to embrace values, motivations and social commitments derived from the traditional indigenous culture of the offender group' (p. 41). Also, the Department has developed a treatment programme specifically for Pacific Island offenders.

Culture-Based Programmes

Te Piriti Special Treatment Unit

The Te Piriti Special Treatment Programme was designed for the rehabilitation of both indigenous and non-indigenous child sexual offenders. It combines a cognitive behavioural approach with tikanga Māori (which translates as customs and traditions based on a Māori world view). A comprehensive evaluation of the programme was carried out in 2003 by Nathan and colleagues (Nathan, Wilson and Hillman, 2003). The evaluation reported that: 'The Te Piriti model works to produce a tikanga Māori context that enables a supportive environment within which to operate cognitive-behavioural based programmes' (p. 13). The Te Piriti Programme provides intensive group-based treatment within a therapeutic community within a prison. Treatment involves sessions (four times per week) for about six months.

Interestingly, the Departmental 2003 evaluation (non-Māori $N=133$ and Māori $N=68$) (Nathan, Wilson and Hillman, 2003) of the Te Piriti programme found that it was effective in reducing recidivism in both Māori and non-Māori sexual offenders. The treated sample, who had spent an average of 2.4 years in the community post-treatment, were found to have a sexual recidivism rate of 5.47%. In contrast, the control group (which was made up of

281 men who had not completed sexual offender treatment in prison and who were matched on variables such as age and ethnicity) were found to have a sexual recidivism rate of 20.8%, which was a statistically significant difference. There was a small difference between treated Māori and non-Māori in rates of sexual recidivism but it was not statistically significant. However, there was a statistically significant difference between treated Māori and non-Māori in the rates of general reconviction; 41.18% for Māori and 26.32% for non-Māori. Unfortunately, there was no control group available for comparing the Te Piriti attendees to non-treated offenders in regard to their general offending.

Māori Focus Units and the Māori Therapeutic Programme

Along with the development of culture-inclusive treatment programmes, a number of Māori Focus Units (MFUs) have also been developed in New Zealand. These are essentially prison-based therapeutic communities which are steeped in Māori culture and traditions, some of which offer culture-based treatment. As mentioned earlier, there is some emerging evidence that therapeutic communities are effective in reducing the risk of reoffending. An evaluation of the MFUs (at five different prisons) conducted by the New Zealand Department of Corrections (2009b) used a range of data acquisition methods, including, interviews with participants, focus groups with participants, and psychometric measures; specifically, the Psychological Inventory of Criminal Thinking Styles (Walters, 2006) and the University of Rhode Island Change Assessment Scale (McConnaughy, Prochaska and Velicer, 1983). Of the 51 MFU participants, 69% were serving sentences for either sexual or violent offences. The evaluation found that placement in an MFU led to the acquisition and development of cultural knowledge and culture-centred skills. Further, spending time in the MFU seemed to enhance an offender's sense of cultural identity.

Another important finding was that the family-focused approach which is an important aspect of MFU involvement appeared to strengthen familial ties and improve relationships with family members. The Department highlighted the importance of this finding, pointing out that research has shown that good relationships with family members and a stable family environment lead to a reduction in the likelihood of reoffending. The evaluation also found that participation in Māori-focused activities led to reductions in the presence of antisocial attitudes and beliefs. However, the recidivism data was less clear, perhaps because of the small sample size and limited statistical power. Although, the MFU participants reoffended at a lower rate than those in the matched control group, the difference was not statistically significant.

The Māori Therapeutic Programme (MTP) is the key treatment programme which is provided in the MFU (New Zealand Department of Corrections, 2009b). As explained by the Department, the MTP takes place over 10 weeks and involves several group-based sessions per week. The programme content is very similar to the content of the mainstream programmes; it follows a relapse prevention model and aims to enhance offenders' understanding of the interaction between thoughts, feelings and behaviour. However, the MTP places special emphasis on Māori concepts, values and practices. The aforementioned evaluation included analysis of outcomes of 39 individuals who completed the Māori Therapeutic Programme. This analysis indicated that participants had learnt a number of useful skills, such as emotional regulation and behavioural management strategies; however, there was no evidence that this learning would be utilized in real-world situations.

Similar to the results of the MFU evaluation, although MTP participants were found to have lower levels of recidivism than the matched controls, the difference in recidivism was not statistically significant. However, the researchers noted that the lack of statistical significance may have been due to the relatively small sample size. Also, with regard to both the MTP and MFU results, they point out that a significant number of the offenders in the MFU would have been assessed as having a low risk of recidivism, which would have made it more difficult to measure any drop in recidivism. Another important finding of the evaluation was that combining the MTP and MFU (in other words, undertaking the MTP in the MFU) appeared to be particularly beneficial.

Saili Matagi Like Māori, Pacific Island people are over-represented in the New Zealand Corrections system. While they make up 6% of the general population, they comprise 11% of individuals in prison (New Zealand Department of Corrections, 2005). Therefore, a programme designed specifically to meet the needs of Pacific Island people has been developed. This programme, termed Saili Matagi (translated as 'in search of winds') is a prison-based violence prevention programme which combines Western cognitive behavioural therapy and 'Pacific values, beliefs and concepts that are familiar to Pacific offenders' (New Zealand Department of Corrections, 2005, p. 4). Similar to the MTP, the Saili Matagi is delivered in a Pacific Focus Unit; thus, involvement in the programme is supported by involvement in a Pacific-based therapeutic community.

As explained by the Department (2005), the three key objectives of Saili Matagi are to: (i) assist Pacific Island offenders in identifying and changing the attitudes and beliefs that contributed to their offending, (ii) enhance the responsivity of Pacific Island offenders so that they are better prepared for participation in mainstream criminogenic programmes, and (iii) reduce the likelihood of future violence and future offending. The Saili Matagi programme is a 180 hour group-based intervention for high-risk offenders, which runs over 28 weeks. It is delivered by two trained facilitators who are familiar with the relevant Pacific Island cultural concepts and ideas (New Zealand Department of Corrections, 2005).

Although it appears that Saili Matagi has not yet been formally evaluated, preliminary research by the New Zealand Department of Corrections found that prison staff reported that individuals involved in the programme demonstrated noticeable improvements in their behaviour within the prison environment.

The Australian Approach

Similar to other colonial nations, including Canada, the Aboriginal people of Australia are over-represented in the Australian criminal justice system. While indigenous people make up less than 2% of the total Australian population, they comprise about 20% of the prison population (Howells *et al.*, 2004; see also Chapter 22, this volume) and they are 10–14 times more likely to be incarcerated than non-indigenous Australians (Jones *et al.*, 2002). However, there are significant differences in percentages of Aboriginal people across the different Australian states. For example, in the Northern Territory, indigenous people comprise about 32% of the total population and about 82% of the prison population (Jones *et al.*, 2010).

In recent years, the Australian government has attempted to improve the situation for Aboriginal people and to make amends for past injustices. For example, in 1991, the Council for Aboriginal Reconciliation Act was passed and this represented the beginning of a process of reconciliation between colonists and the indigenous people (Short, 2003). This commitment to social justice contributed to widespread changes within Australian government departments, including the Australian Departments of Justice (of which each state has their own). For instance, the Victorian Department of Justice has an agreement with the Koori people and their web site refers to: 'The development of an agreed direction for delivering a culturally-responsive justice system for Koories, encapsulated in the *Victorian Aboriginal Justice Agreement* (AJA), evolved as part of a more extensive dialogue to address inequality on a national level' (Victorian Department of Justice, 2011).

Researchers have observed that there are a range of challenges in providing culturally appropriate treatment to Aboriginal Australians. For instance, Howells and colleagues (Howells *et al.*, 2004) report that there are more than 600 different tribal groups in Australia and that it is therefore important not to assume that all Aboriginal people have the same needs. Furthermore, Howells and colleagues (2004) suggest that treatment programmes for offenders need to be designed with this diversity in mind. Other challenges are also identified by these researchers, including the fact that indigenous offenders tend to receive short sentences, that they tend to drop out of programmes and that they are often uncomfortable with non-indigenous facilitators. Other researchers have pointed to the lack of relevance of traditional correctional models. For example, Jones *et al.* (2010) state that Australian Aboriginal offenders have multiple unique needs which do not fit within the predominant 'criminogenic needs' model and that the GLM may be a better fit. For example, they suggest that indigenous offender's needs may manifest on a variety of levels – individual, community and historical – and that they are therefore better accounted for by a Good Lives conceptualization.

As illustrated later, only a handful of indigenous treatment programmes have been developed to date and very few evaluations have been completed. With regard to the limited research that is available, Heseltine and colleagues (Heseltine, Sarre and Day, 2010, p. 84) have stated: 'There is an urgent need for Australian evaluations of Indigenous offender rehabilitation programs.' One interesting aspect of the situation in Australia is the differences in the number and types of programmes that have been developed across different states, to some extent, probably reflect the location of indigenous populations. While Western Australia has four different programmes, Tasmania has none and Northern Territories and South Australia have only one each (Heseltine, Sarre and Day, 2010). As explained by Heseltine and colleagues, across Australia there are programmes for substance abuse, violence, sexual offending, and there are interventions which aim to develop cognitive skills. As mentioned earlier, it was considered useful to include Australia in this discussion because it is a good example of a jurisdiction that is in the early stages of indigenous programme development.

Programmes for Indigenous Offenders

The Indigenous Family Violence Offender Program

As outlined by White (2006), the Indigenous Family Violence Offender Program (IFVOP) is a 50 hour group-based programme which is delivered in the community in the Northern Territory and in Western Australia. The programme is available as an alternative sentence to imprisonment for individuals who commit domestic violence offences. It covers a range of topics, including: values and beliefs, intergenerational violence, anger management, motivation to change, and relationships. Further, the IFVOP is delivered by trained indigenous facilitators. Interestingly, separate programmes are available for both males and females and they also offer support groups for partners of perpetrators. Also, the information provided by White (2006) suggests that the programme depends on communication and cooperation between a range of agencies and organizations, including, the Police, the Court system and Community Corrections.

Unfortunately, there is little information available that describes the cultural elements of this programme, although White states that one of the key elements is educating offenders so that they come to understand that family violence is incompatible with indigenous culture and traditions. It appears that no systematic evaluations of this programme have been conducted to date; however, feedback from those involved in the programme has been positive (Calma, 2007). Also, White (2006) states that of the more than 40 men who had completed the programme at that time, only three had reoffended.

Indigenous Sexual Offender Programmes

The Indigenous Sexual Offending Programme is available to Aboriginal and Torres Strait Islander men who have committed a sexual offence (Queensland Corrective Services, 2009). As explained by Queensland Corrective Services, depending on their unique rehabilitative needs and risk levels, participants spend up to nine months engaged in the programme. The Indigenous Medium Intensity Sex Offender Programme (IMISOP) is a 22-week programme, while the Indigenous High Intensity Sex Offender Programme (IHISOP) is a 39-week programme (Smallbone and McHugh, 2010). The programme combines cognitive behaviour therapy with indigenous concepts and customs with the aim of promoting a pro-social lifestyle. A cultural advisor is included in the delivery team, in order to monitor the integrity of the cultural content. Interestingly, this programme utilizes a rolling format, which means that individuals gain entry to the programme when another participant leaves. According to Heseltine, Sarre and Day (2010), a similar programme is available in Western Australia.

Queensland Corrective Services (2009) reported the results of a small preliminary evaluation which looked at the involvement of 21 participants who participated in either the IMISOP or the IHISOP. The evaluation involved analysis of the participants' pre-test and post-test scores across three risk domains: coping skills, long-term goals and release plans. Results showed that in all three domains there was statistically significant improvement, although some problems in all of these areas were still evident. Immediately before treatment, the indigenous offenders were generally found to have impracticable release plans and some unobtainable long-term goals. In contrast, post-treatment it was found that the participants' release plans and long-term goals were more realistic and achievable, with fewer obstacles. No other factors were included in the evaluation.

Conclusion

There are a number of components that are similar across the diverse programmes that have been described herein. All of the programmes that have been included in this chapter combine cultural content with traditional cognitive behavioural therapy. They generally take a holistic approach to conceptualizing human behaviour; that is, they emphasize the interrelatedness of various aspects of human psychology. Furthermore, they typically see family and community as being especially important in peoples' recovery, and they therefore attempt to reconnect participants with their families and communities. Also, they tend to include a spiritual component which encourages participants to consider the meaning and purpose of their lives. Perhaps more obviously, they all include the use of cultural concepts and traditions which the participants are likely to be familiar with.

According to both the RNR model and the Good Lives approach, including a cultural focus should be a useful addition to cognitive behavioural treatment approaches, and the limited research available to date suggests that this is the case. The few evaluations that have been carried out provide preliminary evidence that the programmes are effective; offenders who take part appear to show improvements in terms of their rehabilitative needs and their risk of reoffending. However, while the results of the various evaluations are consistent, they are too limited in their scope to provide any definitive answers at this point. Also, while a number of studies have included control and comparison groups, some of these groups were simply matched on variables such as ethnicity and age and did not provide an alternative form of treatment. Thus, in regard to some evaluations, it remains unclear if the results found were due to the cultural aspects of treatment or simply to treatment per se. Clearly, there is a pressing need for further analysis in this area. In particular, studies that utilize larger samples, monitor reoffending over greater time periods, and include control groups would be particularly beneficial.

Another important area for future research is the investigation of the various factors that contribute to treatment efficacy. For example, it would be interesting to explore whether the use of cultural concepts is particularly important or whether treatment gains are related to enhanced engagement. For instance, it may be the case that engagement is improved if facilitators come from a similar cultural background as the participants. Alternatively, treatment gains may be associated with improvements in self-concept and self-identity due to the prominence that is given to the participants' cultural understandings. At this point, it remains unclear what is contributing to the apparent efficacy of culture-focused programmes; thus, this remains an important area for future research.

References

Andrews, D.A. and Bonta, J. (1998) *The Psychology of Criminal Conduct*, Anderson Publishing, Cincinatti.
Andrews, D.A. and Bonta, J. (2003) *The Psychology of Criminal Conduct*, 3rd edn, Anderson Publishing, Cincinatti.
Barbaree, H. (1991) Denial and minimization among sex offenders: assessment and treatment outcome. *Forum on Corrections Research*, 3 (4), 30–33.
Brazil, A. (2009) *The Aboriginal Offender Substance Abuse Program: A Holistic Intervention*, Addictions Research Centre, Correctional Service Canada, Ottawa.
Calma, T. (2007) Communities Confronting Family Violence: Promising Practices and Valuable Lessons. *Social Justice Report*. http://www.hreoc.gov.au (accessed 26 December 2012).
Correctional Service of Canada (2011) Healing lodges for Aboriginal offenders. http://www.csc-scc.gc.ca (accessed 26 December 2012).
Durrant, R. and Thakker, J. (2003) *Substance Use and Abuse: Cultural and Historical Perspectives*, Sage Publications, Thousand Oaks.
Glover, M. (2005) Analysing smoking using Te Whare Tapa Wha. *New Zealand Journal of Psychology*, 34, 13–19.

Green, B.L. (2010) Culture is treatment: considering pedagogy in the care of aboriginal people. *Journal of Psychosocial Nursing*, 48, 27–34.

Hanson, K. (2001) A structured approach to evaluating change among sexual offenders. *Sexual Abuse: A Journal of Research and Treatment*, 13 (2), 105–120.

Heseltine, K., Sarre, R. and Day, A. (2010) *Prison-Based Correctional Offender Rehabilitation Programs: The 2009 National Picture in Australia*, Australian Institute of Criminology, Canberra.

Howells, K., Heseltine, K., Sarre, R. *et al.* (2004) Correctional Offender Treatment Programs: The National Picture in Australia. Report for the Criminology Research Council. http://www.criminologyresearchcouncil.gov.au/reports/200203-04.html (accessed on 16 January 2013).

Huriwai, T., Robertson, P.J., Armstrong, D. *et al.* (2001) Whanaungatanga – a process in the treatment of Māori with alcohol- and drug-use related problems. *Substance Use and Misuse*, 36, 1033–1051.

Jones, R., Masters, M., Griffiths, A. and Moulday, N. (2002) Culturally relevant assessment of indigenous offenders: literature review. *Australian Psychologist*, 37, 187–197.

Jones, T., Munro, B., Rowbottom, G. and Creighton, W. (2010) Indigenous specific programs. *Australian Journal of Correctional Staff Development*, 5, 1–7.

Kirmayer, L.J., Brass, G.M. and Tait, C.L. (2000) The mental health of aboriginal peoples: transformations of identity community. *Canadian Journal of Psychiatry*, 45, 607–616.

Kuhn, T. (1962) *The Structure of Scientific Revolutions*, The University of Chicago Press, Chicago.

Kunic, D. and Varis, D.D. (2009) *The Aboriginal Offender Substance Abuse Program (AOSAP): Examining the Effects of Successful Completion on Post-Release Outcomes*, Research Branch, Correctional Service of Canada, Ottawa.

Manna, L. (2001) *Bi-culturalism in Practice, "Te Pounamu:" Integration of a Māori Model with Traditional Clinical Assessment Processes*. The Proceedings of the National Māori Graduates of Psychology Symposium. Waikato, New Zealand.

Marie, D., Forsyth, D. and Miles, L.K. (2004) Categorical ethnicity and mental health literacy in New Zealand. *Ethnicity and Health*, 9, 225–252.

Martel, J., Brassard, R. and Jaccoud, M. (2011) When two worlds collide: aboriginal risk management in Canadian corrections. *British Journal of Criminology*, 51, 235–255.

Maruna, S. (2001) *Making Good: How Ex-Convicts Reform and Rebuild Their Lives*, American Psychological Association, Washington, DC.

Maruna, S. and Roy, K. (2007) Amputation or reconstruction? Notes on the concept of "knifing off" and desistance from crime. *Journal of Contemporary Criminal Justice*, 23, 104–124.

Maynard, K., Coebergh, B., Anstiss, B. *et al.* (1999) Ki te Arotu: toward a new assessment – the identification of cultural factors which may pre-dispose Māori to crime. *Social Policy Journal of New Zealand*, 13, 43–58.

McConnaughy, E.A., Prochaska, J.O. and Velicer, W.F. (1983) Stages of change in psychotherapy: measurement and sample profiles. *Psychotherapy: Theory, Research, and Practice*, 20, 368–375.

Merriam-Webster Dictionary (2011) Culture. www.Merriam-Webster.com (accessed 26 December 2012).

Monchalin, L. (2010) Canadian aboriginal peoples victimization, offending and its prevention: gathering the evidence. *Crime Prevention and Community Safety*, 12, 119–132.

Nathan, L., Wilson, N. and Hillman, D. (2003). Te Whakakotahitanga: an evaluation of the Te Piriti Special Treatment Programme for child sex offenders. http://www.corrections.govt.nz/research (accessed 26 December 2012).

New Zealand Department of Corrections (2005) Ministerial review of Department of Corrections Saili Matagi (Pacific Violence Prevention Programme). http://www.corrections.govt.nz/research (accessed 26 December 2012).

New Zealand Department of Corrections (2008) Reducing re-offending through Te Ao Māori. http://www.corrections.govt.nz/news-and-publications/statutory-reports/business-improvement-initiatives/maori-strategic-plan-2008-2013/reducing-re-offending-through-te-ao-hurihuri.html (accessed on 16 January 2013).

New Zealand Department of Corrections (2009a) What works now? A review and update of research evidence relevant to offender rehabilitation practices within the Department of Corrections. http://www.corrections.govt.nz/research (accessed 26 December 2012).

New Zealand Department of Corrections (2009b) Māori Focus Units and Māori Therapeutic Programmes: *Evaluation Report*. http://www.corrections.govt.nz/research (accessed 26 December 2012).

Nielson, M.O. (2003) Canadian aboriginal healing lodges: a model for the United States. *Prison Journal*, 83, 67–89.

Oxford English Dictionary (2011) Culture. www.oxforddictionaries.com (accessed 26 December 2012).

Prochaska, J.O., DiClemente, C.C. and Norcross, J.C. (1992) In search of how people change. Applications to addictive behaviors. *American Psychologist*, 47, 1102–1114.

Queensland Corrective Services (2009) Indigenous sexual offending program: fact sheet. http://www.healthinfonet.ecu.edu.au/key-resources/programs-projects (accessed 26 December 2012).

Rudolph, S.M. and Epstein, M.H. (2000) Empowering children and families through strength-based assessment. *Reclaiming Children and Youth*, 8, 207–209.

Short, D. (2003) Australian 'Aboriginal' reconciliation: the latest phase in the Colonial Project1. *Citizenship Studies*, 7, 291–312.

Smallbone, S. and McHugh, M. (2010) Outcomes of Queensland Corrective Services Sexual Offender Treatment Programs. Unpublished report. Griffith University.

Stewart, L.A., Hamilton, E., Wilton, G. *et al.* (2009a) An Examination of the Effectiveness of Tupiq: A Culturally Specific Program for Inuit Sex Offenders. *Research Rep. no. R-213*. Correctional Service Canada, Ottawa.

Stewart, L.A., Hamilton, E., Wilton, G. *et al.* (2009b) An examination of the effectiveness of Tupiq: a culturally specific program for inuit sex offenders. Research at a glance. http://publications.gc.ca/collections/collection_2011/scc-csc/PS83-5-R213-eng.pdf (accessed 26 December 2012).

Trevethan, S., Moore, J.-P. and Naqitarvik, L. (2004) *The Tupik Program for Inuit Offenders: A Preliminary Investigation*, Research Branch, Correctional Service of Canada, Ottawa.

Trevethan, S., Moore, J.-P. and Allegri, N. (2005) *The "In Search of Your Warrior" Program for Aboriginal Offenders: A Preliminary Evaluation*, (R140), Correctional Service Canada, Ottawa.

Valor-Segura, I., Exposito, F. and Moya, M. (2011) Victim blaming and exoneration of the perpetrator in domestic violence: the role of beliefs in a just world and ambivalent sexism. *Spanish Journal of Psychology*, 14, 195–206.

Victorian Department of Justice (2011) Aboriginal Justice. http://www.justice.vic.gov.au (accessed 26 December 2012).

Walters, G.D. (2006) Proactive and Reactive Composite Scales for the Psychological Inventory of Criminal Thinking Styles (PICTS). *Journal of Offender Rehabilitation*, 42, 23–36.

Ward, T. (2002) Good lives and the rehabilitation of sexual offenders: promises and problems. *Aggression and Violent Behavior*, 7, 513–528.

Ward, T. and Gannon, T.A. (2006) Rehabilitation, etiology, and self-regulation: the Good Lives Model of sexual offender treatment. *Aggression and Violent Behaviour*, 11, 77–94.

Ward, T. and Stewart, C.A. (2003) The treatment of sexual offenders: risk management and good lives. *Professional Psychology: Research and Practice*, 34, 353–360.

Ward, T., Mann, R. and Gannon, T. (2007) Good Lives Model of offender rehabilitation: clinical implications. *Aggression and Violent Behaviour*, 12, 87–107.

Ward, T., Melser, J. and Yates, P.M. (2007) Reconstructing the Risk Need Responsivity Model: a theoretical elaboration and evaluation. *Aggression and Violent Behavior*, 12, 208–228.

Ward, T., Gannon, T.A. and Yates, P.M. (2008) The treatment of offenders: current practice and new developments with an emphasis on sex offenders. *International Review of Victimology*, 15, 179–204.

Ware, J., Frost, A. and Hoy, A. (2009) A review of the use of therapeutic communities with sexual offenders. *International Journal of Comparative Criminology*, 54, 721–742.

Wayland, S. (1997) Immigration, multiculturalism, and national identity in Canada. *International Journal on Group Rights*, 5, 33–58.

White, D. (2006) Indigenous Family Violence Offender Program: the Ngiu experience. http:// yodelaustralia.com.au/sites/5530 (accessed 26 December 2012).

Whitehead, P., Ward, T. and Collie, R. (2007) Time for a change: applying the good lives model of rehabilitation to a high-risk violent offender. *International Journal of Offender Therapy and Comparative Criminology*, 51, 578–598.

Willis, G.M., Yates, P.M., Gannon, T.A. and Ward, T. (2012) How to integrate the Good Lives Model into treatment programs for sexual offending: an introduction and overview. *Sexual Abuse: A Journal of Research and Treatment*.

Wilson, R. and Yates, P. (2009) Effective interventions and the good lives model: maximising treatment gains for sexual offenders. *Aggression and Violent Behaviour*, 14, 157–161.

Wong, Y.J. (2006) Strength-centred therapy: a social constructionist, virtues-based psychotherapy. *Psychotherapy: Theory, Research, Practice, Training*, 2, 133–146.

22

An Australasian Approach to Offender Rehabilitation

Andrew Day[1] and Rachael M. Collie[2]

[1]Deakin University, Australia
[2]University of Minnesota, USA

Introduction

The development of offender rehabilitation programmes in Australasia has, in many ways, paralleled that which has occurred in other Western countries. Not only is public support for rehabilitative ideals now more clearly enshrined in public policy than perhaps at any time in the past, but recent years have seen significant developments in the provision of offender rehabilitation programmes in both prison and community settings. In addition to the suite of correctional[1] programmes that are now routinely offered to sexual, violent and substance using offenders, a range of diversionary options are also available for lower-risk offenders through specialist or problem-oriented courts, such as drug courts, family or domestic violence courts, Indigenous courts and mental health courts (Lim and Day, 2013; Payne, 2005). This chapter offers an overview of the offender rehabilitation programmes currently offered by correctional services and considers some of the key challenges that currently face rehabilitation providers. We start by providing an overview of Australasian jurisdictions, before outlining the types of programme that are currently offered. We conclude the chapter with a discussion of some of the distinctive features of offender rehabilitation in Australasia, and comment on some of the challenges that face service providers in this area.

Australasian Jurisdictions: An Overview

Australasia is a term used to refer to Australia, New Zealand and neighbouring islands in the South Pacific. Correctional services in the Pacific Islands have yet to develop rehabilitation policies and so are not considered in this chapter. Although there are a number of similarities between Australia and New Zealand, there are also distinctive jurisdictional and demographic

---

[1] In Australasia, correctional services have responsibility for both custodial (prison) and community (probation and parole) programmes.

What Works in Offender Rehabilitation: An Evidence-Based Approach to Assessment and Treatment,
First Edition. Edited by Leam A. Craig, Louise Dixon and Theresa A. Gannon.
© 2013 John Wiley & Sons, Ltd. Published 2013 by John Wiley & Sons, Ltd.

differences, and approaches to offender services in each country have developed independently. As such, it is not possible to make direct comparisons between either the legal systems or types of rehabilitation that are offered in each country. Perhaps most significantly, Australia is a much larger country than New Zealand which is divided into seven states and territories. Parliamentary authority for the delivery of correctional services across Australia changes markedly from jurisdiction to jurisdiction, sometimes appearing in the relevant criminal statutes, sometimes in correctional legislation, and sometimes in the various Acts related to sentencing. In addition, policy specifics in some jurisdictions are left principally to departmental development and implementation (see Heseltine, Sarre and Day, 2011). In contrast, New Zealand has national legislation and only one correctional service agency.

Australia, with a total population of just over 22 million, has almost 85 500 adult persons serving correctional services orders, with just under one-third of these in prison (September 2009 figures, Australian Bureau of Statistics, 2010). In New Zealand (with a total population of 4.4 million), there were over 47 000 persons on correctional sentences and orders in the same year, although over half of these were serving community work sentences (New Zealand Ministry of Justice, 2010). These imprisonment rates across Australasia exceed those of many other Western countries (Sarre, 2009), and continue to rise (Australian Bureau of Statistics, 2009) with offenders now serving longer sentences than at any time in the past (Freiberg, 2005; New Zealand Ministry of Justice, 2011). The recent introduction of legislation in both countries to allow mandatory minimum sentences, consecutive (and in some circumstances indefinite) sentences and increased maximum penalties is expected to ensure that these trends will continue.

A particularly distinctive feature of the Australasian correctional population is the over-representation of Indigenous cultural groups, and the development of culturally appropriate programmes is a significant aspect of rehabilitation in these jurisdictions (see also Chapter 21). The term 'Indigenous' is most commonly used in Australia to refer to both Aboriginal and Torres Strait Islander peoples (groups which comprise more than 600 different cultures and tribal groups), and in New Zealand to those who identify as from Māori descent. Rates of Indigenous imprisonment vary considerably across jurisdiction. However, the latest figures show that just over one quarter (26%) of all prisoners in Australia identify as from Indigenous cultural backgrounds, meaning that Indigenous adults were 13.9 times more likely to be imprisoned in Australia during 2009 than those from other cultural backgrounds (Australian Bureau of Statistics, 2010). In New Zealand, Māori make up approximately 15% of the population, but 50% of the male and 60% of the female prison populations (New Zealand Department of Corrections, 2007; New Zealand Ministry of Justice, 2010). The rates are lower, but still elevated, for those who are serving community-based sentences (New Zealand Department of Corrections, 2010). Māori offenders are also more likely to be re-convicted and re-imprisoned than their New Zealand European and Pacific counterparts (Nadesu, 2009a, b) and are disproportionately over-represented in high-risk offender groups (Wilson, 2004).

Australasian Rehabilitation Programmes

The similarities in service provision between States and Territories in Australia are great; most, if not all, offer programmes that are dedicated towards reducing risk in sexual and violent offenders, as well as addressing more general causes of offending. Each of the jurisdictions has made a policy commitment to the delivery of programmes that are congruent with the

Risk-Needs-Responsivity (RNR) model described in this book. Over the last five years in particular, it has been observed that there appears be an increased confidence, and indeed success, in moving from theory to policy and through to practice, especially in relation to the delivery of intensive sexual and violent offender treatment programmes (Heseltine, Sarre and Day, 2011). To illustrate, four Australian jurisdictions currently offer intensive violent offender treatment programmes (over 180 hours face-to-face contact), with some also offering moderate-intensity programmes (between 100 and 130 hours). Each jurisdiction offers sexual offender treatment programmes, with specialist programmes also available for offenders with cognitive disabilities, Indigenous offenders, and those who deny their offences (Heseltine, Sarre and Day, 2011).

In New Zealand, the Department of Corrections has developed a number of specialized prison-based programmes to address sexual and violent offending over the last 20 years, with more recent emphasis given to the development of standardized general offender and drug treatment programmes for medium- and high-risk recidivist offenders. Within New Zealand prisons, special treatment or 'focus' units are the predominant model for the delivery of high-intensity or specialized programmes. Currently, two special treatment units for child sexual offenders exist, four units for high-risk violent or generally recidivist offenders, nine drug treatment units, five Māori focus units, one Pacific focus unit, and three youth units. Each unit accommodates between 30 and 60 inmates, with placement contingent on participation in the relevant programmes. In contrast, programmes for medium-risk offenders are delivered as stand-alone programmes in mainstream facilities throughout most prisons. The programmes that are offered in New Zealand are illustrated in Table 22.1, compiled from information available in the public domain (New Zealand Department of Corrections, 2006, 2011) and the second author's knowledge of the programmes. The New Zealand programmes are also representative of the types of programme that are available in Australia which are described in full by Heseltine, Sarre and Day, 2011).

The high- and medium-risk offender programmes that are currently available in both Australia and New Zealand typically cover the following content areas (with higher-risk programmes spending longer on the same material than the medium-risk programmes, allowing greater time for practice and attention to group process and motivational issues): (i) Orientation (i.e., group formation, goal setting and introduction to mindfulness skills); (ii) Offence Mapping (i.e., activities to aid identification of individual risk factors and patterns, and development of a personalized programme treatment plan); (iii) Cognitive Restructuring (i.e., psycho-education and activities to facilitate identification and questioning of antisocial attitudes and distortions); (iv) Distress Tolerance Skills; (v) Managing Emotions (i.e., emotion regulation and mindfulness skills); (vi) Substance Abuse (i.e., psycho-education to facilitate substance abuse recognition and coping strategies); (vii) Relationship Skills (i.e., examination of the role of pro-criminal associates as well as communication and conflict resolution skills); and (viii) Safety Planning (i.e., revisiting relapse prevention skills learnt in the programme and developing safety plans). A module on Māori mental health is also included in some of the New Zealand special treatment unit programmes.

Although the Good Lives Model (Ward and Stewart, 2003; Chapter 17, this volume) is often referred to in programme theory manuals and appears to be having an influence on programme design and delivery, it is the RNR model (Andrews and Dowden, 2007) that is the dominant paradigm underlying offender rehabilitation in both New Zealand and Australia. For example, in keeping with the *risk principle*, programmes are (in the main) intended for medium- and high-risk offenders with treatment intensity (duration) matched to the assessed

Table 22.1 Overview of New Zealand sexual, violent, general offending and motivational enhancement programmes (Information summarized from New Zealand Department of Corrections, 2011)

Programme	Target	Intensity	Other information
Special Treatment Units For Child Sexual Offenders (Kia Marama and Te Piriti Programmes)	Imprisoned men with convictions for sexual offences against children (i.e., victims 16 years or under) and identified as low-medium or greater risk for sexual re-offending	*Programme 1 (Kia Marama):* approximately 300 hours of group treatment (33 weeks, three sessions per week, 2½ to 3 hour sessions) *Programme 2 (Te Piriti):* open group format, men stay until their identified sexual offending rehabilitation needs have been adequately addressed	Delivered at two special treatment units that also operate a modified therapeutic community and include pre-treatment and maintenance groups An adapted programme is offered each year at Te Piriti for sexual offenders with intellectual difficulties
Adult Sexual Offender Treatment Programme (ASOTP)	Imprisoned men convicted of sexual offence against an adult victim and identified at medium/high or greater risk of sexual re-offending	300 hours of group treatment delivered in 120 sessions (2½ hour sessions typically four times per week) over eight-months	Delivered within the three high-risk offender special treatment units
Community-Based Sexual Offender Programmes (Safe Network and STOP Programmes)	Offenders with convictions or sexual offences against children (i.e., victims 16 years or under) who are serving community-based sentences	12–24 months of weekly group-based treatment alongside other intervention modalities (e.g., individual, family)	Range of youth and other specialized programmes provided at the various programme sites Delivered by independent (non-government) organizations with funding from Community Probation referrals amongst other sources
Violence Prevention Unit Rehabilitation Programme (VPU)	Imprisoned men with pattern of serious violence and identified as high risk of re-offending	300 hours of group treatment delivered in 120 sessions (2½ hour sessions typically four times per week) over eight-months	Delivered at one special treatment unit (Te Whare Manakitanga) in which a modified therapeutic community model is in development
Special Treatment Unit Rehabilitation Programme (STURP)	Imprisoned men identified as at high risk of re-offending who do not meet criteria for inclusion in specialized violent or sexual offender rehabilitation programmes	300 hours of group treatment delivered in 120 sessions (2½ hour sessions typically four times per week) over eight-months	Delivered at three special treatment units

(Continued)

Table 22.1   (cont'd)

Programme	Target	Intensity	Other information
Medium-Intensity Rehabilitation Programme (MIRP)	Imprisoned and community-sentenced men identified as medium risk of re-offending	100 hours of group treatment delivered in 53 sessions (2½ hour sessions typically four times per week) over three-months	Delivered in mainstream Prison and Probation settings
Kowhiritanga Women's Rehabilitation Programme	Imprisoned and community-based women offenders identified as medium risk of re-offending	100 hours of group treatment delivered in 40 sessions (2½ hour sessions typically four times per week) over 10 weeks	Up to 10 participants are included in a group that is co-facilitated by a licensed psychologist and trained facilitator
Maori Therapeutic Programme (MTP)	Imprisoned men who reside within specialist Maori Focus Units within five mainstream prisons	100 hours of group treatment delivered in 40 sessions over 10 weeks (2½ hour sessions typically four times per week)	Similar content to the other rehabilitation programmes but delivered by a Maori facilitator within Maori Focus Unit
	Sexual and high-risk offenders are expected to attend the more intensive rehabilitation programmes instead of or in addition to this programme		Programme includes greater cultural concepts and processes and is intended to follow completion of a Tikanga Maori (Customs and Traditions) Programme at the unit
Sali Matagi (Pacific Men's Violence Prevention) Programme	Imprisoned Pacific Nation men who have violent convictions and are identified as medium to high risk of violent re-offending	216 hours of group treatment delivered in 72 sessions (2½–3 hour sessions, three to four times per week)	Delivered at one prison site within a specialist Pacific Focus Unit. Similar in focus to the mainstream rehabilitation programmes but delivered by Pacific Nation facilitators using Pacific concepts and practices.
Short Rehabilitation Programmes for Men and Women (SRP-M and SRP-W)	Imprisoned and community-based men and women offenders identified as medium risk of re-offending who cannot complete medium-intensity programmes due to short sentence length or unavailability of programmes	45 hours delivered in 18 sessions (2½ hours per session typically four per week) over 4½ weeks	Delivered in mainstream Prison and Probation settings to same-sex small groups of up to three participants

Table 22.1 *(cont'd)*

Programme	Target	Intensity	Other information
Drug Use Treatment Units	Imprisoned men and women identified as medium or high risk of re-offending with substance abuse problems When an offender's substance abuse problem is identified as the primary rehabilitation need referral to a DTU programme is prioritized	Six-month programmes are offered at six prison sites, one of which is a women's prison, whilst three-month programmes are offered at three other sites.	Operate as therapeutic communities (TCs) with structured programming delivered within the TC model Delivered by contracted community-based alcohol and drug treatment agencies Can be completed before or after other rehabilitation programmes where multiple needs identified and time available within sentence
Focus Youth Offender Programme	Imprisoned male youth residing in the specialist youth units (i.e., all under 18-year-old and vulnerable 18–19-year-old prisoners) who are identified as medium risk of re-offending	Three independent but linked group-based modules (i.e., motivation focus, basic focus, and advanced focus) each 10–12 weeks duration (1½ hour sessions two to four times a week)	Delivered by a licensed psychologist or trained facilitator
Short Motivational Programme	Imprisoned and community-based men and women offenders who are unwilling to attend a rehabilitation programme to address their identified rehabilitation needs	5 hours (weekly 1-hour sessions for five weeks)	Individual sessions with a licensed psychologist or trained facilitator that, amongst other things, examine simple offence chains, the costs and benefits of offending and creating a Change Plan that involves referral to appropriate programmes
Tikanga Maori (Customs and Traditions) Programme	Imprisoned and community-based men and women offenders who identify as Maori and are assessed as having motivational needs, although most offenders who choose to do so can have referral to this programme included in their sentence plan	60–80 hour group-based programme	Delivered by a Maori cultural provider or agency that covers Maori philosophy, values, knowledge and practices. The intention is that through the regeneration of a pro-social Maori cultural identity, values and esteem, offenders will have increased motivation for achieving pro-social change through rehabilitation programme participation

level of risk of re-offence. The high-risk offender programmes, for example, provide up to three times the treatment contact hours as the medium-risk offender programmes. In keeping with the *need principle*, the programmes seek to address dynamic risk factors (e.g., antisocial attitudes, problematic thinking and emotions, problem-solving difficulties, substance abuse, relationship issues including criminal associations and, in the case of sexual offenders, deviant sexual arousal and victim empathy).

The focus is the same for those rehabilitation programmes delivered within the specialist cultural units in New Zealand (i.e., Māori Focus Units and Pacific Focus Unit) and for Indigenous offenders in Australia (see Chapter 21). In the main, Indigenous ethnicity is approached as a treatment *responsivity* issue that, when appropriately addressed, ought to allow offenders to benefit more from mainstream rehabilitation programmes. In practice, culturally safe terms, concepts, metaphors, and to a limited extent, processes are provided or substituted for their (roughly) Western psychological equivalent.

There is increasing recognition that female offenders have distinctive areas of criminogenic need that influence their rehabilitative needs (see Van Voorhis *et al.*, 2008). Gender-responsive risk factors that have been proposed include dysfunctional relationships, family conflict, parental stress, child abuse and adult victimization, and mental health issues. Australian programmes for female offenders include POISE (a 120 hour substance use programme offered in New South Wales), the Women's Substance Use Programme (Western Australia) targeting substance use, and 'Out of the Dark' (offered in New South Wales and Victoria), a programme that targets issues associated with domestic violence victimization. General offender ('Making Choices'), cognitive skills, and substance use programmes have also been adapted for use with female prisoners (see Heseltine, Sarre and Day, 2011). In New Zealand, a medium-intensity general offending programme, a drug treatment programme and a short-rehabilitation and motivational programme are available (see Table 22.1) and provided in a women-only group format. Thus, in contrast to programming for male offenders, no offence-specific programmes are provided for women with serious violent or sexually violent index offences in Australasia. Rather, individual psychological assessment and treatment appear to be the main approach in these instances.

In keeping with the evidence supporting the use of cognitive-behavioural treatment methods (Lipsey, Landenberger and Wilson, 2007), all of the moderate- and high-intensity therapeutic programmes utilize cognitive behavioural treatment strategies. Finally, increased awareness of the importance of maintaining high levels of treatment integrity (Andrews, 2006) has seen the development of programme standards, programme theory and delivery manuals, and standardized programme facilitator training across all jurisdictions in both countries. Formal accreditation processes and professional and cultural supervision models are available in New Zealand, whereas in Australia several jurisdictions have independently developed programme accreditation guidelines and programme standards.

Programme evaluations

A common shortcoming of many of the programmes described earlier is a lack of evaluation. The majority of programmes that are offered in Australia and New Zealand have either not been evaluated or evaluations have been undertaken but not published. Methodological problems have been evident in a number of internal evaluations, including those related to sampling and design procedures, the psychometric properties of outcome measures, the use of small or unrepresentative samples, an inadequate description of demographic information, and the absence of a comparison group or random allocation.

In Australia, although evaluation remains firmly on the agenda for most correctional agencies, very few evaluations have been completed or released into the public domain. Further, a review of the evaluation results from both adult and adolescent sexual offender treatment programmes in Australia and New Zealand treatment programmes (Magregor, 2008) concluded that 12 out of the 13 programmes were effective in reducing sexual recidivism, although the methodological limitations in some of these evaluations were acknowledged, especially in relation to obtaining comparison groups of untreated sexual offenders. There have been only three published outcome studies of sexual offender treatment in Australia, the most recent of which was the evaluation of the Victorian Sex Offender Program (Owen *et al.*, 2007). This study examined the recidivism rates of 330 offenders who entered the programme and were subsequently followed up for an average period of 4.5 years. A lower sexual recidivism rate was reported for programme completers (4%) than for non-completers (20%) and those who were removed from the programme (10%). Several one-off evaluations of New Zealand offender rehabilitation programmes have been conducted, although with few exceptions the findings have only been released in government reports. These have reported positive treatment effects for the two prison-based child sexual offender treatment programmes (Bakker *et al.*, 1998; Nathan, Wilson and Hillman, 2003) and the three main community-based sexual offender treatment programmes (Lambie and Stewart, 2003). Magregor (2008) does note, however, that a proportion of sexual offenders do bypass treatment, including high-risk violent sexual offenders and those who categorically deny responsibility for their offences. She suggests that the development of more community-based programmes for high-risk sexual offenders released on bond (or license) could help to address such gaps in treatment, especially given that this group is more likely to be subject to extended detention/supervision orders on release from custody.

A recent evaluation of the New Zealand Violence Prevention Unit programme for high-risk violent offenders by Polaschek (2011) reported the recidivism outcomes for the first 112 participants who undertook the programme since it opened in 1998 (over the first five or so years of operation). Fifty-six percent of the men who started the programme were of Māori ethnicity; however, the findings were not further disaggregated by ethnicity. The results showed that high-risk offenders who completed the programme ($n = 56$) had significantly fewer re-convictions for any offending than their matched untreated comparison group (83% versus 95%; $\varphi = 0.19$; $\chi^2(1) = 4.25$, $p = 0.04$) over an average of three and a half years of post-release follow-up. In actual case numbers, this translates to six fewer treatment completers re-offending than the comparison group. However, although the high-risk completers had fewer violent reconvictions than their control group (62% versus 72%; $\varphi = 0.11$), the difference did not reach statistical significance. Here, time to failure analyses found no significant differences between the treatment completers and the control comparison groups. Evaluation of high-risk offenders who failed to complete treatment indicated treatment non-completion had no significant deleterious effect on recidivism rate. No statistically significant effects of treatment were found for the smaller group of medium-risk offenders ($n = 26$) who also completed the programme during the evaluation period. In many respects, the impact of this intensive treatment programme for high-risk offenders is disappointing. Although a 10% reduction in any reconviction was achieved, there was no measurable impact on violent reconviction. In summary, most of the treatment completers were reconvicted, with nearly two-thirds of the treatment completers being convicted for further violence and close to half being returned to prison. As Polaschek (2011) notes, however, the programme stands out as one of the few attempts to systematically treat and measure effectiveness with such a high-risk, difficult-to-treat, offender group.

The need to establish whether programmes that are delivered in Australasia are effective is highlighted when one considers the genuine uncertainty that exists about the extent to which current programmes successfully rehabilitate offenders who identify as from Indigenous cultural backgrounds. Heseltine, Sarre and Day (2011), when discussing programmes for Australian Aboriginal and Torres Strait Islander offenders, note that:

> There are inherent difficulties in custodial environments in the development and implementation of programmes for Indigenous offenders. These include, but are not limited to, short custodial sentences, serving sentences away from family and community support networks, mental health and substance use co-morbidity, language barriers and low level of English literacy, educational difficulty, grief and loss issues, trans-generational trauma, kinship difficulty with group composition, and the lack of Indigenous facilitators (p. 48).

Concerns have also been expressed about the appropriateness of current correctional case management processes for Indigenous offenders. For example, the use of actuarial risk assessments has been questioned, with emerging findings that not all risk assessment instruments have the same predictive validity with Canadian Aboriginal offenders (Rugge, 2006) and that the variables that may predict treatment dropout differ between Aboriginal and non-Aboriginal offenders (Nunes and Cortoni, 2006). Similar issues have been raised in an Australasian context (Hsu, Caputi and Byrne, 2009), although, once again, more research and scale validation is required before any firm conclusions can be drawn.

There is much scope for the development of evidence-based programmes here. Berenger, Weatherburn and Moffatt (2010) have shown that a 20% reduction in the rate of reappearance in the court system would halve the number of Indigenous to non-Indigenous court appearances in Australia from 1 in every 9.6 cases to 1 in every 18.6 cases. The first step for Australian rehabilitation providers in particular is to develop culturally appropriate programmes (Allard, 2010), although New Zealand corrections have probably made more progress in this area (see Chapter 21). There is some empirical support for the practice of delivering a Western approach to sexual offender treatment alongside attention to cultural knowledge and processes (Nathan, Wilson and Hillman, 2003) and equivalent treatment effects have been shown for Māori and non-Māori offenders (Bakker *et al.*, 1998; Lambie and Stewart, 2003; Nathan, Wilson and Hillman, 2003). However, it does seem that there are some critically important differences in how treatment is framed, how social and cultural issues are incorporated and in how the practitioner should relate to programme participants (see Day, forthcoming). Although there is clearly much work to be done, there are perhaps grounds for some optimism that properly designed and culturally safe programmes for offenders can have a meaningful impact on the safety of both the individual clients and the communities in which they live.

Overview

In many respects, rehabilitation programmes in Australasia have developed in ways that are consistent with those in other Western countries, and these are described in detail throughout this book. The growing evidence base supporting the positive effects of many programmes on re-offending (see Chapter 2) has led to significant investment in offender rehabilitation and correctional services in both Australia and New Zealand. Both countries currently offer a range of offence-focused rehabilitation programmes which are delivered from within broad policy frameworks that are strongly influenced by the RNR principles. Many of the challenges to the further development of offender rehabilitation in Australasia, such as the inconsistent and fragile political and public support for offender rehabilitation, will be familiar to those from other parts of the world (e.g., Wormwith *et al.*, 2007). Others, such as the challenges in delivering services to rural and geographically remote areas, are more locally specific. A notable aspect of service delivery in Australia, for example, is the size of the jurisdictions served by each administration. To illustrate, the largest Australian state, Western Australia, whilst having a population of only 2.3 million people, covers a geographical area of nearly one million square miles (roughly twice the size of Western Europe). Whilst the majority (75%) of the Western Australian population resides within one metropolitan area (the city of Perth), rehabilitation services are provided across the entire state, including to areas that are geographically remote.

Recent years have seen significant concerns expressed about both the quality and integrity of many rehabilitation programmes (e.g., Andrews, 2006; Andrews and Dowden, 2007). One review by Morgan *et al.* (2007, cited by Andrews and Bonta, 2010) of 374 North American programmes concluded that the majority (61%, *n* = 230) failed to reach even a 'basic level of adherence to good practice principles' (p. 51). It is not clear how Australasian programmes would fare if they were subjected to a rigorous assessment using audit and accreditation schemes such as the Correctional Program Assessment Inventory (CPAI-2000, Gendreau and Andrews, 2001), although in recent years the quality of programmes offered does appear to have improved substantially. In their review of Australian programmes, for example, Heseltine, Sarre and Day (2011) identified a number of areas of programme improvement over the last five years, including in relation to assessment and case management processes: the delivery of programmes of greater intensity in a custodial environment, commitment to staff training, supervision and ongoing professional development, information exchange and sharing of resources, and programme review and evaluation. Whilst the most intensive programmes (for sexual and violent offenders) probably have higher levels of integrity, stand-alone brief psycho-educational programmes continue to be routinely delivered in Australia. These programmes are commonly seen as a way of providing rehabilitation to greater numbers of offenders or as preparatory programmes for more intensive rehabilitation.

There is clearly much work to be done in the area of evaluation and quality assurance in Australasian correctional systems. Despite widespread recognition of the need to evaluate programmes in both Australia and New Zealand (especially the more intensive programmes), there is still very little published data on programme outcomes, particularly for Australian programmes. The dilemma for jurisdictions surrounds the political sensitivity of in-house evaluations, which appears to inhibit wider dissemination. Those evaluations of programmes which have been published, such as Polaschek's (2011) evaluation of the New Zealand Violence Prevention Programme, illustrate how evaluation is a key component of any continuous improvement process. Following this evaluation, significant changes were made to the programme. These sought to utilize developments in the theories about high-risk offenders to address several perceived weaknesses in the programme design and delivery (e.g., too much emphasis on offence specialization, insufficient attention to some core dynamic risk factors, not specific enough targeting of offence-related cognition, programme integrity challenges and lack of specific aftercare). Ongoing evaluation is required if any judgement is to be made about the impact of these revisions.

The issue of offender throughcare and how rehabilitation programmes should interface with pre-release, transitional and post-release services as well as inform case management in community settings (Bonta *et al.*, 2008) has been identified as requiring development for Australasian correctional services. There is some uncertainty about how the RNR framework might be applied to the range of support programmes that are commonly offered to offenders who are released from prison, and some services have seen the Good Lives Model as offering a more appropriate model of service delivery (Day, Ward and Shirley, 2011). There is no robust evidence base from which to make definitive statements about what might be considered to be good practice in this area – Borzycki (2005), for example, identified 185 different post-release interventions for prisoners in Australia and New Zealand of which only seven evaluation reports were available, none of which had been published in peer-reviewed journals. Indeed, even a cursory search of the literature in this area reveals a predominance of government reports and local evaluations, many of which do not meet the methodological standards that are required for inclusion in any systematic review of evidence-based practice (see also Chapter 21). In addition, in some parts of Australasia, these programmes are delivered by non-government organizations which typically aim to achieve multiple goals, of which a reduction in risk of re-offending is just one. As such, even the apparently simple task of describing what a re-integration programme means is far from straightforward (Borzycki and Baldry, 2003).

In conclusion, this chapter has sought to highlight the way in which offender rehabilitation in Australasia has developed over recent years. In many ways this account will be familiar to those who work in other countries; both Australia and New Zealand have developed systems of service delivery that ensure that most offenders who are identified as at medium or high risk of re-offending receive a criminogenic or offending behaviour programme. There is a need to conduct further controlled evaluations of the effects of these programmes, particularly given that a high proportion of participants will identify as from Indigenous cultural backgrounds and the distinctive (and socially important) outcomes associated with effective treatment in this area. In addition, the relatively small population of both Australia and New Zealand means that resources for programme development tend to be restricted, and as a consequence some offender groups (such as female offenders or those from other minority groups) and those who live in geographically remote areas are not currently well served. In addition, there is a need to further develop quality assurance processes in both countries, and consider ways in which treatment can continue following release into the community. Nonetheless, the commitment to rehabilitating offenders is well-established in public policy across Australasia, and it would appear that systems of service delivery are reasonably well developed across both custodial and community settings.

References

Allard, T. (2010) Understanding and preventing indigenous offending. *Research Brief 9*. Indigenous Justice Clearing House, Department of Justice and Attorney General, Sydney.

Andrews, D.A. (2006) Enhancing adherence to risk-need-responsivity: making equality a matter of policy. *Criminology and Public Policy*, 5, 595–602.

Andrews, D.A. and Bonta, J. (2010) Rehabilitating criminal justice policy and practice. *Psychology, Public Policy, and Law*, 16, 39–55.

Andrews, D.A. and Dowden, C. (2007) The Risk–Need–Responsivity model of assessment and human service in prevention and corrections: crime-prevention jurisprudence. *Canadian Journal of Criminology and Criminal Justice*, 49, 439–464.

Australia Bureau of Statistics (2009) *Report 4512.0 – Corrective Services, Australia*. Australian Bureau of Statistics, Canberra.

Australia Bureau of Statistics (2010) *4517.0 – Prisoners in Australia, 2010.* Australian Bureau of Statistics, Canberra.

Bakker, L., Hudson, S., Wales, D. and Riley, D. (1998) *And There Was Light: Evaluating the Kia Marama Treatment Programme for New Zealand Sex Offenders Against Children*, New Zealand Department of Corrections, Christchurch.

Beranger, B., Weatherburn, D. and Moffatt, S. (2010) Reducing indigenous contact with the court system. *Bureau Brief: Issue paper no. 54*, NSW Bureau of Crime Statistics and Research, Sydney.

Bonta, J., Rugge, T., Scott, T. *et al.* (2008) Exploring the black box of community supervision. *Journal of Offender Rehabilitation*, 47, 248–270.

Borzycki, M. (2005) *Interventions for Prisoners Returning to the Community*, Australian Institute of Criminology, Canberra.

Borzycki, M. and Baldry, E. (2003) *Promoting Integration: The Provision of Prisoner Post-Release Services.* Trends and Issues in Crime and Criminal Justice no. 262. Australian Institute of Criminology, Canberra.

Day, A. Culturally responsive CBT in forensic settings, in *Forensic CBT: A Practitioner's Guide* (eds R.C. Tafrate and D. Mitchell), Wiley-Blackwell, New York, forthcoming.

Day, A., Ward, T. and Shirley, L. (2011) Reintegration services for long-term dangerous prisoners: a case study and discussion. *Journal of Offender Rehabilitation*, 50, 66–80.

Freiberg, A. (2005) Sentencing, in *Crime and Justice in Australia* (eds P. Wilson and D. Chappell), Butterworth's, New South Wales, pp 139–167.

Gendreau, P. and Andrews, D. (2001) *Correctional Program Assessment Inventory (CPAI-2000)*, University of New Brunswick, St John.

Heseltine, K., Sarre, R. and Day, A. (2011) Prison-Based Correctional Offender Rehabilitation Programs: The 2009 National Picture in Australia. *Report for the Criminology Research Council*, Australian Institute of Criminology, Canberra.

Hsu, C., Caputi, P. and Byrne, M. (2009) Level of service inventory-revised: assessing the risk and need characteristics of Australian Indigenous offenders. *Criminal Justice and Behaviour*, 36, 728–740.

Lambie, I. and Stewart, M. (2003) *Community Solutions for the Community's Problem: An Outcome Evaluation of Three New Zealand Community Child Sex Offender Treatment Programmes*, New Zealand Department of Corrections, Auckland.

Lim, L. and Day, A. (2013) Mental health diversion courts: some directions for further development. *Psychiatry, Psychology and Law*. Forthcoming.

Lipsey, M.W., Landenberger, N.A. and Wilson, S.J. (2007) Effects of cognitive-behavioural programs for criminal offenders. *Campbell Systematic Reviews*, 6, 1–30.

Magregor, S. (2008) Sex offender treatment programs: effectiveness of prison and community based programs in Australia and New Zealand. *Brief 3.* Indigenous Justice Clearing House, Attorney General's Department of NSW, Sydney.

Morgan, R., Flora, D., Kroner, D. *et al.* (2007) Treatment of mentally disordered offenders: a research synthesis. Paper presented at the North American Conference of Correctional and Criminal Justice Psychology, Ottawa.

Nadesu, A. (2009a) Reconviction Patterns of Offenders Managed in the Community: A 60-Month Follow-Up, *New Zealand Department of Corrections Report*, Wellington. http://www.corrections.govt.nz/research/reconviction-patterns-of-offenders-managed-in-the-community-a-60-months-follow-up-analysis3.html (accessed 17 December 2012.).

Nadesu, A. (2009b) Reconviction Patterns of Released Prisoners: A 60-Month Follow-Up, *New Zealand Department of Corrections Report*, Wellington. http://www.corrections.govt.nz/research/reconviction-patterns-of-released-prisoners-a-60-months-follow-up-analysis2.html (accessed 17 December 2012.).

Nathan, L., Wilson, N.J. and Hillman, D. (2003) *Te Whakakotahitanga: An Evaluation of the Te Piriti Special Treatment Programme for Child Sex Offenders in New Zealand*, New Zealand Department of Corrections, Christchurch.

New Zealand Department of Corrections (2006) *Violence Prevention Unit: Programme to Reduce Re-Offending (Manual)*, New Zealand Department of Corrections, Wellington.

New Zealand Department of Corrections (2007) Over-Representation of Māori in the Criminal Justice System: An Exploratory Report, Department of Corrections, Wellington. http://www.corrections. govt.nz/research/over-representation-of-maori-in-the-criminal-justice-system/executive-summary. html (accessed on 16 January 2013).

New Zealand Department of Corrections (2010) *Annual Report 1 July 2009 – 30 June 2010*, New Zealand Department of Corrections, Wellington, http://www.corrections.govt.nz/__data/assets/ pdf_file/0004/480820/Annual_Report_09-10.pdf (accessed 17 December 2012).

New Zealand Department of Corrections (2011) *Programmes for Offenders*, New Zealand Department of Corrections, Wellington, http://www.corrections.govt.nz/about-us/fact-sheets/managing-offenders-in-the-community/programmes_for_offenders/programmes-for-offenders.html (accessed 17 December 2012).

New Zealand Ministry of Justice (2010) *An Overview of Conviction and Sentencing Statistics in New Zealand 2000 to 2009: Statistical Bulletin*, New Zealand Ministry of Justice, Wellington. http://www. justice.govt.nz/publications/global-publications/c/conviction-and-sentencing-2000-to-2009/ Publication (accessed 17 December 2012).

New Zealand Ministry of Justice (2011) Justice Sector Forecast 2011–2021. http://justice.govt. nz/publications/global-publications/f/forecast-2011-2021-justice-sector/documents/2011-2021-JSF-detailed-report-pdf (accessed on 26 December 2012).

Nunes, K.L. and Cortoni, F. (2006) Estimating Risk of Dropout and Expulsion from Correctional Programs. *Correctional Services of Canada Research Report No 177*, Correctional Services of Canada, Ottawa.

Owen, K., Coates, H., Wickham, A. *et al.* (2007) *Recidivism of Sex Offenders: Base Rates for Corrections Victoria Sex Offender Program*, Victoria Department of Justice, Melbourne.

Payne, J. (2005) Specialty Courts in Australia. *Report to the Criminology Research Council*, Canberra.

Polaschek, D.L.L. (2011) High intensity rehabilitation for violent offenders in New Zealand: reconviction outcomes for high and medium-risk prisoners. *Journal of Interpersonal Violence*, 26, 664–682.

Rugge, T. (2006) *Risk Assessment of Male Aboriginal Offenders: A 2006 Perspective*, Correctional Services Canada, Ottawa.

Sarre, R. (2009) The importance of political will in the imprisonment debate. *Current Issues in Criminal Justice*, 21 (1), 154–161.

Van Voorhis, P., Salisbury, E., Wright, E. and Bauman, A. (2008) *Achieving Accurate Pictures of Risk and Identifying Gender-Responsive Needs: Two New Assessments for Women Offenders*, US Department of Justice, National Institute of Corrections, Washington, DC

Ward, T. and Stewart, C. (2003) Criminogenic needs and human needs: a theoretical model. *Psychology, Crime & Law*, 9, 125–143.

Wilson, N. (2004) New Zealand High-Risk Offenders: Who Are They and What Are the Issues in Their Management and Treatment? *New Zealand Department of Corrections Report*, http://www. corrections.govt.nz/__data/assets/pdf_file/0006/177027/high-risk-offenders.pdf (accessed 17 December 2012).

Wormwith, J.S., Althouse, R., Simpson, M. *et al.* (2007) The rehabilitation and reintegration of offenders: the current landscape and some future directions for correctional psychology. *Criminal Justice and Behavior*, 34, 879–892.

23

Criminogenic Needs of Sexual Offenders on Community Supervision

R. Karl Hanson[1] and Andrew J.R. Harris[2]

[1]Public Safety Canada, Canada
[2]Forensic Assessment Group, Canada

Introduction

Like other law breakers, individuals who commit sexual crimes violate strong social prohibitions and risk serious legal consequences. Sexual crimes, however, raise special problems. Whereas we have little difficulty appreciating the goals (if not the means) of bank robbers and thieves, not everybody wants to fondle pubescent boys, expose their genitals to strangers or have sexual intercourse with their step-daughter. Consequently, there is broad consensus that the risk factors for sexual crime can be divided into two broad categories: factors associated with general criminality and sexual-crime-specific factors (Barbaree *et al.*, 2009; Hanson and Bussière, 1998; Quinsey, 1984, 1986). In order to help visualize this distinction, consider a paedophilic teacher or priest, who may score low on risk scales designed for general offending, but, nonetheless, could present substantial risk for sexual recidivism due to persistent, sexually deviant preoccupations.

Risk factors predict recidivism because they are markers for enduring, risk-relevant propensities. Static, historical factors can be valid and useful indicators of these propensities, as can be information gleaned through interviews, case histories, questionnaires, or specialized testing (e.g., phallometric, viewing time). It is much more helpful, however, to know the psychological meaning of the indicators (e.g., deviant sexual preferences) than to simply know that a risk factor is present (e.g., never married, boy victims). The most well-established psychologically meaningful risk factors for sexual recidivism among sexual offenders are presented in Table 23.1 (based on Mann, Hanson and Thornton, 2010).

Not surprisingly, the major sex-crime-specific risk factors concern deviant sexual interests and problems with sexual self-regulation. There are also certain relationship problems unique to sexual offenders. Perhaps the most distinctive is emotional congruence with children

The views expressed are those of the authors and not necessarily those of Public Safety Canada.

Table 23.1   Psychologically meaningful risk factors for sexual recidivism

---

Sexual-crime-specific factors

Sexual preoccupation

Any deviant sexual interests

   Sexual preference for children (phallometric assessment)

   Sexualized violence

   Multiple paraphilias

Sex as coping

Sexual offence supportive attitudes

Emotional congruence with children

Hostility towards women

General risk factors

Never married

Conflicts in intimate relationships

General self-regulation problems

Impulsivity/recklessness

Unstable employment

Poor cognitive problem solving

Non-compliance with supervision/helpers

Grievance/hostility

Negative social influences

Callousness/lack of concern for others

(Wilson, 1999), which increases the risk of sexual recidivism for child molesters. It is unlikely that such unique factors would be addressed in programmes designed for general offenders.

Risk factors for general recidivism also increase the risk of sexual recidivism. General risk factors are common among sexual offenders, and sexual offenders are more likely to recidivate with a non-sexual crime than a sexual crime (e.g., Hanson and Bussière, 1998). Readers familiar with Andrews and Bonta's (2010) 'Big Four' and 'Central Eight' risk factors will recognize all the factors listed in the lower section of Table 23.1. Even though some of the 'Central Eight' are not represented, the missing items can largely be attributed to lack of research evidence rather than to substantive differences in empirical findings between sexual offenders and other offenders. Consequently, many sexual offenders would be expected to benefit from both generic and specialized correctional programmes.

Evaluators wishing to assess the criminogenic needs of sexual offenders are encouraged to use a structured risk assessment procedure. Structured risk assessments are more reliable and valid than unstructured professional judgements (Hanson and Morton-Bourgon, 2009; Heilbrun, Yasuhara and Shah, 2010; Monahan, 2007), and are widely used with sexual offenders (Archer *et al.*, 2006; McGrath *et al.*, 2010). Static-99 (Hanson and Thornton, 2000) and its variants (see www.static99.org) are by far the most popular risk assessment procedures for sexual offenders. Unfortunately, Static-99 focuses exclusively on static, historical factors. There are, however, a number of specialized risk tools that aim to identify psychologically meaningful risk factors for sexual offenders. These measures include the Violence Risk Scale – Sexual Offender version (VRS-SO; Olver *et al.*, 2007), the Sexual Violence Risk – 20 (SVR-20; Boer *et al.*, 1997), the Structured Risk Assessment scheme (SRA; Thornton, 2002) and STABLE-2007 (Hanson *et al.*, 2007). Each of these instruments has shown moderate to large predictive accuracy (discrimination) and has been cross-replicated in independent samples

Table 23.2   Distribution of STABLE-2007 items for males at first assessment ($n=790$)

STABLE-2007 items	STABLE risk factors		
	No problem % scoring '0' (sample size)	Maybe % scoring '1' (sample size)	Problem % scoring '2' (sample size)
1. Significant social influences	58.7% (464)	26.6% (210)	14.7% (116)
Intimacy deficits			
2. Capacity for relationship stability	22.9% (181)	43.2% (341)	33.9% (268)
3. Emotional identification with children	80.6% (637)	15.6% (123)	3.8% (30)
4. Hostility towards women	70.1% (554)	23.9% (189)	5.9% (47)
5. General social rejection/loneliness	40.4% (319)	40.3% (318)	19.4% (153)
6. Lack of concern for others	57.3% (453)	31.9% (252)	10.8% (85)
General self-regulation			
7. Impulsive acts	57.2% (452)	28.0% (221)	14.8% (117)
8. Poor cognitive problem solving	42.9% (339)	38.7% (306)	18.4% (145)
9. Negative emotionality/hostility	64.2% (507)	26.7% (211)	9.1% (72)
Sexual self-regulation			
10. Sexual preoccupations/sex drive	55.1% (435)	33.7% (266)	11.3% (89)
11. Sex as coping	64.1% (506)	22.5% (178)	13.4% (106)
12. Deviant sexual interests	42.9% (339)	40.8% (322)	16.3% (129)
13. Non-cooperation with supervision	69.9% (552)	21.1% (167)	9.0% (71)

Percentages may not sum to 100 due to rounding. Cases were excluded if any STABLE-2007 items were missing.

Table 23.3   Distribution of ACUTE-2007 ratings for 744 male sexual offenders

	No problem % scoring '0' (sample size)	Maybe % scoring '1' (sample size)	Problem % scoring '2' (sample size)	Intervene now % scoring '3' (sample size)
Sex/violence factors				
Victim access	65.3 (4592)	31.4 (2210)	2.7 (190)	0.5 (36)
Sexual preoccupations	83.2 (5822)	13.4 (936)	3.1 (217)	0.3 (24)
Hostility	83.3 (5842)	14.5 (1019)	1.9 (136)	0.2 (15)
Rejection of supervision	82.8 (5809)	13.9 (977)	2.5 (175)	0.7 (51)
General factors				
Collapse of social supports	81.2 (5700)	16.3 (1145)	2.4 (170)	0.1 (4)
Substance abuse	87.8 (6156)	9.1 (641)	2.7 (191)	0.4 (26)
Emotional collapse	71.9 (5043)	24.4 (1714)	3.3 (235)	0.3 (24)
Highest rating per session				
Sex/violence factors	48.8 (3450)	42.6 (3011)	7.5 (530)	1.1 (80)
Only general factors	60.1 (4250)	33.0 (2334)	6.2 (438)	0.7 (48)
Any acute	36.3 (2566)	50.9 (3602)	11.2 (794)	1.5 (109)

Sample size varies between 6999 and 7071 assessments depending on missing data.

(Eher *et al.*, 2012; Hanson and Morton-Bourgon, 2009). The current chapter focuses on STABLE-2007 and ACUTE-2007 (Hanson *et al.*, 2007; Harris and Hanson, 2010).

STABLE-2007 and ACUTE-2007 were developed to address the dynamic (changeable) risk factors of sexual offenders on community supervision. STABLE-2007 assesses relatively enduring characteristics that would be unlikely to change without deliberate effort (i.e., treatment targets). ACUTE-2007 assesses the rapidly changing states and circumstances associated with imminent risk. The STABLE-2007 and ACUTE-2007 items are listed in Table 23.2 and Table 23.3, respectively. Although specifically developed for offenders in the community, we believe the risk factors assessed by these measures to be relevant to sexual offenders in both institutional and community settings.

STABLE-2007/ACUTE-2007 are the products of an ongoing programme of research (Harris and Hanson, 2010). The early studies (Hanson and Harris, 1998, 2000b; Harris and Hanson, 2003) were influenced by social cognitive theory (e.g., Bandura, 1974), relapse prevention theory (e.g., Laws, 1989), and Quinsey's studies of *dynamic antisociality* (Quinsey *et al.*, 1997). In order to create measures applicable to applied practice, we also spent considerable time interviewing community supervision officers. We asked them to describe the differences between recidivists and non-recidivists, as well as the visible changes in recidivists just prior to reoffending (Hanson and Harris, 2000b). The relatively enduring (but potentially changeable) propensities that distinguished between recidivists and non-recidivists we called *stable dynamic* risk factors. The observable changes within recidivists were called *acute dynamic* risk factors. These stable and acute factors were combined into our first needs measure, the Sex Offender Need Assessment Rating (SONAR; Hanson and Harris, 2000a, 2001).

Even before the SONAR publication appeared, however, we had replaced it with STABLE-2000 and ACUTE-2000 (Harris and Hanson, 2003). One motivation to create two separate scales was that stable and acute factors inform different decisions. Stable factors were intended to identify treatment targets and inform moderate to long-term recidivism potential. In contrast, knowledge of acute factors is essential to managing cases on community supervision, but has little utility if the offender lacks the opportunity to offend. The other motivation to replace SONAR with STABLE-2000 and ACUTE-2000 was to benefit from new research findings. In particular, we were impressed with the work of Beech (1998), Thornton (2002), Wilson (1999), Cortoni (1998) and Cortoni and Marshall (2001) who had all made significant contributions to identifying psychologically meaningful risk factors for sexual offenders.

STABLE-2000 and ACUTE-2000 were examined in a prospective longitudinal study involving 805 sexual offenders, 156 community supervision officers and 16 jurisdictions (all 14 Canadian correctional jurisdictions plus the US states of Alaska and Iowa; Hanson *et al.*, 2007). The results of the 2000–2007 Dynamic Supervision Project (DSP) were encouraging; however, certain items did not work or did not work as intended (e.g., non-linear relationships with the outcome of interest). Consequently, the DSP results were used to revise the measures and create STABLE-2007 and ACUTE-2007 (Hanson *et al.*, 2007; Harris and Hanson, 2010).

STABLE-2007

STABLE-2007 is a structured rating scheme completed by the evaluator based on file review and an interview with the offender. Each of the 13 items (12 for offenders without a child victim) is rated on a 3-point scale: 0 – no problems, 1 – some problem/unsure, and

2 – definite problem. The overall score is the simple sum of the items, with scores of 0–3 considered 'low', 4–11 considered 'moderate', and scores of 12 or more considered 'high'. These interpretative ranges were based on defining the moderate range as ± 1 standard deviation of the mean (Z scores of ± 1; mean=7.5; SD=4.9). Each of the 13 items will now be briefly described.

Significant Social Influences rates the people in the offender's life who are not paid to be with him. Typically, offenders list between two and four people. The evaluator then rates whether each person is a positive influence, a negative influence or a neutral influence. Among general offenders, the existence of negative peer associates is one of the strongest predictors of recidivism (Gendreau, Little and Goggin, 1996). The same pattern is found with sexual offenders. Sex offenders know other sex offenders (Hanson and Scott, 1996) and negative social involvement is a well-established predictor of sexual recidivism (Mann *et al.*, 2010).

The next STABLE-2007 item concerns the *Capacity for Relationship Stability*. It has two parts. The first part is whether the offender has ever spent two years in a marriage-like relationship (identical to the Static-99 item; Harris *et al.*, 2003). The second part considers whether the offender currently has an intimate partner, and, if so, rates the stability and quality of that relationship. The presence of a mutually satisfying, stable, sexually intimate relationship is a well-established protective factor for sexual recidivism (Hanson and Bussière, 1998; Hanson and Morton-Bourgon, 2004). A satisfying intimate relationship can provide a positive social influence, increase rewards for 'going straight', increase motivation for sexual self-regulation, and limit the amount of unstructured leisure time. Conversely, there is some evidence that the lack of a stable relationship is an indication of atypical sexual interests (Blanchard and Bogaerts, 1997).

The next STABLE-2007 item, *Emotional Identification with Children*, is rated only for offenders with at least one victim under the age of 14. That child molesters feel particularly comfortable around children has been observed for many years (Araji and Finkelhor, 1986; Hammer and Glueck, 1957). Wilson (1999) elaborated the modern concept of emotional congruence with children. According to Wilson, child molesters, particularly those with victims outside the family, often feel that their relationships with children are more emotionally satisfying than their relationships with adults. Subsequent research has supported this variable as a risk factor (Hanson and Morton-Bourgon, 2004). It is, however, one of the few risk factors that uniquely apply to child molesters but not rapists (Hanson *et al.*, 2007; Knight and Thornton, 2007).

Hostility towards Women refers to negative and/or hostile beliefs that impair the offender's ability to form warm, close and egalitarian relationships with women. These deficits can be expressed as sexist attitudes, stereotypically traditional beliefs about women and their roles, or simple outright hatred for women. There is strong evidence that such attitudes increase the risk of sexual aggression among community males (Malamuth *et al.*, 1991, 1995). The research evidence with correctional samples is more limited. In a retrospective correlation study, Thornton (2002) found that hostile beliefs about women were more marked among sexual recidivists than first-time offenders. In the DSP (Hanson *et al.*, 2007), we found a significant linear relationship between hostile attitudes towards women and all recidivism outcomes, with an area under the curve (AUC) of 0.58 for sexual recidivism.

General Social Rejection/Loneliness is common among sexual offenders, particularly child molesters (average d=1.02; Whitaker *et al.*, 2008). Although loneliness did not predict recidivism in six previous studies (see summary by Hanson and Morton-Bourgon, 2004), the STABLE-2007 item did show the expected relationship with recidivism in the DSP (d=0.35). In contrast to the other STABLE-2007 items, *General Social Rejection/Loneliness* is primarily scored from the offender's perspective. Even if there are people in the offender's life who care about the offender, if the offender feels rejected and lonely, then the offender is scored as rejected and lonely.

Lack of Concern for Others identifies the small subgroup of offenders whose interactions are utilitarian, selfish, ruthless and indifferent to the rights and well-being of others. Most people are capable of being cruel or indifferent to enemies and adversaries while simultaneously caring for their in-group. Some people have relatively small in-groups, comprising their immediate family and friends; others have large in-groups, identifying themselves broadly with their communities, or even saint-like identifications with all of 'humanity'. An individual who displays pervasive lack of concern for others acts as though his in-group is very small, namely, himself. This item overlaps substantially with the construct of callous/unemotional traits, which is a well-established correlate of general and violent offending (Frick and White, 2008), and may have distinctive neurobiological correlates (Hodgins *et al.*, 2009). Lack of concern for others has predicted sexual recidivism in two studies, including the DSP study (Hanson *et al.*, 2007; Knight and Thornton, 2007).

Impulsive Acts identifies offenders who exhibit impulsive behaviour across a number of settings (e.g., financial, vocational, leisure, accommodation, personal relationships). It is not simply represented by a history of sexual offending, but is generally evident from an early age. Lifestyle impulsiveness (a lifestyle dominated by impulsive, irresponsible decisions with a lack of realistic long-term goals) is one of the most well-established correlates of criminal behaviour (Gottfredson and Hirschi, 1990). Lifestyle instability predicted sexual recidivism in Hanson and Morton-Bourgon's (2004) meta-analysis, and the STABLE-2007 item predicted all types of recidivism (sexual and non-sexual) in the DSP.

Offenders are at increased risk for sexual and general recidivism if they have difficulty identifying and solving everyday problems (STABLE-2007 item: *Poor Cognitive Problem Solving*). Offenders with high scores would be expected to have difficulties identifying problems, generating and evaluating alternatives, choosing a course of action, and evaluating the outcome. It is not uncommon for such offenders to view their situation as 'normal' and attribute their immediate difficulties to other people's behaviour. Poor cognitive problem solving showed a significant linear relationship to all recidivism outcomes in the DSP (Hanson *et al.*, 2007). When the DSP results are combined with three previous studies, poor cognitive problem solving showed a statistically significant, although small, relationship with sexual recidivism (average $d = 0.22$; Mann *et al.*, 2010).

Negative Emotionality/Hostility refers to the tendency to feel victimized and mistreated by others, and to respond with anger and hostility to life's challenges. Some offenders have excessively negative reactions to routine problems, and their negative emotions provoke rash behaviours, such as reactive aggression, verbal outbursts and poorly considered decisions (e.g., quitting a job). For other offenders, their negative emotionality manifests as a simmering grievance which may or may not have obvious links to current events. The key elements are that the negative emotion is intense (or disproportional to the triggering events), externalized towards others, and interferes with the offender's personal and social functioning.

Hostility and grievance are common features of offenders and these personality traits have been shown to precede the onset of crime in longitudinal studies (Krueger *et al.*, 1994). When averaged over 11 follow-up studies (3139 sex offenders), there is a small, significant relationship between grievance/hostility and sexual recidivism ($d=0.20$; Mann *et al.*, 2010). In general, other types of personal distress (e.g., depression, anxiety, worry) have little or no relationship to the onset of crime (Krueger *et al.*, 1994) and are unrelated to long-term recidivism potential (Hanson, 2009). The contribution of negative emotions to criminal behaviour seems to be mediated by externalizing coping strategies.

Many of the characteristics discussed so far apply to all offenders and increase the risk for both sexual and general recidivism. The next three risk factors are particularly important for sexual offenders: *Sex Drive/Preoccupation*, *Sex as Coping*, and *Deviant Sexual Interests*. *Sex Drive/Preoccupation* concerns the *frequency* of sexual outlets, *Sex as Coping* concerns *when* sex occurs, and *Deviant Sexual Interests* concerns *what* is sexually interesting to the offender. Although conceptually distinct, each of these factors is empirically correlated with one another (Kafka, 2010; Långström and Hanson, 2006). Consequently, it is possible that these items represent manifestations of global problems with sexual self-regulation (Hanson, 2010).

Sex Drive/Preoccupation focuses on both the frequency of sexual thoughts and behaviours, and the degree to which they interfere with interpersonal and/or pro-social functioning. The frequency would be considered excessive based on the offender's self-report of difficulty controlling sexual drive, interference with work or relationships, or if the rates are so high that they are statistically rare (top 5–10% of the general male population). This item concerns impersonal sex, and is not concerned with high rates of sexual activity in the context of a loving relationship (e.g., the 'honeymoon' phase of new lovers). The STABLE concept of sexual preoccupation would substantially overlap with the constructs of sexual compulsions, sexual addictions (Marshall *et al.*, 2008) and hypersexual disorder (Kafka, 2010).

Early theories of sexual offending assumed that sexual offenders were sexually inhibited (e.g., 'blockage' in Finkelhor, 1986); however, subsequent research suggests that the opposite is more likely to be true. Sexual offenders are typically more interested in sex and more sexually active than non-offending males (Lalumière *et al.*, 1996), and high rates of impersonal sex are associated with paraphilic interests, such as exhibitionism, voyeurism and masochism/sadism in the general male population (Långström and Hanson, 2006). The general construct of sexual preoccupation significantly predicted sexual, violent and general recidivism in the Hanson and Morton-Bourgon's (2004) meta-analysis.

Sex as Coping concerns sexual offenders who think about sex or engage in sexual activity to manage emotions. The sexual thoughts or behaviours may be normative or deviant, but the key is that the offender relies on sex to self-soothe or mitigate unwelcome feelings of tension, anger, hostility or anxiety (Cortoni and Marshall, 2001). Research has shown that 10–20% of the general non-criminal population is sexually aroused by negative emotions (Bancroft *et al.*, 2003a,b). These individuals were both more likely to engage in high-risk sexual behaviours (Bancroft *et al.*, 2003a,b) and are over-represented among child molesters (Whitaker *et al.*, 2008) and other sexual offenders (Cortoni and Marshall, 2001). This STABLE-2007 item was a significant predictor of sexual recidivism (AUC=0.62) in the DSP study.

It is easy to imagine how sexualized coping could increase the risk of sexual offending. For most people, the victims' distress and the perpetrators' shame would be experienced as aversive. But what if negative emotions are a sexual turn-on? In this case, the suffering associated with sexual victimization would not inhibit the assault; instead, the offender would be motivated to seek comfort and release by going further into an already compromised sexual encounter.

Deviant Sexual Interests concerns arousal by activities, situations, people or objects that are illegal, inappropriate or highly unusual. The most common deviant sexual interests are children, non-consenting adults, voyeurism (peeping), exhibitionism (flashing) and fetishes (e.g., shoes, underwear, cross-dressing). An 'interest' is something that the offender would choose if he had unhindered selection over his sexual activity. Note that this STABLE-2007 item includes legal paraphilias (e.g., fetishism), not just paraphilias that, if acted upon, would result in sexual crimes. The score of the STABLE-2007 *Deviant Sexual Interest* item is primarily based on offence history and self-report, although specialized testing is also considered when available (e.g., penile plethysmography; viewing time).

All sexual offenders have engaged in sexually deviant behaviour; however, only a minority should be expected to have clear, enduring deviant sexual interests. In the DSP study, 16% were identified as having deviant sexual interests (scores of 2), and an additional 41% were identified as having some indications of deviant sexual interests (scores of 1; see Table 23.2). Deviant sexual interests is one of the most well-established predictors of sexual recidivism (Hanson and Bussière, 1998; Hanson and Morton-Bourgon, 2005). In addition, the presence of multiple paraphilias is associated with increased risk of sexual recidivism (Hanson and Morton-Bourgon, 2004; Mann *et al.*, 2010).

The final STABLE-2007 item, *Cooperation with Supervision*, concerns the extent to which the offenders are 'working with' or 'working against' professionals charged with helping them go straight. In the DSP project, this item was rated by community supervision (probation or parole) officers. The concept, however, is intended to also apply to other interveners, such as therapists, teachers and institutional staff. Non-cooperation comes in several forms, including disengagement (just going through the motions), overt manipulation (lying, playing the system) and non-attendance. Non-compliance with rules and authority is a core feature of criminal conduct, and a reliable predictor of both sexual and general recidivism (Hanson and Morton-Bourgon, 2004; Mann *et al.*, 2010).

As previously stated, the primary purpose of the STABLE-2007 items is to identify treatment targets. According to Table 23.2, the most common criminogenic needs for sexual offenders are relationship problems, loneliness, poor cognitive problem solving, and deviant sexual interests. There are well-established programmes that address many of these common needs (Marshall *et al.*, 2011; McGrath, Hoke, and Vojtisek, 1998; Robinson, 1995). Experts may debate the extent to which deviant sexual interests are changeable (Marshall, 1997; Quinsey, 2003); however, nobody questions their relevance for sexual offender treatment and community supervision.

STABLE-2007, on its own, is not intended to provide a global evaluation of absolute recidivism risk. It can, however, be combined with a STATIC risk assessment tool (e.g., Static-99, Static-99R, Static-2002, Static-2002R) to provide relative risk rankings as well as estimated recidivism rates for sexual, violent and general offending.[1] These estimates appear reasonably consistent across settings (Eher *et al.*, 2012).

ACUTE-2007

Acute risk factors are intended to guide decisions concerning community management of sexual offenders. Ratings for the ACUTE-2007 factors are based on current behaviour, which, in practice, means behaviour during the past month, or less (if the offender was seen

---

[1]   Static-99/STABLE-2007 tables are presented in Hanson *et al.* (2007). STABLE-2007 Tables for Static-99R, Static-2002, and Static-2002R are available upon request.

more recently). In contrast to stable factors, which address global dispositions, the acute factors address current manifestations. In order to appreciate this distinction, consider the difference between alcoholism, defined as the chronic propensity for problematic drinking, and drunkenness. It is quite possible for a currently sober individual to be an alcoholic (a stable factor); similarly, being drunk (an acute factor) does not necessarily mean that the individual is an alcoholic.

The seven items in ACUTE-2007 (see Table 23.3) were developed from previous studies of high-risk behaviours and the immediate precursors of sexual reoffending (Hanson and Harris, 2000b, 2001; McKibben, Proulx, and Lusignan, 1994; Pithers *et al.*, 1988; Proulx, McKibben and Lusignan, 1996). ACUTE-2007 includes all the items of the original ACUTE-2000, with one exception. In ACUTE-2000, officers were encouraged to rate a unique factor that was important only for the specific offender (e.g., medication compliance for an offender with major mental disorder). These unique factors, however, turned out to be unrelated to recidivism, and, consequently, were removed from ACUTE-2007. Each of the ACUTE-2007 factors is rated on a 4-point scale: no problems, maybe/unsure, definite problem, and intervene now. The *intervene now* category signals that the problem is sufficiently severe and obvious that immediate action is required (e.g., offender arrives drunk, absconds, child molester moves in with a single mother with young children).

In the DSP project, 7050 acute ratings were obtained for 744 male offenders. The number of ratings per offender ranged from 1 to 70, with a median of 7 (mean=9.5; SD=9.2). Based on item correlations and relationships with different types of recidivism, the items were grouped into two sets. One set contained *Victim Access, Sexual Preoccupations, Hostility*, and *Rejection of Supervision*; all items consistently predicted sexual and violent recidivism. The other set predicted general recidivism and contained all seven factors (the first set of four plus *Emotional Collapse, Collapse of Social Supports*, and *Substance Abuse*). The offenders at highest risk for sexual recidivism were perceived as rejecting supervision, having problems with sexual self-regulation, and making efforts to meet or groom victims. In contrast, *Emotional Collapse, Collapse of Social Supports*, and *Substance Abuse* appeared more related to technical violations than to new crimes. It was as if these offenders were unable to cope with life more generally, and were not uniquely channelling their distress into criminal behaviour.

Although the presence of acute factors meaningfully increased the risk of sexual and general recidivism, the absolute recidivism rate in the month following any particular assessment was low. Out of a total of 7050 acute assessments, only 17 were within 45 days of a new sexual crime (approximately 1 in 400) and only 93 preceded any recidivism (including breaches; approximately 1 in 75). Consequently, evaluators can use acute ratings to identify relative risk (riskier than before, riskier than other offenders), but the acute ratings did not have sufficient discrimination to identify specific months in which an offender would be more likely than not to reoffend.

Another important finding was that the average of the acute ratings for the past six months was a better predictor of recidivism than was most recent assessment considered in isolation. This can partially be explained by appreciating the inherent error in any given acute rating. When a person is observed over multiple occasions, utilizing all observations will provide a better (more reliable) indication of how he or she is doing than any single observation (Epstein, 1979). It also should not be surprising that offenders with chronic problems are riskier than offenders with only recent problems. The DSP findings, however, suggest a different way of thinking about acute factors. Originally, acute factors were only considered as indicators of imminent risk (i.e., the timing of reoffending). However, the DSP results suggested that the

ACUTE items should be considered to be current manifestations of enduring risk-relevant propensities. When these propensities are active, offenders would be expected to show problematic behaviours in the community; when the propensities are inactive, muted or no longer present, offenders' current behaviour would be expected to be less risky.

Research on STABLE-2007 and ACUTE-2007

Although STABLE-2007 and ACUTE-2007 have face validity and are widely used in both institutional and community settings (McGrath *et al.*, 2010; Watson and Vess, 2009), it is important to consider the extent to which they are supported by research evidence. Given that STABLE-2007 and ACUTE-2007 are relatively new, there is still more research on STABLE-2000 than there is for STABLE-2007. The STABLE-2007 research that is available, however, suggests that it is an improvement over STABLE-2000 (Eher *et al.*, 2012; Hanson *et al.*, 2007).

The interrater reliability of the STABLE-2007 was found to be high in two studies. Fernandez (2008) reported an intra-class correlation coefficient (ICC) of 0.92 for the total scores ($n=55$) based on independent ratings by experienced evaluators working for the same intake assessment unit in Canada. Similarly, Eher *et al.* (2012) reported an ICC of 0.90 for the total scores ($n=15$) between graduate students and experienced clinicians in Austria. Given that the standard deviation of STABLE-2007 is 4.9 (mean of 7.5), the standard error of measurement would be expected to be about 1.5 points ($4.9 \times [1 - 0.90]^{1/2}$), with a 95% confidence interval of 6.1 points. Consequently, two raters would be expected to be within 3 points 68% of the time (2×1.5 points), and within 6 points 19 times out of 20 ($1.96 \times 2 \times 1.5$ points). Exact agreement is unlikely, even among well-calibrated teams. Consequently, evaluators should consider measurement error when interpreting individual results and base their conclusions on the plausible range of 'true' scores.

Not all studies have found high interrater reliability. Nicholls *et al.* (2010) found unacceptably low interrater reliability (ICC of 0.14) when 10 anonymous case files were rated by 18 different raters (police officers, probation officers and certified DSP trainers). The reasons for the low reliability are unknown, and may have been an artefact of the research method (unusually long and complex files, restriction of range). It is possible, however, that common training and feedback, as well as conscientiousness, are required to obtain acceptable levels of reliability across diverse professional groups.

There have been four studies of the predictive accuracy (discrimination) of STABLE-2000 (Eher *et al.*, 2012; Lussier, Deslauriers-Varin and Râtel, 2010; Saum, 2007; Webb, Craissati and Keen, 2007), all of which have found AUC values similar to those reported in the original DSP study. There has, however, only been one recidivism study of STABLE-2007 (Eher *et al.*, 2012). Eher *et al.* (2012) followed 263 Austrian sexual offenders for an average of 6.4 years. STABLE-2007 scores were calculated retrospectively from STABLE-2000 scores, Static-99 scores and case file information, all of which were collected prospectively between 2001 and 2005. In comparison to STABLE-2000, STABLE-2007 demonstrated a greater ability to discriminate between recidivists and non-recidivists (AUCs of 0.62 versus 0.71, respectively). The calibration (fit between expected and predicted values) was also good: there were no meaningful differences between the original Static-99/STABLE-2007 sexual recidivism estimates and the rates found in the Eher *et al.* (2012) sample. Further research is needed, however, to determine the extent to which STATIC/STABLE-2007 scores predict recidivism in other samples.

The STABLE-2007 items were not only intended to be risk factors, but to be *dynamic* risk factors. Empirical justification that a characteristic is a dynamic risk factor requires evidence that it can change, and that change is associated with increases or decreases in recidivism risk (Kraemer *et al.*, 1997). Currently, there is only weak (and mostly indirect) evidence supporting the STABLE-2007 factors as dynamic risk factors. In the DSP study, there was relatively little change in STABLE-2007 scores over a six month period, and that change was unrelated to recidivism risk. Few of the offenders in the DSP study, however, would have received effective correctional treatment. In contrast, Nunes, Babchishin and Cortoni (2011) found a statistically significant reduction in STABLE-2000 scores for offenders completing the National Sex Offender Programs offered by the Correctional Service of Canada. The absolute change, however, was small – averaging 1 point (pretest mean of 5.6 versus a post-test mean of 4.5). The effect was also counter-intuitive, with offenders receiving low-intensity treatment showing greater reductions than offenders receiving the moderate intensity programme.

Further research is required to determine the conditions under which meaningful changes in STABLE-2007 can be observed. There is strong evidence that factors similar to those included in STABLE-2007 add incrementally to static, historical factors (Beggs and Grace, 2010; Craig *et al.*, 2007; Olver and Wong, 2011; and see meta-analysis by Hanson and Morton-Bourgon, 2005). Furthermore, treatment programmes that target these psychologically meaningful risk factors reduce the recidivism risk of sexual offenders, whereas programmes that target other, non-criminogenic needs have no effect on recidivism (Hanson *et al.*, 2009). We do not know, however, the rate at which these factors change (with or without intervention), or the duration of observations needed to create a new baseline (Hanson, 2006).

We also need to learn more about what is being assessed by STABLE-2007. The descriptions of the STABLE items are sufficiently clear that acceptable levels of agreement are found between trained raters (Eher *et al.*, 2012; Fernandez, 2008; Hanson *et al.*, 2007). However, it is hard to predict the overlap between particular STABLE-2007 items and other measures with similar labels. For example, Nunes and Babchishin (2012) found that the correlation between *Social Rejection/Loneliness* (STABLE item) and the UCLA Loneliness scale (Russell, Peplau and Cutrona, 1980) was only $r=0.34$. In contrast, there was a substantial correlation ($r=0.81$) between the STABLE-2007 *Deviant Sexual Interest* item and the Screening Scale for Pedophilic Interests (SSPI; Seto and Lalumière, 2001). Further research is needed to examine the extent to which STABLE items correlate with other measures of purportedly similar constructs, and which aspects of these constructs are most strongly associated with the recidivism risk of sexual offenders.

Given that the STABLE-2007 items show moderate to high internal consistency (Cronbach alpha=0.80), it may be preferable to interpret subscales of multiple items rather than focus on individual items in isolation. Exploratory factor analyses suggest that the items can be easily grouped into the familiar dimensions of general criminality and sexual-crime-specific factors (Hanson and Helmus, 2009). Positioning offenders on these latent dimensions may better represent offenders' recidivism risk than would a total score on STABLE-2007, or the total score of other existing measures.

Conclusion

Risk assessments of sexual offenders need to consider factors related to general criminality as well as sexual-crime-specific factors. STABLE-2007 and ACUTE-2007 are presented as a structured approach to evaluating the enduring propensities and current problems associated with the risk for sexual recidivism. Although initial results with these measures are encouraging, further research is needed to: (i) clarify the constructs assessed by these measures, and (ii) determine the extent to which these constructs function as genuinely *dynamic* risk factors. These questions could be profitably addressed by cross-sectional assessment studies and by intervention studies designed to reduce the risk-relevant propensities of sexual offenders.

Acknowledgement

We would like to thank Kelly Babchishin for comments on an early version of this manuscript.

References

Andrews, D. and Bonta, J. (2010) *The Psychology of Criminal Conduct*, 5th edn, LexisNexis Metthew Bender, New Providence.

Araji, A. and Finkelhor, D. (1986) Abusers: a review of the research, in *A Sourcebook on Child Sexual Abuse* (eds D. Finkelhor, S. Araji, L. Baron, L. *et al.*), Sage, Beverly Hills, pp. 89–118.

Archer, R.P., Buffington-Vollum, J.K., Stredny, R.V. and Handel, R.W. (2006) A survey of psychological test use patterns among forensic psychologists. *Journal of Personality Assessment*, 87, 84–94.

Bancroft, J., Janssen, E., Strong, D. *et al.* (2003a) The relation between mood and sexuality in heterosexual men. *Archives of Sexual Behavior*, 32, 217–230.

Bancroft, J., Janssen, E., Strong, D. *et al.* (2003b) Sexual risk-taking in gay men: the relevance of sexual arousability, mood, and sensation seeking. *Archives of Sexual Behavior*, 32, 555–572.

Bandura, A. (1974) *Social Learning Theory*. Prentice-Hall, Englewood Cliffs.

Barbaree, H.E., Langton, C.M., Blanchard, R. and Cantor, J. (2009) Aging versus stable enduring traits as explanatory constructs in sex offender recidivism. *Criminal Justice and Behavior*, 36, 443–465.

Beech, A.R. (1998) A psychometric typology of child abusers. *International Journal of Offender Therapy and Comparative Criminology*, 42, 319–339.

Beggs, S.M. and Grace, R.C. (2010) Assessment of dynamic risk factors: an independent validation study of the Violence Risk Scale: Sexual Offender Version. *Sexual Abuse: A Journal of Research and Treatment*, 22, 234–251.

Blanchard, R. and Bogaert, A.F. (1997) Additive effects of older brothers and homosexual brothers in the prediction of marriage and cohabitation. *Behavior Genetics*, 27, 45–54.

Boer, D.P., Hart, S.D., Kropp, P.R. and Webster, C.D. (1997) *Manual for the Sexual Violence Risk – 20: Professional Guidelines for Assessing Risk of Sexual Violence*. British Columbia Institute on Family Violence and Mental Health, Law, & Policy Institute, Simon Fraser University, Vancouver.

Cortoni, F. (1998) *The relationship between attachment styles, coping, the use of sex as a coping strategy, and Juvenile sexual history in sexual offenders*. Unpublished doctoral dissertation. Queen's University, Kingston.

Cortoni, F. and Marshall, W.L. (2001) Sex as a coping strategy and its relationship to juvenile sexual history and intimacy in sexual offenders. *Sexual Abuse: A Journal of Research and Treatment*, 13, 27–44.

Craig, L.A., Thornton, D., Beech, A. and Browne, K.D. (2007) The relationship of statistical and psychological risk markers to sexual reconviction in child molesters. *Criminal Justice and Behavior*, 34 (3), 314–329.

Eher, R., Matthes, A., Schilling, F. *et al.* (2012) Dynamic risk assessment in sexual offenders using STABLE-2000 and the STABLE-2007: an investigation of predictive and incremental validity. *Sexual Abuse: A Journal of Research and Treatment*, 24, 5–28.

Epstein, S. (1979) The stability of behaviour: I. On predicting most of the people much of the time. *Journal of Personality and Social Psychology*, 37, 1097–1126.

Fernandez, Y. (2008) An examination of the inter-rater reliability of the STATIC-99 and STABLE-2007. Poster presentation at the 27th Annual Research and Treatment Conference of the Association for the Treatment of Sexual Abusers, Atlanta, October.

Finkelhor, D. (1986) Abusers: special topics, in *A Sourcebook on Child Sexual Abuse* (eds D. Finkelhor, S. Araji, L. Baron *et al.*), Sage, Beverly Hills, pp. 119–142.

Frick, P.J. and White, S.F. (2008) Research review: the importance of callous-unemotional traits for developmental models of aggressive and antisocial behavior. *Journal of Child Psychology and Psychiatry*, 49, 359–375.

Gendreau, P., Little, T. and Goggin, C. (1996) A meta-analysis of the predictors of adult offender recidivism: what works! *Criminology*, 34, 575–607.

Gottfredson, M.R. and Hirschi, T. (1990) *A General Theory of Crime*. Stanford University Press, Stanford.

Hammer, E.F. and Glueck, B.C. (1957) Psychodynamic patterns in sex offenders: a four-factor theory. *Psychiatric Quarterly*, 31, 325–345.

Hanson, R.K. (2006) Stability and change: dynamic risk factors for sexual offenders, in *Sexual Offender Treatment: Issues and Controversies* (eds W.L. Marshall, Y.M. Forandez, L.E. Marshall, and G.A. Serran), John Wiley & Sons, Ltd, Chichester, pp. 17–31.

Hanson, R.K. (2009) The psychological assessment of risk for crime and violence. *Canadian Psychology/ Psychologie Canadienne*, 20, 172–182.

Hanson, R.K. (2010) Dimensional assessment of sexual deviance. *Archives of Sexual Behavior*, 39 (2), 401–404.

Hanson, R.K. and Bussière, M.T. (1998) Predicting relapse: a meta-analysis of sexual offender recidivism studies. *Journal of Consulting and Clinical Psychology*, 66, 348–362.

Hanson, R.K. and Harris, A.J.R. (1998) Dynamic Predictors of Sexual Recidivism. *User Rep. no. 1998-01*. Department of the Solicitor General of Canada, Ottawa.

Hanson, R.K. and Harris, A.J.R. (2000a) The Sex Offender Need Assessment Rating (SONAR): A Method for Measuring Change in Risk Levels. *User Rep. no. 2000-01*. Department of the Solicitor General of Canada, Ottawa.

Hanson, R.K. and Harris, A.J.R. (2000b) Where should we intervene? Dynamic predictors of sex offense recidivism. *Criminal Justice and Behavior*, 27, 6–35.

Hanson, R.K. and Harris, A.J.R. (2001) A structured approach to evaluating change among sexual offenders. *Sexual Abuse: A Journal of Research and Treatment*, 13, 105–122.

Hanson, R.K. and Helmus, L. (2009) Methods for combining historical and psychological risk factors: an example using Static-2002 and STABLE-2007. Presentation at the 28th Annual Research and Treatment Conference of the Association for the Treatment of Sexual Abusers, Dallas.

Hanson, R.K. and Morton-Bourgon, K. (2004) Predictors of Sexual Recidivism: An Updated Meta-analysis. *Corrections User Rep. no. 2004-02*. Public Safety and Emergency Preparedness Canada, Ottawa.

Hanson, R.K. and Morton-Bourgon, K.E. (2005) The characteristics of persistent sexual offenders: a meta-analysis of recidivism studies. *Journal of Consulting and Clinical Psychology*, 73, 1154–1163.

Hanson, R.K. and Morton-Bourgon, K.E. (2009) The accuracy of recidivism risk assessments for sexual offenders: a meta-analysis of 118 prediction studies. *Psychological Assessment*, 21, 1–21.

Hanson, R.K. and Scott, H. (1996) Social networks of sexual offenders. *Psychology, Crime & Law*, 2, 249–258.

Hanson, R.K. and Thornton, D. (2000) Improving risk assessments for sex offenders: a comparison of three actuarial scales. *Law and Human Behavior*, 24, 119–136.

Hanson, R.K., Harris, A.J.R., Scott, T. and Helmus, L. (2007) Assessing the Risk of Sexual Offenders on Community Supervision: The Dynamic Supervision Project. *Corrections User Rep. no. 2007-05*. Public Safety Canada, Ottawa.

Hanson, R.K., Bourgon, G., Helmus, L. and Hodgson, S. (2009) The principles of effective correctional treatment also apply to sexual offenders: a meta-analysis. *Criminal Justice and Behavior*, 36, 865–891.

Harris, A.J.R. and Hanson, R.K. (2003) The dynamic supervision project: improving the community supervision of sex offenders. *Corrections Today*, 65 (5), 60–64.

Harris, A.J.R. and Hanson, R.K. (2010) Clinical, actuarial, and dynamic risk assessment of sexual offenders: why do things keep changing? *Journal of Sexual Aggression*, 16, 296–310.

Harris, A.J.R., Phenix, A., Hanson, R.K. and Thornton, D. (2003) Static-99 Coding Rules: Revised 2003. *Corrections User Rep. no. 2003-03*. Department of the Solicitor General of Canada, Ottawa.

Heilbrun, K., Yasuhara, K. and Shah, S. (2010) Violence risk assessment tools: overview and critical analysis, in *Handbook of Violence Risk Assessment* (eds R.K. Otto and K.S. Douglas), Routledge, New York, pp. 1–17.

Hodgins, S., de Brito, S., Simonoff, E. *et al.* (2009) Getting the phenotypes right: an essential ingredient for understanding aetiological mechanisms underlying persistent violence and developing effective treatments. *Frontiers in Behavioral Neuroscience*, 3, 1–10.

Kafka, M.P. (2010) Hypersexual disorder: a proposed diagnosis for DSM-V. *Archives of Sexual Behavior*, 39, 377–400.

Knight, R.A. and Thornton, D. (2007) Evaluating and Improving Risk Assessment Schemes for Sexual Recidivism: A Long-Term Follow-Up of Convicted Sexual Offenders. *Document no. 217618*. U.S. Department of Justice, Washington, DC. http://www.ncjrs.gov/pdffiles1/nij/grants/217618.pdf (accessed 24 December 2012).

Kraemer, H.C., Kazdin, A.E., Offord, D.R. *et al.* (1997) Coming to terms with the terms of risk. *Archives of General Psychiatry*, 54, 337–343.

Krueger, R.F., Schmutte, P.S., Caspi, A. *et al.* (1994) Personality traits are linked to crime among men and women: evidence from a birth cohort. *Journal of Abnormal Psychology*, 103, 328–338.

Lalumière, M.L., Chalmers, L.J., Quinsey, V.L. and Seto, M.C. (1996) A test of the mate deprivation hypothesis of sexual coercion. *Ethology and Sociobiology*, 17, 299–318.

Långström, N. and Hanson, R.K. (2006) High rates of sexual behavior in the general population: correlates and predictors. *Archives of Sexual Behavior*, 35, 37–52.

Laws, R.D. (ed.) (1989) *Relapse Prevention with Sex Offenders*, Guilford, New York.

Lussier, P., Deslauriers-Varin, N. and Râtel, T. (2010) A descriptive profile of high-risk sex offenders under intensive supervision in the province of British Columbia, Canada. *International Journal of Offender Therapy and Comparative Criminology*, 54, 71–91.

Malamuth, N.M., Sockloskie, R., Koss, M.P. and Tanaka, J. (1991) The characteristics of aggressors against women: testing a model using a national sample of college students. *Journal of Consulting and Clinical Psychology*, 59, 670–681.

Malamuth, N.M., Linz, D., Heavey, C.L. *et al.* (1995) Using the confluence model of sexual aggression to predict men's conflict with women: a 10-year follow-up study. *Journal of Personality and Social Psychology*, 69, 353–369.

Mann, R.E., Hanson, R.K. and Thornton, D. (2010) Assessing risk for sexual recidivism: some proposals on the nature of psychologically meaningful risk factors. *Sexual Abuse: A Journal of Research and Treatment*, 22, 191–217.

Marshall, W.L. (1997) The relationship between self-esteem and deviant sexual arousal in non-familial child-molesters. *Behavior Modification*, 21, 86–96.

Marshall, L.E., Marshall, W.L., Moulden, H.M. and Serran, G.A. (2008) The prevalence of sexual addiction in incarcerated sexual offenders and matched community nonoffenders. *Sexual Addiction and Compulsivity*, 15, 271–283.

Marshall, W.L., Marshall, L.E., Serran, G.A. and O'Brian, M.D. (2011) *Rehabilitating Sexual Offenders: A Strength-Based Approach*, American Psychological Association, Washington, DC.

McGrath, R.J., Hoke, S.E. and Vojtisek, J.E. (1998) Cognitive-behavioral treatment of sex offenders: a treatment comparison and long-term follow-up study. *Criminal Justice and Behavior*, 25, 203–225.

McGrath, R.J., Cumming, G.F., Burchard, B.L. *et al.* (2010) *Current Practices and Emerging Trends in Sexual Abuser Management: The Safer Society 2009 North American Survey*, Safer Society, Brandon.

McKibben, A., Proulx, J. and Lusignan, R. (1994) Relationship between conflict, affect and deviant sexual behaviors in rapists and child molesters. *Behaviour Research and Therapy*, 32, 571–575.

Monahan, J. (2007) Clinical and actuarial predictions of violence, in *Modern Scientific Evidence: The Law and Science of Expert Testimony* (eds D. Faigman, D. Kaye, M. Saks *et al.*), West Publishing Company, St. Paul, pp. 122–147.

Nicholls, C.N., Callanan, M., Legard, R. *et al.* (2010) *Examining Implementation of the Stable and Acute Dynamic Risk Assessment Tool Pilot in England and Wales.* Ministry of Justice Research Series 4/10. Ministry of Justice, London.

Nunes, K.L. and Babchishin, K.M. (2012) Construct validity of the STABLE-2000 and STABLE-2007. *Sexual Abuse: A Journal of Research and Treatment*, 24, 29–45.

Nunes, K.L., Babchishin, K.M. and Cortoni, F. (2011) Measuring treatment change in sexual offenders: clinical and statistical significance. *Criminal Justice and Behavior*, 38, 157–173.

Olver, M.E. and Wong, S.C.P. (2011) A comparison of static and dynamic assessment of sexual offender risk and need in a treatment context. *Criminal Justice and Behavior*, 38, 113–126.

Olver, M.E., Wong, S.C.P., Nicholaichuk, T. and Gordon, A. (2007) The validity and reliability of the Violence Risk Scale – Sexual Offender Version: Assessing sex offender risk and evaluating therapeutic change. *Psychological Assessment*, 19, 318–329.

Pithers, W.D., Kashima, K., Cumming, G.F. *et al.* (1988) Relapse prevention of sexual aggression, in *Human Sexual Aggression: Current Perspectives* (eds R. Prentky and V. Quinsey), New York Academy of Sciences, New York, pp. 244–260.

Proulx, J., McKibben, A. and Lusignan, R. (1996) Relationship between affective components and sexual behaviors in sexual aggressors. *Sexual Abuse: A Journal of Research and Treatment*, 8, 279–289.

Quinsey, V.L. (1984) Sexual aggression: studies of offenders against women, in *Law and Mental Health: International Perspectives*, vol. 1 (ed. D.N. Weisstub), Pergamon Press, New York, pp. 84–121.

Quinsey, V.L. (1986) Men who have sex with children, in *Law and Mental Health: International Perspectives*, vol. 2 (ed. D.N. Weisstub), Pergamon Press, New York, pp. 140–172.

Quinsey, V.L. (2003) The etiology of anomalous sexual preferences in men. *Annals of the New York Academy of Sciences*, 989, 105–117.

Quinsey, V.L., Coleman, G., Jones, B. and Altrows, I. (1997) Proximal antecedents of eloping and reoffending among supervised mentally disordered offenders. *Journal of Interpersonal Violence*, 12, 794–813.

Robinson, D. (1995) The Impact of Cognitive Skills Training on Post-Release Recidivism among Canadian Federal Offenders. *Report no. R-41.* Correctional Service Canada, Correctional Research and Development, Ottawa.

Russell, D., Peplau, L.A. and Cutrona, C.E. (1980) The revised UCLA loneliness scale: concurrent and discriminant validity evidence. *Journal of Personality and Social Psychology*, 39, 472–480.

Saum, S. (2007) A comparison of an actuarial risk prediction measure (Static-99) and a stable dynamic risk prediction measure (STABLE-2000) in making risk predictions for a group of sexual offenders. *Dissertations Abstracts International*, 68 (03), B. (UMI No. 3255539).

Seto, M.C. and Lalumière, M.L. (2001) A brief screening scale to identify pedophilic interests among child molesters. *Sexual Abuse: A Journal of Research and Treatment*, 13, 15–25.

Thornton, D. (2002) Constructing and testing a framework for dynamic risk assessment. *Sexual Abuse: A Journal of Research and Treatment*, 14, 139–153.

Watson, T. and Vess, J. (2009) Risk assessment of child-victim sex offenders for extended supervision in New Zealand. *Journal of Forensic Psychiatry & Psychology*, 18, 235–247.

Webb, L., Craissati, J. and Keen, S. (2007) Characteristics of internet child pornography offenders: a comparison with child molesters. *Sexual Abuse: A Journal of Research and Treatment*, 19, 449–465.

Whitaker, D.J., Le, B., Hanson, R.K. *et al.* (2008) Risk factors for the perpetration of child sexual abuse: a review and meta-analysis. *Child Abuse & Neglect*, 32, 529–548.

Wilson, R.J. (1999) Emotional congruence in sexual offenders against children. *Sexual Abuse: A Journal of Research and Treatment*, 1, 33–47.

24

Multi-agency Approaches to Effective Risk Management in the Community in England and Wales

Sarah Hilder and Hazel Kemshall

De Montfort University, UK

Introduction

Multi-Agency Public Protection Arrangements (MAPPA) were designed to enable responsible authorities, including the National Probation Directorate, HM Prison Service and England and Wales Police Forces, to effectively manage offenders who pose a serious risk of harm to the public, including violent and sexual offenders. MAPPA have been set up in 42 areas of England and Wales in line with the police services, following the implementation of measures contained in the CJCS Act (2000) and the CJA (2003).

The multi-agency management of high-risk offenders in the United Kingdom began in the late 1990s in West Yorkshire with police and probation exchanging information to enable more effective community management of sexual offenders (see Maguire *et al.* (2001) and Nash and Williams (2008) for a history). Further partnerships quickly developed across the country and the initiative was given momentum and statutory force by the CJCS Act (2000). Section 67 of this act placed a statutory responsibility on police and probation to:

Establish arrangements for the purpose of assessing and managing risks posed in the area by:

1. relevant sexual and violent offenders, and
2. other persons, who, by reason of offences committed by them (wherever committed), are considered by the responsible authority to be persons who may cause serious harm to the public (CJCS Act 2000: Section 67 (2)).

The CJCS Act (2000) in effect made both police and probation 'Responsible Authorities' with a statutory duty to set up MAPPA to exchange information, and carry out joint risk assessments and joint risk management planning on individual offenders through public protection panel meetings comprising representatives of each agency. This process was designed to facilitate

What Works in Offender Rehabilitation: An Evidence-Based Approach to Assessment and Treatment,
First Edition. Edited by Leam A. Craig, Louise Dixon and Theresa A. Gannon.
© 2013 John Wiley & Sons, Ltd. Published 2013 by John Wiley & Sons, Ltd.

information exchange before, during and after meetings in order to ensure more robust risk assessment and better targeted risk management plans (Kemshall and Wood, 2008).

These initial arrangements were given further statutory force by the CJA(2003), which placed a statutory duty on the Prison Service to become a Responsible Authority, alongside police and probation, and a range of other agencies such as education, housing and social services, who were given a 'duty to co-operate'. Thus, the partnerships became truly multi-agency and were given legislative duties and obligations. Three categories of offenders are considered under the remit of MAPPA. Namely, those who have committed violent and sexual offences, those who are listed on the sex offender register and other offenders considered by the police and probation services to pose a serious risk to the public and others (MoJ, 2009). The Criminal Justice and Immigration Act (2008) amended Schedule 15 of the CJA (2003) to require MAPPA to also consider categories of terrorist and extremist offences (see Section 16 and 15.2 of *MAPPA Guidance* for detailed information (MoJ, 2009)), who are considered to pose a high risk of harm.

Within MAPPA, offenders are managed at three different levels, a reflection of both their level of risk but, more importantly, the level of management and services required to manage them safely in the community. In brief these are:

Level 1 – ordinary risk management Where the agency responsible for the offender can manage risk without the significant involvement of other agencies. This level of management is only appropriate for category 1 and 2 offenders who are assessed as presenting a low or medium risk.

Level 2 – local inter-agency risk management Where there is active involvement of more than one agency in risk management plans, either because of a higher level of risk or because of the complexity of managing the offender. It is common for Level 3 cases to be 'referred down' to Level 2 when risk of harm deflates. The permanent membership of Level 2 should comprise those agencies that have an involvement in risk management. Responsible Authorities should decide the frequency of meetings and also the representation, taking an active role in the convening of meetings and quality assurance of risk management.

Level 3 – Multi-agency Public Protection Panel (MAPPP) For those defined as the 'critical few', the MAPPP is responsible for risk management drawing together key active partners who will take joint responsibility for the community management of the offender. An offender who should be referred to this level of management is defined as someone who:

1. is assessed under OASys (Offender Risk Assessment System) as being a high or very high risk of causing serious harm; *and*
2. presents risks that can only be managed by a plan which requires close cooperation at a senior level due to the complexity of the case and/or because of the unusual resource commitments it requires; *or*
3. although not assessed as a high or very high risk, the case is exceptional because the likelihood of media scrutiny and/or public interest in the management of the case is very high and there is a need to ensure that public confidence in the criminal justice system is sustained (From the *MAPPA Guidance*, MoJ, 2009: para 4.11–4.15).

This chapter aims to summarize the current issues associated with multi-agency approaches that are in use to manage high-risk offenders in the community in England and Wales. It will focus on important recent developments since 2007, following the most current evaluation of

MAPPA by Wood and Kemshall (2007). In particular, it will discuss the improved standards for risk management, the increased emphasis on engaging high-risk offenders in risk management plans, responding to issues of diversity, and important issues for the future development of MAPPA such as the greater inclusion of third sector agencies in the supervision of offenders since 2007.

The Position Post 2007

Following its inception, early evaluations of MAPPA (Maguire *et al.*, 2001; Kemshall *et al.*, 2005) have highlighted concerns about the differing participation levels from agencies, a lack of accurate and detailed recording of information at various stages, inconsistencies in levels of MAPPA management and the misappropriation of resources as relevant to the level of offender risk. This, in turn, has led to additional developments in legislative frameworks and centralized guidance (see CJA, 2003; Home Office, 2004; MoJ, 2007, 2009). Whilst there has been evidence of subsequent improvements and good practice, the joint police and probation thematic inspection report into the community management of sex offenders in 2005 (HMIP and HMIC, 2005) found that risk management plans were still not routinely implemented, with poor systems for review and follow-up, and with many Police MAPPA functions operating on very limited resources (Kemshall, 2010).

The 2005 inspection also noted that the overuse of restrictive measures, a trend of enforcement and control which had characterized MAPPA risk management up until that point, could serve to exacerbate issues of social isolation and hinder efforts to re-integrate offenders successfully (see Levenson and Cotter, 2005). Wood and Kemshall's (2007) evaluation of MAPPA supervision practice, commissioned under the Child Sex offender review (Home Office, 2007), provided a more detailed exploration of the role of quality interventions and supervision as an integral component of effective risk management. MAPPA Guidance in 2007 and 2009 reflected this shift, moving beyond an internalized focus on processes and systems to the wider benefits of quality in community-based interventions and pro-social supervision (MoJ, 2007, 2009). This concentration on offender engagement and securing compliance has been paralleled and influenced by developments in thinking on pathways to desistance from crime (Farrall, 2002; Maruna and Immarigeon, 2004; Ward and Maruna, 2007). Alternative strategies have emerged which harness both restorative principles (Circles of Support and Accountability (COSA)) and strengths-based approaches to re-integration, such as the Good Lives Model (Ward and Gannon, 2006).

Information sharing and disclosure

Information sharing and disclosure are critical to the effective operation of MAPPA (Maguire *et al.*, 2001; Kemshall *et al.*, 2005). Information sharing pre, during and post panel meetings ensures robust and evidenced risk assessments and close monitoring that risk management plans are being delivered as required (Kemshall *et al.*, 2005; MoJ, 2009).

However, difficulties still remain. The flow and exchange of information between key agencies can be limited. Agencies do not necessarily have access to each other's databases, and professional misunderstandings about confidentiality, roles and responsibilities can prevent information exchange from going smoothly (see Maguire *et al.*, 2001 for a detailed description). This has been exacerbated by limited access to the police Violent and Sex

Offender Register (VISOR) system. VISOR is a national confidential database of sexual, violent and other potentially dangerous offenders. It was first introduced as a tool for the police in 2005 following the murder of two Soham school girls by Ian Huntley, with limited access being provided to Probation in 2007 and to the Prison Service in 2008. In effect, there is no single MAPPA management information system accessible to all MAPPA agencies locally. This issue will potentially be exacerbated further by the growing contribution of third sector organizations to offender risk management (discussed later). In addition, group decision making can be tainted by 'group think' and 'problematic processes' with group participation and information exchange constrained by power hierarchies and cultural transference (Peay, 2003).

Misplaced concerns over human rights legislation, information sharing, and disclosure have also inhibited prompt and useful information exchange, and on occasion limited disclosure to third parties to achieve required levels of safety (HMIP, 2006; Kemshall and Wood, 2008). However, MAPPA Guidance is clear on information sharing and disclosure, with the Guidance stating that:

> The appropriate exchange of information is essential to effective public protection. This Guidance, therefore, clarifies the principles upon which MAPPA agencies may exchange information amongst themselves and where the RA may disclose such information to other persons or organisations outside the MAPPA, for example, voluntary hostel or tenancy support projects who are actively working with offenders and need to be aware of the potential risk of harm they present. The Guidance applies only to information that relates to living individuals, i.e. personal information, as it is this type of information to which the law confers heightened protection. The principles contained in this Guidance on information sharing and disclosure take into account the common law duty of confidence, the Data Protection Act (1998) and the European Convention on Human Rights (as incorporated into domestic law by the Human Rights Act (1998)) (MoJ, 2009, p. 60).

The Guidance also argues that information sharing must:

- have lawful authority;
- be necessary;
- be proportionate and done in ways that
- ensure the safety and security of the information shared; and
- be accountable (MoJ, 2009, p. 61).

However, the Guidance does acknowledge that whilst Section 115 of the Crime and Disorder Act (1998) allows any person to pass on information to certain agencies in order to prevent crime, it does not allow those agencies to pass on information to anybody or to non-duty to cooperate bodies, that is, agencies not covered by the requirements of the CJA (2003). Paragraph 5.5 of the Guidance (MoJ, 2009) outlines the difficulties this can present for those agencies involved in risk management, but who are not duty bound to cooperate agencies or Responsible Authorities. For example, this could include voluntary agencies providing drug or alcohol treatment, or those providing domestic violence intervention programmes. The Guidance indicates that other statute or common law might allow this, and that legal checks should be made, or that in some limited circumstances the offender's consent may need to be sought. Disclosure can be made to a third party in order to protect the public, and the Guidance provides clear principles and a protocol (MoJ, 2009). It is likely that third sector, private and voluntary agencies working with offenders may receive disclosures under this protocol if, for example, their staff or other service users are at risk. However, whether this would allow for general disclosures about offenders to these agencies is not clear and may require testing.

MAPPA in the 'Age of Austerity'

In 2010, the newly elected Coalition Government announced significant cuts for the Criminal Justice sector. The MoJ is reducing its budget from £10 billion in 2009/10, to £8.9 billion in 2010–2011, and to £7.9 billion by 2012–2015 (MoJ, 2010a). These cuts have impacted, and will continue to impact, police and probation, with police cuts amounting to some 20% (*The Guardian*, 2011a, b). These cuts should be viewed within the context of a large UK deficit, with borrowing running at some £159.8 billion and amounting to some 11.4% of gross domestic product in 2010, with a total debt currently running at some £1000.4 billion (ONS, 2010). As a consequence, individual Probation Trusts and Police Services are required to manage significant reductions in budget. The implications for MAPPA are both central and local. Centrally, the MoJ and NOMS recognize the need to 'streamline' current MAPPA procedures and processes, and to reflect a more resource-lean and efficient approach to MAPPA within central guidance.[1] The process is recognized as resource-intensive, with significant commitment of senior staff time to meetings, and at times overly intensive and burdensome risk management plans. In going forward, Police Services and Probation Trusts will struggle to continue to service MAPPA at pre-2010 levels. 'Streamlining' is likely to comprise a review and the possible reframing of the MAPPA eligibility criteria in addition to stricter operation of management levels with less resources targeted at management levels 1 and 2. The devalued term 'critical few' may at last recapture its original meaning.

Paralleling this, both the NOMS central MAPPA unit and local MAPPA areas are reviewing risk management planning and delivery, with attention increasingly focused on resource-lean and efficient risk management plans coupled with enhanced compliance to ensure lower attrition and failure. This provides an opportunity to replace the current lengthy lists of unco-ordinated actions with a few critical and well-targeted interventions. The MAPPA evaluation in 2007 found increased attention to motivational and engagement work (Kemshall and Wood, 2007; Wood and Kemshall, 2007). More recently, Her Majesty's Inspectorate of Probation joint thematic report argued for the 'Right Mix' between controlling and restrictive measures, and interventions that address offender need and inculcate self-risk management (HMIP and HMIC, 2010).

In this climate, audits of practice and a tighter focus on evaluation outcomes will be necessary. Proving positive outcomes against the resources invested, and demonstrating both the economic and social value of MAPPA will be important. This will require more sophisticated evaluation of the cost benefits of MAPPA, meeting the criteria set out by Dhiri and Brand (1999), with greater attention to the measurement of outcomes and benefits – for example, the number of high-impact crimes prevented and the number of children protected. This is likely to require the development of more sophisticated evaluation techniques than currently used for MAPPA auditing and reporting, and attention not only to immediate benefits (e.g., increased surveillance of high-risk offenders), but attention to medium-term benefits in

---

[1]   At time of writing, Guidance for 2011–2012 was in preparation.

the prevention of repeat victimization, and long-term benefits around crime reduction within the MAPPA offender population.

At present, MAPPA annual reports do not routinely state the costs of MAPPA, or provide a comparison of unit costs of operation against the outcomes achieved. Within a climate of 'value for money', MAPPA will have to provide data in order to justify its resources. To date, local MAPPA have presented limited evaluation material in annual reports, focusing on inputs to MAPPA (e.g., how many offenders of what type), outputs (number of panels, volume of offenders managed at particular levels), and some limited outcome material, usually in the shape of positive case stories, and where obtainable reconviction data (for area reports see: MoJ, 2011). In 2010, the Ministry of Justice attempted to aggregate area statistics into an overarching annual statistical report (see MoJ, 2011) but more sophisticated and long-term evaluations of MAPPA impact are required and more in-depth attention to outcome data locally.

More sophisticated evaluation does present challenges; not least in demonstrating a direct correlation between MAPPA management and reduction in reoffending. In the absence of a rigorous control group, this is particularly acute. Proxy measures may assist, for example, a comparison of the OASy, Offender Group Reconviction Score (OGRS) or Risk Matrix 2000 risk scores overtime; reductions in problematic behaviours with robust comparisons at differing time points; enhancement of protective factors compared over time; and increases in motivation, compliance and risk management. Audits of good practice can also supplement such outcome evaluations, by helping to develop measures, and by highlighting those interventions that appear to have the most benefit (Kemshall, 2010).

MAPPA Going Forward

Three key strands are identified for the development of MAPPA work going forward. These are not the only issues facing MAPPA, but they are prioritized here as they reflect current issues in work with offenders and the requirement for MAPPA to make an effective contribution to the 'rehabilitation revolution' (MoJ, 2010a). They will now each be discussed in turn.

Responding appropriately to issues of diversity and effectively engaging with a range of offenders and offence types

The importance of valuing diversity and responding to the diverse needs and experiences of victims and offenders is firmly embedded into the policy rhetoric of all statutory criminal justice agencies. However, as Mitchell (2010) highlights, the concept of diversity itself eludes any definitive grip, with a resulting array of organizational beliefs and understandings of its meaning and purpose. The language and characteristics of the anti-discriminatory thread, which formerly ran through probation practice, for example, is not routinely recognized elsewhere, with the police and health services more frequently utilizing the language of equality. Therefore, as Mitchell (2010) continues, 'Whilst the stated commitment to valuing and addressing diversity may seem to be a strong starting position for multi agency work and high-risk public protection arrangements such as MAPPA, partner members are unlikely to come to meetings with a universally agreed understanding of what this actually means and what they are seeking to achieve in this respect' (p. 58).

To a limited extent, MAPPA has attempted to recognize the importance of diversity. For example, the MoJ (2009) Guidance states:

> In undertaking its work, MAPPA agencies will be sensitive and responsive to people's differences and needs and will integrate this understanding into the delivery of their functions to ensure that nobody is disadvantaged as a result of their belonging to a specific social group. To assist in achieving this, each RA (risk assessment) will ensure that:

> * MAPPA is explicitly referenced in its constituent agencies' Diversity Plans;
> * The MAPPA Strategic Management Board has its own Diversity Plan;
> * All staff actively engaged in MAPPA work are trained in diversity;
> * All MAPPA data has the capacity to be broken down by race, ethnicity, gender, age, disability and sexual orientation;
> * MAPPA offenders have access to interpreting and translation service;
> * There is sensitivity to the membership of level 2 and 3 MAPP meetings in relation to the diversity of the local MAPPA population;
> * There is consultation with women, black and minority ethnic offenders, and offenders with disabilities over means to maximise inclusion and their understanding of the processes;
> * There is a formal process for dealing with complaints; and
> * MAPPA information and leaflets are produced in languages appropriate to the local population (p. 32).

However, MAPPA continue to operate within the challenging context of ever-changing levels of tolerance, conceptualizations and characterizations of risk. Practitioners engaged in the assessment and management of high-risk offenders need to understand the pressures and tensions inherent in their practice, where broader social constructions of those who are seen to be the most dangerous are frequently linked to misconceptions of diversity and identity.

A proactive stance towards an exploration of diversity issues is vital to the process of securing good-quality risk assessment and risk management strategies. An approach which fails to question certain factors or behaviours on the grounds that to do so would be disrespectful to the tradition and practices of a community or group is as alarming as an approach which readily attributes risk signifiers on the basis of widely held assumptions and stereotypes about the 'riskiness' of certain minority groups and identity facets (Parekh, 2000). The extent to which power, prejudice and hate towards different groups in society is the motivation for the commission of an offence, or series of offences, also needs to be recognized. Only then can appropriate assessments of the risk of serious harm be determined, with the provision of a context and understanding of different victim behaviours, and identifying appropriate strategies for victim support and reductions in the potential for re-victimization (Grieve, 2010).

Whilst the discussion which follows here pursues examples relating to concepts of race, religion and faith, parallels may be drawn with a variety of other experiences of approaches to 'difference', including mental health, disability, age, sexuality and gender. It is recognized that no individual can be defined by a singular facet of diversity from which all other issues and needs are determined. It is also noted that roles, identities, self-perceptions and the perceptions of others are open to influence, flux and change.

The potential for subjectivity and bias to occur in clinical assessment is well documented (Kemshall and Wood, 2007; Kemshall, 2008). In addition, the various ways in which the power structures of organizations and hierarchical roles may impact upon the exchange of information in multi-agency settings have also been examined (Kemshall *et al.*, 2005;

Kemshall, 2008; Nash, 2010). In this respect, it is quite easy to envisage that panel members may feel particularly anxious about openly raising issues of diversity and discrimination in a multi-agency public protection forum, for fear of having their values, beliefs and knowledge, or lack of, exposed and challenged. However, if a climate conducive to the constructive exploration of such issues is not fostered, the potential for cultural transference becomes greater. Cultural transference between organizations working in partnership is described as the merger and shift in individual organizational identities and philosophies to those of the dominant host organization (Nash, 2010). Bhui (2006) and Cole (2008) highlight that this is a particular strategic barrier to effective partnership working with smaller, voluntary and charity organizations from minority sectors who may become resigned to a subservient tolerance of the dominant ideologies and perceptions of the larger, statutory organizations.

MAPPA also clearly operates within the broader shifting sands of ever-changing socio-political calls for public safety and national security as new emerging 'threats' are identified. The Criminal Justice and Immigration Act (2008) introduced acts of extremism and terrorism into the MAPPA framework. It is important that the concept of 'dangerousness' as being particular to the 'critical few' is retained during such developments. Nevertheless, practitioners may still be susceptible to a dialogue on risk in this context, which perpetuates notions of an exaggerated prevalence of the 'terrorist other' centred predominantly on negative perceptions of religion and Islam. Whilst such risks as radicalization and terrorism should be addressed, an approach which engages in a social construction of those considered to pose the greatest risk can have an oppressive and discriminatory impact (Mythen, Walklate and Khan, 2009). For example, in their survey of the experiences of racism of a group of British Muslim youth of Pakistani heritage 18–26 years in the North West of England, Mythen, Walklate and Khan (2009) found that the young people viewed the negative portrayal of Muslims to extend far beyond the concept of radicalization and extremism, with media attention also fixating on other stereotypical negative images such as honor killings, arranged marriages and spousal abuse.

Marranci (2007) examined the security and scrutiny of Muslims in prison, and concluded the suspicion that religious practices incurred, due to the association with a construction of risk, could serve to marginalize the individual even further and render them more vulnerable to recidivism. Therefore, it is vital that an individual's diversity and identity be seen as part of a holistic picture of assessment, rather than giving weight to particular identity factors or behaviours in isolation.

Other studies have demonstrated that effective statutory, voluntary partnership work which engages with minority communities has much to offer in terms of challenging mainstream orthodoxy, providing more detailed insight into the complex nature that issues of diversity and identity may have on victim experiences, levels of risk and offender engagement in programmes of intervention (e.g., Mills, 2009). However, the recent evaluations of voluntary sector involvement in four Integrated Offender Management pilots (Wong and Hartworth, 2009) highlighted that engagement with some black and minority ethnic groups remained problematic. Addressing this was seen as a priority for future work, reflecting on the disproportionate over-representation of individuals from some of these groups within the offender population.

However, it is arguably the very knowledge of the disproportionate representation and well-documented (Macpherson, 1999), routinely experienced issues of prejudice and institutionalized discrimination of already marginalized groups at the hands of statutory criminal justice sector agencies that serves to influence such resistance. The involvement of voluntary and community sector agencies in the delivery of risk management can inevitably be seen as a further step towards the co-option of the third sector into the delivery of primary functions of punishment and public protection, where there is already significant evidence that the process of 'justice' and punishment is not administered fairly to all (Gough, 2010). Therefore, for some voluntary sector providers this partnership may be a step too far, yet as other independent sources of funding start to rapidly disappear, for others it may be the only chance of survival. It also introduces frameworks of coercion and enforcement to agencies which have evolved from a basis of volunteerism and consensual engagement (Skinner, 2010).

There may, however, also be alternative models. Spalek (2002) explored work which was being undertaken between the police and Muslim communities in relation to extremism, emphasizing the importance of community empowerment in the first instance with information sharing with the authorities as a secondary function (Spalek, 2002). Grieve (2010) also highlights the model of community-empowered public protection illustrated by the Jewish programme, Community Security Trust (Grieve, 2010). Developments in restorative methods have also been examined as a response to Hate Crime, as illustrated by the Southwark mediation centre initiative (Southwark Mediation, 2002). However, as Britton (2004) suggests, explorations of minority group experiences of crime are still far more readily applied to issues of criminality within a community rather than issues of victimization. If funds are only routinely mobilized when it is the former rather than the latter, then the social constructions of the criminality and dangerousness of those groups are simply likely to persist, and the distrust of statutory interventions by both offenders and victims from those communities is likely to remain.

Developing constructive work on engagement with high-risk offenders

The importance of effective offender engagement in the management and reduction of risk is receiving renewed attention (Wood and Kemshall, 2007), influenced by the growing interest and research into the complex ways in which desistance from crime is achieved. McNeill and Weaver (2010) explored the links to be made between desistance theory, the Good Lives Model and offender management as part of the current NOMS Offender Engagement project. In relation to the management of high-risk offenders, this has seen the recognition of the need for an effective balance between restrictive measures and rehabilitative methods, as further endorsed by the 2010 Joint Police and Probation Inspection report (HMIP and HMIC, 2010).

The 2010 Joint Police and Probation Inspection found some evidence of poor communication between police and probation staff still remained, and that 10 years on, the term 'risk' was still often used without any clarification of context or meaning (HMIP and HMIC, 2010). Issues of inappropriate resource allocation to less serious cases were also still apparent. The supervision of sex offenders was primarily viewed by probation practitioners to refer to an individual's participation in the Core Sex Offender Treatment Programme (SOTP) with little confidence expressed by the majority of staff interviewed as to how they might work with an offender without an SOTP requirement, or indeed one who was in complete denial. Delays in the commencement of the SOTP were noted with concerns that pre-programme preparation work was often not fully completed. Access to VISOR was restricted for Probation staff and the quality of data found there was inconsistent (HMIP and HMIC, 2010).

Whilst there were some good examples of the use of community-based re-integration initiatives such as the COSA, the provision of other services which may have aided the re-integration of high-risk sex offenders were generally seen to be poor. In particular, assistance in acquiring appropriate move on accommodation and an understanding of the educational, training and employment needs of offenders were not forthcoming (HMIP and HMIC, 2010).

Interventions with this group of offenders therefore continue to centre on the use of cognitive behavioural accredited programmes. This approach was strongly endorsed by the recent MoJ/NOMs position statement (MoJ, 2010b) and MoJ paper *What Works with Sex Offenders?* (MoJ, 2010c) which relayed the successes of the core SOTP, particularly for those assessed as medium risk. The extended SOTP designed for high-risk offenders in custody has yet to be evaluated. The MoJ (2010c) paper draws primarily on international research to establish the credibility of cognitive behavioural methods with this offender group, acknowledging the current limitations of any robust evaluations of the impact on recidivism in the United Kingdom. Nevertheless, there are a number of reported improvements in relationship skills and a reduction in pro-offending attitudes for SOTP participants (MoJ, 2010c). What is significantly lacking, however, is any extensive comparative analysis with alternative methods of intervention, albeit that many, such as the Good Lives Model which will now be discussed, remain in their infancy.

Advocates of the Good Lives Model approach to the supervision of sex offenders consider that simply to work on the acquisition of skills to aid the offender in managing their own risk factors and high-risk scenarios is not enough (Ward and Gannon, 2006). Long-term desistance can only be achieved if they are also provided with the opportunity to develop and sustain a personal identity which is satisfying and rewarding. The acquisition of human 'primary goods' is key to the formation of a constructive sense of self (see Ward and Gannon 2006 for further details). Under the Good Lives Model, therefore, the successful rehabilitation of an offender is achieved via the exploration of the skills and opportunities required to achieve these 'human' goals via appropriate and positive means. This is as opposed to a perpetual rehearsal of an image of the offender which is totally subsumed by an assessment of risk, seen only to warrant control and isolation. The Good Lives approach to a reduction in recidivism views the offender as a proactive agent of change, rather than a passive recipient of strategies of risk management, surveillance and control (Lacombe, 2008). It also promotes engagement and compliance through the recognition of the offender as someone who has strengths and skills which can be utilized and developed constructively and not someone who is wholly constrained by the status their offending imposes. Simply put, the Good Lives Model focuses on what individuals can do and achieve rather than purely what they must not do and should avoid.

Diversity and the Good Lives Model Diversity and responsivity issues remain key here too, because in order to maximize motivation, engagement and compliance, offender interventions and management strategies need to be informed by an understanding of the different social contexts within which 'choices' are made and opportunities occur (Bottoms and Shapland, 2011). The desire for the acquisition of human primary goods and key pathways to desistance will strike similar chords for many offenders, but the instrumental means and resources available to achieve such goals will vary considerably. The practitioner's minimization or denial of the different contexts within which change is to occur is likely to render its failure.

Although McNeill and Weaver (2010) highlight studies which have examined gender, ethnicity and the impact of religion on desistance, such avenues of exploration remain in their infancy and relatively little is still known about how desistance may work for specific subgroups within society. However, advocates of desistance and Good Lives Models (Maruna, 2001; Ward and Gannon, 2006; McNeill and Weaver, 2010) stress the need to recognize that gendered identities, cultural aspirations, religious and spiritual well-being, indeed all of the constitute elements which may lead to the formation of a 'good life', can be realized in a variety of constructive ways. It is important that their pursuit is offender-driven in a manner which is realistic and achievable. In addition, it is also necessary that the impact of experiences or expressions of dominance, discrimination and prejudice will resonate at different levels for different individuals, and that their significance is not over or underplayed by practitioners in their assessment and management of risks. Engaging effectively in the offender's narrative and examining the significance and meaning they attach to issues of diversity, power and discrimination becomes one of the key tools of insight for risk assessment and risk reduction methods.

The role of the third sector and relationship to MAPPA

The Coalition Government has signalled a greater interest in a 'mixed economy' of criminal justice provision, particularly around supervision, interventions and treatment of offenders (Clarke, 2010; Blunt, 2011) (and all the party manifestos were committed to this development to some degree). In particular, the private and third sectors (generally defined as not-for-profit, charitable or voluntary sector providers) are seen as significant providers (Blunt, 2011), and private providers such as Group 4 security services, are likely to increase their market share through the provision of community payback, and intervention programmes to offenders. Larger providers are likely to harness economies of scale and extend the reach of their provision, a pattern that is already evident in the prison sector. This may also signal a move from largely locally based partnerships with a focus on accessibility, welfare needs, and desistance issues, to traditionally core probation tasks around community sentence delivery. The contracting out and marketization of offender provision is likely to break down existing parameters of responsibility.

Both private and third sectors are already key providers, usually through partnership or commissioning arrangements with local Probation Trusts, providing a range of services and interventions to offenders, such as drug and alcohol treatments, domestic violence programmes, education and training, housing, and employment services. More recent initiatives on Integrated Offender Management (IOM) and Community Payback (CP) will see the sector as a direct national competitor to Trusts for the provision of key services, including treatment programmes and group-based interventions. Perhaps most significant is the introduction of 'Payment by Results' (PbR) in the 2010 Green Paper (MoJ, 2010d), that is, paying providers if they reduce reoffending. This will apply to all providers of services to offenders by 2015. For example, Collins (2011) has stated that PbR:

> ....represents a shift of focus from processes to outcomes, which is intended to drive innovation and creativity by enabling providers to explore new ways of reducing reoffending, free from process-based targets prescribed by central government. It has the added benefit of requiring commissioners to be unambiguous in setting out what they want to achieve, addressing the potential contradictions within the CJS between public protection and reducing reoffending (p. 19).

This shift from outputs to outcomes is significant for all providers, as is the tighter focus on costs of activities. For MAPPA, this will require a shift from the current reliance on process targets and output data, to a more sophisticated measurement of outcomes. However, what will constitute appropriate outcome measures for high-risk offenders under MAPPA? For example, will such a measure be based on long-term reconviction data (one year or longer), or will short-term and interim measures also be developed? Will short-term measures based on completion of treatment programmes, responses to supervision, securing accommodation or gaining employment be appropriate? Will interim measures around reductions in the frequency and severity of offending be useful (Hayes, 2010; Dicker, 2011)? If measures are not chosen with care then 'cherry picking' by private and third sector providers is bound to occur (Collins, 2011). The remaining cases will inevitably result in an evermore difficult and challenging probation and MAPPA caseload. Outcome measures are also likely to be skewed by context – areas of the country with considerable social and economic disadvantage will present more re-integration and resettlement challenges to offenders, particularly high-risk offenders post custody. The 'playing field' is thus far from level.

This re-structuring of provision has implications for the management of high-risk offenders in the community, and more particularly for MAPPA. In essence, offender management characterizes both police and probation offender managers as facilitators, brokers and arrangers of services provided by others, and in this case by private and third sector organizations (e.g., domestic violence, violence reduction programmes, sex offender treatment programmes). Such providers have considerable face-to-face contact time with offenders (and increasingly more than Offender Managers). In this climate, they are likely to provide the specific treatments/ interventions designed to reduce risk; and they may be more directly involved in compliance and engagement issues. However, the statutory and legal powers upon which MAPPA is founded, and which govern information exchange, and the duty to risk assess and risk manage, do not include private or third sector organizations. Such organizations are not likely to be included in local MAPPA Memorandum of Understanding which locally governs MAPPA set-up and operation, and whilst they might be invited to multi-agency public protection panel meetings, they do not necessarily have the right or the duty to attend. Whilst sections 115–117 of the Crime and Disorder Act (1998) provide the legal duty and right to disclose in order to prevent crime, this does not necessarily mean that third sector organizations will, and private providers are likely to, resist the costs involved in such participation. Tensions between third sector organizational values, user confidentiality, and MAPPA public protection concerns are also bound to arise. These tensions will be particularly acute where third sector organizations adopt a value frame prioritizing user needs and rights above public protection, or where internal risk policies and procedures are inadequate for managing offender risk (see, e.g., the prosecution of Mental Health Matters for the work-related death of Ashleigh Ewing in Community Care (2010)).

Conclusions

These are challenging times for MAPPA, not least in the areas of diversity, resource constraint and outcome measures. Prins (2010) and Howard (2010) advocate that the support, supervision and evaluation of those engaged in MAPPA should not only seek to ensure the defensible and equitable nature of the decisions made there, but also provide the opportunity for the generation and development of knowledge and shared learning, particularly around issues of diversity and responsivity, with opportunity for joint reflection. Whether 'streamlining' MAPPA and predicted reviews of eligibility criteria will enable this to occur has yet to be seen.

Developments in the discussion of community protection, public awareness and community re-integration have seen the emergence of 'blended approaches', such as Thames Valley where the COSA has been co-opted into the MAPPA process (Kemshall, 2008). There has also been an increased recognition of the value of pro-social supervision that extends beyond the provision of accredited cognitive behavioural work alone, such as the Good Lives Model approach (Ward and Maruna, 2007). However, Kemshall (2008) highlights that, as yet, there is no formal long-term strategic commitment to exploring this complementary approach to 'protective integration'. Further evaluation and dissemination of learning is therefore necessary to explore a strategy which provides both safety for victims and offenders, and secures long-term secondary desistance from crime.

Dealing with high-risk offenders is also potentially costly, with a number of hidden costs such as additional risk assessments, increased liaison with other agencies, and more intensive supervision (Maguire *et al.*, 2001). Cost pressures on the third sector may mitigate against effective risk management (see, e.g., the case of Clear Springs and bail hostel accommodation, BBC News, 2009) or result in the sector only engaging with lower-risk offenders, or those deemed to be a 'good bet'. Rather than ensuring a greater range of 'flexible' services to offenders, an unintended consequence may be a withholding of services from the most risky and the most problematic. Consequently, offender managers may find less time and resources available for high-risk offenders rather than more. To reiterate, it is a challenging time for MAPPA. The system has expanded greatly since its original inception in 2000, and it must now explicitly prove its worth. Increased attention to quality, effective risk management and positively evaluated outcomes, away from labour-intensive systems and processes, will help.

References

BBC News (2009) Bail hostel Clear Springs 'may lose contract', November 28. http://news.bbc.co.uk/1/hi/uk/8383591.stm (accessed 26 December 2012).

Bhui, H.S. (2006) Anti racist practice in NOMS: reconciling managerialist and professional realities. *Howard Journal*, 45, 171–190.

Blunt, C. (2011) Rehabilitation revolution. Paper presented to the Social Market Foundation Rehabilitation Revolution Conference, January 25. http://www.justice.gov.uk/news/features/features-250111a (accessed 9 January 2013).

Bottoms, A.E. and Shapland, J. (2011) Steps towards desistance among male young adult recidivists, in *Escape Routes: Contemporary Perspectives on Life After Punishment* (eds S. Farrall, R. Sparks, S. Maruna and M. Hough), Routledge, London, pp. 43–80.

Britton, N.J. (2004) Minorities, crime and criminal justice, in *Student Handbook of Criminal Justice and Criminology* (eds J. Muncie and D. Wilson), Cavendish, London, pp. 81–93.

Clarke, K. (2010) *The Government's vision for criminal justice reform. Speech to the Centre for Crime and Justice Studies*, 30 June 2010, Ministry of Justice, London.

Cole, B. (2008). Working with ethnic diversity, in *Addressing Offending Behaviour, Context, Practice and Values* (eds S. Green, E. Lancaster and S. Feasey), Willan, Cullompton, pp. 402–426.

Collins, J. (2011) Payment by results in the criminal justice system: can it deliver? *Safer Communities*, 10, 18–25.

Community Care (2010) Mental health matters fined over Ashleigh Ewing's death. http://www.communitycare.co.uk/articles/02/02/2010/113704/mental-health-charity-fined-30000-over-support-workers-killing.htm (accessed 9 January 2013).

Crime and Disorder Act (1998) http://www.legislation.gov.uk/ukpga/1998/37/contents (accessed 26 December 2012).

Criminal Justice Act (CJA) (2003) http://www.legislation.gov.uk/ukpga/2003/44/contents (accessed 26 December 2012).

Criminal Justice and Court Services Act (CJCS) (2000) http://www.legislation.gov.uk/ukpga/2000/43/contents (accessed 26 December 2012).

Criminal Justice and Immigration Act (2008) http://www.legislation.gov.uk/ukpga/2008/4/section/140 (accessed 26 December 2012).

Dhiri, S. and Brand, S. (1999) *Analysis of Costs and Benefits: Guidance for Evaluators*, Home Office, Research and Statistics Directorate, London.

Dicker, J. (2011) *Payment-by-Outcome in Offender Management*, 2020 Public Services Trust, London.

Farrall, S. (2002) *Rethinking What Works with Offenders: Probation, Social Context and Desistance from Crime*. Willan, Cullompton.

Gough, D. (2010) Multi agency working in corrections: cooperation and competition in probation practice, in *Multi-agency Working in Criminal Justice. Control and Care in Contemporary Correctional Practice* (eds A. Pycroft and D. Gough), Policy Press, Bristol, pp. 21–34.

Grieve, J. (2010) Policing, public protection and minority groups, in *Handbook of Public Protection* (eds M. Nash and A. Williams), Willan, Cullompton, pp. 399–416.

Hayes, C. (2010) *Payment by Results: What Does It Mean for Voluntary Organisations Working with Offenders*, Clinks, London.

Her Majesty's Inspectorate of Probation (HMIP) and Her Majesty's Inspectorate of Constabulary (HMIC) (2005) *Managing Sex Offenders in the Community: A Joint Inspection on Sex Offenders*, Home Office, London.

HMIP (2006) *An Independent Review of a Serious Further Offence Case: Damien Hanson and Elliot White*. London: HMIP.

HMIP and HMIC (2010) *Restriction and Rehabilitation: Getting the Mix Right*, Home Office, London.

Home Office (2004) *MAPPA Guidance (Version 2)*, Home Office, London.

Home Office (2007) *MAPPA – The First Five Years: A National Overview of the Multi-Agency Public Protection Arrangements*, Home Office, London.

Howard, J. (2010) The beauty of reflection and the beast of multi agency cooperation, in *Multi-agency Working in Criminal Justice. Control and Care in Contemporary Correctional Practice* (eds A. Pycroft and D. Gough), Policy Press, Bristol, pp. 231–244.

Kemshall, H. (2008) *Understanding the Community Management of High Risk Offenders*, Open University Press, Berkshire.

Kemshall, H. (2010) Community protection and multi-agency public protection arrangements, in *Handbook of Public Protection* (eds M. Nash and A. Williams), Willan Publishing, Cullompton, pp. 199–216.

Kemshall, H. and Wood, J. (2007) High-risk offenders and public protection, in *Handbook of Probation* (eds L. Gelsthorpe and R. Morgan), Willan, Cullompton, pp. 381–397.

Kemshall, H. and Wood, J. (2008) Public protection in practice: multi-agency public protection arrangements (MAPPA), in *Private and Confidential? Handling Personal Information in the Social and Health Services* (eds C. Clark and J. McGhee), Policy Press, Bristol, pp. 111–128.

Kemshall, H., Wood, J., Mackenzie, G. *et al.* (2005) *Strengthening Multi-Agency Public Protection Arrangements (MAPPA)*, Home Office, London. http://rds.homeoffice.gov.uk/rds/pdfs05/dpr45.pdf. (accessed 26 December 2012).

Lacombe, D. (2008) Consumed with sex: the treatment of sex offenders in risk society. *British Journal of Criminology*, 48, 55–74.

Levenson, J. and Cotter, L. (2005) The impact of the sex offender residence restrictions: 1,000 feet from danger or one step form the absurd? *International Journal of Offender Therapy and Comparative Criminology*, 49, 168–178.

Macpherson, W. (1999) *The Stephen Lawrence Inquiry*, Stationary Office, London.

Maguire, M., Kemshall, H., Noaks, L. and Wincup, E. (2001) Risk Management of Sexual and Violent Offenders: The Work of Public Protection Panels. *Police Research Ser. Paper no. 139*. Home Office, London.

Marranci, G. (2007) Faith, ideology and fear. The case of current and former Muslim prisoners. IQRA Annual Lecture, House of Lords, 26 June 2007.

Maruna, S. (2001) *Making Good. How Ex-Convicts Reform and Rebuild Their Lives*, American Psychological Association, Washington, DC.

Maruna, S. and Immarigeon, R. (eds) (2004) *After Crime and Punishment: Pathways to Offender Reintegration*, Willan, Collumpton.

McNeill, F. and Weaver, B. (2010) *Changing Lives, Desistance Research and Offender Management*, Scottish Centre for Crime and Justice Research, Glasgow.

Mills, H. (2009) *Policy, Purpose and Pragmatism: Dilemmas for Voluntary and Community Organisations Working with Black Young People Affected by Crime*, Centre for Crime and Justice Studies, Kings College London, London.

Ministry of Justice (MoJ) (2007) *MAPPA Guidance 2007 Version 2.0. Produced by the National MAPPA team, National Offender Management Service Public Protection Unit*. Ministry of Justice, London.

Ministry of Justice (2009) *MAPPA Guidance 2009. Produced by the National MAPPA team*, National Offender Management Service Public Protection Unit. Home Office, London.

Ministry of Justice (2010a) *Business Plan 2011–2015*, Ministry of Justice, London.

Ministry of Justice/NOMS (2010a) *Position Statement for the Assessment, Management and Treatment of Sex Offenders*, Ministry of Justice, NOMS, MAPPA and Sexual Offending Group, Public Protection and Mental Health Unit, London.

Ministry of Justice/NOMS (2010b) *What Works with Sex offenders?* Ministry of Justice and NOMS, London.

Ministry of Justice (2010b) Breaking the Cycle: Effective Punishment, Rehabilitation and Sentencing of Offenders. http://www.justice.gov.uk/consultations/consultation-040311 (accessed 9 January 2013).

Ministry of Justice (2011) MAPPA Annual Reports. http://www.justice.gov.uk/publications/corporate-reports/mappa-reports (accessed 9 January 2013).

Mitchell, M. (2010) Diversity and the policy agenda in criminal justice, in *Multi-agency Working in Criminal Justice. Control and Care in Contemporary Correctional Practice* (eds A. Pycroft and D. Gough), Policy Press, Bristol, pp. 51–54.

Mythen, G., Walklate, S. and Khan, F. (2009) "I'm a Muslim, but I'm not a terrorist": victimisation, risky identities and the performance of safety. *British Journal of Criminology*, 49, 736–754.

Nash, M. (2010) The politics of public protection, in *Handbook of Public Protection* (eds M. Nash and A. Williams), Willan, Cullompton, pp. 60–82.

Nash, M. and Williams, A. (2008) *The Anatomy of Serious Offending*, Oxford University Press, Oxford.

Office for National Statistics (ONS) (2011) *Economic and Labour Market* Review, 5 (4). www.ons.gov.uk/ons/.../economic-and-labour-market-review.pdf (accessed 9 January 2013).

Parekh, B. (2000) *Rethinking Multiculturalism: Cultural Diversity and Political Theory*. Palgrave Macmillan, Basingstoke.

Peay, J. (2003) *Decisions and Dilemmas Working with Mental Health Law*, Hart Publishing, Oxford.

Prins, H. (2010) Dangers by being despised grow great, in *Handbook of Public Protection* (eds M. Nash and A. Williams), Willan, Cullompton, pp. 15–39.

Skinner, C. (2010) Clients or offender? The case for clarity of purpose in multi-agency working, in *Multi-agency Working in Criminal Justice. Control and Care in Contemporary Correctional Practice* (eds A. Pycroft and D. Gough), Policy Press, Bristol, pp. 35–50.

Southwark Mediation (2002) *Southwark Mediation Centre*. Hate Crime Project, Southwark Mediation Centre, London.

Spalek, B. (2002) *Islaam, Crime and Criminal Justice*, Willan, Cullompton.

The Guardian (2011a) Police Cuts Will Mean 10,000 Fewer Officers Says Labour, 6 February 2011. http://www.guardian.co.uk/uk/2011/feb/06/police-cuts-labour-research-officers (accessed 26 December 2012).

The Guardian (2011b) Police Chiefs: We Will Lose 28,000 Staff, 7 March 2011. http://www.guardian.co.uk/uk/2011/mar/07/police-chiefs-lose-28000-staff?INTCMP=SRCH (accessed 9 January 2013).

Ward, T. and Gannon T.A. (2006) Rehabilitation etiology and self regulation: the comprehensive good lives model of treatment for sex offenders. *Aggression and Violent Behavior*, 11, 77–94.

Ward, T. and Maruna, S. (2007) *Rehabilitation*, Routledge, London.

Wong, K. and Hartworth, D. (2009) *Integrated Offender Management and Third Sector Engagement. Case Studies of Four Pioneer Sites*. NACRO, London.

Wood, J. and Kemshall, H. (with Maguire, M., Hudson, K. and Mackenzie, G.) (2007) The Operation and Experience of Multi-agency Public Protection Arrangements (MAPPA). *Online Rep. no. 12/07*. Research and Statistics Department, Home Office, London. http://www.caerdydd.ac.uk/socsi/resources/MAPPA1207.pdf (accessed 9 January 2013).

25

Group or Individual Therapy in the Treatment of Sexual Offenders

Geris A. Serran, William L. Marshall, Liam E. Marshall and Matt D. O'Brien

Rockwood Psychological Services, Canada

Over the years, efforts have been made to make treatment programmes for sexual offenders more effective. Sexual offender programming has shifted from focusing solely on deviant sexual interests in the 1960s to more comprehensive interventions over the years. More recently, theorists such as Ward (2002), Ward and Stewart (2003) and practitioners such as Marshall *et al.* (2011) have emphasized the importance of adopting a positive approach to treatment, a shift from a primarily avoidance or relapse-based focus. Therapists working with sexual offenders can find articles and books outlining various strategies and approaches to such strength-based approaches (see Linley and Joseph, 2004 and Snyder and Lopez, 2005).

Interestingly, little attention is paid in the literature to specific procedural issues, such as optimal numbers in the group, therapist factors and group composition. Encouraging clients to participate in intervention can be challenging, especially sexual offender clients, who may be reluctant to enter a treatment programme. Potential challenges might include the setting (e.g., clients might fear being identified as sexual offenders), confidentiality issues, trust in professionals, negative experiences in therapy, fear of being judged and concerns about the expectations of therapy.

This chapter focuses specifically on the issue of group versus individual treatment in sexual offender intervention. The general clinical literature will be examined, followed by sexual offender-specific research. Most importantly, process issues will be discussed in relation to individual or group therapy. Here, attention will be paid to examining which type of therapy – if any – is most likely to foster the development of fundamental process principles associated with effective treatment (see Marshall and Burton, 2010).

General Clinical Literature

The efficacy of group treatment is well established in the literature; Fuhriman and Burlingame (1994) conducted a review of 700 group therapy studies, concluding that group therapy consistently produces beneficial results, regardless of the problem, disorder or treatment modality.

What Works in Offender Rehabilitation: An Evidence-Based Approach to Assessment and Treatment, First Edition. Edited by Leam A. Craig, Louise Dixon and Theresa A. Gannon.
© 2013 John Wiley & Sons, Ltd. Published 2013 by John Wiley & Sons, Ltd.

Empirical research comparing the effectiveness of both individual therapy and group therapy suggests that either approach is significantly more effective than no treatment regardless of therapeutic orientation, client group or presenting problem (Bednar and Kaul, 1994; Fuhriman and Burlingame, 1994; Lambert and Bergin, 1994).

Various meta-analyses have compared outcomes in group and individual therapy. Fuhriman and Burlingame (1994) indicated that, generally, both individual and group therapy are equally effective although some of the studies in earlier meta-analyses were characterized by confounds which could serve to limit the conclusions. Tillitski (1990) conducted a meta-analysis including only studies that directly compared group and individual therapy with either an active or inactive control group. He found no differences, again, between group and individual therapy in terms of overall effectiveness. Some issues and concerns identified with this meta-analysis however were that: (i) child and adolescent clients were combined with adults, (ii) the meta-analysis did not include important methodological criteria which might affect the results, and (iii) the meta-analysis did not clearly define 'group therapy' (McRoberts, Burlingame and Hoag, 1998).

As a result, McRoberts, Burlingame and Hoag (1998) conducted a meta-analysis evaluating the differential outcome between individual and group therapy addressing previously identified methodological issues. In addition, this meta-analysis examined whether and under what circumstances one modality may be preferred. In terms of inclusion criteria, studies had to use both group and individual therapy, groups had to meet regularly with an identified therapist, clients had to exhibit a clinical problem requiring mental health intervention, the study had to be experimental or quasi-experimental with matching or random assignment to groups and effect size estimates needed to be calculated. Twenty-three studies remained for the analysis. Variables examined included treatment variables (theoretical orientation, treatment setting, therapy dosage, frequency and length of sessions), client factors (diagnosis, client gender and age, problem chronicity) and therapist factors (gender, level of training and experience, and presence of a co-therapist).

McRoberts, Burlingame and Hoag's (1998) findings were similar to previous meta-analyses and empirical studies; both individual and group therapy were found to be equally effective. The authors noted, however, that under some circumstances, differential outcomes may be obtained depending on the format used. Individual therapy (cognitive behavioural) was deemed more effective for treating depression when compared to cognitive behavioural group therapy. On the other hand, group therapy appeared more effective in treating clients with substance use problems (Burlingame *et al.*, 1995; Miller *et al.*, 1995; Stinchfield, Owen and Winters, 1994), and various stress syndromes. Group therapy also seemed more effective than individual intervention in short-term (10 or less sessions) interventions. The authors highlight the fact that statistical power is problematic in all of the meta-analyses in this area. They also express concerns that so few studies have been conducted, especially given the fact that group therapy is increasingly being recommended as a cost-effective form of treatment across a wide variety of client populations (MacKenzie, 1995).

Some specific empirical studies suggest that group or individual therapy is preferred for specific problems. For example, a randomized controlled trial compared individual cognitive therapy to group therapy and a wait list control in the treatment of social phobia. Clients were 71 men and women who met the DSM-IV (American Psychiatric Association, 2000) criteria for a diagnosis of social phobia. The intervention was based on a specific treatment manual, and pre–post assessments were conducted. Significant improvements were noted in both group and individual cognitive therapy although on several assessment measures, individual clients showed more improvement than those participating in group therapy. On the other hand, 75 obese clients were assigned to either group or individual therapy and it was found that group therapy produced significantly greater reductions in body mass and weight, regardless of preferred type of intervention. Looking at research studies which compared group versus individual intervention across mental health issues such as past trauma, social phobia, psychotic disorders, stress, anxiety disorders, depression, OCD, and aggression, typically there were no significant differences in effectiveness between modalities.

Shechtman and Ben-David (1999) compared outcomes and group processes in group and individual psychotherapy with aggressive children. The authors noted that group therapy is recommended because it might be less threatening than individual therapy, can provide modelling of positive values and norms, and provide an important context for interpersonal interaction and psychoeducation. However, they suggest it might be difficult to manage aggressive children in a group setting. Participants consisted of 101 grade school students who were randomly assigned to treatment (individual or group) or control conditions. The therapy was based on bibliotherapy and motivational interviewing techniques. Results indicated that group and individual therapy were equally effective in reducing aggressive responses. The authors note that four times as many clients can be treated at any one time in group treatment, suggesting this makes groups beneficial and cost-effective.

Sexual Offender-Specific Literature

Group therapy with sexual offenders is utilized far more frequently by treatment providers than individual intervention. In a 2003 survey of North American sexual offender programmes, 89.9% were group based (McGrath, Cumming and Burchard, 2003). Two large-scale meta-analyses examining treatment outcome with sexual offenders (Hanson *et al.*, 2002; Lösel and Schmucker, 2005) found that out of 112 reports, only 8 were solely focused on individual work and another 8 used primarily individual sessions. Minimal empirical work has explored whether one modality is more effective than another, however. In one study, Abracen and Looman (2004) examined the efficacy of the Regional Treatment Centre (Ontario) Sex Offender Program, which included a combination of group and individual work versus individual therapy alone. The treatment sample was a group of high-risk, high-needs sexual offenders. According to this study, many of the same issues presented in the group treatment programme were addressed in individual therapy although the concepts appear to have been simplified for lower-functioning clients. Follow-up analyses revealed no significant differences between clients who received individual treatment and those who received group treatment. The researchers conclude that there might be a benefit to some clients participating in individual therapy or to integrate individual and group therapy.

In another study, Di Fazio, Abracen and Looman (2001) described treatment options for high-risk sexual offenders within a prison-based programme. Individual treatment was offered to offenders suffering severe Axis 1 disorders or significant cognitive deficits whereas all other offenders were treated in groups. The authors found that offenders who received the full treatment programme benefited to the same extent as clients who participated solely in individual therapy. In fact, clients in the individual sessions received two hours of therapy with a psychologist on a weekly basis, which was less therapy than those in group. Post treatment recidivism rates did not differ.

The limited research conducted specifically in this domain fits with the findings in the general clinical literature. In terms of practical matters, some clients report a preference for individual therapy given their anxiety about confidentiality and the need to disclose private information in a group setting. As therapists, it is our experience that anxiety levels typically dissipate after spending time in the group setting. Group members often feel a sense of relief in the support they gain from others. Glaser and Frosh (1993) noted that group treatment allows group members to realize they are not alone. Groups also provide the opportunity for learning, sharing, relating and building interpersonal skills. At times, however, it can be challenging to spend sufficient time on each client's issues, especially if a therapist is running a closed programme that is more psychoeducational and structured in nature.

Brown (2005) expressed concerns that group therapy could encourage worsening of deviant arousal from discussing offence details as well as the possibility of setting up networks of peer relationships with other sexual offenders which might facilitate subsequent offending. It should be noted that there is no evidence to suggest either of these possibilities might occur. Again, however, these are process issues; in our group programmes, we do not discuss the specific details of the offence in detail nor do we utilize behavioural strategies in which group members would be required to disclose details of deviant fantasies. There is no evidence to suggest any therapeutic benefit in doing so. Thus, by focusing more generally on the offending behaviour and more specifically on dynamic need areas, there should be no concerns about this issue in group therapy.

Implications

The question may not be so much whether group or individual therapy is more effective, but what is it about the process of treatment that makes it effective? For example, while both group and individual treatment seem to be equally effective with respect to outcome, not all group interventions, or individual interventions, for that matter, will be effective with all clients. Not accounting for responsivity or therapeutic process, it seems, will significantly reduce the benefits of intervention. As a result, it appears fitting to present a discussion of therapeutic process issues. Regardless of whether a therapist is working individually or in a group setting, if therapy is to be effective and beneficial, it is necessary to have a strong foundation in the empirical research associated with process issues and possess good therapeutic characteristics.

Therapeutic Process

The general clinical literature is far ahead of sexual offender-specific literature in the exploration of various aspects of therapy, including process issues. Given that therapeutic process is deemed critical, and we suggest especially in sexual offender therapy, this issue should be given some consideration. There appear to be conflicted ideas amongst researchers as to whether there are therapeutic factors that differ between group or individual treatment. It has been suggested that group therapy involves different processes and therapeutic factors from individual therapy (Bednar and Kaul, 1994; Fuhriman and Burlingame, 1994; Yalom, 1995). For example, Fuhriman and Burlingame (1994) argued that some therapeutic factors were common to both individual and group therapy, such as insight, catharsis, reality testing, hope, disclosure and identification. They suggested that vicarious learning, role flexibility, universality, altruism, family re-enactment and interpersonal learning were unique to group therapy. Hill (1990), however, argued that there are no therapeutic factors unique to group treatment. Mallinckrodt (2000) suggested that one form of therapy might emphasize certain factors compared to another.

Holmes and Kivlighan (2000) examined potential differences in therapeutic factors, using the Group Counseling Helpful Impacts Scale (Kivlighan, Multon and Brossart, 1996) finding that the Relationship-Climate and Other versus Self-Focus dimensions were more evident in group therapy while the Emotional Awareness-Insight and Problem Definition-Change were more evident in individual therapy.

Interestingly, the therapist's role in group therapy differs from that of individual therapy. Group members identify feedback from other group members and not from the group leader as the most important source of therapeutic help (Yalom, 1995). Therefore, the group therapist needs to be able to develop a strong group alliance. Kivilighan and Tarrant (2001) found that group leaders' influence on group members' outcome was indirect and mediated through group climate. Those conducting individual therapy, on the other hand, need to focus specifically on developing therapeutic rapport with the individual client.

What Makes Effective Therapy (Group or Otherwise)?

The therapeutic alliance

Numerous studies have demonstrated that the therapeutic alliance predicts psychotherapeutic outcome (Martin, Garske and Davis, 2000). Yalom (1980) suggests that the relationship between therapist and client generates healing power, therefore building a strong therapeutic alliance is considered critical. The relationship between client and therapist is considered the foundation of therapeutic work, one of the main tools for achieving client change (Luborsky, 1994; Klerman *et al.*, 1984). The quality of the client–therapist relationship accounts for about 25% of the variance in treatment effectiveness (Morgan *et al.*, 1982). Furthermore, several meta-analyses demonstrate a moderate effect size between alliance and outcome. Horvath and Symonds (1991) reported an average effect size of 0.26 and similarly Martin, Garske and Davis (2000) reported an effect size of 0.22. In fact, Norcross (2002) demonstrated that the application of specific therapeutic techniques only accounted for 15% of the treatment-induced changes whereas the therapeutic relationship generated 30% of the benefits derived from treatment.

Specific to group therapy, Yalom (1995) reports that group climate affects outcome. Karterud (1988) found that among the six group programmes he examined, the highest functioning group had supportive leaders who were non-aggressive and who encouraged clients to interact in a supportive way. Similarly, Nichols and Taylor (1975) demonstrated that the most important factor in group treatment involved the leader facilitating active participation by all group members, referred to as 'cohesiveness'. Group cohesiveness predicts the amount of between-session work as well as the degree of participation during sessions (Budman *et al.*, 1993). Yalom (1975, 1995) has repeatedly claimed that group cohesiveness is essential to effective treatment.

The quality of the therapeutic relationship also serves to decrease dropouts (Beckham, 1992; Piper *et al.*, 1999; Samstag *et al.*, 1998; Tyron and Kane, 1990, 1993). In sexual offender treatment, offenders who drop out of treatment have higher reoffence rates than those who refuse to enter treatment (Abel *et al.*, 1988; Seto and Barbaree, 1999). Failure to create a therapeutic alliance leads to non-compliance (Eisenthal *et al.*, 1979) and poorer outcomes (Alexander and Luborsky, 1986). Therefore, in either individual or group therapy, it is critical that therapists working with sexual offenders develop a strong interpersonal alliance or group climate.

Client perception

Horvath (2000) notes that the client's perception of treatment significantly influences outcome which is important given that Davis (1984) found that clients regard therapist technique as secondary even in cognitive-behavioural treatments. McLeod (1990) found that therapists who displayed interest, offered encouragement and reassurance, instilled hope and offered practical assistance in increasing problem-solving and coping were seen by clients as most helpful. Saunders (1999) found that clients' perceptions of the therapists' confidence, involvement, focus, emotional engagement and positive feelings for them determined their view of the value of treatment and the degree to which they were willing to engage in the therapeutic process. Clients' perception of their therapists affects whether they show improvements in treatment or not. For example, therapists who are seen by clients as directive (Schindler *et al.*, 1983), confident and persuasive (Ryan and Gizynski, 1971), and sincere (Ford, 1978) generate greater treatment benefits than do therapists who are not perceived to possess these qualities.

Bachelor (1995) examined the therapeutic relationship from the perspective of the client. Given that clients and therapists often view the alliance differently, both views require consideration. Much research has supported the notion that the view of the client needs to be taken into account. For example, Free *et al.* (1985) showed that therapists were inaccurate in estimating client perceptions of therapist empathy. In fact, it was the client rating of therapist empathy that predicted treatment benefits. Similarly, Orlinsky, Grawe and Parks (1994) reviewed various studies and found that in the majority, it was the clients' estimate of therapist features that correlated with beneficial treatment outcome. Based on these results, client perception should be measured, both in group and individual settings (Burns and Auerbach, 1996).

Therapist features that facilitate change

Certain therapist qualities are essential in forming strong therapeutic relationships. Rogers (1957) suggested that warmth, empathy and genuine behaviour on the part of the therapist were both necessary and sufficient qualities. Since then, much research has focused on the impact of these qualities as displayed by the therapist and also examined other important attributes. Empathy, warmth and genuineness have been shown to influence outcome in the cognitive-behavioural treatment of various psychological disorders (Keijsers, Schaap and Hoogduin, 2000). Empathy was a positive predictor of both abstinence and controlled drinking in clients with alcohol addiction (Miller, Taylor and West, 1980) and was related to more effective coping in patients with panic disorder (Matthews *et al.*, 1976) and reductions in depression (Burns and Auerbach, 1996). Warmth is displayed as acceptance, caring and support, which encourages clients to examine their problem behaviour (Safran and Segal, 1990). Orlinsky and Howard (1999) in their comprehensive review concluded that warmth was predictive of positive outcome and positive client ratings. Genuineness is portrayed by the therapist as being 'real', consistent, nondefensive, comfortable, honest and interested (Egan, 1998). Similarly, both sincerity and respect are linked to treatment benefits (Rabavilas, Boulougouris and Perissaki, 1979).

Rewardingness is evidenced through encouragement, reinforcing statements and recognition of client effort and progress. Adopting a reinforcing approach increases clients' self-efficacy, enhances positive expectations about treatment (Miller and Rollnick, 2002) and reduces resistance and aggression among clients (Bandura, Lipsher and Miller, 1960). Clients should be reinforced for small steps and changes early in treatment and gradually for more complex and expanded behaviours (Martin and Pear, 2007). By behaving in a supportive and encouraging fashion, therapists increase client self-efficacy, enhance positive expectations about treatment (Miller and Rollnick, 2002) and reduce any aggression and resistance from the client (Bandura, Lipsher and Miller, 1960).

Directiveness encourages clients to practice skills outside of the session (Schaap *et al.*, 1993) and helps more concrete-thinking clients develop problem-solving skills (Elliot *et al.*, 1982). Being directive with clients provides structure, helps establish an effective working relationship and leads to improved therapeutic outcome. Flexibility is critical; there are clients who require increased structure (e.g., quiet and submissive clients or clients who tend to digress) while others benefit from a more reflective approach (e.g., aggressive or rigid clients) (Ashby *et al.*, 1957; Beutler, Pollack and Jobe, 1978).

Other important skills, for both group and individual therapy, include encouraging active participation, use of humour and self-disclosure. Encouraging active participation is associated with both successful completion of treatment and positive outcomes at follow-up (Garfield and Bergin, 1986). Some argue that therapist self-disclosure should not occur in therapy, especially when working with sexual offenders, as there seems to be a belief that personal information should never be shared. However, while excessive or irrelevant self-disclosure may undermine client confidence in the therapist (Curtis, 1982), appropriate self-disclosure increases trust (Braaten, Otto and Handelsman, 1993). Mahoney and Norcross (1993) suggest that therapists who present as perfectly adjusted may be discounted while clients feel more understood by those who admit the occasional faux pas. We in our therapy encourage the use of occasional and appropriate self-disclosure as a therapeutic tool, as well as a means of building rapport with clients and demonstrating good social skills and relationship boundaries. Although little research has been conducted on the use of humour, Rutherford (1994) concluded that the appropriate use of humour increases clients' interest and helps them view things from a more tolerant perspective. Humour creates a positive and open atmosphere (Greenwald, 1987) and helps relieve tension (Falk and Hill, 1992). We have also found in our experience and from client feedback that use of humour is appreciated. Given the difficult subject matter we deal with in therapy, clients appreciate the light moments in group and report increased cohesion as a result. Of course, humour needs to be appropriate and used with care, as some clients might be sensitive or other clients might use humour as an avoidance strategy (e.g., covering up problems).

Therapist features that impede change

The most important problem in therapist behaviour to emphasize is harsh confrontation. Harsh confrontation, defined as aggressive, critical, hostile and sarcastic behaviour, is very damaging to clients. Unfortunately, confrontational styles have been particularly popular in programmes targeting substance abuse (Miller and Rollnick, 2002) and those treating sexual offenders. This approach is in conflict with evidence suggesting that confrontation is especially harmful to clients in the 'precontemplation' stage, where many of our clients are initially. Annis and Chan (1983) and Beech and Fordham (1997) found that using a confrontational approach with offenders who have low self-esteem harms them even further. Cormier and Cormier (1991) found that clients who perceive the therapist as confrontational either discredit or forcefully challenge the therapist, devalue the issues or agree on the surface but fail to make changes. Overall, a confrontational approach is counter therapeutic (Lieberman, Yalom and Miles, 1973) and ineffective.

Hudson (2005) found that sexual offenders reported when the therapist was confrontational and pressured them to conform to the programme, they simply learned to say what they perceived the therapist wanted to hear rather than participating honestly in treatment. Williams (2004) found that a coercive approach by the therapist reduced the effective participation of offenders in treatment. Furthermore, Harkins and Beech (2007) demonstrated that confrontation by the therapist reduced the positive quality of the group climate that has been demonstrated as crucial for generating effective changes in sexual offenders.

Evidence on factors that impede treatment progress indicate that when therapists are confrontational, defensive and inconsistent, an increased number of offenders dropped out of treatment whereas when the therapist was supportive, empathic, warm and genuine, almost all offenders completed treatment and achieved goals such as increased social skills, victim empathy, better coping strategies and problem-solving skills (Simons, Tyler and Lin, 2005). Preston (2001) reported that therapists with poor relationship skills failed to reduce offenders' resistance to treatment, whereas Stewart, Hill and Cripps (2001) found the most positive effects from treatment occurred with therapists who formed a warm and supportive bond with offenders. Therefore, focusing on therapeutic process is highly relevant, if we want our intervention to be effective.

Process Issues with Sexual Offenders

Andrews, Bonta and Hoge (1990), in their meta-analysis of offender treatment outcomes, generated a set of principles of effective offender treatment (those being risk, needs and responsivity). The 'responsivity' principle is most relevant to process issues and consists of a general responsivity (employing powerful change strategies) and a specific responsivity (adjusting to each client's unique learning style and personality). Dowden and Andrews (2004) showed that unless therapists had the skills necessary for responsivity (i.e., warmth, empathy, respectfulness), treatment benefits were diminished. Therapists need to be considerably flexible in order to adjust treatment to the needs of each client. Importantly, Hanson *et al.* (2009) found the same effective correctional features also applied to sexual offender treatment. Not surprisingly, it was the responsivity principle that was most powerfully predictive of positive treatment change and reductions in subsequent recidivism, not only for sexual recidivism but also nonsexual recidivism.

Our research (Marshall *et al.*, 2002, 2003) involved a series of studies examining the influence of the therapist's behaviour and style on treatment change with sexual offenders. The treatment programmes were conducted in a group setting and run by different therapists who followed a detailed treatment manual and monitored for compliance. The therapists received extensive training in running this manualized programme and treatment was therefore standardized across programmes that all use the same extensive pre- and post-treatment assessment battery.

Initially, we determined whether therapist behaviours and qualities could be reliably identified from the videotapes. Twenty-seven therapist features were derived from an extensive literature review, and 18 features of this list were reliably identified from the videotapes, with inter-rater agreement ranging from 0.57 to 1.00 (Marshall *et al.*, 2002). We then evaluated the influence of the therapist on behaviour change. Correlational analyses between the ratings of the therapists and behaviour change scores revealed significant relationships on measures of a variety of coping skills, various indices of perspective-taking ability and several aspects of relationship skills. Warmth, empathy, rewardingness and directiveness were the most important features influencing change. Importantly, harsh confrontation by the therapists was negatively correlated ($r = -0.31$) with indices of behaviour change.

The results of these studies were incorporated into developing a training programme, and another evaluation of programmes was conducted. Again, the critical therapist qualities influencing behaviour change were warmth, empathy, rewardingness and directiveness (Marshall *et al.*, 2002). Correlations between these characteristics and indices of behavioural change ranged between $r=0.32$ and $r=0.74$ for warmth; $r=0.45$ and $r=0.65$ for empathy; $r=0.35$ and $r=0.57$ for rewardingness; and $r=0.42$ and $r=0.61$ for directiveness. Confrontation, importantly, was not present among the therapists, likely due to the changes in the training programme.

Drapeau and his colleagues (Drapeau, 2005; Drapeau *et al.*, 2004), in a series of studies combining qualitative and quantitative approaches, found that sexual offenders judged the role of the therapist to be crucial to any benefits they derived from treatment. Effective therapists were those who were honest and respectful, caring, non-critical and non-judgemental. Confrontational therapists led clients to withdraw, while clients disengaged from treatment if they perceived the therapist as unsupportive. Those who worked collaboratively with the offenders elicited their full engagement.

The recent emphasis on process issues has at least focused attention on the importance of this issue. With respect to group cohesion, which we know from the general literature is a key component in the success of group treatment, Beech and Fordham (1997) examined the influence of group cohesiveness on behaviour changes among sexual offenders. Using Moos's (1986) Group Environment Scale to assess client's perceptions, Beech and Fordham ranked the 12 sexual offender treatment groups in terms of perceived group cohesion. Measuring treatment-induced changes across groups, Beech and Fordham found that the group with the highest cohesiveness scores generated the greatest degree of change across all measures. The group with the lowest cohesiveness score displayed minimal change.

Beech and Hamilton-Giachritsis (2005) again found that group cohesiveness predicted treatment-induced benefits ($r=0.65$). In addition, they reported that the degree of emotional expression during treatment was related to beneficial changes ($r=0.65$). Pfäfflin *et al.* (2005) also demonstrated that the expression of emotion during sexual offender therapy sessions is a significant predictor of treatment outcome. These benefits were greatest when emotional expression was associated with an intellectual understanding of the issue at hand.

Thornton, Mann and Williams (2000) compared prison-based groups led by a warm and supportive therapist with a therapist who displayed hostility towards the clients. Although both groups improved on several measures (e.g., reduced denial and minimization), only the group led by the warm and supportive therapist demonstrated changes across all measures.

Implications for treatment

The overall goal of treatment for sexual offenders is to prevent reoffending, and recent evidence suggests treatment is reducing long-term recidivism (Hanson *et al.*, 2002). Marshall and Serran (2000) proposed a number of ways to improve treatment efficacy with sexual offenders, specifically by enhancing therapeutic skills. Drapeau (2005) suggests that an effective alliance between therapists and clients plays a major role in generating treatment benefits and that therapists should be carefully chosen based on their ability to effectively adapt to the personal style and ability of each client, and to demonstrate the skills that characterize effective therapists.

Therapist flexibility is therefore critical; not only is it more effective than a rigid approach that follows strict procedures (Ringler, 1977) but flexibility is also essential to good therapy. Therapists who can adjust their style and tailor their approach to suit individual clients appear to generate more positive results (Kottler, Sexton and Whiston, 1994).

In our treatment programme, the role of emotion in the therapeutic relationship is considered critical. Research suggests that successful treatment outcome is related to the degree to which clients are given the opportunity to be emotionally expressive (Cooley and LaJoy, 1980; Orlinsky and Howard, 1986). Empathy and acceptance by the therapist contributes to affect regulation by providing interpersonal soothing and encourages the ability to regulate emotion. A validating relationship is viewed as crucial to affect regulation; people with under-regulated affect have been shown to benefit from interpersonal validation as much as from the learning of emotion regulation and distress tolerance skills (Linehan, 1993). The therapist's communication of emotion (through facial and verbal expression) creates emotional climate. Saunders (1999) demonstrated that the expression of feelings by clients determines the impact each treatment session has and found that these expressions were best facilitated by emotional expressiveness of the therapist. Providing a safe and responsive emotional climate facilitates emotional processing. In fact, encouraging emotional expression facilitates treatment change (Klein, Mathieu-Coughlan and Kiesler, 1986; Orlinsky and Howard, 1999). Attitudes and beliefs are affected by emotional states, and interpersonal schemas which are strongly held by clients are often only accessed and ultimately changed when activated through emotional expression.

All of these reviews and research provide concrete ideas to therapists working with sexual offenders. Specifically, focusing on procedure and skills while ignoring the role of the therapist is contraindicated. Flexibility, sensitivity, support and warmth are essential to behaviour change, and those who are confrontational at worst or even indifferent should not provide treatment to sexual offenders. Directive, supportive challenges can encourage behaviour change.

Offenders can be a challenging population to work with not only because of the many issues they often have but also because they may be unmotivated to address their problem areas. Unfortunately, there are therapists who believe that a confrontational approach will be effective, and there are others who adopt an unconditionally positive approach where they fail to challenge problematic behaviours in their clients (Marshall, 1996). Neither of these strategies is effective. Since resistance is increased by a confrontational approach, adopting a motivational stance (Miller and Rollnick, 2002) seems to enhance client involvement in treatment sessions. Motivational therapists encourage change by expressing empathy, avoiding argument, rolling with resistance, creating dissonance between the clients' view of the future and the likelihood of achieving these goals, and supporting self-efficacy (Miller and Rollnick, 2002).

As well, adopting a positive and motivation approach to treatment is more likely to meet with success than former relapse-prevention approaches which focus solely on risk reduction. Mann (1998) suggests that helping clients pursue approach goals (i.e., pro-social goals that help clients live a healthy and meaningful life) results in active participation in treatment. Clients are also more likely to practice new skills outside of session when a new, positive behaviour is targeted rather than focusing on a reduction of a negative behaviour (Cullari, 1996).

In a recent Delphi study focused on working with lesbian, gay and bisexual clients, Godfrey *et al.* (2006) concluded that therapists need to possess certain values, qualities and sensitivities. Furthermore, it was generalized that therapists working with specific groups need to be open-minded, have awareness and control over their personal biases and issues, and have a strong understanding of theories and issues related to specific populations. We argue that this is definitely true for those working with sexual offenders. Therapy is going to be more effective when a therapist believes in the treatment approach while lack of commitment or belief in the therapy will jeopardize treatment outcomes (Davis and Piercey, 2007a, b; Wampold, 2001). Therefore, therapists working with sexual offenders not only must believe in their therapeutic approach but also must believe that their clients can be successfully treated. It is encouraging that more professionals are exploring aspects of therapeutic process such as group climate, clients' views of intervention and emotion. This avenue of sexual offender work is both necessary and exciting to the field, and will only serve to improve our interventions.

Conclusions

So, what is the bottom line? It appears that both group and individual therapy can be equally effective based on the general clinical literature, although in the sexual offender field, research remains sparse. There are benefits to running group therapy that make it somewhat different than individual therapy, in that therapists can treat far more clients, usually for a lower cost, clients benefit by learning from one another, developing trust and social support from a group, and deal with issues they may have such as social anxiety, shame and feeling alone. On the other hand, if a therapist is working in a venue where running group therapy is not an option for whatever reason, he or she should feel free to treat the client on an individual basis, as effective work can be done. Regardless of whether a therapist is conducting group or individual intervention, the therapist's characteristics and their ability to develop an alliance is paramount as to whether the intervention will be effective or not.

References

Abel, G.G., Mittelman, M., Becker, J.V. *et al.* (1988) Predicting child molesters' response to treatment. *Annals of the New York Academy of Sciences*, 528, 223–234.

Abracen, J. and Looman, J. (2004) Issues in the treatment of sexual offenders: recent developments and directions for future research. *Aggression and Violent Behavior: A Review Journal*, 9, 229–246.

Alexander, L.B. and Luborsky, L. (1986) The Penn helping alliance scales, in *The Psychotherapeutic Process: A Research Handbook* (eds L.S. Greenberg and W.M. Pinsof), Guilford Press, New York.

American Psychiatric Association (2000) *Diagnostic and Statistical Manual of Mental Disorders* (Text Revision), American Psychiatric Association, Washington, DC.

Andrews, D.A., Bonta, J. and Hoge, R.D. (1990) Classification for effective rehabilitation: rediscovering psychology. *Criminal Justice and Behaviour*, 17, 19–52.

Annis, H.M. and Chan, D. (1983) The differential treatment model: empirical evidence from a personality typology of adult offenders. *Criminal Justice and Behaviour*, 10, 159–173.

Ashby, J.D., Ford, D.H., Guerney, B.G. and Guerney, L.F. (1957) Effects on clients of a reflective and leading type of psychotherapy. *Psychological Monographs*, 453, 71.

Bachelor, A. (1995) Clients' perception of the therapeutic alliance: a qualitative analysis. *Journal of Counseling Psychology*, 42, 323–337.

Bandura, A., Lipsher, D.H. and Miller, P.E. (1960) Psychotherapists' approach-avoidance reactions to patients' expressions of hostility. *Journal of Consulting Psychology*, 24, 1–8.

Beckham, E.E. (1992) Predicting drop-out in psychotherapy. *Psychotherapy: Theory, Research, and Practice*, 29, 177–182.

Bednar, R. and Kaul, T. (1994) Experiential group research: can the canon fire? in *Handbook of Psychotherapy and Behaviour Change* (eds A.E. Bergen and S.L. Garfield), John Wiley & Sons, Inc., New York, pp. 631–663.

Beech, A.R. and Fordham, A.S. (1997) Therapeutic climate of sexual offender treatment programs. *Sexual Abuse: A Journal of Research and Treatment*, 9, 219–237.

Beech, A.R. and Hamilton-Giachritsis, C.E. (2005) Relationship between therapeutic climate and treatment outcome in group-based sexual offender treatment programs. *Sexual Abuse: A Journal of Research and Treatment*, 17, 127–140.

Beutler, L.E., Pollack, S. and Jobe, A.M. (1978) "Acceptance," values and therapeutic change. *Journal of Consulting and Clinical Psychology*, 46, 198–199.

Braaten, E.B., Otto, S. and Handelsman, M. (1993) What do people want to know about psychotherapy? *Psychotherapy: Theory, Research, and Practice*, 30, 565–570.

Brown, S. (2005) *Treating Sex Offender: An Introduction to Sex Offender Treatment Programmes*, Willan, Devon.

Budman, S.H., Soldz, S., Demby, A. *et al.* (1993) What is cohesiveness? An empirical examination. *Small Group Research*, 24, 199–216.

Burlingame, G.M., Fuhriman, A., McRoberts, C.H. *et al.* (1995) Group psychotherapy efficacy: a meta-analytic review, in *Group Psychotherapy Efficacy: A Meta-Analytic Perspective* (ed. A. Fuhriman). Symposium conducted at the 103rd Annual Convention of the American Psychological Association, New York, August.

Burns, D.D. and Auerbach, A. (1996) Therapeutic empathy in cognitive-behavioural therapy: does it really make a difference? in *Frontiers of Cognitive Therapy* (ed. P. Salkovskis), Guilford Press, New York, pp. 135–164.

Cooley, E.J. and LaJoy, R. (1980) Therapeutic relationship and improvements as perceived by clients and therapists. *Journal of Clinical Psychology*, 36, 562–570.

Cormier, W.H. and Cormier, L.S. (1991) *Interviewing Strategies for Helpers*, Brooks/Cole, Pacific Grove.

Cullari, S. (1996) *Treatment Resistance: A Guide for Practitioners*, Allyn and Bacon, Boston.

Curtis, J.M. (1982) The effect of therapist self-disclosure on patient's perceptions of empathy, competence, and trust in an analogue psychotherapeutic interaction. *Psychotherapy: Theory, Research, and Practice*, 19, 54–62.

Davis, M. (1984) Nonverbal behaviour and psychotherapy: process research, in *Nonverbal Behaviour: Perspectives, Applications, Intercultural Insights* (ed. A. Wolfganf), Hogrefe & Huber, New York, pp. 203–228.

Davis, S.D. and Piercey, F.P. (2007a) What clients of couple therapy model developers and their former students say about change, part I: model–dependent common factors across three models. *Journal of Marital and Family Therapy*, 33, 318–343.

Davis, S.D. and Piercey, F.P. (2007b) What clients of couple therapy model developers and their former students say about change, part II: model–independent common factors and an integrative framework. *Journal of Marital and Family Therapy*, 33, 344–363.

Di Fazio, R., Abracen, J. and Looman, J. (2001) Group versus individual treatment of sex offenders: a comparison. *Forum on Corrections Research*, 13, 56–59.

Dowden, C. and Andrews, D.A. (2004) The importance of staff practice in delivering effective correctional treatment: a meta-analytic review of core correctional practice. *International Journal of Offender Therapy and Comparative Criminology*, 48, 203–214.

Drapeau, M. (2005) Research on the processes involved in treating sexual offenders. *Sexual Abuse: A Journal of Research and Treatment*, 17, 117–125.

Drapeau, M., Korner, C.A., Brunet, L. and Granger, L. (2004) Treatment at La Macaza clinic: a qualitative study of the sexual offenders' perspective. *Canadian Journal of Criminology and Criminal Justice*, 46, 27–44.

Egan, G. (1998) *The Skilled Helper: A Problem-Management Approach to Helping*. Brooks/Cole, Pacific Grove.

Eisenthal, S., Emery, R., Lazare, A. and Udin, H. (1979) "Adherence" and the negotiated approach to patienthood. *Archives of General Psychiatry*, 36, 393–398.

Elliot, R., Barker, C.B., Caskey, N. and Pistrang, N. (1982) Differential helpfulness of counsellor verbal response modes. *Journal of Counselling Psychology*, 29, 354–361.

Falk, D.R. and Hill, C.E. (1992) Counselor interventions preceding client laughter in brief therapy. *Journal of Counseling Psychology*, 39, 39–45.

Ford, J. (1978) Therapeutic relationship in behavior therapy: an empirical analysis. *Journal of Consulting and Clinical Psychology*, 46, 1302–1314.

Free, N.K., Green, B.L., Grace, M.D. *et al.* (1985) Empathy and outcome in brief focal dynamic therapy. *American Journal of Psychiatry*, 142, 917–921.

Fuhriman, A. and Burlingame, G.M. (1994) Group psychotherapy: research and practice, in *Handbook of Group Psychotherapy* (eds A. Fuhriman and G.M. Burlingame), John Wiley & Sons, Inc., New York, pp. 3–40.

Garfield, S. and Bergin, A. (eds) (1986) *Handbook of Psychotherapy and Behaviour Change*, John Wiley & Sons, Inc., New York.

Glaser, D. and Frosh, S. (1993) *Child Sexual Abuse*, 2nd edn, Macmillan Press, Basingstoke.

Godfrey, K., Haddock, S.A., Fisher, A. and Lund, L. (2006) Essential training components of curricula for preparing therapists to work with lesbian, gay, and bisexual clients: a Delphi study. *Journal of Marital and Family Therapy*, 32, 491–504.

Greenwald, H. (1987) The humor decision, in *Handbook of Humor and Psychotherapy: Advances in the Clinical Use of Humor* (eds W.F. Fry and W.A. Salameh), Professional Resource Exchange, Sarasota, pp. 41–54.

Hanson, R.K., Gordon, A., Harris, A.J.R. *et al.* (2002) First report of the collaborative outcome data project on the effectiveness of psychological treatment of sex offenders. *Sexual Abuse: A Journal of Research and Treatment*, 14, 169–194.

Hanson, R., Bourgon, G., Helmus, L. and Hodgson, S. (2009) The principles of effective correctional treatment also apply to sexual offenders: a meta-analysis. *Criminal Justice and Behavior*, 36, 865–891.

Harkins, L. and Beech, A.R. (2007) A review of the factors that can influence the effectiveness of sexual offender treatment: risk, need, responsivity, and process issues. *Aggression and Violent Behavior: A Review Journal*, 12, 615–627.

Hill, C.E. (1990) Is individual therapy process really different from group therapy process? The jury is still out. *Counseling Psychologist*, 18, 126–130.

Holmes, S.E. and Kivlighan, Jr., D.M. (2000) Therapeutic factors in group and individual treatment. *Journal of Counseling Psychology*, 47, 478–484.

Horvath, A.O. (2000) The therapeutic relationship: from transference to alliance. *Journal of Counseling Psychology/In Session: Psychotherapy in Practice*, 56, 163–173.

Horvath, A.O. and Symonds, B.D. (1991) Relation between working alliance and outcome in psychotherapy: a meta-analysis. *Journal of Counseling Psychology*, 38, 130–149.

Hudson, K. (2005) *Offending Identities: Sex Offenders' Perspectives of Their Treatment and Management*, Willan Publishing, Portland.

Karterud, S. (1988) The influence of task definition, leadership and therapeutic style on inpatient group cultures. *International Journal of Therapeutic Communities*, 9, 231–247.

Keijsers, G.P.J., Schaap, C.P. and Hoogduin, C.A.L. (2000) The impact of interpersonal patient and therapist behaviour on outcome in cognitive-behaviour therapy. *Behaviour Modification*, 24, 264–297.

Kivilighan, Jr., D.M. and Tarrant, J.M. (2001) Does group climate mediate the group leadership-group member outcome relationship? A test of Yalom's hypotheses about leadership priorities. *Group Dynamics*, 5, 220–234.

Kivlighan, Jr., D.M., Multon, K.D. and Brossart, D.F. (1996) Helpful impacts in group counselling development of a multidimensional rating system. *Journal of Counseling Psychology*, 43, 347–355.

Klein, M.H., Mathieu-Coughlan, P. and Kiesler, D. (1986) The experiencing scales, in *The Psychotherapeutic Process: A Research Handbook* (eds L.S. Greenberg and W. Pinsoff), Guilford Press, New York, pp. 21–71.

Klerman, G., Weissman, M., Rounsville, B. and Chevron, E. (1984) *Interpersonal Therapy of Depression*, Basic Books, New York.

Kottler, J.A., Sexton, T.L. and Whiston, S.C. (1994) *The Heart of Healing: Relationship in Therapy*, Jossey-Bass, San Francisco.

Lambert, M.J. and Bergin, A.E. (1994) The effectiveness of psychotherapy, in *Handbook of Psychotherapy and Behaviour Change*, 4th edn (eds A.E. Bergin and S.L. Garfield), John Wiley & Sons, Inc., New York, pp. 72–113.

Lieberman, M.A., Yalom, I.D. and Miles, M.B. (1973) *Encounter Groups: First Facts*, Basic Books, New York.

Linehan, M. (1993) *Skills Training Manual for Treatment of Borderline Personality Disorder*, Guilford Press, New York.

Linley, P.A. and Joseph, S. (2004) *Positive Psychology in Practice*, John Wiley & Sons, Inc., Hoboken.

Lösel, F. and Schmucker, M. (2005) The effectiveness of treatment for sexual offenders: a comprehensive meta-analysis. *Journal of Experimental Criminology*, 1, 117–146.

Luborsky, L. (1994) The benefits to the clinician of psychotherapy research: a clinician-researchers view, in *Psychotherapy Research and Practice: Bridging the Gap* (eds P.F. Talley, H.H. Strupp and S.F. Butler), Basic Books, New York, pp. 167–180.

MacKenzie, K.R. (1995) Rationale for group psychotherapy in managed care, in *Effective Use of Group Therapy in Managed Care* (ed. K.R. MacKenzie), American Psychiatric Press, Washington, DC, pp. 1–26.

Mahoney, M.J. and Norcross, J.C. (1993) Relationship styles and therapeutic choices: a commentary. *Psychotherapy: Theory, Research, and Practice*, 30, 423–426.

Mallinckrodt, B. (2000) Attachment, social competencies, social support, and interpersonal process in psychotherapy. *Psychotherapy Research*, 10, 239–266.

Mann, R. (1998) Relapse prevention? Is that the bit where they told me all the things I couldn't do anymore? Paper presented at the 17th Annual Research and Treatment Conference of the Association for the Treatment of Sexual Abusers, Vancouver, October.

Marshall, W.L. (1996) Assessment, treatment, and theorizing about sex offenders: developments during the past twenty years and future directions. *Criminal Justice and Behavior*, 23, 162–199.

Marshall, W.L. and Serran, G.A. (2000) Current issues in the assessment and treatment of sexual offenders. *Clinical Psychology & Psychotherapy*, 7, 85–96.

Marshall, W.L., Serran, G.A., Moulden, H. *et al.* (2002) Therapist features in sexual offender treatment: their reliable identification and influence on behaviour change. *Clinical Psychology and Psychotherapy*, 9, 395–405.

Marshall, W.L., Fernandez, Y.M., Serran, G.A. *et al.* (2003) Process variables in the treatment of sexual offenders: a review of the relevant literature. *Aggression and Violent Behavior: A Review Journal*, 8, 205–234.

Marshall, W.L., Marshall, L.E., Serran, G.A. and O'Brien, M.D. (2011) *The Treatment of Sexual Offenders: A Positive Approach*, American Psychological Association, Washington, DC.

Marshall, W.L. and Burton, D. (2010) The importance of therapeutic processes in offender treatment. *Aggression and Violent Behavior: A Review Journal*, 15, 141–149.

Martin, G. and Pear, J. (2007) *Behavior Modification: What Is It and How to Do It*, 8th edn, Pearson Prentice Hall, Upper Saddle River.

Martin, D.J., Garske, J.P. and Davis, M.K. (2000) Relation of the therapeutic alliance with outcome and other variables: a meta-analytic review. *Journal of Consulting and Clinical Psychology*, 68, 438–450.

Matthews, A.M., Johnston, D.W., Lancashire, M. *et al.* (1976) Imaginal flooding and exposure to real phobic situations: treatment outcome with agoraphobic patients. *British Journal of Psychiatry*, 129, 362–371.

McGrath, R.J., Cumming, G.F. and Burchard, B.L. (2003) *Current Practices and Trends in Sexual Abuser Management: Safer Society 2002 Nationwide Survey*, Safer Society Press, Brandon.

McLeod, J. (1990) The client's experience of counselling and psychotherapy: a review of the research literature, in *Experiences of Counselling in Action* (eds D. Mearns and W. Dryden), Sage Publications, London, pp. 66–79.

McRoberts, C., Burlingame, G.M. and Hoag, M.J. (1998) Comparative efficacy of individual and group psychotherapy: a meta-analytic perspective. *Group Dynamics: Theory, Research, and Practice*, 2, 101–178.

Miller, W.R. and Rollnick, S. (eds) (2002) *Motivational Interviewing: Preparing People to Change Addictive Behaviour*, 2nd edn, Guilford Press, New York.

Miller, W.R., Taylor, C.A. and West, J.C. (1980) Focused versus broad-spectrum behaviour therapy for problem drinkers. *Journal of Consulting and Clinical Psychology*, 48, 590–601.

Miller, W.R., Brown, J.M., Simpson, T.L. *et al.* (1995) What works? A methodological analysis of alcohol treatment outcome literature, in *Handbook of Alcoholism Treatment Approaches*, 2nd edn (eds R.K. Hester and W.R. Miller), Allyn & Bacon, Boston, pp. 12–44.

Moos, R.H. (1986) *Group Environment Scale Manual*, 2nd edn, Consulting Psychologists' Press, Palo Alto.

Morgan, R., Luborsky, L., Crits-Christoph, P. *et al.* (1982) Predicting outcomes of psychotherapy by the Penn helping alliance rating method. *Archives of General Psychiatry*, 39, 397–402.

Nichols, M. and Taylor, T. (1975) Impact of therapist interventions on early sessions of group therapy. *Journal of Clinical Psychology*, 31, 726–729.

Norcross, J.C. (2002) Empirically supported therapy relationships, in *Psychotherapy Relationships That Work: Therapist Contributions and Responsiveness to Patients* (ed. J. C. Norcross), Oxford University Press, Oxford, pp. 3–10.

Orlinsky, D.E. and Howard, K. (1986) Process and outcome in psychotherapy, in *Handbook of Psychotherapy and Behaviour Change*, 3rd edn (eds S.L. Garfield and A.E. Bergin), John Wiley & Sons, Inc., New York, pp. 311–381.

Orlinsky, D.E. and Howard, K.I. (1999) Process and outcome in psychotherapy, in *Handbook of Psychotherapy and Behaviour Change*, 3rd edn (eds S.L. Garfield and A.E. Bergin), John Wiley & Sons, Inc., New York, pp. 311–384.

Orlinsky, D.E., Grawe, K. and Parks, B.K. (1994) Process and outcome in psychotherapy – noch einmal, in *Handbook of Psychotherapy and Behaviour Change*, 4th edn (eds A.E. Garfield and S.L. Garfield), John Wiley & Sons, Inc., New York, pp. 270–376.

Pfäfflin, F., Bohmer, M., Cornehl, S. and Mergenthaler, F. (2005) What happens in therapy with sexual offenders? A model of process research. *Sexual Abuse: A Journal of Research and Treatment*, 17, 141–151.

Piper, W.E., Ogrodniczuk, J.S., Joyce, A.S., McCallum, M. *et al.* (1999) Prediction of dropping out in time limited interpretive individual psychotherapy. *Psychotherapy: Theory, Research, and Practice*, 36, 114–122.

Preston, D. (2001) Addressing treatment resistance in corrections, in *Compendium 2000 on Effective Correctional Isming* (eds L.L. Motiuk and R.C. Serin), Ministry of Supply and Services Canada, Ottawa, pp. 47–55.

Rabavilas, A.D., Boulougouris, I.C. and Perissaki, C. (1979) Therapist qualities related to outcome with exposure in vivo in neurotic patients. *Journal of Behaviour Therapy and Experimental Psychiatry*, 10, 293–294.

Ringler, M. (1977) The effect of democratic versus authoritarian therapist behaviour on success, success-expectation and self-attribution in desensitization of examination anxiety. *Zeitschrift fur Klinische Psychologie*, 6, 40–58.

Rogers, C.R. (1957) The necessary and sufficient conditions of therapeutic personality change. *Journal of Consulting Psychology*, 21, 95–113.

Rutherford, K. (1994) Humor in psychotherapy. *Individual Psychology: Journal of Adlerian Theory, Research, and Practice*, 50, 207–222.

Ryan, V.L. and Gizynski, M.N. (1971) Behavior therapy in retrospect: patients' feelings and their behavior therapies. *Journal of Consulting and Clinical Psychology*, 37, 1–9.

Safran, J.D. and Segal, Z.V. (1990) *Interpersonal Process in Cognitive Therapy*, Basic Books, New York.

Samstag, L.W., Batchelder, S.T., Muran, J.C. *et al.* (1998) Early identification of treatment failures in short-term psychotherapy: an assessment of therapeutic alliance and interpersonal behaviour. *The Journal of Psychotherapy Practice and Research*, 7, 126–143.

Saunders, M. (1999) Clients' assessments of the affective environment of the psychotherapy session: relationship to session quality and treatment effectiveness. *Journal of Clinical Psychology*, 55, 597–605.

Schaap, C., Bennun, I., Schindler, L. and Hoogduin, K. (1993) *The Therapeutic Relationship in Behavioural Psychotherapy*, John Wiley & Sons, Ltd, Chichester.

Schindler, L., Revenstorf, D., Hahlweg, K. and Brenglemann, J.C. (1983) Therapeuten-verthalten in der Verhaltenstherapie: Entwicklumg eines instruements zur Beurteilung dunch den Klienten. *Partnerberaturing*, 20, 149–157.

Seto, M.C. and Barbaree, H.E. (1999) Psychopathy, treatment behavior and sex offender recidivism. *Journal of Interpersonal Violence*, 14, 1235–1248.

Shechtman, Z. and Ben-David, M. (1999) Individual and group psychotherapy of childhood aggression: a comparison of outcome and processes. *Group Dynamic: Theory, Research, and Practice*, 3, 263–274.

Simons, D., Tyler, C. and Lin, R. (2005) Influence of therapist characteristics on treatment progress. Paper presented at the 24th Annual Research and Treatment Conference of the Association for the Treatment of Sexual Abusers, Salt Lake City, November,.

Snyder, C.R. and Lopez, S.J. (2005) *Handbook of Positive Psychology*, Oxford University Press, Oxford/New York.

Stewart, L., Hill, J. and Cripps, J. (2001) Treatment of family violence in correctional settings, in *Compendium 2000 on Effective Correctional Isming* (eds L. Motiuk and R. Serin), Correctional Service of Canada, Ottawa, pp. 87–97.

Stinchfield, R., Owen, P.L. and Winters, K.C. (1994) Group therapy for substance use: a review of the empirical research, in *Handbook of Group Psychotherapy* (eds A. Fuhriman and G.M. Burlingame), John Wiley & Sons, Inc., New York, pp. 458–488.

Thornton, D., Mann, R.E. and Williams, F.M.S. (2000) *Therapeutic Style in Sex Offender Treatment*, Unpublished manuscript available from Offending Behaviour Isming Unit, HM Prison Service, London.

Tillitski, L. (1990) A meta-analysis of estimated effect sizes for group versus individual versus control treatments. *International Journal of Group Psychotherapy*, 40, 215–224.

Tyron, G.S. and Kane, A.S. (1990) The helping alliance and premature termination. *Counseling Psychology Quarterly*, 3, 233–238.

Tyron, G.S. and Kane, A.S. (1993) Relationship of working alliance to mutual and unilateral termination. *Journal of Counseling Psychology*, 40, 33–36.

Wampold, B.E. (2001) *The Great Psychotherapy Debate: Models, Methods, and Findings*, Erlbaum, Mahwah.

Ward, T. (2002) Good lives and the rehabilitation of offenders: promises and problems. *Aggression and Violent Behavior*, 7, 513–528.

Ward, T. and Stewart, C. (2003) Good lives and the rehabilitation of sexual offenders, in *Sexual Deviance: Issues and Controversies* (eds T. Ward, D.R. Laws and S.M. Hudson), Sage, Thousand Oaks, pp. 21–44.

Williams, D.J. (2004) Sexual offenders' perceptions of correctional therapy: what can we learn? *Sexual Addiction & Compulsivity*, 11, 145–162.

Yalom, I.D. (1975) *The Theory and Practice of Group Psychotherapy*, 2nd edn, Basic Books, New York.

Yalom, I.D. (1980) *Existential Psychotherapy*, Basic Books, New York.

Yalom, I.D. (1995) *Theory and Practice of Group Therapy*, 4th edn, Basic Books, New York.

Index

What Works in Offender Rehabilitation: An Evidence-Based Approach to Assessment and Treatment,
First Edition. Edited by Leam A. Craig, Louise Dixon and Theresa A. Gannon.
© 2013 John Wiley & Sons, Ltd. Published 2013 by John Wiley & Sons, Ltd.